Philosophical issues in Aristotle's biology

...there are gods here too.

(PA 1. 645a21)

PHILOSOPHICAL ISSUES IN ARISTOTLE'S BIOLOGY

EDITED BY

Allan Gotthelf and James G. Lennox

The right of the
University of Cambridge
to print and sell
all manner of books
was granted by
Henry VIII in 1534.
The University has printed
and published continuously
since 1584.

Cambridge University Press

Cambridge

New York   New Rochelle   Melbourne   Sydney

Published by the Press Syndicate of the University of Cambridge
The Pitt Building, Trumpington Street, Cambridge CB2 1RP
32 East 57th Street, New York, NY 10022, USA
10 Stamford Road, Oakleigh, Melbourne 3166, Australia

First published 1987

Printed in Great Britain by the University Press, Cambridge

British Library cataloguing in publication data
Philosophical issues in Aristotle's biology.
1. Aristotle–Contributions in biology
2. Biology–History
I. Gotthelf, Allan II. Lennox, James G.
574′.092′4   QH31.A7

Library of Congress cataloguing in publication data
Philosophical issues in Aristotle's biology.
Bibliography.
Includes index.
1. Biology–Philosophy. 2. Biology–Philosophy–
History. 3. Aristotle. I. Gotthelf, Allan, 1942–
II. Lennox, James G.
QH331.P465 1987   574′.01   86–24423

ISBN 0 521 32582 x hard covers
ISBN 0 521 31091 1 paperback

Contents

Notes on contributors

DAVID M. BALME is Professor Emeritus of Classics at Queen Mary College, University of London, and former Fellow of Clare College and Jesus College, Cambridge. He is the author of *Aristotle's De Partibus Animalium I and De Generatione Animalium I* (Oxford 1972; repr. 1986). He has published numerous articles on Aristotle's biology, natural philosophy and metaphysics, and has edited and translated *Aristotle: Historia Animalium VII-X* in the Loeb Classical Library (forthcoming). He is currently at work on a critical edition, with commentary, of the whole of *HA* for Cambridge University Press.

ROBERT BOLTON is Associate Professor of Philosophy at Rutgers University, and has taught at Michigan, MIT, Pittsburgh, and Virginia. He studied ancient philosophy with Gregory Vlastos at Princeton, where he was awarded the McCosh Prize for a thesis on Plato, and with G. E. L. Owen at Oxford as a Rhodes Scholar. He has published articles on Aristotle's scientific method and philosophy of language in classical and philosophical journals.

WILLIAM CHARLTON is Senior Lecturer in Philosophy at the University of Newcastle upon Tyne. He is author of *Aristotle's Physics Books I and II* (Oxford 1970) and *Aesthetics, An Introduction* (London 1970), and numerous articles and reviews on ancient philosophy, metaphysics, and aesthetics.

JOHN M. COOPER is Professor and Chairman, Department of Philosophy, Princeton University and author of *Reason and Human Good in Aristotle* (Cambridge, Mass. 1975) and many articles and reviews in classical and philosophical journals.

CYNTHIA A. FREELAND is Associate Professor of Philosophy at the University of Houston, having taught for eight years at the University of Massachusetts at Amherst. She has published articles on Aristotle's natural philosophy and philosophy of action, and is currently working on a book on Aristotle's philosophy of science. In addition

vii

to her work in ancient philosophy, she has written on topics in aesthetics and psychoanalysis.

MONTGOMERY FURTH is Professor of Philosophy at the University of California, Los Angeles (UCLA). He has written on Frege, Leibniz, the Eleatics and Aristotle, and has recently published a translation of the central books of Aristotle's *Metaphysics* (Indianapolis 1985). His *Substance, Form and Psyche: an Aristotelean Metaphysics*, from which the extract in this volume is taken, is forthcoming from Cambridge University Press. At present he is working on a book about the Presocratics.

ALLAN GOTTHELF (co-editor) is Associate Professor of Philosophy at Trenton State College, and life member, Clare Hall, Cambridge. He is editor of *Aristotle on Nature and Living Things* (Pittsburgh and Bristol 1985), the Festschrift for David Balme, and organizer or co-organizer of several international conferences on the philosophical significance of Aristotle's biology. He has published articles and reviews on ancient philosophy, chiefly on Aristotle and Theophrastus.

L. ARYEH KOSMAN is Professor and Chairman, Department of Philosophy, Haverford College and former Junior Fellow of the Center for Hellenic Studies. He is the author of many articles on the philosophy of Plato and of Aristotle.

JAMES G. LENNOX (co-editor) is Associate Professor of History and Philosophy of Science at the University of Pittsburgh. A former Junior Fellow of the Center for Hellenic Studies and Fellow of the Center for Philosophy of Science at the University of Pittsburgh, he has published numerous articles and reviews in the history and philosophy of biology, especially on Aristotle's philosophy and biology.

G. E. R. LLOYD is Professor of Ancient Philosophy and Science at the University of Cambridge and a Fellow of King's College, where he has taught since 1960. He has published numerous books and articles on topics in ancient philosophy and science, including most recently *Magic, Reason and Experience* (1979) and *Science, Folklore and Ideology* (1983). The Sather Classical Lectures that he delivered at Berkeley in 1984 are to be published shortly by University of California Press under the title *The Revolution of Wisdom*.

PIERRE PELLEGRIN is Chargé de Recherche at the Centre National de la Recherche Scientifique in Paris, and author of *La Classification des animaux chez Aristote: statut de la biologie et unité de l'Aristotelisme* (Paris 1982; rev. edn. in English translation by A. Preus, Berkeley 1986), and of numerous articles and reviews in Greek philosophy. He is co-director of an Aristotle fragment translation project in France.

Preface

Aristotle's biological writings have happily been the subject of an increasing amount of attention of late. This interest has developed primarily among scholars of ancient philosophy, and has focused in the main on the lessons these treatises might provide for our understanding of central areas of Aristotle's general philosophical thought. In the book before you we present some of the most interesting recent work in this vein, in hopes of stimulating yet wider and deeper attention to this still largely untapped core of Aristotelian writing.

Though the book is addressed primarily to students of Aristotle's philosophy, its extensive attention to the whole of the biology, in matters both of detail and of general purpose and direction, should make it of interest to historians and philosophers of biology as well. We hope this is so, as we think that additional attention from these quarters to Aristotelian biology, and its relations to Aristotelian philosophy, would be beneficial both for Aristotelian studies and for the history and philosophy of biology. As in most other areas, there is much in Aristotle here that remains alive, even vital, for contemporary study. But the focus of this volume is, as we say, on the lessons of Aristotle's biology for our understanding of his philosophy.

There are sixteen essays in this collection, by eleven authors. Of the sixteen, ten appear here for the first time. Three more combine previously published essays with substantial new material, and a fourth is a thorough revision of an earlier study. Of the remaining two, one integrates two previously published essays in a fresh way, so that only one piece is a straightforward reprint of an earlier publication. And all of the material reprinted is itself quite recent, only three of the pieces having appeared in their original form before 1980.

This collection has a long history, and its editors have received assistance from several quarters, to which, and to whom, we would like to express our gratitude. Among institutions, the Center for Hellenic Studies, Washington, D.C., has a special, if symbolic, place: Gotthelf was a junior fellow of the Center in 1979–80 when he first conceived the idea for a collection of essays on Aristotle's teleology from which the present book eventually grew; and much of the editorial work was completed during Lennox's tenure at the Center in 1983–4. Discussions with David Balme and Rob Bolton, after Lennox joined Gotthelf as co-editor in 1982, contributed to its structure. The primary influence here, though, was Jeremy Mynott, who wisely urged that we prune and shape our initial list, and expand our introductory material, in the direction of a work of much greater unity. We hope his influence shows.

Our contributors are to be thanked as well, both for their participation and for their unfailing cooperation, as is Tony Preus for his informed and sensitive translation of Pierre Pellegrin's original French. David Balme should be singled out here: his pioneering work over the last 25 years has been a stimulus and an inspiration to all who have explored these issues. The range of his work, and our sense of its importance, is evidenced by the appearance in this volume of four pieces by him, one in each of its Parts.

Much of the work collected here shows the effect of lively and valuable discussions at two recent conferences, and we would like to thank all those who participated in these discussions, as well as those who made the meetings possible. Williamstown, Massachusetts, saw the first of these, eponymous with the present collection, during ten exciting days in summer 1983. Organized by David Balme and Allan Gotthelf, and directed by Gotthelf, the conference was sponsored by the Council for Philosophical Studies, and funded by the Research Division of the National Endowment for the Humanities (RD-20351). To Alan Mabe, Executive Secretary of the Council, working at a distance, goes credit for keeping the Williamstown wheels oiled, with his imaginative and tireless work. The 'Cambridge/Trenton Conference on Aristotle's Philosophy of Biology', organized by Geoffrey Lloyd and Allan Gotthelf, and funded by Trenton State College and Cambridge University's Faculty of Classics, ran for three days at King's College, Cambridge in June 1985; a special thanks to Tony DiGiorgio, Vice-President for Academic Affairs, Trenton State, for his support. Each of the contributors to this book attended at least one of the conferences, and four, including the editors, were at both; more than half of the essays received preliminary airing at one or the other of these very rewarding meetings.

Our editorial endeavors, as well as work on our own essays, have been supported in various ways from various sources. In addition to the Center for Hellenic Studies already mentioned, Gotthelf is especially grateful to Trenton State, and Clare Hall, Cambridge (where much editorial work was done in 1984 and 1985), and Lennox to the University of Pittsburgh. The support of friends and family has been invaluable, and Pat and Cressie, Aristotelians both, deserve a very special thanks. We are most grateful to Mathesis Publications for their kind permission to reprint several recently published items. In the final stages of editorial work, David Charles and Joan Kung have provided some very useful advice, and our editor, Pauline Hire, and subeditor, Susan Moore, have both been especially helpful and patient.

Though the first-named editor has kept the guiding hand, what you have before you is a fully collaborative endeavor, and we both take responsibility for the whole of the final result.

Allan Gotthelf
Cambridge, England

James G. Lennox
Pittsburgh, Pennsylvania

June 1986

Introduction

And just as Heraclitus is said to have spoken to the visitors, who were wanting to meet him but stopped as they were approaching when they saw him warming himself at the oven – he kept telling them to come in and not worry, 'for there are gods here too' – so we should approach the inquiry about each animal without aversion, knowing that in all of them there is something natural and beautiful.

(*PA* 1. 645a17–23)

In his famous exhortation to biological study in the last chapter of *Parts of Animals* 1, Aristotle offers his students several reasons for pursuing the study of plants and animals.

While the study of the heavens has the superior objects, he begins, the information about living things is 'better and more plentiful', and *their* study thus 'take[s] the advantage in knowledge (*epistēmē*)' (645a1–2).

This study is also, Aristotle continues, a source of 'wonder' and 'immeasurable pleasures', since 'the non-random, the *for-something's-sake*, is present in the works of nature most of all, and the end for which they have been composed or have come to be occupies the place of the beautiful' (a9, 17, 23–6). The *epistēmē* that this study of living things offers is an understanding of *final causes*, and the pervasiveness, and perspicuousness, of the final cause among plants and (especially) animals is another source of the biology's value.

Finally,

Just as in any discussion of parts or equipment we must not think that it is the matter (*hulē*) to which attention is being directed or which is the object of the discussion, but rather the conformation as a whole (*hē holē morphē*) (a house, for example, rather than bricks, mortar, and timber), in the same way we must think that a discussion of nature is about the composition (*sunthesis*) and the being as a whole (*hē holē ousia*), and not about parts that can never occur in separation from the being (*ousia*) they belong to. (a30–6)

The study of living things is thus of value because of the more extensive *epistēmē* it provides, the final causes it exhibits, and the fact

I

that it deals not just with matter and organic parts, but with the unity of matter and form in whole substances.

If these are the features and preoccupations of Aristotle's biological writings, might not important light be shed on these features and preoccupations by a close examination of those writings? Might not a close look at the biology's 'more extensive' *epistēmē* teach us something about the character of *epistēmē* itself, and the demonstrations and definitions in which it is expressed? Might not an examination of the pervasive use of the final cause in the biological treatises shed light on Aristotle's *notion* of a final cause, and show us precisely how its operation in nature is interwoven with the operation of material necessity? And might we not, from his attention to the unity of form and matter in whole substances, learn something about his view of the nature of that unity, and of the nature of substance itself?

Such has been the view of a number of scholars who have been exploring the biological works of late, and such is the theme of this book.

Much of the most exciting recent work on Aristotle's biology and its philosophical significance has concentrated precisely on these three sets of issues which Aristotle singles out for us in *PA* 1.5 – definition, demonstration, and the nature of science; teleology and necessity; and such metaphysical themes as substance, and the unity of matter and form. It seems fitting, then, for this collection to divide into four Parts:

I.   Biology and philosophy: an overview
II. Definition and demonstration: theory and practice
III. Teleology and necessity in nature
IV. Metaphysical themes.

The introduction to each Part places its essays in relation to each other and to the wider issues of their Part, and where appropriate ties them to the essays and issues of other Parts. Aristotelian scholars are too well aware of the way work on one issue leads inexorably out to others. This is particularly the case with the issues of this book, and cross-references are thus frequent throughout.

The essays in Part I, by three scholars who have spent many years with Aristotle's biology, were commissioned or selected especially for their introductory and, we hope, motivational value. They help us to understand the nature, content, and simultaneously theoretical and empirical character, of these treatises, and identify reasons why their study might be expected to yield philosophical fruit.

For centuries, as Jonathan Barnes recently remarked, 'learned Aristotelians sought and found the influence of the *Posterior Analytics* on the scientific [treatises]' (Barnes 1981 : 58). More recently, the tide has been towards denying that connection, but the contributions to Part II (and M. Pellegrin's in Part IV), challenge us to return to the tradition, and bring to bear on the controversy a rich acquaintance with the biological treatises in particular. It is not that the *Posterior Analytics* itself must have shaped biological practice: David Balme's discussion of chronology in Part I leaves the direction of influence quite open. Their claim is rather that elements of the theory expounded in the *Analytics* are at work in the biology, and that close study of one can be expected to illuminate the other.

That the biology might help in our understanding of Aristotle's views on teleology and necessity in nature is no surprise, and the results of such use are already in the mainstream of scholarly work on this topic. We reprint two of the most influential studies that have made important use of the biology (both modified in different ways for this volume), and print one new study also in this vein. These studies point back, to the theory of science discussed in Part II, and forward, to some of the 'Metaphysical themes' of Part IV.

Our resignation to that very general title for Part IV is perhaps testimony to the range of topics and texts that its contributions deal with. What unites these essays is their use of specifically biological texts at key points in their arguments. Overall, they show the biology making rich use of Aristotle's metaphysical terminology in its rich technical senses, and together, we think, argue for a unity of philosophical spirit between the metaphysics and the biology.

The theme of this collection, then, is the value of Aristotle's biology for the study of his philosophy, and readers will forgive us, we hope, if mention of it appears once too often. This is the perhaps inevitable consequence of our enthusiasm for this theme, and of the character of a collection of essays, with self-contained introductions to each of its Parts.

There has been no attempt to give a full cross-section of the work in this area, or to represent all points of view. We have decided instead to select essays whose central themes and arguments we, the editors, have found most convincing and illuminating, to make the best case for our larger theme that we think can at present be made. The selection is our responsibility alone, as are the claims of the introductions that appear in the book; beyond general sympathy with our overall theme, the individual authors should not be taken as necessarily in agreement with either, and their views should be inferred only from their own contributions.

The essays break new ground, and are aimed as much at stimulating further work in this vein as at establishing specific interpretative conclusions. If readers should find themselves turning to the biology to dispute the conclusions of these essays, and thereby arguing, even successfully, against these conclusions, that would give us and, we are sure, our contributors as well, nothing but pleasure. For we think the biological works deserve a central place in every Aristotelian scholar's arsenal, and that Aristotelian studies will be the better for their coming to have that place.

PART I

BIOLOGY AND PHILOSOPHY:
AN OVERVIEW

... For even in the study of animals unattractive to the senses, the nature that fashioned them offers immeasurable pleasures in the same way to those who can learn the causes and are naturally lovers of wisdom (*philosophoi*).

(PA I. 645a7–10)

Introduction

The biological writings constitute over 25% of the surviving Aristotelian corpus. There are, first of all, the 'big three': *Parts of Animals*, *Generation of Animals*, *History of Animals* (usually referred to here by its Latin name, *Historia Animalium*). These comprise, respectively, some 58, 74, and 146 Bekker pages.

Then there are the smaller works, really monographs or even papers: *Progression of Animals* (*De Incessu Animalium*), 10 pages; *Motion of Animals* (*De Motu Animalium*), 7 pages; and the essays collected as *Parva Naturalia*, the 'little nature studies', of which the last two are especially 'biological': *On Length and Shortness of Life*, 3 pages; *On Youth and Old Age, Life and Death, and Respiration*, 13 pages. (*Resp.* is sometimes treated as a separate work.) Other essays in *PN* have a clearly biological element, especially *On Sleep and Waking*, though scholars have tended to treat them only as 'psychology', placing them rather with the *De Anima* than with the biology. *De Anima* itself is something of a bridge between the biology and the more familiar treatises such as the *Metaphysics* and the *Ethics*, and though it certainly belongs with the latter so far as amount of study received is concerned, it was at some point probably intended to provide a theoretical framework for the biological studies.

But 'biological' is *our* label: Aristotle has no such term, and speaks rather of the general study of nature (*phusikē*), and within that, of the study of plants, or of animals, or of the capacities of soul. Nor must we assume that we can straightforwardly map these studies as

5

Aristotle conceived them onto *portions* of our own general biology, or botany, or zoology (or embryology, or comparative anatomy, etc.) – or even assume that they are science *rather than* philosophy (or philosophy *rather than* science). We need instead to approach them fresh, on their own terms, to come to see what their aims are, and their methods, and their contents, and what their relation is to (and how they might be of use in the understanding of) Aristotelian philosophy itself. The three essays in Part I deal with these and related questions.

In his provocatively titled 'The place of biology in Aristotle's philosophy' David Balme asks us to reconsider the aims of these treatises: they are not just primitive counterparts to our own biology, they grapple with philosophical issues, make contributions to the resolution of these issues, are in a sense philosophical treatises themselves. This is an exciting if controversial thesis, made more exciting by an argument which dates the work they embody, or much of it, to Aristotle's time in the Academy. For, the evidence of the place-names which assigns the biology to Aristotle's middle period applies primarily to *HA*, and Balme argues that *HA* is the latest, not the earliest, of the three major treatises. He summarizes the argument for this, which is to be presented at greater length in the introduction and appendices to his forthcoming edition of *HA*, and then offers a picture of how the likely progression, *PA* II–IV, *PA* I, *GA*, *HA* might evidence certain developments in Aristotle's metaphysical thinking. In the course of this discussion, Balme introduces some of the themes of his interpretation of the *Metaphysics* developed in his contribution to Part IV, including his understanding of individual form in Aristotle.

Montgomery Furth, too, has turned to the biology for help in understanding Aristotle's *Metaphysics*. We excerpt from his forthcoming book-length study of Aristotle's theory of material substance a discussion aimed at motivating his strategy, and outlining those features of Aristotle's biological world view salient to his metaphysical enterprise. If 'the actual Aristotelian substances are pre-eminently the biological objects, living things' one might expect his biological studies to reveal those features most characteristic of substances, 'as they are to be found in the real world: the manner of their construction, how they come into existence, their modes of self-sustenance, how they relate to the remainder of the world surrounding them, what is specifically meant by a substance's decline and eventual ceasing-to-be, *et cetera*'. This is the more so, Furth suggests, if his hypothesis is right that the metaphysics of substance itself 'was

to a great extent motivated...as a deep theoretical foundation...
for the biological sciences'.

It therefore becomes important to understand what Aristotle was
up to in the complicated enterprise which is his biology, and Furth
spends some time giving us an overview of 'Aristotle's biological
universe'. The context is set, Furth explains, by the presence of highly
organized, sharply demarcated biological *units*, countable 'thisses',
against a background of non-structural basic matter obeying a *mass*
logic. Furth goes on to identify seven fundamental facts about these
objects which biological theory has to explain, and identifies
Aristotle's notion of biological form as the fundamental innovation
designed to do just that. He then traces the successive levels of
increasing organization and complexity from the elements or elementary powers, through inorganic compounds to uniform parts of
animals, and then gradually – through an important if little noticed
intermediate stage – to non-uniform parts and then whole organisms. Furth's close look at the biological facts, as Aristotle understood
them, generates important morals for our understanding of the
conceptions of matter and form which are at work in the *Metaphysics*,
morals difficult to extract from the latter treatise alone, yet crucial
to its understanding.

Though it will be of interest to contrast Furth's insistence that
Aristotelian form is primarily *specific* with Balme's that it is individual,
we offer this excerpt rather as an introduction to (some aspects of)
the biological theory from which our contributors attempt to draw
their various philosophical morals, as well as for Furth's own very
valuable moral-drawing. His stress on the way the limitations of the
matter theory generate Aristotle's distinctive concept of biological
form, helps to illuminate one central thrust of the interpretations of
Aristotelian teleology argued in the contributions to Part III. And the
discussions of the unity of form and matter in several essays in Part
IV are likewise illuminated by his explanation of the way biological
form puts rigid constraints on biological matter.

(To facilitate reference between this excerpt and its appearance
in Furth's book, we use the same part and section numbers to be used
in the book, and preserve the cross-references.)

If Balme and Furth are right in finding the biology so rich in
philosophical content, we are entitled to ask if it is after all empirical
science, and if so, what precisely its relationship as such is to
Aristotle's 'theoretical interests and preoccupations'. Geoffrey Lloyd
discusses just this question in the excerpt we present from his
important study of the development of science in Ancient Greece,

Magic, Reason, and Experience (Cambridge 1979). Lloyd's book surveys
the interplay between empirical research, dialectic and demonstration in the development of Greek science, and places Aristotle's work
in biology (as well as in other areas) in the context of that
development. Lloyd shows that Aristotle's biological treatises *are* the
result of empirical research, that in fact they embody 'the first
generalized program of inquiry into natural science'. These researches,
Lloyd argues, with a rich range of examples, are 'guided throughout'
by Aristotle's theoretical commitments. On occasion these commitments even shape 'what he reports he has seen'. But, Lloyd observes,
'there are other occasions when the theories themselves appear to
depend on, and may in some cases even be derived from, one or more
observations'.

Lloyd's work points to the biological treatises as rich sources for
reflection on the *nature*, as well as the history, of science, and invites us
to join him in attempting to articulate the principles of Aristotle's
research program. It also invites further questions about the relationship between research into causes and the exposition of its results,
and thereby about the connections between the practice in the
biological treatises and the theory of science expounded in the
Analytics and elsewhere, issues treated in contributions to Part II
below. But, quite apart from that, Lloyd's discussion joins those of
Balme and Furth in giving us a valuable picture of the nature and
content of Aristotle's biological studies and of their various relationships to his philosophical thought.

The place of biology in Aristotle's philosophy

D. M. BALME

The first difficulty in reading Aristotle's biological treatises, as often in reading Aristotle, may well be to decide exactly what their purpose is. They are so factual and so comprehensive that it is easy to mistake them for descriptive information, an animal encyclopaedia, as the ancients regarded them. Modern readers have tried to assimilate them to present-day categories, classifying the *HA* as natural history, the *PA* as comparative anatomy, the *PN* as physiology, the *GA* as embryology. But this assimilation does not fit. One can test it by looking for the facts about any given animal in *HA*. Without an index (which ancient readers did not have) the facts can only be found by reading through the whole treatise, for they are distributed all over it; and when found they may seem strangely inadequate. A striking example is the blind mole-rat, *aspalax*, which Aristotle quotes in the *De Anima* as an interesting case.[1] He twice describes a dissection of its concealed eyes.[2] But the only other fact that he reports is that it is viviparous – not what kind of animal it is, how many legs, what its coat or feet or tail are like, how it lives, nothing. His aim is clearly not to give a natural history of the mole, but to show how it differs from other animals: it is his only case of sightlessness combined with viviparousness.

The other treatises will equally fail the corresponding tests. The *PA* is not primarily comparative. When it discusses the difference between long-legged and short-legged birds, its interest is not anatomical – not in how the legs compare or how they work – but in what they are for, and why some birds have longer legs, some animals more stomachs.[3] *PA* II–IV surveys each tissue and organ, explaining the function that each serves and the necessary interactions of the air, earth, fire and water out of which they are formed. Book I, which is an introduction to biology, first discusses teleology – arguing that necessary interactions alone cannot produce animal

---

[1] III. 425a11.   [2] *HA* I. 49:b28, IV. 533a3.
[3] Birds' legs: IV. 694b12, cf. 692b20; animals' stomachs: III. 674a22.

parts unless final causation is also present – and then discusses the proper way to define animals by genus and differentia. The *PA* therefore is primarily concerned with some large problems that are still of interest: how is teleology to be reconciled with material-efficient causation, is the final cause really an objective factor or is it only a heuristic device of the biologist? If we pigeon-hole the treatise as comparative anatomy, about which we know infinitely more than Aristotle, we run the risk of putting him down and closing our eyes to the possibility that he might have something interesting to say on the philosophical level where he is not less competent than us, to put it mildly.

Those of the *PN* that are biological do raise physiological quest-ions, it is true. But again if we test them, something more interesting than archaic physiology emerges as their real subject. In Aristotle's physiology, as one finds it throughout the biological works, the most important elements are the blood and the by-products of nutrition (*perittōmata*); out of these, by various processes of which the chief is concoction (*pepsis*), the tissues develop with their different charac-teristics. But the *PN*, while using these elements and processes, are not a discussion of them but of the vital heat: how it is moderated and preserved by breathing or other means. In other treatises Aristotle declares that vital heat is the critical index of the differences between higher and lower animals.[4] The *PN* are special studies, therefore, subsidiary to the great question of how animals differ, indeed why they differ. If their function, as both we and Aristotle think, is to eat, survive and reproduce, why can they not all do it in the same way? To this simple-minded question we have not yet a satisfactory answer, either on the empirical level or on the philosophical. Aristotle has much to say about it. The *PN* form an explanatory footnote or appendix to a major problem that is still with us.

In *GA* Aristotle considers how a parent's form is transmitted to its offspring, and how accidental characteristics are produced. This is perhaps the most exciting of this group of treatises, because its argumentative quality is more intense and sustained, and it tackles a problem that is not discussed in the *PA*, namely how does teleology actually work, by what physical means is a final cause imposed upon the material. Aristotle's explanation is that form is conveyed into the embryo from the male parent as a complex of movements which continue to control the embryo's development. The male contributes only these formative movements, nothing somatic. By this explana-tion Aristotle not only translates form and finality into physical

[4] E.g. *PA* iii. 668b34, iv. 686b28; *GA* ii. 732b27.

terms, but he makes the parent's form to be its own individual form and not the form of its species. He takes a clear position on the problem over which he agonizes in *Metaph.* Z, how can the subsistent individual animal – the Socrates – be formally definable when it contains matter.[5]

The same position is detectable in *HA.* Its intention is stated near the beginning: to grasp the differentiae that properly belong to animals, together with their accidental characteristics.[6] It is not an investigation of animals as animals, but of the means by which one may distinguish and define them. The differentiae that it examines occur at every taxonomic level down to sub-specific races and odd individuals.[7] In this latter respect it resembles *GA* v, which explains inessential accidents (like grey hair) that are due only to material interactions and not to final causes, and vary with individuals and not necessarily with species. The *HA* therefore is the way into the defining of *this* visible animal.

This last question evidently concerned Aristotle in his logic and metaphysics more acutely than the others that I have mentioned, like teleology (in which our problems do not seem to have troubled him). But teleology nevertheless is the primary subject of *PA*, and the other treatises likewise have primarily theoretical purposes. They are not just empirical studies in which some philosophical concepts are put to use. We go less far wrong if we regard them as studies of these concepts made through empirical data.

This suggests the possibility that we might gain light upon these concepts – such as substance, form, species, essence, *logos* – by examining their reference in biology, together with the arguments around them. Judging from Aristotle's own discussions, it would seem that form, *eidos*, and its relation to the individual, was a crucial problem for him; it produces the paradoxes of *Metaph.* Z, the apparent conflict between the *Metaphysics* and the *Categories*, and a possible tension in Aristotle's philosophy which many people have commented on. If it is true, as I for one accept, that Aristotle intended his answer to the puzzle of *Metaph.* Z to be found in H.6, – namely that at any given moment an object's form and matter are one, so that definition of the individual is logically possible even though it changes from moment to moment – then this could be a theory that biology might illustrate, since its business is to analyze and account for the visible animal. In this case, is there any sign of a reciprocal influence

---

[5] See below 18, and ch. 11, 292, 305. For references to the *GA* theory of reproduction see ch. 11, nn. 2–14.

[6] *HA* I. 491a9.   [7] *HA* v. 556a14; VIII. 605b22f.; IX. 617b28, 632b14.

between Aristotle's metaphysical discussion and his biology? One
thing can be said immediately, that *PA* examines animals in classes,
while *GA* examines them as individuals. Does this reflect a movement
from class to individual in Aristotle's ontology? Does the biology
suggest any movement in other concepts?

Before we can show any such movement, and in particular before
we can speak of an interaction between the metaphysical and
biological treatises, it is vital to have a plausible chronology for
them. Too many ambitious schemes aimed at mapping Aristotle's
development have come to nothing because they were forcing
chronology to match an imaginary intellectual progress: one need
only mention Jaeger, or Nuyens. This trap must be avoided. But the
dating of the treatises is uncertain because of their present state, for
since they were written they have twice undergone major rearrangement. The first apparently happened when they were made
into teaching courses at the Lyceum in the last phase of Aristotle's
career. The biological treatises betray this more clearly than most,
for they form a homogeneous group in which frequent references to
each other indicate the order in which they are meant to be studied.
Some of these references are reciprocal, showing that at least one of
a pair was inserted after the work was written. Nearly all can be
removed without upsetting the syntax of the sentence in which they
occur; not one contributes anything needed by the context, either
as data or as argument. It is quite possible therefore that they are
all additions to the original text, and the most likely time of their
insertion would be when the lecture courses were set up. If this is so,
they are not evidence for the order of composition, but only for the
order of teaching.

The second rearrangement was the editing by Andronicus two
centuries after Aristotle's death. We are told in a famous story
originating from Strabo, which I have not yet found sufficient reason
to disbelieve, that Andronicus was given charge of the newly
rediscovered manuscripts, edited them, and 'arranged them by
subjects' – an alarming expression. There is little doubt that his
recension was the archetype of the manuscripts that we now have.

So Aristotle's original version has been, as Düring used to say,
'churned like butter', and any evidence that it may have contained
about order of composition has probably been obliterated. However,
there is a little that can be said, and it may be just enough to support
a hypothesis sufficient for our present purpose. We know that after
Aristotle left the Academy at Plato's death in 347, he went now aged
40 for a year or two to Assos on the Ionian Asia Minor coast, and

then for two more years across to Lesbos where Theophrastus lived. D'Arcy Thompson, in the preface to his Oxford translation of the *HA*, pointed out how many references there are to the lagoon of Pyrrha (now Kalloni). Lee followed this up in 1948 with a more thorough analysis of place-names, and concluded that not all, but a considerable part, of Aristotle's biology was probably indebted to information obtained in that area.[8] Ross and Guthrie, and probably most scholars, accepted this dating, which is of course one more death-blow to Jaeger's theory that Aristotle did all his so-called empirical studies in the Lyceum after completing his philosophical work.

Now the place-name evidence applies more strongly to the *HA* than to the other treatises; in fact in the others these references are so few that they can be attributed to common information, for Ionia and the islands were in close touch with Athens. But there is something else too that can be said about the *HA*. There is considerable internal evidence suggesting that it may have been written after the others, but written by Aristotle and not by Theophrastus or anybody else. It has usually been taken for granted that the *HA* came earlier, because in it Aristotle says that it is to contain the investigation of facts which must precede the investigation of causes, and this procedure agrees with what he says in the *APo.* and *PA* I.[9] But this statement comes in the introduction to *HA* and clearly refers to the order of lecturing. Naturally one also expects Aristotle to collect facts before working out a theory, but they do not have to be these facts; for the other treatises, which are concerned with the causal explanations, themselves contain all the facts that they need. Their data appear also in *HA* together with many more. When the two sets of data are compared, there are two very interesting results. First, the passages in *HA* which report the same facts as the other treatises are often much briefer than the corresponding passages, sometimes so brief that they cannot be easily understood unless one consults the corresponding passage; they strongly suggest that they are extracts from the others, or summaries of them. Secondly, among the data that *HA* alone reports, there are many that conflict with the explanations given in the other treatises, and ought to have modified them if they were known at the time.[10]

There is a very large quantity of these comparable passages, which means that any general conclusions that can be drawn from them

[8] Lee 1948; see also his 1985.   [9] *HA* I. 491a11.

[10] In what follows I summarize evidence presented in greater detail in a forthcoming edition of *HA*.

must constitute weighty evidence; one is not relying on odd lines or even paragraphs, which could so easily have been interpolated into a work such as *HA*, but on quantities of the following order – about 40% of Book I, as measured by counting Bekker lines, of which one-third has the appearance of being summarized from the accounts given elsewhere; in Book II 44%, of which nearly half appears to consist of summaries; in III and IV about 35%, of which one-third appears to be summarized or extracted. In later books the percentages drop away as would be expected, for they no longer discuss parts but animal activities which are less the concern of other treatises. Here are a few examples of comparison.

HA I. 490a26. Aristotle says that all animals move themselves at four or more points or fulcra, the sanguineous at four only, the bloodless at more, and gives as examples man, birds, quadrupeds, fishes, without further specification. Now *IA* has a long discussion of this question, saying first (at 707a18, b5) that the sanguineous are moved at either two or four points, but eventually (709b22) deciding that they all use four, while the bloodless all use more than four. *PA* IV says (693b5) that the sanguineous use four points. Both *PA* and *IA* quote as examples man, birds, quadrupeds, fishes, specifically describing the movements of muraina, water snake, land snake, eel, kestreus, flatfish. The *HA* account therefore gives only the general conclusion, occupying nine lines, while the *IA* discussion occupies 40 and the *PA* discussion 25. Moreover the specific data quoted in *IA* and *PA* are not quoted in *HA* (except for one cryptic remark elsewhere, 489b28, that the muraina uses the sea as snakes use the land, a remark that also occurs in *IA* and *PA* during the discussion; but in *HA* it occurs irrelevantly in a comparison of the numbers of fins).

I. 492b8. 'Breathing takes place as far as the chest; it cannot be done by the nostrils alone, because it comes from the chest past the uvula and not out of the head; it is possible to live without even using the head.' This too is cryptic. But there is a fuller and more intelligible version at *Resp.* 473a19; 'Breathing is both through the windpipe out of the chest and through the nostrils, but one cannot breathe by the nostrils themselves without the windpipe. Animals prevented from breathing through the nostrils do not suffer, but if prevented by the windpipe they die... For breathing is not a property of the nostrils but goes along the passage beside the uvula, where the roof of the mouth ends, some of the breath going this way through the nostril apertures and some through the mouth, both going in and going out.' This account in *Resp.* is not adding a causal explanation to data taken from *HA*; it is itself the full account of the data which *HA* merely summarizes in a manner that is barely adequate unless supplemented by the *Resp.* account.

II. 498a3. Aristotle compares the ways animals bend their legs, again appearing to summarize a much longer account in *IA* (chs. 12-16). For instance he says here 'the viviparous quadrupeds bend the front legs frontwards and the back legs backwards, and have the concavities of the circumference mutually opposed'. Not many would understand this without consulting *IA*, which explains it fully with a diagram (712a1).

Many of the common passages are so close as to be doublets, in which one cannot tell which of the two came first. But if the fact that over a third of these passages are apparently summarized in *HA* allows us to infer that the others also originated in the other treatises, then a very large proportion of the early books of *HA* would have to be later than those treatises. It suggests that when Aristotle set about collecting the data for *HA* he began by extracting everything relevant from his previous work, and then went on to add new information. This is where the second significant point becomes evident: the data that are not paralleled in the other treatises include a good many that conflict with those treatises. For example, the passage just quoted (I. 490a26) about animals' movement goes on to add a report of a four-footed insect, also reported in v (552b20), which defeats the theory of both *IA* and *PA* that all bloodless animals must have more than four feet. Both I. 487b9 and v. 548b10, 549a8 give evidence that the sponge has sensation, which qualifies it to be an animal, whereas *PA* IV. 681a17 with its doublet at *HA* VIII. 588b20 calls it 'completely plantlike'. I and VI report a kind of half-ass that is fertile (491a2, 577b23, 580b1), an exception to the sterility of mules which is taken as universal in *GA* and used for an important argument there (*GA* II. 747a25). Another argument in *GA* presumes that birds have no external genitalia; but *HA* III and v report them (*GA* I. 717b16; HA III. 509b30, v. 541a2). There are many more such data which should have modified the conclusions stated in the other treatises.[11]

HA also reports diagnostic features which are not noticed in the other works, such as the occurrence of the crest in some birds,

---

[11] E.g. animals that naturally swim backwards (*HA* I. 489b35, 490a3, IV. 524a13; cf. *IA* 706b30); cephalopods have a brain (I. 494b27, IV. 524b4; cf. *PA* II. 652b23, IV. 686a6); chameleon's brain connected with its eyes (II. 503b18; cf. *PA* II. 652b3); oviparous selachians beside the fishing-frog (VI. 565a22-8; cf. *GA* III. 754a25); and many others.

'hair-like' structures in marine animals (probably the gills), and many others that one would think required causal explanation.[12] On the other hand the other treatises contain nothing more that ought to be in a collection of differentiae but yet is not in *HA*.

In general the *HA* knows a great deal more, for example about the brain and the vessels leading to it.[13] Of the 560 animal species reported in Aristotle altogether, 390 are mentioned only in *HA*. While the other treatises do not really show more knowledge than could be expected of the ordinary citizen, *HA* includes specialist information from stock farmers, bee-keepers, eel-breeders, bird-fanciers, and many others. It shows a big advance both in the effort of collecting data and in sophistication of handling them, for example in distinguishing significant features in marine animals, upon which it is far better informed.

I have found no evidence however, that fundamental theory is different in *HA*. Some critics have suggested that it supports views on teleology, on the ladder of nature, on reproduction, on the physiology of *pneuma*, that conflict with *PA* and *GA*. Such conflicts, if they existed, would be more far-reaching than the minor corrections that I have been quoting. In the past I had thought they were evidence of non-Aristotelian authorship. But a more careful examination has satisfied me, at any rate, that on these fundamental matters *HA* agrees with the others. Obviously no one can be sure that the *HA* is free of interpolations; but there is no good evidence of spuriousness on a large scale. Moreover the plan of the whole work is too coherent to permit the insertion of complete new sections, as Joachim and Dittmeyer suggested of IX and large parts of II and VIII. Their suggestion that Theophrastus was the author is prima facie implausible because of the difference in style between these books and the *HP* and *CP*. VII has been rejected as a compilation made partly from *GA* and partly from Hippocratic treatises. The debt to the *GA* is obvious enough, accounting for 40%; but the debt to Hippocratics is simply not there: on the contrary it makes statements that conflict with Hippocratic views. As for the suggestion that *HA* originally consisted of Books I-VI, or even only Books I-III$\frac{1}{2}$, no evidence of this has ever been put forward to my knowledge, and yet one sees it quoted by respectable scholars. Much of this criticism arose in the nineteenth and early twentieth centuries from armchair naturalists

---

[12] Crests: I. 486b13, II. 504b9, IX. 617b20; 'hair-like' structures: IV. 524b21, 529a32, b30. Others include: certain 'dark' structures (*ta melana*): IV. 529a22, 530a34, b13, 31 (cf. *PA* IV. 680a14); stone-like structures (*chalazae*): VI. 560a28; differences in nipples or dugs (*thelai*): II. 499a18, 500a17, 25, 30, 502a34, 504b23, VI. 578b31.

[13] E.g. I. 494b29, III. 519b2; cf. *PA* 652b30.

who disbelieved Aristotle's reports and thought them too silly for a great philosopher – the same kind of criticism that Athenaeus made in a famous passage which time has proved to be wholly misconceived.[14] Aubert and Wimmer's edition of 1868 and Ditt-meyer's of 1907 are the high points of such criticism. The modern camera has taught us better. I confess that I was still blaming Aristotle for swallowing the story about buffaloes projecting their dung at enemies, until in 1983 I saw a picture on television of hippopotamuses doing just that.

What one can admit to the critics is that *HA* remained unfinished and untidy at Aristotle's death, and he had evidently been treating it as a filing cabinet to store new information whenever it came in: this can account for some of the isolated complete descriptions, as of the ape and chameleon in II.

All the hard evidence that we have then, such as it is, makes it a plausible hypothesis that *HA* was written by Aristotle during and following his stay on Lesbos, and after writing the other biological treatises. This gives us far more room for manoeuvre than if we have to place *HA* first. For not only is *HA* the heavyweight which would have taken Aristotle a good few years to collect, but if the Lesbos evidence correctly puts it into the middle period, then the other biological treatises would have to be later still and so could hardly coincide with the development of his metaphysics; for I doubt if anybody now accepts Jaeger's thesis that Aristotle was a Platonist for twenty years until he left the Academy.

So far as the other biological treatises are concerned, the evidence can only be impressionistic. *PA* II-IV recalls Plato's *Timaeus*, both in the dual causation by the good and the necessary, and in its view of the scala naturae with its associated value judgments. *IA*, which is a special study of locomotion, more detailed than *PA* but agreeing with it, gives even more emphasis to value judgments: man is not just more advanced, but better; right is better than left. *PA* I is like *Ph.* II in its analysis of finality and hypothetical necessity, while its analysis of logical division agrees with *Metaph.* Z.12 and goes a little further. *GA* is generally felt to be more mature and to come after *PA*; while I share this feeling, I must say that I can put up no objective evidence for it. The *PN* are special studies like *IA* but now surely more mature, probably belonging with *GA*. So a defensible order of writing could be (1) *IA* and *PA* II-IV early in the Academy; (2) *PA* I in the

---

[14] 'From what Proteus or Nereus rising from the deep did Aristotle learn what fishes do or how they go to bed or spend the day? For those are the sort of things he wrote about, for fools to marvel at...' (VIII. 352d).

area of *Ph.* ii and *Metaph.* Z.12; (3) *PN* and then *GA*, still in the Academy; (4) *HA* begun perhaps in the Academy but mostly written later, Aristotle now being aged in the 40s.

At any rate there is no chronological obstacle to considering whether there is reciprocal influence between the biological and the metaphysical treatises, for instance in the reference of the big problematic concepts like substance and so forth. Other studies in this volume explore these possibilities, and so I will not say more now about them except for the one case I have already touched on: individual form in *GA*.

Aristotle argues that the male contribution to the fetus is form and movement only, nothing somatic.[15] It starts movements in the fetal matter which are evidently simple at first but then develop in complexity, controlling the diversification of the embryo. These movements are the embryo's soul, located at first in the heart when that is the only part so far produced, but then located in all parts as their entelechy. To show how this might be possible, Aristotle uses the model of automata – not puppets as some commentators have thought, in fact anything but puppets: on the contrary these are automatic toys which work independently without strings, developing a routine once they have been set going. They show three things: (i) that a movement can be continued after the mover has let go; (ii) that a movement can be actually simple but have potentially greater complexity latent within; (iii) that a complex of movements can control and direct itself. These movements have been transmitted from the male parent's blood via the *pneuma* in the semen; they are the movements of his blood in its final stage of concoction before becoming bodily parts. There is no further material influence working upon the movements between this moment and their particularization; therefore they are already individual, so that what is conveyed to the new foetus is a potentiality for this actual individual's form. Later in the treatise, when discussing the transmission of personal likenesses, Aristotle emphasizes that the individual male parent is the dominant formal influence: 'the generator is not merely male but such-and-such male, i.e. Coriscus or Socrates...What generates is both the individual and the kind (*genos*) but chiefly the individual; for that is the real being (*ousia*)' (iv. 767b24). In the same discussion he says that the likeness of the species is a consequential (768b13, *akolouthei*).

In this theory Aristotle seems to demonstrate that the solution of the *Metaph.* Z puzzle works in practice: one can formalize individual

---

[15] For references cf. above n. 5.

material states and accidents. Two small points need to be added. In his long discussion of likenesses in *GA* IV. 3 Aristotle does not use the word *eidos*. He speaks only of *genos, idion, kath' hekaston, kath' holou*, which are unambiguous here. He may have avoided *eidos* precisely because of its ambiguity of reference between class and individual. The other point is the reason given in *GA* II.1 for reproduction, namely the attempt to survive: since the animal cannot persist in number (i.e. as a subsistent individual) but can in form, it persists in the way possible for it; hence there is always its kind. This is sometimes quoted to show that species is eternal and that the individual acts for the sake of the species. But I myself do not find that here. Rather the individual is seeking to preserve its own form, and it can only do this by handing it on; that is why its kind persists.[16] This more simple and less ambitious interpretation agrees, I think, with the discussion at the end of *GC*. In *HA* the aim is evidently to collect and analyze differentiae so that animal forms can be defined, and such definition will be able to be individual. For some of the differentiae are variable accidents, such as the geographical variations in sheep, goats, cattle, and changes in birds' coloration and note, and many are sub-specific, like the occurrence of the divided abdomen in some cicadas. *HA* does not distinguish between *sumbebēkota kath' hauta* and *mē kath' hauta*. This does not imply that the distinction has been abandoned, but rather (i) that what is *kath' hauto* to one sort of animal may be *mē kath' hauto* to another; since the subject is the differentia and not the animal, the distinction becomes irrelevant; (ii) more important, whether essential or not, accidents of every kind can be formalized and explained, like the *pathēmata* in *GA* V. The introduction of *HA* links it with the discussion of division in *PA* I.2-4. There Aristotle concludes that *diairesis* can grasp the form if it is used not dichotomously as Plato used it but by applying all the relevant differentiae to the genus simultaneously; after that he explains the ways in which animal features should be compared so as to set up differentiae – by analogy as between kinds (*genē*), by the more-and-less as between the forms comprised within a kind (*eidē*). *HA* restates this and then proceeds to analyze general kinds of differentia, those of parts, activities, lives, characters; the whole treatise from books I through IX follows this analysis. The grasp (*lambanein*: *PA* I. 642b5) of the animal this permits, the obtaining of its genus together with all its differentiae, would not be classificatory (for it does not gain its meaning from its place in a classification), but ostensive – that is by correctly exhibiting the differentiae that belong to an

[16] Cf. ch. 10 below, and Balme 1972: 93–8.

animal. Clearly it cannot claim rigorous force. But it can claim the unity that was desiderated in *Metaph.* **Z**.12. Therefore when the differentiae have received their causal explanation, that explanation will have explained the whole animal as an instance of the way life is realized in nature; for the explanation by the four causes must be oriented towards the final causation of the animal in terms of *PA* 1.5, all parts being related teleologically and necessarily. The way would now be clear for a formal definition. In this way *HA* brings Aristotle's analysis to its fruition. None of his logical or metaphysical theory has collapsed, but he has solved a grave problem in it. For what has now collapsed is the paradox of *Metaph.* **Z**, of the snub nose, of the indefinable individual. It may be that, if this picture of Aristotle is right, we lose a clumsy natural historian and a confused encyclopedist; but we gain a greater philosopher of living nature.[17]

---

[17] On division, definition, and the role of *HA* see further ch. 4; on the metaphysical issues see ch. 11.

2

Aristotle's biological universe: an overview

MONTGOMERY FURTH

The following is taken from an extended work on Aristotle's theory of material substances that is forthcoming from Cambridge University Press. The course of developments leading up to the present extract is, briefly and roughly, as follows. Part I of the work (§§1–5) deals with the metaphysical theory of substance in the Categories, *which is a considerably simplified and scaled-down version of the complete theory as found in various other writings of Aristotle. The most considerable simplifications are (1) the total absence of the notion of matter (8a9–11 is of no theoretical significance), and (2) a certain lack of explicitness as to whether the* eidos *(in the* Categories, *usually Englished as 'species') of a substantial individual is something essential to that individual, so that anything describable as its ceasing to have or belong in that* eidos *is tantamount to that individual's ceasing to exist. The question then naturally arises why these features of the full theory, as usually interpreted, should be thus effaced in the* Categories *version, if, as seems to me highly probable, the* Categories *is an authentic and mature Aristotelian work; and some suggestions are hazarded along these lines.*

Part II (§§6–8) is a 'first approximation' of the complete theory of substance, necessarily somewhat attenuated and abstract in the absence of a rich intuitive conception of what a 'full' substance actually is – something that the Cat-egories *cannot possibly furnish. But the exercise is a useful one, particularly in fixing upon some of the features that carry over from the* Categories *version. Two of these should be mentioned here, albeit sketchily, for they come up at the beginning of the excerpt that follows. (i) In both the restricted and the full versions, a material substance is what Aristotle calls 'some this' (tode ti), which means (in one of its several significations) that a substance is a discrete and unitary entity in some way sharply marked out as one something, as 'individual and numerically one' (atomon kai hen arithmōi), 'the individual man', 'the individual horse' (thus 1b3–7). In the work, the term adopted for this phenomenon, a deliberate neologism, is the 'synchronic individuation' of substance; the term is meant to connote that at any given moment, the population of substances consists of such 'thisses'. (ii) In both the restricted and the full versions, a substantial individual F's being F is necessary or essential to it,*

21

in the sense that its coming-to-be is the coming to be of an F; its ceasing-to-be-F is its ceasing-to-be altogether; and its persistence as one and the same (to the extent that it does persist) is its persisting as one and the same F – whatever in detail that may consist in, or our criteria for its satisfaction may be. This phenomenon about substance is called its 'transtemporal' or 'diachronic individuation'. (I do not hesitate to put this interpretation on the restricted treatment in the Categories, *despite the lack of explicitness on the point mentioned earlier.)*

Part III opens with the sections that follow. The original section-numbering is retained.

THE ZOOLOGICAL UNIVERSE

9. *Methodological reorientation*

We have noted in §4* that in the *Categories*, the substantial individuals are (as it was put) 'methodologically opaque', so pro-digiously 'atomic' as to display no internal structure. And we saw (also in §4*) that the treatment of both the synchronic and the diachronic unity or 'oneness' of substantial individuals is unusually terse and obscure: synchronically, the explanation of the 'this'-hood of substance quickly gets into deep trouble. And diachronically, the requirement that a substantial individual have a permanent essential nature which it cannot 'migrate' out of while remaining the same and numerically one, is at most insinuated there by some not very luminous outgivings about 'definition', rather than made unmis-takably explicit. Subsequent to that, some few main features of substantial individuals according to the *Metaphysics* concept have been sketched out, in a rather schematic way; but we have not yet tried to see very deeply into their internal structure, to conceptualize with any vividness what 'substantial being' comes to. To get further, we must try to do this.

However, the best way to do this is not, I believe, to try to wring an intuitive understanding directly out of Aristotle's own positive outgivings on the topic, particularly those coming down to us as the *peri tēs ousias*, 'On Substance', i.e., *Metaphysics* ZHΘ. That is an abstruse and imperspicuous work, as is well-known in itself and well-attested-to by the notably uneven successes of the interpretive tradition, and this tends to discourage such a frontal approach; but besides, for an *intuitive* understanding there is a better way in, one that can for now circumvent some of the perplexities of the

---

* Asterisked references are to sections of the parent work not included in this volume. They
have been minimized as far as possible.

metaphysical writings, and that may later enable us, as it were, to come up beneath them under our own power.

It consists in following up the consequences of the hypothesis, first, that the actual Aristotelian substances are pre-eminently the biological objects, living things – which means, in practice, the higher animals, metazoans, the ones he could see. (Higher plants, metaphytans, are not excluded – to the contrary, much of what will be said here applies to them as well – but they do not seem to have been the focus of nearly the intense concern that the animals drew. Of course he had no inkling of microbial forms of any sort.) Thus, let us take seriously and in earnest the tender concerning Population, that 'plants and animals are substances *malista*, most of all' (Z.8, cf. §§7–8*), and look to his biological studies for both the common 'principles' and the distinguishing 'differences' most characteristic of substances, as they are to be found in the real world: the manner of their construction, how they come into existence, their modes of self-sustenance, how they relate to the remainder of the world surrounding them, what is specifically meant by a substance's decline and eventual ceasing-to-be, *et cetera*.

Second, in studying the nature of these 'beings' and endeavoring to analyze the 'causes' that are at work in bringing them about and endowing them with their immensely absorbing and unique characteristics, we are embarking (in Aristotle's tracks) on a highly ambitious enterprise of biological *theory*, in which a number of deep and difficult problems must be faced and resolved: theoretical problems, we shall see, that are not at all primitive, or naive, or superannuated, but that are in large part still unresolved today, and go to the very nature of life itself.

Third, these problems, and the theoretical framework that Aristotle devised to deal with them, raise in turn very important general issues of a foundational character – in fact, it is my belief that Aristotle the biologist asked himself a series of very profound questions about the animal kingdom, and at this point enters my thought, as was mentioned in §0*, that the metaphysics of substance was to a great extent motivated (and that hence 'The Metaphysics of Substance' should to a great extent be approached) as a deep theoretical foundation, a 'methodology' in Tarski's sense, for the biological sciences, much as the work of Frege and his successors was to stand to the 'deductive sciences' two millennia later.

The present work does not masquerade as a free-standing original dissertation on Aristotelian biology; nor can all the biological problems he contended with be discussed here, nor his attempted resolutions be definitively evaluated. But if this general perspective is at all sound, it suggests that only by grasping at least the basics of this complicated subject can we hope to acquire a good intuitive view of what he was up to. Or more positively, perhaps by tracing his ideas as to the manner in which the complex biological objects are constructed and what they are like, we may not only lay a firm grasp on the strands that form some of the snares of ontology, but even see to some of their unraveling.

So let us now use our imagination. We now must truly try to put our feet in Aristotle's tracks. Let us go all the way back to first principles, and consider from scratch.

(i) We are endeavoring to understand the fundamental character of the natural world at a time when its *micro structure* was quite unknown. The (perhaps better, *an*) atomic theory of matter has been stated, with luminous clarity and precision by Democritus, yet seems quite impossible to accept. Why? – all the way back to first principles: it asks us to found everything on unobservables, which is contrary to sound scientific practice; it requires the existence of a *void* – an endless source of paradox and absurdity; and it asserts the *law of inertia*, which is patently falsified by experience. Thus we are moved to accept instead an Empedoclean concept of matter, whose 'elements' are stuffs, bulks, fluids, gases ('Earth', 'Air'), and where 'combination' of elements therefore is likened to the squeezing-together of pigments by a painter (Empedocles, fr. 23 Diels).[1] Thus the logic of our matter, if such a phrase be permitted, is inescapably a *mass* logic; and there is the related, most radical consequence that 'combination' is not structural but chemical in nature – the elements can mingle and merge, but of itself, on its own (*kath' hautēn*), the nature of this basic matter is not to build up *into* complex structures and superstructures in the way that can be made at least intuitively plausible on, for one example, an atomic basis.

This nonstructural character of the basic matter is very significant. I believe it goes to the fundamental reason why Aristotle makes much ado about Form in connection with organic substances.

Put the other way, the material elements are such that, the deeper we go into the infrastructure of the world, the more homogeneous and 'uniform' (technically, *homoiomeres* – see §11 below) its character becomes, and the less structure it manifests – there is in this matter-

---

[1] It will be seen that here and below (especially §12), I do not hesitate to take an Aristotelian view of Empedocles, and do not trouble much whether this view does justice to the historical personage of that name. In the final analysis I think the injustice is not altogether and impossibly gross, but I acknowledge that such an analysis is not provided here.

theory nothing corresponding to the notion of an atomic and molecular architecture; rather at that level discreteness gives way to continuity, and organization of components to commingling, blending, alloying of ingredients in a mixture.[2]

(ii) In the light of this, the occurrence in the megascopic world of these endlessly repeated, specifically identical, highly organized, sharply demarcated, integral structures or systems (*sustēmata*, he calls them, or *sustaseis*) – the biological objects which are the substantial individuals, each one a unitary individual entity or 'this', each one exemplifying over its temporal span a sharply defined complete specific nature or substantial kind – stands out as a remarkable fact of nature which invites explanation. 'Invites', not 'defies' – how *do* such entities come to take shape, out of the Empedoclean swirl of mixing and unmixing, clumping and unclumping?[3]

This phenomenon, '(ii)', will be enlarged upon shortly; but even going no further than this, there is already a real question here, not less real in contemporary than in ancient terms, and it seems that Aristotle saw it very clearly: how is it, what principles must be at work to make it the case, that in the environmental circumstances that terrestrially prevail, the world of bio-organic substances takes this form of numerous species of independent, integral *units* – the individual men, dogs, chambered nautili, catfish, grasshoppers, whales? That 'how is it?' answers to Aristotle's 'why?': why this, rather than, say, a general bio-organic swamp, or some other organic distribution built on a completely different principle from that of the *constantly repeated individual*? This stupendous superquestion of course resolves into a great many subquestions, to which even today only the dimmest beginnings of answers are apparent; and *we* know that even these beginnings of the answers that are currently unfolding are possible only through the resurrection of the atomic theory, and then (among much else) the beginning comprehension of the molecular bond, the successful analysis of the proteins, the decipherment of nucleic acid, and the interweaving of all these factors with what is known of evolution. Of all this Aristotle of course knew nothing

---

[2] For Aristotle's awareness of this distinction in principle, *sunthesis* versus *krasis* or *mixis*, see e.g. *GC* I.10 328a6–15, and §12 below.

[3] I do not suggest by any means that a similar question cannot or should not be asked about the occurrence of such entities as higher animals on the basis of an atomic as opposed to an Empedoclean matter theory; obviously the reverse is true, as indicated below. The point is rather that whereas in dealing with such objects on an atomic view of matter, the need for a concept like Aristotelian *form* – as opposed to the possibility of completely reductionistic explanations in terms of micro-states of elementary matter – is at least debatable, on an Empedoclean view of matter it is in principle inescapable. As Aristotle indeed argues, often and at length, against Empedocles himself; cf. §12 below.

whatever; most of it was unknown to anyone before yesterday afternoon. But he did know, and constantly reiterates, that much more must be involved in the construction of these intricate specifically identical units than the Empedoclean clumping and commingling of material stuffs. On the basis of this (perfectly correct) insight, he evolves a theory of the (onto)logical working-up of materials into a unity, through a succession of progressively more complex stages ('parts', as his language makes him call them), from the mass-logic level of the original materials to the count-logic level of the completed individual. This occurs through the progressive advent of *form*, and to Aristotle's mind would be totally unintelligible without it.

As can be seen from these remarks but should be made explicit, my hypothesis is that the philosophical concept of substantial form should basically be seen as an *invention*: as a conceptual instrumentality deliberately fashioned in the course of seeking a theoretical understanding of the agencies (or 'causes') responsible for the simultaneous unity and complexity of biological objects, in the setting of an Empedoclean physics and chemistry (if we may call it that) of itself nowhere nearly powerful enough to accomplish such a task.[4] This does not imply that it is devoid of contemporary value – the question of its possible applicability today, at least in part, to biological questions of the kind that interested Aristotle, is a separate one. The important thing is the task it was devised to do at the time it was devised – a *task* that is still with us.

It will now be useful to look more closely at some of the biological *phainomena* that Aristotle was endeavoring to deal with, since my claim is that he was deeply impressed by a number of extremely basic and pervasive 'facts of nature' concerning the biosphere which should strike observers today as equally notable. They are all of course totally obvious (at least once formulated), yet, ridiculously banal as such points as the following appear when one troubles to state them, a first perception of them and of their potentially profound implications was a feat of no mean biological intuition: they are indeed banal, but they are also global. Although hard to formulate without using some words that have been preempted at

---

[4] The line I am here suggesting is thus in contrast to the view in Rorty 1973: 399, in that I take Aristotle to be *introducing* a concept in a theoretically self-conscious way, rather than defending a common-sense concept in everyday use against 'reductionist attack' from materialists and Platonists. In terms of the (dubious, to me) distinction of revisionary versus descriptive metaphysics, my Aristotle is much more revisionary than is generally assumed. If his 'metaphysical arguments' sometimes strike *us* as 'attempts to defend something like a common-sense view of the world' (Hartman 1977: 51, and many others), I would say that (a) that does not mean they played that role for Aristotle, (b) we should not underestimate the extent to which our common sense has been shaped by Aristotelian influence.

one time or another for some philosophical or scientific purpose, I take them to be thoroughly untechnical in principle.

Fact 1. Biological objects are individuals or 'thisses'; as observed above, for some reason the animal kingdom (i.e., mainly the metazoans, as was said) comes in the form of countable, repeated specifically identical unitary parcels, *tade tina*, each one a *tode ti*: the individual *F*'s, *G*'s, and so on.[5] Simultaneously,

Fact 2. Each one of these biological individuals is permanently endowed with a highly definite specific nature, a characteristic specific constitution, which it shares with other individuals (the ones we say are *homogenē*, of its kind, co-specific) and which incorporates a very large number of features and aspects of its make-up, among these: (a) an overall physical structure of the living thing as a whole, and underlying this, very typically fashioned subassemblies, substructures and subcomponents, extending down to quite minute details of its construction – its minute as well as gross anatomy and physiology – and to a considerable extent even including the kinds of basic materials that compose its various parts; all of this apparently specifically determined. And founded on this structure, (b) also incorporated in its specific character is a characteristic lifestyle, a total pattern of functioning typical for its species – including, e.g., a manner of growth and development, manner of nutrition at different stages of development, mode of reproduction, mode of homemaking, mode of relationship to co-specific individuals, to potential enemies, to the general animal population, to the total circumambient environment. For discussion of these millions of features of structure and function that specifically typify any biological object, Aristotle takes over and adapts to the purpose an old technical term from the Academy, calling them the object's *differentiae* (*diaphorai*);[6] in any concrete case their comprehensive description would fill volumes. Indeed it is notable and deserving of separate mention, that:

Fact 3. These biological individuals are by a wide margin and without exception the most complex and highly organized objects to be found on the Earth; in particular, they display to a marked degree a hierarchical structure of *levels* of organization, in which what is a 'whole' at one level is a 'part' at the next, and in which the part–whole relationship

---

[5] It should be remembered that this is not the *only* meaning of *tode ti* in Aristotle, cf. e.g. §4*, §15*.

[6] In actual usage these are usually called differentiae of the species rather than of the individual; however a species being after all simply a kind of individual (= a kind in which they come, cf. §4*, §8*), in effect they are really differentiae of every individual of the species. On that understanding, the terminologies are equivalent. The development of the 'logical' idea of differentia discussed in the Organon into the biological idea introduced here, is treated in §13(ii) below.

itself assumes a variety of forms beyond that of ingredience in a mixture, or aggregation into a bulk or a 'heap'. In complexity of behavior, too: these objects are strikingly more elaborate in what they *do* than are non-living objects such as stones and lakes, even than are rivers and fires (which so impressed Heraclitus). In particular, they are constantly and at all levels engaged in natural processes and routines that are *future-oriented*, i.e., ones that are aimed at natural *telē*, 'completions' (this is not unique to them, but is very highly characteristic). Such future-directed processes and activities need not involve conscious planning and explicit purposes, which is only one variety found in higher forms,[7] although that case can sometimes be used (with great care) as an illustrative model for the non-conscious natural processes that aim at a *telos*. (It is noteworthy that although the dimension of transtemporal persistence through change was identified as 'most distinctive' of substances in the *Categories*, the aspect of future-directedness, of the utmost import for organic substances, is there entirely absent; cf. §16*.)

Fact 4. Yet, all these complexities granted, *the intricate constitutive nature that typifies such things is very highly species-specific, to the extent that a detailed examination of relatively few specimens is sufficient to smooth out the variation attributable to environmental influence* and ascertain the basic character of all, past, present and future, species members.[8] A fact of some significance: it suggests (particularly in view of the fact about complexity) that the causal agencies at work must be extremely stable and regular, so much so that the underlying mechanisms involved must be extremely reliable and so, in the end, intelligible[9] – the patterns are too deeply systematic for chance or random influences to lie at their basis. This leads us to:

Fact 5. Offspring virtually invariably share their specific character (are *homogenē*) *with a pair of parents, and vice versa*: more fully, (a) with a few

---

[7] Explicit purposes with respect to the future and memory with respect to the past are found only in those animals that can perceive time, *Mem.* 1 449b28–30.

[8] It is a consequence of this that the living substances can be discussed *at the level of* infima species, the usual practice in Aristotelian biological writings. 'The ultimate species are the substances [*sc.* with which we deal]; the individual specimens, like Socrates and Coriscus, are not further differentiated (*adiaphora*) with respect to species', *PA* 1.4 644a23–5 (a much contested passage). Another outcropping of the 'substance means a this' problem, cf. §8*. Cf. also Balme 1972: 73–4 *ad* 639a16.

[9] A formula stating the complete formal nature of an animal species is known technically as a '*definition*' (*horismos* or *logos*), and that which is formulated by such a definition (better, from our standpoint, by the definiens) goes by the name of '*essence*' (*ti ēn einai*); in these terms, Fact 4 is our first encounter here with the possibility of getting understanding of the essences of living things by deep and careful study of the living specimens. See next §11.

explicable exceptions, the existence of an animal is *invariably* traceable to a pair of parents specifically identical with it; (b) with a few explicable exceptions, a pair of animals that generate offspring at all are *invariably* specifically identical with one another and generate offspring specifically identical with themselves. This fact is perhaps the most remarkable of all: 'Human being begets human being', as he repeatedly reflects,[10] *never* horse or squirrel or ant; from which can be immediately gathered with great probability that there must be a *copying mechanism*, highly reliable and very accurate, guaranteeing the transmission of specific nature identical and intact from one generation to the next.[11] Remarkable, to say the least.

Fact 6. These natural types are profuse in number and of enormous diversity; the biosphere presents literally thousands upon thousands of species, representing all sorts of extremes of morphological and functional variation; and the variety reflects a corresponding range of habitats and of choices of function – in fact, so amazingly prodigal is Nature with species, and so extreme, even bizarre, are the capabilities of functional adaptation, that it seems that hardly an ecological space or 'niche' is to be found that some queer creature or other doesn't flourish in.

Fact 7. These objects are subject to temporal as well as spatial limitations; even barring accidental misadventure, they invariably decline with time and eventually perish. That there seem to be no exceptions whatsoever to this phenomenon, of death, is another striking and surely significant fact of nature; why then is it, what can be learned from the fact, that living things apparently must have a specifically characteristic temporal as well as spatial size?

Our interest here is philosophical, and I have already disavowed the aim of furnishing a full-fledged independent treatise on Aristotelian biology. It is also beside our main purposes to get into comparisons,

---

[10] *Metaph.* Z.7 1032a25, Z.8 1033b32, Θ.8 1049b25, Λ.3 1070a28, Λ.4 1070b31; *Ph.* II.1 193b8, II.2 194b13, II.7 198a27, III.2 202a11; *PA* I.1 640a25, 641b26ff., II.1 646a33; *GA* II.1 735a21; *de An.* II.4 415a28, b7 (cf. §16(ii)*), etc. Compare *GC* II.6 333b7–9: 'What's then the cause of *from man, man* (either always or mostly), and *from wheat, wheat,* and *not* an olive tree?', cf. *Ph.* II.4 196a31–3.

[11] The fact that the generation of animals *is*, normally, reproduction, is of course *no tautology*, but a very highly significant *a posteriori* truth. Its recognition by Aristotle as the leading phenomenon to be saved by his theory of generation inclines me to think that François Jacob is mistaken in saying, 'Only towards the end of the eighteenth century did the word and the concept of reproduction make their appearance to describe the formation of living organisms. Until that time living beings did not *reproduce*; they were *engendered*.' (Jacob 1973: 18, emphasis mine.) He may possibly be right about the word; but not the concept, which in Aristotle is prominent, explicit and self-conscious.

favorable or otherwise, between Aristotle's attempt to put together
a comprehensive and scientifically adequate explanatory rationale
that would account for such 'facts' as the foregoing, and our present-
day understanding of such matters, such as it is. But two remarks
are in order, of which one seems approximately self-evident,
and the other, it is hoped, will be borne out by the ensuing discussion.
First, it is evident that his questions – the quest for a causal account
that would make sense of such phenomena as those just set out – had
a certain rightness about them; to put it one way, any inquiry
motivated by questions that good must be worthwhile. Second, while
we are not primarily concerned with his biological theories, of which
(as would be expected) parts are basically sound and other parts are
basically completely mistaken, there are a number of points at which
matters of substantive biology do seem to have an impact that is
direct and considerable on the metaphysical theory of substance.

Let us then lay out a rapid summary of the overall structure of
Aristotle's biological universe and the organisms that compose it.

A. Elements of morphology

10. *Empedoclean infrastructure*

For expository convenience we start with the most elementary
materials and work 'upward' to successive levels of formedness, but
it should be emphasized that in an important sense it reverses the
true order of things to proceed in this way. This is especially worth
stressing in a contemporary philosophical/scientific setting in which
the idea of all things' being 'built up' from elements into which they
are ultimately 'reducible' has wide if not universal currency (even
though this is not the same as acceptance). It had some currency in
Aristotle's time also, and his attitude towards it is thorough disap-
proval. The basic Aristotelian intuition, of course, is one of a form's
informing a matter; but this should be thought of more in terms of
a form 'reaching down' into the matter than of the matter being
'built up' into the form. It must never be forgotten that when
Aristotle speaks of form as a kind of *cause*, he is speaking literally and
in earnest, and not of something that can be reduced away.

(i) 1st level: the simples (*ta hapla*).
The world is wholly saturated with Empedoclean matter, ranging
from extremely dense to extremely fine; nowhere is there any 'void'.
The simplest types of 'body' – according to the *Physics*, *ta hapla tōn*

sōmatōn[12] – are the four elements, Earth–Water–Air–Fire; although according to an extremely ingenious theory put forth in the work *On Coming-to-be and Passing-away* (*GC* II.1–4), these four only appear to be simple (they are *hapla PHAINOMENA sōmata*, 330b2), but in reality are 'mixed' (*mikta*, 330b22), breaking down into combinations of the two pairs of contraries *moist* v. *dry* (*hugron*, *xēron*), and *hot* v. *cold* (*thermon*, *psuchron*); then

$$\text{dry} + \text{cold} \quad = \text{Earth}$$
$$\text{cold} + \text{moist} = \text{Water}$$
$$\text{moist} + \text{hot} \ = \text{Air}$$
$$\text{hot} + \text{dry} \quad = \text{Fire.}$$

This last analysis, reaching what may be called the very deepest-lying 'ultrasimples' of the world, is not directly relevant to or required for understanding of biological objects and processes, for which the four elements are as deep as we need go; but I will return to it later. For the 'ultrasimples', as such, represent Aristotle's view of that which is the most ultimate matter of things, or 'prime matter' as it is sometimes called. This has been a focus of furious scholarly contention over many years, but I shall suggest that his actual position on it, as lofted in the *GC*, is quite a bit cleverer and more interesting than any of those which the scholarly contenders have attributed to him. (See §22(iii)*.)

These four elements, then, are the most basic to figure in the explanation of biological phenomena; sometimes in the biological works they are called *dunameis* ('potencies', 'powers', 'strong substances').[13] At *PA* II.2 648b9 they are the 'principles of the natural elements', *archai tōn phusikōn stoicheiōn*.

At this level it is a world of *masses*, of stuffs and quantities thereof, and its logic a mass logic (cf. §9). The kind of *unity* that comes in is not the more advanced kind that goes with counting, but the cruder one characterized as a sense of *hen* in the paragraph of *Metaph. Δ.* 6 where

the subject isn't differentiated in kind (*tōi eidei adiaphoron* – not differentiated by a species?), where not-differentiated means that the kind (species?) isn't divided-off according to perception (= in a perceptible way),…e.g. *wine* is 'one' in this sense, and *water*, and all juices (lit. = things poured), like oil, and wine, and things (that are or can be) melted down – these because the ultimate subject of them all is the same; for they're *all* water or air (1016a17–24).

---

[12] *Ph.* II.1 192b10. Here and throughout this work I am concerned only with what goes on in the sublunary realm, i.e. within the moon's orbit or so-called 'sphere', thus ignoring for the most part all such matters as the aetherial element, planets and stars, Unmoved Motor, etc.

[13] Cf. *PA* II.1 646a15, and Peck's introduction to *PA* (1961: 30–1), and to *GA* (1963: xlix–li).

Here a straightforward attempt to formulate the minimal amount of 'unity' (in the sense that interests us) that comes with a mass term, is at the end crossed with an interjection of Aristotle's own physical speculation, about what everything (if I may say so) boils down to.[14]

Each of the elements, taken in itself and disregarding the further reduction proposed in the *GC*, is 'homogeneous' and 'uniform', in the sense that a quantity of Water, for example, divides into parts that are also Water; any part of it is of the same nature as the whole and as any other part. In accordance with this intuition, Aristotle's word for something with this kind of uniformity is *homoio-meres*, 'of *like parts*'. And although the term is used by him and by later writers (Aetius, Diogenes, etc.) in explaining theories of Eleatics, Anaxagoras, and Empedocles, there is every indication that the term itself, and the developed technical distinction of the uniform *versus* the *non-uniform*, or *an-homoio-meres*, where a whole is composed of parts 'un-like' each other and/or the whole, originates with Aristotle and not earlier. (But the germ of the idea is once stated clearly by Plato.[15])

(ii) 2nd level: compounds (*suntheta*).

These basic material elements combine in various ways and proportions to form more complicated compounds (*suntheta sōmata*, *PA* II.1 646a17, etc.), but the latter are still *homoiomerē*, uniform and 'having like parts' from a molar standpoint. *Examples*: (from the *Meteorologica*) 'metallic stuffs (*metalleuomena*, lit. = stuffs dug out of mines) – bronze, gold, silver, tin, iron, stone and other suchlike' (*Mete.* IV.10 388a13ff.); other examples would be wood, glass, coal, wine, honeywater. These are compounds that can exist as such (= as wood, as gold) *on their own*, *kath' hauta*, and accordingly by one criterion[16] could be termed 'substances': namely, being 'what they are' on their own rather than by way of being said of something else, and as opposed to the cases where 'what something is' connotes being part of an organic whole – cases to be encountered in §11. But as already noted, such compounds are elsewhere rejected as substantial candidates on grounds of failing the individuative test;[17] and to the

---

[14] Anything meltable is water; Δ.4 1015a10, 24 1023a28; *Mete.* IV.8 *fin.*

[15] *Prt.* 329d4–8, 'You mean (that Virtue has "parts") as the parts of a face are parts – mouth and nose and eyes and ears? Or like the parts of the gold, which don't differ from one another, or from the whole, except in size?' And a related idea clearly underlines the distinction between a *pan* (which is an unstructured aggregate) and a *holon* (which is a structured unity), as 'bravely' but unavailingly maintained by Theaetetus against Socrates' browbeating at *Tht.* 204a8–205a7. For *homoiomerēs* as applied specifically to the four elements as understood by Aristotle, *Metaph.* A.9 992a7.

[16] That of *Metaph.* Δ.8 1017b10–11, 13–14, 23–4; recall above, §6*.

[17] *Metaph.* Z.16 1040b8–10; cf. again §6*.

extent that the substances are the individual *animals*, it is Aristotle's explicit and emphatic contention that the existence of such objects as these cannot so much as be intelligibly described, let alone explained, solely in terms of Empedoclean material elements – even together with cosmic forces driving the processes of their commingling and separation, i.e. so-called 'efficient' or 'moving causes' – whether Love and Strife, as Empedocles maintains, or something thermodynamically more standard. Rather, the present level is the upper limit of what, according to Aristotle's view, can come-to-be or can *be* at all by the agencies of *matter* and *force*; to get beyond this point requires the further agencies of *form* and *end*.

Details of Aristotle's criticism of Empedocles are deferred to §12(iii), for it falls in the category of moral-drawing rather than exposition of the Aristotelian biological universe itself; but it must be noted that an important divide is transited here: that is, since these complex individual units with their complex parts do exist, in no chance or erratic fashion and in great profusion over and above the 'heaps', the inference is inescapable that constitutive substantial forms must be systematically at work in the world; at the next level upward we see the lowest traces of their agency.

11. *From mass to individual: anatomy and physiology, the Parts of Animals*

(i) 3rd level: uniform parts of animals (*ta homoiomerē*)

Now, there are also 'uniform' compounds that come about as part of the formation of living things. *Examples*: (from the *Parts of Animals*[18]) blood, serum, lard, marrow, semen,[19] bile, milk, flesh, also bone and sinew (but those typified by these last two introduce complications, see '4th level' to come). These compounds, however, unlike those of level 2, *cannot* exist as such, as 'what they are' (= as blood, etc.) on their own; rather, apart from their functioning *as* part of a complete living organism, they cannot be these things (= blood, etc.) except homonymously, by a mere ambiguity, merely in name.[20] Why is this? A complicated matter of which there will be more to say, but briefly and partially: because their nature, their being 'what

---

[18] Though the *Meteorologica* list also includes a number of these, as do other passages throughout the natural writings. Citing here *PA* ii.2 647b10ff.

[19] But he changed his mind about this one's being a 'part' in the *Generation*, on important theoretical grounds: cf. 1.18 724b23–31, and §14* below.

[20] A frequent theme: of the non-uniform parts, e.g. *PA* i.1 640b34–641a3, but extended to all parts 641a3–6, 18–21; cf. *Metaph.* Z.16 1040b5–10. A like consideration figures interestingly in discussing the formation of semen in *GA* i.18 722b33–723a1.

they are', includes fitness to a certain function or *work* (e.g., 641a3, 655b18–21), something not true of (say) *rock*, or *water*. Not only are these parts not that (= blood, etc.) apart from the body of which they are parts, but in addition, the moment the body of which these uniform parts are parts ceases to be enpsyched by the psyche (see §16* on this), these parts, like those of levels 4 and 5 cease to be that, and all that is left is EWAF.

(ii) 4th level: uniform to non-uniform
Now we are at a very delicate point; for about here begins an interface between the mass-system prevailing below, and the count-system prevailing above.

For there are certain sorts of 'part' that on one hand consist of a *single* uniform nature, and for this reason divide into 'like parts' and thus seem even as wholes to meet the condition for the uniform, yet on the other hand simultaneously have some further structure and form to them, hence partaking of the nature of the non-uniform as well. Such bi-polarity is first called to our attention for

certain of the Viscera, which on one hand are complexly structured (*polumorpha tois schēmasin*), yet, consisting of a body that's uniform, also are in a manner of speaking simple (*PA* ii.1 646b30–4);

soon thereafter we learn that the Heart is also like this:

the Heart divides into homoeomeries, just as does each of the other Viscera, but owing to its shaped configuration (*morphē tou schēmatos*), it is also anhomoeomerous (ii.1 647a31–3).

In such cases, of which (a) Vein (*phleps*)[21] is another example,

in one way the part is homonymous[22] with the whole, for example a part of Vein is Vein [as with the uniform], but yet in another way it's *not* homonymous [as with the non-uniform – i.e., a part of *a* Vein is not generally *a* Vein] (ii.2 647b18–19).

It may sound odd to us; but it seems we are being told that certain 'parts' are *proto*-structural, of an intermediate nature or at an

---

[21] I adopt 'Vein' for *phleps*, rather than 'blood-vessel' as Peck and Platt, just because it seems better to reflect the required ambiguity as between the uniform, *vascular stuff*, and the non-uniform, *thing with a structure* (viz., '*a* Vein'); to me at least, 'blood-vessel' too strongly suggests the latter.

[22] Pellegrin (1982: 188) cites this passage as marking the connection of division and differentia and with reason calls it 'very difficult to translate'; but a very important concept lurks in it. Evidently, 'homonymous' here has to mean merely having the same name, and not also to entail (as in the *Categories*) that the formula of definition must be distinct. Thus this use of 'homonym' does not exclude homonyms from being also some kind of synonyms – as in this instance they certainly are (see on Hoof and Horn below); the *Categories* sense of '(merely) homonymous' corresponds here to *homōnumon MONON*, e.g. *GA* i.19 726b24. Similarly *Metaph.* Z.9 1034a22. (In the final analysis of this case they will actually turn out to be a new and different kind of *paronyms*: see §20(ii)*.)

interface between uniform and non-uniform: the same nature somehow doubling as *stuff* and as *structure*. In *PA* II.9, something of the
same sort apparently is intimated about Bone, but the bi-polarity
here seems to be between the uniformity of 'bony stuff' (i.e., the E_2
W_2 A_0 F_4 of Empedocles, cf. §12(iii)) and a non-uniformity that is
seen not so much at the level of '*a* bone', as it is at the level of the
whole 'system of bones', the skeletal structure of the whole animal
(the entire chapter should be studied):

654a32 The case is similar between the nature of the Bones and that of the Veins.
For each of them is a connected system originating from one thing; and there's no
bone itself by itself,[23] but either as a connected part or else attached and bound into
it, so that nature can make use of it (654b) both as one and continuous and as two
and divided, for flexing. Likewise there's no *vein* itself by itself, but they're all part
of a unity. b3 For if a Bone were something separated, it couldn't do the work for
whose sake the nature of bones exists – for it couldn't be the cause of either any
flexing or any straightening, being not connected but at a remove – it would even
be harmful, like some thorn or projectile lodged in the flesh. b7 Again, if a Vein
were something separated and not connected with the origin, it couldn't preserve
the blood inside it, for the heat from that origin prevents its congealing, as appears
when separated blood goes bad. b11 The origin of the Veins is the Heart, and of
the Bones is what's called the Spine, in all animals that have Bones, from which the
nature of the other Bones is continuous; for the Spine is what holds together the
length of the animals and makes them straight. b14 But since the animal in motion
must flex its body, [the Spine] is *one* because of the continuity, but *polymer* by the
division of the vertebrae.

After some more about the integration of the 'system of Bones', the
'unity' of the skeletal system (654b16–655a4) and related matters,
some of which will concern us below, the discussion returns to the
theme of bi-polarity between uniform and non-uniform, and puts
the idea with great clarity:

655b2 Very close to the Bones in characteristic feel are also these sorts of parts, such
as Nails, and Hoofs and Talons and Beaks, i.e. those of birds [as opposed to the snouts
of swine, which *rhunchē* also covers?]. Animals have all these for the sake of defense.
b5 For *the complete structures composited out of these and synonymous with the parts* – e.g.,
the complete Hoof, the complete Horn – have been contrived for the self-preservation of
each of these [creatures]. Of this kind is also the nature of Teeth...b15 related parts
are Skin and Bladder and Membrane and Hairs and Feathers and parts analogous
to these...b21 in all these (which strictly are non-uniform), nonetheless *the parts are
synonymous with the wholes*.[24]

A mass-versus-count ambiguity is being exploited here, of the kind
that exists in English in (Quine's example) 'Mary had a little *lamb*'

---

[23] Cf. *HA* III.7 516a10, 'no such thing as Bone all on its own'.

[24] The same point recurs for Horn at *HA* I.1 487a8–9: *not* an 'unimportant parenthesis'
(Thompson), *nor* 'secludenda' (Peck). Pellegrin 1982: 22, n.26, quoting the *PA* II.9 passage
about Bone: 'Here again Aristotle has *chosen* a point of view that is not our own' (his
emphasis).

(followed her to school one day, *versus* for supper one evening). We might say, e.g., that the mollusc's shell is made out of shell, or the pearl out of pearl, even if we are not inclined to say with Aristotle that the complete horn is made out of horn, or the tooth out of tooth (i.e., horny or toothy stuff).

In any event, it is at this level in the upward sequence that the formulation passes to, and remains with, the count-system.

Once this transition-point is formulated, it is available for exploitation with great vividness: the 'system of Bones', the structure, is analogized to the armature used by modellers in clay – the framing that 'subserves', he says (and 'is for the sake of') the fleshy parts that are built around it.[25] Similarly with the 'system of bloodvessels', the articulation-out (*diarthrōsis*) of which also plays a significant role in his account of early embryonic development, as we shall see in §14*.

These transitional semistructural 'parts' too are defined in part through their function ('work'), which is the reason why even being a portion of Bone, or Vein – the uniform pole of the ambiguity – really and truly so being, that is, requires being integrated into a *system* of Bones or Veins – the non-uniform pole of the ambiguity.[26]

(iii) 5th level: non-uniform parts of animals (*ta anomoiomerē*)
Head, ears, limbs, digits, organs of all kinds, external and internal (in fact, *ta an-homoiomerē* = *ta organika*, flatly, at several points[27]). Here the whole part has the name, and its parts in turn not at all. The germ of the conception, we have seen, was known from Plato's day (cf. the 'face' case in the *Protagoras*); Aristotle's remark shows the transition complete: we can go either way with Vein, which in one sense has 'like parts' – but what about with Face? Is part of a face a face? *Oudamōs*, 'no way' (*PA* II.2 647b21; cf. also *Cael.* III.4 302b25).

Yet still as before, these parts too do not 'have their names', are

---

[25] 654b27–34. As for Veins, see *HA* III.5 525a34ff., *GA* II.6 743a2.

[26] By 'viscera' (*splanchna*) is meant the so-called bloodlike viscera (heart, liver, spleen, lung and the like); they are all *haimatika*, 647a35, b7–8, 655a29, 667b3, and Peck on *PA* III.4 (p. 232 n.); LSJ[6] also opposes them to *entera* (intestines). It would be tempting to think of *phleps* (Vein) as centered on the uniform side and *splanchna* (Viscera) on the non-uniform; but the ambivalence is too pronounced: see respectively 647b17–19 and 647a31–b9.

[27] *GA* II.1 734b28; 1.18 722b30; *PA* II.1 647a4. At the outset of *HA* (486a5),
    asuntheta = *hosa diairetai eis homoiomerē*, e.g. *flesh*
    suntheta = *hosa eis anomoiomerē*, e.g. *hand* and *face*.
Many writers point out the similarity of the uniform–nonuniform dichotomy to the nineteenth-century physiologists' distinction between 'tissues' and 'organs'.

not 'what they are' (= hands, etc.), except as operating according to their fashion in a functioning living being; separated from it, or if the animal dies, these parts may still look like 'what they are' in their (superficial, here) 'outward configuration' (*morphē tou schēmatos*), but they no more really *are* these things than a carved hand, or a painted one.[28]

(iv) 6th level: animals (*ta sunestoka hola*)
Finally the non-uniform parts are found assembled, organized and integrated into the complete living organism, the individual this or that. (For 'this or that' naturally substitute his species, cf. §8*.) The migration-barriers in the species take the form already sketched, that Socrates' (say) coming-to-be-Man is identical with his coming-to-exist, and when he ceases-to-be-Man, that individual ceases-to-exist (dies, presumably; for as field zoologists – as opposed to metaphysicians – we have no thought of, having never observed, such bizarre modes of extinction and genesis as were imagined in §7*). When Socrates does die, what remains is not a man: 'the corpse has the same superficial outward configuration [*scilicet*, as did the living being with which it is spatiotemporally continuous], but all the same it is *not* a man',[29] no more than the doctor in the drawing can be said to heal – at best, homonymously. And as already noted, this homonymy extends to the deepest of the underlying parts: the non-uniform organs are no longer organs, the intermediate Bone(s) and Vein(s), etc., no longer Bone and Vein, and the uniform Blood and Bile no longer Blood or Bile.

B. Moral-drawing (1): some first principles of morphology

12. *First principles of matter*

Now we are in a position to do some philosophical anatomy and physiology on the concepts that are involved in Aristotelian anatomy and physiology of animals. For the concept of *form/matter* that figures in the integrative assembly of Aristotelian biological individuals, as just quickly sketched, involves several quite interesting points of theory.

[28] *PA* I.I 640b34–641a3, a18–21, etc.; *Metaph.* Z.11 1036b30–2, and of course 'finger', *Metaph.* Z.10 1035b11, 24, 'eye', *de An.* II.1 412b20–2, etc. We can, though, *know* it's a head or hand without knowing whose head or hand it is, *Cat.* 7 8b15–21.

[29] *PA* I.I 640b34. At *Int.* 11 21a23, though not that I have noted in the biological writings, 'dead man' is actually called self-contradictory.

(i) Hierarchical organization

One is this: the construction of an individual (ontologically speaking[30]) is by way of a hierarchical structure of stages, each of which is thought of as underlying the next as a 'matter' for an 'enmattered form' – thus the primary elements for the compound masses,[31] these for the uniform parts, etc., all the way up;[32] each stage is also described as existing 'for the sake of' that above it (e.g. *PA* II.1 646b10–12), and all 'for the sake of' the complete individual.[33] Such talk as this last, I would suggest, is not so much teleological as it is functional: beyond the inorganic compounds like wine and the like, which can be 'what they are' *kath' hauta*, the nature of the uniform and non-uniform parts of animals invariably includes fitness to a 'work', i.e. a specific contribution to the life of the total organism, separated from which the part no longer retains that nature or 'is what it is' except by ambiguity; the 'for the sake of' terminology is a variant on the same idea.[34] And regarding the terminology just now of 'all the way up': in the vertical depiction we are sketching, the direction of 'matter-to-end' can be represented as upward, but the direction of *formal* 'causation' is *downward*: specific form determining overall organization, through the nature of the non-uniform structures so organized, 'all the way down' through the particular sorts of uniform matters required to support these structures.[35] We shall return to this shortly (§12(ii) *fin.*).

[30] This is to allow for the divergence at certain points between the hierarchy as discernible in the finished product and the *temporal* sequence of stages in embryonic development – in which the earliest 'parts' to articulate out (*diarthrousthai*) are actually the ontologically intermediate transitional or 'interface' semistructures (level (iv) in the enumeration of §11), principally the primitive embryonic cardiovascular system. So far as possible, developmental topics and the biological ramifications of Fact 5 will be dealt with in §14*; but owing to the many points of overlap with topics of structure and the ramifications of Facts 1 – 4, embryological matters inevitably creep in to a degree prior to then. For Aristotle on the methodological correctness of dealing with 'being' before taking on 'coming-to-be' (thus morphology before morphogenesis) cf. *PA* I.1 639b11ff., 640a10ff.

[31] Recall that *mixis* or *krasis* is already a rudimentary species of 'form', cf. n. 2.

[32] *GA* I.1 715a9ff., *PA* II.1 646b5ff., etc. Cf. *GC* I.5 321b19ff., where each of the 'parts' is *ditton*, 'double in its nature', both matter of what's over it, and form of what's beneath; also Joachim's note thereon (1922:129–30). Also *Ph.* II.2 194b9: 'Matter is a relative term: to each form there corresponds a special matter' (after Hardie and Gaye).

[33] At *PA* I.5 645b15ff. the whole *body* exists 'for the sake of some complex (or complete) activity', *praxeōs tinos heneka polumerous* (or *plērous*). Cf. also Bonitz, *Index*, 62a23ff. (s.v. *anomoiomerēs*), and §16*.

[34] The etymological derivation of *organon*, *organikon*, etc. from *ergon* and their accordant sense of 'instrumental', has been frequently remarked; cf. also on *energeia*, §16*.

[35] Kosman 1984: 143 appreciates this point, from a slightly different vantage. See also ch. 14 below.

(ii) Complexity of matter

Beyond this, however, we need to mark also both a complexity and a degree of theoretical abstractness or attenuation in the form/matter notion, particularly in the notion of matter, in this biological theory that go considerably past anything in Empedocles, Aristotle's matter-concept's nearest ancestor – especially once we are past the interface between mass and count (concerning which there is shortly more to be said also). An aspect illustrative of this, which has many further ramifications also, is the following.

Beginning at the most primitive level, the 'stuff' or 'oatmeal' stage, we are used to the matter/form notion's intuitively including the idea of certain forms' *entailing restrictions on the sort of matter that will 'take',* as we say, *that form*: at the crudest level, where matter = stuff and form = shape, we know that a statue of Socrates, say,[36] can be formed from such materials as wood, marble, soap, bronze, snow, clay; whereas candidates like olive oil, air, dry sand, wine, mercury will infallibly frustrate even the craftiest of Moving Causes. So much is plainly *endoxon*, unquestioned lore ('can't make a saw of wool or of wood' – *Metaph.* H.4[37]). But now beyond this, at the higher, more complicated stages, where matter = successively more complex structures and form = function or 'work', an analogous relationship continues to prevail: the uniform tissues and non-uniform structures must be adapted to their functions and not only will not just anything do, but the requirements become exceedingly exacting and detailed: if a function is *in-* and *di-*gestion, for example, then teeth and esophagus and stomach(s) need to be thus-and-so constructed; again, some structures are required to contribute to more than a single function (as teeth, for catching, for chewing, for defense); again, if an animal's specific manner of reproduction is of this or that kind, the requisite reproductive organs are accordingly restricted in their potential variety; again, the innumerable particular varieties of self-propulsion impose requirements of a very precise kind upon the structural layout and articulation of the skeletal and muscular systems involved; and so on indefinitely.[38] At the level of the finished product, that of the

---

[36] Taking it that to be a statue of Socrates is pure-and-simple to be an inanimate solid having a surface conformation resembling to a sufficient degree the surface of Socrates (what is 'sufficient' is of no concern here), and is independent of sculptor's or modeler's intent, circumstances of production etc. (Here 'solid' excludes e.g. clouds; 'inanimate', e.g. Socrates' lookalike twin Xocrates.)

[37] 1044a29. Likewise *Ph* II.9 200a10, b5.

[38] Thus 'can't walk without feet', *adunaton badizein aneu podōn*, *GA* II.3 736b24. These forms of explanation so permeate the works on animals that detailed references would be either

completed individual animal body, it too underlies as 'matter'[39] a 'form': the total lifestyle lived by individuals of that species, their total range of function; and thus constraints exist on the body as 'matter' as a whole:

Take an illustration: A hatchet, in order to split wood, must, of necessity, be hard; if so, then it must, of necessity, be made of bronze or of iron. Now the body, like the hatchet, is an instrument; as well the whole body as each of its parts has a purpose, for the sake of which it is; the body must therefore, of necessity, be such and such, and made of such and such materials, if that purpose is to be realized.[40]

As is easily seen, a number of important strands come together at this locus or 'topos' – namely, the idea of forms' either explicitly specifying, or else implicitly placing restrictions upon, the type of matter in which they are to be, can be, embodied; the unraveling of these strands is one of the central businesses of Aristotelian metaphysics.[41] To that we shall attend; but we cannot so much as commence unless it is clear that in speaking of 'matter' in the present theoretical context, Aristotle can no longer be counted upon to mean the simple sort of thing we familiarly understand, lumps of rock, quantities of Water or Earth. Rather, depending on the context the relevant 'matter' may be, or include, something as complicated and highly organized as a complete organic system (cardiovascular, gastrointestinal, respiratory, skeletal-muscular, etc. *ad lib.*), or, ultimately, may be one of those most remarkably intricate total objects, against whose biological description in detail (even yet to be given) Aristotle issues that poignantly terse paper draft (even yet to be cashed), 'an organized body, potentially having life in it'.

> interminable or largely random; for some further interpretive comment about them cf. §13(ii) below.

[39] *de An.* II.1 412a16ff., cf. §16*. I speak typologically of the 'lifestyle', meaning that complex set of capacities *for* the various activities, so-called 'first actualization'.

[40] *PA* I.1 642a9–13 (Peck); cf. n.33 above. Also *PA* I.3 643a24–7.

[41] The case of a form's restricting, without explicitly specifying, the type or the properties of the matter is discussed at numerous points in the biological writings in the terminology of 'conditional' or 'hypothetical necessity'; cf. the use of 'of necessity' in the passage just quoted, and Peck's note thereon with further references; also *PA* I.1 639b21–640a9, and Balme's commentary (1972:76–82). The difficulty of the distinction between explicit and implicit restrictions by form on matter is all too apparent in the notorious *Metaphysics* chapters devoted to the problem What Sorts of Parts Belong to the Form, and What Sorts Aren't Parts of the Form but of the Compound (*Metaph.* Z.10–11). And the critical importance of the problem is of course attested to by (among other things) Aristotle's well-known morbid preoccupation with the snub-nose – no fetish, but in this context illustrative of a serious crux: *concavity* carries no restrictions beyond surfaces in general, perhaps even including immaterial (= geometers') ones, cf. *Metaph.* E.1 1025b28ff., but *snubness* has to be concavity in a nose, and thus becomes a persistently-returned-to study object, for the very good reason that according to the theoretical framework that Aristotle is endeavoring to elaborate (*Metaph.* E.1 *ibid.*) '*all* the natural things "are said" (or "are called [what they are]"') like the snub, e.g. nose eye face flesh bone, and generally *animal*; and leaf root bark, and generally *plant* – for the formulae of none of these things are independent of movement but always include a matter'.

The point is not difficult in principle, and would not require such emphasis here were it not for a pair of mutually opposing factors: on one hand the importance of the point in the actual application of the form–matter analysis to the biological objects that are the substances, and on the other a tendency among interpreters to stoutly persevere in reading 'matter' as *stuff* or oatmeal or 'goo', wherever encountered and regardless of level; to instance only one distinguished interpreter, Sir David Ross in an otherwise laudable note on an important paragraph in *Meta.* Θ.7 (which we too shall examine – cf. §20(ii)*), abruptly compromises the central intuition in his final clause:

> The difference which Aristotle here points out is that between two levels at which the cleavage between substratum and attributes may be made. You may distinguish accidental attributes from their subject, and in this case the subject is a substratum containing certain essential characteristics [= in *Categories* language, is a primary substance; cf. §4*, 6*, 8*]; or again you may distinguish the essential characteristics from the substratum to which they belong, and in this case the substratum is *bare unqualified matter*.[42]

Not in the least: the idea involved is neither scientifically so simple-minded nor philosophically so disreputable as that last suggests (in my view there is in this theory no such thing as 'bare unqualified matter' – nor, for all of that, in any other theory known to ancient Greek thought prior to Stoic physics – unless it be, possibly, Anaximander's[43]). Not that it cannot ever be simple; it is simple enough with the bronze and the statue, or the letters and the syllable, hence their usefulness as study objects. But with the biological objects that are the real substances, it is always exceedingly complicated, and terminology like 'featureless' or 'unqualified' in connection with the concept of a matter is at very best unhelpful.

Another way of seeing the question is this. We can think of an individual organism as built up by way of the series of stages just described – though, as was cautioned at the beginning of §10 and just now in §12(i), what we are really looking at is the 'reaching down' of the specific form as a whole. That is a determination of the whole nature of the organism: of all its 'parts', through the non-uniform, through the semistructural, all the way to the uniform. Of course, at the base of the hierarchy, the organism is composed of E and W and A and F – everything in our sublunary region is so composed;

---

[42] Ross 1924; II 257 (*ad* 1049a26, my italics). Both the basic mistake and a step in the direction necessary to correct it are made just earlier, 256 (*ad* 1049a24–7).

[43] Certainly Earth, Water etc. are not 'bare and unqualified'. And what is taken as 'prime' is itself relative to the context of inquiry: in the context of biological objects, Aristotle more than once nominates for 'prime matter' (however tentatively) the 'natural constitution of the *katamēnia*', *GA* I.20 729a33; cf. *Metaph.* H.4 1044a34–5. Also *PA* II.1 646a34; Peck 1963: xi–xii, 110 n.

the elements are not 'used up' when the animal comes-to-be (for more about this aspect, cf. §20(iii)*). But recall that all the *organic* parts (in our sense of 'organic', i.e. 'living') are tied to the existence of the whole (no blood or bone or hand except as parts of a living whole), and *all the 'matters' above the EWAF are tied to their being formed by the whole form* – when death occurs, not only is the whole no longer (e.g.) an individual sheep, but with it disappear the organ systems and the organic matters, everything that was '*ditton*' (n. 28). Looked at in this way, the entire hierarchy is within the form, and disappears from the matter as a whole with the form, and what is left is as close as we can get in Aristotle to 'bare unqualified matter'[44]. This is one of the points at which the 'metaphysics of the biology' is more subtle and complex than the 'metaphysics of the *Metaphysics*': for the organic matters that are '*ditton*' *do* come-to-be and pass away, whereas *Metaphysics* Z.8–9 says flatly that matter does not come-to-be or pass away; the reason, of course, is that Z.8–9 is thinking of simple matters like bronze. (It is even wrong about that, since bronze, an alloy of copper and tin as was known to the ancients, obviously is creatable and destructible. When he wrote his theory of interelemental change in the *GC*, Aristotle even believed that EWAF themselves could come-to-be and pass away.) This topic will recur frequently (§17(iii)*, §19*, §22*, §23*, §24*).

(iii) FORM needed to get above the 2nd level: criticism of Empedocles
We saw in §10 that the material elements under the influences causing mixing and unmixing can build up in the way of 'compounds' to compound *bulks* or masses – what Aristotle calls 'heaps' – of a primitive order of differentiation, but no farther. Let us try the thought-experiment of imagining with Aristotelian imagination what the sublunary world would look like if the Empedoclean elements and the forces ('moving causes') driving their mixing and separation were all that there was. Those agencies could build up to rocks and rills, templed hills, puddles, ponds and oceans, earth and sky, the minerals and other materials *in* the earth, the clouds and other ephemera *of* the sky. (In fact, the Empedoclean elements and the efficient forces could very likely build up to the condition of the pre-biotic Earth, much as it is nowadays believed that it would have

---

[44] This may not be quite right as it stands; for although the dead body has none of the parts or materials of the *living* body, it might well be thought to have more form to it than just a heap of EWAF. There is no science of necrology, in the requisite sense, to which to appeal for an answer to this.

looked to the unaided vision of a time-traveler or other visitor, perhaps over 3×10^9 years ago, or to the condition of present-day Mars.) But that is the limit to what can be achieved by the 'mixing together' and 'distilling out' of homogeneous masses; in Aristotle's view, if there were no constitutive properties in the sense of §8*, the sort of world described thus far in this paragraph would have to be all that there was: not a bad sort of world, with a certain amount going on in it by way of both 'alteration' and 'coming-to-be and passing-away'[45]: transformation of compounds, seasonal changes, lunar, solar and planetary motions, weather, erosion, *et al.* (think again of present-day Mars). But the leap is immense from here to such phenomena as Fact 1 (a world swarming with sharply defined biological individuals), and Fact 2 (having intricate specifically determined development, form and function), and Fact 3 (their demonstrated degree of complexity and organization), a jump that to Aristotle plainly requires a further and higher-order type of explanatory rationale than 'mixing' and 'unmixing'; hence the hypothesis of a distinct type of causal agency, called form.[46]

That this is indeed Aristotle's outlook comes out especially clearly in his reaction to Empedocles' own attempt to account for the building-up of the natural-world-as-we-find-it, using a theoretical framework having only the four material elements and the two forces, Love and Strife, that drive processes of commingling and separation. His story is of *evolution*: according to it, in the portion of the cosmic cycle leading down to our own day,[47] the four elements began by being wholly Mixed together (we may call this *Phase E-1*), under the total ascendancy of Love, as undifferentiated as possible (DK B27,

[45] As Joachim pointed out long ago (1922: xxxvi–xxxvii), the work *GC* is in fact mainly concerned with generation and destruction at this level, of *homoiomerē*, and thus at most in a preliminary way with substances in our sense. The distinction between *genesis* and *alloiōsis* in I.3 uses an anti-migration condition (319b6ff.) not supplemented with a condition concerning individuativeness, and the examples in the ensuing discussion oscillate between 'the body' (which might imply such a condition) and 'the bronze' (which presumably does not). It is stated that it is the *material* cause that is being sought (318a2, 9–10), and the governing sense of *ousia* in the work is stated in II.8 to be one in which Earth is *contrary* to Air, and Water contrary to Fire, *hōs endechetai ousiāi enantion einai*, 'in the sense that a substance can be contrary to a substance' (335a5) – in evident conflict with *Cat.* 3b24, were the explanation not to hand, that we are dealing with the material substructure of the organic world and not with the complex organic substances themselves, as 'composited by nature' (*hai phusei sunestōsai ousiai*, II.1 328b32; cf. Joachim's note thereon, 191–3). (On the 'contrariety' point, Joachim follows Philoponus' rationale: that the opposition involved is that of the deeper-underlying 'moist versus dry', etc – 218 *ad* 331a1–3, and §22(iii)*.)

[46] Technically, again, *mixis* or *krasis* is already a primitive or rudimentary species of 'form', cf. *Metaph.* H.2 1042b16, 23; *GC* I.10 328a6–15 etc.; above nn. 2, 31.

[47] In order to get on with the account, I pass over a number of difficult and controversial issues in the interpretation of the 'Cycle'.

B29). Then (*Phase E-2*) Separation began to occur, owing to Strife (DK B30, B31), and different regions of the cosmos began to have different local mixtures of elements – that is, mixtures differing in the *ratio* or *proportion* of elements; at that point (*Phase E-3*) the influence of Love was found in local regions where elements were *drawn* together to form compounds, both inorganic and (*Phase E-4*) organic, such as Blood or Bone, whose formula (for this see below) is (B96):

$$E_2 W_2 A_0 F_4.$$

The next evolutionary step (*Phase E-5*) was when these bits of organic matter, as commingled at E-4, in turn mixed up into miscellaneous animal 'parts' on their own ('faces without necks', 'arms without shoulders', DK B57); these 'parts' then in turn (*Phase E-6*) mixed up into random combinations, or 'Scrambled Animals' ('ox-kind with human faces', 'of human form with ox-heads', DK B61, B59). Most of these monsters were of course functionally maladapted and did not survive, or even if otherwise successful, died off because unable to reproduce (DK B61.3–4). But (*Phase E-7*) in a very small fraction of cases, creatures were thus 'mixed together' that happened to be both well-adapted and reproductively viable; these are those that have survived, and their progeny are among us – and *include* us – today.

   The key to this account is of course the idea that compounds and complexes of elements are defined by the '*formula*' or '*ratio*' or '*proportion* of the mixture', *logos tēs mixeōs*; it is uncertain whether the actual phrase is Empedocles', for it is found earliest in allusions by Aristotle.[48] But there is no question that the idea is active in the *Peri Phuseōs*; the statement of the formulae of Bone and of Blood (DK B96, B98) is explicit, including the assignment of numerical values. On what ground, then, does Aristotle, departing from his usual level-headed language, call Empedocles' theory such immoderate names as 'inconceivable', 'clearly impossible', 'absurd', 'fantastic'[49]? *Not* because it is evolutionary, deviating from the true view that present-day species are eternal, did not come-to-be, have always been and will always be;[50] the problem is more fundamental: the account evinces *no* appreciation of the difference between *mixture* and *structure*.

---

[48] *PA* II.I 642a18–24; *de An.* 1.4 408a13–18; cf. *Meta* A.10 993a17–18.

[49] These epithets being variously drawn from *GA* 1.18 722b17–30, *Ph.* II.8 198b34, *Cael.* III.2 300b25ff. Observe that in the last, *dunaton ē* should be omitted in line 26, as it is by the OCT and Budé, and is not by the Oxford translator. The words, which are in neither MS E nor either the lemma or the paraphrase of Simplicius, in any case subvert the sense.

[50] *GA* II.I, *de An.* II.4 cf. §16* – reference is to the genetic capacity of individuals *as* a sort of threptic capacity of the eternal species.

We can accept for argument's sake (though it is clear from §11(i) that it is more complicated than this) that the Blood of some species of animal, say, Horse, is accurately defined by an Empedoclean formula, of the type $E_x W_y A_z F_w$; there is an obvious sense in which that *is* a simple mixture of elements, in the proportion x–y–z–w (even though, to Aristotle, that is *not* what blood *is* – i.e., the point that nothing can be blood that is not enpsyched by the psyche of a complete living thing. Leaving that aside, then): such a compound can be called homogeneous (or with Aristotle, homoeomerous), in no particularly technical way but in the sense that any portion of it is much like any other portion – as a consequence, a small sample of it will serve as an adequate representative of the whole mixture (this is why a 'blood sample' is all that is needed to diagnose the condition of *all* the blood of a given horse).[51] Mixture, the same throughout, is all there is to it, and Empedocles' analysis is adequate (so far as the present contrast is concerned, not that Aristotle has no further objections, see §11).

But when we come to deal with a complete animal, that is something else. A *horse* is obviously more than a mixture, and not homogeneous at all: it has a *structure* without which the same elements in the same proportions certainly do not add up to a horse. This is easily seen by the simple if distressing expedient of putting the horse through a large grinder, and carefully preserving all the material coming out the other side – whereby are obtained exactly the four elements composing the original horse, in exactly the same ratios as before; but no one will mistake that quantity of matter for a horse. For the *structure* has been destroyed. In this sense the horse is *heterogeneous* – consisting of diverse parts, that have to be organized in a particular and very definite manner. This is a higher-order compound than a mixture. (There is no such thing as a 'horse-sample', on the order of a 'blood-sample'.) A similar point holds for such 'parts' of animals as head, neck, thorax, leg – these are structural also, not just mixtures like blood.

The point of belaboring the obvious at even this little length is that this difference, between mixture and structure, is evidently entirely unapparent to Empedocles, who goes straight from *blood* and *bone* as material mixtures of elements, to *heads* and *legs* as further material mixtures of elements, to *whole organisms* as still further material mixtures of elements, without seeming to notice the conceptual difference and added dimension of complexity that comes in with the latter type of case, and certainly without making it explicit.

---

[51] *Pace PA* ii.2 647b33–5. (Here I am ignoring the thesis that 'drawn blood is not blood'.)

This is the point of Aristotle's severe and even vitriolic criticism: Empedocles' scheme of *elements* and *ratios* is the earliest clear prefiguring of the scheme that Aristotle means to exploit to the uttermost, of *matter* and *form*. But Aristotelian *form* means *structure* – that is, *biological* structure – and that concept is altogether lacking in Empedocles.[52] As long as simple 'mixing' is all that is recognized, Aristotle argues, there is no rational explanation of the repeatable 'complete organic structure', *hē holē morphē*, of 'subcomponents and substructures', *moria kai skeuē*, the 'composition and substance of the whole', *hē sunthesis kai tēs holēs ousia*.[53] The '*logos* of the mixture' is only the crudest beginning.

In sum, to fail to realize that causal agencies beyond the mixing of uniform elements are required to explain the most basic features of the biosphere, is to miss completely the significance of Facts 1–3. Beyond this, Empedocles' theory of generation and animal development fails to come to grips with Facts 4 and 5:

So, Empedocles was wrong when he said that many of the characteristics belonging to animals are due to some accident in the process of their formation, as when he accounts for the vertebrae of the backbone by saying, 'the fetus gets twisted and so the backbone is broken into pieces': he failed to realize (a) that the seed which gives rise to the offspring must have within itself the appropriate type of power; and (b) that the producing agent was preexistent: it was prior not only in formula, but in time: that is, *human being begets human being*, so that it's because the former is such as he is, that the latter's coming-to-be goes as it does.[54]

(There is a notable parallel between Aristotle's physico-biological argument against Empedocles, and the argument for 'forms as causes' at *Phaedo* 96–102. Both operate in the framework of a broad contrast between moving/material 'causes' on one hand and formal/final ones on the other; and for both, the two are related as 'the real cause' (here, form) and 'that without which the real cause couldn't cause' (here, matter) (cf. *Phaedo* 99b, and §19(ii)*).)

13. *First principles of form*

(i) Uniform and non-uniform: a closer look

A conspicuous feature of the succession of stages that are descried in the constitution of a biological object is the advent of 'non-uniform parts'. Now we must look a little more deeply into the concept of

[52] At least, from the evidence we have – but also, from the evidence Aristotle had, which presumably was more than we have. It is plain that he went through Empedocles' verses thoroughly, looking for that concept, and that he did not find it. And he knew what he was looking for.
[53] Thus *PA* 1.1 640b22–9, 1.5 645a30–6 (whence the quoted expressions).
[54] *PA* 1.1 640a20–7 (partially after Peck).

'non-uniformity', the an-homoeomerous, for it is at the core of our concern.

Aristotle nowhere addresses himself to a full-scale analysis of this important idea, being apparently content to convey its gist with schematic intimations of the form, 'such as resolve into parts unlike the whole', together with examples (of the kind already cited in §11). From his practice, however, we can make out some of the features that seem to figure significantly in his understanding of it. (1) The simplest and most obvious feature of something non-uniform in Aristotle's sense is *spatial* heterogeneity or regionalization: differences among its spatial portions; in the case of higher organisms as wholes, animal bodies tend to be organized, and component organs tend to be distributed, along geometrical axes of orientation with respect to which they display characteristic symmetries and (especially) asymmetries – (a) an antero-posterior axis, for the most part associated with the direction of locomotion and orientation of the digestive apparatus, along which animals are generally asymmetrical with respect to fore and aft, (b) a dorso-ventral axis, for the most part associated with the direction of gravity, along which animals are generally asymmetrical with respect to top and bottom; finally (c) a plane of (for the most part) bilateral symmetry, right and left.[55] Similar geometrical characteristics are found in the various organic parts, although some terminological conflation is evident in Aristotle's discussion of this instance between the bipolarity of any linear axis and the bilateral symmetry of certain organ pairs (Kidneys, *et al.*) or of organs that tend to come in halves (Brain, *et al.*).[56] For both organic parts and organic wholes, however, such geometric distributions are highly pervasive, and are in natural objects one source of the fact that dividing the object results in 'parts unlike the whole'.

(2) Closely connected with this in anything non-uniform is the presence of properties that are in various ways irreducibly structural, in the sense of originating in the way in which parts are organized or distributed or related or composed, and not attributable to the same parts in a different arrangement, nor dependent directly

<hr>

[55] Bipolarity with respect to each of three axes (Aristotle calls it being *diphuēs*, or *dimerēs*), *PA* III.5 667b31–4; III.7 669b18–21; *IA* 2 704b17ff.; symmetry and asymmetry, *HA* 1.15 493b17–25. Cf *isophuēs*, *HA* 1.13 493a23. Not all forms manifest these differences along three axes, e.g. the radially-arranged sea-urchin, *PA* IV.5 680b9; and the first two are interchanged in Man, who walks erect, *HA* II.1 498b11 (more accurately, of course: the other forms deviate from the organization in Man, which is the most natural, *PA* II.10 656a10–13). (I continue to leave aside plants, cf. §9.)

[56] *PA* III.7 669b13–670a7.

(though almost always indirectly or mediately, cf. §12(ii) above) on the more elementary materials involved. It is this aspect which Aristotle, unlike ourselves perhaps, seems to conceive of as coming in stages or degrees: there are the fully structural non-uniform parts of animals ('Head, Hand') which resolve into parts different not only from the whole but also from one another; then there are the semistructures ('Bone, Bloodvessel') which, according to him, have parts that *are* like one another and that (for that reason?) can be said 'in a way' to be like the whole as well.[57] In either event, the further factor that is invariably present in any non-uniform entity (of whatever 'grade') – whether it be arrangement, organization, composition or (in biological cases) some highly complex 'form' consisting of a number of these – is not yet another part, but goes to the integration of the parts – in Aristotle's language, not another 'element', but a 'principle'. It comes in enormous variety ('there are *many* differentiae', *Metaph.* H.2 1042b15–25), and is of course *the* central preoccupation of the metaphysics.[58]

(3) A third conspicuous aspect of the non-uniform as manifested in higher organisms is specialization of various regions or tracts of animal bodies to furnish highly specific adaptedness to specific functions: different 'parts' being given over to locomotion, ingestion, digestion, reproduction, sensation and so forth, each in a very definite and particularized manner according to the species in question. The phenomenon is that of *differentiation*, and Aristotle's knowledge of the gross features thereof accessible to megascopic anatomical and physiological observation in a great variety of species is vivid and detailed. (He is quite unaware of the underlying cellular basis of *cyto*-differentiation, knowing, as he does, nothing of cells themselves, and equally unaware of the evolutionary mechanisms involved in bringing about the phenomenon in its currently observable state in the animal kingdom, knowing nothing of organic evolution as well.) His interest in the phenomenon is twofold. Chiefly, first, to understand the 'causes' responsible for these observed facts, *why* it is that the organic parts subserving the various functions in the various particular species are shaped and formed just as they are, and *how* it is that the functional differences of habitat, lifestyle, diet, methods of reproduction and so forth in each species are causally related to the manner of construction of the whole body and its parts of the animal of that species and to one another. A second interest is differentiation in the embryological sense: the processes of genera-

[57] Cf. §11(ii). and the passages from *PA* II there cited (646b30ff., 654a32ff., for 'Viscera', 'Vein', 'Bone').   [58] See §24*, and §13(ii) *fin.* below.

tion, by which pairs of species members produce offspring that are specific replicas, differentia by differentia, of themselves; this motivates a study of the course of events in embryonic development through which the offspring gradually assume specific form over time from conception to completion, and a theoretical inquiry into the 'causal' factors that must be at work here; also, *why* it happens thus.

Not everything that eventuates from Aristotle's pursuit of these two subjects is germane to our philosophical purposes here; those points which are so will occupy the remainder of this and the following two sections. Also, the biological topic of differentiation itself is exceedingly deep and complicated; if we are to avoid drowning in the depths and wandering among the complications it is necessary that we restrict our attention to a few essential points of principle. On that understanding, however, it is useful to pursue the topic a little further; for the fact is that Aristotle does apparently come to conceptualize what he calls 'differentia' in a way that is comparable (as well as contrastable) with the concept that is current today in speaking of the differentiation of tissues, tracts and organs, meaning, specification and specialization of function through adaptive-in-effect articulation and diversification of structure, and this fact has a consequential impact on the advanced metaphysical theory of substance. It also seems as if the Aristotelian notion of differentia may have undergone some noteworthy changes, as between its character in such more programmatically-oriented works of his as the *Topics* and *Analytics* and the (maturer, very likely) form in which we are considering it; failure to appreciate these developments can foster some troublesome and persistent interpretive misconceptions that need to be circumvented if we are to proceed.

(ii) Something important has happened to differentia

The idea of differentia is, if not commonplace, familiar; it goes away back before Aristotle to the Academy and the method of dichotomous Division, according to which by importation of successive qualifying characters a generic kind is subdivided and subdivided again, resulting finally in smallest kinds of which the whole procedure is thus supposed to constitute an analysis or 'definition'. It needs no chronicling here that this technique is discussed, refined and elaborated at length by Aristotle in the *Organon*, and that his celebrated resulting theory of definition and classification, *per genus et differentiam*, passed down through his own text and the influence of Porphyry, the Greek commentators and the medieval tradition, heavily influenced the classical systematic taxonomy associated with Linnaeus that is widely familiar in natural-history connections today. Partly for this reason perhaps (abetted, in this century, by the Jaegerian *Entwicklungs*-scenario and his accompanying chronology of the treatises), it has frequently been thought that a main objective of Aristotelian biology must have been systematic taxonomy too, and the biological treatises the record of its beginnings at ordering, classifying and cataloguing the natural-historical data. However, recent work on this topic points in a quite different direction; and this provides a useful setting for the hypothesis I wish to pursue, that there may have occurred a considerable transformation in the Aristotelian concept of differentia itself, from its original provenance in the Academy and its aspect in such early contexts of discussion as the *Topics* and *Analytics*, to its employment here.

(*Note added for this volume: Since much of the work just referred to is reprinted in this book, the rest of my discussion can be greatly abbreviated. The reader is referred to Balme's ch. 4 below, for a clear account of the treatment of differentia in the* Organon, *for some difficulties in seeing this program as applied to taxonomic concerns in the biological works, and for the beginning of an alternative answer to the question, in his phrase, 'What then was he doing with all these differentiae?' Balme's thesis is that Aristotle is concerned with the* causal *significance of the various found combinations of differentiae, thinking that the systematic interrelatedness of the differentiae constitute a valuable clue to the real nature of the species in the sense of its specifically typical manner of interactive functioning ('doing business') with its environment. All of this is in my estimation correct and valuable. I adopt it here and go further, as follows.*)

The other aspect to differentia in the biological connection is this. The original, 'logical' concept of differentia is basically that of a 'difference from';[59] suppose Number as a genus divides into Odd and Even as species,[60] then the differentia of Even (say, Factorable By Two) represents a difference of Even *from* Odd, something that distinguishes this *from* that co-ordinate kind. It is in this meaning, of contrariety or opposition, that differentia is appropriately seen as 'a sort of otherness';[61] and the idea goes over naturally to the case of the animals: a differentia would be a respect in which this type of animal is different *from that* one. (Here we are close to the original idea of 'definition', as a quasi-literal 'drawing of boundaries' that

---

[59] Cl. Pl. *Tht.* 208cff., *et al.*   [60] Pl. *Euthphr.* 12c, *Top.* 142b10.
[61] *Metaph.* Γ.2 1004a21; cf. Bonitz, *Index* 192b23ff. (s.v. *diaphora*). (Cf. also the everyday use of 'variety'.)

will in principle 'include' what is defined and 'exclude' all else; also related is the notion of obtaining definitions by the 'dividing' (*diairesis*) or 'cutting' (*dichotomē*) of kinds; and indeed in some early works of Aristotle the concepts of both 'definition' and 'differentia' are more or less equated with that of Division.[62])

Now, in the writings with which we here have mainly to do, this intuition, of so-to-speak *horizontal* differentiation of co-ordinate kinds, 'this from that', certainly is not lost. But I think it is also joined by a new and so-to-speak *vertical* dimension, in which it bears something nearer its modern sense, namely what we are calling adaptive-in-effect articulation and diversification of structure: it connotes a manner in which relatively undetermined, only generically characterized structures are variously specialized and specified – in this sense the focus is accordingly upon what a given differentia is a difference *of*: here, of *an underlying generic potentiality, and the differentiae are the particular manners in which that potentiality is found to be restricted or reduced.* Accordingly, the notion of differentia has moved somewhat from its older association with ideas like 'dividing' and 'cutting' with respect to kinds, toward something more like an 'articulating-out', 'articulation' (*diarthrōsis*) of a specifically typical structure in a specifically typical organism, from a lesser-defined substrate potential receiving that finishing-off as final form. Differentia comes to connote determination as well as discrimination, shaping as well as sorting. Cloven-footed is differentiated *from* not-cloven; but both are differentiae *of* foot.[63]

This shift in the central focus of differentia, from being basically a classificatory concept to being one of the construction as well, is of considerable import and needs to be borne steadily in mind. (Yet it is no complete surprise in principle. It was already foreshadowed in a point made about 'constitutive properties' in §8* – we do not in this theory assume automatically to hand a stock of completed individuals that are just 'there', for us merely to 'sort'; rather, there is a problem about how such things are built up: it is necessary to understand their construction as well as their discrimination. The later concept of differentia comes to be a key factor in the theory of 'Formal Causation' meant to deal with this requirement.) Looking ahead momentarily to the advanced stage of development of the theory represented by *Metaphysics* H.2, the constructional or organizational moment in differentia is quite marked:

[62] E.g., *APo.* II.13; cf. the Oxford translator's note on 97a1.
[63] *Metaph.* Z.12 1038a14–15. Difference not otherness: *Metaph.* I.3 1054b23ff. Cf. Pellegrin 1982: 45–6 and below ch. 12, 319–20.

Evidently though, there are *many* differentiae, e.g., (i) some things are constituted [lit. 'are said'] by a composition of the matter, as are such things as are constituted ['said'] by *blending*, like honeywater, (ii) others by *tying*, like a bundle, (iii) others by *gluing*, like a book, (iv) others by *nailing*, like a box, (v) others by more than one of these, (vi) others by *position*, like a threshold or lintel (for these 'differ' by being placed thus-and-so), (vii) others by *time*, like dinner and breakfast, (viii) others by *location*, like the winds, (ix) others by the affections [proper] to sensible things, like hardness and softness, and density and rarity, and dryness and wetness, and [of these], some by some of these [affections], others by them all, and in general, some by excess, others by defect...Of some things the 'being' (*to einai*) will even be defined by all of these [marks], in that some [parts] are mixed, some blended, some bound, some solidified, and some employing the other differentiae, as are Hand, or Foot. (*Metaph.* H.2 1042b15–31; cf. §24(i)*)

By laying such heavy emphasis on the structural character of differentiae I do not mean to suggest that all the differentiae Aristotle
discusses are morphological; he devotes much attention as well to
functional and ethological characteristics, 'differentiae with respect
to manners of life and dispositions and activities' (*kata tous bious kai
ta ēthē kai tas praxeis*, *HA* I.1 487a10, etc.) – habitat, nutrition, social-
ization, breeding characteristics, etc. – the whole range of complex
behavior that so sharply distinguishes the zoological objects from
everything else in the world (cf. Fact 3).[64] But the structural
ones are primary, the functional ones presuppose them, and he
frequently points out the dependence of animals' behavioral works
and deeds, *erga* and *praxeis*, upon their possession of the requisite
highly diversified non-uniform 'parts' with which to perform
them.[65,66]

---

[64] By 'sharply' is meant strikingly, not that there are not gradations of 'activity' between the most active species and non-living things, cf. *PA* IV.5 681a12, esp. *HA* VIII.1 588b4–589a2. Also Balme 1972: 81, 97.

[65] *PA* II.1 646b12–17, 22–5. Plants have fewer such 'organic' parts than animals do because they do fewer things; animals possess more and more varied such parts and a *polumorphoteran idean*, *PA* II.10 655b37–656a8. The 'active faculties' (*poiētikai dunameis*) have to be located in the non-uniform, *HA* I.4 489a27; *GA* I.2 716a23ff, I.18 722b30; *de An.* II.1 412a28; Balme 1972: 88–9 (*ad PA* 641a17).

[66] When this extract was prepared for the present volume (in November 1984), I had not yet read Pierre Pellegrin's *La Classification des animaux chez Aristote* (1982, referred to occasionally above), which intersects with many of the themes touched upon here. I have since done so. Some integration of Pellegrin's ideas with my interpretation is undertaken, after-the-fact, in the parent work (pp. 21–2 above); but in the extract for this volume, I have not tried to update the references to Balme in §13(ii). However, I particularly applaud Pellegrin's emphasis, which accords well with my closing suggestion here, upon divisions and differentiations as fundamentally focused upon the animals' *parts* (see pp. 62–3, 125, 143, 153–4, 188–9 (the 'moriologie étiologique')).

3
Empirical research in
Aristotle's biology*

G. E. R. LLOYD

The range of Aristotle's investigations in zoology is such that a discussion of his use of empirical methods has to be drastically selective. Yet the need to come to some assessment of his performance in this field is all the more pressing in that it has been subject to such divergent judgments. Some of the most extravagant praise, but also some of the most damning criticisms, have been directed at his empirical researches in zoology.[1]

The massive array of information set out in the main zoological treatises[2] can hardly fail to impress at the very least as a formidable piece of organization. But both Aristotle's sources and his principles of selection raise problems. As we have already noted in connection with his use of dissection, it is often impossible to distinguish Aristotle's personal investigations from those of his assistants, although, given the collaborative nature of the work of the Lyceum, that point is not a fundamental one. It is abundantly clear from repeated references in the text that he and his helpers consulted hunters, fishermen, horse-rearers, pig-breeders, bee-keepers, eel-breeders, doctors, veterinary surgeons, midwives and many others with specialized knowledge of animals.[3] But a second major source of information is what he has read, ranging from Homer and other poets, through Ctesias and Herodotus to many of the Hippocratic authors.[4] In general he is cautious in his evaluations of all this

* This selection is excerpted from Lloyd 1979: ch. 3, 'The development of empirical research', pp. 211–20.
[1] Contrast the evaluations in, for example, Bourgey 1955 and Lewes 1864.
[2] The authenticity of some of the later books of *HA* (vii, viii and ix) is open to doubt, but I shall treat the whole (with the exception of x, which most scholars treat as un-Aristotelian) as evidence for work organized and planned by Aristotle, if not carried out by him. Recently D. M. Balme has argued for the authenticity of i–ix, as a whole (Introduction to Balme forthcoming, and ch. 1 above, 16–17) and, as an earlier work not part of *HA*, of x (Balme 1985).
[3] There is a convenient analysis of Aristotle's principal sources in Manquat 1932:31ff., 49ff., 59ff. Cf. also Lones 1912, Le Blond 1939:223ff., Bourgey 1955:73ff., 83ff., Louis 1964–9:xxxiv ff., Preus 1975:21ff., Byl 1980.
[4] See Manquat 1932: chs. 4 and 5, and cf. the analyses of the relationship between Aristotle and the Hippocratic treatises in Poschenrieder 1887 and Byl 1980.

secondary evidence. He points out, for example, that hunters and fishermen do not observe animals from motives of research and that this should be borne in mind.[5] He recognizes, too, the need for experience – a trained eye will spot things that a layman will miss[6] – though even experts make mistakes.[7] He frequently expresses doubts about the reports he has received, emphasizing that some stories have yet to be verified,[8] or flatly rejecting them as fictions[9] – though understandably there are tall stories that he fails to identify as such[10] – and on some occasions the different degrees of acceptance exhibited in different texts may suggest some vacillation on his part.[11] He is particularly critical of some of his literary sources, describing Ctesias as untrustworthy[12] and Herodotus as a 'mythologist'.[13] Yet he sometimes records baldly as 'what has been seen' something for which his principal or even his only evidence may be literary. Thus when at *HA* III. 516a19–20 we read that an instance 'has been seen' of a man's skull with no suture, his (unacknowledged) source may be the famous description of such a case on the battlefield of Plataea in Herodotus (IX 83). When we are told that lions are found in Europe only in the strip of land between the rivers Achelous and Nessus[14] the authority for this may again be a passage in Herodotus (VII 126) which makes a similar suggestion, though the river Nessus appears by its alternative name Ne*s*tus.

Aristotle's use of these sources and of his own personal researches is, naturally, guided throughout by his theoretical interests and preoccupations. The very thoroughness with which he tackles the task of the description of animals reflects his declared aim to assemble

[5] See, e.g., *GA* III. 756a33.
[6] See, e.g., *HA* VI. 566a6–8 (outside the breeding season, the sperm-ducts of cartilaginous fish are not obvious to the inexperienced), 573a11ff., 574b15ff.
[7] E.g. *GA* III. 756b3ff.
[8] E.g. *HA* I. 493b14ff., VI. 580a19–22. That further research is necessary is a point repeatedly made in other contexts as well.
[9] E.g. *HA* VI. 579b2ff., VIII. 597a32ff. *PA* III. 673a10–31 is a careful discussion of stories about men laughing when wounded in the midriff: he rejects as impossible the idea that a head, severed from the body, could speak (since voice depends on the windpipe) but accepts that movement of the trunk may occur after decapitation.
[10] E.g. *HA* V. 552b15ff. on the salamander extinguishing fire.
[11] As in the notable case of his reports on the phenomenon now known as the hectocotylization of one of the tentacles of the octopus, recorded without endorsement at *HA* V. 541b8ff., cf. 544a12ff., and apparently accepted at IV. 524a5ff., but rejected at *GA* I. 720b32ff. Such divergences may, of course, indicate not a change of mind, but inauthentic material in, or plural authorship of, the zoological works.
[12] *HA* IX. 606a8.
[13] The context suggests that the term *muthologos*, used of Herodotus at *GA* III. 756b6ff., there carries pejorative undertones.
[14] *HA* VI. 579b5ff., cf. VIII. 606b14ff.

the 'appearances' (*phainomena*), the differentiae of animals and their properties, before proceeding to state their causes.[15] As we have noted, this very program obliges Aristotle to be comprehensive in his account, and certain features of the way he implements it stand out. His stated preference for the formal and final causes, rather than the material, dictates greater attention being paid to the functions of the organic and inorganic parts than to their material composition, although the latter is also discussed, indeed sometimes, as in the case of blood,[16] at some length. More importantly, the form of the living creature is its *psuchē*, life or soul, and his psychological doctrines influence his investigations not only in insuring a detailed discussion of, for example, the presence or absence of particular senses in different species of animals in the *De Sensu*, of the different modes of locomotion in the *De Motu* and *De Incessu*, and of the fundamental problem of reproduction in the *De Generatione Animalium*, but also by providing the general framework for his description of the internal and external parts of animals in the *Historia*.

Thus at *PA* II.655b29ff. and *Juv.* 468a13ff. he identifies the three main essential parts of animals as (1) that by which food is taken in, (2) that by which residues are discharged, and (3) what is intermediate between them – where the *archē* or controlling principle is located: in addition animals capable of locomotion also have organs for that purpose, and in the corresponding passage in *HA* I.2 and 3 he further adds reproductive organs where male and female are distinguished.[17] In his detailed account of the internal and external parts of the four main groups of bloodless animals (cephalopods, crustacea, testacea and insects) in *HA* IV.1–7 he evidently works quite closely to this broad and simple schema. Thus he regularly considers such questions as the position of the mouth, the presence or absence of teeth and tongue or analogous organs, the position and nature of the stomach and gut and of the vent for residue, as also the reproductive organs and differences between males and females. A series of passages shows that he actively considered whether or not certain lower groups produced residue and attempted to identify and trace the excretory vent.[18] But while the whole course of the alimentary canal is thoroughly discussed in connection with each of

[15] See *PA* I. 639b8ff., 640a14–15, *HA* I. 491a9ff. especially.
[16] E.g. *PA* II.4 and cf. the subsequent chapters on fat, marrow, brain, flesh and bone. *PA* II.2 discusses the problems posed by the ambiguity of hot and cold and stresses the difficulty of determining which substances are hot and which cold.
[17] *HA* I. 488b29ff., especially 489a8ff., and cf. also *PA* II. 650a2ff.
[18] See *HA* IV. 530a2ff., 531a12ff., b8ff.

the bloodless groups,[19] he has little or nothing to say about the brain[20] or about the respiratory (or as he would say refrigeratory) system.[21] Again while the external organs of locomotion are carefully identified and classified, the internal musculature is ignored throughout.[22] It would certainly be excessive to suggest that his observations are everywhere determined by his preconceived schema: yet the influence that that schema exercised on his discussion is manifest.

In other cases too it is not hard to trace the influence of his theoretical preoccupations and preconceptions on his observational work, not only – naturally enough – on the questions he asked, but also – more seriously – on the answers he gave, that is on what he represents as the results of his research. His search for final causes is an often cited example, though it is not so much his general assumption of function and finality in biological organisms, as some of his rather crude particular suggestions, that are open to criticism: moreover he is clear that not everything in the animal serves a purpose[23] and that it is not only the final cause that needs to be considered. But many slipshod or plainly mistaken observations (or what purport to be such) relate to cases where we can detect certain underlying value judgments at work. The assumption of the superiority of right to left is one example that has been mentioned before.[24] His repeated references to the differences between man and other animals, and between males and females, are two other areas where errors and hasty generalizations are especially frequent. Man is not only marked out from the other animals by being erect – by having his parts, as Aristotle puts it, in their natural positions[25] – and

---

[19] *HA* IV. 527b1ff. concludes that the stomach, esophagus and gut alone are common to bloodless and blooded groups (the passage is considered suspect by some editors, but it sums up Aristotle's position well enough). In the strictest sense in which the term *splanchnon* is reserved for red-blooded organs, the bloodless animals have no viscera at all, but only what is analogous to them: *HA* IV. 532b7ff., *PA* III. 665a28ff., IV. 678a26ff.

[20] In *HA* IV.1–7 the brain is mentioned only at 524b4 and in a probably corrupt passage, 524b32. Cf. *HA* I. 494b27ff., and *PA* II. 652b23ff.

[21] In *Resp.* 475b7ff., however, he says that the crustacea and octopuses need little refrigeration and at 476b30ff. that the cephalopods and crustacea effect this by admitting water, which the crustacea expel through certain opercula, that is the gills (cf. also *HA* IV. 524b21ff.).

[22] This point can be extended also to his descriptions of the blooded animals. Although his account of the external organs of locomotion in *IA* is, on the whole, quite detailed, he has almost nothing to say of the disposition and functioning of the muscles. Similarly his osteology (with the exception of his description of the limbs) is in general crude: even though he writes in praise of the hand, remarking on the importance of the opposition of thumb and fingers for prehension (see *PA* IV. 687a7ff., b2ff., 690a30ff.) he limits his account of its bones to remarks on the number of fingers and toes in the forelimbs of different species.

[23] There is an explicit statement to this effect at *PA* IV. 677a15ff., for example.

[24] The main examples of anatomical doctrines influenced by his beliefs that right is superior to left, up to down, and front to back, are collected in Lloyd 1973.

[25] E.g. *PA* II. 656a10ff., *IA* 706a19–20, b9–10.

by possessing the largest brain for his size, hands and a tongue adapted for speech:[26] Aristotle also claims, more doubtfully, that man's blood is the finest and purest,[27] that his flesh is softest,[28] and that the male human emits more seed, and the female more menses, in proportion to their size.[29]

While his general distinction between male and female animals relates to a capacity or incapacity to concoct the blood,[30] he records largely or totally imaginary differences in the sutures of the skull,[31] in the number of teeth,[32] in the size of the brain,[33] and in the temperature,[34] of men and women. His view that in general males are better equipped with offensive and defensive weapons than females[35] is one factor that leads him to the conclusion that the worker bees are male.[36] To be sure, he sometimes notes exceptions to his general rules, as when he remarks that although males are usually bigger and stronger than females in the non-oviparous blooded animals the reverse is true in most oviparous quadrupeds, fish and insects,[37] and while he goes along with the common belief that male embryos usually move first on the right-hand side of the womb, females on the left, he remarks that this is not an exact statement since there are many exceptions.[38] But although there are certainly inaccuracies in his reported observations besides those that occur where an *a priori* assumption is at work, those where that is the case form a considerable group.[39]

We can document the influence of his over-arching theories on what he reports he has seen: but there are other occasions when the theories themselves appear to depend on, and may in some cases even be derived from, one or more observations (however accurate or

[26] See, e.g., *PA* II. 653a27ff., IV. 687b2ff., II. 660a17ff. and Lloyd 1983: 26ff.

[27] See *HA* III. 521a2ff., cf. *PA* II. 648a9ff., *Resp.* 477a20–1.

[28] *PA* II. 660a11, cf. *GA* V. 781b21–2.

[29] See *HA* III. 521a26–7, *HA* VII. 582b28ff., 583a4ff., *GA* I. 728b14ff.

[30] See *GA* I. 728a18ff., IV. 765b8ff. and Lloyd 1983: 94ff.

[31] See *HA* I. 491b2ff., *HA* III. 516a18ff., *PA* II. 653b1.

[32] See *HA* II. 501b19ff.

[33] See *PA* II. 653a28ff. (on which see Ogle 1882: 167).

[34] E.g. *GA* IV. 765b16–17, 775a5ff.

[35] E.g. *HA* IV. 538b15ff., *PA* III. 661b28ff.

[36] See *GA* III. 759b2ff.

[37] *HA* IV. 538a22ff., V. 540b15–16, *GA* I. 721a17ff.

[38] See *HA* VII. 583b2ff., and 5ff., and cf. further below, p. 59, on *GA* IV. 764a33ff. Cf. also *HA* VII. 584a12ff. on exceptions to the rule that women have easier pregnancies with male children.

[39] Another important group of mistakes relates to exotic species (for which parts of *HA* especially show some predilection) where he was, no doubt, relying more on secondary sources or hearsay. Thus many of his statements about the lion are erroneous (see Ogle 1882: 236). See also the mistakes mentioned by Bourgey 1955: 84–5 (there are inaccuracies in those listed by Lewes 1864: 164ff.).

inaccurate) which accordingly take on a particular significance for his argument. Undoubtedly the most striking example of this[40] is his often repeated statement that the heart is the first part of the embryo to develop. This is introduced at *Juv.* 468b28ff. as something that is 'clear from what we have observed in those cases where it is possible to see them as they come to be'. At *PA* III. 666a18ff. he says that the primacy of the heart is clear not only according to argument, but also according to perception,[41] and in reporting his investigation of the growth of hen's eggs in particular he remarks that after about three days the heart first appears as a blood spot that 'palpitates and moves as though endowed with life'.[42] The circumstantial detail of this and other accounts show that they are based on first-hand inspection, although the conclusion Aristotle arrived at is not entirely correct: as Ogle put it, 'the heart is not actually the first structure that appears in the embryo, but it is the first part to enter actively into its functions'.[43] However the consequences of Aristotle's observation were momentous. This provides the crucial empirical support for his doctrine that it is the heart – rather than say the brain – that is the principle of life, the seat not just of the nutritive soul, but also of the faculty of locomotion and of the common sensorium. As in the physical treatises, so too in his biology, Aristotle often constructs a general theory largely by extrapolation from a slight – and sometimes insufficiently secure – empirical foundation.

Destructively, however, his deployment of observations to refute opposing theories is often highly effective. This can be illustrated first with some fairly straightforward examples. (1) The idea that drink passes to the lungs is one that we know to have been widely held,[44] although it is attacked by the author of the Hippocratic treatise *On Diseases* IV.[45] At *PA* III. 664b6ff. Aristotle dismisses it primarily on the

[40] Two others would be (1) his claim to have verified that the brain is cold to *touch*, *PA* II. 652a34–5 (not true of a recently dead warm-blooded animal) – which was no doubt a major factor in contributing to his theory that the primary function of the brain is to counterbalance the heat of the heart and (2) his reported observation that a bull that had just been castrated was able to impregnate a cow (*GA* I. 717b3ff., cf. *HA* III. 510b2ff.) – which presumably influenced his doctrine that the testes are mere appendages, not integral to the seminal passages (e.g. *GA* I. 717a34ff.).

[41] Again at *GA* II. 740a3ff. he says that not only perception but also argument shows that the heart is the first part to become distinct in actuality. Cf. also *PA* III. 666a8ff., *GA* II. 740a17–18, 741b15–16.

[42] *HA* VI. 561a6ff., 11–12, *PA* III. 665a33ff.

[43] Ogle 1897: 110 n. 24, and cf. 1882:193.

[44] This we know from *Morb.* IV ch. 56, Littré VII 608.17ff. The view is found in Plato, *Ti.* 70c, is attributed to Philistion by Plutarch (*Quaest. Conv.* VII 1, 698A ff., at 699c) and after Aristotle was the subject of an attempted experimental demonstration in *Cord.* ch. 2, Littré IX 80.9ff.

[45] The nine proofs, *historia*, that this author adduces are a very mixed bag: they include not only a reference to the epiglottis and its function (VII 608.23ff.) but also arguments that

simple anatomical grounds that there is no communicating link
between the lungs and the stomach (as there is between the stomach
and the mouth, namely the esophagus), and the confidence with
which he rebuts the theory is clearly seen in his concluding remarks:
'but it is perhaps silly to be excessively particular in examining silly
statements'.[46] (2) At *GA* II. 746a19ff. he refutes the view that human
embryos are nourished in the womb by sucking a piece of flesh: if that
were true, the same would happen in other animals, but it does not,
as is easy to observe by means of dissection. And while that remark
is quite general,[47] he follows it with a specific reference to the
membranes separating the embryo from the uterus itself.[48] Dissection
again provides the evidence to refute (3) those who held that the sex
of the embryo is determined by the side of the womb it is on,[49] and
(4) the view that some birds copulate through their mouths.[50]

In such instances an appeal to easily verifiable points of anatomy
was enough to undermine the theory. But more often no such direct
refutation was possible, and Aristotle deploys a combination of
empirical and dialectical arguments to attack his opponents' positions. One final example of this is his extended discussion, in *GA* I.17
and 18, of the doctrine that later came to be known as pangenesis,
that is the view that the seed is drawn from the whole of the body.[51]
Here most of what passed as empirical evidence was agreed on both
sides, and the strengths of Aristotle's discussion lie in his acute
exploration first of the coherence of his opponents' doctrine, and
secondly of the inferences that could legitimately be drawn from the
available data.

One of the principal arguments he mounts against pangenesis poses
a dilemma:[52] the seed must be drawn either (1) from all the uniform

if drink went to the lungs, one would not be able to breathe or speak when full, that another
consequence would be that dry food would not be so easily digested, that eating garlic
makes the urine smell, and other often inconclusive or question-begging considerations,
see VII 606.7ff.

[46] *PA* III. 664b18–19.
[47] Some of Aristotle's general appeals to what would be shown by dissection are clearly
hypothetical and were not followed up: thus at *PA* IV. 677a5ff. he dismisses the view of
Anaxagoras' followers that the gall-bladder causes acute diseases with the claim that those
who suffer from such diseases mostly have no gall-bladder and 'this would be clear if they
were dissected'.
[48] *GA* II. 746a23ff. says that this is true for all embryos in animals that fly, swim and walk.
[49] *GA* IV. 764a33ff., cf. 765a16ff.; yet he is prepared to allow that males often move first on
the right-hand side (*HA* VII. 583b2ff.; cf. b5ff.), and also that, given that the right-hand
side of the body is hotter than the left, and that hotter semen is more concocted, seed from
the right side is more likely to produce males (*GA* IV. 765a34ff., but cf. b4ff.).
[50] *GA* III. 756b16ff., especially 27ff.
[51] Our principal original sources for the pangenesis doctrine are the Hippocratic treatises,
Genit., *Nat. Puer.* and *Morb.* IV. See Lesky 1951:70ff and Lonie 1981.
[52] *GA* I. 722a16–b3.

parts (such as flesh, bone, sinew) or (2) from all the non-uniform
parts (such as hand, face) or (3) from both. Against (1) he objects
that the resemblances that children bear to their parents lie rather
in such features as their faces and hands, than in their flesh and bones
as such. But if the resemblances in the non-uniform parts are not due
to the seed being drawn from *them*, why must the resemblances in the
uniform parts be explained in that way? Against (2) he points out
that the non-uniform parts are composed of the uniform ones: a hand
consists of flesh, bone, blood and so on. Moreover this option would
suggest that the seed is not drawn from *all* the parts. He tackles (3)
too by considering what must be said about the non-uniform parts.
Resemblances in these must be due either to the material – but that
is simply the uniform parts – or to the way in which the material is
arranged or combined. But on that view, nothing can be said to be
drawn from the *arrangement* to the seed, since the arrangement is not
itself a material factor. Indeed a similar argument can be applied to
the uniform parts themselves, since they consist of the simple bodies
combined in a particular way. Yet the resemblance in the parts is
due to their arrangement or combination, and has therefore to be
explained in terms of what brings this about,[53] and not by the seed
being drawn from the whole body.

A series of further arguments follow, for example that the seed
cannot be drawn from the reproductive organs at least, because the
offspring has only male or female organs, not both (*GA* I. 722b3ff.),
and again that the seed cannot be drawn from all the parts of both
parents, for then we should have two animals (b6ff.). At *GA* I.
722b30ff. he considers how the uniform and non-uniform parts are
to be defined, namely in terms of certain qualities and functions
respectively. Thus unless a substance has certain qualities it cannot
be called 'flesh'. But it is plain that we cannot call what comes from
the parent *flesh*, and we must agree that that comes from something
which is not flesh.[54] But there is no reason not to agree that other
substances may do the same, so again the idea that all the substances
in the body are represented in the seed fails.

At the same time it is notable that he not only challenges the scope
and significance of the evidence his opponents cite, but also shows
some ingenuity in collecting other data that pose difficulties for them.
One of the main arguments they used depended on the supposed fact

[53] The semen has just such a function, as supplying the efficient cause, in Aristotle's own theory.
[54] He is led from this to consider Anaxagoras' theory that none of the uniform substances comes into being.

that mutilated parents produce mutilated offspring, and among the evidences (*marturia*) they cited was that of children born with scars where their parents were scarred, and a case at Chalcedon of a child of a branded father born with a faint brand mark: it was claimed, as Aristotle puts it, that children resemble their parents in respect not only of congenital characteristics (*ta sumphuta*) but also of acquired ones (*ta epiktēta*).[55] But this he counters simply by pointing out that not all the offspring of mutilated parents are themselves mutilated, just as not all children resemble their parents.[56] Among the evidence he brings against pangenesis he cites (1) that many plants lack certain parts (they can be torn off, and yet the seed thereafter produces a new plant that is identical with the old, *GA* I. 722a11ff.) and (2) that plant cuttings bear seed – from which he says it is clear that even when the cutting belonged to the original plant the seed it bore did not come from the *whole* of that plant (*GA* I. 723b16ff.).

But the most important consideration, in his view, is (3) what he claims to have observed in insects (*GA* I. 723b19ff.). In most cases, during copulation the female insect inserts a part into the male, rather than the male into the female. This by itself looks quite inconclusive, but Aristotle believes that in such cases it is not semen, but simply the heat and the *dunamis* (capacity) of the male that brings about generation by 'concocting' the fetation.[57] He remarks quite cautiously that not enough observations have been carried out in such cases to enable him to classify them by kinds, and his remark that the males do not have seminal passages is introduced with *phainetai* in the tentative sense, 'appears' rather than 'it is evident'.[58] Yet this erroneous observation is not only his 'strongest evidence'[59] against pangenesis, but also one of the crucial pieces of 'factual' support that he cites for his own view that the role of the male in reproduction is to supply the efficient cause, not to contribute directly to the material of the offspring.[60] In the main the arguments mounted against pangenesis are telling ones, and they draw on well known, and some not so well known, data to good effect: even so, the chief point that derives from Aristotle's personal researches in these chapters is one where, under the influence, no doubt, of his general

[55] *GA* I. 721b17ff., and 28ff.

[56] *GA* I. 724a3ff., cf. *HA* VII. 585b35ff.

[57] See especially *GA* I. 729b21–33, and cf. other references to species that do not emit seed in copulation, 731a14ff., II. 733b16ff.

[58] See *GA* I. 721a12, 14ff.   [59] *GA* I. 723b19.

[60] See *GA* I. 729b8–9 and 21–2, where in both cases there is a contrast between *logos* and *erga*. Cf. also b33ff. with some equally doubtful evidence such as the supposed fact that a hen bird trodden twice will have eggs that resemble the second cock.

theories, he assumed too readily that his observations yielded a
conclusion that supported them.

It is apparent that much of Aristotle's biology – like his physics –
does not live up to his own high ideals. His drawing attention to the
inadequacy of certain of the information available to him and to the
need to survey all the relevant *huparchonta* ('data'),[61] does not prevent
him from being less than persistent in his research in some areas, nor
deter him from some highly speculative theories in others. Where he
remarks on other writers' inexperience of internal anatomy, for
example,[62] or charges them with not taking what is familiar as the
starting-point of their inquiries,[63] with generalizing from a few cases
or otherwise jumping to conclusions on inadequate evidence,[64] or
with guessing what the result of a test would be and assuming what
would happen before actually seeing it,[65] in each case similar
criticisms could be leveled at him to some – if not the same – extent.

Nevertheless two simple but fundamental points remain. First, if
he does not always live up to his own methodological principles, at
least they are stated as the principles to follow. The end is defined
in terms of giving the causes and resolving the difficulties in the
common assumptions: he is no fact-collector for the sake of fact-
collecting. But as means to his ends the appeal to the evidence of the
senses is allotted its distinct role, alongside the reference to generally
accepted opinions and the use of reasoned argument, and he makes
it clear that in certain contexts at least it is the first of these that is
to be preferred. Moreover his is the first *generalized* program of inquiry
into natural science: his doctrine of causes identifies the kind of
questions to be asked, and he provides an explicit protreptic to the
study of each branch of natural science as far as each is possible.[66]

Secondly the limitations of his observational work should not lead
us to ignore the extrordinary scope of what he did achieve in the
various departments of the inquiry concerning nature. An analysis
of what he says he has observed and of how he uses this to support
his theories sometimes reveals the superficiality of his empirical
research. Yet as the first systematic study of animals, the zoological
treatises represent a formidable achievement, not only in the individual discoveries that are recorded, but also in the patient and

[61] Apart from *PA* I. 639b8ff., 640a14ff., *HA* I. 491a9ff., see also, e.g., *GA* II. 735b7–8, 748a14ff.
[62] See, e.g., *Resp.* 470b8–9, 471b23ff.
[63] E.g. *GA* II. 747b5–6, 748a8–9, IV. 765b4–5.
[64] E.g. *PA* IV. 676b33ff., *GA* III. 756a2ff., b16ff., v. 788b11ff., 17ff.
[65] *GA* IV. 765a25–9.
[66] *PA* 1.5 644b22ff.: the study of the heavenly bodies and of animals each has its own
attractions.

painstaking amassing of a vast amount of data concerning many different species and in the ingenious interplay of data and arguments in his assault on such obscure problems as those connected with reproduction.

PART II

DEFINITION AND DEMONSTRATION:
THEORY AND PRACTICE

...for it becomes apparent from [this *historia*] both *about which things* and *from which things* the *apodeixis* must proceed.

(*HA* I. 491a13–14)

Introduction

Some years ago, Jonathan Barnes introduced a discussion of 'Aristotle's theory of demonstration' with the following statement:

This, then, is the problem: on the one hand we have a highly formalised theory of scientific methodology; on the other a practice innocent of formalisation and exhibiting rich and variegated methodological pretensions of its own. How are the two to be reconciled? (Barnes 1975b:66)

Barnes argued against three traditional attempts at reconciliation, and provided a radical diagnosis for these failures: the scientific treatises report the tentative explorations of ongoing inquiries, while the *Posterior Analytics* provides a theory of how to *present* already acquired knowledge. On this view, the attempt to shed light on the *APo.* theory of scientific knowledge by a close study of the biological treatises is doomed at the outset.

Barnes has himself drawn back from this conclusion (1981), reviving Friedrich Solmsen's thesis that there is a presyllogistic theory of demonstrative science within *APo.*, which may after all be reflected in the scientific treatises. Both of these papers presuppose that unless one first accounts for the absence, in Aristotle's zoological explanations, of an overtly syllogistic form, one cannot proceed any further in exploring the relationship between his theory of science and his scientific practice.

The four papers in this Part may lead to a reconsideration of this presupposition. For they argue for the place in Aristotle's biological thinking of five subjects which are at the heart of his philosophy of

65

science as presented in the *Analytics*: division, explanation, dialectic, definition, and axiomatic structure. And they do so while largely bracketing the issue of the role of syllogistic in Aristotelian science.

David Balme's contribution joins to his classic study of 'Aristotle's use of differentiae in zoology' (1961; rev. 1975) an examination of the reforms of Academic division (*diairesis*) undertaken by Aristotle. It draws and expands upon material in Balme 1972, incorporating the important results of Pierre Pellegrin's work (summarized by Pellegrin in his contribution to Part IV below), and introduces Balme's most recent thoughts on a number of issues.

Balme's earlier paper took the aims of *Historia Animalium* as its primary subject, and showed that it was neither natural history nor taxonomy: the data were highly selective and organized not around animals but around their differentiae, and there was no systematic attempt to construct or define intermediate genera. Rather, Balme argued, its aim, in line with the recommendation of *APo*. II.14, was 'the significant, causal grouping of differentiae' as a necessary preliminary to a full study of causes.

More recently, impressed by the connections between the opening of *HA* and the analysis in *PA* 1.2–4, he has come to think that *HA* has in addition a more immediate purpose, more directly related to definition. Causal explanation presupposes a grasp of the exact nature of the differentiae to be explained (and of those that do the explaining), and a pre-causal (or as Balme calls it, non-rigorous or non-formal) account of animal kinds. This, as much as the grouping for purposes of causal explanation, he argues both here and at the close of his contribution to Part I, is the aim of *HA*, and this too makes it a deeply theoretical treatise.

To help place *HA* in the context of these theoretical concerns, Balme traces a series of reforms of Platonic *diairesis* from the *Topics* through the *Analytics* and *Metaphysics* Z to the critique of dichotomy and the presentation of the concept of simultaneous, multi-axis division in *PA* 1.2–4. This 'final reform of *diairesis*' embodies the earlier reforms but reflects an attempt to apply them to the more complex objects typical of biological inquiry.

James Lennox's contribution develops Balme's suggestion that *APo*. II.14 is a key text in solving the puzzle of the relationship between division and demonstration in Aristotle's scientific method. Central to the theory of the *APo*. is the articulation of a distinction between incidental and unqualified understanding. Unqualified understanding requires locating the widest kinds to which differentiae belong universally: this allows explanations of why sub-kinds of

these widest kinds have the differentiae in question, and identifies
those features which are either essential to the kind, or explicable as
consequences of its essence. Lennox argues that *APo.* II.14–18
explores the nature of explanation based on this insight. Finally, and
these are the primary aims of his argument, Lennox suggests that *HA*
organizes information about animals in accordance with this
methodology, and that *PA* provides explanations of both sorts.

The picture of the aims of *HA* defended by Lennox differs from
Balme's earlier one in finding a much more central and systematic
place in *HA* for the 'grouping of differentiae', but remains very
much in its spirit. As such, it can take its place beside Balme's
more recent emphasis on the preliminary definitional aims of
HA. The identification and grouping of differentiae make possible
the discovery of their causes, and thereby their 'formal' or causal
definition. The question then remains how these causal definitions,
crucial to a science organized on Aristotelian lines, are to be
established. This, and related issues, are the subject of Robert
Bolton's contribution.

In 'Definition and scientific method in Aristotle's *Posterior Analytics*
and *Generation of Animals*', Bolton first gives careful consideration to
the commonly held view that dialectic, in the sense of reasoning
based on common or noted opinions (*endoxa*), was Aristotle's primary
method of establishing results in the study of nature. He argues,
against G. E. L. Owen's claim in his influential ' *Tithenai ta phainomena*' (1975), that even in the *Physics* Aristotle's method is *empirical* in
ways that dialectic cannot be; and he shows that this result holds
generally for Aristotle's method in biology and the other physical
sciences. He insists that the dialectical consideration of a subject's
endoxa is at best a necessary accompaniment to empirical investigation and is never sufficient for the grounding of one's scientific
starting-points.

Building on his own previous work on *APo.* II.7–10, Bolton insists
that 'a fairly full picture of what paths scientific inquiry normally
takes' can be gleaned from Aristotle's account of the different types
of definition, and their relationship to each other. The reader is then
led through the analysis of the principles of generation in *GA* I, prima
facie the most 'dialectical' passage in the biology, focusing on the
account of the nature of *sperma*. Bolton finds that there is a gradual
articulation of a basic causal account of *sperma* from an initial
definition much closer to common experience. He argues that this
development conforms to the pattern of inquiry elaborated in *APo.* II
but not to anything required by dialectic. Insofar as dialectic has

a role to play, it is as part of the argument 'against the received doctrine', where that is inadequate, serving thereby, 'to fix what is obvious to us at the initial stage of inquiry'. The essay closes with a suggestion that the pattern found here may well be repeated in other scientific treatises.

Finally, Allan Gotthelf faces head-on the question of whether the *Parts of Animals* exemplifies anything approaching an axiomatic structure, a central necessary condition for a science organized on *APo.* lines. Are there, in short, first principles at the base of its complex explanatory structure? And is there a discernible order of priority in the explanatory strategy of this work? Like Bolton and Lennox, Gotthelf distinguishes these questions from that of whether *PA*'s explanations have syllogistic form, though he has something to say about this issue at the end of his essay. There is, it turns out, such a structure, and Gotthelf spends some time trying to bring it out, giving special attention to the role in that structure of (i) postulations of animal forms as ends, (ii) propositions about the nature of the matter that constitutes the organism, and the part, under discussion, and (iii) partial definitions of animal kinds. He concludes with some suggestions regarding the relationship between this structure and the structure proposed for a proper science in *APo.*, and some remarks on what the practice in *PA* might suggest for our understanding of the character of *APo.* itself.

Aristotle's theoretical discussions of the nature and methodology of proper science are often programmatic, elliptical, even downright obscure, on subjects central to their argument. If, then, the overall thrust of the papers in this Part is correct, the biological works may help put flesh on those skeletal accounts, and we may once again be ravished, not exasperated, by those 'Sweet Analytics'.

4
Aristotle's use of
division and differentiae

D. M. BALME

I. The reform of *diairesis*

Aristotle's comments on logical division (*diairesis*) evidently refer to
a more regular method than the examples given in Plato's late
dialogues, but unfortunately no reliable evidence survives of Academic practice between the dialogues and Aristotle's *Topics*.[1] We
cannot know how much of the rules that Aristotle lays down may
represent a codification of existing methods, and how much is
correction of them. It is clear, however, that the criticisms and rules,
which he sets out with great profusion of detail in the *Topics* and
Analytics, are intended to ensure a good method, not merely to
demolish bad ones, so that the picture which they build up may be
taken as the form of *diairesis* of which he himself approved. It is very
different from that set out by Plato, and the difference is exactly what
we should expect after the change in philosophical viewpoint from
Plato's theory of forms to Aristotle's theory of the substantial *tode ti*.
Aristotle presents three major innovations: (i) the ontological
distinctions between genus, differentia, species, property, essential
and inessential accident, and other formal categories, which Plato
did not distinguish; (ii) the insistence on successive differentiation,
to preserve the unity of definition; (iii) division by a plurality of
differentiae simultaneously, instead of by one at a time. These
improvements are made respectively in (i) *Topics* and *Categories*; (ii)
Posterior Analytics and *Metaphysics*; (iii) *De Partibus Animalium* I. Quite
possibly this is in fact their chronological order; but in any case they
represent a continuing refinement of *diairesis*, not a rejection of it.

Platonic division

Plato's original description of *diairesis*, at *Phaedrus* 265d, presents it
as the second stage of a logical procedure which he names 'dialectic'

[1] Cf. Cherniss 1944: 1–82; Balme 1962b: 81; Kullmann 1974: 342.

and treats as very important. The first stage is 'collection', in which disparate objects are grouped according to their 'form' (*idea*). The second stage is 'division', in which a general group is divided into different forms, and these forms are further divided until one reaches the object of definition. For example, (*Politicus* 263e), after deciding that our object has the form 'animal', we might divide animals into tame and wild, then the tame into gregarious and solitary, the gregarious into aquatic and terrestrial, the terrestrial into horned and hornless, and so on until we narrow it down to a class which contains only our definiendum. Then by recalling all the divisions we can show the forms in which it participates – it is animal, tame, gregarious, terrestrial, hornless, etc. During the second stage Plato emphasizes that we must verify the 'cuts' against the natural divisions, and not chop across the joints like an unskillful butcher (*Phaedrus* 265e): the division therefore corrects the original collection. It is the same inductive–deductive procedure that Aristotle sets out at *APo.* II. 97b7.

Plato's most elaborate examples are in the *Sophist* and *Politicus*, which show that he would construct several separate divisions to reach the same definiendum, and would then extract from them together what seemed to be the best characterizations (e.g. *Sph.* 221–31). This strongly suggests that his aim was not to classify but to define – to 'track down' (*thēreuein*) a given object and 'discover what exactly it is' (*heurein hoti pot' estin, Sph.* 221c). Aristotle, who uses the same metaphor of hunting, makes it clear that his aim in *diairesis* is definition, not classification; for at *APo.* II. 97a6 he argues that in order to secure the definiendum it is necessary to ensure that it is wholly contained within the classes taken, but not necessary to know the contents of the excluded classes. Here he is opposing Speusippus, who had argued that it is impossible to be sure of some differentiae without knowing all, an argument that would necessitate setting up a comprehensive classification.

Plato's examples also show that each stage of division is in fact preceded by a new inductive grouping, so that a new form is added to the list. In the example already quoted from *Plt.* 263e, the division of tame animals into gregarious/solitary really represents a new grouping of all animals, since wild animals too divide into gregarious/solitary. Plato has divided the whole class animal twice, into tame/wild and into gregarious/solitary. He offers no reason why one of these divisions should precede the other. What he achieves is to select those animals that are both tame and gregarious (and terrestrial and hornless, etc.). This is not therefore a progressive differentiation, but a succession of independent collections and divisions. Each form is added arbitrarily by intuition, and there is no order of priority nor hierarchy among them. Obviously it is important that the list should be complete, as he says at *Plt.* 267c; but there is no way of guaranteeing this except by inspection (as exemplified at *Sph.* 231c ff.). This method was to be criticized by Aristotle as 'accidental' or false division. For Plato's purposes, however, it is adequate, since he regards each form as independent, not as a class enclosing other forms: if man is animal-biped-wingless, this means for Plato that the form of man combines (*sumplokē*, *koinōnia*) with the forms animal, biped and wingless.

Plato's dialogues indicate no firm technical terminology for *diairesis*. He calls each class indifferently a kind, a form, a part (*genos*, *eidos*, *meros*). This indifference confirms that he was not distinguishing the status of different forms, nor asserting any relationship or hierarchy among them. For his purpose it was important to assign an object correctly to its kind; so he is parodied by the comic poet Epicrates as exercising himself over the assignment of a gourd (Epicr. fr. 11, 11. p. 287 K). The combining of forms was a serious problem for him (*Prm.* 129e; *Sph.* 251d), but it did not lead him to the grand classifications of reality that were later proposed by the neoplatonists. Although the 'Divided Line' in *Republic* VI suggests a hierarchy of orders of intelligibility, it does not produce either a class-inclusion analysis or the categorical distinctions that Aristotle made between genus, differentia, species and attribute.

The reforms

These latter distinctions, which are primarily ontological, became necessary after Aristotle's abandonment of the theory of subsistent forms which combine together: to explain the natural sense-perceived object, he needed to distinguish its essential being from its adventitious attributes, and its general nature from its particular characteristics. He achieves this analysis in the *Topics*, which have been rightly said to consist largely of rules for the control of *diairesis*. They are his first and crucial reform of Plato's method, transforming it from a study of the 'combining of forms' into an analysis of the substantial unitary object's 'being' – not what forms it participates in but what it itself is. Fundamental to the *Topics* is the theory of categories of being, which distinguishes the status of genus, species, differentia, qualification, essential and inessential accidents, and the rest. Genus is now reserved for the general kind to which an object

belongs, that is its basic nature in the sense that a horse is basically
a quadruped animal, so that the explanation of a horse's nature must
start from this premise. But genus is no longer a subsistent form:
quadruped animal exists only as a horse or a cow, that is it exists
only in its own 'forms' (*eidē*). A *genos* therefore is a kind that collects
different forms, while an *eidos* is one of the forms of a kind. The *genos*
itself may be a member of a wider *genos* collecting similar genera,
in which case Aristotle speaks of 'kinds under each other', *genē hup'*
allēla; similarly an *eidos* may be divisible into *eidē*, in which case it may
be regarded as a *genos* in this respect (*Ph.* v. 227b11). Such a division
might contain several stages between the widest genus and the infima
species, while another division might require only few: to proceed
from animal to viviparous dogfish will need at least three more stages
than to proceed from animal to man. But this is not significant for
Aristotle, for he does not carry the framework of division across the
board as in a classification, nor does he create a terminology of orders,
families, etc., as Linnaeus did to establish such a framework. As I
argue more fully in section II of this chapter, modern taxonomists
have been mistaken in seeking a classificatory system here. For in
biology Aristotle uses only two taxonomic concepts, the *genos* and the
forms of a *genos*, and all attempts to find regular intermediate classes
have notoriously failed. In fact he does not even provide enough
genera to exhaust the animal kingdom, but after naming the chief
kinds he then draws attention to animals that fall outside them.
Furthermore, *genos* and *eidos* differ not merely in that the one class
includes the other, but more significantly in that each is a different
way of grouping and analyzing animals. The *genos* is an exclusive
group whose members share the same essential features (e.g. wings),
these features not being shared by other groups (e.g. fishes have fins
instead, quadrupeds have forelegs). The *eidos* is one of the different
forms within a single *genos* (e.g. swan, eagle). Now if it becomes
necessary to treat a form as if it were a kind, in order to distinguish
forms within it (e.g. to divide selachian fishes into oviparous and
viviparous), such a procedure asserts that the selachians exclusively
share certain features but also exhibit certain differences among
themselves. The *genos*/*eidos* analysis can therefore be useful at various
levels of generality, for they are different concepts or tools of analysis.[2]
Aristotle shows this by using both terms at all levels from the most
general 'bloodless' animal down to varieties of the species 'dog'. The
neoplatonist commentators were seriously wrong to present his
analysis as a classification of orders of generality in which genus and

[2] Cf. Pellegrin 1982: 73ff.; and ch. 12 below.

species are two among many levels, as in the 'tree of Porphyry'. And of course when they went even further, and tried to endow genus and species with the real subsistence that Plato had believed, they lost Aristotle altogether.

Aristotle's second fundamental innovation was the requirement for successive differentiation, intended to ensure that the final differentia should entail its predecessors.[3] For example, 'footed' can properly be differentiated as quadruped or biped, but not as gregarious or solitary, which are not sorts of footedness. Moreover, footed does not exist in nature until it has been determined as four-footed, etc. Intermediate differentiae are therefore only analytical steps towards the final determination, and the final differentia entails them and renders them 'redundant' as Aristotle puts it. The resulting definition consists of two terms, the genus and the final differentia. Since the genus too can only exist in a differentiated form as one of its own species,[4] the naming of genus with differentia will denote a single thing, the unified substantial *tode ti* which for Aristotle is the object of definition. Here again his change of procedure follows directly upon his philosophical movement away from Plato's theory of forms. Now his requirement for the unity of definition produces the difficulties of *Metaph.* Z. But they are not primarily logical difficulties, but metaphysical. The problems of individuation and of including material accidents within the formal definition, although vitally important to the theory of biological form and species, do not in fact affect the procedure of *diairesis*. For the definiendum which a division aims to reach can be at any level of generality, so long as it is treated as not further divisible. So far as logic alone is concerned, therefore, successive differentiation adequately secures the unity of the definition as representing the unity of its object.

The procedure at once becomes inadequate, however, to characterize any but the simplest objects. An animal is a complex of attributes, which cannot be presented in a single line of differentiation drawn as strictly as Aristotle insists. This is the main point of *PA* I. 2–3 where, during his introduction to biology, he makes his third reform of *diairesis* by showing that it must be conducted by a plurality of differentiae applied simultaneously. The genus – e.g. animal – must be differentiated straightaway by all the differentiae that are exhibited by the definiendum. If it is a species of bird, then it is biped, winged, has beak, neck, tail, etc; these are its generic differentiae. Having stated all of these, we must then further differentiate each – the legs are long/short, the wings are broad/

---

[3] *Metaph.* Z. 1038a19; *APo.* II. 97a28. [4] *Top.* VI. 144b16.

narrow and long/short, etc. – until the species is uniquely characterized. He points out the insuperable difficulties that are inevitable
if we try to divide by one differentia at a time, the method which
he here calls 'dichotomy'. His criticisms do not hold against dichotomy in the sense of division into two classes, nor indeed was this
always Plato's practice. They hold against division by one differentia
at a time, whether dichotomous or polytomous; for instance, to
divide animal into land/water/air incurs the same difficulties as
dividing it into land/water, unless all the other necessary differentiations are made at the same time. Plato did divide by single
differentiae, whether into two or more classes, and presumably this
was the Academy's method. Aristotle aims his criticisms at 'the
dichotomists' and 'the written divisions', and his target could be
either Plato or the Academy. Plato himself commonly calls *diairesis*
a 'cutting into halves' and can even call the divided class a 'half'.
In reviewing the objections to this so-called dichotomy, Aristotle
provides his most comprehensive set of rules for *diairesis*. Far from a
rejection of *diairesis*, it is a methodical demonstration that it should ·
be conducted by multiple differentiae but must yet be rigorous and
avoid introducing differentiae in an illicit and 'accidental' way. This
section of *PA* I falls into eight parts, each giving one criticism or rule.
These are by no means the only rules of *diairesis*, many more of which
are to be found in the *Topics* and *Analytics*; but they conveniently
summarize what seems to be Aristotle's most mature view of logical
division as it should be applied to the definition of animals.

Rules *of* diairesis *quoted in* PA *1. 2–3*

(1) 642b7. Dichotomy produces only one final differentia. This is
the crux of the matter. Aristotle amplifies this difficulty in section 8
(643b26). Single-differentia division must be either inadequate or
invalid. For, as he will argue presently, its final differentia cannot
be made to include sufficient characteristics except by 'accidental'
or false division.

(2) 642b10. Dichotomy splits natural kinds. If we divide animals
into terrestrial and aquatic, then we cannot go on to divide either
side into blooded/bloodless or polypod/footless, since there would
have to be some of each on each side. Why does this matter, and how
should it be remedied? It matters because polypod, for example,
would appear under both terrestrial and aquatic, so that at the end
we should not show whether our polypod form is a terrestrial or
aquatic animal. This is cross-division, and the only remedy for it is

to recognize from the outset both polypod-terrestrial animals and polypod-aquatic animals. But that means using not single differentiae but multiple, as Aristotle is going to argue.

(3) 642b21. Dichotomy cannot use negative differentiae ('privations', *stereseis*). A negative, e.g. 'footless', cannot be further differentiated; for there are no forms of not-*X*, but only of the subject to which not-*X* belongs. If we purport to divide the footless into snakes and fishes, what we are really dividing is not footless but those animals that are footless. Aristotle argues that a privation cannot stand either (a) as a general differentia or (b) as a particular differentia; and (c) since it cannot be further divided, it blocks the division at that point, so that the forms to be defined will outnumber the final differentiae that can be available.[5] Once again, the remedy is to use multiple differentiae, recognizing footless among many others, of which the positive ones can be further divided while the negatives are carried down.

(4) 643a27. We should not divide by essential accidents, but by differentiae that are in the being (*ousia*). Although we may uniquely mark out the triangle by saying that its interior angles add up to two right angles, this statement does not grasp the triangle's nature: to do that, we must say 'plane figure having three angles'. This criticism holds against Plato, who did not distinguish between categories of form, and probably also against Speusippus, who apparently grouped 'similars' without analyzing the grounds of similarity. It illuminates the difference in Aristotle's approach, showing that his aim is not simply to mark out and identify but to grasp the substantial being of the object.

(5) 643a31. We should divide only by opposites. Here Aristotle criticizes the kind of empirical division that would be made if, in defining a colorless fish, we were to divide animals into swimming and colored. This would produce a cross-division by changing the *fundamentum divisionis*, since there may be animals that both swim and are colored. Then at the next stage, when we divided swimmers into swimmers *A* and swimmers not-*A*, we should not show whether we had divided all swimmers, since some may be on the colored side as well. At the end we could not guarantee that the final differentia is exclusive to our object. In the *Topics* (VI. 143a36, 144b13) Aristotle calls this mistake a dividing of two separate genera of differentiae (locomotion and coloration). Here he says merely that 'opposites divide', implying that the cross-division is not a division. Although

---

[5] The interpretation of Aristotle's argument here is disputable: see my note in Balme 1972: 110.

it is an elementary mistake, the risk of it would be greater for both
Plato and Aristotle than for modern dichotomists. For it is customary
now to divide by *A* and not-*A*, which both avoids cross-division
and ensures exhaustiveness; but Plato and Aristotle regularly used
positive attributes (e.g. land/water rather than land/not land),
presumably to ensure that the definiendum is included on one side
and excluded from the other.

(6) 643a35. We should not divide by the common actions of the
body and of the soul.[6] Actions such as walking and flying, or wild
and tame behavior, may not mark real divisions. For example, ants
are sometimes winged and sometimes not; many animals can be
tamed, but we do not then consider them to be different forms from
the wild ones. This rule would apply only to animals, which can
change their actions. Perhaps this is why the rule appears only here;
it has only limited application, and Aristotle does not state it
elsewhere. It is intelligible if confined to the limited sense of his
expression here: if walking and flying are taken merely as bodily
actions (or wildness and tameness merely as psychic behavior), they
do not mark out the animal's essential being. When walking and
flying result from the animal's real nature (as with quadrupeds or
birds), they are proper bases of division: so in his interesting
discussion of amphibia in *HA* VIII.2 the question at issue is not the
actions of limbs but the animal's basic nature (which is found to
depend upon its original constitution – what stuff it is made of).
Similarly wildness and tameness do not differentiate animals merely
because these have been tamed and those have not, but because these
are basically tameable (e.g. elephants) while others are not; again
the difference must be one of 'being', not merely of superficial
actions.

(7) 643b9. Division by single differentia must either fail (by

---

[6] The Greek is ambiguous between (i) the actions common to body and soul – i.e.
psychosomatic; (ii) the common actions of the body and the common actions of the soul.
In Balme 1972: 116 I preferred (i), since it is the usual meaning of this expression (cf. *Sens.*
436a7, b2; *Somn.* 453b13; *de An.* III. 433b20). But James Lennox has pointed out that the
argument is better served by (ii) if taken in the sense that both of the opposed common
actions may belong to animals in one group. In this case 'common' means 'common to
many', as at 643a8. Aristotle restricts it to *ta g' empsucha* because only animate objects could
change their actions (as from walking to flying). 'Actions' or 'deeds' (*erga*) here should
not be generalized to 'attributes' as I did in my note in Balme 1972, nor even to 'functions',
which might imply permanent states. Nor is it necessary to write *mē* for *men* at 643b7; for
Aristotle's point, as Cherniss argued (1944: 57 n. 47), is that if wild and tame made a
differentia, then man and horse would be equivocal names; yet they have not been divided,
as they would have been in that case. Meyer 1855: 89, followed by Cherniss 1944: 50 and
Kullmann 1974: 65, 320, argued for (ii) on the grounds that Aristotle intended to exclude
functional differentiae from species; but this seems difficult to maintain in the face of his
practice in both *HA* and the other treatises.

causing cross-division or by producing an inadequate final differentia) or compel us to divide per accidens; therefore we should divide initially by many differentiae. Here Aristotle for the first time announces his solution: to apply all the relevant differentiae to the genus simultaneously at the beginning of the division. He does not say here that we should then proceed to divide all the differentiae simultaneously, but this must be assumed from his explanation of 'difference' in chapters 4 and 5 and in *HA* I: the difference between forms within a genus is 'the more and less' (short feathers, long feathers). Presumably therefore the initial differentiae are to be further divided by differences of the more-and-less, as necessary to reach a specification of the particular definiendum. The only other way to produce enough final differentiae is to add a new attribute at each stage, as Plato does (e.g. *Sph.* 223b, 224d, 226a, where at the end of the division he collects up all the differentiae mentioned en route). But at *Metaph.* Z. 1038a12, 26, Aristotle calls that dividing per accidens, and here he calls it discontinuous. If for example feathered is divided into tame/wild, the unity of the definition is lost since tame is not a sort of featheredness; therefore we fail to show that the final differentia is a determination of an attribute belonging to the object's genus. Aristotle's method begins by recognizing that the genus bird possesses various differentiae (limbs, coloration, etc.) and ends with a cluster of determinations of these differentiae which can be seen to belong together in the species because they belong together in the genus. It does not prove the definition – he is careful to refute the claim that *diairesis* proves its conclusion (*APo.* II. 91b12) – but it is 'useful in finding it' (96b25). Accidental or discontinuous division, on the other hand, provides no generic basis for the conclusion; it fails therefore to show that the final differentiae flow from the animal's basic nature. Although the initial recognition of generic differentiae is empirical and intuitive (implied at 643b11), the method that Aristotle will display in collecting and grouping the differentiae and then seeking causal explanations of them (cf. *HA* I. 491a9) will give them a theoretical foundation that cannot be claimed for the purely empirical method of 'the dichotomists'.

(8) 643b26. A single final differentia, as produced by correct dichotomy, must be inadequate. Aristotle now explains that this inadequacy, which he had merely asserted in general terms at 642b7, is not remedied by reciting all the intermediate differentiae together with the final differentia, since they are already entailed by it. No animal is so simple that a single line of successive division could define it; therefore dichotomy must always fail to obtain a particular animal

form. He restricts this refutation here to animal forms, although at
one point earlier (643a17) he had said that dichotomy cannot obtain
'any other kind either'. That is disputable, however, since really
simple concepts (such as some ethical concepts, e.g. liberality, *EN* IV.
ʍ 19b22), which because they are not complexes have only one
fundamentum divisionis, may well be satisfactorily divided by single
differentiae. Otherwise, wherever more than one kind of differentia
is involved, Aristotle's criticisms both in this and in the preceding
sections are well-founded. It is interesting that they should not have
emerged during his extensive critique in the logical treatises, but
should have been provoked by biology.

How to recognize genera and differentiae

This final reform of *diairesis*, evidently made in the light of Aristotle's
thinking about biology, clears away the logical difficulties in defining
animal forms *per genus et differentiam*. (The metaphysical difficulties
are not mentioned, but *PA* I makes the innocent assumption of
Metaph. Z. 1034a8: that Socrates and Coriscus are the same in form
(644a25) and the form is the enmattered final differentia (643a24).)
It remains now to show how to recognize genera and differentiae.
In chapters 4 and 5 Aristotle says that we should accept the genera
that have been marked off by popular usage and possess a single
nature in common, that is that the recognition must be intuitive.
Having listed them, he then points out that some animal forms do
not fall under genera but must be dealt with individually: here he
mentions man, while *PA* IV treats the bat, seal and ostrich as peculiar forms, and *HA* II adds snakes and some marine animals.[7] The
differentiae that mark off a *genos* are to be compared analogically
with those of other genera, e.g. feathers compared with scales, while
those that mark off a form within a *genos* differ by the 'more and less',
that is by size or shape or bodily affections such as hard/soft and
rough/smooth. He comments that most similarities among animals
are analogical (644a23), and that the popular genera have been
marked off mainly by morphology (644b7). Both comments have led
to misunderstandings, through being taken for either more or less
than precisely what he says. For if 'analogy' is confined to the nine
listed genera (which he does not say), it could not be true that most
similarities are analogical; but since the practice of the *HA* does in
fact make more use of analogy than of 'more and less' at all levels,

[7] *HA* II. 505b5; (also apparently 505b31, but there the text is dubious; cf. Peck 1965: 124
n. 5).

it would follow that Aristotle abandoned his own method.[8] And in the other case, if Aristotle means to rely on morphology, the practice of both *HA* and the other treatises belies this. But in both cases the practice of *HA* is in fact the best guide to what Aristotle intends by these comments. For its long introduction (486a5–491b26) explains its method in close agreement with *PA* I. 4–5, and then lays out a plan for the whole treatise based on this method. It begins by analyzing the ways in which animals should be compared. Their parts are either homoeomerous or anhomoeomerous, that is either tissues or organs, and should be compared either analogically as between genera or by 'the more and less' as between forms of a *genos*. *HA* I extends 'the more and less' to include possession and non-possession of a feature, and its position. Then Aristotle distinguishes animal differentiae under the general headings 'lives, activities, characters, parts', so making it clear that his comment on morphology in *PA* I refers to the popular criteria but not to his own. The rest of the treatise follows according to these four headings, within which the animal examples are taken *genos* by *genos*, special attention being given to peculiar animals and peculiar attributes. In comparing differentiae, Aristotle often calls them analogical within a single animal *genos*, e.g. nail and hoof within viviparous quadrupeds (486b20), bone and cartilage in fishes (516b14). But while there are occasional lax uses of this and other technical terms including *genos* and *eidos*, most cases can be defended on one of two provisos: (i) when Aristotle is considering an *eidos* as an exclusive group, he may by his own method treat it as a *genos* (*Ph.* 227b11); (ii) he may group attributes together because they belong to one *genos* of attribute – bone with bone, cartilage with cartilage – and not necessarily because they belong to one *genos* of animal. This flexible usage is only possible because he is not attempting a classification system but applies the concept of the *genos* with its forms freely to all levels of generality and to all objects of definition, whether whole animals or parts.

When read in the light of *PA* I, *HA* evidently sets out on what would be Aristotle's final task preliminary to the defining of animal differentiae. At the end of the introduction, in an explanatory passage for students, he says that the task is to collect the differentiae and attributes of all animals, and then to discover their causes (491a9). Presumably the causal explanations referred to are to be

---

[8] As I argued in Balme 1962b: 84ff. But Pierre Pellegrin (above n. 2) has corrected me on this point and I am glad to accept his interpretation that Aristotle uses *genos* and *analogon*, at all levels of generality, consistently in *HA* and in *PA* I and the logical works.

found in the other treatises.[9] The role of the *HA* would be to collect, screen, distinguish, and describe correctly the differentiae requiring explanation. Such a role presupposes the critique and reform of *diairesis*, especially the observations in *PA* 1 about the selecting and comparing of differentiae, and would be thought to yield the 'grasp' of the animal forms spoken of there, the formal definition coming later with the causal analysis. The *HA* remains unfinished, with evidence that new items were constantly being added. It is of course unfinishable, for there is no end to the recognition of fresh significant attributes. In view of this we may indeed doubt whether Aristotle maintained this aim when his experience as a naturalist increased, for it is a somewhat naive one. But the correct identification and grouping of differentiae is far more important, leading directly to the fundamental causes of animals' attributes and differences. This might well have seemed the best way towards a methodical *apodeixis* of living nature.

II. Aristotle's use of differentiae in zoology

The *Historia Animalium*, as I have said, is a comparison not of animals but of animal differentiae. They are grouped under four headings: bodily parts, life histories, activities, character (i.e. psychology). Within these headings the animals are quoted in ten main groups which Aristotle calls the 'major genera': man, viviparous quadrupeds, oviparous quadrupeds, birds, fishes, cetaceans, molluscs (i.e. cephalopods), crustaceans, testaceans, insects. The first six are called 'blooded' (i.e. red-blooded), the other four 'bloodless'. But additionally, in discussing the animals Aristotle uses a great many group-names, such as *scaly, horned, carnivorous, ruminant*. The question has been whether he used them to group the animals in sub-genera, and if so how.

Evidence that Aristotle did not classify sub-genera

Widely different answers have been given to the above question. Aristotle seems to use the group-names in so contradictory and confused a way (if looked at from the viewpoint of taxonomy) that no two scholars ever agreed upon the details of his supposed classification. Scaliger (1619) ambitiously tabulated *suprema genera denominata – summa genera – media genera non nominata – media genera*

---

[9] The passage probably introduces the order of lecturing; I have argued above (ch. 1, 12–18) that *HA* was most likely written after the extant explanatory treatises.

nominata – species. At the other end of the scale, Whewell (1837) denied that there was any scheme at all, and those who followed him have tended to conclude that the *HA* was simply a collecting-box of observations. The best and most complete study of the subject is still that by J. B. Meyer (1855). He tried to get rid of the contradictions, but to save Aristotle as a systematist, by distinguishing between certain group-names which (he thought) Aristotle intended as genera, and the great majority which Aristotle used only as descriptions. By examining Aristotle's actual use of each, Meyer showed that most of the important differentiae which had been regarded as genera by previous scholars (and, one might add, by some subsequent scholars, e.g. Aubert and Wimmer) were not *in practice* used as genera by Aristotle. The following are those which Aristotle uses most commonly and treats as especially significant:

> blooded, bloodless
> terrestrial, aquatic, flying, stationary
> viviparous, ovo-viviparous, oviparous, larviparous, spontaneous
> multiparous, pauciparous, uniparous
> solid-hoofed, cloven-hoofed, fissiped
> footless, biped, quadruped, polypod
> fish-scaled, horny-scaled, feathered, hairy
> social, solitary, wild, tame
> differentiae of teeth, tusks, horns, alimentary canal, diet

All of these, and hundreds more, are plausibly shown by Meyer *not* to be sub-genera. He concludes that Aristotle had turned against 'artificial' classification by division, and was seeking instead a 'natural' classification by inductive grouping; that most of the group-names denoted not genera but diagnostic characters; and that Aristotle used a plurality of them to give a commensurate definition of each genus and sub-genus. Meyer has to admit that Aristotle, for want of information, did not go far with the scheme, but claims to recognize some 60–65 groups comprising about 200 out of the 550 animals which Aristotle distinguishes.

Meyer's result, however, is seriously reduced when one considers the actual groups so recognized. Only 15 of them are sub-genera in the sense of being intermediate between the major genus (e.g. bird) and the common species (e.g. hawk); all the rest are sub-divisions of common species, i.e. varieties of hawk, etc. Now to distinguish different varieties of the bird named 'hawk' is by no means the same operation as to group the birds named 'hawk' and 'eagle' in a single class. It is the latter operation that is required for a natural inductive classification, but there is very little to be seen of it in Aristotle's zoology.

Even the few intermediate groups found by Meyer are open to objection. They are as follows:

Viviparous quadrupeds:	*lophoura* (horse, ass, mule)
	simians (apes, monkeys)
Oviparous quadrupeds:	none
Birds:	taloned
	web-footed
	long-legged
	terrestrial non-flying
	(i.e. the gallinaceous birds)
Cetaceans:	none
Fishes:	selachians: (*a*) shark types
	(*b*) rays
	(*c*) the fishing frog
	egg-layers
Cephalopods:	none
Crustaceans:	none
Testaceans:	spiral-shelled (snails)
	bivalve (mussels, oysters)
	univalve (limpets)
Insects:	coleoptera (chafers)
	apiform (bees, wasps)
	diptera (flies, gnats)
	long polypods (centipedes)

These groups have some obviously unsatisfactory aspects, which show up the nature of the problem. First, some of the gaps are surprising, if we are to believe that Aristotle was engaged in creating groups. The quadrupeds, for example, are scantily represented, although Aristotle reports more information about them than about any other class. It seems strange to acknowledge *lophoura* while rejecting the solid-hoofed and cloven-hoofed, which were traditional divisions frequently quoted by Aristotle and clearly given greater significance by him than he gives to *lophoura*. They must be rejected because pigs belong to both (*HA* II. 499b11). Secondly, some of these groups have little systematic effect. Among birds, the species of 'the long-legged' are never named. Among fishes, while the selachians clearly comprise the cartilaginous types (16 named), the egg-layers are merely 'the remainder' (112 types). Among testaceans, the spiral-shelled and bivalves are clear enough (one need not be an Aristotle to see them), but the univalves include only the limpets and the grouping means only that they are not bivalves (hence some scholars have made them include the spirals, but Meyer gives good reasons against this). Thirdly, some of the larger groups not only lack precise definition but even defy it. For example, Aristotle often discusses together those birds that have bulky bodies, fly little, lay eggs on the ground; they are prolific, their diet is greenstuff, they have thick skin and therefore blink with the lower lid only. But the birds that he wishes to discuss do not answer to all these descriptions. The pigeon is bulky, but does not lay eggs on the ground nor fly little; the lark lays on the ground and flies little, but is not bulky; some water birds are bulky and fly little, but do not lay on the ground; the partridge eats snails; the pigeon blinks with both lids, and lays not many eggs but often – to explain which, Aristotle has to say that the pigeons combine bulk with much flying. This really makes nonsense of the 'group', and so Meyer in order to save it cuts out the 'bulky' birds; but then the group is left with only the domestic fowl, partridge, and ostrich, which is not only ridiculous but contradicts *PA* IV. 694a7, where the bulky birds are explicitly put together with the others. (For Aristotle's discussions of this group cf. *HA* VI. 559a1; VIII. 593a15; IX. 621a1; *PA* II. 657b7; IV. 694a5; *IA* 710a12; *GA* III. 749b13; Meyer 1855: 299.) Again, the taloned birds, which make otherwise a more distinguishable group, incongruously include the parrot, who upsets many of its descriptions (*HA* VIII. 597b25, not discussed by Meyer). Among insects, both the coleoptera and the apiform are suspect. Aristotle quotes them at *HA* IV. 531b22 to show that 'some related kinds do not share a common name', and often refers to both; but in the only other passage where he discusses the grouping of either, namely the bees and wasps at *HA* IX. 623b5, he confines himself to the group of honeycomb-makers, which cannot be a genus because it includes only one of the wasps and therefore splits a recognized type (causing cross-division). All these cases show how Aristotle's observation of associated characters may lead towards recognition of systematic groups; but they show also how far he was from any clear definition of such groups.

   The conclusion begins to emerge that a 'natural' classification is no more to be found here than an 'artificial' one. This antinomy is in fact unreal, for animal classification cannot be other than inductive; division was always preceded by the collection of species, and from the beginning Plato emphasized that in dividing we must not miss the natural joints like an unskillful cook (*Phdr.* 265e, *Plt.* 287c). The question is simply whether Aristotle either had or was making a classification of animals, and the answer is no. Even Meyer's modest results are obtained by Procrustean methods. And the 'major genera' themselves were not intended to exhaust the animal kingdom, for Aristotle tells us that certain species do not fall under them. Two examples will show the consequences of ignoring this warning. Both the snakes and the sea-anemones and sponges are left under no generic heading; the snakes are compared sometimes with lizards and sometimes with fishes, the sea-anemones and sponges with testaceans. Now modern zoology has indeed shown a relationship between snake and lizard, and accordingly Meyer argued that Aristotle classed them together with the tortoise under oviparous quadrupeds. But Aristotle does not argue thus, nor does he create the concept *reptile* to cover so paradoxical a grouping. Without such overarching concepts, a man who could class the viviparous footless viper under oviparous quadrupeds, or 'the unshelled' (*HA* v. 548a23) under testaceans, as Meyer supposed, would stick at nothing.

The belief that there must be a classification in the background rests on the assumption that Aristotle, like every good pre-evolutionary zoologist, put systematics first in zoology and morphology first in systematics. But better sense can be got out of the evidence if this dual assumption is removed. Aristotle's aim was not taxonomy, nor did it involve one; the comparison of differentiae had other purposes. In examining his use of the more important differentiae, Meyer shows that they were never used *in practice* as systematic genera. But he fails to make the point that they are *incapable* of being so used: they cannot form a hierarchical system because they cross-divide. This was evident to Aristotle, for he points it out several times. At *HA* I. 490b19–27, discussing the major genera, he shows how a neat scheme distinguishing *quadruped-viviparous-hairy* from *footless-oviparous-scaly* is upset by the viviparous footless viper and selachians, so that all that can be got out of these groupings is the non-convertible proposition that hairy animals are viviparous. At *GA* II. 732b15 he shows similarly how the divisions *quadruped/ biped/ footless* and *viviparous/oviparous* cut across each other, and remarks that 'much overlapping occurs between kinds'. He gives other examples of overlapping at *GA* II. 733a27; III. 749b20; IV. 774b17; *HA* II. 501a22.

Whereas an overlap between genera must mean that the genera have not been adequately defined (as Aristotle remarks at *HA* VIII. 589b13; cf. *GA* II. 732b26), it does not matter if differentiae overlap generic boundaries, as of course they often must. One of Aristotle's arguments against dichotomy is that it cannot allow an overlap of differentiae without incurring cross-division, since it takes only one differentia at a time (e.g. if it divides *terrestrial/aquatic*, it cannot also divide *quadruped/polypod*, for polypods occur both on land and in water, *PA* I. 642b18). Therefore when he states the need of a new group-name which overlaps or splits genera, it is clear that he is naming a differentia and not a genus. This is the case when he suggests that *lung-possessors* could be recognized as a *kind of animal* (*PA* III. 669b9); he often makes use of this category, but he himself provides the reasons why it could not be a systematic division (*HA* VIII. 589a10ff.). Similarly his statement that honeycomb-makers are a *kind* implies splitting the wasps, as has been seen (*HA* IX. 623b5). In both cases he uses the word *genos* for 'kind', but this does not necessarily signify 'genus' unless the context requires it. In the zoological treatises *genos* may signify not only any genus or species, but any differentia-class (e.g. 'Man overlaps all the kinds, being both uniparous and multiparous and pauciparous'; *GA* IV. 772b1). Even on those occasions when he systematically distinguishes verbally between kind, form, and differentia it is not for taxonomic reasons, as explained in section 1 above (78–9). And in practice he does not base zoological arguments upon taxonomy. True, he sometimes appeals to similar types, as at *HA* IX. 629a24 where he considers whether certain wasps must have stings like others. But the comparison with others does not lead him to an opinion, and there is even less sign of reasoning from the characteristics of the genus to those of the member species. Nor is there much sign of the reverse process. In recording the varieties of ordinary types (varieties of lion, or of hawk) he gives the differences but not the similarities: we are not told what entitles the various eagles (both land and sea types) to the common name *eagle*.

The search for causal differentiae

What then was Aristotle doing with all these differentiae, and how can his practice be reconciled with his theory? At the close of section 1 above, I suggested that he was after the correct identification and grouping of differentiae, and said something about the former process. Here I would like to elaborate on the latter.

In the discussion at *GA* II. 732b15 (quoted above), where he shows how certain divisions cut across each other, he concludes that 'this is not the way to divide' and proceeds instead to look for a differentia which is 'the cause' of the division *viviparous/oviparous*. He finds it in the lung, which is the sign of a hotter and more perfect nature. But this too encounters a difficulty in the ovo-viviparous fishes which 'tend to both sides' (viviparous and oviparous, hot and cold). Aristotle gives many examples of 'tending to both sides', and seems even to go out of his way to emphasize the difficulty of precise grouping (cf. *PA* III. 669a9; IV. 681b1, 689b32, 690b22, 697b1,

697b14; *GA* I. 719a7, 731b9; IV. 772b1, 774b18; *HA* I. 488a1; II. 499b12; IV. 529b20; VIII. 598a15). These cases are not dismissed as exceptions that prove a rule, nor are they assigned to both sides of a division (for that is impossible, *HA* VIII. 589b12); since they seem to have some characteristics of each side, they compel a 'more precise definition' (*ibid.*). But their proper grouping is rarely decided, and they seem to be brought into the discussions, not in order to be classified, but in order to bring out sharper distinctions in the differentiae concerned, or more precise statements of the ways in which the differentiae can be combined.

Such discussions show how differentiae are essentially associated or divergent, and this is the real use that Aristotle makes of them in *PA* and *GA*. In his arguments about causes there, he appeals largely to the interrelationship of differentiae which appear to belong together. He seeks the significant, causal grouping of differentiae. He does not use them as a method of reference to animals in a cataloging system: if he did, he would be bound to quote them in some regular manner. On the contrary, he selects just those differentiae which appear relevant at the moment, as offering a clue to the problem under discussion. Hence their order is immaterial, and it makes no difference whether he speaks of 'ovipara among quadrupeds' (*GA* I. 717b5) or 'quadrupeds among ovipara' (*GA* I. 718b16) or 'oviparous quadrupeds among scaly animals' (*GA* I. 719b11). Contrast this with the importance of the order of differentiae in classification (*APo.* II. 96b30). His method in fact is what he briefly describes at *APo.* II. 98a14–19: by looking for those characteristics which are regularly associated we may detect their cause. A few examples will show the method in operation.

(1) *PA* III. 664b22: 'the epiglottis occurs in all that have lungs and a hairy skin, and are not scaly or feathered'. The reason why the scaly and feathered lack the epiglottis is found to lie in the dryness of their flesh and skin (665a1). They take in less liquid (671a13).

(2) Lungs have further associations. *PA* III. 668b33: 'they have lungs because they are terrestrial'. The connection is that they are blooded and therefore hotter; fishes are cooled by water, but land animals need to take in air to cool their blood, hence the lungs. Then what about the dolphin, which takes in air? 'It tends to both sides' (669a9). The comparative heat of aquatic and terrestrial animals exposes an ambiguity in 'hot', which requires further definition (*PA* II. 648a25, b1).

(3) *PA* III. 670b13: 'in the oviparous quadrupeds the spleen is small and firm, because the lungs are spongy and the animals drink

little and the excess residue is diverted to flesh and scales...but in animals that have a bladder, and whose lungs contain blood, the spleen is moist'. This is not a straight contrast between ovipara and vivipara, since animals with a bladder include the tortoise, as he points out. No systematic sense is derived from this division. But the distinction between 'causes' is made clear: the former group (being cooler) is associated with the 'spongy' (i.e. drier and bloodless) lungs and with drinking little, while the latter is associated with blood-filled lungs and an excess of liquid residue which helps to make a bigger and moister spleen. (The different kinds of lungs have been explained at 669a24.)

(4) In the viviparous quadrupeds there is a connection between feet, teeth, horns, and stomachs. This has caused much ink to flow among Aristotelian systematists, all to no purpose since the characteristics of pig, camel, and Indian ass (rhinoceros) block all solutions, as Aristotle himself keeps pointing out (*HA* II. 499b12, 501a14; *PA* III. 663a19, 674a32; *GA* IV. 774b18). These characters form no systematic divisions, but they are called in, in various combinations, to point the way to causes. *PA* III. 662b30: the fissipeds have no horns, but they have claws or teeth unlike the horned animals. The connection is defense. The horned animals have defensive horns at the expense of their upper incisors; therefore they need more stomachs to complete mastication (674a30). But the camel, who has no horns, also has no upper incisors. The connection is nutrition: he eats thorns, which take more digesting; hence more stomachs, hence fewer teeth (because he does not need both). Then his defense? He gets it from greater bodily size, like the elephant (663a1).

(5) *PA* IV. 688a32. Why do horned animals have two udders near the hind legs, while fissipeds have more than two on the abdomen? The connection lies in rate of growth and number of young. The horned animals are cloven-hoofed, hence larger, hence pauciparous (*GA* IV. 771b2); hence two udders suffice; and they are placed further back because the animals grow more in front, therefore the surplus residue is found further back. The fissipeds are multiparous, hence they need more udders, which they have in the more natural position because nothing prevents it. But the lion is fissiped and yet has only two udders. The connection is nutrition: she is carnivorous, therefore gets less to eat, therefore has less residue available, therefore does not produce much milk (*PA* IV. 688a32–b5).

The differentiae from which Aristotle argues are all 'essential'; it is not possible to disregard some as 'accidental' in order to make a tidy system. In *GA* v he discusses the causes of accidents like color, voice pitch, hair quality, and distinguishes between those which vary with the individual and those which belong to the kind (778a22, 785b24). In *HA*, where these differences are recorded, only those belonging to the kind are discussed, and individual variations are noticed (if at all) as mere exceptions.

Nor is it possible to say that Aristotle differentiated the animals solely by morphological characters. They are admittedly the most important (*PA* I. 644b7; *HA* I. 491a15), but his whole teleological view of animals depends upon his belief that bodily parts are explainable by activities, not vice versa (*PA* I. 645b14). In practice he is just as ready to argue from habitat or nutrition or behavior or breeding characteristics; in short, from all the kinds of differentia which he distinguishes in the *HA* under the headings of 'parts, lives, activities, character' (*HA* I. 487a11).

Aristotle's purpose in *PA* and *GA* is made clear: to find the 'causes' of animals' parts, and of their generation and growth. In doing so, it seems that an important part of his method is to look for significant differentiae and combinations of differentiae; he constantly groups and regroups them to focus on particular problems. The purpose of *HA*, however, is perhaps not clearly enough stated for a modern generation whose natural history is rooted in systematics. We find it extraordinary, for example, that Aristotle can describe a dissection of the blind mole's concealed eyes (*HA* IV. 533a3), and yet tell us nothing else about it except that it is viviparous, not even how many legs it has. To any reader looking for information about given genera or species, the *HA* seems an incoherent jumble. Yet Aristotle does state his purpose: 'first, to grasp the differentiae and attributes that belong to all animals; then to discover their causes' (*HA* I. 491a9). The *HA* is a collection and preliminary analysis of the *differences* between animals. The animals are called in as witnesses to differentiae, not in order to be described as animals. What is interesting about the blind mole is precisely that, though viviparous, it is blind – the only case of this combination of characteristics known to Aristotle, who quotes it often. Its other characteristics are not different enough to be worth mention. But the whole collection is still incomplete. For the treatise ends abruptly; and it contains occasional complete descriptions of animals, no doubt inserted at convenience and awaiting breakdown and distribution to the appropriate chapters (e.g. 11.8 and 11, listing the characteristics of the apes and of the chameleon). And so the discussion of causes that *HA* is to precede was never reached. (Ancient editors took the *HA* to be Aristotle's first zoological treatise, containing the data, and the other treatises to be the promised discussion of causes. But this is mistaken, first because it is the causes of *all differences*, not merely of parts or generation, that will be discussed according to 491a9; and secondly because internal evidence suggests that most, perhaps all, of *HA* is later than the other treatises.[10]) What form that discussion would have taken, we can only guess. But since the *HA* begins with the analysis of generic and specific differences that was argued in *PA* I. and since we know Aristotle's theory of dividing by multiple differentiae and can see how he looked for causes by examining combinations of differentiae, it is likely that he would have wanted to pick out the significant generic combinations and to show the specific differentiae flowing from them. Before he could do this, he must collect *all* the differentiae. But, however that may be, if the *HA* is read, not as an encyclopaedia nor as a collection of simple natural history, but as being itself to some extent a theoretical treatise – namely a study of differentiae – then much of its apparent incoherence disappears.

[10] See ch. 1 above, 12–18.

5
Divide and explain:
The *Posterior Analytics* in practice

JAMES G. LENNOX

I

A longstanding problem concerning Aristotle's philosophy of science is the extent to which there is a serious conflict between the account of scientific explanation and investigation in the *Posterior Analytics* and the explanations and investigations reported in treatises such as the *Historia Animalium, Parts of Animals*, and *Generation of Animals*.[1] I shall not here mount a frontal attack on this question, preferring instead a rearguard action. This will consist of (i) articulating a familiar epistemological distinction between unqualified and sophistic or incidental understanding, which plays a fundamental role in Aristotle's philosophy of science; (ii) relating that distinction to the methodological recommendations of *Posterior Analytics* II.14; and (iii) presenting three sorts of evidence from the *PA* and *HA* indicating that the zoological works owe a great deal both to the above epistemological distinction and to its methodological implications. The evidence for (iii) will consist of the organization of information found in the *HA*, the relevance of that organization to the explanations of *PA*, and the theoretical and practical concern with the way in which lack of an appropriate zoological nomenclature can hamper the achievement of understanding. The evidence points to a much more direct relationship between the *APo.* and the biology than recent commentators have suggested.[2]

II

The distinction between incidental and unqualified understanding first appears in the preliminary account of understanding (*epistēmē*) which opens *APo.* I.2.

We think we understand a thing without qualification and not in the sophistic fashion, that is, incidentally, whenever we think we are aware both that the

---

[1] For two recent, but quite different, attempts to deal with this problem, along with valuable surveys of the history of the problem in recent times, cf. Barnes 1975b; 1981.

[2] Cf. Kullmann 1974; Barnes 1981: 58; and Bolton, ch. 6 below.

explanation because of which the fact is is its explanation, and that it is not possible for this to be otherwise.

This distinction is clarified in *APo.* 1.5, which is primarily devoted to indicating circumstances under which we will fail to demonstrate 'universally and primitively' that a predicate holds of some subject. There are three sources of such failures discussed and exemplified (74a6–32), and the chapter closes with a brief methodological suggestion for determining 'when you know without qualification'.[3]

I shall confine myself to the second case in Aristotle's list. Here, while the same feature is predicated distinctly of a variety of different sorts of entity, and that feature actually belongs to each of them in virtue of their being of some wider kind, this fact about them goes unrecognized, owing to the more general kind lacking a name (74a8–9, 74a17–25). In addition, 74a26–33 provides an example where there is a name designating the common kind in virtue of which the feature belongs, but where it belongs to each sub-kind because of its being an instance of the general kind. That is, there would seem to be two distinguishable sources of error of this sort: lack of a general term may be the source of a failure to grasp the wider kind; or the wider kind may be grasped, without the realization that the predicate in question belongs per se to the wider kind and only incidentally to the sub-kinds.

Later in the paper I will take up the issue of the epistemological and methodological problems which arise from the lack of general terms when they are needed, and will discuss 74a17–25 in that context. Prior to doing so, however, I want to discuss the way in which the distinction between unqualified and incidental understanding is developed from 74a26–33.[4]

For this reason even if one demonstrated, for each triangle, either by one or by a different demonstration, that each has two right angles, separately for the equilateral, scalene, and isosceles, you would not yet know that the triangle has two right angles, except sophistically; nor do you know it of the triangle as a whole, even if there is no other triangle besides these. For you do not know [that it has two right angles] as triangle, nor do you know it of every triangle, except in a numerical sense; but you do not know it of every one according to kind, even if there is none which is not known.[5]

[3] Cf. Barnes 1975a: 122; Ross 1949: 324.
[4] The importance of the distinction between incidental and unqualified *epistēmē* to the argument of the *Analytics* is brought out forcefully by Myles Burnyeat in his 1981. I am following the original suggestion of Kosman 1973: 374, insisted upon recently by Burnyeat, that *epistēmē* is better served translated 'understanding' than 'knowledge'.
[5] This last sentence is interesting for reasons I explore in ch. 13 below, namely its use of the distinction between numerical and formal sameness in characterizing the

The general notion of a subject to which a predicate belongs universally (*katholou*), per se (*kath' hauto*) and as such (*hēi auto*), developed in the previous chapter, is assumed here (cf. 73b25–74a3). There are many expressions which may truly identify the bearer of some property such as having interior angles which are equal to two right angles (*2R*). For example, it may be a bronze object, an isosceles figure, a triangle, and a plane figure. Which of these expressions identifies that about it in virtue of which it possesses *2R*? Answering this question is crucial in advancing toward unqualified understanding. For, if *2R* is in fact an immediate consequence of being a triangle, we will only have a sophistic sort of grasp of why every isosceles figure has it if we do not realize this. There are, as Aristotle notes, extensional marks that can guide one to the correct identification (74b1, 73b39); things which aren't isosceles also have *2R*, so it can't be because it's an isosceles figure that it has this feature.[6]

But as Aristotle makes clear in the above passage, this is not ultimately an issue that can be understood in extensional terms. It is, as the language of *qua* (*hēi*) and in virtue of (*kata*) makes clear, the intensional grasp, the identification of the subject *as* the appropriate sort of thing, that is crucial to achieving unqualified understanding. Knowing of every sort of triangle that each has *2R*, while missing the fact that it is *qua* triangle that each has it, is to have only an incidental grasp of the predication in question. You grasp it incidentally, because you know all the things which have *2R* but you don't know that they have *2R* because they are triangles. As *APo.* 1.1 71a17–29 implies, you would be better off knowing that *2R* belongs to whatever it does *qua* triangle while lacking experience of certain sorts of triangles – at least then, once these sorts are familiar, you will instantly grasp the fact that they have *2R*. (This implication is drawn out explicitly at 86a26–8.)

The realization that different *eidē* of a *genos* have certain features in virtue of those features belonging primitively to that *genos* points toward a sort of demonstration, which I will simply refer to as 'type A'. An A-type explanation of the above predication would be,

relationship between three *kinds* of a more general kind. This is the only passage I know of in which a kind, as opposed to a countable individual, is said to be one in number relative to the unity constituted by it and related kinds.

[6] These 'marks' are interestingly similar to the constraints on what can be an adequate *aitia* in the *Phaedo*; cf. 97a7–b3, 101a6–b2, and the discussions in Gallop 1975: 186–7 and Nehamas 1979: 93ff.

A. 2R belongs to every triangle.

Being a triangle belongs to every isosceles figure.

2R belongs to every isosceles figure.[7]

The syllogistic formulation paints over the explanatory force here, but it can be brought out as follows. 2R flows from the very nature of triangularity *as such*, and this is the general nature of isosceles figures. To reveal the isosceles figure as a sort of triangle, and 2R as a primitive attribute of triangles, implies that the isosceles figure must, in the nature of things, have 2R.

I wish to contrast such explanations with another sort, which will be labeled 'type B'. Let me highlight the differences between them by presenting parallel accounts of their basic features.

A. 1. The predication to be explained is the predication of a feature which belongs to its subject necessarily, but to other subjects as well, what Aristotle describes in *APo.* as the least restricted sort of *kata pantas* predicate: as 2R belongs to isosceles triangles.

2. The predication is explained by showing that the subject is an instance of the kind to which the predicate belongs primitively and as such: as 2R belongs to triangle.

3. Thus, were one to syllogize the explanation, the middle term would identify the proximate kind of the subject, with respect to the predicate in question.

B. 1. The predication to be explained is the predication of a feature which belongs to its subject primitively and as such: as 2R is predicated of triangle.

2. This primitive predication is explained by identifying some aspect of the subject's specific nature as responsible for it.

3. Thus the middle term identifies, *not* a wider kind of which the subject is a sub-kind, but an aspect of that subject's *specific* nature, i.e., something *idion* to it which makes it that sort of thing.

Aristotle is ambivalent toward A-type explanations. There are times when he seems to reserve the concept of demonstration for explanations of per se predications.[8] But in these contexts he is typically contrasting per se predications with incidental predications

---

[7] For now I must sidestep the issue of how well this example fits the account of *kath' hauto* predication in chapter 4. A useful recent survey of the issues and literature is Tiles 1983: 1–16. I will refer to predicates which belong to all and only some kind but which can be explained by reference to what the kind is as 'primitive' or 'belonging primitively to the kind'. The complex and fluid language Aristotle uses to describe various sorts of predicates and modes of predication in the *Topics, Analytics* and *Metaphysics* is nicely discussed in Ferejohn 1981.   [8] E.g. 75a18–22, 75b1–2, 76a5–16.

in the weakest sense, i.e. those which hold only contingently. He gradually develops a terminology for the predications which figure as the explananda of A-type explanations: he speaks of certain predicates which belong in virtue of something common,[9] or which stretch beyond their subject, but not beyond their subject's kind.[10]

APo. 1.9 is a prime example of this ambivalence toward A-type explanations. A strong contrast is drawn between unqualified and incidental demonstrations, the former being B-type alone. That is, only those explanations in which the conclusion states a primitive predication (of the subject *qua* that subject), and is explained by reference to *archai* of that subject, are unqualified demonstrations (cf. 76a4–9).

On the other hand, even here 'incidental' demonstrations include those in which harmonic properties are explained by reference to their purely mathematical features (76a9–10; cf. 75b15–21), and such demonstrations share at least some of the features of A-type explanations.

This ambivalence may arise from an ambiguity in Aristotle's language. Take the remark, 'That bird has a beak in virtue of being a bird.' There are two ambiguities here. First, it is unclear whether the subject is being identified as a *sort* of bird or simply as a *bird*. Second, it is equally unclear whether 'in virtue of being a bird' implies knowledge of those features of a bird's life which necessitate its having a beak, or merely knowledge that beaks, for whatever reason, are an *idion pathos*, a feature unique to, the birds.

When the subject is viewed as a sort of bird, and 'in virtue of' implies nothing more than knowledge of the kind to which the feature in question belongs per se, A-type explanations are a possibility; when the subject is considered as a bird, and 'in virtue of' implies knowledge of what it is about being a bird that necessitates a beak, the above remark may point toward a B-type explanation.

The distinction can be put in historical terms as well. We may occasionally learn that a feature belongs to every *A*, then that it belongs to every *B*, and *C*..., and not yet notice that *A*, *B*, and *C* share a common nature (*K*) in virtue of which they all have that feature. In fact, I learned that chimpanzees, great apes, humans and orangutans were each tailless before I realized these were all members of a group, the hominoids, of which this is a peculiar feature. I learned this, in turn, before I learned that the hominoids share a common ancestor in the late Miocene era.

---

[9] 1.23 84b7–8.
[10] 1.22 84a25; 1.24 85b7–15; 11.13 96a24–31; 11.17 99a18–21, 24.

Now it is sometimes supposed that the intermediate stage of cognitive development in the above sort of sequence only gives the illusion of the capacity for explanation. At the zoo, my daughter asks why chimpanzees don't have tails, and I say it is due to their being hominoids, one of the oddities of which is lacking tails (always with the implied context of a wider group for which tails are the norm, of course). The person next to us, overhearing this conversation, may silently accuse me of sophistry – but Aristotle, I think, would not. For I have accomplished two very important tasks with this explanation. First, I have identified hominoids at the appropriate level of generality with respect to gaining a further understanding of the lack of tails – my daughter now knows the kind which has the feature *as such*. Second, even without pursuing this further question, she has gained a picture of the unity of the primates which the partial knowledge that chimpanzees and humans don't have tails did not provide. A-type explanations, then, are a crucial stage in the acquisition of understanding about a domain.

These two sorts of explanation are distinguished quite clearly in *APo.* II.16–17. This is not surprising, for these chapters explore just those issues of counter-predication and of the role of definitions in explanation where the distinction between A- and B-type explanations becomes important. I simply wish to draw on this discussion to mark the distinction on which I have been insisting.

The primary goal of *APo.* II.16–17 is to establish that, within a given subject kind, a scientific demonstration involves a middle term which is extensionally equivalent with, causally prior to, and part of the definition of, the predicate to be demonstrated (98a35–98b4, 98b14–24, 99a1–4, 99a21–2). The following passage summarizes the main features of this discussion.

...the middle term is an account of the first extreme: that is why all understanding comes about through definition. E.g. shedding leaves follows together with the vine [kind] and extends beyond it; and with the fig [kind] and extends beyond it – but it does not extend beyond all, but is equal in extent to them. Thus if you were to take the primitive middle term, it is an account of shedding leaves. For there will be a middle term in the other direction (that all are such and such); and then a middle for this (that the sap solidifies or something else of this sort). What is shedding leaves? The solidifying of the sap at the connection of the seed. (99a21–9)[11]

---

[11] This passage applies a set of principles argued for in *APr.* 1.27 concerning selecting predicates for premises of syllogisms (esp. 43b11–38). As here, the context is how to select terms relative to a specific *problēma* (*APr.* 1.26 42b29, 43a18; 27 43b34, 28 44a37), and the first principle enunciated is, 'It is necessary to select *not* the things which follow some part, but whatever follows the whole thing, e.g. not what follows a sort of human, but what follows *every* human' (43b11–13). The passage goes on to counsel against selecting predicates which follow from a kind *as* following from a form of it – in such cases, one

This complex and difficult passage is an attempt to distinguish the
two sorts of explanation I have been discussing. Shedding leaves is
here the feature to be explained. It is noted that it belongs to all of
various kinds, extends beyond each kind, but is equal in extension
to their conjunction.

Thus there are two initial problems: why does shedding leaves
belong to every vine?, and why does shedding leaves belong to every
fig tree? Philoponus suggests that the enigmatic reference to 'a
middle term in the other direction' is a reference to an earlier
example, in which the middle term is a 'such and such' over various
sorts of plants which shed leaves, namely 'broad-leaved plants' (cf.
98b5–16).[12] If this suggestion is correct, the explanations which
emerge through this middle term are A-type explanations of why fig
trees or vines shed their leaves.

Now, however, we are introduced to the idea of a more basic
middle *for this*, that is, for why broad-leaved plants shed their leaves
(as such). This will, we are told, be a *logos* of shedding leaves. The
parallel explanation we might build on his hints would look like this:

> B. Shedding leaves belongs to everything which undergoes
>   solidification of sap at the seed connection.
>   Solidification of sap at the seed connection belongs to
>   every broad-leaved plant.
>   _____
>   Shedding leaves belongs to every broad-leaved plant.[13]

In this explanation, the explanandum involves a predicate which
belongs to its subject 'in itself'. But it doesn't belong primitively; that
is, there is a cause of its belonging. Shedding leaves is a process
resulting from a more basic process of solidification.[14] In such

---

should select *idia* of the form, for the predicates of the kind apply to its forms implicitly
(43b22–9). What is entirely missing in the *APr.* discussion is the identification of the middle
term as identifying the cause of the predication to be explained. Cf. my forthcoming 1987.

[12] *CIAG* xiii.3 429.32–430.7. John Ackrill suggests that in such cases 'the only explanation
why *S*s are *P*s is the explanation why *G*s in general are *P*s' (1981b: 380). But *APo.* 1.5 and
APo. ii.14 state that, while we will ultimately want the explanation why *G*s are *P*s, noting
that *G*s in general are *P*s and that *S*s are sorts of *G*s is a respectable explanation of why
*S*s are *P*s.

[13] It is worth noting, because of its affinity to the actual practice of the biology, that this
explanation is not stated syllogistically in the text, but rather as the answer to a *problem*
about why leaves are shed. Stated in this way, the appropriate answer is just to provide
the reason why (e.g. 'This is so, because certain processes take place in these plants'), not
an argument with 'Shedding leaves belongs to every broad-leaved plant' as a conclusion.

[14] The research strategy this theory of explanation suggests is to ask, when one has the same
predicate belonging to distinct subjects, whether these distinct subjects share in a common
nature in virtue of which the predicate belongs. An important question, approached
repeatedly in *APo.* ii.16, 17, is whether this *must* be the case, and thus whether this strategy
is *always* appropriate (cf. 98b25–39, 99a1–16, 99b4–7).

explanations, that close relationship between answers to *ti esti* and *dia ti* questions argued for in *APo*. II. 1–10 is clearly revealed. For this causally basic process is both what shedding is, and the cause of certain plants shedding their leaves.[15]

To reiterate then: in A-type explanations, a universal predication of a subject is accounted for by noting the primary *genos* of that subject relative to the predication to be explained, i.e. by reference to the kind which has the predicate per se. In B-type explanations, such per se predications are accounted for by understanding what it is about being that kind which immediately necessitates it having that predicate. This sort of explanation answers the primitive question relative to the predicate under scrutiny – why does it belong to the things it belongs to *as such*?

III

The distinctions between incidental and unqualified understanding, and between A-type and B-type explanations, have a number of methodological implications. If there are ways of organizing our true propositions about a subject so that A-type explanations will be more readily apparent, which in turn will reveal those per se predications which will need to be explained by reference to peculiar, differentiating features of a subject, then one ought to so organize one's true propositions. This, I suggest, is the subject of *APo*. II.14. One of the features of that chapter which gives prima facie plausibility to this suggestion is that, as in *APo*. I.5, the subject of how kinds are related to their *eidē* leads directly to the issue of *eidē* which have much in common but no common name. Again, the issue of nomenclature will be put off until a later section of the paper.

APo. II.14 suggests how to use 'dissections and divisions' in grasping *problēmata* (98a1).[16] *Problēma* is used here in a technical sense defined at *Topics* I. 101b17: 'Problems are the things about which there are deductions.' Scientific problems are in the form of requests for explanations – *dia ti p*? The discussion in *APo*. II.14 recommends, developing arguments of *APr*. I.27, that the investigator is

---

[15] For discussion of these issues cf. Ackrill 1981b and Bolton, ch. 6 below, 139–46.

[16] Jonathan Barnes (1975a: 240) rightly argues that the likely reference of 'dissections' here is a lost work referred to regularly in the biological treatises. Cf. *PN* 456b2, 474b9, 478b1; *HA* 497a32, 509b22–4, 510a29–35, 511a13, 525a8–9, 530a31, 565a12–13, 566a14–15; *PA* 650a31, 666a9, 668b29–30, 674b17, 680a2, 684b4, 689a19; *GA* 719a10, 740a23–4, 746a14–15, 764a35, 779a8–9. Diogenes Laertius v.25 lists a *Dissections* in eight books and one book of *Selections from the Dissections*. The notion of a *problēma* here is paralleled at *GA* I. 724a7 and II. 746b16; cf. *APo*. 88a12–16 and *APr*. 43a18.

to select thus, positing the kind common to all; e.g., if the subjects of study are animals, [select] what follows all animals, and having grasped these, again what follows all the first remaining things, e.g. if this is bird, what follows every bird, and thus always [ask what belongs] to the nearest kind.[17]

A full evaluation of this chapter would involve placing it in the wider context of the relevance of division to definition and explanation, and of the general rules for constructing scientific syllogisms in *APr*. 1.27–30.[18] For the moment, I merely wish to draw attention to its relevance to the issue of formulating A-type explanations and hitting on per se predications.

In considering the above quotation, it is crucial to remember that it assumes a set of divisions of a subject domain ready at hand, and divisions, the example suggests, organized along Aristotelian lines. But as Aristotle makes clear in *APr*. 1.31, the investigation of a subject S cannot move to an explanatory stage via division alone. We may recognize that S belongs to a kind K, and know that K is differentiated into sub-kinds F_1 and F_2; but that only allows us to infer that S is either F_1 or F_2. We need first to grasp empirically, as a problem, which of the differentiae belongs to our subject $(F_2 a S)$, ask why every S has F_2, and search for a middle not wider in extent than F_2. Divisions are useful, however, as a potentially exhaustive *source* of predicates from which to select appropriate predications (cf. *APr*. 1.31 46a31–b19).

APo. II.14 is thus suggesting how best to make use of such information. The suggestion is that we begin with the most common kind relative to the object being investigated and select or pick out what follows necessarily and what it follows necessarily before proceeding. Again, assuming our divisions have been properly made, we can proceed to the *first* remaining group, i.e. to the immediately next level. As an example we are given a *megiston genos* which is common coinage, bird, and we are told to collect all the features common to *every* bird. We are to apply this methodology iteratively throughout our division, presumably until we get to the indivisible kinds.

Why are we doing this?

For it is clear that we shall now be in a position to state the reason why what follows the items under the common kind belongs to them – e.g. why it belongs to man or horse. Let A be animal, B what follows every animal, and C, D, E sorts of animals. Well it is clear why B belongs to D, for it does so because of A. (98a8–12)

---

[17] *APo*. II.14 98a2–8; cf. Balme 1972: 72, Kullmann 1974: 196–202.
[18] Allan Gotthelf and Myles Burnyeat independently pointed out the relevance of these chapters to *APo*. II.14. It indicates that the method of II.14 may be simply an application of a more general theory about the use of systematically organized information in framing explanations. Cf. n. 11 above.

To use a concrete example: suppose we are examining the peregrine falcon, and are asking why it possesses a hooked beak. We recognize it is a bird, and, consulting our divisions we see that having a beak follows on being a bird, that beaks are differentiated in many ways, that having hooked beaks follows on having crooked talons, strong wings, soaring flight, being carnivorous (all under *other* divisions). We are now in a position to formulate an explanation:

> Having a hooked beak belongs to every crook-taloned bird.
> Being a crook-taloned bird belongs to every peregrine falcon.
> _____
> Having a hooked beak belongs to every peregrine falcon.[19]

Further, should one find features which belong to all and only one sort of bird such as hooked beaks belonging *only* to birds with crooked talons, one will know that, while these may be demonstrated to belong to less extensive kinds, such predications cannot themselves be explained through the subject's membership in a wider kind. Nor can we know, simply by consulting this information, whether a middle term is just part of what it is to be this kind of thing, or a per se incidental feature to be B-explained, but we know that determining *that* is what is at issue.[20]

What this downward division/correlation methodology accomplishes, then, is to provide a collection of propositions which will play various roles in explanation, to reveal in certain cases the A-type explanation for kinds having certain features, and to direct, or redirect, inquiry to the appropriate level for B-type explanations of certain more primitive predications.

But this, it shall now be contended, is rather like what we find in the *Historia Animalium*, and thus this chapter may provide clues to the aims of that work, and to its relationship with the other zoological works. It is now time to look to the biological works for indications that the epistemological and methodological recommendations of *APo.* to which I have drawn attention play an important role in the organization of investigation and explanation in that domain.

---

[19] Thus the constant stress that division is valuable as a means of insuring that the intermediate kinds are not left out in articulating the nature of a kind, e.g., 96b35–97a6. This is simply a methodological consequence of the point made at *APo.* 1.1 71a18–71b9, that if one knows the predicates which hold at the universal level, acquaintance with a new instance of the universal will directly provide understanding of it. The centrality of division in the overall program of the *APo.* is stressed in Ferejohn 1982/3.

[20] In either case, even if it is known that the predicate belongs to all and only the members of a certain kind, it does not follow that one will know whether it is a primitive incidental or *idion* of the subject, or an aspect of what the subject is.

IV

About to launch into a discussion of the bloodless animals in *HA* iv, Aristotle looks back self-consciously on the preceding discussion.

We have said previously, about the blooded animals, which parts they have in common and which are peculiar to each kind; and about the non-uniform and the uniform parts, which they have externally and which internally. Now we must discuss the bloodless animals. (523a31–b2)

This is a careful summary. The second half of the sentence reflects precisely the order of the composition of *HA* 1.7-iii, which within extensive kinds has surveyed first the external non-uniform and internal non-uniform, and then the external uniform and internal uniform, parts. Likewise, the first part of the sentence points to a pervasive feature of the earlier discussion. For within each extensive kind, there is a tendency to move from the consideration of what this kind has in common with previously considered kinds, to the isolation of the distinctive features of that extensive kind, and then to the noting of what is distinctive to various sub-kinds.

Considered within the context of contemporary biological classification, the purposes of the *HA* are difficult to fathom. Many attempts to construct an organized taxonomy out of its materials have failed, and for the first half of this century it came to be viewed as a loosely organized natural history.[21] David Balme began serious re-evaluation of *HA*'s scientific function by stressing the way in which it draws attention to closely related groups of differentiae:

...if the *HA* is read, not as an encyclopaedia nor as a collection of simple natural history, but as being itself to some extent a theoretical treatise – namely a study of differentiae – then much of its apparent incoherence disappears.[22]

Both Balme and, recently, Pierre Pellegrin have stressed the role of the *HA* in providing the materials for scientific definition. Pellegrin, in addition, has furthered the work on the meaning of Aristotle's classificatory concepts, *genos*, *eidos* and *diaphora* begun by Balme, showing how the apparent chaos in the use of these terms in the biology is largely dissipated when they are viewed within the context of the logic and metaphysics of division.[23] With these insights as background, Professor Allan Gotthelf and I decided to read continuously through the *HA* with two eyes (one each) on the details of

---

[21] The most painstaking study is that of Meyer 1855; his argument has been carefully critiqued by Balme in ch. 4 above, 81–5.

[22] Balme, in ch. 4 above, 89.

[23] Pellegrin 1982; cf. below, ch. 12. Balme, in ch. 4 above has in general endorsed Pellegrin's conclusions on this matter.

organization and structure of that work. Part of our concern was to test some preliminary speculations I had ventured at an N.E.H. Research Conference directed by Gotthelf, about the relevance of the *APo.*'s theory of explanation to Aristotle's biological practice.[24] The provisional results of this joint venture are reported here and in Professor Gotthelf's 'Philosophical lessons of Aristotle's *Historia Animalium*' (cf. Gotthelf 1987a), and a first attempt shall be made to tie them to those wider concerns about explanation and scientific methodology.

In outline, the argument of this section of the paper is that a reasonably constant focus of *HA* is the indication of the widest class to which a feature belongs universally, and drawing attention to cases where a feature predicated universally of a *megiston genos* belongs to other extensive kinds as well. There is a persistent concern to distinguish these features from those which are *idia* of the kind in question. And where some common feature of a kind is differentiated in unique ways in sub-divisions of that kind, this is noted, and a list of other features peculiar to the sub-kind is usually provided. The organization, that is, is sufficiently akin to the ideas in *APr.* 1.27–30 and *APo.* II.14 to make one suspicious that that sketch is in the background.

And not too far in the background, perhaps. Consider *HA* 1.6 491a7–14.

These things have been said in this way now as an outline, to provide a taste of the things, however many they may be, about which we must study, in order that we may first grasp the differences and the incidental features in every case. (We will speak in more detail in what follows.) After this we must attempt to discover the causes of these [differences and incidental features]. For to pursue the study in this way is natural, once there is an investigation (*historia*) about each kind; since it becomes apparent from these investigations both about which things and from which things the demonstration (*hē apodeixis*) ought to be carried out.

This is a pivotal text. The previous chapters have given a theoretical account of the nature of similarity and difference of animal parts, distinguished four types of zoological differentiae (parts, lifestyle, activities, and character traits), and given a carefully selective analysis of how various widely different animals can be said to differ according to features of these four sorts. (It is also shock therapy for those who would use such differentiae as wild/ tame, winged/wingless, land-dweller/water-dweller, indiscriminately.) The first half of chapter 6 then lists what he takes to be established as extensive kinds, and argues for additions and limits to

[24] 'Aristotle's *Posterior Analytics* and the biological works.'

that list.[25] It closes with the above account of this investigation's place in the zoological enterprise.

What does this account tell us? It apparently alludes to the first five chapters as providing a taste of the sort of investigation which will be carried on in a more *akribēs* fashion afterwards. On the other hand, it could be referring to the immediately preceding discussion of the extensive kinds, for there is explicit reference to a discussion of the number of things to be studied, i.e. to the question how many kinds there are.

The first task, we are told, is to grasp the differences and the incidental features that belong in each case. This may allude to two aspects of the 'divide and select' methodology of *APo.* II.14, that is, the division of a kind into its immediate sub-kinds and then the 'grasping' of what belongs to each. But the phrase is admittedly enigmatic, and is best left relatively uninterpreted until the actual method has been examined.

Whatever precisely this first stage comes to, it is called a *historia* and is said naturally to precede the attempt to discover the causes of these, which I take it refers to these differences and incidental features of kinds. The *historia* will make apparent the about whiches (the *explananda*) and the from whiches (the *explanans*) of our scientific explanations (*apodeixeis*). This last sentence is self-consciously worded in the language of the *Posterior Analytics*.[26] Notice that it does not say merely that the investigation of difference and incidentals is a preliminary to causal investigation. Rather, it says that differentiation of *explanans* and *explananda* becomes clear as a consequence of this investigation. This, I suggest, makes it more likely that the organization of *HA* will reflect the needs of Aristotelian explanations.[27]

Is this passage *post hoc* methodological window-dressing, or does it actually describe *HA*'s procedures? And is the methodology of *APo.* II.14 behind *HA*'s organization, if it has one?

Our preliminary results suggest that it is. The evidence from the

---

[25] This passage has been insightfully discussed in Gotthelf unpublished (1).

[26] Besides the reference to *apodeixis*, the description of the components of demonstration as that *about which* and that *from which* is reminiscent of the description of demonstrative understanding at *APo.* 1.10 76b12–23, esp. 76b22–3. Cf. 1.12 77a40–b3. The use of *historia* here as the appropriate name for the pre-demonstrative investigation of a subject is likewise reminiscent of *APr.* 1.30 46a18–28; esp. 46a24–8. Cf. Lennox forthcoming 1987.

[27] I don't intend this to suggest that Aristotle conceived of science in a Baconian fashion. Division is a way of organizing information for the sake of explanation/definition, not a method of discovering information. Furthermore, it is often discussed in *APo.* as if it were as much a method of *testing* antecedently organized information for completeness as it is a method for organizing previously unorganized propositions; cf. 96b27ff.

HA alone is suggestive, but not conclusive. But when it is combined with an examination of explanations in *PA*, that evidence gains in power. In the following sections I shall focus exclusively on *HA* ii-iv and *PA*.[28]

HA ii opens[29] with a seemingly innocuous remark which none-theless takes on significance against the background of the method-ology of *APo*. ii.14:

Some of the parts of the other [i.e. non-human] animals are common to all of them, just as was said before, while others are common to certain kinds. (497b6–9)

Select what's common to the widest kind first, and then to the next widest, may be the suggestion. He then reviews the earlier discussion of sorts of likeness and difference, and proceeds according to the summary quoted earlier from the opening of Book iv. Let us begin with a wide-angle shot of the terrain and then 'zoom' in on certain sections to study the details.

Summary: HA ii–iv

ii.1–7:	external non-uniform parts of viviparous quadrupeds
8–9:	apes, baboons, monkeys – tending both toward biped and toward quadruped
10:	external non-uniform parts of oviparous quadrupeds
11:	chameleons
12:	external non-uniform parts of birds
13:	external non-uniform parts of fish
14:	external non-uniform parts of serpents
15–17:	the internal non-uniform parts considered one part at a time in all the blooded kinds.
iii.1:	genitalia (which are not neatly divisible into internal or external, and which differ considerably between male and female)
2–4:	blood vessels
5–22:	sinew, fibre, bone, cartilage, nail, hoof, claw, horn, hair, skin, feathers, membrane, omentum, bladder, flesh, fat, suet, blood, marrow, milk, semen
iv.1:	comparison of four bloodless kinds cephalopods, external and internal parts
2:	crustacea, external and internal parts
3:	testacea, external and internal parts
4:	hermit crabs which tend both toward crustacea and toward testacea
5:	sea urchins and odd testacea
6:	the odd ones, sea squirts and sea anemones
7:	insects, external and internal parts rare unclassified creatures
8:	sense organs across the animal kingdom
9:	noises across the animal kingdom
10:	sleep and dreams across the animal kingdom

[28] *HA* ii–iv.7 deals exclusively with parts-differences.

[29] The beginning of a new 'book' does not signal a lack of continuity with i.17, as the *de* of the first sentence of Book ii contrasting with the *men* of the last sentence of Book i shows.

11 : male and female across the animal kingdom, which neatly points
toward v-vii on reproductive behavior

Even at this level of resolution there are some interesting variations
to be noted. While the discussion of the external parts of the blooded
animals takes the form of an account of each part in one kind, and
then a new account of each part in the next kind, each of the internal
and the uniform parts is discussed as it appears *throughout* the blooded
kinds, and then discussion moves to the next *part*.

Yet another shift in method occurs in *HA* iv. Aristotle returns to
discussing the parts of each bloodless kind, kind by kind, again. But
now *both* the external and internal parts are discussed for one group
before proceeding to the next.

These shifts, and more subtle ones that occur more regionally, are,
I suspect, thought out, not arbitrary.[30] But, as David Balme has so
forcefully brought home, if one were looking for a systematic
treatment of kinds of animals, kind by kind, organized by one
uniform method of classification, one could only be disappointed.

Nonetheless, the above summary does suggest that the 'extensive
kinds' do have an importance as a locus of a number of similarities
and differences among parts. Yet if understanding of the sort
envisaged in *APo.* is Aristotle's ultimate goal, these can't be the
primary focus. What we will want to know is the widest group to
which a particular *feature* belongs, and how that feature differs or is
differentiated in sub-kinds, and what the widest group is to which
each of these differentiated features belongs. Focusing on such
questions will not suggest an encyclopedia of animals with a full and
complete non-comparative description, of each kind. Nor will it
recommend remaining with one principle of organization as the
features being examined change.

Let us now narrow our focus in on one passage from each of the
methodologically distinct discussions mentioned. *HA* ii.12 discusses
the external organs of birds. It begins with a review of parts which
belong to birds but extend more widely:

the birds as well have some parts similar to the animals already discussed [viviparous
and oviparous quadrupeds]; for all birds have a head, neck, underbelly, and an
analogue of the chest. (503b29–32)

[30] It seems plausible that these shifts are dictated by differences in the manner in which
different sorts of parts are distributed and differentiated among the extensive kinds. For
example, given that the introduction to the bloodless kinds stresses the fact that hard and
soft parts are external/internal in some, internal/external in others, it makes sense both
to stress this mode of difference and to discuss what is internal and what external in each
kind before proceeding to the next.

In addition, they are bipedal, like humans, but the legs bend more as those of the quadrupeds do (503b33–4). Various features are marked as *idia* of birds – feathered wings (503b35), a long haunch bone (504a1), beak (504a21), quilled feathers (504a31–2). Certain features, while common to the birds, are found in distinctive ways in various sub-kinds. Crook-taloned birds have the largest and strongest chests (504a4–5); all have numerous clawed toes, but swimmers have them with webbing (504a8), and high flyers all have *four* toes. Of this latter group, most have three forward and one behind ('instead of a heel'), but a few, such as the wryneck, have two front and two rear, an *idion* of theirs (504a10–13). All long-legged or web-footed birds have short rumps and extend their legs when in flight (504a33–6); good flyers have no spurs, while the heavy birds do (504b7–10). Some have feathery crests, but the domestic cock's is peculiar in being flesh-like (504b11–12).

What prevents this material from being an extremely spotty, random assortment of observations is its consistent focus on the following questions:

1. What features of birds 'extend beyond' to a wider class?
2. What are the *idia* of birds, features belonging to all and only the birds?
3. What differences does one find among the birds – can we find a group to which such differences belong uniquely?[31]

The first concern is indicated by the fact that every separate consideration of a *megiston genos* begins by taking up the issue of which parts it has in common with other such groups – the opening of the discussion of the external parts of the oviparous quadrupeds, for example, is a review of features which are 'just as the vivipara among quadrupeds' (502b29–32). The focus on the extensiveness of a feature is often remarkable.

All the quadrupeds have bony, fleshless and sinewy limbs; in fact, this is generally (*holōs*) true of all the other animals which have feet, excepting man. (499a31–2)

This feature not only extends to all the quadrupeds (this remark occurs during a discussion of viviparous quadrupeds), but to birds as well – to all blooded, footed animals except man.

Let us turn briefly to a consideration of a discussion of the internal organs. Remember that Aristotle has here abandoned the methodology of remaining within a kind for each part and is reviewing a number of related organs throughout the blooded animals.

---

[31] One might compare the discussions of elephants (497b22–498a12), camels (499a13–30), seals (498a32–b4), or river crocodiles (503a8–15). Discussion of passages of similar import can be found in Gotthelf 1987a.

Now those which are quadrupedal and viviparous all have an esophagus and windpipe, and it is positioned in the same way as in humans; and whichever of the quadrupeds are oviparous are alike in this respect; in fact the situation is similar among the birds, but there are differences in the forms of these parts. Generally speaking (*holōs*), all which take in air by inhaling and exhaling have a lung, windpipe and esophagus... Not all the [blooded] animals have lungs; for example, fish do not, nor if there are any other animals which have gills.[32]

When one compares this with the discussion of these organs in *PA* its acausal, a-explanatory nature is truly remarkable. But notice – he is seeking the highest level of generality possible for these features; schematically the passage reads 'in K_1, in K_2, also in K_3, in fact, in all the Ks that breathe: not in *all* the blooded Ks, however, for fish don't have lungs.' Now at this point he could easily have said. 'For gills perform the same function as lungs, namely cooling blooded animals, but fish, living in water, cool themselves with water rather than with air.' This he clearly avoids. Notice, however, that we are told what else, besides lungs, breathers have in common, and are provided with a mark of the widest unnamed class with these features. We have moved from knowing that isosceles, equilateral and scalene each have $2R$, to knowing that triangles do, so to speak. Thus, while *HA* stops short of actual explanations, it has organized the facts in such a way as to direct us toward A-type explanations for sub-kinds having a lung (by identifying the kind to which it belongs primitively); and B-type explanations for the possession of a lung (by noting its correlation with the inhaling and exhaling of air). In fact, Aristotle devotes an entire work to these features, or perhaps part of a treatise.[33]

Certain innards are dealt with rather summarily.

All the viviparous quadrupeds have kidneys and a bladder; none of the non-quadrupedal ovipara have them, neither the birds nor fish, while the sea turtle alone among the oviparous quadrupeds has these in proportion to its other parts. (506b25–8)

Occasionally, however, while a part may be common to all the blooded kinds, it will be differentiated in a markedly different manner at some level: 507a30–508a8 is an extensive discussion of the stomach and gut of the ruminants (as we should say), and features correlated with these differences.

The first uniform part taken up (for it is most common in the

---

[32] *HA* II.15 505b32–506a11. While he insists that no animal will have both lung and gills, he is quite open to the possibility of kinds other than fish turning up which have gills. In fact he treats the newt as such; cf. *HA* VIII. 589b27–9, *PA* IV. 695b25, *Juv.* 476a6.

[33] *De Juventute* 7–27 (*De Respiratione* 1–21). I agree with Ross (1955: 50–60) that there is no good reason to view this as a separate treatise.

blooded animals and has the appearance of being an *archē*) is the system of blood vessels. This discussion is atypical, both because it contains long quotations and extensive discussion of previous views, and because his own account is explicitly generalized so as to be applicable to all blooded kinds.

The facts about the starting-points and the great blood vessels are thus in all the blooded animals, though the other numerous blood vessels are not alike in all; for they neither have the parts in the same way, nor do they all have the same ones... (515a16–19)

Thus the account provided can be applied to *any* of the blooded kinds, *qua* blooded. Any more detailed description would have to take into account the different organization of vessels reflecting the different organization of the other parts, kind by kind.

Finally, one passage will be examined from Aristotle's account of the bloodless animals (*HA* IV.1–7). The discussion begins with an overview of the four main kinds, especially focused on which have the hard parts inside and which outside, and the nature of those parts. Let us focus on the *cephalopods*.

First is the *genos* of the so-called softies or cephalopods – this consists of those which are bloodless and yet have their fleshy part outside, while if they have any hard part it is inside, just as with the blooded animals – for example, the *genos* of cuttlefish. (523b1–5)

The specific discussion of the cephalopods first notes four external parts which they all have in common ('select the common kind first, and what follows this'), and proceeds,

Now all have eight feet, and all these have a double row of suckers, except one kind of octopus. But the cuttlefish and the small and large calamary have, as a peculiarity (*idia*), two long tentacles (*proboskidēs*), at the end of which is a rough part having two rows of suckers, by means of which they acquire nourishment and take it into the mouth... (523b28–32)

Again, there is clear movement from those features which belong to the cephalopods as such, to those which belong to a group which again has no single name, but a number of features in common (cf. 524b22–4). When Aristotle moves on to a discussion of the octopuses (a kind with many *genē* – 525a13) he again notes first common features and then those peculiarities of the sub-kinds, e.g. the *heledōnē* which is 'alone in having a single row of suckers [on each tentacle]' (525a17).

Professor Balme has pointed out the oddity, from the standpoint of natural history, of Aristotle's treatment of the blind mole, mentioned often, but as if it had only two features, being viviparous and having rudimentary eyes below the skin.[34] But from the standpoint of Aristotelian explanation, it makes perfect sense. As with the *heledōnē* above, only features *not* common to the wider group are worth noting – all others are to be explained at the wider level of generality.

Balme has also drawn our attention to discussions which read as reports about various kinds which have not been parceled out to the appropriate section of *HA*.[35] One of these is the discussion of the apes and baboons (502a17–b27). In some sense, Balme is clearly right; both character traits and internal parts are referred to (although only by the way), and there is no discussion of their behavior or character elsewhere in *HA*. On the other hand, this material is certainly well placed, for it appears after creatures which are either clearly viviparous bipeds or clearly viviparous quadrupeds, and opens by announcing

Some animals are allied in nature both to man and the quadrupeds, for example, apes, monkeys and baboons. (502a17–18)

Accordingly, throughout the discussion, their features are allied either with the bipeds or with the quadrupeds. The focus thus remains on identifying the widest class in virtue of which a feature belongs. Let me direct the discussion toward actual explanation by comparing a statement about the ape's hindquarters with an A-type explanation from *PA*.

...and as a quadruped [the ape] has no buttocks, while as a biped, it has no tail. (502b21–2)[36]

But the ape, owing to its tending to both sides with respect to its shape, that is, to its being neither sort and yet both – owing to this, it has neither a tail nor buttocks; as a biped no tail, as a quadruped no buttocks. (*PA* iv.10 689b31–4)[37]

Now of course, as it stands, this is not a fully satisfactory explanation of either feature – it is, as I have characterized them, an A-type explanation. In order to understand why quadrupeds lack buttocks, a B-type explanation is required, which might point to aspects of the life of quadrupeds which would make buttocks useless or harmful. (In fact such an explanation precedes the above quoted passage.) To explain why *apes* lack them, one needs only to be reminded that they are, *in this respect*, built like quadrupeds.

---

[34] Cf. Balme, ch. 1 above, 9.

[35] Balme, ch. 4 above, 88.

[36] ...καὶ οὔτ᾽ ἰσχία ἔχει ὡς τετράπουν ὂν οὔτε κέρκον ὡς δίπουν...

[37] Ὁ δὲ πίθηκος διὰ τὸ τὴν μορφὴν ἐπαμφοτερίζειν καὶ μηδετέρων τ᾽ εἶναι καὶ ἀμφοτέρων, διὰ τοῦτ᾽ οὔτ᾽ οὐρὰν ἔχει οὔτ᾽ ἰσχία, ὡς μὲν δίπους ὢν οὐράν, ὡς δὲ τετράπους ἰσχία. Here and elsewhere I have adopted David Balme's suggestion to translate ἐπαμφοτερίζειν as 'tending to both sides'.

More will be said about such explanations in a moment. Here I want to close the discussion of *HA* by stressing the relationship between these two texts. The *HA* gives us the relevant descriptions of the features of the animal in question, assigns those features under the appropriate wider kind, and leaves it up to *PA* to do just what it says it will:

> From what parts and how many parts each of the animals are composed has been shown in greater detail in the histories about them. Now we must investigate the causes through which each is the way it is, separating these off by themselves from what was said in the histories. (646a8–12)

The hypothesis that *HA* has, as one of its primary aims, the purpose of finding and characterizing the groups to which various features belong primitively, even when those groups have no common name, makes its organization reasonable, and squares well with the recent work of both David Balme and Pierre Pellegrin showing its non-taxonomic nature. In addition, the use of the information that one finds in *HA* in the *PA* strongly suggests that these generalizations were used as interim explanations of lower-level kinds having certain features, and as the focus of the more basic explanations of that work.

V

The *Parts of Animals* is a work of sustained scientific explanation. Its explanations are typically worded as answers to 'problems', i.e., questions of the form, 'Why do these animals have this part?' They can be fairly cleanly divided into A-type and B-type explanations, the latter subsuming both explanations by reference to a creature's material make-up and by reference to its lifestyle or activities.

The A-type explanations are exemplified well in the following example:

> But even the dolphin has, not fish spine, but bone; for it is viviparous. (664a16–17)

There are two facts specified about dolphins: they *are* viviparous, and they *have* bones. These important facts about dolphins are remarked on in the *HA* (that they have bone at 516b11; that they are viviparous at 489b2 and 566b3–26). Having bones rather than fish spine is a necessary, but not a primitively universal, feature of dolphins. Bone *tout court*, however, *is* a primitively universal feature of the vivipara; indeed, it is while pointing this out in the *HA* (516b12) that Aristotle there remarks, 'But the dolphin also has bone, *not* fish spine.' The above explanation, then, directs us to the lives of vivipara for an understanding of their having bony skeletons.

But it also tells us that, whatever that explanation might be, *dolphins* have them because they are a sort of viviparous animal.

The interaction between these two types of explanations can be seen clearly if we remain with cetaceans for a moment. *PA* III.6, on lungs, opens with the following broad explanatory generalization:

> Any *genos* of animals has a lung due to its being a land-dweller (*dia to pezon einai*). (668b33–4)

As we saw earlier, four of the five *megista genē* of blooded animals have lungs. It thus can't be because they are *blooded* that they have this structure, for then *all* blooded ones would. Aristotle here sanctions an A-type explanation for any of them in terms of their being 'land-dwellers' (*peza*).

The term *pezon* normally means either land-dweller or walker, but either way the above generalization would seem to be in serious trouble when confronted with cetacea. How does Aristotle handle this problem?

> The animals that breathe, on the other hand, produce cooling by air, so that all the breathers have a lung. Further, all the land-dwellers breathe, and so do some of the water-dwellers, as well, e.g., whales, dolphins and all the spouting sea monsters. For many animals have a nature which tends to both sides (*epamphoterizein*), and while among the land-dwellers and those receptive of air, they spend most of their time in the water owing to the blend of materials in their body. And some of those which live in the water participate to such an extent in the land-dwelling nature that the decisive factor in life consists in their breathing (*en tōi pneumati autōn einai to telos tou zēn*). (669a6–13)

There is a thorny nest of problems here, having to do with how Aristotelian division deals with 'dualizers', problems extensively discussed in *HA* VIII.1–2, and alluded to in Balme, chapter 4 above (85–6). Most of them I will not discuss, but will focus on the form of explanation being offered here.[38] The chapter opened, as we saw, with the bald claim that any *genos* of animal has a lung due to its being a land-dweller. In the passage just quoted, however, it is said that (among blooded animals) both land-dwellers *and some water-dwellers* (*enhudra*) breathe. We seem to be in deep trouble here.

The solution which emerges in *HA* VIII.2 lies in distinguishing different criteria for being a water-dweller: for our purposes, a creature may be a water-dweller with respect to nutritive requirements, or with respect to the way it cools itself. Thus Aristotle imagines two lines of division, one under 'cooling organ' and one

---

[38] The line developed somewhat dogmatically in my text has been questioned by Allan Gotthelf in a private communication. For the purposes of this discussion, however, I don't think the differences are crucial.

under 'nutritional nature', with a water-dweller/land-dweller division within each line. In this way, the same animal may be both a land-dweller (in so far as it cools itself by means of inhaling and exhaling air) and a water-dweller (in so far as its bodily nature requires sea food). The porpoises, then, partake in the nature of land-dwellers to the extent that they cool themselves as land-dwellers do, though from the standpoint of their material makeup and nutritive requirements they are water-dwellers. But as they are each according to different criteria, and under different lines of division, we will not have the same animal appearing in more than one line of the same division.

The issue here concerns the nature of lunged creatures *as such*. Aristotle, that is, moves beyond noting the kind to which anything which as lungs must belong to an exploration of the nature of this wider class. These animals all cool themselves by means of inhaling cool air and exhaling warm air – that is they partake in the nature of land-dwellers (*qua* cooling).[39] Here is a clear B-type explanation of why it is that all these creatures have lungs, for lungs are necessary if a creature is to breathe – that is what lungs are for.[40] On the other hand, to apply this understanding to the *genos* of cetacea, one may simply point out that, with respect to cooling, they participate in the land-dwelling nature.

To indicate that this distinction between 'forms' of explanation is neutral with respect to what sort of causation is involved, it is useful briefly to examine examples of the very common double-barreled material/teleological explanations found throughout the *PA*. At the same time, an awareness of what is and is not said about the same features in the *HA* will help focus attention on the nature of the explanations in *PA*. In each of these cases I will look at explanations of features which are *idia* of their kind.

The *HA* has the following to say about the bushiness of the hair on man's head:

---

[39] The rendering given of 669a13 above, and the interpretation of it here, are suggested by a similar turn of phrase at *Juv.* 480b19–20: διὸ κἀκείνοις τοῦ ζῆν καὶ μὴ ζῆν τὸ τέλος ἔστιν ἐν τῷ ἀναπνεῖν. The idea of rendering τέλος in this less technical fashion was suggested by Allan Gotthelf.

[40] Notice that any attempt to syllogize this explanation would eliminate the causal content of the explanation. *APo.* II.11 suggests that the middle term in an explanation may *refer* to a goal. But in order to know *how* a middle term explains, one must understand *the way in which* its referent is responsible for what is being explained. The effect of formulating all predications in a neutral 'belongs to' language is to obscure distinctions between various types of predications (e.g., between 'essential', primitive, and merely 'universal' predications), and distinctions between various causal relationships holding among the predicates in question.

All those animals which are quadrupeds and viviparous are hairy, so to speak, unlike man, who has a small amount of minute hairs except on his head, which is the hairiest of all the animals. (*HA* 498b17–18)

The *PA* tells us why:

The human head is the hairiest of all the animals *from necessity because* of the moistness of the brain and *because* of the sutures in the skull (*for* wherever there is a lot of moisture and heat, there growth will necessarily be greatest), but also *for the sake of safety*, in that the shelter it provides can protect against excess of cold and warmth. (*PA* 658b2–6, emphasis added)

As a human *idion*, one cannot provide an A-type explanation for the fact that it belongs to humans by showing it belongs to a wider kind. (One could use knowledge of its being a human *idion* to account for Persians having it, however.) It is by delving further into man's nature that one will come to understand why it's there. And that is just what Aristotle does, rooting its presence in facts about human physiology (facts provided elsewhere in *HA*: the size and moistness of man's brain at 494a28, the sutures at 491b2–5, 516a12–20 and 517b13–21), and the special need to protect the human brain from climatic extremes so that it may perform its proper function.

Both explanations, however, point to basic facts about human nature in accounting for a per se attribute of human beings. In this respect, they are both complementary B-type explanations of the same fact, one invoking material necessity, the other invoking the function for the sake of which it is there.[41]

The same relationship between *HA* and *PA* is clear in their respective discussions of the shedding of deer horns.

[41] The background to these joint explanations in terms of material necessity and 'the good' is, of course, *Phaedo* 96–100 and the *Timaeus*. This specific explanation is a development of that at *Timaeus* 76a–d (as Cornford (1937:301) notes). On the differences between Plato and Aristotle on the way these two sorts of explanations ought to be integrated, cf. Balme, ch. 10 below, 276–8. On the role of such explanations within Aristotle's teleological framework, cf. Cooper, ch. 9 below. I am inclined to agree with Cooper that, where such explanations are contrasted, as here, with teleological explanation, we need to distinguish the *subsumption* of the necessity associated with a thing's material/elemental make-up under the necessity relative to a goal, from a *reduction* which would eliminate explanations by simple 'element potentials' (Gotthelf, ch. 8 below, 211–13) from biology altogether. For here, excessive hair growth is seen as an instance of what necessarily happens to certain materials under conditions of excessive moisture and heat; and in the example to follow, deer horns are said to fall in part simply because of the weight of their dense, earthy nature. That is, the force of *these* explanations ('because it is heavy stuff, it moves down'; 'because there's excessive heat and moisture here, things grow') is not vitiated by showing that it is also true that this must happen if an organism of a certain sort is to flourish. And in fact, it is not clear that these cases are hypothetically *necessary*: that is, it is not clear that Aristotle believed that if there are to be deer, there must be horn-shedding, or that if there are to be human beings, they must have excessive head hair. (Cf. Cooper, ch. 9 below, 256.)

Deer alone among those having horns have them solid throughout... (*HA* 500a6–7)[42]
Deer alone shed their horns in season, beginning from the age of two, and grow new
ones again... (*HA* 500a10–11)[43]
In deer alone are the horns solid throughout, and deer alone shed their horns, on
the one hand for the sake of the advantage gained in having their load lightened,
on the other hand from necessity, due to their weight. (*PA* 663b12)[44]

The solidity of the horns of the deer is a per se feature, and in fact
is not further explained, but rather plays a role in explaining the
shedding, another *idion* of deer. For, as in the previous example, this
feature happens necessarily, given the weight of solid horns, *and*
because the deer benefit from this happening. Again, there is
reference both to the peculiar material nature of deer, and to the
requirements of their lives, in accounting for the shedding of horns.
The shedding of horns is explained to belong to deer in virtue of more
basic features of their nature; in the context of this discussion, it has
been B-explained.

My last example is an explanation of why the strange wryneck has
one of its peculiar features. It is, of course, a soaring bird, and were
I to wonder why it has four toes, it would be appropriate to simply
point that out.[45] If however I wish to understand the 'idiotic'
arrangement of *its* toes – two fore and two aft – knowing something
about *its* nature will be necessary, such as the following.

In other birds, then, the position of the toes is thus [three fore, one aft] but the
wryneck has only two in the front and two behind; a cause (*aition*) of this is that
its body is less inclined in the forward direction than the body of other birds. (*PA*
iv 695a22–6)

Thus, we may imagine, this particular feature is needed to insure
proper 'balance'. Similar explanations of features found only among
the swimming, wading or soaring crook-taloned birds are also found
throughout this chapter: in each case, some peculiar feature of their
lifestyle is shown to require, or at least be improved by, a structural
difference in parts common to birds.[46]

---

[42] τῶν δ' ἐχόντων κέρας δι' ὅλου μὲν ἔχει στερεὸν μόνον ἔλαφος...
[43] ἀποβάλλει δὲ τὰ κέρατα μόνον ἔλαφος κατ' ἔτος ἀρξάμενος ἀπὸ διετοῦς, καὶ πάλιν
φύει...
[44] Ἔστι δὲ τὰ κέρατα δι' ὅλου στερεὰ τοῖς ἐλάφοις μόνοις, καὶ ἀποβάλλει μόνον, ἕνεκεν
μὲν ὠφελείας κουφιζόμενον, ἐξ ἀνάγκης δὲ διὰ τὸ βάρος.   [45] Cf. 695a15–22.
[46] Cf. ch. 13 below, 356–9. *PA* 1.5 645b15–20 suggests that certain *praxeis* tend to be
fundamental in explaining both various parts and other, less fundamental *praxeis*.
Nonetheless, the evidence gathered by Gotthelf 1985b (and summarized in ch. 7 below,
190–2) suggests one can't take the further step of supposing that only these fundamental
praxeis will be given in an account of an organism's nature. On the basis of Bolton's
suggestions (142–6 below), one might attempt to characterize different sorts of accounts
which approach, to different degrees, a scientific/explanatory definition. Balme has

These texts are representative of a pattern that one finds throughout the *PA*. Often, a part is said to belong to some sub-kind by noting that this part is a common feature of some more general kind. The message of such explanations, which I have referred to as A-type, is that a deep theoretical explanation for this part should be sought at a more general level, but that an explanation for its belonging to this particular kind is that *it* is a form of the kind to which this part belongs primitively and as such. On the other hand, if a feature is identified as peculiar to a kind, the explanation does not take the form of subsuming the kind under a wider kind, but of exploring that kind itself, to see if something basic to its life or material constitution can account for it as a consequence. This seems to be a treatise thoroughly in the spirit of the philosophy of science of the *Posterior Analytics*.

VI

PA I, Aristotle's 'philosophy of zoology', begins by considering whether we should study the most common kinds first or the most specific. It offers what at first sight appear to be rather trivial reasons for choosing the former strategy. But, as David Balme has hinted, *APo*. II.14 is in all likelihood in the background here too.[47] I should like to develop these hints in two directions. First, I want to note in detail the parallel between this strategic recommendation and the ideas I earlier discussed in the context of *APo*. about unqualified understanding. Then I shall return, as promised more than once, to the problem of groups with common features and no common name.

Having distinguished between the actual practitioner of a science and the person with a methodological concern with the principles 'to which one will refer in appraising the method of demonstration' (639a13), Aristotle goes on to consider questions of this latter sort in *PA* I. The first is:

> should one take each being singly and clarify its nature independently (*peri tautēs diorizein kath' hautēn*), making individual studies of, say, man or lion or ox and so on, or should one first posit the attributes common to all in respect of something common (*ē ta koinēi sumbebēkota pasi kata ti koinon hupothemenous*)? (639a16–19, tr. Balme)

The question here is so reminiscent of *APo*. II.14–18 that it is difficult not to see its methodological suggestions in the background. That background would recommend the latter approach, on grounds that if one knew, for example, that lion and ox were each covered with

---

suggested that what might be included in an abstract account of an animal's essence will be quite different from an account of the animal's form at any level of generality. (Balme, ch. 11 below, 294–8.)   [47] Balme 1972: 72; cf. ch. 4 above, 86.

body hair, but hadn't yet recognized that each of these kinds had a common nature, both being viviparous quadrupeds, one would lack a true understanding of why these particular kinds possess this feature. In fact, he goes on to say that, pursuing the first option, a researcher would consistently describe in partial terms (*kata meros*) what belongs universally (639a23). The alternative is summarized as 'studying that which is common to the kind first, and then later the peculiarities (*ta idia*)' (639b5).[48] This is indeed the method he goes on to recommend in chapter 4, wherever there is a common *genos* available (644b1–7; 645b1–12). Further, as I have argued, a plausible construal of the *HA* is that it is organizing animal differentiae according to this method.

The same background in the *Analytics*, which I will now consider, explains both a theoretical and a practical concern over naming animals so that one refers to their nature at the correct level of generality with respect to the problem to be solved.

As I said earlier, one pervasive source of a failure to achieve anything more than incidental understanding according to *APo.* 1.5 is the lack of a name which characterizes a subject at the appropriate level of generality.

And it might seem that proportions alternate for things as numbers and as lines and as solids and as times, as when it was proved separately, though it was possible to prove it of all cases by one demonstration. But because all these – numbers, lengths, times, solids – were not some one named group, and differed in form from each other, they were grasped separately. But now they are proved universally. (74a17–23)[49]

Lacking the appropriate name for the universal common to these various forms of continua, an investigator may fail to recognize that this property belongs to them all in virtue of something common. Nor will he direct his search toward the reason why all continuous magnitudes have alternating proportions.

This will have methodological ramifications, which again are the concern of *APo* II.14.

We are currently speaking according to the traditional common names, but it is necessary to investigate not only in these cases, but also by selecting anything else which is seen to belong in common, and then to investigate what this follows and

[48] Cf. Balme 1972: *ad* 639a15–b7.

[49] A scholium to Euclid, *Elements* v attributes the discovery of a general theory of proportion to Eudoxus (cf. Heiberg 1919: v 280.8), which would account for Aristotle's *nun*: for the discovery would have been made in recent times and within the Academic circle. The scholium is suggested by Heath (1956: 112–13; 1949: 43) to be due to Proclus. Aristotle doesn't give a general name to the subject to which the alternando property belongs per se. For Euclid it was 'magnitude' (*megethē*), but there are good reasons for supposing Aristotle would have resisted this (cf. *Metaph.* Δ.13 1020a7–15). As Heath (1949: 44) suggests, Aristotle would likely have preferred *poson*.

what follows this; for example, the possession of a third stomach follows on having horns as does being without both rows of teeth; and again possessing horns follows after something. For it is clear why (*dia ti*) the thing mentioned will belong to them, for it will belong because of (*dia*) the possession of horns. (98a13–19)[50]

This suggests a method of 'scanning' a set of universal predications to observe correlated sets of differences – to my mind, it sounds much like a description of those passages in the *HA* which read, in effect, 'All *S* has *P*, and indeed all *T* and all *U* – in fact generally whatever is a *K* has *P*', a couple of which were quoted in section IV above. And the above passage notes the A-type explanation that displays this understanding by means of an example which appears in *PA*.[51] To see deer, antelope and oxen as all horn-bearers is to recognize in them a common nature in virtue of which a number of features common to them can be understood.

This particular concern surfaces with some regularity in the biology. *PA* 1.4 opens with an *aporia* about whether the water-dwellers and the flyers should be brought under one common name (*hen onoma*). Aristotle answers that those kinds which differ only by the more and less can be linked under one kind (644a18) – that is

The right course is to speak about some affections in common by kind, wherever the kinds have been satisfactorily marked off by popular usage and possess both a single nature in common and forms not far separated in them – bird and fish and any other that is unnamed but like the kind embraces the forms that are in it; but wherever they are not like this, to speak of particulars, for example about man or any other such. (644b1–7: tr. Balme, but translating *genos* as 'kind' and *eidos* as 'form')

The *HA* often raises the issue of whether a variety of kinds ought to have a common name,[52] and again, given the importance of this problem to the facilitation of explanation and therefore unqualified understanding of the animal world, this is to be expected.

Allan Gotthelf's recent work on substance and essence in the biological works has focused attention on a passage in *PA* III.6 which indicates the variety and complexity of the issues which the lack of common names can raise.[53] In part, the question of the extent to

---

[50] Compare Socrates' injunction to Theaetetus, *Theaetetus* 148d4–7: '...try to imitate your answer about the powers. Just as you collected them, many as they are, in one class try, in the same way, to find one account by which to speak of the many kinds of knowledge' (tr. McDowell). Cf. *APr.* 1.27 on selecting what follows *x* and what *x* follows.

[51] Cf. *HA* II. 507a30–b13, where Aristotle adopts *ta keratophora* as a semi-technical expression; cf. *PA* 674a31. For the relevant background explanations, cf. *PA* 662b35–664a7; 674a30–674b5. The four stomachs are named at *HA* II. 507b1; *ho echinos* is listed as the third.

[52] E.g., at 490a13–14, 505b30, 531b20–5, 623a3. This issue, not surprisingly, comes up in other disciplines as well. Cf. *Poetics* 1447b9–12, *Mete.* IV.9 387b1–5. Cf. Gotthelf unpub. (1).

[53] Cf. Gotthelf 1985b. My understanding of this passage has been greatly helped by discussion with Gotthelf.

which the various *eidē* need to be similar before they can be viewed
as varieties of a *genos* is at stake. Does Aristotle make a rigid
distinction between true kinds and forms which can be grouped
together only for narrow explanatory purposes? Can 'horn-bearers'
or 'crook-taloned birds', for example, be considered a true kind, or
is it merely a convenient grouping in a narrowly prescribed context?
How about 'lung-possessors', a 'kind' we have already discussed?

> Now speaking generally, the lung is for the sake of breathing, but there is also a
> bloodless sort for the sake of a certain kind of animal; but that which is common
> in these cases is without a name, unlike 'bird' which names a certain kind. So, just
> as the being for a bird (*to ornithi einai*) is from something, possessing a lung also
> belongs in the being (*en tēi ousiai*) of these. (669b8–12)

The first sentence here suggests Aristotle has in mind a general kind,
those with lungs for the sake of breathing, which has two forms, a
bloodless-lunged sort and a blooded-lunged sort.[54] Implicitly, it is the
common kind – what is common to these sub-kinds – which lacks a
name. This is contrasted with birds where there *is* a name which
applies to the common kind. There are features which constitute the
being for a bird, in virtue of which the name applies. The suggestion
seems to be that the possession of a lung likewise may (perhaps
partially) constitute the being for breathers. It of course is not
suggested that 'lung-possessor' is the name, any more than we name
birds 'feather-possessor'. What does seem at least to be under
consideration here, however, is the possibility that the lunged group,
which has a good deal in common though diverse in so many ways
(e.g. some fly, some live continuously in the water; some have
feathers, some hair), ought to be considered a kind with its own
name.[55]

From the standpoint of explanation, the value in recognizing the
commonality among these extensive kinds, which Aristotle sees as
crucially bound up with having an expression which refers to this
fact, cannot be denied. The last chapters of *De Juventute*, often
referred to separately as *De Respiratione*, treat as fundamental the
distinction between breathers (air-coolers) and gilled water-coolers.
Aristotle may here be facing the issue of conditions under which
explanation requires (or is at least facilitated by) more general
referring expressions. The account of the development of a general
theory of proportional magnitudes in *APo.* 1.5 shows that Aristotle
was sensitive to this issue *as* a general issue in the philosophy of

---

[54] This distinction is developed in the immediately preceding passage, 669a24–669b8, and
at *Juv.* 7 (*Resp.* 1) 470b13–27.
[55] Whether Aristotle can be seriously recommending this group as a *genos* is discussed by
Balme (ch. 4 above, 84–5; 1972: 120–1) and in Gotthelf 1985b: 31–3).

science. These passages in the biology show him to be facing the practical question of when a more general concept ought to be introduced.

VII

A number of lines of evidence have now been presented suggesting deep affinities between the theory of explanation and understanding in the *APo.* and the zoological treatises. The strongest evidence against this suggestion is, I believe, to be based on the claim that the *Posterior Analytics* recommends a picture of science, at least a science at the stage of providing explanations, at odds with the structure of explanation found in the biology. I have been unwilling to adopt the expedient that *APo.* is primarily a treatise in pedagogy. At the very least it is an exploration of those themes central to the *Theaetetus*: what is scientific understanding, how do we distinguish the person possessing it from the person with opinions, what sorts of facts can we hope to have understanding of, what place do sense perception, causal explanation, definition and division have in our account of understanding? As Myles Burnyeat has pointed out, *APo.* is innocent of our distinction between philosophy of science and epistemology – it explores, as one, issues contemporary philosophy has tended to treat separately.[56] Nor is it easy to distinguish philosophy of science from methodology in this treatise; *APo.* 1.5 at once explores the questions of what unqualified understanding is, the role of the formation of new concepts as it relates to explanation, the close relationship between predication, reference and explanation, closing with methodological recommendations for searching for the appropriate referring expression for a subject relative to identifying it as the bearer of a certain predicate.

The argument of this paper leads me to think that we need to reassess the evidence that has been used to claim that Aristotle would have pictured a science of zoology as an axiomatic system *à la* Euclid's *Elements*, had he based it on the *APo.* Jonathan Barnes has recently suggested that the claim, defended earlier in this century by Solmsen, that the *APo.* was initially innocent of the syllogistic, which was then grafted on to it after its discovery, has a good deal to be said for it.[57] On the other hand, it has also been recently argued that the function of the syllogistic was not primarily viewed by Aristotle as that of structuring explanation, so much as that of testing the logical properties of explanations presented in a natural language.[58]

[56] Burnyeat 1981: 97.   [57] Barnes 1981.
[58] Lear 1980.

Surely there are considerations which, even after the 'discovery of the syllogism', would lead us to reject the claim that Aristotle would have recommended putting scientific explanations into syllogistic form.[59]

All these issues, as well as questions about the nature of hypotheses and definitions as starting-points of explanation and the relationship between definition, division and explanation, are worth exploring within the context of the zoological treatises. It is not safe to assume that those treatises have little to do with the exploration of *epistēmē* carried out in the *Analytics*.[60]

[59] See n. 40 above and Gotthelf, ch. 7 below, esp. 194–6.

[60] This is a revision of a paper delivered at a most exciting NEH Research Conference, 'Philosophical Issues in Aristotle's Biology', July 1983, directed by Allan Gotthelf. I would like to thank all those who offered constructive criticism on that occasion. In addition, I should like to thank L. A. Kosman, Allan Gotthelf and Michael Ferejohn for their careful comments on an earlier draft of this revision. The material in section IV of this paper owes much to the discussions of texts in *HA* I–IV which Gotthelf and I, and occasionally Kosman, engaged in during the fall of 1983, at the Center for Hellenic Studies. Finally I should like to thank Bernard Knox, the staff at the Center and the Trustees of Harvard University for support of the project of which this is part while I was a Junior Fellow at the Center in 1983–84; and the National Science Foundation for support during the summers of 1983 and 1984. The errors and imprecisions which remain are, of course, my responsibility. Some of the ideas of this paper are developed further in Lennox forthcoming 1987.

6

Definition and scientific method in Aristotle's *Posterior Analytics* and *Generation of Animals*

ROBERT BOLTON

> The middle term [in a demonstration] is a definition of the major term. This is why all the sciences are built up through the process of definition.
>
> *Posterior Analytics* II.17 99a21–3

1. Scientific method in Aristotle's biology

The relation between Aristotle's official account in the *Posterior Analytics* of the nature of scientific knowledge and of the means by which it is reached and his actual practice in arriving at the results presented in his special scientific writings has long been a topic of considerable study. In the recent history of attempts to account for the discrepancies between Aristotle's theory and his practice, or to explain away the apparent discrepancies, the biological works have been assigned a special role. In his famous and still influential treatment of this problem, Jaeger saw in what he took to be the thoroughgoing empiricism of the biological works the final step in Aristotle's emancipation from the Platonic view of scientific knowledge and method found in the *Analytics*.[1] Students of Aristotle now agree that Jaeger's general account of Aristotle's 'progress' away from Platonism is untenable. But it is still widely supposed that Jaeger was at least right that there are empirical elements in the method practiced in the biological writings to which no role is given in the *Analytics*.[2]

There has also developed in recent years the widespread view

---

[1] Jaeger 1948. See especially pp. 337–41.
[2] For an important example of Jaeger's influence on this point, see Düring 1943: 22–3. Lloyd 1968: 71–80, 301 offers a concise statement of the current common view. See also Bourgey 1955, e.g. at pp. 121–2.

according to which there is a more basic unresolvable discrepancy between the account of the path to scientific knowledge mandated by the *Posterior Analytics* and the path actually followed in all the scientific writings including the biological. The *Analytics* restricts knowledge to what has been demonstrated from self-evident first principles. The scientific treatises seem to secure their results without such demonstrations. The accepted explanation for this now is that the *Posterior Analytics* does not contain recommendations as to how scientific knowledge is to be pursued or discovered but only an account of how it is to be systematically presented once discovered.[3] The method for scientific *discovery* to be employed in the search for theoretical principles is not the method described in the *Analytics* but rather the alternative to it described in detail in the *Topics*, namely dialectical reasoning.[4]

The main aim of this paper is not to examine the merits of these current views generally. Rather it is to study the relation between the place given in the *Analytics* and in certain passages in the biological works to the crucial vehicle of scientific knowledge for Aristotle, definition. But the comparison of the role assigned to definition in the *Analytics* and in the biological treatises will have a direct bearing on the larger questions mentioned above. To facilitate later consideration of them it is worth commenting, before proceeding to the discussion of definition, on the current treatment of the larger questions.

2. Empiricism and dialectic in Aristotle's scientific method

In the current view of the relation between the method for knowledge acquisition recommended in the *Analytics* and that practiced in the biological works two elements are prominent. The method of inquiry followed in the biological works is supposed to be empirical in a way not envisaged in the *Analytics* and dialectical in contrast with the method of reasoning described in the *Analytics*. Are these two claims mutually consistent? If a method of reasoning to conclusions is without qualification dialectical can it also be fully empirical, as

---

[3] Influential statements of this view are found in two articles by G. E. L. Owen, ' *Tithenai ta phainomena*' (Owen 1975, first published in Mansion 1961) and 'Aristotle' (Owen 1970). A special version of the view is defended in Barnes 1975b.

[4] Anticipations of the current view are perhaps found in Alexander, *in Top.* 30. The main elements are in Le Blond 1939: 46–7, 252ff. See also Weil 1951 (Eng. tr. in Barnes, Schofield and Sorabji 1975; note the editors' approving comment, p. viii); Wieland 1962: 202–30; Brunschwig 1967: xii; Evans 1977: 31ff.; Lloyd 1979: 118; Barnes 1980; Nussbaum 1982b. In Balme 1972 Aristotle's method of inquiry in the *Generation of Animals* is described as 'dialectical' (127).

Aristotle understood these notions?[5] There are good reasons to suppose that this is impossible.

Reasoning is defined in the *Topics* as dialectical 'which reasons from noted opinions (*endoxa*)', where *endoxa* are understood to be 'things which are accepted by everyone or by most people; or by the wise – either by all of them, or by most, or by the most famous and distinguished'.[6] Clearly, new empirical data uncovered by, say, the working expert biologist doing dissections on the members of some heretofore unexamined or improperly examined species could easily fail to fit into any of the sub-classes of *endoxa* permitted to figure in dialectical reasoning. Aristotle himself makes clear in various places that such a researcher might well arrive at, and use in his theory construction, results which contradict all standing opinions or, more often perhaps, results which have not occurred to anyone before.[7] It might be argued that if this biologist happened to be among 'the most famous and distinguished' *any* of his own opinions, including new observational results, would count as *endoxa* and his argument based on them as dialectical. But even if Aristotle was assuming this, which is quite unlikely,[8] if our genuine expert biologist with new empirical

---

[5] There is an obvious need for clarity on what is meant by 'empirical' in this context. The best way to achieve this simply without anachronism is to specify that the empirical is what, in Aristotle's own words, conforms to 'what appears so from perception' (*to phainomenon kata tēn aisthēsin*). For remarks on the significance of this sufficient for our purposes here see below on *Cael.* 303a22–3. The investigation here will not deal with the much discussed question of whether Aristotle lived up to his own empirical methodological standards but only with what those standards were. For discussion of the former question see Düring 1943, Bourgey 1955 and Lloyd ch. 3 above.

[6] *Top.* 100b21–3, cf. *SE* 165b3, 183a39; *Metaph.* 995b23–4; *APo.* 81b18–23. The translation of the term *endoxa* is difficult. In his valuable recent study, Barnes (1980: 498ff.) opts for 'reputable opinions', which has the advantage of connecting the sense of the term with the ordinary sense of *endoxos* (cf. n. 8 below). But not all things 'accepted by... the most famous and distinguished' (e.g. Parmenides and Zeno) are reputable, i.e. in good repute. But these are still *endoxa* (though not dialectical *protaseis* – see n. 12 below). The class is thus wider than 'reputable opinions'. It includes other opinions generally regarded as noteworthy; thus 'noted opinions', which also retains the connection with *endoxos*, seems preferable.

[7] That many results of both sorts are to be expected is clear from Aristotle's criticism of the methods of dissection used by his predecessors and his alternative account of the proper method in *HA* III.2–3 511b13ff. (see especially, b13–23, 513a8–15; cf. *GA* 760b27–33). For a specific example of a new observational result contradicting *all* previous opinion see 513a8–15. See also *GA* 742a16–18, *Resp.* 470b8ff., 471b23ff.

[8] Aristotle does not directly address this question. But he never introduces his own *new* views into argument with others or claims authority for them on the ground that they are the views of the famous expert Aristotle. He uses the *endoxa* as a starting-point in reaching his own distinctive views, not as including them. Moreover, in ordinary use, the term *endoxos* has the primary meaning of *noted* or *esteemed* or *accredited* which indicates that an *endoxon* has achieved already some generally recognized standing. In *APr.* 24b10–13 Aristotle uses *endoxon* adjectivally in this sense in characterizing a dialectical premise as 'what appears so and is accredited'. (Cf. *SE* 170a40.) And in *APo.* 81b18–23 the fact that a proposition is *endoxon* (or most *endoxon*) is taken to imply that it is already accepted in the appropriate circles. The frequent characterization of dialectical reasoning as *kata doxan*, as

data were not yet so lucky as to stand among the most acclaimed biologists neither he nor anyone else would be entitled to use his new results in *dialectical* argument no matter how empirically well-grounded they might be.⁹ This, of course, was Aristotle's own standing when he was actually doing much of his biological research. In addition, new information based on reliable eyewitness reports of *non-experts* in biology – so long as these results are unknown to *most* people – do not count as *endoxa* and thus cannot be accommodated in dialectic either. Yet Aristotle regularly takes account of such data in the course of his biological inquiries, as we should expect he would given his view of the value of the special experience of non-experts (*Metaph.* 981a12–17, 28–9).¹⁰

in this last passage, is further indication of this. (Cf. *GC* 318b27 and below, section 5.) Aristotle does allow views which are 'similar to *endoxa*' to count as dialectical premises on the ground that such a view 'might appear to be *endoxon*' (*Top.* 104a12ff.). But clearly, this will not cover all the new observations to which Aristotle himself appeals (see n. 7 above). And, most importantly, this does not permit observational results to enter in *because* of their observational character but only because they can pass for 'noted opinions' and so be taken as such.

⁹ These results once accepted could be used in *ad hominem* dialectic by the expert himself in testing some thesis of his own or in allowing this to be done by others. (See *Top.* VIII.5 159b1 with b25–7.) In this restricted form of dialectic any opinion of the person being tested is admissible. However, if there is conflict between a long accepted thesis, say, and new observational results *ad hominem* dialectic does not require resolving the inconsistency in favor of the new observations. Aristotle indicates that in this case priority should be given to what is most esteemed and familiar to the person being tested (159b8ff. with 25–7). But what is most familiar to him (and hence most esteemed, 159b13–15) is what he is most accustomed to (*Metaph.* 995a1–3), and this may be his long accepted thesis. (Normal observational results are not regarded as incorrigible by Aristotle: *GC* 318b27ff., *Metaph.* 1010b14ff.) Scientific inquiry requires a different resolution, as we shall see below. Moreover, in any case, this form of dialectic for self-examination is not the one we find Aristotle mainly employing in his treatises. There he is testing the views of others. The views of others may be tested dialectically in two ways, neither of which permits the use of one's own new results, particularly if one is an unestablished expert. One's own new results cannot be used at all in *ad hominem* dialectical testing of the views of another person or group. There the relevant *endoxa* are restricted to the views of the person or group being tested (*Top.* 159b27–35). More importantly, the new results of the unestablished expert cannot be used in the testing of the views of others *via* dialectic proper or *simpliciter*. There the relevant *endoxa* are *endoxa simpliciter* (159a38ff.), the *endoxa* as defined at 100b21–3, and these data obviously do not count as such. (Alexander, *in Top.* 549.22ff., takes the *endoxa simpliciter* to be only the views of all or most people. This would only strengthen the point here but it cannot be right. This would restrict the use of the special views of the wise to *ad hominem* dialectic and this does not fit Aristotle's theory (see *Top.* 104a34–6) or his familiar practice.) The view of some that whatever one can get a respondent to accept is legitimately introduced in dialectic proper or *ad hominem* dialectic is based on a confusion between this form of dialectic and *ad hominem* dialectic. Cf. further, against this view, Owen 1968; 103–7. See also n. 50 below.

¹⁰ Note, for instance, the seriousness with which he treats the unusual observations of 'some experienced fishermen' at *HA* 532b18–26. The discussion of the behavior of bees in *HA* 623b5–629a28 is particularly full of specialized information based on observations attributed to bee-keepers. (Aristotle's extensive reliance on the observations of persons with such specialized experience is well-documented. For a useful catalogue see Manquat 1932.) Such persons are clearly 'experienced' (*empeiroi*) but not 'wise' (*sophoi*) in *biological* matters

These problems are not merely incidental results of Aristotle's
description of dialectic which might be easily ruled out. Aristotelian
dialectic proper is a method for reasoning solely by appeal to types
of *testimony* which, given their source, anyone can and should
recognize the need to take account of.[11] By contrast with the
testimony of a distinguished expert[12] or of the majority of experts or,
even, of the majority, the reported observations of unestablished
experts or of a small group of experienced non-experts, given their
provenance, lack this epistemic standing. Not everyone can be
expected to see the need to take account of such testimony particularly when it conflicts with testimony of the sanctioned types.[13]

(though many of them may be 'masters' in the arts of fishing, bee-keeping and the like
and so be relatively speaking wise *in these practical arts* by comparison with manual workers:
see *Metaph.* 981a24–b6; cf. *EN* 1098a29ff.). Nor is their specialized information accepted
'by everyone or by most people'. So there is no place for appeal to their reports in dialectical
reasoning proper about strictly scientific biological matters by contrast with the matters
which their arts concern.

11 *Rhetoric* 1354a1–6 describes dialectic as like rhetoric in being based on materials 'which it
is in a particular way common to all to recognize and which are not derived from any special
science' – a remark clearly intended to characterize dialectic proper, not *ad hominem*
dialectic. This does not mean that one cannot argue dialectically about scientific questions.
The *Topics* clearly permits this (105b19–29). Rather, it means that in dialectic an argument
cannot be expected to carry weight simply because it is based on scientifically compelling
reasoning or evidence. Only a knowledgeable scientist can be expected to see the force of
this appeal and dialectical premises must carry weight which even a non-specialist can be
expected to acknowledge. Scientific wisdom can have such weight only as the testimony
of a generally accredited source and not as scientific wisdom. In this respect Aristotelian
dialectic corresponds closely to the method which we (like the ancient Greeks) standardly
encounter in everyday reasoning – in the streets, in the media, in the lawcourts. In such
a forum scientific wisdom is typically introduced as, and carries weight which can only
be expected to be grasped as, the testimony of a generally accredited expert source and
not as scientific wisdom. Aristotle's discussion in *Topics* I.10 confirms his understanding of
this. He counts material introduced as consensus expert testimony as a basis (*protasis*) for
dialectical argument 'since anyone would grant the things accepted by those who have
studied the subject, for example the doctor in medical matters' (104a34–6). But he qualifies
this to exclude from *protaseis* all expert testimony, observational or otherwise, which is
contrary to majority opinion 'since anyone would grant what is accepted by the wise unless
it is opposed to the views of the majority' (a11–12; see also the following note). Thus
Aristotle is attempting to codify, in his account of dialectical method, *only* the method of
reasoning used paradigmatically in everyday situations of the type mentioned above.
Failure to take proper account of this may be responsible for recent overestimations of the
value of dialectic for scientific inquiry.

12 Aristotle says that the views of the famous and distinguished (though not of all experts)
even when opposed to the views of the majority may be introduced as dialectical *theseis*
(104b19ff.). *Theseis*, unlike *protaseis*, will not be normally *granted* by anyone but given their
provenance they do compel attention from anyone, which new views from an unestablished
thinker opposing previous views would not (b22–4).

13 Suppose it were a generally accepted and, hence, *endoxon* principle, that (1) one should
accept whatever careful observation reveals. Suppose then that to a certain unestablished
expert in biology, say Aristotle on Lesbos, (2) careful observation reveals such and such
new data. Could he then draw the *dialectical* conclusion that (3) one should accept such and
such new data; and so accept them *via* dialectical argument? Obviously not. In a dialectical
argument all of the premises must be *endoxa* and here the second premise is not.

Scientific inquiry does not operate under any such restrictions, however. In a well-known passage in the *De Caelo* Aristotle carefully distinguishes between *endoxa* and 'perceptual *phainomena*' in order to emphasize that it is the latter, by contrast with the former, by which principles in physical science generally are ultimately to be tested (III. 4 303a22-3 with III.7 306a13-17). The scientist cannot ignore his own observational data or those from other reliable sources whether they count as *endoxa* or not. By contrast, the dialectician does not make direct appeal to observational data as such but only to claims based on testimony of certain sorts. Aristotle contrasts matters where dialectical inquiry is suitable with those where direct perceptual data are what is needed (*Topics* 1.11 105a3-9). To take someone to *see*, or to go to *see* oneself, how things stand is not as such a dialectical move since in such a case one does not rely on argument based on testimony from an accredited source. It is, thus, only to be expected that not one line of argument (*topos*) which Aristotle introduces in the *Topics* for use in dialectic is based on an appeal to the data of perception – a fact which would be quite difficult to explain if appeal to empirical data as such were necessary or legitimate in dialectic as it is in physical science. Those who have wanted to emphasize the empirical element in Aristotle's biological research have argued that Aristotle did draw inferences from new empirical data in ways not in fact countenanced by dialectic and have wanted to count this as indication of the new character of his work. They have not, however, directly faced the difficulty of squaring this with the conviction, held now by many of them, that his method is thoroughly dialectical.

Attention is given to certain aspects of this problem in the influential paper of G. E. L. Owen, '*Tithenai ta phainomena*'. Owen was not primarily concerned with the problem as it relates to the biological works but rather with a form of it which had already been raised with reference to the *Physics* by A. Mansion, among others. In various passages Aristotle draws attention to the role of *phainomena* and of *empeiria* in scientific investigation.[14] Owen followed Mansion in believing that if in these passages the *phainomena* referred to are empirical data, and the *empeiria* based on them generalization from empirical data, then these methodological remarks could not be made to fit with Aristotle's practice in the *Physics* where, as Mansion put it, 'in general everything comes down to more or less detailed conceptual analyses – analyses often guided and illustrated by, rather than founded upon, empirical data'.[15]

[14] See *APr.* 46a4ff., 17ff.; *APo.* 78b39ff., *Cael.* 293a25ff., 306a5ff., *PA* 639b5ff. with 640a13ff., *GA* 760b27ff.   [15] Mansion 1946: 211 as translated by Owen.

Owen moved to resolve this apparent difficulty by pointing out that the term *phainomena*, and the associated term *empeiria*, are in fact often used by Aristotle not for 'the observed facts but the *endoxa*, the common conceptions on the subject which constitute the familiar data of dialectic'. He argued that Aristotle's practice in the *Physics* could be made to fit with his preaching on the role of the *phainomena* and of *empeiria* in science if the data from which the *Physics* starts are understood as 'the materials not of natural history but of dialectic'.[16]

Owen did not bring the problem of the extent to which empirical data *can* be used in dialectic sharply into focus in the manner attempted above. But he did acknowledge that Aristotle makes it clear in the *De Caelo* that not all perceptual *phainomena* count as *endoxa* and that it is the perceptual *phainomena* by which we must finally test the merits of our principles in physical science. Owen moved to square this with his account of the *Physics* by supposing that a distinction could be drawn between 'the *Physics* proper' where Aristotle does not suppose that 'the analyses either start from or are closely controlled by our inspections of the world' and other 'more empirical inquiries', such as biology, where this is a requirement. It is only indirectly, Owen claimed, through empirical confirmation of the results of these latter inquiries that the results of the *Physics*, which are presupposed by them, are themselves subject to any contact with 'our inspections of the world'.[17]

Owen was thus committed by his argument to the view that in biology as opposed to physics proper the method of dialectic is not sufficient. It has recently been more common (largely because of Owen's influence, ironically) to suppose that dialectic is sufficient for reaching the basic principles in biology and all other sciences as well as in the *Physics*. To facilitate evaluation of the latter it is worth seeing the difficulties that arise even for the attempt to secure dialectical method as the method of the *Physics*.

In the *De Caelo* (303a20–4) Aristotle himself refers to the *Physics* as a place where he appeals *both* to noted opinions and to perceptual

---

[16] Owen 1975: 116. Owen adds the qualifier 'for the most part' here but the caution is at crucial points absent. As we shall see below, he argues explicitly for the thesis that the method of arguing from the *endoxa* is taken by Aristotle to be sufficient in the *Physics*. It is this thesis (widely influential: see Barnes, Schofield and Sorabji 1975: viii) which is discussed here, though it does not fit perfectly with everything in Owen's paper.

[17] Owen 1975: 118. Owen does permit the method of the *Physics* to be in an important respect empirical in its reliance on *endoxa*. He emphasizes that '*endoxa* rest on experience, even if they misrepresent it…If they did not Aristotle could find no place for them in his epistemology' (117). However, even if all *endoxa* count as items of *empeiria* not all items of *empeiria*, or all perceptual *phainomena*, count as *endoxa*. This is the point – not disputed by Owen – whose implications are explored here.

phainomena in reaching his results. Since he distinguishes the two in making this claim this indicates that he did not view himself as restricted to the former in 'the *Physics* proper'. In fact, in *Physics* I.1 Aristotle argues that the data which, to use Owen's terms, 'the analyses start from' in any physical inquiry must be perceptual data since these data are the ones which serve to adequately fix what the object is of which later inquiry leads to a deeper understanding (184a16–25, cf. *APo.* 72a1–5).[18] Owen takes as his own prime example of a purely dialectical inquiry in the *Physics* Aristotle's investigation of the nature of place (IV.1–5). In Aristotle's discussion the *initial* data about place, which do 'closely control' the later analysis, are that we are aware of a place as where some real thing is and as that to which and from which things move (208a29–32).[19] These data clearly reflect what is perceptually evident about places. The perceptual data on such a subject as place are, of course, minimal and generally known (208a29). Given this these data, no doubt, also count as *endoxa*. But it is still an important question whether Aristotle regards the data as starting-points and controlling factors *because* they are perceptual and, hence, independently of whether they are also *endoxa*. The function assigned to all such starting-points by *Physics* I.1 is one which depends on their being perceptual and not on how many or what types of people are aware of them. The same result can be inferred from the *De Caelo*. Aristotle emphasizes, as noted above, that in physical science principles must be *finally* judged in the light of 'the always authoritative perceptual *phainomenon*' (306a17). He says this in a context where perceptual *phainomena* have been distinguished from *endoxa* (303a22–3) which implies that the former possess their ultimate authority independently of whether they belong among the latter. As noted above, Owen attempts to restrict the application of 'physical science' (*phusikē*) at 306a17 to the body of physical science taken as a whole so that the results of the *Physics* itself as opposed to the whole, including biology, of which it is the primary part may be taken to be free from direct perceptual constraints. There is, however, no basis for this in the text. Aristotle is not talking there about the totality of physical science. He considers a particular claim – namely that just one element, earth, is exempt

[18] The *Physics* passage is somewhat problematic. But this much is clear: we must start with an understanding of a subject from the point of view of what is clearer and better known to us. This is general information about the subject which we acquire by perception (184a24–5). From this we move to a grasp of the basic principles of the subject and this enables us to achieve a proper understanding of the initial data (a22–4).

[19] These are the most fundamental data – the ones by grasp of which we are aware that place exists (208a27ff.). Other accepted data are introduced as potentially problematic (a32ff.).

from transformation into the other elements (306a3ff.). It is this claim on its own which he says must fit with the perceptual evidence. Then, generalizing, he extends the point to any claim of physical science (a9–17).

Owen relies on two influential arguments to support his view of the *Physics*. The first is that 'as Aristotle says both in the *Physics* and the *Ethics*..."If the difficulties are resolved and the *endoxa* are left standing, this in itself is a sufficient proof.'"[20] This claim and the words quoted in it are clearly found in the *Ethics* (VII.1 1145b6–7). But in the passage in the *Physics* which Owen cites (IV.4 211a7–11) Aristotle says this:

> It is necessary to try to conduct our investigation so that it is determined what place is in a manner such that the difficulties are resolved, and the things which seem to belong to it (*ta dokounta*) do turn out to belong to it, and, further, it will be clear what the cause is of the trouble and the difficulties about it. For in this way is each thing best established.

Unlike the passage in the *Ethics*, this passage does not say that it is a sufficient defense of an account of what something is that 'the difficulties are resolved and the *endoxa* are left standing'. It discusses only what is necessary for the best account, not what is sufficient. Moreover, the passage does not use the term *endoxa*. It uses the term *dokounta* which can apply to data (including empirical data) which do not count as *endoxa*.[21] It might be supposed that the passage in the *Ethics* is by itself enough to make the general point and that it shows how the *Physics* passage is to be understood.[22] But this will not do for Owen. He claims that the requirements in question are sufficient for ethics and for the 'analyses of the *Physics* proper' but not for meteorology or biology. The *Ethics* passage alone does nothing to secure this result. Independently of Owen's special view, moreover, we know that Aristotle believed that the methodology of ethics differs from the methodology of the theoretical sciences (*EN* 1094b11–27 with 1141a16ff.; cf. 1096b30ff., 1102a23ff.). For one to be able to take the *Ethics* passage to cover the *Physics* it would need to be shown that the greater sufficiency of dialectic is not one of the things characteristic of the methodology of ethics as opposed to that of physics. This conclusion, in fact, seems required when one puts

[20] Owen 1975: 116.

[21] At *Topics* 100b21–4 the *endoxa* are defined as a special sub-class of the *dokounta*.

[22] It has been taken to show that the requirements are everywhere sufficient. See Ross' translation of 1145b2–3 and Nussbaum 1982b: 267. But Aristotle does not say 'here, as in *all* other cases...' at b2–3; he says 'as in *the* other cases', where the others are clearly the ones just mentioned – namely virtue, vice, continence, and the other *ethical* traits referred to at 1145a15ff. along with incontinence. This is particularly clear at b5 where the requirements are invoked for *tauta ta pathē*.

together the claim in the *Ethics* that an investigation based on the *endoxa* is sufficient with the fact that in the *De Caelo* Aristotle explicitly distinguishes the *endoxa* from perceptual *phainomena* and emphasizes that in physics the ultimate test of principles is that they should square not with the *endoxa* but with the perceptual *phainomena*.

Finally, it should be noted that whereas the *Ethics* passage requires only that the account to be subsequently offered of incontinence be *consistent* with the chief *endoxa* (as required at *Topics* 100a20–1) the *Physics* requires that it somehow *result* from the account of what place is that the *dokounta* concerning it do hold. We shall see later what the significance of this contrast is.[23]

Owen's second argument involves the common appeal to 'the claim made in the *Topics* that the first premises of scientific argument can be established by methods which start from the *endoxa*' (*Top.* 1.2 101a36–b4).[24] It is again not clear how far Owen can use this point. In particular he makes no attempt to show that the doctrine of the *Topics* would apply to the *Physics* and not to the biology. In the *Topics*, indeed, the point is perfectly general. If it shows that any first principles can be established by use of dialectic alone then it shows that all can, counter to Owen's own view. This itself should make us question the common interpretation of the *Topics* followed by Owen, given the least that is required by the *De Caelo*. When we do look carefully at the *Topics*, in fact, we can see that Aristotle does not say that any principles can be established by dialectic *alone*. In describing the purposes for which dialectic is useful Aristotle says this:

It is useful in connection with the things which are primary in each science. For it is impossible to say anything about them on the basis of principles proper to the science in question since the principles *are* what is primary in relation to everything else. It is necessary in dealing with them to work in each case through the *endoxa*. This task is uniquely, or at least principally, proper to dialectic since it is a method of examination which offers a way for dealing with the principles of all disciplines.

There are many aspects of this important passage which cannot be dealt with here. But one thing is clear. The passage does not say that the method of working through the *endoxa* is *sufficient* to establish the first principles of the sciences. It says only that this is *necessary* and that to do this necessary job dialectic is most useful. This leaves

---

[23] The contrast in the two texts may seem not this hard-edged. The *Ethics* does require one so far as possible *deiknunai ta endoxa* (b4–5); but this goal is immediately glossed as seeing that 'the difficulties [*sc.* for or among the *endoxa*] are resolved and the [main] *endoxa* are left standing'. This indicates what the mode of 'establishing the *endoxa*' (cf. *dedeigmenon*, b7) is in ethics – refuting objections to *endoxa*, and possibly some *endoxa*, so as to leave the main ones in place. The procedure is characterized again in this way at 1146b6–7. As we shall see, the mode of establishing the relevant *dokounta* in physics is quite different.

[24] Owen 1975: 118, cf. 115.

it open that something more is also required. In particular it leaves
it open that, as the *De Caelo* says, in physical science the adequacy
of principles must not only be judged by reference to the *endoxa* but,
ultimately, by reference to their perceptually observable consequences whatever their provenance.

These various considerations show that there are serious difficulties
in the way of defending the view that in physical science, whether
physics proper or biology, Aristotle wanted to hold both that the
method of discovery is dialectic and that principles must be finally
judged by their conformity to perceptual *phainomena*. Hence, they
also raise serious difficulties for the view that the method of discovery
is simply dialectic, since dialectic cannot by itself guarantee that all
of the relevant perceptual *phainomena* are taken proper account of in
theory construction. They do indicate, however, that there is some
necessary role to be assigned to dialectic, and some independent role
for empirical observation as well. We need to determine, then, what
these roles are and, in particular, to determine what methodological
device will guarantee that all relevant perceptual *phainomena* will be
accommodated by scientific theory independently of whether they
are *endoxa*. We need also to investigate what other important
additional elements there may be in Aristotle's method of scientific
discovery.

3. The method of discovery in the *Posterior Analytics*

It is now quite widely accepted that one finds little or nothing in
Aristotle's works on physical science that counts as strict apodeictic
reasoning of the sort delineated in the opening chapters of the *Posterior
Analytics*. The opening chapter of the *Topics* describes the strict
apodeictic method in order to contrast it with another – dialectic.
Given that Aristotle appears there to envisage only these two methods
of reasoning, it is natural that writers have supposed that since the
method used in the works on physical science seems not to be the
apodeictic one it must be the dialectical. If this is unsatisfactory,
where does Aristotle give any indication of how any third device,
alternative to or supplementary to these, might operate? Surprising
as this may seem, it is in the *Posterior Analytics*.

The first book of the *Posterior Analytics* is chiefly concerned with the
theory of strict demonstrative reasoning. But the second book deals
mainly with another subject, definition. It has been supposed that
in his treatment of this subject, Aristotle is mainly concerned with
those first principles of a science which are definitions and how they

figure in the systematic development of the science.[25] This is clearly one focus of what interests him. But Aristotle does not in fact concern himself solely with those definitions which are first principles. He, in fact, distinguishes *three* types of definitions, only one of which consists of first principles (II.10 93b29ff.; cf. 75b31–2). An important part of his discussion concerns how definitions of these three types are related to each other and in the course of this discussion and the discussion which leads up to it Aristotle has a good deal more to say about the process of the acquisition of scientific knowledge than we find in any other place in his works. Given this, it will be worth our while here to pay more attention to the second book of the *Posterior Analytics* than has been paid in the most influential recent discussions of Aristotle's views on the process of scientific discovery.

That Aristotle is deeply interested in the nature of scientific inquiry in Book II of the *Posterior Analytics* is evident from the outset. The book begins:

The things which are searched for are equal in number to the things we know; and we search for four things – that something is so, why it is so, whether something exists and what a thing is…It is when we know that something is so that we search for why it is so…And it is when we know that something exists that we search for what it is.

This remark makes it immediately clear, as do the succeeding remarks in the first two chapters, that Aristotle is going to be concerned with the nature of how we search for and *come* to know the various things that can be known. Instead of discussing this matter in a way which would make it easily accessible to us, however, Aristotle embarks, in chapters 3–10, on a long complex discussion of the relation between the role of definition and demonstration in making clear what a thing is. (See 90a35ff.; cf. 93b15ff.; 94a14ff.) It is not obvious what this has to do with the process of scientific inquiry or discovery as opposed to having to do with the place of definition in the demonstrative reasoning which lays out in finished form the results of this inquiry. It is clear, however, that Aristotle takes this discussion to be relevant to his earlier interest in how we come to know. For this is precisely the point to which he returns when, after the aporetic discussion of chapters 3–7, he begins to try in chapter 8, 93a15ff., to state systematically his views on the matter of the relation of definition to demonstration.

Let us start again from the beginning and say how it is possible [to have a demonstration of what a thing is.] When we are aware that something is so we search for why it is; sometimes both become evident simultaneously, but it is not possible

[25] See Barnes 1975a: xi.

to know why a thing is so before knowing that it is. Similarly, it is clear that it is not possible to know what it is to be something without knowing that it exists. We are sometimes aware in an accidental way that something exists and sometimes by being aware of something of the thing itself (for instance that thunder is a certain noise in the clouds, that eclipse is a certain loss of light, that man is a certain sort of animal or that the soul is that which moves itself). Whenever we know in an accidental way that a thing exists our awareness is necessarily in no way directed toward what it is. For we do not know that it exists. To search for what something is not being aware that it exists is to search for nothing. But whenever we are aware of something [of the thing itself] to that extent it is easier to search. Thus, according to the manner in which we are aware that something exists, so is our awareness directed toward what it is.[26]

Here Aristotle commences his positive account of the relation between demonstration and definition (how it is possible to have a demonstration of what a thing is) with a discussion of the general topic of how we come to discover what something is. He evidently supposes that a proper understanding of the latter is essential for a proper understanding of the former. Of primary interest to us here initially, then, is what he has to say about the general topic.

Aristotle reaffirms, in this passage, his doctrine that we need to know that something exists in order to search for and come to know what it is. He clearly supposes that the search for the knowledge of *what* something is (which he has already identified with the knowledge of why it is, 90a14–15, 93a4) begins from an awareness *that* the thing exists. But he goes on to emphasize that there are different ways of knowing that something exists and that the mode of the search for what a thing is will vary depending on the *way* in which we are aware that it exists. So in order to understand Aristotle's view of how the search for scientific knowledge proceeds it is crucial to understand

[26] Aristotle's unusual idiomatic phrase *echomen pros to ti esti* (93a28–9, a26) has posed difficulties for translators. Mure speaks of 'our knowledge of a thing's essential nature', Tredennick of 'our capacity for discovering what a thing is' – each avoiding literal translation. J. L. Ackrill has proposed to me that the phrase must be literally translated 'we are related to what it is'. In context, however, this does not fit Aristotle's claim at 93a28–9. The manner of one's awareness that something exists is not what determines in general how one is *related* to its essence. This translation misses the crucial point which the other translators see, that in this whole passage *echein* clearly has cognitive force; it signifies having some cognitive grasp or awareness. To translate 'we grasp what it is' would be too strong, however. (For this Aristotle would write *echomen to ti esti*; cf. a17, a27; 92b6.) The grasp in question is clearly supposed to involve sufficient knowledge of the essence to permit a meaningful search for its full nature, but perhaps no more (a24–7). Barnes translates 'we have some hold on what it is'. This has the right flavor but a more precise translation is perhaps possible. With certain verbs connoting awareness *pros* is used in a directional sense, e.g., *idein pros* = to look toward or see in the direction of, without necessarily fully discriminating. (See Kühner–Gerth 1898 II.1, 518.) Here this use is perhaps extended to cognitive awareness which is directed toward but does not necessarily involve full understanding of a certain essence. W. D. Ross apparently had this understanding of *pros* in mind in describing such awareness as that which 'help(s) us *towards* knowing what the thing is' (Ross 1949: 628, my italics. Ross was probably following Themistius here, *in An. Post.* 49.27–9, cf. Philoponus 367.6–8).

what these varieties of knowledge or awareness of existence are. In this passage Aristotle divides them into two general types, awareness that a thing exists which involves a grasp of 'something of the thing itself', and accidental awareness that a thing exists. The latter Aristotle characterizes as awareness which gives us no hold or fix on the essence which would enable us to conduct a meaningful search for its nature (93a24–7).[27] By contrast, non-accidental awareness does give us this sort of fix on the essence (93a27–8). This reflects Aristotle's earlier insistence that when we *know* that something exists in a way that permits us to search for what it is, our knowledge that it exists does involve the knowledge *that* it has an essence (90a5–15; cf. 90a24–5). We shall see how this comes into play in the examples of non-accidental knowledge which Aristotle goes on to immediately introduce.

Aristotle proceeds to offer us a series of examples 'of cases where we are aware of something of what a thing is' and are seeking a full understanding of what the thing is (93a29ff.). The language he uses here is, clearly, a variant on the language just used to characterize the crucial ingredient in non-accidental knowledge of existence ('awareness of something of the thing itself', 93a22, cf. a28). So he is here proceeding to attempt to make it clearer, by example, just how that non-accidental knowledge which he has required as a starting-point for scientific inquiry does facilitate such inquiry. The examples offered are importantly different and Aristotle presumably offers this variety in order to provide a fairly full picture of what paths scientific inquiry normally takes. Though the examples present problems of interpretation which there is not space to fully discuss here, the most important elements of this picture come through unaffected by the details involved in these problems.

The first and least interesting example, at 93a29–36, concerns a case where we discover both *that* something exists and *why* it exists (= what it is) simultaneously.[28] Aristotle describes a situation where

---

[27] It is clear from this that accidental awareness of existence cannot involve even a grasp of the so-called necessary accidents of the thing – that is of the scientifically explicable properties which it has in addition to its basic essence. For Aristotle supposes that a grasp of such properties *does* permit one to conduct a methodical search for the essence (*APr.* 1.30 46a17ff., *de An.* 1.1 402b21ff.). This conclusion is confirmed, as we shall see, by the fact that in his list of cases where we *are* able to search methodically for the essence Aristotle mentions at least one (at 93a36ff.) where our knowledge of the existence of something is based solely on an awareness of one of its explicable accidents. Our review of these cases below will confirm that non-accidental knowledge requires awareness either of a part or the whole of the essence, or of some explicable property of the thing.

[28] The key to the structure of the discussion of the three examples is 93a35–7. The first example, together with the illustration introduced to clarify it at a33ff., is a case of discovering fact and explanation (= definition) simultaneously; the next two of discovering the fact first and the explanation afterwards.

we are initially aware that there are lunar eclipses by being aware of a 'blockage by the earth'.

Let *A* stand for eclipse, *C* for the moon, *B* for blockage by the earth. Here then, seeking whether or not there is an eclipse is just seeking whether or not *B* occurs; and this is no different from seeking whether there is an account of it. If the account should be this [*sc. B*], we can also claim that that [*sc.* the eclipse] occurs.

As Aristotle describes this case, to ask *whether* there is an eclipse is just to ask whether there is a blockage by the earth of the moon's light source. So here we understand an eclipse simply to be such a blockage by the earth.[29] Also, however, asking *whether* the blockage (and thus the eclipse) occurs is said to be equivalent to asking whether there is an account or explanation of the eclipse, and finding that the account is *B* (the blockage) is finding *that* the eclipse occurs. The key to understanding these initially puzzling remarks comes with Aristotle's indication (at a33–6) that he has in mind a case where we learn *that* the eclipse occurs and *why* it occurs simultaneously. That is, knowing *that* the eclipse (= the blockage) occurs in this case is by itself knowing the account of an eclipse. So the proposition that an eclipse is a blockage by the earth is immediate (a36).

This case is, of course, somewhat atypical. It would be unusual for anyone to be first aware *that* there are lunar eclipses by being directly aware of the occurrence of their cause, blockage by the earth of the moon's light source. But an earlier passage where Aristotle evidently considers the same example makes clear that he had gone to the trouble for illustrative purposes to imagine a situation where, as he took it, this was so.

If we were on the moon [during an eclipse] we should not be inquiring whether it was happening nor why. Both would be evident simultaneously. We would come to know this by perceiving the universal. Since perception would indicate that there was now blockage (and since thus it would be evident that there was an eclipse) from this the universal would come to be known. (90a26–30)

This example conforms to Aristotle's prescription that knowing *that* something is in a non-accidental way involves knowing *that* there is a cause for its being (90a5–11), that is that it has an essence (a14–15). Here this requirement is easily satisfied because we are aware that

---

[29] Some commentators suppose that in this case we begin with the unexpressed assumption that an eclipse is 'a certain loss of light' (as at 93a23). We then learn as a separate item of information that this is caused by a blockage by the earth. (See Ross 1949: 631.) But this does not fit the text. Aristotle says initially that seeking *whether* (not why) there is an eclipse is just seeking whether the blockage occurs. If our starting assumption were that an eclipse is a loss of light then seeking *whether* an eclipse occurs would be seeking whether the loss of light occurs. It may be presumed here that loss of light is consequent upon eclipse (= blockage) but that is another matter.

an eclipse exists by directly observing the occurrence of its cause and, thus, the display of its essence. In the two cases of inquiry which Aristotle goes on to discuss which involve knowing that something exists non-accidentally without knowing what its cause or essence is, it will not be so simple to explain how Aristotle can think we still must know *that* the thing has a cause and essence as soon as we know non-accidentally that it exists.

The first of the two cases where we know initially that something exists by being aware of 'something of what it is' but do not know its essence (93a36ff.), is described by Aristotle as follows:

Let *C* be the moon, *A* an eclipse, *B* the inability of a full moon to cast a shadow when it is apparent that there is nothing between us. Then if *B* (inability to cast a shadow when nothing is between us) applies to *C* and *A* (being eclipsed) to *B* it is evident that there is an eclipse but not yet evident why. When it is evident that *A* applies to *C*, to ask why it applies is to ask what *B* is, whether it is a blockage or a rotation of the moon, or an extinguishing. And this is the account of the other extreme, that is, in this case, of *A* – since the eclipse *is* a blockage by the earth. (93a37–b7)

It is clear that what we are presumed to know here about lunar eclipse, when we know *that* it exists but not *what* it is, is that it is 'the inability of a full moon to cast a shadow when nothing [*sc.* no cloud, etc.] is between us'. Aristotle mentions no other fact that we know about eclipses, by grasp of which we understand *that* the moon is eclipsed. Moreover, he says that in looking subsequently for why the eclipse occurs, that is for what an eclipse is, we are looking simply for *what B* – the failure of the full moon to cast shadows – is (93b4–5). So he supposes that, in this case, looking for what an eclipse is, is simply equivalent to looking for what the failure of the full moon to cast shadows is.[30]

---

[30] Some have argued that this example too presupposes a prior understanding of an eclipse as 'a certain loss of light' on the part of the moon. (See Ross 1949: 631; Sorabji 1980: 198.) But Aristotle says nothing which implies this. He mentions various possible explanations of the fact of eclipse as understood here, one of which is 'a rotation of the moon', *sc.* so that its bright side is turned away from us (93b5). In this case the moon would not have *lost* its light.

Of course, awareness of the full moon's failure to cast shadows on a clear night no doubt involves an awareness of a failure of the moon to *manifest* its light on earth. So there is perhaps a sense in which an eclipse here is initially understood to involve a certain failure to manifest light; but this could only be an aspect of the understanding of eclipse as a certain failure to cast shadows. This is required since Aristotle says that in this case to look for *what* an eclipse is, once we know that it exists, is just to look for what *B* – the failure to cast shadows – is. If, as Ross claims, awareness of the moon's inability to cast shadows is only *evidence* for the existence of eclipse (= loss of light) then Aristotle would describe the further seach for what an eclipse is not as the search for what the inability to cast shadows is, but for what the loss of light is. Ross (p. 628) attempts to avoid this conclusion by assigning a meaning to the occurrence of the term *B* at 93b5 different from the original meaning specifically assigned to it by Aristotle at a39 (for which Ross imports a second

Presumably, Aristotle has in mind here the sort of case where, say, a hunter previously ignorant of eclipses knows that it is the night of the full moon and that the weather is clear and plans on a night of hunting. On leaving his house after dark, however, he notices immediately that the moon is unexpectedly failing to produce shadows of trees, and rocks and, most importantly, of moving deer and the like. The moon is failing, that is, to create the normal patterns of light and shade which he had expected on such a night to facilitate his hunting. From this he is aware *that* the moon is eclipsed, understanding an eclipse *simply* as the failure of the full moon to produce shadows of things when it is obvious that the sky is clear. It would be atypical, though certainly not impossible, for this fact about certain eclipses to be *the* item of information by grasp of which eclipses were (non-accidentally) known by anyone to exist. But Aristotle does treat the matter in this way for illustrative purposes.

We need to explore further now how Aristotle can here describe looking for *what* the inability to cast shadows, etc. is as looking for *why* (= what) an eclipse is. Are these not two quite different, if connected, types of events? It is clear that in the case in question, as Aristotle understands it, they are not; and good sense can be made of this in the following way. Aristotle makes it clear that looking for *what* the inability to cast shadows is is looking for what the primary nature or cause of the inability to cast shadows is. This can be the same as looking for what an eclipse is if an eclipse is identified with and known to us simply as the state (whatever its ultimate nature may be) which is a certain inability to cast shadows. This shows us how the case at hand conforms with Aristotle's requirement that knowing non-accidentally *that* something is involves the knowledge that it has a cause or essence. When we know that the full moon is unable to cast shadows, and thereby that there is an eclipse, we do not take the failure as a mere happenstance. We take it, rightly, as a phenomenon with a cause where that cause is in fact the essence of eclipse. So we are aware of the essence of eclipse here – as we must be since we know *that* there is such an essence – but only as the cause of a certain phenomenon.

This second example offers us, quite unlike the first, a case where our initial understanding and grip on the essence of some phenom-

designation, *B'*). In its later occurrence Ross treats *B* as a variable for whatever 'the *real* reason' for the eclipse is. For this there is no justification in the text. Aristotle introduces the one term *B* at a37–9 with a fixed sense (inability to cast a shadow, etc.) and does not change its sense or introduce any new term. Its occurrence at b5 is, moreover, in a sentence where the terms *A* and *C* also reappear. There is no more basis for treating *B* as having a new sense there than *A* or *C*.

enon is based solely on a grasp of explicable properties of the thing and on no generic or other feature of its ultimate essence. In his initial list of examples of non-accidental knowledge of existence where we do have a grip on the essence, Aristotle had already mentioned a case of this sort; namely, awareness of the soul as 'that which moves itself' (93a24). This is, for Aristotle, an explicable accident of certain cases of the soul, nothing more (*Top.* 120b21ff., *de An.* 408a30ff.). So presumably he is using the present example to show in detail how a grasp of features of this sort can in practice facilitate a search for the basic essence.

The next example which Aristotle offers is introduced as follows:

What is thunder? The extinguishing of fire in a cloud. Why does it thunder? Because the fire in a cloud is being extinguished. Let C be a cloud, A thunder and B extinguishing of fire. Then B applies to C (to the cloud), since the fire is being extinguished in it; and A (a noise) applies to B. So B is an account of A, the major term, and if there should be in turn another middle term of this, it will be one among the remaining accounts. (93b7–14)

This is the second example which Aristotle lists in his discussion of cases where we begin our inquiry by knowing non-accidentally *that* something is but not *what* it is. As in the previous case, we are supposed to be initially aware of the existence of something by grasp of a certain fact about it which turns out to be explicable by reference to what the thing is. The explicable fact which Aristotle introduces here is the occurrence of a certain noise in the clouds. A particularly significant feature of this example is Aristotle's use of 'thunder' (*brontē*) and 'noise' (*psophos*) interchangeably. (The term '*A*' is used to stand first for the former, then the latter.) This makes it clear that in looking for an explanation of why *thunder* exists (and thus an account of what it is) we are simply looking for the explanation of a certain type of noise. This makes good sense, assuming that we are, in this case, initially aware of thunder as a certain sort of noise, so that thunder is for us initially that kind of thing which manifests itself in this familiar noise.[31] Awareness of this noise counts as non-accidental awareness of the existence of thunder (cf. 93a22) since, as in the previous case, we are here aware of a kind through a manifestation of it which has a cause which we can methodically look for and when we find that cause we have found what the kind is.

[31] 'Noise' here must be an abbreviation for 'a certain noise' (*psophos tis*) as at 93a22. This is what is equivalent to 'thunder' in the initial usage of the term in question here. Aristotle knows that there are other (loud) noises in the clouds than thunder, e.g. during certain high winds. See *Mete.* 348a24. (He understands the noise of thunder as the familiar rumbling type of noise at *Mete.* 369b1.) So by 'noise' he must mean not just any loud noise occurring in the clouds but a particular well-known type of noise.

The most interesting feature, perhaps, of the third example comes in Aristotle's indication that even when we have found an account of thunder (that is, of that familiar noise which occurs in the clouds) as the extinguishing of fire, there *may* be 'in turn another middle term of this', and if so 'it will be one among the remaining accounts'. The phrase 'in turn' (*palin*) indicates that the new middle would be one which accounts for that by virtue of which the initially grasped fact about thunder was explained. Thus it would explain why thunder is an extinguishing of fire, or why the type of noise we call thunder is produced when fire is extinguished.[32] Aristotle adds that this new account based on the new middle would be 'among the *remaining* accounts'. Remaining accounts of what? A middle term, Aristotle has just indicated (93b6–7, 12), supplies us with an account of the major term, which would be in this case thunder. So this new account would belong to a sequence of remaining accounts of the one thing, thunder, of whose essence we are looking for a final account.[33] We

[32] Cf. Waitz 1844–6: II 397. This interpretation is confirmed by Aristotle's other discussion of such a sequence of middles, in *APo.* II.17 99a21ff. See below. Ross (1949: 629) takes it that the new middle will explain only the term *B*, extinguishing of fire – i.e. why fire is extinguished. But it is not clear how this (a general account of how fire is transformed into other elements) would give us, as Ross rightly supposes it should, a new definition of thunder. Furthermore, if this were what Aristotle had in mind he would hardly use the subjunctive here ('if there should be another middle'). Aristotle had no doubt that the extinguishing of fire has an explanation (*GC* II.4); but he did have doubt whether there is an explanation of why thunder *is* an extinguishing of fire. In the *Meteorology* (II.9), Aristotle in fact argues against this account of thunder and offers an alternative. But it is clear from his discussion there that this account was commonly understood to be basic, and he himself takes it in this way in *APo.* II.11 94b32ff., where he puts the necessity that it thunders when fire is extinguished on a par with the necessity that a stone falls. Finally, the claim that the new middle should be a middle simply of *B* does not fit the context. See the next note.

[33] Numerous interpretations of this brief remark have been offered by commentators. (Zabarella has an extended discussion of many of the ancient and medieval accounts. See *in Post. An.* 1124–8, in Zabarella 1597.) Already by Alexander's time, it seems, two general types of interpretation were being offered (see Moraux 1979: 98ff.). On one – the type followed here – the remaining accounts are further accounts of the same thing as the initial account, namely thunder. They lead us (in one way or another) to a final account of the essence of thunder. See Pacius, Waitz and Ross, *ad loc.* On the other – followed in various versions by Philoponus, Eustratius and Zabarella – the remaining accounts include any premises which occur at a more primitive level in the science of meteorology from which the premises used in the original proof are to be derived (*including* those which would be used if necessary to establish the premise that thunder is an extinguishing of fire and so would provide further accounts of thunder). This difference is perhaps not very significant for our purposes here since the case in focus on the first interpretation is included as a possible sub-case on the second. And it is this possibility which is the interesting and important one for our purposes. Zabarella, however, excludes this sub-case, mainly on the ground that only the minor premise but not the major in a demonstration can be in turn demonstrated since the major gives *the* basic account and definition (and so gives *immediate* properties) of the major term, as he claims Aristotle says here (1125bff. at 1126b–e). But this conflicts directly with Aristotle's remarks in *APo.* II.17 (see the previous note). And Aristotle says here only that '*B* is an account of *A*' (93b12) and he envisages 'another

are, thus, presumed to start with a certain understanding of thunder as the kind of thing which manifests itself as a noise in the clouds. We can find an account of this phenomenon which will give us *an* account of what the kind thunder is. But we may not yet have reached the basic nature of thunder. We may be able to account for the connection between thunder and the extinguishing of fire in terms of some other more basic feature of thunder, and for that feature in terms of some other more basic feature, and so on. Each new account will be, however, *an* account of thunder – that is an account of what the kind is – since each will in turn explain why thunder is, understood as the kind which manifests itself in a certain previously apprehended way. The feature of thunder initially apprehended in this event would only be an explicable accident of thunder (comparable to the inability to cast shadows in the previous example) and not a part of the basic essence.

This extended process is alluded to by Aristotle again in similar language in II.16–17. There he first supposes that we can explain the fact that certain plants shed their leaves through a certain middle term – the broadness of the leaves (98a36ff.). Perhaps he is here working under the assumption that broad leaves are heavy as leaves go and so have a relative tendency to fall off. (Cf. *PA* 663b12 on why some animals shed their horns.) But as he later makes clear the account or definition of leaf loss through this middle is not the end of the story (99a21ff.). There is 'further, a middle of this' (99a27) – that is of the connection between broadness of leaf and leaf loss. Broad-leaved plants experience hardening of the sap at the junction of the leaf stem. This gives us our ultimate explanation and definition of leaf loss – perhaps because hardening of the sap makes the leaf stem dry and brittle so that the broad leaf, given its weight, falls.

Aristotle takes it, then, that the process of scientific inquiry will standardly develop in a certain methodical fashion. We start with an awareness of some easily apprehendable features manifested by some kind. This manifestation may involve the exhibition of the

middle term of *this* among the remaining accounts, where 'this' cannot refer to the minor premise but must refer to the major premise (or to the middle term *B* alone, but against this see the previous note). Aristotle's use of the singular ('this') indicates that he is interested here only in a sequence of middle terms each of which will serve as the middle between the terms in the preceding demonstration which introduce the account of the thing to be explained. That is, he is interested in a sequence of middles all of which furnish accounts of previous major premises and thus of the one thing thunder. This is what the context requires, since this is all that is relevant to the topic of discussion here, namely how an account of a *particular* essence becomes known 'through demonstration' (93b15ff.). The discussion of how such an account and the premises which exhibit it may be *in general* related to other more basic premises would be quite unmotivated and out of place here.

self-explanatory basic essence of the kind (as in the first case in II.8),
or of one part of the essence of the kind which is explicable by
reference to some other part (as is probable in the third case in II.8),
or only of some feature explicable by reference to some more basic
feature and ultimately by reference to the essence (as in the second
case in II.8 and the case in II.16–17). In each of the cases discussed,
these initially apprehended features are directly perceptible. Even in
the case where we are initially aware of the essence simultaneously
with the fact Aristotle goes to the trouble to invent circumstances
where, as he supposes at any rate, we are directly aware of the essence
through perception. This fits with his general doctrine that what we
can most readily perceive gives us our start in scientific inquiry
(100a10–13; cf. 79a2–3, *Ph.* 184a16–26). In case our initial awareness of a kind does not involve an understanding of its essence, we
make progress by finding an account of what the kind is which is
adequate to explain the initially apprehended perceptual features.
And thereafter, if necessary, we make further progress by finding
other accounts each of which in turn explains the features which
figure in the previously discovered account. By this means we come
ultimately to an account of the basic essence of the kind which
exhibits primitive or indemonstrable features of it.[34]

This final stage of discovery is the one on which Aristotle proceeds
to shed further light in II.9. His account there, on one standard
reading, is in apparent conflict with the doctrine of II.8 as described
above, and so needs discussion here. He says, in II.9:

Of some things there is something different which is their cause, of others there is
not. So it is clear that of cases of what a thing is some are immediate and so first
principles, and for these [cases of what a thing is] one must take it as given that
they exist and what they are – or make this clear in some other manner. Just this
is what the arithmetician does, for he takes what the unit is as given, and also that
it exists. But for those [cases of what a thing is] which have a middle, for which there
is some different thing which is the cause of their being, it is possible, as we said,
to display what they are through demonstration (though not by demonstrating what
they are).

On perhaps the most common reading of this chapter Aristotle
here distinguishes two types of *entities*, self-explanatory ones and
non-self-explanatory ones. The latter, which are not immediately
knowable, have their essences displayed 'through demonstration' in
the way detailed in II.8.[35] These are the attributes of the primary

---

[34] This fills in some of the details in the similar picture of inquiry more briefly outlined
in various other places. See especially, *APo.* 1.24 85b27–86a3. See also *APr.* 1.30 46a17–30,
PA 1.1 639b5–10 with 640a13–15, *de An.* 1.1 402b16–25.

[35] A version of this view is laid out by Ross (1949: 78, 633). Cf., earlier, Themistius. An early
version of the type of alternative defended here is offered by Philoponus.

objects of the sciences as distinct from the primary objects themselves (cf. 76b11–16). The self-explanatory objects, which are immediately knowable, are the primary objects, for example the unit in Arithmetic. These, as immediately knowable, come to be known in some other way than by the procedures discussed in II.8. and from our knowledge of them our knowledge of the other things is ultimately derived.

There are numerous difficulties, however, for this reading of II.9. On this reading the only definitions which are immediately knowable are the definitions of the primary objects of the sciences. The other definitions, not being immediate, are to be demonstrated from them. But this is totally unworkable. The primary objects of geometry are points and lines (I.10 76b3ff.). There is, however, simply no way to derive by demonstration the definition of the triangle, say, solely from the definitions of point and line. Aristotle was quite aware of this. In his discussion in I.10 he claims that there is an account not only of what any primary object is which is an indemonstrable first principle but also an account of what the triangle and other secondary objects are (76a31–6, cf. b3–11).³⁶ Aristotle does say there that the *existence* of the secondary objects must be proved (though not demonstrated – *deiknunai*, not *apodeiknunai*). But this proof, whatever it amounts to, cannot involve any proof of the basic definition of the secondary objects, since this cannot be proved (76a31–2). Thus this proof cannot involve even the display of this definition 'through demonstration' since this is regarded by Aristotle as a proof (though not a demonstration) of it (II.10 93b38–94a2).³⁷

This doctrine in I.10 fits the discussion in II.8. There Aristotle treats the secondary object, lunar eclipse, as an entity which *can* be known 'through immediates', that is through characteristics which belong immediately to it (93a29–37 with 90a24–34).³⁸ And Aristotle lists the soul, a primary object of a certain science (*de An.* I.1 402a4–8, II.1 412a19–21), as an example of an entity which we come to a basic

³⁶ In 76a34–5 it is not certain whether *ti* is to be completed by *esti* or *sēmainei*. But it does not matter. Aristotle uses the two types of locutions interchangeably in contexts such as this. See 76b3–11 with 71a11–17 and 72a21–4.

³⁷ The type of definition which becomes clear through demonstration is one which does, as such, 'prove' (*deiknusi*, 94a1) what a thing is by making clear why it is through demonstration. Given this, the account of what a thing is which this type of definition exhibits cannot be one of the things which 'it is not possible to prove' (*mē endechetai deixai*), as the basic definitions of *both* the primary *and* the secondary objects of a science are (76a31–6).

³⁸ The simultaneous grasp of *that* and *why* comes 'through immediates' (93a36) and *nothing* more is required for this simultaneous grasp than awareness that the blockage by the earth of the moon's light source is an eclipse (90a26–30). So this must be an example of an awareness of what eclipse is 'through immediates'.

account of in the same way we do eclipse or the triangle (93a16–30 at a24).[39]

How can II.9 be read so as to conform to Aristotle's previous claims? To begin with, it is important to see that Aristotle does not focus his *main* attention there on two types of entities distinguished in the way supposed by the standard interpretation described above. The main items distinguished in this way are rather two different types of 'cases of what a thing is'. Nothing which he says shows that these cannot be different types of cases of what the *same* thing is. So the most that II.9 requires of a primary object of a science is that there is *some* case 'of what it is' which is immediately knowable. This permits other accounts of what that thing is which are not immediate and permits us to proceed from these accounts to the immediately knowable one in the way indicated in II.8.

What of the objects of a given science other than the primary ones, for instance thunder in meteorology or eclipse in astronomy? Do Aristotle's remarks in II.9 show that there is *no* immediately knowable account of eclipse by contrast with the unit? They do not. All that Aristotle requires is that the basic essence of anything is such that both the existence and nature of this essence must be *either* taken as given *or* made clear 'in some other manner' – where by the latter he particularly means, as he goes on to indicate, in some other manner than 'through demonstration'. This requirement fits the case of the unit since both its basic nature and the existence of this are taken as given without proof. It also fits the eclipse, however, since its basic essence is taken as given without proof and the existence of this is made clear in some other manner than by demonstration.

4. Definition and the process of discovery

In his discussion of the nature of the search for what a thing is, Aristotle has implicitly recognized that there are various quite different sorts of understanding of 'what something is' which one can have at different stages of the search. (See, especially, 93a29, b15–28, and compare 71a11ff., where our initial understanding of an object of inquiry is identified as an account of 'what it is'.) But 'an account of what a thing is' is just the standard description of a definition (II.10 93b29). So Aristotle goes on in II.10 to introduce three types of definition corresponding to the importantly different types of accounts which we can have of *what* some object of scientific inquiry *is* at the different stages of inquiry which he has already dis-

[39] For a detailed account of the way in which Aristotle's own discussion of the soul fits this pattern see Bolton 1978.

tinguished. So, as we shall see in detail below, Aristotle in effect repeats in II.10 his conclusions reached in II.8–9 about the nature of inquiry for what something is recast in the terminology of the theory of definition. On this theory it turns out that any understanding of 'what a thing is' which we have at any stage of inquiry – from the point where we only grasp *that* something is to the point where we know the basic essential features of the thing – counts as a genuine definition (of one sort or other) of the thing. This point remains inadequately appreciated in the literature. Writers who discuss or make claims about particular definitions which Aristotle offers here and there in his works, or who discuss his uses of the notion of definition outside the *Analytics,* almost invariably fail to ask the necessary question: Which of the types of definition which Aristotle distinguishes does he have in mind? We shall shortly consider the import of this point for the interpretation of certain passages in the biological works. It is necessary, however, that we first see more clearly what the three types of definition are. Aristotle's summary account of them is as follows:

One sort of definition is an indemonstrable account of what a thing is; a second is a proof of what a thing is – differing in arrangement from a demonstration; the third is a conclusion of a demonstration of what a thing is. (94a11–14)

These three types of definitions are in effect distinguished, as we shall see, by reference to where they arise in the course of successful scientific inquiry which results in full discovery of how to demonstrate what is demonstrable. They are best discussed in reverse order.

The third type of definition is 'a conclusion of a demonstration' – that is, it is a definition which exhibits only those characteristics of a thing which are explicable by reference to more basic characteristics. Aristotle gives as an example the definition of thunder as 'a noise in the clouds; this is the conclusion of the demonstration of what thunder is' (94a7–9). This example reintroduces the case discussed earlier in Chapter 8, where Aristotle lists our awareness of thunder as ' a certain noise in the clouds' as a case of non-accidental knowledge that something exists which permits a search for the essence, and goes on to show how this feature of thunder comes to figure in the conclusion of a demonstration which displays what thunder is (93a22–3, b7ff.). This indicates what the importance is of a definition of this type. It is a definition of the sort we have when we are at the stage of inquiry where our understanding is based on a grasp of explicable but unexplained features of things. One might infer from this example that definitions of this third type are restricted to those which exhibit the proximate genus of a kind whose presence is entailed and explained by the presence of the final differentia, as perhaps is the case here (see 94a5).[40] But this is clearly not so. As we have seen, Aristotle is prepared to regard any demonstration which explains the occurrence of any manifestation of a kind by awareness of which we are aware of the existence of the kind as a demonstration which gives us an account of what the kind, as previously understood, is (93b3–7). Since the features on which the previous understanding is based are just those which figure in the 'conclusion' of such a demonstration, any such features can serve as the basis for a definition of this type. So the understanding of an eclipse as the failure of the moon to cast shadows – the second case from Chapter 8 discussed above – also provides the basis for a definition which is a 'conclusion of a demonstration'. Aristotle does not directly discuss an initial account of what a thing is based on a *number* of its explicable features each of which might figure in some (but not the same) 'conclusion of a demonstration'. But, clearly, such an account would be, in principle, an account of this third type.

The second type of definition is 'a proof of what a thing is', or 'an account which displays why a thing is' (93b39). It is 'an account of what a thing is' which exhibits some explicable features of the thing defined of the sort which figure in definitions of the third type and also other features through which one can explain and demonstrate the occurrence of the explicable features. Thus, it is 'like a demonstration of what something is, differing in arrangement from a demonstration' (94a1–2). A sample definition of thunder of the second type is: 'Noise due to fire being extinguished in the clouds' (94a5–7). This definition makes clear *why* thunder – understood as a certain noise in the clouds – exists. It repeats the definition which Aristotle gave earlier as an example of an account of what something is which we have when we have come to know not only that something exists but why (93b7ff.). As with the third type of definition, Aristotle's description of the second type would cover accounts where some feature other than the proximate genus of the final differentia of a thing is in focus and connected with the feature which explains it. He even leaves it open, as we have noted, that this particular definition of thunder may not be one of that sort (93b8–14). It would nevertheless still be *an* account or definition which makes clear why thunder (understood as 'a certain noise in the clouds') exists, even if it is not an account which brings all questions as to why to an end (b12,14).[41]

Again, Aristotle does not say directly how he would classify a single complex account of what a thing is which listed a number of explicable features of the thing, each of which were explicable by reference to *some* other feature mentioned in the account (whether or not the account contained the ultimate indemonstrable features of the thing). He speaks earlier (93b13–14) only of the situation where we might successively uncover a sequence of different accounts together exhibiting such a collection of explicable and explaining features – no doubt because he wants primarily to indicate in simple form the stages by which discovery normally occurs. But clearly a *single* account of this sort would be essentially of the same type as the account which exhibits some features as due to another. So such an account would count as a definition of the second type.

The first type of definition can now be easily understood. It is 'an indemonstrable account of what a thing is' or 'a definition composed of the immediate characteristics [of a thing]' which is 'an inde- monstrable posit (*thesis*) of what a thing is' (94a9). That is, it is 'an account of what a thing is' which exhibits just the feature(s) of it which cannot be accounted for or demonstrated to belong to it by reference to other more basic features, but rather those by reference to which all of the explicable features of the thing are, ultimately, accounted for. At 93b8ff. Aristotle mentions an example which belongs to this type: 'Thunder is the extinguishing of fire in a cloud.' This is not an alternative to 'Thunder is the noise due to fire being extinguished in the clouds' (94a5), such that one need worry over which, in Aristotle's view, is the true definition of thunder. Each is a genuine definition but the two belong to different types distinguished by reference to the stages in the process of scientific discovery at which they become apparent. The grasp of, and awareness that one has, a definition of the first type does nevertheless mark the completion of a certain process of inquiry and, hence, attainment of the final stage in the understanding of what something is. Later, in II.19, Aristotle will argue that this type of understanding is 'more accurate' than any other including, hence, that where our grasp of the thing is essentially based (at least in part) on awareness of explicable demonstrable features of the thing.

We can now restate Aristotle's views on the normal way in which scientific inquiry proceeds and scientific discovery takes place, put in the terms introduced by his discussion of definition. (1) We nor- mally begin with a definition or account of the kind which is our object of inquiry which exhibits the features or manifestations of it which are perceptually most accessible. Typically, such features are not fundamental features of the kind in terms of which others can be explained, but rather explicable by reference to the more fundamental ones and, thus, features which figure in 'conclusions of demonstrations'. (2) Inquiry proceeds by moving from an understanding of some thing based on a definition of this sort to an understanding where we have an account or definition which exhibits why the thing has the characteristics which figure in the former type of definition. (3) We continue our inquiry to determine whether there is yet a further account or definition which explains the features already used to explain the features initially grasped, and so on, until we have a definition based on the feature or features most basic from the point of view of explanation.

5. Dialectic and definition in the *Analytics*

This is the general theory found in *Posterior Analytics* II.8–10 of the proper method to follow in scientific inquiry.[42] Does Aristotle's practice in his special scientific works, particularly in his biological works, conform to this theory? Putting Aristotle's recommendations in the terms introduced by his theory of definition is of direct use in answering this question, since the search for and the setting out of accounts or definitions frequently plays a dominant role in Aristotle's practice of inquiry in his scientific works. But before investigating instances of that practice, it is worth drawing attention here to the bearing of the results reached to this point on the claim discussed above, that Aristotle's recommended method for inquiry in science is dialectic, and on the claim often connected with it that the production of demonstrations is not the aim of scientific inquiry but only a way of exhibiting the results of such inquiry.

To begin with the latter claim, while it is obvious from our discussion thus far that Aristotle does not suppose in *Posterior Analytics* II that inquiry proceeds by starting with a grasp of immediate first principles and then generating demonstrations from them, it is also clear that inquiry is nevertheless directly aimed at the securing of demonstrations. Inquiry into some kind is directed at uncovering more and more basic features of it by reference to which the earlier grasped features can be demonstrated to belong to it. Inquiry is not complete concerning some kind until we are in possession of genuine demonstrations of what is demonstrable concerning it based on a grasp of its basic non-demonstrable essential features. The reason for this is not simply that we need to produce these demonstrations for

[42] These are not the only recommendations on the method of discovery in the *Analytics*. For some of the others, which can be integrated into the general theory outlined here, see James Lennox, ch. 5 above. For still others see section 8 below, at n. 56.

the purpose of exhibiting the knowledge which it is the aim of inquiry to acquire. Without these demonstrations we do not know *why* the initially grasped features of the thing in question occur, and without knowing that we do not yet *have* the knowledge which it is the aim of scientific inquiry to acquire (74b26–32, 93b3–7 with 71b9ff., and *Metaph.* A.1 981a24ff.). It is on this basis that Aristotle concludes that we cannot actually come to know what a thing is where some of the elements in what it is are demonstrable from others without producing the appropriate demonstration (93b18–19).

To what extent does Aristotle's recommended method of inquiry here conform to the method of dialectic? According to *Posterior Analytics* II inquiry should follow a path which moves from a definition which is a 'conclusion of a demonstration' to one which is 'like a demonstration' to one which is an indemonstrable starting-point for demonstration. More generally, inquiry moves from a grasp of definitions based on the perceptually available explicable facts to definitions which exhibit the explanations for those facts or the features by which those facts are explained. However, Aristotle's own handbook for the conduct of dialectic, the *Topics*, contains nothing which suggests that dialectic should or even might follow such a path. In particular, there is nothing at all in the sections of the *Topics* which deal with definition (mainly in Books VI–VII) which suggests that there are the three types of definitions discussed in the *Analytics* or that the adequacy of a definition must be judged by reference to the stage of inquiry at which the definition is offered.

Aristotle does recognize in the *Topics* that definitions can be attempted either by reference to what is more intelligible to us or by reference to what is more intelligible absolutely (VI.4 141b3ff.). And this distinction can be used to help distinguish the preliminary from the other types of definition in the *Analytics*. But in the *Topics* Aristotle argues at length that a definition by reference to what is more intelligible to us does not satisfy the requirements for a definition and he concludes that 'it is clear that one should not define by reference to things of this sort' (142a6–7). The only use for this mode of defining which Aristotle recognizes in the *Topics* is in discussion with those who are incapable of coming to possess genuine scientific knowledge (141b15–19). In the *Analytics*, by contrast, such definitions are viewed as essential starting-points for those who *can* come to possess scientific knowledge. Finally, and most importantly, there is nothing in the *Topics* which corresponds to the doctrine much emphasized in the *Analytics* that advanced definitions of the sort that are more intelligible absolutely are adequate only to the extent that they can be used to *explain* those perceptible and other characteristics of things which figure in initial definitions. In the *Analytics* all three types of definition are themselves *defined* by reference to their role in such explanations, while in the *Topics* this is not the basis even for a single line of argument *(topos)* by reference to which one can test the adequacy of the proposed definition.[43]

It might, of course, be argued that these facts only show that Aristotle changed his mind about definition after writing the sections on definition in the *Topics* and came to develop more complex views on the subject while working on new questions in the philosophy of science in the *Analytics*. If he had rewritten the relevant sections of the *Topics* after that, one might argue, his remarks on the dialectical treatment of definition would have been revised to accommodate the new ideas of the *Analytics*. We have ample reason to reject this proposal, however, even ignoring the difficulties for the assumptions about the dating of the works of the *Organon* which the proposal requires.[44]

---

[43] In *Top.* VI.8, in the course of explaining how to improve certain defective definitions reached by division, Aristotle says: 'When someone defines...the wind as a movement of the air, it is necessary to add in what quantity and of what sort [and where?] and from what source *(hupo tinos)*...since one who leaves out any differentia whatever does not state what it is to be something' (146b27–32). A closely related passage in *Mete.* II.4 makes clear what is meant by *hupo tinos* here: 'It would be absurd if this air around us should become a wind simply when it moves no matter from what *(hothen)* its movement may come. Just as we do not take water which flows in any fashion to be a river, even if there is a large quantity of it, but only if the flow is from a source *(pēgaion)* so too with the winds. A great quantity of air could be moved by some large falling object, but have neither a point of origin *(archē)* nor a source *(pēgē)*' (360a27–34). It is clear that the proper definition by division of a river which Aristotle has in mind here is: a large quantity of water flowing *from a source (pēgaion)*. Similarly a wind is a large quantity of moving air arising from a certain standard point of origin (viz. the earth, 361b1). This indicates that it is wrong to translate *hupo tinos* here as 'by what cause', following some translators. A river is not, for Aristotle, a body of moving water caused to flow by a certain source. The cause of its flow is that it lies downhill from its source (353b27–9). Similarly, winds are not caused to move by their point of origin but because they are hot air, and hot air rises and is then carried horizontally by the motion of the upper spheres (361a23–8). This makes it apparent that the definitions of wind and river here which mention source or *hupo tinos* as a differentia are not definitions of the second type listed in *APo.* II.10 in which certain features of the thing defined are described as due to some cause which functions as a middle term through which the connection between those features can be demonstrated. The *Topics* mentions no example of such definitions. So though Aristotle's language at 146b could be construed so as to cover such definitions (see *Metaph.* H.4 1044b9–20) there is clear indication that he does not intend this in the *Topics*. More importantly, there is in any case no suggestion at all in the *Topics* of any interest in testing definitions by reference to their ability to explain the full range of phenomena which, according to the *Analytics*, adequate final definitions must be able to explain.

[44] It is often supposed that Books I and VII.3ff. of the *Topics*, which do contain discussions of definition, *are* later than the *Analytics*. And the date of the original formulation of the essentials of the theory of demonstration used in *APo.* II.8–10 is uncertain. These are, for one thing, found in the *Protrepticus* (fr.5 Ross). See also nn. 46, 47 below.

At the beginning of *Topics* VIII.13 (162b31ff.). Aristotle introduces his discussion of the topic of begging the question with the remark that the subject 'has been discussed in accordance with truth (*kat' alētheian*) in the *Analytics*; now it is necessary to describe it in accordance with received opinion (*kata doxan*)'. This remark and the discussion it introduces were evidently written, or revised, *after* the completion of the *Analytics*.[45] And the remark makes it clear that the account of the guidelines (*topoi*) for the testing of claims in the *Topics* cannot go beyond what is proper in a discussion restricted to appeal to received or noted opinions as a basis for argument.

Some of the differences between what is appropriate in the discussion of a subject 'in accordance with received opinion' and the discussion of it from the point of view of truth are illustrated by the differences between the treatment of begging the question found in the *Topics* and the treatment 'in accordance with truth' given in the *Analytics*. The most striking point of difference is that in the *Prior Analytics* (II.16) the account draws heavily on material from the technical theory of the figures of syllogistic proof (65a1–35) and on material from the theory of demonstration (64b35ff.; 65a10ff.). The latter material, at least,[46] could not be included in the account in the *Topics* (whether or not it had already been worked out) because it treats the subject in a way inappropriate to dialectical discussion. The special definition of begging the question given in the *Analytics* itself establishes this point: 'To beg the question is to prove by means of itself what is not self-evident' (65a26, cf. 64b34ff.). This definition could not be given in the *Topics*, since it refers to a type of evidence – the self-evident – not relevant in argument based only on

---

45 It has been argued that this opening line contrast is a later addition. See Brunschwig 1967: lxxxv n. 1. But whether or not it is, the particular distinction drawn here between the point of view of the *Topics*, that is the dialectical point of view, and that of the *Analytics* is standard both in the *Topics* and *Analytics* (*Top.* 105b30–1, *APr.* 46a8–10, 65a35, *APo.* 81b18–23). Brunschwig argues for the later addition on the ground that the line brings 'into the domain of the problems of dialectical method the opposition of truth to opinion, otherwise used to characterize the dialectical method of the treatment of problems. (Cf I.14 105b30–1.)' But this contrast is a false one. Dialectical method does require that one treat a problem by arguing 'in accordance with received opinion'. But this not only means that one's premises must be *kata doxan* but also that one's entire method, including the *topoi* or guidelines for testing claims, must be appropriate for the type of argument which is restricted in this way. Contrary to Brunschwig's claim, Aristotle also uses the distinction between *kat' alētheian* and *kata doxan* to emphasize the latter point at *APr.* 65a35–7 as we shall see below.

46 Could the former be included? (While 65a1–25 concerns the first figure, a26–35 concerns mainly the second and third. The details are spelled out by the commentators. See, e.g., Ross 1949: 463–5.) Not clearly. The technical theory of the syllogism is Aristotle's own discovery and is, thus, not in accord with any received opinion. If this is right then the absence of this theory from the *Topics* is not the basis it is usually assumed to be for arguing that the *Topics* is earlier than the *Prior Analytics*.

appeal to noted opinion. What is begged in dialectical proofs must be what is not a matter of noted opinion (since noted opinion *may* there be assumed without proof), rather than what is not self-evident (since the self-evident may be assumed without proof in genuine demonstrations but not in dialectical proofs if it is not noted opinion).

> In demonstrations begging the question concerns things which stand in a certain way in accordance with truth, in dialectical proofs it concerns things which stand in a certain way according to received opinion. (65a35–7)

So the definition of begging the question given in the *Analytics* simply cannot be used to test whether begging the question has taken place in a dialectical argument.

The corresponding point holds of the definitions of definition in the *Analytics*. Just as with begging the question, the discussion of definition in the *Analytics* is based heavily on material from Aristotle's contributions to the theory of demonstration. As we have seen, the three types of definition or accounts of what a thing is are themselves defined by reference to the way in which each figures in genuine demonstrations. But occasion for appeal to what does or does not play a certain role in a genuine demonstration does not arise in dialectical discussion.

> It is clear that those who are reasoning *kata doxan*, that is only dialectically, should only consider this, whether their argument proceeds from the most accredited (*endoxotatōn*) premises possible. Thus, although a term is not in truth the middle term between *A* and *B*, if it is taken (*dokei*) to be then one who reasons through it has reasoned dialectically. But with a view to truth it is necessary to proceed from what actually holds.

This remark from *Posterior Analytics* 1.19 (81b18ff.) introduces the same contrast as the opening lines of *Topics* VIII.13. It makes it clear that the requirement of II.10 that a definition figure in one way or another in a genuine demonstration could not be a requirement for the adequacy of a definition in dialectic. A demonstration must proceed through a truly explanatory middle term, and dialectic has no interest in and no means to guarantee that, or even to determine whether, an argument is of this sort. It can and need only determine for a given term whether it is taken by appropriate persons as a middle term. So Aristotle would not have included the requirements for definition from the *Analytics* in the *Topics* whenever he wrote it. In *Topics* VII.3, he points out himself that 'it is the business of another discipline to explain accurately both what a definition is and how it is necessary for something to be defined; for now, we will only go so far as is requisite for present needs' (153a11ff.). The needs in question are, of course, those determined by the goal of the discipline at hand which is to lay out the method for reasoning *kata doxan*. This licenses Aristotle to go on to say without further qualification that a syllogistic proof of a definition is possible (153a13ff.), since a *dialectical* syllogistic proof clearly is possible (cf. *APo.* 93a14–15), whereas a strict demonstration is impossible (*APo.* II.4–6).[47]

The main importance of this result for our present purposes is this: if we find that Aristotle, in his scientific works, is following a pattern of inquiry leading to the discovery of definitions which is based on the special requirements for definitions reflected in his account of the types of definition in the *Analytics* then that pattern of inquiry is not dialectical. Since the biological works are the ones generally supposed to be farthest away in method from anything recommended in the *Analytics*, by virtue of being both more dialectical and more empirical, it will be of interest to determine what application this result may have to these works. Among these works the most mature and complete is by common consent the *Generation of Animals*; so it will perhaps be of special interest to determine what application the result has for this work.

6. Scientific method in the *Generation of Animals*

The *Generation of Animals* opens with a discussion which leads up to the identification of the chief factors in animal reproduction: the female, the male, and sperma. Aristotle argues that of these the female and the male are the most basic (716a4ff.), but a dominant aim of the whole of the work is to discover the nature and definition of each of these factors in a way that brings to light the role of each in animal reproduction. The discussion of sperma, to which Aristotle assigns a special importance (716a7–13), is the most compact and clearly organized, so we may conveniently concentrate our study of Aristotle's search for definitions on it.

Aristotle's main investigation of sperma[48] begins in *Generation of*

---

47 Cf. Cherniss 1944: n. 28. The rejoinder of Brunschwig, 1967: lxvii n. 1, following A. Mansion, fails to properly distinguish a syllogistic proof from a demonstration.

Many scholars have taken the view that Aristotle makes it clear a few lines later in *Topics* VII.3 that he had, when he wrote this section of the *Topics*, *already* formulated the views on definition found in *Posterior Analytics* II. (See Solmsen 1929: 151–2; Cherniss 1944: 35; Brunschwig, lxvii n. 1.) Aristotle says there: 'It is clear, therefore, that it is possible for there to be a proof of a definition. It has been more precisely determined elsewhere from what materials it is necessary to construct a proof, but the same lines of argument (*topoi*) are useful for our present method' (153a23ff.). The reference here to a more precise discussion cannot, however, be to *Posterior Analytics* II since the 'same lines of argument' which Aristotle goes on to list are not found there. Nor are they found earlier in the *Topics* as H. Maier supposed (1896–1900: II.2 78ff.). The reference may be to one of the lost works listed in Diogenes Laertius v.24.

48 There is no exact English equivalent for Aristotle's term *sperma*. See Balme 1972: *ad GA* 716a4. Aristotle indicates clearly enough what significance the term has in the passages discussed here, however, so it is sufficient simply to transliterate it – sperma.

Animals 1.17 721a30 and runs through 1.23 to the end of the book. It resumes at important points in II.1–5. The discussion opens in the following way:

> Some types of animals obviously emit sperma (for example, all whose nature it is to be blooded – it is unclear in which way the insects and cephalopods act). Therefore, we must investigate this: whether all males emit sperma, or not all; and if not all, what sort of cause is it by virtue of which some do and others do not; and whether females contribute a kind of sperma; and if not sperma, whether they contribute nothing else at all or something but not sperma. Then we must also ask, further, what those who emit sperma contribute through their sperma to generation and, generally, what the nature of sperma is (and also of the so-called menses in those animals which emit this fluid).

This paragraph, which at first seems only a rather rambling introduction to Aristotle's later discussion, is in fact very carefully organized. It falls into three distinct parts. First there is the claim that a certain fact obviously obtains. Second, there is the claim that the obviousness of this fact impels us to investigate a certain group of related questions. Finally, there is the claim that, as a further step, we must find the answer to another pair of questions (and a third related one) of which the second is in some way the more general.

What is Aristotle's reason for this particular organization of his inquiry? As we noted earlier, according to the *Posterior Analytics* inquiry into some subject begins with a grasp of the fact that the thing exists, based on what is most apparent to perception. This provokes a search for an understanding of why the thing so understood exists, which is the same as a search for what it is. Clearly this doctrine exercises a heavy influence on Aristotle's pattern of thought here. That it is obvious that certain animals emit sperma is, in effect, the claim that we are in a certain way aware *that* sperma exists. (Aristotle has in mind here, of course, certain perceptually apparent cases.) And the ultimate two questions to which we are led finally by this awareness of the existence of sperma are, in effect, *why* does sperma exist (= what does it contribute to generation) and *what* is sperma (which is, according to the *Analytics*, just a general way of putting the question we are asking when we ask *why* sperma exists).

What is the purpose of the intervening material – the questions initially provoked by our awareness of the existence of sperma? Here again the *Posterior Analytics* offer a clue to the answer. According to that work our initial awareness of the existence of something may be better or worse. As we have seen, it is better to the extent that we are by virtue of it in the best position to learn *what* the thing is, and we are in such a position to the extent that we are aware of the existence of the thing *via* a grasp of those non-accidental features of it which can be ultimately demonstrated to belong to it (cf. *de An.* 1.1 402b16ff.). If we consider carefully the import of the initial group of questions we will see that their answers function to put us in a much better position to determine what sperma is than we are initially by giving us better non-accidental knowledge *that* sperma exists.

This can be best seen by asking what Aristotle supposes we know about sperma at the point at which it is first initially obvious to us that it exists. We can determine this by finding out what is, in Aristotle's questions, presupposed as already understood and what is presumed to need investigation. We know that sperma is a fluid which sometimes makes some contribution to generation. This much at least is presumed as already understood by the final group of questions (721b2–6). But those questions also presuppose that we do not know in general *what* contribution sperma makes to generation which means that we do not know when it contributes and when it does not. We also know that sperma is emitted by members of certain species – the blooded ones (721a30–1). But we do not know whether it is emitted by all the members of these species who may contribute to generation. Aristotle says we need to inquire whether *all* males emit sperma (a33), which presumes that we are aware that at least some males of the blooded species do. But we do not know whether or not it is emitted by any females and so we need to inquire about this (a33–5). We do not even know whether it is the only material from which generation can take place since we do not know whether the so-called menses is a type of sperma or another type of fluid which contributes to generation or whether it makes no contribution to generation at all (b1–2, 4–6 with 726a28–b1). Nor do we know whether the only way males can contribute to generation is through emitting sperma, since we do not know why some do and some do not – assuming some do not emit sperma, as for all we know they may not (a33–4). So, for all we know at the beginning, generation may take place without sperma from either male or female. The initial knowledge which we are, thus, presumed to have of the existence of sperma is very thinly based. We are aware that sperma exists as a material which is at least one contributing factor in at least some cases of generation and a material of the type to which the normally generative material contributed by at least some blooded males belongs. More simply, we know that sperma exists because we can identify certain clear cases of it. We know that the type of generative material emitted by certain males (in fact the most familiar cases of males to us) is sperma. So we know one set of sufficient conditions for being sperma. This gives us non-accidental knowledge of the existence of sperma since it gives us *one* fact about sperma which our final account of its essence will, as we shall see, enable us to explain. This permits us to look for the essence. However, it does not yet put us in a good position to investigate generally what the function of sperma is in generation, i.e., to say generally why it exists and, hence, what it is. We need to know more about what the other cases of sperma are if there are others. And we need to know what the general relation is between sperma and generative material. Is sperma always generative? Is it the only generative material? If not, what are the exceptions and what else is involved?

7. The place of dialectic in Aristotle's inquiry

Aristotle begins his further discussion with a review of a certain received doctrine which incorporates an answer to the initial set of questions which he has claimed are open questions: 'It is held that all animals come from sperma and that this sperma comes from those that generate' (721b6–7). On this view (1) sperma is necessary and sufficient for animal generation and (2) sperma is emitted by *all* those that contribute to generation (and so by both males and females in species which have both). Aristotle is himself opposed to both parts of this view but it is the second only which he is interested to consider here – presumably because he thinks the first is easily rejected by appeal to the commonly admitted fact of spontaneous generation to which he has already devoted attention. (See, e.g., 715b2–30.) He investigates the second through a review of the so-called pangenesis theory – the theory that 'sperma comes from every part of the body' of its producers – because, as he explains, he thinks that to undermine this theory will be to undermine the dominant received basis for believing that *both* sexes contribute to generation by emitting sperma (721b6–10; 724a7–11). The main point of this extended discussion is, thus, to show that despite certain received views to the contrary, the main questions initially supposed to be open (at 721a30ff.) are indeed open.

The role which the examination of pangenesis plays in Aristotle's discussion of sperma deserves close attention since this examination is entirely dialectical in character. Aristotle undertakes to show that the denial of this received doctrine 'is more apparent' (722a1–2) than the doctrine itself. To do this he argues against the received doctrine solely by reference to other *endoxa* – either by appealing to obvious commonly accepted views to show that the arguments cited to support this doctrine are without force (as at 722a2ff.); or by showing that the doctrine has consequences which anyone will admit are 'plainly impossible' or 'absurd' (as at 722b6–30, 723b9ff.). Aristotle's arguments presume no technical information or theory. They rely on nothing which Aristotle could not expect to be much more widely accepted and, indeed, 'more apparent' than the premises and assumptions on which the doctrine of pangenesis is based.[49] The latter are even in some cases, Aristotle says, 'quite beyond us' (723a22). The function of the dialectical discussion here is thus to indicate where we stand as a result of a review of received opinions in which the more generally apparent and accredited are allowed to take precedence over others where there is a conflict. As such, dialectic serves here only to fix on what is most obvious to us about sperma and nothing beyond. This is just what is to be expected from a dialectical investigation. In his account in *Topics* viii.5–6 of the rules to follow in serious dialectical inquiry (as opposed to a mere competition, 159a25–37) Aristotle lays it down that 'one who reasons well demonstrates his projected result from what is more accredited and more familiar' (*ex endoxoterōn kai gnōrimōterōn*) than the thing he wishes to establish or reject (159b8–9, cf. 160a14–16, 161b34–162a3, *APo.* 81b18ff.).[50]

8. Aristotle's initial definitions of sperma

That the dialectical review of received opinion relevant to the doctrine of pangenesis has not got us beyond the theoretically thin but most obvious understanding of what sperma is which was initially presumed is clear from the succeeding discussion (1.18 724a14ff.). Aristotle begins his further investigation of the questions which remain open with the following remarks:

The starting-point of this investigation and those that follow is to first say what we take for granted (*labein*) concerning what sperma is. For proceeding in this way we will be much better able to inquire into its functions (*ta erga*) and into the derivative

---

[49] Just once Aristotle suggests that one might counter pangenesis *if* another expert view, that of Empedocles, were correct (723a23). But, significantly, he explicitly declines to draw conclusions from this and prefers to appeal instead to what 'is apparent' (a26). At 723b19 Aristotle appeals to 'what we have sufficiently observed in insects'. These are not his own new observations but what has been quite generally observed and accepted.

[50] These passages confirm that contrary to what is frequently supposed it is neither necessary nor sufficient for Aristotle's purposes in dialectic that the premises from which he reasons are accepted by his opponent. (See, e.g., on this passage, Balme 1972: 141.) This is a requirement only for *ad hominem* dialectic, whose best result can only be to show that *the opponent* should reject a view. Here Aristotle wants to show dialectically that the view should be rejected generally. For this purpose Aristotle's premises must be more esteemed in general or absolutely than the view he wants rejected and the opponent's own views as such are irrelevant. See further n. 9 above.

facts (*ta sumbainonta*) about it. And sperma is understood to be in its nature the sort of thing from which the things which are naturally formed come in the first place into being.

Aristotle here distinguishes three things concerning sperma. There is an account of 'what it is' which we take for granted, there are its functions and there are the derivative facts about it. How do these differ? In describing the first, Aristotle uses the language of and draws on the doctrine of the *Analytics*. Any learning about something requires that we take for granted (*lambanein*) *some* account of what it is (76a31–b22; cf. 71a11ff.).[51] Ultimately, when inquiry is finished the account taken for granted of what a thing is is an indemonstrable first principle (76a31ff.). But we are in no position to posit such an account concerning sperma here. Rather, the account must be of the sort with which we initially begin. At this stage too some account of what a thing is must be taken for granted (71a12ff.; cf. 71b33ff. with *Topics* VI.4 141a26–b14). Given this, the distinction here is not one between an ultimate definition of sperma and other matters but one between the definition from which inquiry starts and other matters. The preliminary account of what sperma is, moreover, is carefully framed so as to reflect no more than we were earlier presumed to know about it. Sperma is not that from which *all* animals are formed, as some suppose (721b6). It is only *the sort of thing* (*toiouton*) from which naturally formed things originally arise. This leaves it open that there may be other things similar in kind, though not sperma, from which living things in some way originally arise, such as that from which spontaneously generated animals arise, or menses (cf. *to toiouton morion*, 716a11). Since some things of the sort in question are not sperma, or might not be, for all we know here, it is not enough, in order for us to be aware non-accidentally *that* sperma exists at this point, that we are aware of the existence of *something or other* of this sort. Aristotle must here still be relying on our awareness of the most familiar cases of sperma. Strictly speaking, what we most clearly understand sperma to be is the type of original generative source emitted by certain familiar blooded males.[52] It is only after further study of this that the status of menses and other things similar to the male emission will be settled.

The other matters introduced in the above passage concern the 'functions' of sperma and the 'derivative facts' about it. How are

[51] Writers on *GA* seem to have missed the connection with the *Analytics* here. This has led to the mistranslation of *labein* as 'discover' (Peck) or the undertranslation of it as 'grasp' (Balme).

[52] Thus the initial definition conforms to the pattern prescribed for such definitions in the *Analytics*. See Bolton 1976.

these related? The latter are for Aristotle the low-level, preferably perceptually based, data we gather which we expect to be explained or accounted for by the principles of our final theory, including our ultimate definitions. (See, e.g., III.10 760b27–33.) This suggests that, by contrast, the account of the 'functions' of sperma will have to do with the theoretical principles by reference to which the 'derivative facts' are explained. This conforms to Aristotle's familiar doctrine that in biology the account of a thing's function is a relatively basic item of theoretical information about it (*PA* I.1 639b14; cf. 648a16). Thus Aristotle's account here of the procedure to follow in investigating sperma conforms to his recommendations in the *Analytics*. We begin with a preliminary account of sperma which reflects the common understanding of it on which our initial knowledge *that* sperma exists is based. We then work our way toward the ultimate definition which will explain the features of it which figure in the preliminary account together with other explicable facts about it which we may uncover. We must now see to what extent Aristotle actually follows such a pattern of investigation.

Before proceeding Aristotle pauses to settle a final preliminary matter. It is not made clear in our initial account what is meant by the claim that a thing comes '*from* sperma'. So Aristotle begins his further investigation with a review of the relevant possible ways of understanding this locution (724a20ff.). Since these are all based on ordinary usage it is clear that Aristotle is still working to get clearer on what the initial ordinary understanding of sperma is. However, he is unable to settle the matter in question on this basis alone. All that ordinary understanding permits us to say is that something is generated 'from' sperma in one of two ways, 'either as *from* a material or as *from* a proximate agent' (724a35).

> Therefore, we must find out in which of these two ways sperma should be understood, whether as a material, i.e. a passive thing, or rather as a kind of form, i.e. an active thing – or even as both. (724b4–6)[53]

To solve this problem, Aristotle undertakes an investigation the point of which is to 'now say what the primary nature is of that which is called sperma' (724b21–2).[54] This language further confirms the

---

[53] Aristotle's notions of matter and form here are not (as Balme suggests, 1972: 145) his special technical notions. He remains here at the level of ordinary understanding, as his explicative glosses on these notions in line with the ordinary usage just introduced make clear.

[54] This remark is excised by A.L. Peck along with the immediately preceding definitions as 'inappropriate' or 'incorrect' (Peck 1963: 76). This may be true of at least some of the definitions but it is not true of the remark which serves quite appropriately to introduce the subsequent discussion. Balme has qualms about the definitions (1972: 145) but leaves them in the text and, without argument, excises only this remark.

point that our earlier account of sperma has served to specify only what it is that we *call* sperma, which is to say that it is an account or definition based on our initial common understanding of the entity by contrast with an account which displays its nature and function. (See *APo.* II.10 93b29ff.)[55]

Aristotle begins to work his way to a new account of the nature of sperma or of 'what sperma is' (cf. 726a26–8) with the following argument.

> It is necessary that everything which we find in the body is either a natural part – and in that case either a non-homoeomerous or a homoeomerous part – or an unnatural part (such as a growth), or a residue, or a colliquation, or nourishment. (I call the surplus of nourishment *residue* and the secretion by unnatural decomposition from the material added in growth a *colliquation*.) Clearly, sperma cannot be a part. For, although it is homoeomerous nothing is composed out of it as things are from sinew and flesh. Neither is it distinct, but all the remaining parts are. Nor is it unnatural or a deformity since it is originally present in all the parts and the nature of the thing comes into being from it. And nourishment is obviously imported from without. It is necessary, therefore, that sperma is either a colliquation or a residue...But a colliquation is something unnatural and nothing natural comes into being from what is unnatural. It is, therefore, necessary that sperma is a residue. But every residue is either composed of useful or useless nourishment. I call useless that from which nothing further is contributed to the thing's nature, and which is harmful if too much is used up; the opposite, useful. That sperma is not of the former sort is obvious. For those in the worst condition because of age or sickness have the most residue of that sort and the least sperma...Sperma, is, therefore, a certain part of a useful residue; and the final residue is most useful and so that from which each of the parts comes directly into being. (724b23ff.)

The most striking thing about this new argument is the extent to which in it, by contrast with the earlier discussion, Aristotle leaves behind the realm of received opinion. The initial premise of the argument – which offers an exhaustive survey of everything found in the animal body – is not something which 'we say' (as earlier at 724a22, 25) nor something which is 'held' or 'appears so' (as earlier at 721a30, b6, 25; 722a1, b15; 723a26) but rather something which is 'necessary'. So this premise must be taken as already established in a way that guarantees its necessity. (For the opposition of the necessary to *endoxa* see *APr.* II.27 70a7; *APo.* II.5 91b15–7.) It clearly is a part of more general physiology and thus theoretically prior to the present inquiry, as are the definitions of the technical terms 'residue' and 'colliquation' which Aristotle adds as footnotes to it.[56]

55 Aristotle's language here provides evidence for identifying the account of what we call by some name (the 'account of what the name signifies', 93b29–30) with the sort of account which serves as 'the conclusion of a demonstration' in the way explained above, sections 3–4. See, further, Bolton 1976: n. 14.
56 Aristotle nowhere in his extant writings establishes that this starting premise is necessary. Related material is, however, found at *PA* 647b21ff., 677a11ff. Our passage here illustrates effectively how material from one science may be used in a subordinate science.

None of the other premises in the argument are introduced as what is said or held or what appears so, or by use of any of the standard expressions which Aristotle uses to introduce *endoxa*. They are all based either on equally prior material from general physiology or physics, or on what we originally take it sperma is or on facts which are available to perception in the way our initial presumption is. Sperma is not a natural part of the organism. It is (as is, presumably, perceptually apparent) homoeomerous or uniform in character and thus would be, if anything, a homoeomerous part. But (as general physiology tells us) none of the non-homoeomerous parts – i.e., the organs – are made out of it as is standardly the case for homoeomerous parts, for instance flesh and sinew. Furthermore (as our initial grasp of sperma indicates) it is not distinct in function or nature, as are all the other parts, but rather the whole organism with all its parts, somehow, arises from it at least in the most familiar cases of generation.[57] It is not an unnatural part since (as our initial understanding again indicates) at least in certain cases it is originally related to all the parts in such a way that the whole nature of the thing somehow comes from it. It is not nourishment given (our theoretically prior knowledge) that nourishment is not emitted by the body but introduced from outside. It is not a colliquation since a colliquation (given its definition) is contrary to nature and (given the prior general principle that) nothing natural comes from something unnatural. So sperma '*must* be a residue' (725a3). Moreover (given the perceptually apparent fact that normal sperma is not produced in persons in whom useless residues are produced in quantity) it must be a useful residue. In fact, it must be 'the final residue' of useful nourishment *since* the final residue is 'most useful and so that *from which* each of the parts comes *directly* into being' (725a11–14). In the last crucial move which Aristotle makes here he alludes back to the main feature of sperma which figured in the initial account of it – that it is 'the sort of thing *from which* naturally constituted things come *in the first place* into being' (724a17–18: the phrase 'from which' is repeated and 'in the first place' corresponds to 'directly' in the later passage). He introduces his new account of what sperma is – 'a residue from the final form of useful nourishment' (726a26–7) – as the one which explains this feature of sperma. The final form of nourishment is that from which every part of an

---

[57] This need not and, of course, should not be taken to mean that the whole organism comes *from* sperma as matter. That point is not yet settled and the argument here requires only that the whole organism come *from* sperma in one of the ways which our initial understanding permits. This holds for the subsequent arguments as well.

organism, and thus the whole organism, can somehow directly develop.

By this argument Aristotle reaches his second account or definition of sperma. Unlike the first definition the second is not described as an account of what is *called* sperma. Rather it is an account of what sperma must be given that our account of its nature must fit with the theoretically prior content of general animal physiology and other perceptually obvious facts in such a way that the initially apprehended features can be explained by it. Specifically, the new account is presented as offering the key to the explanation of why an animal can, as a whole, develop *from* sperma – the point on which our initial understanding focuses. However, this criterion for the adequacy of the new account is not, as we have seen, one dictated by dialectic as presented in the *Topics* or elsewhere. Rather it fits with the conditions of adequacy for post-preliminary definitions which we have found displayed in the *Posterior Analytics*. Further confirmation that this is what interests Aristotle comes immediately in the text. He goes on to defend the adequacy of his new account on the basis that given it various other low-level facts (*ta sumbainonta*) about sperma can be readily explained (725b4–726a25). Again this is not required by dialectic. Insofar as these facts may be *endoxa* it is at most required by dialectic that our account of sperma be not inconsistent with them (*Topics* I.1 100a18–21). But Aristotle is after a stronger connection; he shows that 'these things result *because* the nature of the residue is such as this' (725b5–6). The *Analytics* expects this of the most accurate definitions, the *Topics* does not. Moreover, though some or all of the low-level facts which Aristotle considers here may be matters of received opinion it is again significant that he does not speak of accounting for the *endoxa* but rather for the low-level facts with no restriction as to the source of our awareness of them. This makes it clear how perceptual data can serve as the final test of a scientific theory even when they are not *endoxa*. The theory must *explain* all such data whatever their level of acceptance.

Our new definition gives us a better understanding of sperma. It helps us to understand *how* sperma can contribute to generation. But it clearly is not yet an account which fully reveals to us *why* sperma exists, or *how* it contributes to generation, since it does not yet make clear whether animals develop *from* sperma as material or as active agent. From the *Analytics* and Aristotle's initial remarks on sperma at the opening of chapter 17, we should expect him to now work further toward such an account.

9. The final definitions of sperma

Aristotle began with a commitment to the existence of sperma which only clearly extended to the most obvious cases. His deeper account of what sperma is in these cases, however, puts him in a position to consider in 1.19 the merits of other cases which are thought by some to be cases of sperma, in particular the menses. (See 726a28–b1; 727b5ff.) By a pattern of argument the same as he has just used – which combines a consideration of the theoretically prior material (as at 726b1ff.) and the low-level facts (as at 726b6ff.), with both of which any new results must fit – Aristotle argues that 'sperma is clearly a residue from the final stage of nourishment, which takes the form of blood, which is being distributed to all the parts' (726b9–11). This gets us directly a bit closer to seeing *how* sperma is an originative source of generation. Since it is even more potent – because even more of a concentrate from food – than blood (which is already as nourishment potentially all of the parts of the whole animal) it is clearly all the parts potentially (726b11–17). But we cannot yet answer the question raised initially at 724b4–6 whether it is such because 'the body of the sperma is the cause of generation or whether it has a certain disposition, a source of movement which is generative' (726b19–21).

We can, however, directly see from another combination of prior theoretical matters (726b30ff., note 'necessary', b30, 32, 35; note 'impossible', a26) plus derivative facts to be explained (727a4ff.; a31ff.) that the thesis which fits with the prior theory and which with it best explains the derivative facts is that the menses (being blood but not as hot or, hence, as highly concocted as the male sperma) are a residue of nourishment which is not sperma but is closely similar to it and which, given its character, can and does contribute to generation by providing the matter used in the process whereby the whole animal – with all its parts – is produced (727b31–2; cf. 729a20ff.).

This result serves to put Aristotle directly in a position, in chapter 21, to reach his goal, stated earlier (721b2–3), of saying what the function of sperma is in generation and, thereby, of saying in the most revealing way what sperma is. Since it is only the male that emits sperma, to say this comes now to the same thing as saying 'how the sperma from the male is the cause of the thing generated' (729b1–2). If the female emission contributes only matter in generation – 'that which gets set and receives the form' – then the other ingredient, sperma, must be the active ingredient which does the setting and provides the form (729b6–8). This is the only result which will fit with the previously established or evident material to account for generation. Prior results do not indicate whether sperma *also* contributes *some* matter; but Aristotle proceeds to argue that this is not the case. He does so in two quite different ways. His main argument (729b21ff.; note 'the best indication', 729b33ff.) follows the previous pattern. The supposition that sperma contributes form but not matter is the one that best accounts for various low-level facts (*erga*, most importantly the supposed fact that sperma acts on bird and fish eggs already formed and in process of development in a way that does not involve any contribution to their nourishment and growth or, hence, to their matter, 729b33ff.).

However, Aristotle argues for his result in another way as well (729b8ff.). He appeals to certain 'general' (*katholou*) considerations which show that this result is 'in accordance with reasoned argument' (*kata logon*). The argument which he produces here is dialectical – it does not rely on theoretically prior material nor on the explanatory power of the result. It relies on endoxical information, most notoriously on the claim that 'the female *qua* female is, of course, passive and the male *qua* male is active' (729b12–14), and on received views concerning the relation between active and passive contributors to any results which are too general and analogical to form a part of any special science. Given this, this argument lies outside the procedures for the justification of scientific results laid down in the *Posterior Analytics*, and is introduced here for rhetorical purposes.[58] But this serves again to point up, this time by way of contrast, how the main line of argument continues to conform to the requirements of the *Analytics*. Interestingly enough, it is the nonscientific argument – which is quite independent of the sustained scientific discussion – which contains the claims often thought to be most morally and otherwise objectionable in Aristotle's discussion here.

---

[58] The contrast here between arguing *epi tōn ergōn* and *kata ton logon katholou* is matched later, in II.8 747b27ff., by the contrast between argument *ek tōn huparchontōn* (748a14–15) and argument which is *logikē* and as such *katholou mallon*. There Aristotle explains the difference. The former is, unlike the latter, based on materials which are proper to the specific science in question and is thus not 'excessively general' (747b27–30, 748a7–14). Arguments of the latter sort appear to be based on the facts (748a9) and thus may be more rhetorically effective (747b27–8) even though they are without value (748a8–9). Aristotle thus specifically opposes a method which is *logikē* to that which is required in physical or other science (748a13–14). Hence this contrast is basically the same as his more frequent contrast between a method which proceeds *logikōs* and that which proceeds *phusikōs* or, more generally, *analutikōs* (*APo.* 84a8, *Ph.* 204b4, 264a7, *GC* 316a11). Aristotle also substitutes *dialektikōs* for *logikōs* in making this type of contrast (*de An.* 403a2; cf. a29). This fits the discussion here and gives us a measure of the inferiority of the argument *kata ton logon*. (Balme 1972: 152–3 offers without discussion a reverse assessment of the merits of the two lines of argument.)

We have now reached a more fundamental account of what sperma is, based now for the first time on an understanding of its function. This Aristotle is able to provide only when he has reached the point where he has improved our knowledge *that* sperma exists to the point where he can say whether the menses are or are not sperma. On the new account, sperma is that which has the power to set the menses by contributing the initial motion and form to that which is generated. What is the relation between this new account and the previous one? Are they related as explanans and explanandum, as the *Analytics* suggests they should be? We are not yet in the best position to say since the new account gives us only a partial statement of the functional definition of sperma. The account does not yet make fully clear why it is that sperma has its special power. It does, however, provide enough information to enable Aristotle to explain what the role of the male is in generation and, hence, to explain how the male and female operate in cases where sperma is *not* emitted (730b8ff.,; cf. 738b9ff.). This permits him to make further progress in his account of the nature of male and female begun in 1.2 (cf. ii.1 732a24–5). He does not return to the consideration of the function of sperma until ii.1 (733b16ff., *passim* through ii.5). When he does return, however, he directly takes up the question of how sperma can set the menses and contribute the initial motion to the fetation which makes it a living developing thing. The answer which he gives is that this is due to the motion of the special heat of the pneuma which sperma can be shown to contain (736b33ff., 737a18ff.; see also ii.2 and 739b20ff.). So the full revealing functional account of the nature of sperma becomes this: sperma is a fluid emitted by males which has the motion of the heat of the pneuma which it contains, and so is able to set the menses and contribute the initial motion and form to that which is generated(737a18ff.). The interest of this is that it does enable us now to account for the previous definition of sperma as a residue from nourishment in its final form, i.e., from blood. If sperma does contain the level of pneumatic heat (beyond that of blood) which is required to give it its power then this shows why it must be a residue from blood or nourishment in its final form. For this is required for the body to produce emittable material with this level of pneumatic heat. (See 728a17ff.)

Aristotle does not himself take the time to explicitly produce this explanation in Book ii. By the time he comes to directly discuss the pneumatic character of sperma in ii.2–3, he is preoccupied with the relevance of this doctrine for explaining the facts of embryology. But from the distinct anticipations of this later development in the earlier discussion (as at 728a17ff., 729b25ff.) we can see that he did pull things together, in his own mind, in this way.

Aristotle's final functional definition of sperma (737a18ff.) is picked up again in a later passage in iv.3 where he draws on his earlier discussion.

It makes no difference whether we speak of the sperma[59] or the motion which causes each of the parts to develop (or whether we speak of what causes them to develop or what sets them from the beginning). For the account of the movement in question [the movement of pneumatic heat derived from the male] is the same in each case. (767b18–20)

The functional definition of sperma expressed earlier and alluded to here has the form of the second type of definition listed in *Posterior Analytics* ii.10 – the one which is 'like a demonstration'. It mentions certain features as caused by or explicable by others (cf. 736b33–5). In the *Analytics* the causally primary element in such definitions is regarded as an indemonstrable first principle. Here the principle would be: sperma is a bodily emission with the motion of pneumatic heat.

The upshot of our analysis of the pattern to which Aristotle's inquiry into the nature of sperma conforms will now be quite apparent. Simply put, it is that Aristotle follows a general pattern of inquiry leading to discovery which is laid out in the *Posterior Analytics* but neither recommended nor required by the canons of dialectic. It will be noticed, however, that in describing this pattern and Aristotle's conformity to it, no mention at all has been made of the syllogism. No attempt has been made here to determine to what extent the explanations of less by more fundamental theoretical information about sperma which Aristotle offers can be cast into syllogistic form. What the correct interpretation is of the role assigned to the syllogism in the *Posterior Analytics* is uncertain and too large a topic to consider here. These results are based on attention to methodological features of Aristotle's theory of inquiry in the *Posterior Analytics* which by themselves set it apart from the methods of dialectic, independently of reference to the role of the syllogism.

10. Scientific method in the *Analytics* and *Physics*

It is worth asking finally whether the degree of conformity to the *Posterior Analytics* of the passages we have considered in the *Generation of Animals* is matched widely by other passages in this work and

---

[59] Aristotle uses the term *gonē* here, but clearly as a synonym for *sperma* in the sense in focus earlier, as, e.g., at 723b26. Cf. 724b12ff., where *gonē* is used when *sperma* is assigned another sense.

elsewhere in Aristotle's special scientific treatises. It would be easy to show that it is.[60] But a special question remains concerning the *Physics*. Owen argued, as noted above, that it was the *Physics*, in particular, by contrast with the biological works and others, which employs dialectic as its method. In making this claim Owen wanted, primarily, to contrast the dialectical method of the *Physics* with a more empirical method in the biological works. We have already found reason to doubt that Aristotle was committed to this contrast. But Owen also meant to contrast the dialectical method of the *Physics* with the method of the *Posterior Analytics*. One reason for doubting that this contrast can be maintained is that the brief recommendations on method found in the opening chapter of the *Physics* conform to those spelled out more fully in the *Posterior Analytics* but not to anything required by dialectic.[61] More specifically, it can also be shown that the discussion which Owen took to be primary confirmation of his view – Aristotle's inquiry into the nature of place in *Physics* IV – conforms at crucial points to those distinctive methodological requirements of the *Analytics* which are exhibited in the *Generation of Animals*.

Aristotle opens his inquiry by specifying the questions which he wants to answer: 'whether or not place exists, and how it exists and what it is' (208a27–8; cf. *APo.* II.1). He first indicates, as he does in his inquiry into the nature of sperma, how we grasp initially *that* place exists.

Everyone takes it for granted (*hupolambanousi*)[62] both that the things that are are somewhere...and that the most common and ordinary change is change of place – what we call movement. But the question *what* place is presents many difficulties. (208a29–33)

Thus, we are all initially aware of the existence of place by being aware of where things are and of their movements to and from places (cf. 208b1–2, 32–3, 211a12–13). However, 'from all the data (*tōn huparchontōn*) the same thing is not apparent (*phainetai*) to all those who study the subject' (208a33–4). Various further data sometimes taken to also manifest the existence of place as a thing of a certain sort (208b1–209a2) or to indicate to what general kind (*genos*) it

---

[60] For example, Aristotle introduces sequences of definitions of the other main *archai* in *GA*, male and female, which correspond in type to the sequence of definitions of sperma. Briefly, in I.2 716a13–31 Aristotle starts by indicating what 'we say' a male and a female are. His accounts focus on the familiar distinctive functions associated with the familiar distinctive sexual parts of the two sexes. By IV.1 766a16–b26 he has reached his theoretically basic account of sex differentiation (based on the difference in heat of the seminal residues of the two sexes) on the basis of which he can explain why the sexes have these separate functions and these parts to accomplish them in the familiar cases.

[61] See above at n. 18.

[62] The terminology here is, again, that of the *Analytics*. See 71a12 and above at n. 51.

belongs (209a2–b17) give rise to conflicts and puzzles. This is just to say, in the terminology of the *Analytics*, that the mode of our knowledge *that* place exists (cf. 208a29) is not yet adequate to best facilitate the search for what it is. Aristotle critically reviews these further data which are based on received views in *Physics* IV.2–3. He argues against certain received views mainly by appeal to others that are more obvious. For example:

> The place of each thing is neither a part nor a state of it but is separate from it. For place is taken to be something such as a jar is – since a jar is a movable place. But a jar is no part of the thing. (209b27–30)

> How could a thing be moved to its proper place if place were its matter or its form? It is impossible that what has no reference to movement nor to up or down could be place. Place must be looked for among things with such properties. (210a2–5)

The result of this dialectical review is to settle on certain things about place which 'we can take it for granted (*labōmen*) seem truly (*dokei alēthōs*) to belong to it in its own right (*kath' hauto*)' (210b32–4). This section of Aristotle's discussion of place thus corresponds to the second section of Aristotle's discussion of sperma, where he reviews received opinions to determine just what it is on which our knowledge *that* sperma exists is properly based. He characterizes the features in question here as properties of place 'in its own right', invoking the terminology of the *Analytics* (84a12ff.) to indicate that these are at least explicable properties of place and, as such, ones which facilitate the search for *what* the thing is (93a21ff.; cf. *de An.* 402b21ff.). This leads us to expect that the subsequent account of *what* place is will be one which explains *why* these properties characterize place. This is just what we do find (see, for instance, 212a20–30 with 210b34ff.), as Aristotle himself indicates we will (211a7–9).

This brief overview of some of the main structural features of Aristotle's discussion of place is not intended to account for every significant methodological aspect of it. It does, however, isolate features of the discussion which conform to the procedures for scientific inquiry laid down in the *Analytics* but are not based on anything appropriate in dialectic. Aristotle's critical review of received opinion is clearly dialectical but as with his corresponding discussion of sperma his main aim is to find not simply an account of place which is *consistent* with a certain dialectically defensible body of received opinion about it – which is the most that dialectic requires – but also an account which explains *why* these things are true of it.[63]

---

[63] David Charles, Wolfgang Detel, Cynthia Freeland, Allan Gotthelf, James Lennox and Richard Sorabji made very helpful contributions to this paper.

7
First principles in
Aristotle's *Parts of Animals*

ALLAN GOTTHELF

Introduction

It is often maintained that Aristotle's practice in such explanatory treatises as the *Parts of Animals* does not correspond to the theory of science presented in the *Posterior Analytics*. Two major respects in which this is so, it is held, are (i) the absence in *PA* of the explicit syllogisms in which, according to *APo.*, the explanations are to be cast, and (ii) the absence in *PA* of the axiomatic structure of explanation *APo.* calls for.

Writing of the second point in his little book on *Aristotle* (1982), Jonathan Barnes explains that

Aristotle's scientific treatises are never presented in axiomatic fashion. The prescriptions of the *Posterior Analytics* are not followed in, say, the *Meteorology* or the *Parts of Animals*. These treatises do not lay down axioms and then proceed to deduce theorems; rather, they present, and attempt to answer, a connected series of problems. (37)

Barnes' formulation makes it clear that he takes the requirement that proper science have an axiomatic structure to mean that it is to be *presented* in a certain way – with its first principles presented first, and labeled as such, and its deductions following sequentially, 'in the geometrical manner'. Similarly, the requirement of the full theory of *APo.* that the deductions be syllogistic in form, Barnes and others take to be a requirement that they be presented in explicit syllogisms. The absence of explicit syllogisms and of an explicit axiomatic structure is the basis of the twofold discrepancy between the *APo.* theory and the *PA* practice. How is this discrepancy to be explained?

In 'Aristotle's theory of demonstration' (Barnes 1975b), Barnes proposed that while the *APo.* theory was a theory of how to present and impart a completed science, the biological (and other scientific) treatises were a record of 'research', 'progress-reports', 'the sharing of tentative...explorations'. As such they had a 'rich and variegated' methodology of their own, neither syllogistic in form nor axiomatic in structure.[1] Since the scientific treatises did not aim to be the sort of thing *APo.* described, there was no conflict. One problem with this view, which scholars familiar with the biological treatises noticed, was that these treatises did not seem very tentative, and that they were less the presentation of 'research' into facts than of explanations of facts previously gathered, and that as explanations they invited, after all, comparison with the theory of explanation in *APo.*

In 'Proof and the syllogism' (1981), Barnes argued that a pre-syllogistic theory of demonstration could be detected in *APo.*, and that the lateness of the development of the syllogistic would explain its absence in the biological works; this invited anew consideration of the relationship between the theory of demonstration (now shorn of the syllogism) and the scientific practice.[2] This pre-syllogistic theory would of course require of Aristotelian science an axiomatic structure, but on the apparent absence of this in the scientific treatises Barnes said nothing in this paper. However, in his *Aristotle*, Barnes offered a new solution:

Why are the *Meteorology* and the *Parts of Animals*, say, not presented axiomatically? The answer is disconcertingly simple. Aristotle's system is a grand design for finished or completed science...Since the treatises are not the final presentations of an achieved science, we should not expect to find in them an orderly succession of axioms and deductions. Since the treatises are intended, in the end, to convey a systematic science, we should expect them to indicate how that science is to be achieved. And that is exactly what we do find: Aristotle was a systematic thinker; his surviving treatises present a partial and unfinished sketch of his system. (38–9)

Barnes offers no argument for this view of *PA* (and the other scientific treatises), but he does raise for us a question rarely given much attention: *is* there in fact an implicit axiomatic structure, or the outlines of one, in treatises such as *PA*, which might reflect movement towards a system of the sort *APo.* calls for? If the solution to the apparent discrepancy between theory and practice in Aristotelian science is to be found in the relationship between an achieved ideal and its partial realization, we will need a very full picture of the practice, to see if in fact it is a realization, even if only partial, of that ideal. We will need to take a close look at the actual

[1] Barnes 1975b: 77, 84.
[2] 'For centuries, learned Aristotelians sought and found the influence of the *Posterior Analytics* on the scientific πραγματεῖαι; more recently, impressed by the Syllogistic content of the *Posterior Analytics*, scholars have tried to divorce that work from the rest of the Aristotelian corpus. If, instead, we liberate Apodeictic from the shackles of Syllogistic, we may again look for the influence of the *Analytics* on Aristotle's scientific and philosophical practice...I do not pretend to know how much we shall find; but I now think, as I once did not, that the search is worth undertaking' (Barnes 1981: 58).

explanations in *PA*, at their internal structure and their premises, and at their connections to each other. We will need to ask if there is, even implicit in the treatise, anything like an axiomatic structure to these explanations, and anything like the principles which such a structure demands. It is these questions I would like to address in this paper.

This is a large inquiry, and I can only make a first entry into it. I will attempt to show that there *is* an implicit axiomatic structure to the explanations in the *Parts of Animals*, and will attempt to identify the sorts of first principles embedded in this structure. Such an examination will inevitably use many of the concepts and categories of the *Posterior Analytics*, but I want so far as possible to avoid, at least in the bulk of this paper, the many interpretative controversies that burden the study of that difficult treatise, and to focus instead on *PA* itself, and the explanatory structure to be found there. In the last part of this paper I will make some general remarks about possible connections between the two treatises, focusing especially on the question of the absence of both explicit syllogisms and an explicit axiomatic structure in *PA*, but these will be brief and largely independent of the analysis I offer of the structure of *PA* itself.

In asking whether there is an implicit axiomatic structure to the explanations in *PA*, we need to start with a quite general notion of such a structure, so as to be open to the variety of sorts of 'axioms' we might find. In general, we are asking, roughly, whether the explanations to be found in *PA* are based on first principles, i.e. on facts about the animal kinds whose possession of certain features are being explained, which facts are not themselves explained by reference to more basic facts. To take one possible variety, are there, for instance, features of an animal kind that explain other features of that kind without themselves being explained by features of that kind? Aristotle's theory of science would call for such features, and in *APo.* he treats statements expressing the possession by entities of such features, when properly formulated, as definitions, and includes such definitions among the first principles of a science. But are there animal definitions in *PA*, and do they play such roles? It has often been claimed, and not without reason, that there are no definitions of animal kinds in *PA*, or anywhere in the biological treatises. That the theory of science calls for such definitions does not entail that they will be present in the scientific practice. Aristotle might, for instance, have come to believe after doing his biological work that explanations are not linear and directed in the way just described but, say, circular, animal features being explained ultimately in terms of each

other, or in a highly localized and contextual way. I have already
implied that I do not myself believe this, but that is the sort of
alternative our argument will have to exclude.

Biology as demonstrative science: *PA* I and *GA* II.6

Though I have referred to *PA* as a whole, it is strictly only the last
three books, *PA* II–IV, that offer explanations of biological phenomena, and can be counted as 'biology proper'. *PA* I is, as David Balme
has called it, 'a string of papers', a series of methodological discussions, probably put together as an introduction to the zoology
as a whole.[3] Its use cannot be a substitute for a close look at the actual
workings of II–IV. At this stage, I want to draw on *PA* I only for a
picture of how Aristotle himself conceived the nature and structure
of his enterprise in II–IV and the rest of the biology proper, and then
turn immediately to II–IV themselves.

It seems clear from *PA* I, we may note first, that Aristotle himself
saw *PA* II–IV as offering (and not just aimed at) *epistēmē*, in the sense
of a systematic knowledge of causes, and as containing demonstrations.

The famous motivating passage of 1.5, for instance, recommends
attention to the lectures that are immediately to come – such as the
PA series, one would presume – first of all on grounds of the greater
epistēmē it offers (645a2) in providing what is an immeasurably
pleasant knowledge of *causes* (a9–10). Though the heavenly bodies
are much greater in value than the living things 'which grow beside
us', these living things, because 'the information about them is better
and more plentiful, take the advantage in *epistēmē*' (645a1–2).

The enterprise being introduced and characterized in 1.1 is called
phusikē epistēmē at 640a2,[4] where the mode (*tropos*) of demonstration
(*apodeixis*) and of necessity which its contents possess are distinguished
from those of the *theorētikai epistēmai* (probably, or primarily, the
mathematical sciences[5]). The immediately preceding paragraphs,
and in fact most of 1.1, make clear that this *epistēmē* embraces a
knowledge of causes, and the fact that the contrast between biology
and mathematics comes parenthetically within a discussion of the
necessity that obtains in nature, and the way the contrast is characterized, ensure that the *apodeixeis* of *phusikē* are no less *apodeixeis*

---

[3] Balme 1972: v, 69. Because of its methodological character, *PA* I can serve as a bridge
between the general theory of *APo.* and the practice in *PA* II–IV and the rest of the biology
proper. See, e.g., below 188–9 and James Lennox, ch. 5 above, 114–15.
[4] Only 'in effect', if *epistemōn* does not as noun carry back all the way to *phusikēs*, but the
enterprise is in any case explicitly called *epistēmē* at 639a3.   [5] Cf. Grene 1985.

(if somewhat different in character) than those of mathematics.[6] And we can connect these characterizations of the explanations of natural science to *PA* II–IV via the specification at 640a33ff. of the modes of explanations of the parts of animals required by their hypothetically necessary (or generally teleological) character. That these are the proper modes is inferred (*dio*: 640a33) from the arguments for teleology which surround the discussion of necessity in nature; and as we will see later, these are in fact the major modes of explanation used in *PA* II–IV.[7]

Both Wolfgang Kullmann and James Lennox have pointed us to the serious use of *apodeixis* (with its *peri hōn* and its *ex hōn*) in *HA* I.6.[8] We might also note a most interesting passage in *Generation of Animals* II.6 (beginning at 742b17), where Aristotle criticizes people 'like Democritus' who accept the observation that 'this is how they are always formed' as a sufficient explanation of certain matters on the grounds that they are eternal and thus can have no prior principle:

[b23] On this line of argument...there will be no demonstration (*apodeixis*) of any single one of the 'eternal' things. It is obvious, however, that demonstrations of many of these (some of them things which *always* come to be, some things which *always* are) do in fact exist. For instance the angles of a triangle are *always* equal to two right angles, and the diagonal of a square is *always* incommensurable with the side; in both of these cases we have something 'eternal', yet there is a cause for them and they are demonstrable (*estin autōn aition ti kai apodeixis*). Thus it is right to say that we cannot undertake to try to discover a starting-point (a first principle) in all things and everything; but it is not right to deny the possibility in the case of all the things that *always* are and that *always* come to be; it is impossible only with the first principles of the eternal things, for of course the first principle does not admit of demonstration (*apodeixis*) but is apprehended by another mode of cognition. Now with those things that are 'immutable' (*en tois akinētois*) the first principle is the essence (*ti esti*); but in the things which come into being, immediately there are several, and another manner of principle and not all the same.[9] Among them the source whence the movement comes must be reckoned as one, and that is why the heart is the first part which all blooded animals have...(742b23–36; tr. Peck, with one change, noted)

This is an important passage for our purposes. First of all, Aristotle speaks clearly and self-consciously of the presence of demonstration

[6] See 'Additional note on *PA* I.1 639b21–640a9', below 197–8.
[7] See below 188–9 and the essays in Part III (*passim*).
[8] 491a13–14. Cf. Kullmann 1974: 81 n. 8 and Lennox ch. 5 above, 101–2.
[9] Here I have softened Peck's translation, which reads: 'but as soon as we begin to deal with those things that come into being through a process of formation, we find there are several first principles – principles, however, of a different kind and not all of the same kind'. The Greek of the last clause is τρόπον δ' ἄλλον καὶ οὐ πᾶσαι τὸν αὐτόν, and means that the *additional* principles in this case are of another manner from the *ti esti*, and that these additional ones are different from each other. There is no reason to exclude the *ti esti* from being one of the principles of *gignomena*.

(*apodeixis*) not only in mathematics but also in natural science, and in the study of animals in particular ('things which always come to be': 742b30–1). Furthermore, he makes clear that the demonstrations in both cases have *first principles* (*archai*); it must be stressed that the reference is not only to *archai* of the subject matter but also to *archai* of the demonstrations: as Peck notes *ad loc.*, there is a clear reference in the words *tēs gar archēs allē gnōsis kai ouk apodeixis* to standard Aristotelian doctrine about the first principles of demonstration in the *Posterior Analytics*, *Metaphysics*, and *Nicomachean Ethics*. Finally, the passage suggests (as one might well expect) that propositions about the *archai* in the sense of the *causes* of a subject matter will be *archai* of the demonstrations regarding that subject matter, and that this is so as much in biology, where several causes are operative, as in mathematics, where only one is.[10]

In sum, it seems clear that Aristotle himself is happy to speak the language of *epistēmē*, *apodeixis*, and first principles in talking of his existing biological work.

This language is too pervasive and self-conscious to be dismissed, but we are entitled to ask with how much precision and technical richness it is being used. And it is here that we must turn to the biology itself, exploring the reference of the language directly as our best guide to its sense.

The overall structure of *PA* II–IV

Let us begin with a descriptive overview of the whole of *PA* II–IV, so that we may see features of the structure of the whole, and place our discussions of individual passages and explanations properly within that structure.

PA II begins with the three *suntheseis* (Peck: 'levels of composition'): of elementary powers into simple compounds, of these into the uniform parts of animals, of those into the non-uniform parts.[11] After

[10] This passage is interesting for at least one other reason as well. As discussed in my 'Additional Note on *PA* 1.1 639b21–640a9' (below 197–8), it seems to reveal Aristotle's sensitivity to the issue of how non-eternal objects could be the subject of a demonstrative science, and suggests, as I propose in that Note, his solution: though we do not have objects which 'always are' we do have objects which 'always come to be', and that will somehow be sufficient to guarantee the reference of the subject term in the propositions of the science. For details, see below 197.

There are other places in the biology where Aristotle betrays sensitivity to concerns expressed in the *Posterior Analytics*. E.g., at 747b27–748a14 (and ff.) he considers and rejects an explanation of the sterility of mules on grounds that it does not proceed from the principles proper to the subject matter. (The explanation also rests on premises that are false, but that is a *second* difficulty.) Here too the term *apodeixis* is used, for what this proffered explanation would be if successful.

[11] The immediate beginning places *PA* II–IV relative to the *historiai* concerning the animals (probably, though not necessarily, our *HA*), as investigating (*episkepteon*) 'on account of

some arguments (reminiscent of 1.1) that each level is for the sake of the succeeding, Aristotle turns to the last two levels, as the basic division between parts which controls the structure of the three books. He first explains why animals must have uniform parts at all, and non-uniform parts at all (cf. 646b35ff.), then explains why sense-organs must be uniform, and why viscera (especially the heart) must be in one way uniform and another non-uniform, thus distinguishing them from the true organs (*organika*), which are simply non-uniform.

At this point (our[12] ch. 2) begins the study of the uniform parts, which are immediately divided into the soft and fluid, and the hard and firm. The various sorts of cause the uniform parts may have (as matter or as nutriment for the non-uniform, or as residue of nutriment) are listed, and the existence of differences within each type noted, with the observation that we should expect (*hupolēpteon*) them to be explained as required for the functions and in general the *ousia* of the animals that have them, or as making their working better than it would be without them.[13] The part-by-part review then begins, and blood is first, but Aristotle is not long into the discussion when he announces the need to distinguish the various ways in which things can be hotter or colder, and more solid (or dry) or fluid, for the reason (to be discussed below) that 'the nature of many things is referred to these'.

Finally the review actually commences. Returning to blood, Aristotle discusses one by one across chs. 3–9 first the more fluid, then the more solid uniform parts, stating 'what each is and on account of what causes' (e.g. 651b13–19, 652a19–21). From 11.10 until the end the focus is on the non-uniform parts, with the sequence as

what causes' the parts of each animal are as they had been said there to be. The passage has the ring of the lecture room, and may well be placing 11–1v relative to a previous course based on (something like) our *HA*. But it is interesting that we are asked to put aside (*chōrisantas kath' hauta*) what was said there, since as David Balme has observed, 11–1v quotes all the data which it explains (referring us to the *historia* or the *historiai* only for additional descriptive information not relevant to the present explanatory task).

12 I say 'our' because the chapter divisions have no ancient authority, and are not found in the manuscripts, nor in any printed edition before the second Basel edition of 1539. The Basel divisions, which were taken over by Bekker, are identical to those in the 1492 Venice edition of Theodorus Gaza's Latin translation of the biology, *De Animalibus* (= *HA*, *PA*, *GA*), in which we are told that 'Sebastianus Manilius Romanus recognouit & per capita disposuit'. The great majority of these mirror the unnumbered divisions produced via enlarged initials in the first printed edition (Venice 1476), prepared just before G.'s death, though R. redid a significant minority. Whether G. himself produced the 1476 division, however, is unclear. (My thanks to the British Library for making all these wonderful editions so easily available.) It is worth remembering that our chapter divisions are the construct of late Medieval or Renaissance editors, and not Aristotle's own, and reading the text right through them to see if its import changes. Sometimes it does.

13 ...τὰ μὲν πρὸς τὰ ἔργα κὰι τὴν οὐσίαν ἑκάστῳ τῶν ζῴων, τὰ δὲ πρὸς τὸ βέλτιον ἢ χεῖρον...(648a15–16; cf. 647b29–30).

follows. Aristotle begins by identifying the 'most necessary' (non-uniform) parts in all animals[14] – that which receives food, that which expels residue, and that in between, 'in which is the *archē* of its life' (655b37). The increasing complexity of animals, as we compare them with plants and move up the scale to man, is noted, and man's sharing in the divine, the relative familiarity of his external parts, and the correspondence of his 'up' and 'down' with the normal 'up' and 'down' of spatial direction are given as reasons for beginning with him. (It is not that all of man is done first, but that the list is taken from man, and for each part man's is dealt with first, then others, accordingly as they are essentially the same, or different from man's.[15]) Though he does not say he is doing so, Aristotle considers for the time being only the blooded animals, leaving the bloodless for much later.

The review of non-uniform parts starts at the top and works down. Aristotle takes a portion of the body at a time, first the head, then the neck, and looks outside then inside.[16] Within each portion the order is mostly, but as we will see later, by no means completely, from top down. Having finished the internal parts in the neck area, he moves not to the chest, or the trunk generally, but directly to the internal parts in that area – the viscera. In each case, the tendency, as James Lennox has shown above,[17] is to start with common features, and with the widest class possessing them, then with differences – e.g. first with the possession of horns as such as in the class of animals that have them (carefully delineated), then with why some have one horn, some two, etc. Existing animal groupings are made use of to facilitate the identification of the widest classes possessing each feature. For instance, the classification into *megista genē* (cf. *HA* 1.6 *init.*), and the broad divisions between vivipara and ovipara, and between land and water animals, are in evidence, but the review within a part is not rigorously by any one of these divisions. Rather, the animals are, as David Balme has said (above p. 88), 'grouped and regrouped', according to the needs of widest-class generalization for each difference of that part.

---

[14] The subject of the sentence is actually all 'complete' (*teleia*) animals, but see below nn. 38, 43.

[15] Cf. *HA* I. 491a19–25 on doing man first and going top to bottom. The 'up' and 'down' of spatial direction is given, of course, by the outermost sphere and the center of the earth. Biological 'up' and 'down' is given functionally (*ergōi*): the 'up' is the direction of 'the part from which is derived the distribution of nutriment and [thus] the growth of each thing', the 'down' 'the part in which it finally ends'. In animals, then, the 'up' is where the mouth is, in plants, where the roots are. Cf. *IA* 4 705a27–b8 and Lennox 1985b.

[16] In his Loeb edition (1961: 15–18) Peck tabulates the parts discussed.

[17] Ch. 5 above, 109–14; cf. Gotthelf 1987a.

After completing the viscera and related internal parts, Aristotle moves to the bloodless animals, introducing them by their lack of viscera. He offers an explanation of that lack, deriving it from their nature as bloodless, notes the four main kinds, and begins a review of their internal parts part by part (or area by area), apparently using the cephalopods as the standard (comparable to man in the blooded), and perhaps going top down, but looking first at the parts concerned with nutrition (681b13–15), then those that serve as sense organs. At 682a30–4 we are told that we have now completed our discussion of the internal parts of animals, and are ready for the external, first in the bloodless, then in the blooded, picking up where we left off with the latter only after the shorter discussion required of the bloodless.[18] That is what we get, in a general review, largely across *megista genē* (plus man), but often moving down to differences within large kinds, of head and neck, overall layout and degree of uprightness, limbs, breasts, trunk features, excretory organs, rear parts and feet. After overall layout and degree of uprightness, the discussion was restricted to the vivipara, so it now proceeds to the ovipara, focusing first on the quadrupeds and snakes, then birds, then fish. The cetacea are introduced as animals that, with respect to being water or land animals, 'tend to both sides',[19] and that invites a brief explanatory review of the external parts of some others – seals, bats, and the Libyan ostrich. *PA* ii–iv then closes with the notice that 'We have discussed, concerning the parts of all of the animals *kath' hekaston* (Peck: [taken] severally), on account of what cause each is present to them. Having determined that, the next thing in order is to deal with the things that pertain to their modes of generation.'

This is a complicated structure, but in essence it is: part by part, first uniform, then non-uniform; within the non-uniform, separating the blooded and the bloodless animals, then proceeding top to bottom (as measured by man), moving from external to internal and back. Within a part it moves from the general explanation of why its possessors have it at all to an explanation of why possessors of one type have that type and those of another that other. There is nothing prima facie axiomatic about this structure, but I would like us to take a closer look at some of its features.

1. If explanations in a (sub-branch of a) science depend on premises drawn from a prior (branch of that) science, it would be

[18] This may be lecture-preparer's glue, as may 685b27–8, introducing the resumption of discussion of externals in the blooded, since the latter discussion has the feel of a self-contained essay, with striking echoes of the *Timaeus*, and our *PA* ii–iv could well be an amalgam, as i + ii–iv surely is, but this does not matter for our purposes.
[19] David Balme's rendering of *epamphoterizein*. Peck's 'dualizing' is misleading, as the animals do not in fact fall into both of the two contrary groups.

no surprise if those premises were presented first, especially if the scientist were sensitive to the logical order of his explanations. There is some reason to think this is why Aristotle distinguishes the three *suntheseis* as early as he does, and why he discusses first the elementary powers, then uniform parts, then non-uniform parts. As we saw, he says explicitly that his reason for discussing the elementary powers is that 'the nature of many things is referred to these'. And that is the case in his own explanations. Thus at 649b20ff. he makes use of his discussion of the various ways things can be hotter, colder, more fluid or solid, with a statement of the way in which blood is hot, thus permitting the establishment of (part of) the definition of blood, which is part of his aim. The establishment of this partial definition is not of course a demonstration, but the definition plays a role in the explanation of some of the features of blood,[20] and makes possible the explanation of certain psychic differences (e.g. in intelligence, and readiness to anger) in terms of differences of fluidity or heat in the blood.[21]

When a sense of 'hot' or 'fluid' plays a role in explanation, it does so by way of a premise regarding the actions of the power conceived in that sense. Thus certain fluids when deprived of heat congeal, other thicker ones when deprived of heat thin out; moist earth is in the former category: 'the cold expels the heat and makes the fluid evaporate'. 'Passion produces heat; and solids, when they have been heated, give off more heat than fluids.'[22] Premises about the elementary powers also occur in explanations of the presence or features of several of the uniform parts besides blood. Thus, suet congeals because it is earthy, lard does not because it isn't.[23] Things that are brittle or fluid cannot pass without a break right through something like a whole spine.[24] Appropriate amounts of hot and cold will balance in an intermediate position.[25] A certain process occurs according to the principles involved in rain-showers.[26] Heat does not pass as easily through thick earthy as through thinner fleshy material.[27] And so on.[28]

---

[20] E.g. that it congeals when separated from the body (649b28–9). At 651a5ff. basic facts about hot and cold help to explain how congealing takes place, and why some blood (i.e. the blood of some animals) congeals more than (that of) others.

[21] II.4 *passim.*

[22] 649b28ff.; 651a7–10 (and surroundings); 650b35–6 (and surroundings).

[23] 651a27–9, 33–6.   [24] 651b32–6.

[25] 652a31–3, and II.7 *passim.*   [26] 652b34–653a8.   [27] 654a3–8.

[28] As I discuss below (188–9), in most cases in *PA* II–IV, premises about the matter function in explanation only in conjunction with premises about the final cause. But, as John Cooper shows below, all explanations that appeal to hypothetical necessity, and most teleological explanations generally, do make use of distinct premises about the nature of the matter. (Ch. 9 below, 255–64, with which cf. David Balme, ch. 10 below, 283–5.)

2. The order of discussion of the uniform parts is not without explanatory purpose. Blood is surely discussed first because it is an *archē* for the rest. It is explained as present to provide nourishment to the other parts, being the *eschatē trophē* (Peck: final form which the nourishment assumes).[29] Lard and suet are blood that has gone through certain types of concoction, as is marrow, and the explanation of marrow's presence draws explicitly on the prior explanation of blood's.[30] Bone and certain other hard materials are for the sake of supporting flesh or its analogue, itself necessary to all animals as the organ of the defining sense of touch.[31]

3. Surely at least part of the reason that non-uniform parts are discussed after uniform is that explanations of the former sometimes make use of facts about the latter. Thus, the explanation of blood-vessels and of the heart presupposes that of blood, as does one part of the explanation of the liver and spleen.[32]

4. The reason the bloodless are treated separately from the blooded is probably that most of their parts are the same as those of the blooded only by analogy. They are treated after the blooded probably because the blooded are better known and understood (compare the explanation for treating man first among the blooded), as evidenced by how many of their parts have no name of their own

---

[29] 650b2–3, 651a15. In the latter passage Aristotle says this makes the blood the matter of the (blooded) living thing. For an interesting discussion of this see Cynthia Freeland, ch. 15 below, 398–404. The argument that concludes with 650b2–3 seems an example of one that establishes blood's function rather than one that uses that knowledge to explain its presence: surely blood isn't the final form of nourishment *because* (explanatorily) it is the only fluid in the blood-vessels. That is what helps us to *know* that blood must be nourishment, but does not *explain* it. The demonstration itself is probably signaled by the *heneka* in b2, but is not actually given. Cf. below, 179 and n. 34.

[30] Lard and suet: 651a20–4; cf. 651b28–30, 652a7–10. Marrow: 651b20, 652a2–23. Note the definition of marrow which results (a19–23) from the investigation: it mentions material, final, efficient, and (as some combination of the preceding) formal causes. This is a fairly rare paradigm of the sort of definition of a part that each of the discussions of the uniform parts, and probably of the non-uniform parts as well, is aimed at. It presupposes, and can probably be seen as embedded in, the explanation of the presence of marrow that precedes, and as such has at least an affinity with the second of the three types of definition in *APo.* II.8–10. Cf. Robert Bolton's discussion of the three forms of definition in ch. 6 above, 142–6, and cf. below 179 (with n. 34) and 181.

[31] Flesh and its analogue: 653b20–30 (cf. b22–3:...*ton logon...horizometha*). Bone and its analogues: 653b30–6 and ff. (to end of II.8), 654b27–9 (and most of II.9).

[32] Heart and blood-vessels: 665b9–16, and III.4–5 *passim*. Liver and spleen: 670a20–1. Here too, many facts about the presence of uniform parts will be explained by reference to the needs of the non-uniform parts, and someone might therefore expect discussion of the latter to precede discussion of the former. But, as noted above (n. 28), these explanations via hypothetical necessity presuppose certain facts about the uniform parts, and it is certainly reasonable that these facts should be stated first. (Certain facts about the matter will only be explained teleologically, by reference to the needs of the whole organism, and the irreducible *dunameis* for the fulfillment of those needs, but again those explanations will presuppose the sort of facts about the matter given in the early parts of *PA* II.)

but are called '*x*-analogue', where '*x*' is the name in the blooded case.

5. Finally there is surely an explanatory basis to treating the common features of a part (including its presence at all) before treating the differences in that part. For instance, horns are present in animals which have them because they have no other suitable defense and there is earthy material available to make them. The explanation why some animals have one horn, others two, presupposes that horns as such come from earthy material, and refers to the amount of such material available. Where there can be only one, its placement in the center is explained by reference to the generic defensive function.[33]

In sum, then, *PA* II–IV has a structure which is at least amenable to exhibiting relations of priority among demonstrations, and may well have been in part designed for such a purpose.

A representative explanation: the multiple stomachs of ruminants

To see more clearly the different sorts of premises that may appear in the explanations in these books, and to observe the structure more microscopically, it will be useful to look at a particular stretch of text. The discussion of the multiple stomachs in ruminants (in the first part of III.14) will be an interesting test case, as the explanation is unobvious, and referred to in *APo*. (II.14). Before embarking on this, however, I need to make an important general observation about *PA* II–IV.

---

[33] III.2, esp. 662b27, b30–663a8. Aristotle seems to me not to have progressed as far in his explanation of horns as he has with most other organs, since he does not seem to be able to isolate the class of horn possessors, and so has to describe it as including animals that have no means of defense other than horns. It may be that he has independent explanations for why these others have the means of defense they do, and why horn-possessors cannot have any of those, and believes that horns are the only possible means left. But there is no indication of that, and we probably have an example of an obvious way in which *PA* II–IV is incomplete (and was probably thought to be so). But we can see how this sort of incompleteness does not in the least stop the treatise from having the structure which it would have if it were complete in this sense. There is just a gap, and a temporary filler, where the ultimate explanatory differentia(e) of horned animals qua horned will go. But it is worth noting that the filler is not without explanatory value. At its present stage the demonstration has the form 'Horns belong to all vivipara that are not polydactylous which have no other means of defense; viviparousness without polydactility and no non-horn means of defense belongs to all horn-possessors.' ('Horn-possessors': where there isn't a ready-made name for the widest class that possesses a feature *x*, Aristotle often describes the group as 'those which have *x*', and often summarizes by saying 'we have now discussed on account of what causes those which have *x* have *x*'.) As for the useless horns in the deer, Theophrastus was puzzled too: cf. his *Metaphysics* 9 10b11–14 (Ross and Fobes 1929), discussed in Lennox 1985b: 148–9.

Though I have been arguing, and will continue to argue, that *PA* ii–iv has a broadly axiomatic structure, with demonstrations based on first principles, I should make it clear that I do not think that that is all these books contain. A fair amount of the time, what we get are systematic discussions – arguments, actually – aimed at *establishing* what the cause (generally, the function) of the part in question is. Both of these are tasks of Aristotelian science – to establish non-demonstratively the causes and then to demonstrate that they are the causes – and *PA* ii–iv takes them on together, sometimes doing one, sometimes the other.[34] I mention this in part for its place in a picture of the structure of the whole of *PA* ii–iv, and in part because it will help us to understand certain portions of the passage in which Aristotle explains why some animals have one stomach, others more than one, to which we now turn.[35]

It is a long passage, but with apologies I quote it in full, in Peck's translation, so that we can have it before us, and I can refer to it in numbered portions.

[(1) 674a9–12] Below the diaphragm is the stomach, which is placed where the esophagus ends (if there is an esophagus; if not, immediately next to the mouth). Next after the stomach and continuous with it is what is called the 'gut'.

[(2) a12–16] It must be obvious to everyone why all animals have these parts. It is a necessity for them to have some receptacle for the food they take in, and to expel it again when its moisture has been extracted from it; and there must be two different places for these two things – the unconcocted food and the residue; there must also be another place in which the change from one to the other is effected.

[(3) a16–21] Two receptacles, then, one for the incoming food, one for the residue which is no more use – as there is a separate time for these so there must be a separate place. However, it will be more appropriate to go into these matters in our work

---

[34] The arguments aimed at *establishing* what the cause of the part in question is amount, I believe, to attempts to establish the definitions of these parts, in the spirit of *APo.* ii.8–10, much as Robert Bolton explains it in his contribution to this volume (ch. 6 above). According to *APo.*, these arguments should not, of course, be demonstrations of the definitions they establish, and it would be interesting to explore their form in *PA* ii–iv, as Bolton has done above for some of the arguments in *GA* i–ii. Bolton argues, with respect to the theory of *APo.* and the practice of *GA* i–ii, that the definition-establishing arguments are not essentially dialectical, though they may contain dialectical parts, because they rely on empirical data in ways not permitted or countenanced by dialectic proper, and appeal to explanatory relations not properly introduced in dialectic. *Endoxa*, according to Bolton, are often brought in as alternative hypotheses to be examined against, and refuted by, the empirical data, and I now think this is right for the cause-establishing arguments in *PA* ii–iv. (Cf. n. 41 below.) In a very interesting unpublished paper, 'Scientific method in Aristotle's *Meteorology*', Cynthia Freeland has attempted to show the same thing for *Meteorology* i–iii.

[35] Our passage will exhibit one more dimension to the exposition in *PA* ii–iv. In addition to arguments establishing the causes, and demonstrations that exhibit them, will be stretches of text expounding the facts whose explanations are to be given. (Cf. n. 11 above.) Finally, in understanding what is going on in *PA* ii–iv, it must not be forgotten that what we have are lecture notes, or memoranda for students, and not really finished 'treatises', as we are wont to call them.

on generation and nutrition. [(4) a21–7] At the present we must consider the variations (*diaphorai*) that are to be found in the stomach and its subsidiary parts.

The stomach differs both in size and appearance in different animals. Those of the blooded vivipara which have front teeth in both jaws have one stomach; e.g. man, the dog, the lion, and the other polydactyls; so also those that have solid hoofs, e.g. the horse, the mule, the ass; and those which although they are cloven-hoofed have front teeth in both jaws, e.g. the pig – [(5) a27–b7] unless, because of a large body and the character of its food, being, say, not easy to concoct but thorny and woody, it has several, such as the camel. So also have the horned animals, as they have not front teeth in both jaws. Thus also the camel has not the two rows of front teeth either, although it has no horns; this is because it is more necessary for the camel to have several stomachs than to have all these front teeth. So, as it resembles the animals which lack the upper front teeth in that it has several stomachs, therefore the arrangement of its teeth is that which normally accompanies the multiple stomachs: in other words, it lacks these front teeth, as they would be no use to it. And also, as its food is thorny, and as the tongue has of necessity to be of a fleshy character, the nature has made use of the earthy matter saved from the missing teeth to make the roof of the mouth hard. Again, the camel ruminates as the horned animals do, because it has stomachs that resemble theirs. [(6) b7–15] Every one of the horned animals (such as the sheep, the ox, the goat, the deer, and the like) has several stomachs; and the purpose of them is this (*hopōs*): Since the mouth is deficient in teeth, the service which it performs upon the food is deficient; and as one stomach after another receives the food, which is quite untreated when it enters the first stomach, more treated in the next, completely treated in the next, and a smooth pulp in the next. And that is why these animals have several such places or parts, the names of which are (1) the paunch (*rumen*), (2) the net or honeycomb-bag (*reticulum*), (3) the manyplies (*omasum*), (4) the reed (*abomasum*). [(7) b15–17] How these stand in relation to each other as regards position and appearance must be studied both from the *historia* dealing with animals and from the dissections. (674a9–b17; tr. Peck, modified slightly)

The beginning portion, labeled (1), names the next two subjects in the roughly top-to-bottom survey of the viscera in blooded animals, but also notes their physical connections, to each other and to other organs already discussed.[36] This is relevant because such connections are often evidence of causal relation, and of function, or of their lack.[37]

The general explanation for the presence of stomach and gut follows immediately, in portions (2) and (3): (2) explains why there is a need for the organs to do what they do, and (3) explains why there are two separate ones. What these organs do, Aristotle says, is quite obvious to everyone, and the explanation, informally expressed, amounts only to one sentence: 'All animals must have a place where unconcocted food is received for concocting and a place for the residue of concoction prior to its expulsion.'[38] But this statement,

---

[36] The esophagus has already been said to be continuous with the mouth at 650a15 and again at 664a21–5. [37] For an example, cf. n. 41 below.

[38] Peck's translation, and the second *te* in a16 make it sound as if we are getting an explanation for the esophagus as well as the stomach and intestines, but that cannot be right. The esophagus is always described as a *passage* for the food (*poros, di' hou poreutai*; cf. n. 36 above),

simple as it sounds, packs in a great deal, and it will be worth taking some time to see that. Actually, what Aristotle says is obvious to all is not this statement, but an assumed one (or two) which we could supply as follows: 'The stomach is the place for unconcocted food ready for concoction; the gut is the place for the residue of concoction prior to its expulsion.' This is the (joint) fact apparent to all which we are being asked to explain, and we can note that it is a sort of definition of its subject, which serves also, in one form or another, as the conclusion of the explanatory deduction, much as Aristotle says of 'Thunder is noise in the clouds' in *APo.* II.8–10.[39]

I say 'in one form or another' because, as the conclusion in the latter case is sometimes given as 'There is noise in the clouds' (or perhaps: 'Noise belongs to some clouds'), so in our text it is given first as 'All animals have a stomach and intestines', then as 'All animals have a place for unconcocted food ready for concoction and a place for the residue of concoction prior to concoction.' But in our case the second is a scientific advance on the first. The second feeds into the conclusion the identification of what the stomach and intestines do, so that the explanation can go on to show what about the animals that have them (i.e. have organs that do what they do) *necessitates* that they have them, and thus explains *why* they have them.[40]

If it were not 'apparent to all' what stomachs and intestines do, we would probably have been given an argument for this being its function, an argument which would not itself be a demonstration, and which, as indicated above, would combine dialectical examination of alternative hypotheses and appeals to empirical evidence, including the physical connections, or absences thereof, mentioned above.[41] This discovery of what these organs do would at that point have been fed into the original 'nominal'[42] definitions of stomach and

---

as is the mouth at 650b15. Perhaps *einai te tina dei topon en hōi metaballei* is an alternative characterization of the *topon tēs apeptou*. Though the subject of this sentence is the unrestricted 'all animals', what Aristotle says elsewhere may imply a restriction to 'complete animals' (*teleia zōia*) – cf. n. 43 below. Since the discussion from II.10 to IV.4 is in any case focused on the blooded animals, so too may be the quoted proposition.

[39] E.g. 94a7–9. On this see, again, Bolton's discussion, above 143–4, and in Bolton 1976.

[40] A lesson of this is that identifying what an organ does is not sufficient to explain its presence. One must go on to show why the organisms which have it *need* something that does what it does (or are otherwise better off for having it rather than not). It seems too that for Aristotle to call what some organ does its *function* (*ergon*) is for him to say both that it does that, *and* that it is necessary (or better) for the organism that it do that. This has interesting parallels with the contemporary account of functions given by Larry Wright, on which see Section III of my 'Postscript 1986' to ch. 8 below.

[41] For an example see the discussion of the function of the windpipe at 664a35–b19 (and note yet another of Aristotle's humorous plays on words in his concluding sentence).

[42] If Bolton is right to view the 'nominal' definition as involving an assertion of existence: cf. above, 158 n. 55 and Bolton 1976.

intestines, to give the fuller statement that appears in the text, although (and this is important) without any mention of necessity. The assertion of necessity is what makes the statement as we have it part of the explanation.

Interestingly, it is still strictly the conclusion of the explanation but now in proper, modal form. The actual explanation – i.e. of why animals must have such places – is simply assumed, because – I want to suggest, getting back finally to our main purpose – the various premises have been given (and demonstrated) earlier for it to be simple to construct it. For, what is the full explanation? Why must all animals have a place for unconcocted food ready for concoction and a place for the residue of concoction prior to its expulsion? The answer clearly must be first that: 'It is not possible to be (*einai*) or to grow (*auxanesthai*) without food' (655b30–2). The discussion of non-uniform parts, as we noted in our overview, opens, in II.10, with one of Aristotle's usual 'fresh starts', 'beginning first with the things that are first'. And what is first about non-uniform parts is the question of what parts are most necessary (*anankaiotata*) to all animals.[43] The first two mentioned are 'that by which food is received and that by which residues are eliminated',[44] and they get the explanation just quoted. (The third, 'intermediate between these two, is the part in which is the *archē* of its soul'.)

The surrounding context of this premise (viz. that it is not possible to be or to grow without food) makes clear that its intended application is to all living things. Plants we are immediately told get their food from the soil, already concocted, and thus have no place for useless residue. Nor do they have any stomach. (The earth, in effect, is their stomach he says at 650a22.) So the fact about animals

[43] As noted above in n. 14, the subject of the sentence is actually all 'complete' (*teleia*) animals. It is hard to see what the restriction is due to. In his note to 655b29–30, Peck suggests, with references to *GA*, that only the viviparous animals are *teleia*. At 682a34, however, all of the blooded seem to be so called. But then most even of the bloodless have these three 'most necessary' parts, with soul-source in the middle, and even most of the testacea (cf. 681b31–682a2). One has to go, it seems, to the lowest of the low, the poor ascidian (*tēthua*), to find an animal which, though it has distinct openings by which it takes in fluid matter for food and lets out the surplus moisture, 'has no evident residue like the other testacea'. These, and some equally (or more) primitive creatures, the sea-anemones ('the ones called *knides* or *akalēphai*, which are not testacea but fall outside of the *genē* which have been divided off', 681a36–b2), Aristotle says, are barely animals, having as they do several features that make them plant-like, including the lack of residue. The sea-anemones 'tend towards the plants because they are incomplete (*atelēs*) and quickly attach themselves to rocks; and further, because they have no apparent residue though they have a mouth' (681b6–8). Could Aristotle have had (only) *these* creatures in mind when he qualified his statement in II.10?

[44] At this level Aristotle is probably talking more about 'systems', e.g 'mouth–esophagus (if present)–stomach–liver–etc.' and 'intestines–kidney–bladder–etc.' than specifically and only about stomach and intestines.

which distinguishes them from plants, and is central to their mode of nutrition (their 'threptic' soul) is that they concoct their food inside themselves. The argument thus starts with a basic fact about all living things, then adds a basic fact about (in effect) animal soul, then derives the need for certain organ-systems. All this is a general framework within which existence of the stomach and organs is explained, as the organs which perform these necessary functions.

But we should note also another twofold assumption that is made here, and taken over in the explanation of stomachs and intestines, about the metabolic process, namely that food must be *processed* (and in particular 'concocted'), and that the processing leaves a *residue*. These are physiological facts, as it were, having to do (at least in part) with the nature of the uniform parts of which the non-uniform parts are constituted, and with the principles of interaction of the elementary powers. This puts it into a part of *phusikē* wider than the study of animals, the part dealt with in *Generation and Corruption* and in *Meteorology* IV, two treatises in fact referred to early in *PA* II as sources on such issues.[45]

So the initial, general explanation of the presence of stomachs and intestines in the animals that have them makes use of premises (i) about the basic nature of all living things, (ii) about the basic nature of all animals, and (iii) about the interactions of elementary powers, and these with foodstuff and with the uniform parts of animals, which are themselves conclusions of explanations in prior parts of the study of nature.

The part of our passage from III.14 marked (3) attempts to explain why there are two separate organs doing what stomachs and intestines respectively do. It is a brief and cryptic argument, based on the premises that [1] the storing of unconcocted food ready for concoction, and the forming of the residue ready for expulsion, take place at different times, and [2] different times require (or render more advisable) different places. There is some spelling out to be done here, at least of the second premise. But let us pass over that for now, to move on to the explanation of the difference in number of stomachs among animals.

The part of our passage marked (4) identifies two types of difference, then peculiarly moves on to discuss a third; the first two

---

[45] See below 186. Part of the physiological story had been noted already in *PA* II–IV, in connection with the nutritive function of blood, at 650a2ff.: 'Everything that grows must of necessity take food. This food is always supplied by fluid and solid matter, and the concoction and transformation of these is effected by the agency (*dunamis*) of heat...' This is in line with the already noted frequent use of facts about the elementary powers and their interaction throughout the discussion of uniform parts.

are not discussed until much later in the chapter. The third has to do with the number of stomachs. The general explanation spoke as if stomachs come in ones (*hē koilia*); now we learn that while many animals do indeed have only one, many others have several. The question is why, but the first question is which: what correlates with each possibility. First Aristotle catalogues those animals that have one stomach – I have marked that part (4) – then (at the start of (5)) those that have several, noting what each have in common and how they differ. He looks first at how the number of stomachs correlates with the number of rows of teeth and the presence of horns, then at how it correlates with type of feet. Those with one stomach have teeth in both jaws. Those with several stomachs have teeth in only one jaw, and with one exception are all horned. Those with one stomach include all the polydactyls, and all the solid-hoofed, and all those with several stomachs are cloven-hoofed, but the pig is cloven-hoofed and yet has only one stomach, so the decisive factor must be not 'being cloven-hoofed' but 'having one row of teeth'. All we need now is an explanation of the connection between having only one row of teeth and having several stomachs, and that would be easy, since Aristotle has already (III.1) noted that teeth are for mastication, and less mastication should mean that more concoction is required than the normal one stomach can handle. But instead of going on to give that explanation (which he does, finally, in (6)), he spends a good deal of time with the camel.

The reason seems clear: the camel does not have horns, and we know from our discussion of horns (III.2) that it is when an animal needs the limited upper earthy material for horns that it loses one of the two rows of teeth. Yet here is the camel, which does not need horns because its large size provides sufficient defense, and thus it does not have any horns, yet it is missing that row of teeth. It seems as if we have got to understand why the camel has those several stomachs *before* we explain why the rest do, in order to insure the soundness of the latter explanation. And so Aristotle proceeds. The camel, Aristotle seems to infer, would need several stomachs even if it had two rows of teeth, for its food is thorny and woody and thus hard to concoct. That is the source of its need of four stomachs, not its teeth. If it has one row of teeth, it is that given the four stomachs, it no longer needs the second row – and one row tends to go with four stomachs,[46] and anyway, given that hard food, we could use some hard containing material in the mouth, and the tongue has got

---

[46] It would not be amiss to see a vague developmental hypothesis in the background: if they are correlated in being, their production in the generative process is probably connected.

to be fleshy, so let us put it on the roof of the mouth. 'A nature does nothing without a point but always the best from among what is possible to the being of the thing.' O.K. Now we can go on to the several stomachs in the horned animals, and in (6) we finally get that explanation. For details, now, on the other differences among the stomachs of vivipara, we are referred to something like our *HA*, though after some discussion of features of the stomachs of birds and fish which have related explanations to that just given, Aristotle actually turns to the other differences among vivipara.[47]

Three types of first principles

Instead of following Aristotle any further in these explanations, let us step back and take a look at the premises that have been mentioned, alluded to, or otherwise made use of in the explanation of multiple stomachs, and note their provenance. In the general explanation, Aristotle draws on the connection between horns and teeth, demonstrated earlier. That earlier explanation itself drew on the fact that the larger vivipara, though they alone have *some* earthy material available in the developmental process for the construction of hard parts in the upper area, have only a limited amount of such material. The explanation of the camel's stomachs depends on the fact of what it eats, which is a given for this explanation (and not derived, for example from what an antecedently given stomach might be able to process). And the explanation of *its* one row of teeth, and of the hardness of the roof of its mouth, seems to make use of the principle that nature always operates for the best from among what is possible in the construction of a living thing.

Since the 'nature' which operates for the best is just the natures of particular organisms, the application of that premise to the camel presupposes that a camel nature exists. That is to say, teleological explanation of features of camels requires that we posit the existence of camels as ends, on the basis of which we can establish the necessity (or 'at least best'-ness) of those features which are explained by reference to this end. (I will elaborate on this shortly.)

There seem to me to be several groups of premises at work here, which bear on our theme.

   1. There are premises about the elementary powers and their

---

[47] If someone were to argue that a separately written discussion of birds and fish, and the reference to 'the animal *historia* and the dissections' were both inserted between a continuous discussion of stomachs in vivipara, he would get no objection from me, though these things are always hard to decide. (On 'dissections' cf. above 97 n. 16.)

interactions with various uniform compounds of them – and these appear drawn from prior parts of the study of nature. Early in the presentation in *PA* II, as mentioned in our overview above, Aristotle announces the need to distinguish the various ways in which things can be hotter or colder, and more solid (or dry) or fluid, explaining that these are *archai* 'to which the nature of many things is referred' (648a23).

There is almost the identical wording in Theophrastus' *De Causis Plantarum* at 1.21.4. In both Aristotle and Theophrastus these words introduce a review of the different ways in which things can be said to be, or known to be, hotter or colder than each other. To further motivate his discussion of the elementary powers, Aristotle writes a few lines later that it will be important to make this review (and a comparable one for 'dry' and 'fluid'),

> since it seems clear that indeed these (but not roughness and smoothness, or heaviness and lightness, or any such things) are pretty much causes (*aitia*) of death and life, and also of sleep and waking, prime and old age, sickness and health. And this makes good sense, for, as was said previously elsewhere (*en heterois*), these – hot, cold, dry, fluid – are *archai* of the natural elements (*phusikōn stoicheiōn*). (648b4–10; tr. mine, with help from Peck)

The 'elsewhere' is probably *Generation and Corruption*, though the thesis is made use of in *Meteorology* I–III, and IV. (Cf. *GC* II. 2, where we are given an argument for the priority of these contraries over the others, a thesis only asserted here.) The reference to another work at 649a33 is, as Peck notes, almost certainly to *Mete.* IV. Here we have Aristotle drawing on facts established in a prior portion of the general study of nature, in just the way one might expect of a linear, axiomatic-like structure of explanations.[48]

2. There is also here, as I have said, a general principle that for anything with a (formal) nature, its nature does nothing without a point but always acts for the best within what is possible to its being – and there are the posits of the individual natures for all the kinds of animals there are (known to be). Since explanation can take place at various levels of generality, these natures too can be posited

---

[48] When one begins to make close comparisons between the practice in the biology and the theory in *Posterior Analytics*, one will want to ask whether the study of *animals* (or for that matter, animal *parts*, animal *generation*, etc.) is the unit *epistēmē*, or rather the whole study of nature (*phusikē*, 'second philosophy'), or whether in the end it doesn't much matter. At that point one will want to consider the relationship between the studies of the elements in such treatises as *GC* and *Mete.* IV *and* the biology, and perhaps to compare that relationship with the *APo.* account(s) of the relationship between 'superordinate' and 'subordinate' sciences. The biology clearly draws causes from the prior (portion of the) science, though here the borrowed (material) causes are secondary to the (final) causes which belong to the biology itself. See also Bolton, ch. 6 above, 158 n. 56.

at various levels. Thus, the explanation of beaks for example depends on the positing of a bird nature; this would not of course exist separately but only as a component of the natures of the individual bird-forms. Nonetheless, explanation at the level of birds would require the positing specifically of that generic aspect of these individual forms. We thus have the positing not only of the *genos* of animal as such (since some explanation takes place at that level), but also of all the sub-kinds of animals the parts of which get explanations at the level of those sub-kinds by reference to the natures of those sub-kinds. Such posits, even if not given explicitly, are embedded in the use of teleological explanations for the kind in question, and are thus central to the enterprise of *PA* II–IV.[49]

I mentioned that in addition to the posit of the individual formal natures there is a general posit to the effect that these natures do nothing without a point but always for the best. Aristotle himself makes this very observation in a rare explicit identification of first principles in the study of nature, in *IA* 2. At 704b12–17, the principle that 'a nature makes nothing without a point but always the best from among the things possible to the *ousia* for each kind of animal' is said to be among the things we must here posit (*hupothemena*) as we customarily do in *phusikē* when studying 'the works of nature'.[50]

Teleological explanation is licensed jointly, then, by two posits:

[49] I sidestep here some complicated, if fascinating, questions about these posits. First of all, there are many explanations in *PA* where the class of animals whose possession of a feature is being explained does not constitute a *genos* and does not have a name. One example is the class of animals whose possession of four stomachs is being explained in our *PA* III.14 passage; another (a subset of that class) is the widest class of possessors of four stomachs which gets a single explanation, the horned animals. They are identified by a description, and not a name, a common practice in the biology, as David Balme shows in ch. 4 above. I will need to make clear what sort of nature is being posited in such cases.

Now, it may be that the fact that explanation takes place at the level of horned animals is grounds for viewing them as a *genos*, and that raises the question generally of how *genē* are fixed in Aristotle. Here *PA* I.4 is of utmost importance, stating as it does that one should take as one's *genē* those classes which 'have been satisfactorily marked off by popular usage and possess a single nature (*mia phusis*) in common and forms not far separated in them – bird and fish and any other that is unnamed but like the kind embraces the forms that are in it...' (644b1–7, tr. Balme, with 'kind' and 'forms' in place of 'genus' and 'species'). But there is a question of whether *PA* I.4 refers primarily to the initial stages of a science, before causes have been systematically identified, or refers equally to the developed stages. Lying behind this are questions about what counts as a 'single nature', how one grasps these natures initially, and how one establishes that what one took as single natures really are. Some of these issues are discussed in Gotthelf unpublished (1), and in Charles unpublished; cf. also ch. 4 above, 78–89.

[50] ἀρχὴ δὲ τῆς σκέψεως ὑποθεμένοις οἷς εἰώθαμεν χρῆσθαι πολλάκις πρὸς τὴν μέθοδον τὴν φυσικήν...Aristotle names two additional sets of *hupothemena*: the six directions, and the fact that the *archai* of change of place are 'thrusting and pulling' (Peck). In the discussion of family resemblance in *GA* IV.3 Aristotle identifies three *katholou hupotheseis* (768b5–6) required for the discussion, two of which derive from the general theory of interaction presented in *GC* (as the apparent reference at 768b23–4 suggests).

the existence of formal natures (really a set of posits), and the fact
that these natures make nothing without a point but always for the
best among what is possible to the organisms of that form.

That such formal natures are posited in teleological explanation
is made very clear by Aristotle's language in *PA* I. The material
necessity which operates in the living world, Aristotle explains at two
places, is not simple but *ex hupotheseōs*.[51] As John Cooper explains in
his discussion of hypothetical necessity below (ch. 9), 'the hypothesis
relatively to which a hypothetical necessity, in Aristotle's usage, is
necessary is always a goal posited or set up (*hupotethen*) as something
to be achieved' (243). Since Aristotle believes that biological natures
act for an end, Cooper explains, 'the concept of hypothetical
necessity will apply also to natural formations' (244). The application of hypothetical necessity to the explanation of the parts of
animals thus depends *both* on the existence of formal natures *and* on
their acting for the sake of something, i.e. for the best from among
what is possible to things of that formal nature.[52]

We thus have, at the basis of the explanations in *PA* II–IV,
principles pertaining to the matter of animals, drawn from the prior
study of that matter, and principles pertaining to their form and final
cause, embedded in posits of the formal natures of individual animals
(plus a general teleological principle about formal natures). Cooper's
study points the way to an understanding of how these two sorts of
principles interact in these explanations, and thus how these explanations may be understood as demonstrations in a fairly strong sense.

Though, as we have seen, Aristotle is happy to acknowledge with
respect to the elementary powers which constitute the first level of
the matter of animals that 'the nature of many things is to be referred
(*anagetai*) to these *archai*', he is very unhappy with those of his
predecessors who referred *all* things to them.[53] For material natures
by themselves are insufficient to generate the complex plant and
animal forms we find around us; the existence of form is a separate

[51] 639b24, 642a9; cf. 642a33 and *Ph.* II.9 199b34ff.
[52] Cooper rightly makes a distinction between strict hypothetical necessity, which explains
some feature of an animal as *necessitated* by the being or essence of the kind in question,
and explanation by reference to what is better for the kind from among several alternatives
all of which are possible to it. I take it, though, that in the *ouden matēn* principle quoted
in its fullest form in *IA* 2 but mentioned frequently elsewhere (cf. Bonitz 836b28ff.),
Aristotle means to collapse the two sorts of explanation into one. If a nature always makes
what is best from among what is possible to the being of a kind of animal, then surely if
there is only one alternative possible to that being, it will choose that one (rather, say,
than some alternative which would make the animal's being impossible). Cf. Gotthelf
1985b: 44–5 for an occurrence of the principle in which this seems pretty clearly to be
the case.
[53] 639b22, 640b4ff., *GA* v.8 789b2–4, *Ph.* II.8 198b12ff.

principle, and one which acts for the sake of something.[54] Explanations of parts must thus (*dio*, 640a33) begin not from the material natures of the elements which constitute these parts, and the animals of which they are parts, but from the natures of the animal forms themselves:

> Hence we should if possible say that because this is what it is to be a man, therefore he has these things; for he cannot be without these parts. Failing that, we should get as near as possible to it: we should say altogether that it cannot be otherwise, or that it is at least good thus. And these follow...(640a33–b1, tr. Balme)

I substantially follow David Balme (1972: 87) and Cooper (below 254) in finding three teleological and one non-teleological mode of explanation in this passage.[55] The three teleological modes are: (i) of a part as necessary given an essential function because it is *the* organ which performs it; (ii) of a part as necessary given an essential function because it makes some necessary contribution to the performance of that function; and (iii) of a part as not necessary but 'at least' best, given an essential function, because it is one among the possible contributors to some necessary function, and the best of that group. The fourth mode, derivative from these, is of a part (usually a residue or other byproduct) as a materially necessary consequence of the production of parts explained in one of the prior ways.[56]

3. The passage just quoted in which Aristotle outlines the various modes of explanation of the parts of animals (640a33ff.) starts not only from a posit of the existence of an animal kind (in Aristotle's example, man), but from a statement of (some aspect of) *what it is to be* a member of the kind in question (*epeidē tout' ēn to anthrōpōi einai*). This cannot but bring to mind the claim of the *Posterior Analytics* that among the first principles of a demonstrative science are *definitions*. Putting aside again for now the various controversies concerning the *APo.* prescription, let us ask if the explanations of *PA* II–IV rest on definitions.

In our stomachs passage we saw explanations going back to what I loosely called 'the basic nature' of this or that. But does Aristotle in his biology in fact believe that there are features that can be called basic, i.e. features of a kind that explain other features of that kind without themselves being explained by features of that kind? As I

---

[54] Cf. Montgomery Furth, ch. 2 above, 24–5 (with n. 3), 33, and the essays in Part III below.

[55] For further details see Gotthelf 1985b: 28–9 and n. 5.

[56] Other views of this passage may be found in Kullmann 1974: 37 and Sorabji 1980: 155–6. The Balme–Cooper alternative seems supported by the rough parallel at 1.5 645b 28–33, with modes two and three collapsed into this passage's second way, as well as by Aristotle's practice in distinguishing modes (i) and (ii), as Cooper argues. I give some further evidence for this in Gotthelf 1985b, esp. n. 5.

mentioned towards the beginning of this paper, he might, for instance, have come to believe after doing his biological work that explanations are not linear and directed in that way but, say, circular, features being explained in terms of each other, or highly localized and contextual. I think in fact that this is not the case, and that the biology speaks firmly to the existence of such basic features for each authentic kind.

This is a large subject, and there is not space to deal adequately with it here. In outline, the evidence is this. First, there are some eight passages in *PA* II–IV, and one more in *IA*, in which Aristotle explicitly says that some feature of an animal kind is in the *ousia*, or in the *logos ousias*, etc. of that kind, and in every case that feature so identified is at work explaining some other feature of that kind. I have discussed these passages in detail elsewhere,[57] and for now can only present them for your examination, in a literal translation.

(1)   II.8 653b19–27: We must now examine the other uniform parts, and first flesh in those that have flesh, and its analogue in the others; for this [*sc.* flesh-or-its-analogue] is of animals an origin and a body in itself. This is clear also from *the logos, for we define an animal by its having sensation, and first the primary sense, which is touch,* and such a part is the sense organ of this – either its primary organ, as the pupil is of sight, or the organ taken together with that-through-which, as if someone took the whole of the transparent together with the pupil.

(2)   III.6 669b8–12: Generally, then, the lung is for the sake of respiration, though it will be bloodless and such [as has just been described] for the sake of a certain animal kind [*sc.* the ovipara]. But there is no common name in the case of those [which have a lung], not like 'bird' is applied in the case of a certain kind. This is why, just as the being (*einai*) for a bird is out of something, also in these cases *having a lung is present in the ousia.*

(3)   IV.5 678a26–34: The commonly called 'softies' [cephalopods] and 'soft-shells' [crustacea] are very different from those [*sc.* the blooded animals], since they have nothing at all of the nature of viscera. Nor, likewise, do *any* of the bloodless animals. (There are two kinds of the bloodless remaining, the 'potsherd-skins' [testacea] and the insect-kind.) For, none of them has that out of which viscera nature is composed – blood – because *some such condition belongs to their ousiai* for *that some animals are blooded, while others are bloodless, will be present in the logos defining their ousia.*

(4)   IV.6 682a35–b32: Now, then, the insects are all many-footed, in order to make their motion quicker and to counteract their natural slowness and coldness, and those that are especially cold on account of their length are very-many-footed, such as the centipede-kind. Furthermore, because they have many origins [of life-activity], they have their 'insections' and are correspondingly many-footed.

They are insected both on account of the aforementioned causes and in order that they may protect themselves by curling up to avoid injury. For those of them that are long coil themselves up, and this could not happen if they were not insected. Those that do not coil up make themselves harder by pulling their sections together. And it is necessary for them to be insected:

[57] Gotthelf 1985b.

for *having many origins is present in their ousia* and in this they are similar to plants. For, just as plants, they also can live when cut up, though the latter live only a while, whereas the former become complete in nature and two or more in number from one.

[(5)   IV.8 684a32–b1: In lobsters only, whether male or female, it is a matter of chance which claw is bigger. The cause of their having claws is that *they are in the kind that has claws*; but they have them irregularly because they are deformed (Balme: 'imperfect') and do not employ them for their natural use but for walking.[58]]

(6)   IV.9 685b12–16: Now, the others [that have suckers] have two rows of suckers, but one kind of octopus has one row of suckers. The cause of this is *the length and slimness of their nature*, for a narrow one will necessarily have only one row. Thus, it is this way not as being the best but as necessary because of *the particular logos of its ousia*.

(7)   IV.10 686a25–31: Now, man, instead of forelegs and forefeet, has, as we call them, arms and hands. For he alone of the animals stands upright, on account of *his nature and ousia being divine, and the function of that which is most divine is to think and reason*; and this would not be easy if there were a great deal of the body at the top weighing it down, for weight hampers the motion of the intellect and the common sense.

(8)   IV.12 693b2–13: Two legs like man, bent inward like quadrupeds and not outwards like man; and the wings, as the forelegs of quadrupeds, with the convex side outward. They are biped of necessity, for *the ousia of a bird is among the blooded*, and at the same time also winged, and the blooded do not move on more than four points. So birds have four attached parts, just as the other [blooded] ones, i.e. the ones that live and move on the ground; but whereas these have arms and legs (quadrupeds having forelegs), birds instead of forelegs or arms have – uniquely – wings, for they are stretchable out with these, and *being a flier is in the ousia of a bird*.

(9)   IV.13 695b17–25: Fishes do not have attached limbs because *their nature according to the logos of their ousia is being a swimmer*, since nature makes nothing either superfluous or pointless. And since *they are according to their ousia blooded*, because they are swimmers they have fins, while because they do not walk they do not have feet, for the addition of feet is useful for moving on the ground. At the same time it is not possible for them to have four fins and feet as well, or any other such limbs, since they are blooded.

(10)   *IA* 8 708a9–20: The cause of the footlessness of snakes is *both* that nature makes nothing pointless, but always with a view towards the best for each thing from among the things which are possible to it, preserving *the particular ousia and essence of each, and* what we have said earlier, that it is not possible for blooded animals to move with more than four points. For, it is evident from these things that *all blooded animals which are disproportionate in length relative to the rest of the bodily nature, as are the snakes*, cannot possibly be footed. For it is not possible for them to have more than four feet (since then they would be bloodless), and if they had two or four feet they would be pretty much unable to move at all; this way their movement would necessarily be slow and useless.

These are of course only *partial* definitions: David Balme and Pierre Pellegrin are certainly right that there are no full definitions of

---

[58]   I argue in the paper cited in the previous note that this is *not* a generic portion of the lobster's definition, so I bracket the passage, but include it for completeness.

animal kinds offered in the biology.⁵⁹ But partial definitions are all
that *APo.* itself requires.⁶⁰ Interestingly they appear at all levels of
generality, from the (unnamed) blooded and bloodless animals down
to a certain kind of octopus. The suggestion seems to be that for every
level at which there is explanation of features of some animals, there
are features basic (causally primary) at that level, features which
define *at that level* one part of the being of the animals that have the
features explained at that level. What this implies for the existence
of kinds (*genē*) at levels identified only descriptively, and for the posits
at those levels, is not clear (cf. n. 49 above), but the metaphysics of
this are less relevant than the fact that we have in the biology
definitions that serve as principles of demonstration.

Once one notes the existence of some partial definitions, one is
tempted to look for features which play the same role but are not
labeled as so doing. I call these features the 'givens' (for any
kind) – features which though not identified as such in fact serve to
explain features of their possessors without themselves being explained. This is to some extent speculative, of course, since the fact
that Aristotle has not given an explanation of some feature does not
establish that he thought there was none to be given, but as one tries
to isolate such features from a close look at the actual explanations
in *PA* ii–iv, a picture begins to emerge which looks plausible to me
at least. For, it includes all the soul-faculties, in their various
differentiated forms, that *De Anima* identifies as part of the *ousia* of
animals generally, and also those (primarily) non-functional features
that appear in the nine *ousia* passages, such as size, and being blooded
(or bloodless – i.e. possessive of that other, nameless, nutritive fluid).
Also frequently serving as 'givens' in *PA* ii–iv are the *bioi* of the
animal kinds – not just their capacities but their capacities in relation
to some environment. They are given by such predicates as 'land-
animal', 'water-animal', 'marsh animal'.⁶¹ One component of a
bios seems often to be the type of food an animal eats, as in the case
of our camel, with its thorny and woody food. Aristotle does not think
that animals eat the food they do because they have the organs that
can process that sort of food – 'nature makes the organ to suit the
function not the function to suit the organ' (694b13–14).

⁵⁹ Balme, ch. 11 below, 310; Pellegrin 1985: 99.   ⁶⁰ Cf., e.g., Barnes 1975a: 247.
⁶¹ The following is a possibly complete list of places in *PA* and *IA* where something labeled
the '*bios*' of some animal kind seems to serve as a given: 657b29, 660b33, 662b6, 662b15,
663b19, 665b3, 682b7, 682b13, 684a5, 691a26, 693a4, 693a5, 693a11, 693a15, 694a2,
694a6 (text disputed), 694a7, 694b7, 694b12, 694b16, 710a27, 713b21, 713b28, 714a10,
714a21, 714a23. Cf. the detailed and elaborate division of *bioi* in *HA* i.1 (487a10–488b10),
and the general discussion of *bioi* and *praxeis* in *HA* viii.1–2 (588a16–590a18) and at the
beginning of viii.12 (596b20–8).

One might take food as a given, but in *HA* VIII.1–2 he states that animals eat food with an elemental blend like their own. The cetacea, though land animals (*peza*) so far as lungs and internal structure is concerned, have a more watery blend than they, and require food that is more watery. Such food being found only in the water (for the same reason, I suppose), they live in the water.[62] The same doctrine is alluded to in *PA* III.6 in the discussion of lungs, to explain why cetacea violate the correlation of lungs with living on land and again in *Resp.* and in *GA* and even in the discussion of growth in *GC*.[63] This suggests that an animal's 'elemental blend', whatever that is exactly, may have been thought by Aristotle to be part of the *ousia* of that animal. While this opens intriguing metaphysical doors, generating reflections on the unity of form and matter, and their relationship in teleological explanation, and so forth – issues I hope to pursue elsewhere – what is relevant to the present discussion is the clear existence of a structure of essential, explaining features on the one hand, and explained ones on the other.

The explanations in *PA* II–IV rest, then, on at least these three sorts of principles – premises about the elementary matter of which animals are composed, premises about the existence of formal natures and their character as ends, and definitions of these formal natures. For this reason, I am strongly inclined to take Aristotle at his word when he asserts, in some of his introductory and methodological discussions, that his biological works offer an *epistēmē* of animals, full of *apodeixeis*, based on a variety of *archai*. Based on our examinations of the overall explanatory structure of *PA* II–IV, and the detailed explanation of the presence of one or more stomachs in animals, and the frequent dependence of later explanations on premises established in earlier explanations, I am equally inclined to see *PA* II–IV as exhibiting the sort of interconnected structure of demonstrations which one typically associates with the Aristotelian idea of science.

This structure may be disguised in part by the fact that the material so structured is unfamiliar to us (both as students of biology and as scholars of Aristotle), and in part by the fact that Aristotle does not in *PA* II–IV appear interested in showing that this material exhibits that structure. He is working not against the background of those who might wonder if his biological material is amenable to the sort of structure that is outlined in the *Posterior Analytics*, but against

---

[62] 589a5–8, 589a29–590a12.
[63] 669a8–13. Cf. *Resp.* 14, *GA* IV.2 767a30–4, and *GC* II.8 335a10. The explanation of the differences in mode of reproduction among types of animals in *GA* II.1 (732a25–733b16) also makes use of differences in elemental blend.

the background of those who have thought that one could explain the nature and generation of animals and their parts by reference to low-level material principles alone. Aristotle's claim is that final causes as well as the necessary natures of the elementary materials are operative in nature, and that their operation is prior to these necessary natures in the sense that it is only on the hypothesis that an animal's formal nature is to be realized as end that these material natures are operative in the genesis of that animal or any one of its parts. These theses are the background for the systematic study of animal parts which is exhibited in *PA* II–IV, and generate much more talk about causes than about premises, and about reasons why than about demonstrations. But the structure is there, and the language is present enough, to warrant our speaking of an axiomatic structure for the theory of these books.

Need the syllogistic and axiomatic structures be explicit?

In making these claims about the epistemic character of *PA* II–IV, I have purposely avoided giving anything like rigorous definitions of such notions as *epistēmē*, demonstration, *hupothesis*, definition. Our major source for these is the *Posterior Analytics*, and I have thought it important in our exploration of *PA* II–IV not to entangle us in the many controversies that surround the interpretation of that terribly difficult text. The attempt to establish the precise relationship between the structure exhibited in a general way in this paper, and the precise theory of the structure *APo.* requires of a properly developed science, is a project in itself. But it is a project which requires as groundwork the sort of examination of *PA* II–IV begun here.

I would like to close, however, with some brief remarks on the relationship between the practice in *PA* II–IV and the theory in *APo.* which do arise directly out of our study of *PA* II–IV as a whole, and which bear on the question of the significance of the absence of syllogistic in *PA* II–IV.

The fact that *PA* II–IV can have the sort of structure I have argued it has, and be declared by Aristotle to be a body of demonstrative understanding, in the face of its clearly (logically) *informal* character, should perhaps give pause to the notion that *APo.* calls for science to be formal.

In his study of 'Aristotle's theory of demonstration' mentioned above, Jonathan Barnes claimed that according to the *Posterior Analytics*, a demonstrative science must be presented in the language and form of the syllogistic. By that criterion, of course, *PA* ii–iv fails miserably. When *PA* ii–iv was thought to be 'tentative', 'exploratory', or 'dialectical', its informal character was no surprise. But what are we to make of a highly structured *explanatory science* that is presented without syllogistic form? Is it awaiting the stage of final science (which it clearly isn't in its present form) before being cast into syllogisms?

In a more recent paper (1981) also referred to above, Barnes argued for the view, maintained years ago by Solmsen, that the central core of the theory of demonstration is independent of the syllogistic, and earlier. It follows from this, of course, as Barnes observes, that scientific treatises written prior to the discovery, or the implementation into apodeictic, of the syllogism, could be demonstrative without containing any syllogisms. Barnes did not, however, say much about the requirements the pre-syllogistic theory of demonstration places on the logical form of demonstrative premises, to help us judge whether *PA* ii–iv would on that earlier theory count as demonstrative science. Nor did he suggest that the pre-syllogistic theory of demonstration does not require proper science to be presented in *explicit* axiomatic form. But I want to suggest that there is reason to think that *PA* ii–iv would count as demonstrative science even on the post-syllogistic theory, or would at least not be debarred from that status by virtue of its lack of an explicitly syllogistic form or of an explicit axiomatic presentation. This has to do with the character of the *Posterior Analytics* itself as a presentation of a theory of science, and it is a point that was first brought to my attention by Aryeh Kosman, in discussion at the 1983 Williamstown conference.

Kosman's thesis is that *APo.* should be understood as offering a formal description of proper science, not a requirement that proper science itself be formal. As he put it in that discussion, it is much like getting the quantifiers in the right place, though here it is the 'formal' operator: a formal description of science not a description of formal science. On this view, the *APo.* theory requires of the natural philosopher only that his exposition be put*able* into the appropriate form, not that it actually be so *put*; and it relieves proper science of a self-conscious concern with that form, allowing it to satisfy its various informal purposes – though it of course does not give the scientist a blank check, since the formalization of a stretch of informal discourse is not an arbitrary matter.

This view finds support, I think, from the analysis of the syllogistic itself in Jonathan Lear's valuable study of *Aristotle and Logical Theory*

(1980). Lear argues that 'Aristotle's project is to provide a formal analysis of the non-formal deductions with which he was familiar.' I take it this implies that there is no suggestion that speakers, to get their logic fully right, should reason in formally explicit syllogisms. Lear reminds us of the ambiguity of the term *sullogismos*, and its match with the ambiguity of our word 'deduction', and observes that 'This ambiguity is tolerable since the value of the formal syllogistic is supposed to derive from the fact that a syllogism in the broad sense can be represented as a syllogism or chain of syllogisms in the narrow sense.'[64] Since the study of the syllogism is announced at the opening of the *Analytics* as a part of the study of demonstration, one might expect Lear's point to transfer over to the theory of science. It would be an interesting question to consider whether there is any explicit support from *APo.* itself for this view of it, but I pass by that for now.

On such a view, which as Kosman has suggested is certainly an intuitively plausible one for Aristotle to take, one would expect *PA* II–IV to have much the logical form it has now. For, whether or not the explanations can in fact be cast into syllogistic form, there is much reason to think that Aristotle himself thought they could be so cast.[65]

But even if this line of approach to *APo.* is not right, and that treatise does call for proper science to be presented in syllogistic form, one will want to ask what constraints syllogistic theory places on the character of preliminary, informal science. For not every form of explanation at the informal level will make later formalization of the appropriate sort possible. And the same can be said for its premises. An informal structure without at least the prototypes of axioms, *hupotheseis*, definitions, etc., or with an essentially circular structure, or with explanations that are highly contextual or piecemeal, will not be axiomatizable in the way required.

Regardless of whether proper and final science is to be formal or

---

[64] Lear 1980: 10–11.

[65] The clearest piece of evidence is, perhaps, Aristotle's actually doing so, for some sample explanations concerned with plants, in the later chapters of the *Posterior Analytics*. For references and discussion, cf. James Lennox, ch. 5 above, 95–6. (I owe the reference to Lear 1980 to Lennox's briefer discussion of this issue at the close of that chapter.) As Alan Code pointed out in the discussion of this paper at the 1985 Cambridge/Trenton conference, the fact that Aristotle does not present his biological explanations in syllogisms, or even that they cannot be so presented (if that too is a fact), should not count against the demonstrative character of *PA* II–IV. After all, Greek mathematics cannot be formalized within the unaugmented syllogistic Aristotle presents, and Aristotle does little to try to show that it can, but that doesn't stop him from using mathematics as an example (if not the paradigm) of a demonstrative science. There is, of course, the question of whether and, if so, how Aristotle thought that the facts of natural science, which are most of them true only 'for the most part', could be syllogized. This is a difficult (but not, I think, insuperable) matter which must await another occasion.

informal, then, we might expect close study of the explanatory structure of such biological treatises as *PA* II–IV to be of help in resolving some of the interpretative logjams that plague the study of *APo.*, as we might expect close study of *APo.* to further illuminate the explanatory structure of *PA* II–IV. Towards those ends the present paper is only a first step, but I hope a useful one.[66]

Additional note on *PA* I.1 639b21–640a9

(See n. 6 above.)

Aristotle's use of *tropos* in *Metaph.* Δ and elsewhere (cf. Bonitz, *Index*, 774b2ff.) suggests that he would not speak of another *manner* of demonstration unless the explanations in natural science referred to *were* demonstrations in no merely homonymous way, and this is borne out by the fuller parallel passage in *Ph.* II.9 (esp. 200a15ff., most probably the 'elsewhere' referred to in 640a2). For, in that passage, while noting the differences between explanations in the case of things that come to be and explanations in mathematics, he focuses as well on their *similarities*, and these can show us why he counts the former as demonstrations.

Here, as in *PA* I.1 (200a13, 639b24), Aristotle begins by insisting that the necessity in things which come to be is only hypothetical, and moves immediately to compare it with the necessity in mathematics. In *Ph.* II.9 he starts with the similarity: necessity appears in both 'in a parallel fashion' (*paraplēsiōs*, 200a16):

> Because the straight is so and so, it is necessary that a triangle should have angles together equal to two right angles, and not the other way round...With things which come to be for something the case [*sc.* though parallel] is reversed: if the end will be or is, that which comes before will be or is... (a16–22; tr. Charlton)

The parallel is that in both cases (if in different ways) the necessity is one-directional, and from *what* some primary subject is to some other feature of the subject whose presence follows from the subject's being that. (The geometrical explanation assumes that straight sides are essential to triangles.) 200a34–b4 brings this home:

> And the end is that for which, and the start is from the definition and the account;...so if this is what a man is, then so and so, and if so and so, then such and such.

---

[66] Some of the main ideas of this paper were developed in an undergraduate seminar at Trenton State College in Spring 1985 which began with nine students. To the three noble souls who survived to the end, Don Angellini, Tom Church, and Laura Italiano, my gratitude, for their stimulating attention and suggestions. Some of these ideas were anticipated in Kullmann 1974. An earlier draft of the paper was read at the Cambridge/ Trenton Conference on Aristotle's Philosophy of Biology, at King's College, Cambridge, in June 1985. I would like to thank all those who participated in an exceptionally valuable discussion, but especially David Balme, Myles Burnyeat, Alan Code, Jim Lennox, Geoffrey Lloyd, and Malcolm Schofield. An initially sceptical response by David Balme to an early outline of the first draft, and his suggestion that I try my thesis out on the stomachs passage, helped shape some of the direction of this paper. I am grateful to him for those comments. I owe thanks, too, to David Charles and Martha Nussbaum, for important discussion outside the Cambridge session, and to Cynthia Freeland, Joan Kung, Mario Mignucci and, especially, Jim Lennox for very helpful written comments.

Though parallel in this way, the cases are 'reversed' (*anapalin*, 200a19). In mathematics, the starting-points are (in some sense) eternal (cf. 639b24), and thus *are* and are *of* (*unqualified*) *necessity*, so that whatever they necessitate is also of unqualified necessity. But with things which come to be, the starting-point of explanation, the end, is *not* necessary (200a13), and thus what this starting-point necessitates is necessary only *on a hypothesis*: '*if* the end will be or is, that which comes before will be or is' (a19–20).

Interpreters have made much of this use of the future tense, especially in the abbreviated *PA* I.1 version, where only the *contrast* between the mathematical and natural-coming-to-be cases is noted, and where it is drawn in terms of tense: 'For the latter begin from what is, the former from what will be' (640a3–4). But these interpreters fail to notice both that the portion of the *Ph.* II.9 passage just quoted that corresponds to 640a3–4 reads 'if the end will be *or is*' (200a21), and that the sample demonstration that in abbreviated form immediately follows 640a3–4 is entirely in the present tense: '"Because health or man is such, it is necessary that this be or come to be"' (a4–5). This illustration makes clear that the demonstrations *both* in the mathematical *and* in the natural cases will typically have the same outward form, and when formalized will be indistinguishable. (Cf. Lennox above, 111 n.40.) Aristotle's use of the future serves rather (and only) to reflect the contrast in the necessary status of the starting-points in the two cases, *and* the temporal order of necessitating and necessitated factors in explanations of coming to be, *and* to allow an economical way of contrasting his own view of the latter case with the view of his predecessors that complex organic features come to be of unqualified necessity from their elemental antecedents (640a6–9).

Thus, in sum, though the difference between demonstrations in mathematics and those in natural science (in the case of things that come to be) is of great significance, it does not lead Aristotle to deny that there *are* demonstrations in natural science, and our *Ph.* II.9 passage helps us to see why. As the passage explains, in both the mathematical and the biological cases the explanation proceeds from *what the subject is* to some less essential attribute of it, and in both cases it proceeds by necessity. These are central features of demonstration for Aristotle, and evidently central enough for their presence in biological explanations to entitle these explanations to be called 'demonstrations'. Their *mode* of demonstration is different from that in the case of mathematical explanations, since the mode of necessity is different (Balme's 'i.e.' for *kai* in 640a1 seems right), but both are demonstrations nonetheless.

(That the individuals subsumed by the minor terms in these biological demonstrations do not exist of necessity will have to be dealt with eventually. To start, we will have to distinguish between the necessary existence (or not) of the subject and predicate terms in demonstrative premises, and the necessity of these premises themselves. Aristotle's concern in the *PA* I.1 and *Ph.* II.9 passages is with the former; the question just raised has to do with the latter. On this question I imagine he would say that while there is no necessity that any particular man, say, should exist, it *is* necessary that some man or other exist, and that this is sufficient to render the relevant universal minor premises necessary in the way appropriate for demonstration, even though their referents are not necessary existents. The passage from *GA* II.6 quoted above (p. 171) seems to support this, suggesting perhaps that the amenability of things which come to be to demonstration lies in the fact that there is an eternal coming-to-be of things of the relevant kind. This is a large problem, but the question will be to understand *why* at *PA* I.1 640a1 Aristotle allows demonstration in natural science; *that* he does is clear from that text and its parallel in *Ph.* II.9.)

PART III

TELEOLOGY AND NECESSITY
IN NATURE

...a nature makes nothing without a point but always the best from among what is possible to the being of each kind of animal.

(*IA* 2 704b15–17)

Introduction

If Aristotle is known for anything it is for his teleology. In the understanding of this issue the biology has proved especially useful, as one might well expect, since the primary subject of teleological explanation for Aristotle is the living thing – its development, structures, and activities.

What, then, is it, according to Aristotle, for a part of a living thing to *be* for the sake of an end, where that end is explanatory of the part's presence in an organism? And what is it for that part, or that organism, to *come to be* or to act for the sake of an end, where that end is not consciously aimed at? Earlier interpreters tended to assimilate the general living case to the human case, and they spoke for instance of potential souls and invisible entelechies guiding organic development – of 'immaterial agencies' of various sorts. But this, as J. H. Randall, Jr. (1960) pointed out, is to turn the final cause into an efficient cause. More recent interpreters agreed, and went on to speak as if the true *causation* involved in teleological processes was all at the material level.

According to this line of interpretation, specification of the end helped to *explain* a part or process, but it did so by describing the phenomenon in terms which helped to make sense of it *to us* (in one way or another), and not by identifying a second causal factor. On this more recent, pragmatic interpretation Aristotle's materialist opponents were right in a way: ontologically speaking, processes teleologically described *were* reducible to processes described non-teleologically, the teleological biology to the (relatively) non-teleological matter theory. Such a reduction would involve loss of some explanatory force, but not loss of ontological content, since the teleological formulation added nothing to the ontological content expressed at the level of matter (unless these subjective explanatory facts were taken to structure the ontology itself, a position difficult to square with Aristotle's realism).

In his Inaugural Lecture of 1965, 'Aristotle's use of the teleological explanation', David Balme spoke of the irreducibility of organic development to the laws of the matter, but rested it on a view of species which he came to 'disown'. Our three contributors, Allan Gotthelf, John Cooper, and Balme himself in a new paper written for this volume, share the view that there is an ontological irreducibility of the teleological to the non-teleological in Aristotle, and offer a wealth of evidence and example from the biological works in support of such a reading of the main theoretical passages in *Physics* II, *Parts of Animals* I, *Generation and Corruption* II, *Metaphysics* A, and elsewhere.

Gotthelf's paper is an updated version of his often-cited 1976 dissertation prize essay, largely retaining the original text but with expanded or added footnotes and a 'Postscript 1986'. Cooper has provided us with an imaginative integration of the central portions of his contribution to the 1982 Owen Festschrift, 'Aristotle on natural teleology', and the whole of his 'Hypothetical necessity' written for the 1985 Balme Festschrift. Balme's 'Teleology and necessity' is, as already mentioned, a new paper, and is notable both for its revision of the views on necessity expressed in his 1972 Clarendon volume, and its interpretation of Aristotle's teleology as essentially cybernetic (though in a manner distinct from that of contemporary cybernetic interpretations of teleology, as will be explained below).

While the three authors agree, as we have said, on the main line of interpretation, their differences are most interesting and instructive. All seem to agree that the finality of organic development is a central case in Aristotle's natural teleology, and all insist that the natures and powers of the living thing's elementary constituents are by themselves insufficient to effect that development. Living things have a form, and a nature *qua* whole in virtue of that form, and it is this formal nature which is the primary cause of organic development, and is so as the goal or end (*telos*) of that development. They differ over precisely how this works, i.e. over what fact is most basic here, over what (as Cooper puts it) 'licenses' teleological explanation.

For Gotthelf all explanation in Aristotle is in terms of natures and potentials. An outcome which is not wholly the result of material necessity – of the natures and potentials of a living thing's elementary constituents – is (or is involved in) the actualization of an 'irreducible potential for form', a potential transmitted from parent to offspring via a certain heat and set of 'movements'. Such a potential is actually at work in teleological processes, and the form which is being realized is responsible for the development – is its *final cause* – as that which the potential being actualized is irreducibly *for*.

Balme agrees, but finds the teleological control not merely in a basic potential borne by the movements, but in its characteristic material base: in the cybernetic character of the 'self-limiting complex' of movements. 'The resulting complex interactions are "reducible" to the primary actions of the elements only in the trivial sense that they consist of them, as a polygon consists of lines and angles, but not in the sense that they come about because of those primary actions and would have resulted automatically.' He maintains, much as he did in his first published paper back in 1939, that matter in Aristotle's sense – here, the simple natures of air, earth, fire and water, and their automatic interactions – is essentially indeterminate or imprecise, and could not by itself produce determinate complexes – e.g. living organisms – in the way that the Greek atomists proposed (cf. Lucretius's *motus convenientes*). Nor, therefore, could it give rise to those 'self-limiting', cybernetic processes which do impart living form, so in this way Aristotle's approach differs from the modern one: these controlling movements can only be inherited from previous possessors. Nevertheless, 'these limiting movements are movements only of the elements', and not some extra-material or magical 'factor'. 'For what he is saying is that there is a cybernetic control in biological processes over and above the simple actions of air, earth, fire, and water, but still consisting only of their interactions within the complex.'

For Cooper, the basic fact which underwrites teleological explanation is rather 'the permanence of the species of living things, not explicable, as Aristotle plausibly thinks, on other natural principles'. One can speak of an 'irreducible potential' for form, but this is not a capacity possessed by the complex of movements, or by the vital heat, in itself, as fire has the capacity to burn certain things, or earth to move downwards. It just sums up the fact that what happens when, say, 'fetal materials coming from a female dog and acted upon by a male dog's sperm are transformed by certain definite stages into a puppy', needs to be explained 'by referring to a fundamental tendency of the natural kinds of living things to be preserved in existence, and recognizing that this process is one of those by which a species, the dog, preserves itself by reproduction'.

Balme and Gotthelf view the permanence of the species of living things as itself a consequence of the prior fact that individual living organisms exist with a capacity, not reducible to capacities of their constituents, to produce other organisms like themselves. This view is outlined in Balme's contribution to this Part but most fully spelled out in his contribution to Part iv, where 'the principles of *inherited form* and *functional advantage*' are argued to be sufficient to explain the existence and permanence of species.

Cooper differs from Gotthelf as well in giving a more central role in understanding Aristotelian teleology to the notion of the 'good'. He suggests that Aristotle has two distinct lines of argument for the irreducibility of teleological explanation, only one of which rests on the insufficiency of material natures to explain the formation of precisely structured outcomes. The other line of argument is the notorious first argument in *Physics* ii.8, which Cooper discusses in some detail. According to this line, even if material natures *were* sufficient in that way, they still would not explain why these outcomes are *good* for the organism which possesses them; on the materialists' view, that they are beneficial would be a *coincidence*. But since species are permanent that would mean a coincidence repeating itself regularly through all time, which is incredible. So irreducibility in the former sense is not as central to Aristotelian teleology for Cooper as Gotthelf would make out, though in fact Aristotle thinks it obtains. Gotthelf explains his own view on this issue in one of his additional notes.

In his discussion of necessity in nature Cooper explains how it is that Aristotle can say that all natural necessity is 'on a hypothesis' without treating material necessity as a *form* of hypothetical necessity, as Balme did in his Clarendon volume (Balme 1972). Balme now agrees in rejecting that part of his 1972 analysis but in his own contribution argues that more needs to be said if hypothetical necessity is to be understood, specifically about *how* the formal nature exerts its teleological control in those cases where the material natures are insufficient by themselves to explain some occurrence. On Cooper's analysis all one need say is that the occurrence happened 'because it is an occurrence by which something good was achieved'. Balme on the other hand insists that there must be a reference to the movements transmitted from parent to offspring, and their capacity to produce form, much as there is in the explanation of species.

But to say this is to remind ourselves of the close ties between the teleological question and issues of metaphysics, and to suggest ties to other issues as well, which make these discussions of teleology an appropriate center of the book. For Balme's discussion of teleology in the closing essay of this Part leads directly into the issues of his opening essay in Part IV. And all three essays on teleology and necessity, as Gotthelf suggests in the closing essay in Part II, raise issues central to the understanding of the *structure* of Aristotelian explanation and of Aristotelian method in the biological sciences generally. It is no accident then that Aristotle is so known for his teleology, and that understanding his teleology is so important for understanding the rest of his thought. We thus go out on a limb in offering three pieces which, whatever their differences, share main lines of interpretation. But we think that these are the right lines, and that they are the lessons of the biology on their issues, and we believe that each contributes important pieces to a large and rich picture which is worth careful study.

8
Aristotle's conception
of final causality*

ALLAN GOTTHELF

I

Aristotle's teleology is a central component of his philosophy, and interpretations of it often heavily influence evaluations of the significance of his thought, both in science and in philosophy. Much has been written about this aspect of his philosophy, but surprisingly little sustained attention has been directed to what is clearly the fundamental question: what, precisely, does Aristotle mean when he asserts that something is, or comes to be, *for the sake of* something?[1]

II

If we are to answer this question with both historical accuracy and philosophical precision, how must we proceed?

The place to begin, of course, is with the text – ideally, with Aristotle's own statement of an answer. One would expect to find, somewhere in the vast Aristotelian corpus, a thorough analysis and explicit definition of this central notion. Surprisingly, it is not there to be found. Readers of the corpus will search in vain for a detailed analysis of what it is to be (or come to be) for the sake of something.

The longest continuous passages on final causality, *Physics* II.8 and (sections of) *Parts of Animals* I.I, while containing much that eventually proves helpful, do not address themselves directly to this issue. In each case, the purpose is to argue for the applicability to nature of a conception of final causality whose precise meaning and statement is largely taken for granted.

In looking for such an analysis outside these chapters, one thinks

---

* This paper is reprinted substantially as it appeared in 1976. A 'Postscript 1986' and some notes have been added for this reprinting; the new notes are placed in square brackets.

[1 Since this essay was published much good work has been done on this issue. I comment on some of it in notes which follow.]

first of the passages in which the final cause – 'that for the sake of which' – is being introduced as one of the four (types of) causes.[2]

The main text is *Physics* II.3 194b32–195a3.[3] A careful reading of these lines, however, shows that here too Aristotle is not introducing or defining the concept of *being for the sake of* in terms of more familiar concepts. Rather, assuming a familiarity with the notion from its ordinary use, he is arguing for its status as a (type of) cause. More precisely, in fact, Aristotle is arguing for the inclusion of the *end* (*to telos*) in the list of causes. In a literal translation, the relevant portion reads:

In yet another way we call [something] a cause as [being] the end; this is that for the sake of which – e.g. of walking, health. For, why does one walk? We say, 'in order to be healthy', and speaking so we think we have given the cause.[4]

Failing to find an explicit account of the nature of final causality in the passages listing the four types of causes, one thinks next of

---

[2] 'That for the sake of which' is a literal rendering of Aristotle's *to hou heneka*. *Heneka* is an ordinary preposition in Greek, appearing mostly in the construction *A–verb–heneka–B*, with *A* the subject and *B* the genitive object (e.g. 'he walks for the sake of his health'). Aristotle formed abstract substantive expressions to designate the terms of the relation (*to hou heneka* for *B*, *to toutou heneka* for *A*) and the relation itself (e.g. *heneka tou*). I follow the traditional rendering of *aitia* and *aition* as 'cause'. I am unconvinced by the arguments against this translation given by Gregory Vlastos in 1969: 292–4. There is much to be said for the view that Aristotle is offering a conception of causality different from the Humean one that has so infiltrated the speech, and structured the intuitions, of many philosophers. One should not equate a particular *conception* of causality with the *concept* of causality as such. I cannot argue this here in any detail, though for some brief remarks see n. 51 below. [See also Gotthelf 1980: 368, and the remarks by John Cooper and David Balme in chs. 9 and 10 below, 273–4 and 281 respectively.]
[3] *Metaph.* A.3 983a31–2 refers us to *Ph.* II.3; Δ.2 is an almost exact duplicate of part of II.3; and *APo.* II.11 merely repeats II.3's illustration.
[4] 194b24, 32–5. In canonical form, the argument runs:

P_1 That for the sake of which is a cause.

P_2 The end is that for the sake of which.

The end is a cause.

P_1 is not actually stated, but is the implicit conclusion of a subsequent argument, embedded in the walking example, which may be put:

P_3 An acceptable answer to a 'why' question states a cause.

P_4 Stating that for the sake of which is an acceptable answer to some 'why' questions.

That for the sake of which is a cause.

Neither P_2 nor P_4 is felt by Aristotle to need explanation or defense, and the wording of the example which generates P_4 makes clear that Aristotle is assuming that his readers are thoroughly familiar with the notion of being for the sake of, at least in its application to human action. Nowhere in the passages describing the four causes is a statement given of what it is to be (or come to be) for the sake of something. (In support of this reading, cf. the summary passage in the same chapter, at 195a24–6, and the similar arguments in the passages listed in n. 3.)

looking through the corpus for passages which contain an explicit statement of conditions necessary and/or sufficient for something's being (or coming to be) for the sake of something. As it turns out, there are ten to fifteen passages which appear to offer this, but, once again, it can be shown that none of them gives what can be considered a definition – an account of what it is to be (or come to be) for the sake of something.[5]

III

Since the text does not provide us with an explicit answer to our main question, some indirect method of determining the answer is required. There are at least three such methods that might profitably be used.

(1) One might examine the passages just referred to in which, at least apparently, Aristotle gives conditions for something's being (or coming to be) for the sake of something, in the attempt to determine what particular conception(s) of final causality, if any, they presuppose.

(2) One might examine the various passages in which Aristotle is presenting arguments for his thesis that final causality is operative in nature, in the attempt to determine what particular conception of final causality is the subject of this thesis.[6]

(3) One might examine relevant texts throughout the corpus in the attempt to determine Aristotle's position on what is now known as the problem of (biological) reduction.

Of course, the manner in which one would proceed to do this last, and the point of such a procedure – i.e., the relevance to Aristotle's conception of final causality of his position on reduction, if he can even be said to have one – are by no means obvious, and eliciting

---

[5] Demonstrating this would require a longer discussion than is possible here. For now, I simply list the passages. There are eight or so distinct statements of conditions, two of which, notably, are repeated several times in different works. They are, in order of Bekker pagination: *APo.* II.11 95a6–9; *Ph.* II.2 194a28–32 (with II.8 199a8–9; b15–17; *PA* I.1 639b27–30; and 641b24–5); *Ph.* II.5 196b21–2; II.8 199a17–20; *de An.* II.4 415b1–2 (with 20–1; *Ph.* II.2 194a35–6; *Metaph.* Λ.7 1072b2–3; and *EE* VIII.3 1249b15); *Metaph.* α.2 994b9–10; *Metaph.* Δ.17 1022a4, 6–8; and *Protrep.* fr. 11 (Ross). [These passages are discussed in chapter 2 of my dissertation (Gotthelf 1975). Cf. also n. 13 below.]

[6] We should expect these arguments to have some such form as: 'Any phenomenon which is such-and-such is for the sake of something; some natural phenomena are such-and-such; therefore, some natural phenomena are for the sake of something.' The first premise, very possibly unstated in the text itself but easily formulable, might well be of some help in identifying what, for Aristotle, it is for something to be for the sake of something, if not itself already such an account.

them would require some sustained discussion. Since this method turns out to be the most fruitful – the others being more valuable for providing possible support to an interpretation already arrived at than for discovering and formulating a new one – let us turn directly to this discussion.

One might come to see the value of this method by means of the following considerations. First, in almost every passage in which Aristotle introduces, discusses, or argues for the existence of final causality, his attention is focused on the generation and development of a living organism.[7] In line with this, then, we ought to direct our attention to organic development and ask our main question of this type of case: what, precisely, does Aristotle mean when he asserts that the coming-to-be (or any stage in the coming-to-be) of a living organism is *for the sake of* the mature, functioning organism which results?[8]

Secondly, in considering this question we should remember that such an assertion is intended by Aristotle to convey an *explanation* of the occurrence and character of the stages in the development (and thus of the development itself), since that which the development is for the sake of is one of its 'causes'. Thus, a condition on any successful account of Aristotelian final causality is that it illuminate why Aristotle thinks reference to the end of a development might serve to explain the existence and character of that development.

This condition takes on a special importance when we remember, further, that in Aristotle's own study of organic development, *Generation of Animals*, he offers a detailed exposition of the 'mechanisms' involved in development, identifying sequences of changes in quality and place of the embryonic materials. In fact, it is often thought that *Generation of Animals* provides conclusive evidence that Aristotle himself believes that it is at least in principle possible to account for the development of a living organism fully in terms of

---

[7] Cf. the passages listed in nn. 3 and 5. While the *Ph.* II.3 passage discussed above (see n. 4) and its counterparts (see n. 3), are restricted to examples of human action, the point of listing and describing the four types of cause is stated to be the contribution knowing the types of causes will make to the investigations of the natural scientist (194b16–23); and in coming to understand that 'The nature is among the "for-the-sake-of-something causes"' (II.8 198b10–11, the chapter's opening lines), what the natural scientist learns is that the development of (the parts of) a living organism is for the sake of (their contribution to) its mature functioning. (Cf. Charlton 1970: 120–1, 122–3 and below n. 41.)

[8] That Aristotle's preoccupation is with organic development's being for the sake of something is no accident. It can be shown, once the correct interpretation of this use of 'for the sake of' is established, that all other uses of it are derived from and partially definable in terms of this one. See below n. 19.

features of the organism's constituent materials, features which make
no reference to the development's outcome.[9]

If this is the case, we may properly wonder what the explanatory
significance is of statements that refer the development's existence
and character to its end, and thus in what precise sense the
development is *for the sake of* the mature, functioning organism which
issues from it. Alternatively, if Aristotle rejects, explicitly or
implicitly, such a reduction, this too might well shed important light
on what it is for a development – or for anything – to be *for the sake
of something*.

Such, in brief, is the rationale for pursuing our main question
through an examination of Aristotle's position on the problem of
biological reduction.[10]

IV

Let us now give a more precise statement of the reducibility question,
first in general, and then as it applies to Aristotle's own philosophical
and scientific context. That will make us better able to discuss
Aristotle's position on the question, and the implications of this
position for our understanding of his conception of final causality.

The problem of biological reducibility is, for our purposes, the
problem of determining the relationship between the laws of action
of organic phenomena and the laws governing the living organism's
material constituents. Specifically, can one account for a particular
living process in terms of laws governing the material involved in the
process, laws which make no mention of the end or goal of the

---

[9] [Expressed most recently, in one form or another, in Nussbaum 1978 and (with
reservations) Sorabji 1980. I have discussed Nussbaum 1978 in Gotthelf 1980 and 1981/2;
for Nussbaum's latest views, see Nussbaum 1980, 1982a, 1983, 1984. I discuss Sorabji 1980
in section II of 'Postscript 1986', below.]

[10] Some contemporary writers distinguish under the general heading of biological reduction
two theses: (1) that teleological explanation can be reduced to non-teleological explanation; and (2) that biology can be reduced to chemistry (or physics, via chemistry). For
example, Ernest Nagel, in a now classic discussion (1961: 398–446), argues that the first
thesis is necessarily true, while the second is an empirical matter which is not currently
known either to be true or to be false. Charles Taylor (1964: ch. 1), on the other hand,
has argued convincingly that Nagel's case for the first thesis presupposes at key steps the
truth of the second thesis. Taylor takes the position that the *first* thesis is an empirical
matter, then argues that the claim that a system is teleological, that it 'inherently tends'
in a certain direction, involves, essentially, the claim that such a reduction *cannot* be
effected. 'It involves, for instance, the assumption that the basic level of explanation has
been reached. For the claim that a system is [teleological] is a claim about the laws holding
at the most basic level of explanation' (18). This view turns out to parallel Aristotle's own
in important ways, and that is one reason the two reduction theses are not distinguished
here. Furthermore, since all of Aristotle's distinctively biological 'laws' are teleological in
character, thesis (2) for Aristotle reduces to thesis (1) (at least with regard to the 'derivability' condition – see the next note).

process? In the case of organic development, can one give an account of the process of development solely in terms of laws of chemical interaction, laws which make no mention of the end to be realized, so that in principle one could give a chronological list of sets of chemical transformations of initial and added material such that the end result is a correct chemical description of the structure of a mature living organism, without any of the laws of transformation making any reference to the end result? Such is the question stated generally.[11]

If one asks this question of Aristotle, one is immediately struck by the fact that Aristotle makes no use, and certainly no explanatory use, of the concept of *law* involved in the formulation of the problem. If we are to understand Aristotle's position on reducibility – and his teleology – we must understand *his* approach to explanation, his alternative to the concept of law, and also the equivalent in his system of what are for contemporary science the laws of physics and chemistry, the laws of the behavior of the material constituents of living organisms.

Now, Aristotle's central explanatory concepts are 'nature' (*phusis*) and 'potential' (*dunamis*). Compressing as much as possible, and simplifying somewhat, we may say that Aristotle's manner of explanation of natural changes and processes goes as follows.[12] Nature consists of individual entities, each of a specific kind, possessing various attributes, moving and changing in various ways. Some are

[11] For a more rigorous and detailed analysis of what might constitute a reduction, see, e.g., Nagel 1961: 345–66, 433–5, summarized usefully in Ayala 1972: 1–6, or Schaffner 1974: 111–18. The problem as I have defined it here corresponds to the condition for a successful reduction which both Nagel and Schaffner call the condition of 'derivability'. Omitted in this essay is a consideration of the Aristotelian position on the second of the two formal conditions these writers lay down (which is called 'connectability' by Nagel and 'referential identity' by Schaffner). While a full-scale treatment of our subject would require discussion of this issue, such discussion is not possible in the present context, involving as it does the questions of the relationships of an Aristotelian entity (*ousia*) and its form, respectively, to the entity's constituent material, and of actions (or identified in terms of) the former to actions (i.e. motions and changes) of the latter. This involves many issues extraneous to our immediate concerns. Determining Aristotle's position on the 'derivability' issue will be sufficient to determine both his position on reduction and his conception of final causality. [On some of those 'extraneous issues' see the papers in Part IV below by Balme, Kosman, and Freeland, the brief discussion of metaphysical issues in ch. 7 above, 189–93, and the fuller study on which the latter discussion is based in Gotthelf 1985b.]

[12] What follows is a fairly standard account, making use of central themes of several of Aristotle's works. The loci classici for 'nature' (*phusis*) and potential (*dunamis*) are respectively, of course, *Ph.* II (with *Metaph.* Δ.4) and *Metaph.* Θ (with Δ.12). The exposition is so familiar that, with only one exception, references are cited only for quotation. The account will be slightly oversimplified in places, so as not to burden it with so many qualifications that the relevant points are lost; on this (and for the exception) see the next note.

living, some not; all are composed of the four simple bodies, the 'elements', which are themselves analyzable into combinations of elementary qualities and some sort of underlying matter. All these things which exist by nature – simple bodies, inanimate compounds, plants, animals and their parts – move and/or change in ways characteristic of themselves if not impeded, which is to say, each has a *nature*. If an entity or material body is acting in such a characteristic way, it is a sufficient explanation of its action to identify that it is acting in accordance with its nature.[13]

Not all motion and change, however, can be explained solely in terms of the nature of the moving or changing entity. Most motion and change, in fact, is due to *interaction*. Things act on other things, and things respond to the action on them of other things, in characteristic ways. In addition to having 'within themselves a source of motion-or-change and rest',[14] each natural thing has within

---

[13] Cf., e.g., *Cael.* IV.3 310b15–19. Omitted here as irrelevant to our immediate purpose are the role of the efficient cause of locomotion to natural place and the role of the Unmoved Mover, for both of which see *Ph.* VIII. [There is a valuable discussion of these matters in Waterlow 1982.] Ignoring the latter, and the *Metaph.* Λ discussion of its role as the final cause of the rotation of the outermost sphere (especially 1072b2–3 and its sister passages – listed in n. 5 above), will be thought by some to be a serious mistake. Space limitations prohibit anything more than the following brief remarks. The passages which identify or refer to two ways in which *to hou heneka* is 'said', are intended to isolate the sense of 'that for the sake of which' which plays a technical role in Aristotle's philosophy from an ordinary use, approximating 'beneficiary', and as such are neither intended to nor do shed light on that technical sense. [For a somewhat different view see Kullmann 1985.] Secondly, the sense in which the action of (the *nous* of) the outermost sphere is for the sake of something is parallel to that in which human action, also directed by *nous*, is. If it can be shown that this sense is derivative from the sense in which organic development is for the sake of something, then an examination of the role of the Unmoved Mover as final cause cannot substitute for the examination undertaken herein – and in fact does not contribute anything to the attempt to answer our main question. On the priority of senses, see n.19. [Charles Kahn has argued for an interpretation of Aristotelian teleology that gives a central role to the Prime Mover as final cause (Kahn 1985). In this interesting paper he maintains that the capacity of most living things to produce offspring one in form with themselves – which will be argued in this paper to be fundamental to Aristotelian teleology – is itself explained teleologically 'from general principles of cosmic perfection' (Kahn 1985: 195, 200). Among other passages, he appeals to *GA* II.1 731b18–732a1, *GC* II.10 336b25–34, and *de An.* II.4 415a23–b7. There is not space to treat the issues Kahn raises at the length his discussion warrants (several are anticipated in Gotthelf 1975: 46–50, 260–1, 304–6 (esp. n. 161), 317–43); I can only make two points here. First, the thrust of these three passages is to assimilate generation to *self*-preservation (not the preservation of the species). (For discussion, see, e.g., Balme 1972: 96–7, Gotthelf 1975: 331–9, Lennox 1985a, and Balme, ch. 10 below, 279–80.) Second, to relate the striving for self-preservation to the general striving for the better is not to make self-preservation an expression of some wider, cosmic goal the striving for which *explains* the striving for self-preservation. The striving for the better over which such passages generalize just *is*, in the end, a striving for self-preservation, and the arguments in each of these three passages *could* be stated without mention of 'the better' or of 'the divine' (cf. nn. 18 and 38 below, with references). But Kahn's wide-ranging paper deserves fuller attention than can be given here.]

[14] *Ph.* II.1 192b13–14.

itself 'a source of being moved-or-changed by another'[15] to which, in each case, corresponds a 'source' in that other of so changing the first – which is to say that in addition to having a nature, each natural thing has *potentials* – potentials to change certain other things in certain ways (which we may call 'active potentials') and potentials to be changed by certain other things in certain ways (which we may call 'passive potentials').[16]

These two concepts, 'nature' and 'potential', are *the* basic explanatory concepts for motion and change in Aristotle's scientific theories, and statements identifying the natures and potentials of things are the closest Aristotelian equivalents of 'laws' in modern science. Every process in nature, every motion or change, according to Aristotle, *is* action in accordance with a nature *or* the actualization of a coordinate pair of active and passive potentials *or* the sum of some combination of these. A natural motion or change is *explained* when it is shown to be the result of: action in accordance with one or more natures and/or actualizations of one or more irreducible potential-pairs. Explanation, to this extent, is for Aristotle subsumption (not under general laws but) under the natures and potentials of the acting and changing entities – and thus in large part consists simply of correctly identifying, in causally fundamental terms, *what* is actually happening.

V

As for the Aristotelian equivalent of modern physical and chemical laws, let us briefly consider the form his account of the action of the material constituents of living organisms takes.

According to Aristotle, the material constituents of bodies, the

---

[15] *Metaph.* Δ.12 1019a15–16; cf. Θ.1.
[16] Any interaction will be, in fact, the actualization of a specific potential pair, an active and a passive, and there will be for any interaction a scientifically fundamental and ultimate way of describing it. We should note that the scientific account may not recognize a distinct potential, even though it might appear to be recognized in ordinary speech. For example, one could describe the collapsing of a row of dominoes as the actualization of the single (passive) potential of the row to be knocked over. This potential, however, consists of – is reducible to – the potentials of each of the dominoes (in virtue of the material of which it is made, and its shape) to be knocked over (and to knock the succeeding one over), and as such would not be, fundamentally or scientifically, a distinct potential. For a clear-cut conception of what for Aristotle would be the ultimate, irreducible potentials of the inanimate world, one would have to examine very closely the physical works, including *Meteorology* (esp. IV, now generally agreed to be authentic (cf. Furley 1983)), *Generation and Corruption* and *De Caelo*. It will always be an empirical matter which potentials are irreducible. (The potential of opium to cause sleep, for instance, would *not* be – for Aristotle or for us – irreducible, and thus ascribing a 'dormitive virtue' to opium would for Aristotle *not* be explanatory.) [There is an interesting discussion of this point in Sorabji 1980: 171–2; I remark on it in my discussion of Sorabji in section II of 'Postscript 1986' (below 236). See also the quotation from Taylor 1964 in n. 10 above.]

'so-called elements' (earth, water, air, fire), each have a nature and
potentials. The nature of a simple body – its characteristic way of
acting if unimpeded – is locomotive, and its potentials – its characteristic ways of interacting with other such bodies – are primarily
qualitative: each has a pair of primary qualities, and it is these that
determine their interactions, including their mutual transformations.[17]

To arrive at the Aristotelian form of the problem of reduction,
then, one need only state the reducibility question in terms of
element-potentials instead of laws of chemical interaction. With this
substitution the question takes the following form: Can one account
for a particular living process completely in terms of the element-
potentials involved in the process, making no mention of the overall
end or goal of the process? In the case of development, can one give
an account of the process of organic development solely in terms of
element-potentials which make no reference to the overall outcome
of the process, viz., the form of the mature, functioning organism?
Or must at least one of the potentials involved in the account be
irreducibly a potential for the development's end, for an organism
of that form? If the latter is the case, one can think of the development
as primarily the actualization of that irreducible potential, and any
element-potentials additionally involved would be viewed as subsidiary to that one. Then, focusing on development and with our
discussion of the Aristotelian approach to explanation of natural
motion and change in mind, we may put the reduction question as
follows: *Is the development of a living organism the result of a sum of
actualizations of element-potentials, or is it primarily the actualization of a
single potential for an organism of that form, a potential the actualization of
which involves the actualization of element-potentials, but is not reducible to
them?*

VI

The answer to this question is the key to understanding the precise
nature of Aristotle's conception of final causality.

It is the thesis of this essay: (1) that Aristotle posed precisely this
question, and that it was on this question more than on any other

[17] To simplify terminology we will designate the locomotive natures and qualitative potentials
of the elements jointly as 'element-potentials'. For various reasons, the difference between
a nature and a potential (though important in certain contexts) is not a great one, and
Aristotle himself licenses this usage at *Metaph.* Θ.8 1049b6–11. (For the relationship between explanation in terms of natures and potentials, the type of Aristotelian explanation
just expounded, and explanation by causes, see n. 51 below. The connection between these
two is, in large part, the deeper theme of this essay.)

that he saw himself differing directly from his 'mechanistic' predecessors; (2) that the evidence of the text – in the metaphysical and physical, as well as in the biological, works – is that Aristotle's response to this question was an unwavering advocacy of the second alternative: that his view was that the development of a living organism is *not* the result of a sum of actualizations of element-potentials the identification of which includes no mention of the form of the mature organism, but *is* in fact the actualization primarily of a single potential for an organism of that form, an actualization which incorporates many element-potentials, but is not reducible to them; (3) that this question and the question of whether a living organism develops *for the sake of* being a mature, functioning organism are *one and the same question*; and thus (4) that the irreducibility to element-potentials of organic development is the core of the meaning of the assertion that the development is *for the sake of* the mature organism, and thus the core of Aristotle's conception of final causality.

In regard to this last, it is thus the thesis of this essay that Aristotle's concept of *coming-to-be for the sake of* may be defined as follows:

A stage in development, A, comes to be for the sake of the mature, functioning organism which results from the development, B, if and only if: (1) A is a necessary (or 'best possible') stage in a continuous change resulting in B, and (2) this change is (in part) the actualization of a potential for B which is not reducible to a sum of actualizations of element-potentials whose identification does not mention the form of B.[18]

---

[18] Two comments on this definition. First, the definition is formulated to apply only to those cases where the mature organism actually results. Since an organic development which does not succeed in reaching its goal is nevertheless for the sake of that end, a definition which applied to these cases as well would have to reformulate condition (1). For these cases, 'resulting in' would have to be replaced by something like 'tending to'. However, since 'tending to' for Aristotle can ultimately only be defined in terms of an irreducible potential for B (cf. Taylor's account, quoted in n. 10 above), there would be no need for condition (1) for these cases. In fact, condition (1) is superfluous, being a consequence of (2), and is included only to stress the contrast of this interpretation with those which do not make irreducibility a necessary condition of final causality for Aristotle. Secondly, the phrase 'best possible' is included to cover those (recognized by Aristotle to be) frequent cases where an organ or action is not actually *necessary* for the organism's life or well-being, but is one of a set of which one is necessary, and the most efficient of that set. This raises a number of considerations outside the scope of this essay, but the phrase needs to be included for completeness. See *PA* 1.1 640a33–b3 and *IA* 2 704b10–17 for two representative texts. [These considerations include: (1) the relationship between explanation by hypothetical necessity and explanation by the principle that 'nature does nothing in vain but always for each thing the best from among what is possible'; (2) the epistemological status of the latter principle; and (3) the relationship between explanations that appeal to 'the honorable' and those that appeal to advantage. On (1), and on hypothetical necessity generally, see n. 32 and chs. 9 and 10 below, and ch. 7 above, 188–9. On (2) see ch. 7 above. On (3) see Balme's note below (277 n. 5) and the discussion in Lennox 1985b: 149–55. They argue that appeals to 'the honorable' are a subset of appeals

It is a corollary of this four-part main thesis that Aristotle's teleology – his doctrine that the development, structure, and functioning of a living organism is for the sake of something – is fundamentally *empirical* in character, and not an a priori doctrine brought *to* his investigation of nature.

The balance of this essay will consist of arguments in behalf of this thesis and its corollary.[19]

to advantage and do not represent a separate principle of explanation. A similar case can be made out, I believe, for appeals to 'living well' (*to eu zēn*). (Cf. also n. 13 above.) Since a naturalistic account can thus be given of the notion of the good with which Aristotle operates in his biology, it seems to me that the fundamental account of the final cause need not make use of that notion. While it is true that accounts more 'familiar to us' start there, it is not the case (contra, e.g., Kahn 1985: 197–8) that Aristotle (in effect, arbitrarily) designates as the aim of a process that stage which he independently wishes to count as good. It is rather that the capacities actually at work *are* capacities for the mature state (*akmē*), where the mature state is identifiable in terms of the presence of maximal powers of self-maintenance without reference to independent normative criteria, *and* that for (what we would call) meta-ethical reasons the good is defined by reference to this same mature state. This raises the question of how one determines which capacities are actually 'at work'. This is a large issue, with important metaphysical dimensions, but surely it is clear that *Physics* II.2's poet spoke ridiculously (194a30–3) for more than one reason: if a living thing's aim were death one could not understand the elaborate process of continuous physical articulation and continuously expanding powers we call its development (the self-maintaining powers at each stage the same as those at earlier ones only more efficacious, etc.). The only question is whether the decline to death that regularly follows development to maturity is to be seen as part of the *dunamis* which is actualized in maturity, or is rather to be attributed to the natures and potentials of the materials of which the organism is made. I take it there are arguments (or premises from which one can construct arguments) in *De Anima, Parva Naturalia, Generation and Corruption* and *Metaphysics* H and Θ in favor of the latter view (though as I say this is a large issue). (For a good discussion of 'self-maintenance' in Aristotle, see Nussbaum 1978: 76–8.) See also the new portion of n. 38 and section I of 'Postscript 1986', below.]

[19] There are two other very controversial corollaries of the main thesis which can only be mentioned here. (1) All uses of 'for the sake of' to be found in the Aristotelian corpus other than to denote the relationship between (a stage in) a development and its outcome are definable, and were understood by Aristotle to be definable, in terms of this primary use. This includes the notions of a *part* of an organism being for the sake of the whole, mature organism (i.e. the notion of a part having a *function*), of anything in the realm of human action – practical or productive – being for the sake of something, and of the action of heavenly bodies being for the sake of something (cf. n. 13 above). [For discussion of this dependence in the case of parts, see now section III of 'Postscript 1986', below.] The natural motions and changes of the simple bodies (earth, water, air, fire) when outside a living organism are *not* for the sake of anything. (While these motions and changes are *to* (*eis*) a place or quality – very infrequently called a *telos* – they are not, and are never said to be, for the sake of anything (*heneka tou*). The latter concept is reserved for those processes of complex entities which are not reducible to element-potentials. Being the actualization of a single element-potential, each elemental motion or change *is*, of course, reducible to a set of element-potential actualizations – viz. the set consisting of that one element-potential actualization! Both *PA* II.1 646b5–9 and *Mete.* IV.12 389b29ff. concern elements as constituents of living organisms. Insofar as 'the movement of each body to its place *is* motion towards its own form' (*Cael.* IV.3 310a33–4), that movement may be thought of as being *for the sake of* reaching that place – in as derivative a sense of 'for the sake of' as that passage's 'form' is derivative of the full-blooded organic forms of *Metaphysics* ZHΘ. No such use of *heneka* is found in the corpus, however.)

VII

A full case for this four-part thesis would contain at least three components: (1) an examination of Aristotle's own account, in *Generation of Animals*, of the nature – and 'mechanisms' – of the generative process in order to put flesh on the so far very skeletal notion of an 'irreducible potential for form' and provide support for the claim that, for Aristotle, organic development can be explained only by reference to such a potential and not solely in terms of element-potentials; (2) an examination, as suggested earlier, of the arguments Aristotle gives for his doctrine that final causality is operative in nature, in the attempt to elicit whatever information we can about the precise conception of final causality which is in fact the subject of this doctrine, against which information the present interpretation can be tested; and (3) an examination of the various apparent statements of conditions necessary and/or sufficient for something's being or coming to be for the sake of something, as also suggested earlier, for the same purpose.

In this essay we will have to limit ourselves to the first two tasks, in order to give them (minimally) sufficient attention. I will begin with a sketch of the theory of generation in *GA*, and a discussion of its implications for the reducibility question and the interpretation of Aristotelian final causality in terms of irreducibility. This will be followed by an examination of arguments to be found in each of the three chapters which are our main sources for Aristotle's arguments for natural teleology. After some brief remarks contrasting the interpretation offered here with the main alternative traditions of interpretation, I will conclude with an argument for the corollary of our main thesis, the claim that Aristotle's teleological doctrine is fundamentally empirical in character.

VIII

The purpose Aristotle sets for himself in *Generation of Animals* is to explain how reproduction – the generation and development of an offspring one in form with its parents – is effected. Across the first book he develops his thesis in a general way, in reaction to common opinion and the views of his scientific predecessors.

His thesis, as it applies to the higher animals, is that the semen of the male acts on a material produced by the female, causing it to 'take shape' in the appropriate way.

Aristotle rejects the preformationist-pangenesis theories of some of his predecessors, to the effect that semen comes from the whole body, parts of the semen deriving from, resembling in miniature, and being directly responsible for parts of the body, generation being the enlargement and articulation of this composite mini-organism. The semen, Aristotle argues, does not contribute any *material* to the offspring. Rather, it carries, embodied in a 'motion', an active 'potential' to act on material supplied by the *female*, in just such a way as is required to effect reproduction to type.[20]

As the artist's tools, while in use, convey in their motions the specific potential to shape the material to the form he intends, so, Aristotle explains, the semen is the tool of (the father's) nature, conveying, in something like a motion, the potential to shape organic material to form, i.e., to a mature adult one in form with its parent.[21]

In Book II Aristotle offers a more systematic and detailed exposition and defense of his thesis. In the main theoretical passage of *GA* (II.1 734b19–735a4) he lays down the fundamental principle of explanation that must be used, then uses it to track down the identity of the 'potential' and 'motion' carried by the semen.

According to 'our first principle',[22] both the external agent of generation (the father) and its internal transmitter (the semen) must be adequate to the product. The former must be (or possess) in actuality that very (aspect of the) effect of which it is to be the cause, and the latter must possess the appropriate 'motion'. What it is for the 'motion' to be appropriate is not stated explicitly, but it seems clear that the purpose of the second part of the passage is to give some clarification of this:

[20] At 729b4–9 Aristotle states his view in the form of a question: '...or is it that the body of the semen takes no part, but the "potential" (*dunamis*) and the "motion" (*kinēsis*) in it does, for this is what is active, whereas that which is formed, which gets shape, is the [useful] remainder of the female residue?' Throughout this essay I have translated *kinēsis* in this way, for lack of any better consistent rendering. But the reader is to be warned that it is not an accurate translation. Not only does it refer to various types of change other than locomotion (change in quality, change in quantity), but in the biological works especially it often refers to an internal 'activity' – as if boiling water just removed from the fire were said to still contain a 'boiling motion'. This becomes especially significant in Book II, where Aristotle identifies the 'motion' in the semen with a special kind of heat; we are to think of this heat, as we are of the heat of the boiling water, not simply as a quality of the semen, but as an essentially active constituent of it. In II.2 Aristotle argues that semen is a kind of foam, with tiny bubbles of heat-bearing air. We have to understand *kinēsis* in such a way that it makes sense to call this heat a *kinēsis*.

[21] Cf. 730b8–23. Conception and development require that the material supplied by the female be appropriate, i.e. possess a passive potential for such an outcome. (For a representative text see II.3 737a24–5.) [As David Balme has pointed out, it is also part of the *GA* theory from the beginning that the female material as well carries 'movements' of its own, which play a role in the generative process. These are the very movements which convert her food into more of herself but which, because of her lesser heat, are unable to produce a new organism. See the new n. 14 in ch. 11 below, 293–4.]

[22] 734b20.

Just as we would not say that fire alone produces an axe or any other instrument, neither [should we say this of] a foot or a hand. Nor, likewise, of flesh, for even this has a certain function. Accordingly, hard, soft, tough, brittle, and all other such qualities belonging to the parts having soul – heat and cold may very well produce these; but never the organization (*logos*) by which one thing is flesh and another bone: only the 'motion' from the generating parent who is in complete actuality what that out of which [the offspring] comes to be is potentially [can produce this] – just as it is with the things which come to be according to an art: heat and cold make the iron hard and soft, but the *sword* [is made by] the 'motion' *of the instruments*, [this 'motion'] having a definition corresponding to the art, [which is] the source *and form* of the product...[23]

The semen's 'motion' is analogous to the motions of the artist's tools. As the motions of the tools have a definition corresponding to the art, i.e., to the form in the mind of the artist, so the semen's 'motion' must have a definition corresponding to the nature, i.e., to the form, of the parent.[24] That is to say, the semen's 'motion' *must be identified by reference to the form it is transmitting.*

To grasp the significance of this, let us recall that for Aristotle any specific 'motion' (and 'motion' as such) is to be defined in terms of its outcome: it 'gets its name rather from that-to-which than from that-from-which' it proceeds.[25] If the respective outcomes of two 'motions' are different in kind, then the two 'motions' themselves are different in kind. By stressing that the outcome of the semen's 'motion' is different in kind from the outcome of fire's heating – viz., an organization (*logos*) and not just a quality or a set of qualities – Aristotle is asserting that the semen's 'motion' itself is different *in kind* from the quality-generating 'motions' of fire. The semen's 'motion' is to be defined by its outcome: it is the fulfillment of the potential to generate an animal of a certain form or *logos*, qua potential; the form or *logos* is an inescapable part of its very definition.

If this is so, then the 'potential' which is manifested in the semen's motion also is to be identified by reference to the form being transmitted: it is, essentially, a potential for form, a potential *distinct from* and *not reducible to* any sum of qualitative and locomotive potentials. For, if it were reducible, so would the 'motion' be, and then heat and cold *could*, in the proper sequence of actions, produce 'the *logos* by which one thing is flesh and another bone'.[26]

---

[23] 734b28–735a3.

[24] That this is the point of the analogy is suggested most strongly by the last sentence of the full passage: 'For the art is source and form of the product, but in *another*; the "motion" of the nature is in [the generated natural thing] *itself*, being *from* another nature, one having the form in actuality' (735a2–4).

[25] *Ph.* v.1 224b7–8. On the definition and individuation of motions see all of *Ph.* v.1–4. For the general definition of 'motion' see *Ph.* iii.1–3. [Waterlow 1982 has some important discussion of these issues and of their relation to Aristotle's teleological commitments.]

[26] 734b33–4. The whole matter of the philosophical implications of Aristotle's theory of generation – his view of the manner in which form is 'transmitted' in generation, the

IX

There is further evidence in *Generation of Animals*, and in related passages elsewhere, that Aristotle viewed the 'potential' the semen carries as an irreducible potential for form, in the manner specified in the formulation of the main thesis of this essay.

In *GA* ii.2–3 Aristotle takes up the question of the physical nature of the bearer of the 'potential' for form. In ii.2 he offers a chemical analysis, as it were, of semen, an identification of its qualitative properties. Semen is 'a combination of *pneuma* and water, and the *pneuma* is hot air'.[27] In ii.3 he asserts that it is the heat in the *pneuma* that is responsible for generation, and compares that heat with the more familiar heats of fire and the sun.

Now, the 'potential' of all soul seems to be associated with a body different from and more divine than the so-called elements, and as the souls differ from each other in value and lack of value, so too this sort of nature differs. For within the semen of everything there is present that very thing which makes the semen fertile, the so-called 'hot'. This is not fire or that sort of 'potential', but the *pneuma* enclosed within the semen, that is, within the foamy part, and more precisely the nature *in the pneuma*, being analogous to the element of the stars. This is why fire generates no animal, and none is seen to be constituted in things subjected to fire, whether wet things or dry. But the heat of the sun and the heat of animals [do generate] – not only the heat conveyed through the semen, but also if there is some other residue of their nature, even this contains a life-source. Such things make plain that this heat in animals neither is fire nor has its origin from fire.[28]

This passage deserves much more attention and space than it can be given here. Its highlights are (1) its stress on the *difference* in character between the 'potential' for soul, and the heat which bears it, on the one hand, and the potentials of the elements and the elemental heat of fire, on the other; and (2) its stress on the similarity of generative heat to the heat from the sun, an analogy or comparison which has puzzled scholars.[29]

The doctrine of this passage nicely focuses the irreducibility question. It makes clear that if there is to be an irreducible 'potential' for form, it will be the 'potential' borne by the heat in the *pneuma*. We know this heat must be such as to act on the female's material in just such a way as to produce an organism of the relevant form. If this 'potential' is to be reducible, there will have to be a way of

nature and character of the 'potential' and motion by which it is accomplished, etc. – deserves more extended treatment. [See now David Balme, chs. 10 and 11 below, esp. 281–2 and 292–3. There is much work yet to be done.]
[27] 735b37–736a1.   [28] 736b27–737a7.
[29] On this and related matters concerning Aristotle's theory of generation, see Balme 1972: 158–65 *ad* 736a24–737a34, and above n.26.

specifying the series of heatings, coolings, and movings around of material in the developing embryo which this heat effects, without referring to the form. On the face of it, the absence of any sort of quantitative chemistry, and the simplicity of the descriptions of qualitative 'potentials' and interactions that Aristotle countenances, make it difficult to believe that he thinks such a specification possible, and there is no evidence in his works that he does.[30]

On the contrary, there is at least one passage that suggests the reverse. In *De Anima* II.4, Aristotle considers whether fire could be the cause of nourishment:

Some think that it is the nature of fire which is the cause quite simply of nourishment and growth; for it appears that it alone of bodies is nourished and grows. For this reason one might suppose that in both plants and animals it is this which does the work. It is in a way a contributory cause, but not the cause simply; rather it is the soul which is this. For the growth of fire is unlimited while there is something to be burnt, but in all things which are naturally constituted there is a limit and a *logos* both for size and for growth; and these belong to soul, but not to fire, and to *logos* rather than to matter.[31]

[30] This also deserves fuller treatment, focusing on an analysis of Aristotle's conception of heat, its nature, potentials, and varieties. Balme 1972: 163–4 is helpful. Of interest is a little-noted passage in Theophrastus' *On Fire*, which clearly makes use of *GA* II.3 736b27–737a7, just quoted.

> Now the heat which is natural to animate bodies, being infused into a comparatively large number of creatures and in a rather special way becomes in a sense alive and capable of generating similar creatures. Even more so the heat from the sun. It is able to create animals and plants. It is mixed, to be sure, with air (occurring rather in it), but by reason of its gentleness (*malakotēti*) and fineness (*leptotēti*) has a certain appropriateness for generating life; it is not, like the heat of fire, hard (*sklēra*) and caustic (*perikaēs*). For that reason seeds subjected to fire do not generate, but those which are warmed by the sun to excess (*huperbolēn*) generate and germinate. (Coutant 1971: §44 28–31.)

There are suggestions in this work of an attempt by Theophrastus to formulate some generalizations pertaining to the varying effects on various materials of varying degrees of (fineness of) heat, but they are not developed enough to indicate clearly a reductionist sympathy on Theophrastus' part, nor *a fortiori* on Aristotle's. (It is sometimes suggested that the analogy of embryonic development to the operation of the 'automatic marvels' (734b10, 741b9; Balme 1972: 157; Nussbaum 1976: 146–52; Balme above 18) makes clear that Aristotle thought of embryonic development as the result of a 'causal mechanism' involving only element-potentials. But it establishes no such thing. Briefly, the analogy is meant to illustrate how the male parent may be the efficient cause of the generation even though not in contact with the embryo (734b10), and that the development is a smooth, uninterrupted process (741b9), and is not meant to suggest anything about the character of the potentials being actualized. The common feature underlying the analogy, as Aristotle notes each time, is a complex but smooth sequence of actualizings of potentials immediately upon a single contact from outside. The analogy is in no way weakened by the fact that in the case of embryonic development some of these potentials will be irreducibly for form (e.g. the potential of the semen's heat to solidify the female-supplied material in just the shape necessary for an organism of that type, and irreducibly so, as we have just seen in our discussion of II.1 734b19–735a4).)

[31] 416a9–19.

There is no mention of *pneuma* here, but readers of the two passages from *GA* just quoted and discussed will find it hard to resist supplying it, especially in view of Aristotle's identification of the nutritive and reproductive faculties.

That this distinction between element-potentials and potentials for form (soul, *logos*, etc.) is at the root of the distinction between explanation in terms of material-efficient causes and explanation in terms of final-formal causes will be argued in the next three sections, as we examine the arguments Aristotle offers for the necessity of employing the final cause, in the study of organic nature.[32]

X

The need for employing the concept of final causality – of being for the sake of something – in the understanding of nature is asserted and defended in three main places in the Aristotelian corpus: *Metaphysics* A.7 (with 3), *Physics* II.8, and *Parts of Animals* I.1. In each case, the conception whose employment is defended is the one attributed to Aristotle by our 'irreducible potential' interpretation.

Metaphysics A. At A.3 983a33–b6, Aristotle explains in advance

---

[32] A fuller examination of the evidence of the biological works would require discussion of the well-known set of passages in which Aristotle states that some part of an embryo or organism comes to be 'on the one hand of necessity, on the other for the sake of something'. I think that the key to understanding these passages is provided (as might be expected given the theoretical centrality of the passage) by *GA* II.1 734b19–735a4, as interpreted above in section VII. My suggestion is that throughout Aristotle's biological works certain (qualitative) aspects of the embryo or organism are explained by element-potentials ('of necessity') and certain (organizational, functional) aspects by a potential for form ('for the sake of something') – and that the same aspect (e.g. the solidity of the bones mentioned in II.6 743a36–b18) is said to be both of necessity *and* for the sake of something only when that aspect contributes to the constitution of an aspect which is not there of material necessity (e.g. the *logos* – the bone itself, qua bone – as in 734b19–735a4). The 'biochemical' basis for the distinction in the type of causality involved in the generation of the different aspects of the embryo is to be found in the different aspects of the semen's 'motion', i.e. of its heat. The qualitative properties of the embryo are explained by the element potentials the *pneuma*'s heat has qua heat, the organizational properties by the 'purity' or 'fineness' (n. 30 above, esp. Balme *loc. cit.*) unique to this sort of heat (which 'fineness' is specifiable – I am arguing – only as being a potential to produce an organism of a certain sort) [See now, on hypothetical necessity, the essays by Cooper and Balme, chs. 9 and 10 below. I take Cooper's thesis regarding the operation of material (or 'Democritean') necessity in organic nature to include, roughly, the following proposition: Certain organic outcomes do not come to be of material necessity; those that do, do so *only* conditionally upon the coming to be of those that don't. This way of putting it shows that Richard Sorabji's criticism (1980: 173–4) of the view expressed in this note was misguided. The deer's shedding of horns (*PA* 663b12ff.) is for the sake not (as Sorabji suggests) of greater lightness *per se* but of the contribution (*heneka opheleias*: 663b13) such lightness can make to the life of the deer, and *that* good when achieved is not achieved of necessity. As Cooper points out (below 265), Aristotle explicitly denies in the theoretical passages (and never asserts in the biology) that (e.g.) individual deer come to be and continue to exist of necessity.]

the purpose of his historical survey of the types of causes that his predecessors have employed: 'we shall either find another kind of cause, or be more convinced of the correctness of those which we now maintain'. What is important to see is that the discussions which follow constitute arguments for the need to employ the four types of causes. If attempts by the best thinkers to account for certain natural phenomena without a given kind of cause are unsuccessful, while attempts making use of it are successful, that is good reason to maintain that this type of causality *is* operative in nature.

The case for the final cause is made in two parts. First, in chapter 3, we are introduced to the phenomena which, according to Aristotle, material factors alone – i.e., the natures and potentials of the elements – cannot account for, and which (therefore) gave rise to an awareness of the efficient cause. Then, in chapter 7, we are shown that the account in terms of the efficient cause was really a misguided attempt to formulate and employ the final cause.

The insufficiency of explanation wholly in terms of material causes became clear fairly soon, Aristotle states:

For it is not likely either that fire or earth or any such element should be the reason why things manifest goodness and beauty both in their being and in their coming to be, or that those thinkers should have supposed it was; nor again could it be right to entrust so great a matter to spontaneity and chance. When one man said, then, that mind was present – as in animals so throughout all of nature – as the cause of order and of all arrangement, he seemed like a sober man in contrast with the random talk of his predecessors.[33]

These later thinkers, however, did not clearly distinguish the final from the efficient cause and thus never clearly saw the need for the former to account for 'goodness and beauty, order and all arrangement'.

For those who speak of mind or friendship class these causes as goods; they do not speak, however, as if anything that exists either existed or came into being for the sake of these, but as if movements started from these...Therefore it turns out that in a sense they both say and do not say the good is a cause; for they do not call it a cause qua good [i.e., qua that for the sake of which] but only incidentally.[34]

The structure of this two-part argument is clear. The phenomenon to be explained is the order, the arrangement, the beauty and goodness to be found in nature.[35] This cannot be explained solely in terms of element-potentials, neither individually ('fire or earth or any such element') nor in combination ('spontaneity and chance');

---

[33] 984b11–18.   [34] 998b8–16.
[35] Though Aristotle does not here say so, it is clear from similar language in *Parts of Animals* that he means both the regularity of the heavenly motions and the organization of living organisms: cf. 1.5 644b22–645a36.

it is unreasonable (un-'sober') to think it could, Aristotle asserts.[36] The only reasonable account, when clearly articulated, is one which acknowledges that the process by which instances of order and beauty come to be, is essentially or inherently a process *to* order and beauty. But, given Aristotle's definition of 'motion' as the actualization of a potential ('as such'), a process, which is *essentially* to some end, is precisely a process which is the actualization of a potential essentially – and thus *irreducibly* – for that end. This, then, is what it is for something to come to be for the sake of something, according to the argument of *Metaphysics* **A**.

XI

Physics II.8. This notorious chapter is the only one in the entire corpus devoted completely and in detail to a defense of natural teleology. It opens with a clear statement of its purpose, sketches the alternative position, then offers a series of arguments and remarks in opposition to this alternative and in support of its own thesis.

The alternative to teleology sketched in the opening section of the chapter is precisely the view that the development of a living organism is the necessary outcome of a sum of actualizations of element-potentials.

> For everyone brings things back to this cause [*sc.* necessity: cf. 198b11] saying that because the hot is by nature such as to be thus, and similarly the cold and everything of that sort, therefore these things [*sc.* natural things: cf. 198b12] of necessity come to be and are...
> The problem thus arises: why should we suppose that nature acts for the sake of something and because it is better? Why should not everything be like the rain? Zeus does not send the rain in order to make the corn grow: it comes to be of necessity. The stuff which has been drawn up is bound to cool, and having cooled, turn to water and come down. It is merely concurrent that this having happened, the corn grows... What, then, is to stop parts in nature too from being like this – the front teeth of necessity growing sharp and suitable for biting, and the back teeth broad and serviceable for chewing the food, not coming to be for the sake of this, but by coincidence? And similarly with the other parts in which the 'for the sake of something' seems to be present.[37]

Thus, when Aristotle announces in the lines immediately following these that this view, though plausible, *cannot* be true, it is the possibility of an account of development solely in terms of element-potentials that he is rejecting.[38]

---

[36] While Aristotle does not argue in behalf of this charge here, he would surely do so along the same lines as he does in rejecting fire as the cause of nutrition in *de An.* II.4 (quoted and discussed in section IX above). See also n. 38 and my analysis of the first argument in *Ph.* II.8, in section XI below.   [37] 198b12–29.

[38] 198b34. That this is so becomes certain if we consider how Aristotle could possibly characterize the alternative view as maintaining both that development is due to *necessity*

While Aristotle here characterizes his own proposal only as the view that development is 'for the sake of something and because it is better', its nature seems clear. For one may ask how Aristotle could conceive an alternative *account* of development – given his general view of explanation sketched above – other than as one which holds the development to involve the actualization of an irreducible potential for form? If every process *is* the actualization of one or more potentials,[39] and organic development is *not* the actualization only of a sum of element-potentials, then it must be the actualization of a potential irreducibly for a mature organism of the relevant form. These two accounts are the only kinds of explanation available to Aristotle.[40]

Thus, the very way Aristotle poses the alternative he is rejecting in the name of final causality suggests his view of its nature and lends support to the 'irreducible potential' interpretation.

So does the first argument Aristotle offers in support of his teleological account of organic development.[41] The argument may be summarized as follows:

> and that it is due to *chance* (in the wider sense which encompasses chance and spontaneity). For a good discussion of this see Guthrie 1965: 163–4 and 414–19. [This language is nicely explained by Cooper (below 251). However, Cooper has maintained (below 250–3) that the line of argument outlined in this passage is independent of Aristotle's thesis that material natures are insufficient to explain the formation of precisely structured living outcomes. According to this line, Cooper claims, even if material natures *were* sufficient in that way, they still would not explain why these outcomes are *good* for the organism which possesses them; on the materialists' view, that they are beneficial would be a *coincidence*. But it is not clear that this is right. The point, I take it, is that even if material factors explained the regular production of, say, just this type of eye, and of just that type of eye-covering, they would not explain why the type of eye-covering produced is just the kind needed for the successful functioning of just the type of eye produced. But, if the material natures were such as to produce, by themselves, just such eyes *and* just such eye-coverings (etc.), then they would be such as to produce just such well-covered eyes (and just such well-organized living things); no *further* explanation would be needed. It is not as if they *could* have produced bad eye-coverings, or none, in this circumstance. Of material necessity, when there are these eyes, there are also those eye-coverings. Once one sees that the material natures are such as to produce such wholes, the only further question one could be asking would be why material things have the natures they do, and as Cooper rightly argues in his discussion of material necessity, this was not a question Aristotle thought one could ask. For this reason, I am still inclined to read this first argument in *Ph.* ii.8 as presupposing the thesis that material natures are insufficient by themselves to generate living organisms or their parts. (On the role of the concept of 'the good' in Aristotle's teleology, see also the bracketed addition to n. 18 above, and section 1 of 'Postscript 1986' below.) James Lennox (1982) has argued that the contrast between sexual and *spontaneous* generation is central to understanding the contrast between teleological and non-teleological processes in Aristotle. I do not think that is right, and have discussed his paper in Gotthelf forthcoming 1987c.]

[39] In the broadened sense that includes natures, as above n. 17.
[40] Cf. Charlton 1970: 114–17.
[41] 198b34–199a7. That the subject of this argument is organic development, and not natural things as such, is argued successfully by Charlton in 1970: 120–1. [David Furley has argued against Charlton on this in Furley 1985. I do not think his argument succeeds, and have given my reasons in Gotthelf forthcoming 1987b.]

Organic development is either for the sake of something or by chance; it is not by chance (since chance outcomes are irregular, organic outcomes regular); therefore organic development is for the sake of something.

More explicitly than in the opening statement of the problem, the available modes of explanation are said to be just two: explanation by element-potentials ('chance'[42]) and explanation by final cause ('that for the sake of which'). The case against the former is given in the parenthetical sub-argument: while the processes leading to a given chance outcome neither always nor for the most part issue in outcomes of the same type, the processes leading to the existence of a mature organism of some type always or for the most part do issue in an organism of that type. Thus the development of a living organism cannot be the result of a series of actualizations of element-potentials. Rather, it is a process for the sake of its outcome, which must mean, if our account of Aristotelian explanation is correct, that it involves the actualization of a potential irreducibly for an organism of that type.

This argument of Aristotle's has often been criticized. It is charged that he equivocates, switching senses of 'chance' from, roughly, 'mechanical sequence' to 'unusual sequence'. His argument is alleged to actually proceed: either for the sake of something or by chance (by 'mechanical' sequence); because usual not by chance (by unusual sequence); therefore, for the sake of something.[43]

I submit, however, that this is not an equivocation, because Aristotle's description of chance outcomes as 'unusual' is not ultimately a matter of language: what appears to be an appeal to ordinary language is in fact a factual claim.

W. D. Ross writes of this premise that, according to Aristotle,

it is of the nature of chance events to be the exception, while *everything* or almost everything in nature has the appearance of adaptation to purpose. That end-like results should be *constantly* produced in the absence of final causation would be too extraordinary a coincidence to be credible.[44]

Ross's last sentence might well have been intended as a summary of the argument for final causality in *Metaphysics* A.3 and 7, and even a restatement of 984b11–15, where, as we recall, Aristotle writes that

it is not likely either that fire or earth or any such element should be the reason why things manifest goodness and beauty, both in their being and in their coming to be, or that those thinkers [*sc.* the early Presocratics] should have supposed it was; nor again could it be right to entrust so great a matter to spontaneity or chance.

[42] Interpreted as above n. 38.
[43] The harshest such criticism is that of Cherniss 1935: 250–2; cf. Charlton 1970: 123.
[44] 1936: 43.

The argument in *Physics* II.8 is neither an equivocation nor an appeal to ordinary language. It is a restatement of the argument in *Metaphysics* **A**.3, and has the same force. Given the simplicity of Aristotle's chemistry, he can only believe that the outcome of organic development is too complex, too orderly, possessing too much of limit, *logos*, and form, to be the result merely of the unlimited, relatively indefinite natural action and interaction of the elements. The development must be *for the sake of* its outcome – i.e., essentially and irreducibly a development *to* order – i.e., to form. The development, in short, must be the actualization of an irreducible potential for form.

XII

Parts of Animals I.1. This chapter is a lengthy and structurally complex one, which develops several themes pertaining to method in biological science.[45] One of its most dominant themes is the importance of final causality for the study of the parts of animals. Though the subject of study is the structure and functioning of the parts of a mature, functioning animal, the argument for the necessity of employing final causality derives from the character of the coming to be of these parts. An examination of Aristotle's argument here should therefore be of value in determining his view of what it is to come to be for the sake of something.

The relevant conclusion is stated near the end of the chapter:

There are then these two causes, the *for-the-sake-of-which* and the of-necessity...
That there are two modes of causation, then, and that we must at least attempt to state both, is now clear, as it is that all those who do not do this say virtually nothing 'about nature', for the nature of a thing is more an origin than its matter...The reason why our predecessors did not arrive at this method of procedure is that the what-it-is-to-be and the defining of the being did not exist.[46]

The position of those who spoke only of matter and necessity was described in some detail in an earlier passage.[47] These were the thinkers who searched 'for the material origin and that sort of cause', explaining everything from the origin of the universe to the formation of nostrils by reference to 'the underlying matter's having some definite nature by necessity, e.g. that of fire, hot, that of earth, cold, the one light, the other heavy'. Clearly, they attempted to explain everything in terms of element-potentials.

But, just as Empedocles did not realize that complex structures do not come about at random, but as the result of the actualization of

---

[45] Balme's masterly analysis (1972) of the structure of this chapter is invaluable here.
[46] 642a1–2, 13–27.   [47] 640b4–28.

a specific potential for a form that includes that structure,[48] so he and
the others did not realize in general that

> if man and the animals and their parts exist by nature, then we must have to say
> of each part – of flesh, bone, blood, and all uniform parts, and similarly of the
> non-uniform ones such as face, hand, foot – in virtue of what each of them is such
> as it is, and according to what sort of potential. For the 'out of which' is not
> enough…we have to speak also of…what sort of thing it is in respect of its form;
> for the nature in respect of form is of more fundamental importance than the
> material nature.[49]

Thus, explanation solely in terms of element-potentials will not
account for aspects of the form; this requires a second 'mode of
causation' – an appeal to that for the sake of which these parts have
come to be – which requires an awareness of the phenomenon of
form and of the proper 'sort of potential'.[50]

The doctrine of *Parts of Animals* I.1 in regard to final causality, then,
is essentially the same as that of each of the other texts we have
investigated – *Generation of Animals* II, *Metaphysics* A, and *Physics* II.
Processes for the sake of something are distinguished from those that
are not by the presence in the one case, and the absence in the other,
of a potential for form. Since reference to this potential is necessary,
and mention only of element-potentials insufficient, this potential is
evidently one which is *not* reducible to element-potentials. Thus, for
a living organism of a certain form to come to be for the sake of
something is precisely for it to result from a sum of actualizations of
potentials, one of which – and the most explanatorily important of
which – is an irreducible potential for an organism of that form, a
potential (transmitted via the male parent's semen) to act on the
material supplied by the female parent in just such a manner as to
produce an organism one in form with the parents.[51]

[48] Earlier at 640a19–27, quoted in the next note.

[49] 640b18–28. Cf. 640a19–27: 'So Empedocles was not right when he said that animals have
many of the characteristics they do because "it just happened this way" in the process of
coming to be – e.g. even the spine, he says, is such as it is because "it happened to get
twisted and thus break". He was unaware, first, that the productive seed must have a
specific (*toiautēn*) potential and, secondly, that the producing agent is prior, not only in
logos but also in time – for a human begets a human, and therefore it is on account of the
parent being of such a sort that the child's coming to be is such as it is.'

[50] Thus, 'the reason why our predecessors did not arrive at this method of procedure is that
the what-it-is-to-be (*to ti ēn einai*) and the defining of the being (*to horisasthai tēn ousian*) did
not exist' (642a24–7).

[51] The argument of these sections (and of this essay as a whole) suggests an account of
Aristotle's four causes in terms of the concepts of potentiality and actuality. Every process
is the actualization of a pair of potentials, active and passive. (A nature may be thought
of as an internalized potential-pair.) The bearer of the active potential (the 'whence the
source of motion') is the efficient cause. When the outcome of a process is so organized
(has a *logos* such that) it has a distinctive manner of acting (an *ergon*) not reducible to the
qualitative changes of its material constituents, then the active and passive potentials must

XIII

Such is the case for the main thesis of this essay. The interpretation of Aristotle's conception of final causality presented here may be designated the 'irreducible potential' interpretation.

Most interpretations that have been offered, heretofore, fall into two main traditions. The first, which may be called the 'immaterial agency' interpretation, maintains that Aristotle understands natural teleology fundamentally on an analogy to human purposive action, in a way that implies that the developing embryo is (or embodies) some sort of conscious or quasi-conscious agent, directing the flow of materials, guiding its development to maturity.[52]

Such a view has little, if any, textual plausibility; it rests heavily on Aristotle's (in fact, quite infrequent) use of the metaphors of striving and desiring, and a somewhat casual reading of the comparisons of nature to an artisan in *Physics* II.8 and the biological works. While this sort of interpretation has the merit of taking Aristotle's teleology seriously and as a real alternative to the mechanism of his predecessors, its insensitive pressing of the nature/art analogy results in an Aristotelian mortal sin. Ultimately, the 'immaterial agency' interpretation makes nature a sub-category of art – i.e., of consciously directed, intentional action – thereby reversing the actual

be irreducibly potentials for form. This form, which must be specified in the identification of these potentials and their actualization (the 'what it is to be' both of the outcome and of its development), is the formal cause. And since the process, the development, is irreducibly *for* that form, that form ('that for the sake of which') is the final cause. Such a conception of causality presupposes, of course, the reality of natures and potentials. Aristotle's case against Hume here may in part be found in *Metaph.* Θ.3, but a fuller and stronger case can be constructed from other texts. [There is an excellent discussion of Aristotle's concept of 'the nature of a thing', and its role in his natural philosophy, by Sarah Waterlow Broadie in Waterlow 1982, esp. chs. 1–2. Professor Broadie does not discuss the implications of her analysis for our understanding of Aristotle's conception of a cause, but it would be well worth someone's trying to draw out those implications. Her analysis, for one thing, provides an explanation of why accounts of *aitia* in Aristotle simply in terms of necessary and/or sufficient conditions must fail (as Sorabji 1980: ch. 2 argues), and why it does not follow that we must fall back on epistemologically-oriented analyses (such as Sorabji offers) which explicate *aitia* in terms of explanation. (Cf. n. 2 above.) I hope to explore this issue elsewhere.]

[52] Advocates include Zeller (1897: 1 459–61) and Collingwood (1945: 83–5). I include in this category interpretations which speak of an 'unconscious desire' on the part of the embryo (e.g. Rist 1965), since 'unconscious desire', as psychologists use the term, is possible only to beings capable of conscious desire. Thus as meant in its ascriptions to embryos, this characterization is actually not metaphorical and illuminating, but self-contradictory. [Robinson 1983 defends a form of the 'immaterial agency' view in the course of a critique of the contrary view in Nussbaum 1978. His argument rests, I think, on a confusion between soul as efficient cause and soul as final cause, and more generally between the *dunamis* which is efficient cause and its object (what the dunamis is *for*) which is final cause. I discuss his argument, and these issues, in Gotthelf forthcoming 1987c.]

Aristotelian priority of nature to art, and thus rendering them both unintelligible.

The second, and more recent, interpretation may be designated the 'explanatory condition' interpretation. It maintains that the 'final cause' is in no sense actually a *cause*, though it plays a role in a certain type of explanation; and that its role in the explanation of organic development is to identify that for which the stages of development are necessary and (thus) that in terms of which they must be identified if they (and the development they constitute) are to be rendered 'intelligible'. The rooting of an acorn, for instance, is *for the sake of* the oak tree which results, according to this interpretation, if and only if the rooting is (1) a necessary condition of the existence of the oak tree and (2) 'intelligible' – fully 'understood' – only if identified by reference to the oak tree (e.g., as the rooting of a seed-for-an-oak-tree).[53]

Such an account works from a textual base that renders it initially plausible, but in viewing the specification of the end as necessary only to facilitate an (undefined) demand for 'understanding' or 'intelligibility', and not as demanded by the irreducible character of the potential actually possessed by the relevant 'seed', this interpretation appears to imply that the existence of final causality is compatible with the reducibility of the development to element-potentials. As a consequence, this interpretation seems to commit an Aristotelian mortal sin of its own: it appears to permit chance events to be for the sake of something. For instance, on this interpretation, it seems, Empedocles' human-headed bull[54] came to be for the sake of something: the coming together of the head and body were necessary for the existence of the bull, and these organic parts seem fully 'intelligible' only if reference to their ability to function in the calf is included in (or entailed by) their account.[55]

Aristotelian teleology, in fact, is neither vitalist and mystical, nor 'as if' and mechanical. The notion of an irreducible potential for form supplies the proper content to the awareness that for Aristotle

---

[53] Randall 1960 is often read this way (and not without warrant), e.g. by Toulmin and Goodfield, who give an admirably clear statement of this interpretation in 1966: 83–5. Cf. Wieland 1962: ch. 16, 'Zum Teleologieproblem' (English translation in Barnes, Schofield and Sorabji 1975).

[54] One of *ta bougenē androprōira* (*Ph.* II.8 198b32; cf. DK31 B61).

[55] My hesitation in attributing this consequence to the interpretation is due to the vagueness of its notion of 'intelligibility'. If a process were taken to be 'intelligible' only in terms of its end if and only if the potential being actualized was irreducibly for that end, then the objection would not hold. Even in that case, however, the 'irreducible potential' interpretation would constitute a significant advance, as I go on to indicate. I am indebted to Richard Schuldenfrei for bringing this possibility to my attention.

organic development is actually direc*tive*, without implying (as the 'immaterial agency' interpretation does) that it is direc*ted*; and it identifies the ontological basis of the awareness that the existence and stages of a development can be understood only in terms of its end – by establishing that the *identity* of the development is its being *irreducibly* a development to that end, irreducibly the actualization of a potential for form.

XIV

Aristotle's teleology – his thesis that the development, structure, and functioning of a living organism are for the sake of something – is a central tenet of his thought. It is a corollary of the 'irreducible potential' interpretation of his conception of final causality that this thesis is *factual* or *empirical* in character: it is a conclusion drawn from observation of nature and not a premise brought to it.

Philosophers of science today are in increasing agreement that the question of reduction is an empirical one; they insist that one cannot legislate the precise form of the laws in which our understanding of nature is expressed. Aristotle's attitude is similar: he does not attempt to legislate a priori the particular form which a successful account of the natures and potentials of living organisms must take. His arguments for his teleological doctrine make this clear. What he insists is that the facts as we have observed them, and the identifications of the natures and potentials of things which these observations have led us to, entail the irreducibility thesis which is at the core of the concept of final causality asserted to obtain in nature. Though the simplicity and the non-mathematical character of Aristotle's chemistry (and physics) eliminates for him any real possibility of a successful reduction to element-potentials of the complexities of the organic world, this makes his thesis no less empirical – for his view of the inanimate world is equally subject to revision. There is nothing in the fundamentals of Aristotle's philosophy, and nothing in his philosophical or scientific method, which would prohibit the adoption of a reducibility thesis, should the scientific evidence be judged to warrant it.[56]

[[56] In an important discussion of teleological explanation in Aristotle (Waterlow 1982: chs. 1–2), which I was delighted to find has much in common with my own, Sarah Waterlow Broadie takes me to task for the exaggeration involved in my 'empiric Aristotle' (91). She argues that the commitment to irreducibility of the sort I have argued here (and on which she has much to say that is highly illuminating) is bound up in the very notions of substance and the nature of a thing. Since these notions are surely among 'the fundamentals of [Aristotle's] philosophy', if teleology goes so go some fundamentals. It is not clear to me, however, that reducibility of the sort Aristotle denies would render the notion of a nature inapplicable at the elemental level or, more importantly, that there would not be other

But Aristotle did not believe that the evidence warranted it. On the contrary, we have seen that he thought that a reduction of biology to chemistry could not be accomplished, and thus that organic development involves the actualization of an irreducible potential for form – which is to say, that it is a process *for the sake of* its end, irreducibility of potential for form being the core of Aristotle's conception of being *for the sake of something*.[57]

Postscript 1986

I

Though I would write this paper somewhat differently if I were writing it today, I still agree with virtually* all of its main claims. There are three that are crucial.

(i) *Ontological irreducibility*. The development, structure, and functioning of living organisms cannot be wholly explained by – *because it is not wholly due to* – the simple natures and potentials of the elements which constitute these organisms. No sum of actualizations of what I have called 'element-potentials' is sufficient by itself for the production of those complex living structures and functionings for which Aristotle offers teleological explanation.

(By 'simple' natures and potentials I mean those whose essential specification does not make reference to the form or nature of the living organism as a whole. I do

grounds on which the substantiality of living things or even their teleological character could be grounded. There are weaker sorts of teleology that we could imagine Aristotle legitimately retreating to, upon being faced with, and coming to accept, a more quantitative and structural chemistry. Such teleologies could certainly give no trouble to his concept of the nature of a thing, and would probably sustain his theory of substance. (The thesis 'T1' that Bradie and Miller (1984) describe as 'the core of Aristotle's teleology' (143) is an example of such a weaker teleology. Their mistake, as I see it, is in claiming that this is the thesis which Aristotle actually argues for, and not the stronger 'T2'. They seem to assume (cf. 142 bottom) that Aristotle wanted to leave open the possibility of there being a deeper level of matter to which potentials for form *were* reducible, but there is surely no evidence for this. What is puzzling is how, if that were Aristotle's position, it could still be classified as 'Irreducible Compatibilism', as Bradie and Miller correctly argue earlier it is, rather than (e.g.) the unwanted 'Supererogatory Compatibilism'. Though I must take issue with them here, I am gratified by their endorsement of many of the claims of this paper.)

The issues raised by Professor Broadie require further investigation. Though I stand by my original statement, I happily concede that in her very rich study she has shown the question more complicated and subtle than I had made it out to be.]

[57 Some of the ideas developed in the Postscript and additional notes, as well as the main themes of this paper, were presented to several meetings of a graduate course I gave with Professor J. L. Ackrill at Oxford University in Trinity Term 1984, on 'Substance and teleology: some issues in Aristotle's biological works'. I am grateful to all those who participated in discussions on that occasion, both inside and outside of class, and especially to Professor Ackrill and to David Charles, both of whom forced me to sharpen some formulations – and some thoughts. In addition, I have benefited over the years, since the original publication of this essay, from discussions of these ideas with more people than I can name, but have benefited most, I think, from exchanges with David Balme, James Lennox and, most recently, David Charles. Warm thanks are due also to Richard Sorabji and Sarah Waterlow Broadie for discussing some of my views in print, especially to Sorabji, who was the first and with whom I had in addition some valuable correspondence.]

* Cf. n. 56 above.

not mean to deny, and am inclined to affirm, that the elements have (irreducible) capacities to be worked up into such wholes, and that such capacities may be seen as part of their natures as the elements they are, on which cf. *Metaph. Z*.16 and *Mete.* IV.12, and below Balme, ch. 10, 284–5, and Kosman, ch. 14, 389.)

(ii) *The dependence of teleological explanation on ontological irreducibility.* If some sum of actualizations of element-potentials *were* by itself sufficient for the production of some outcome, that outcome would *not* be subject to teleological explanation for Aristotle.

(iii) *The way ontological irreducibility generates and legitimates teleological explanation.* This is a two-part claim, involving (a) a thesis about the nature of explanation generally, and (b) a thesis about the form of a teleological explanation:

(a) Explanation, for Aristotle, works fundamentally by identifying the natures and potentials whose actualization actually constitutes, or is producing, the phenomenon being explained.

(b) A teleological explanation explains the presence of some phenomenon by showing it to be necessary for the presence of some complex end which a potential being actualized is irreducibly *for*.

(To be 'teleological', all will agree, an explanation must have some such form as '*A* is present/occurs because *A* is necessary or best for some end *B*'. Typically an 'end' is defined as a good outcome. While it will in fact always be true that an end is something good, this is not, on claim (iiib) here, part of Aristotle's concept or analysis of something's being an end. Rather to be an end is to be what a potential being actualized is actually and irreducibly for. This is a factual or objective matter and does not depend on imported normative notions. (These claims require, and will get, further explanation below, where I also show how (iiib) incorporates the 'best possible' clause.) As above, the potential is 'irreducibly' for some complex end when the production of that end is not due wholly to the actualization of element-potentials.)

Claim (i) is agreed to in one form or another by the other contributors to this Part of the present volume, and by Waterlow (1982), Lennox (1982), Robinson (1983), Bradie and Miller (1984), and Charlton (1985), among others. It was disputed by Nussbaum (1978) and Sorabji (1980), who thus also rejected claim (ii). I discuss Nussbaum's views in Gotthelf 1980 and 1981/2, and examine Sorabji's in section II of this Postscript. The challenge for interpretations which jointly deny (i) and (ii) is to show how teleological explanation could have any force as explanation if a reduction to element-potentials were in principle available. For, given Aristotle's realism, there will not be some merely *pragmatic* function that certain language can perform which other language for the very same aspect(s) of a phenomenon does not; and it seems to me that any authentic explanatory function which the teleological level would be thought to have could be performed instead by the corresponding account at the material level, if a reduction were available (cf., e.g., the new part of n. 38 above). These are, of course, only assertions on my part, and are best taken, as I say, as (friendly) challenges to other interpretations. (For the positions of John Cooper and David Balme on claim (ii), see their contributions in chs. 9 and 10 below.)

My approach to the issue claim (iii) addresses has been to ask why the fact that something, *A*, is necessary for some end *B*, should explain the presence of *A*, and how, thus, *B* would be *responsible* for *A*. I start from claim (iiia) – that explanation, for Aristotle, is essentially by natures (*phuseis*) and potentials (*dunameis*). This seems clear to me both from the *Physics* and *Metaphysics* passages cited in n. 12 above, and from the pervasive use of these concepts in key explanatory passages throughout the scientific treatises, including, especially, *GA* and *PA* i, focused on in this chapter. This being so, we have to ask, for any phenomenon to be explained, which nature(s) and/or potential(s) are being actualized in the course of the phenomenon's generation or functioning. Now, the identity of a nature or potential is given in part by its object or end (i.e. by what it is irreducibly *for*), so we have to ask what that object or end is in each case. If, in accordance with claim (i), the production of a complex organic outcome is *not* the sum of actualizations of element-potentials, then the nature or potential being actualized must be a potential for that outcome (or for some larger end that includes that outcome), in other words: a potential for form. But *that* makes the explanation teleological, because it puts into the explanans an irreducible reference to an outcome for which the explanandum is antecedently necessary.

The use of teleological explanation in cases of complex organic outcomes is thus legitimated by the fact that those outcomes are the result of actualizations of potentials that are in fact for (and thus whose descriptions make inescapable reference to) complex living forms as such. On this picture, the fact that something, *A*, is necessary for some end, *B*, will *explain* the presence of that *A* because (i) a potential for *B* is being realized, and (ii) if a potential for *B* is being realized, anything necessary for *B* is also being realized. (That is part of what it *is* for a potential for *B* to be being realized.) If this account of how teleological explanation is legitimated is to be successful, however, two conditions will have to be satisified. First, it will have to be true, in some objective way, to say that *B* is somehow *responsible* for *A*. Second, the fact that the potential for *B* is being realized will have to be a basic fact, so far as explanation is concerned. Both conditions, I would like to argue, are in fact satisfied, on the picture I have sketched.

It might be said that the first condition is automatically satisfied if there is an explanation since an *aitia* just is that which explains, for Aristotle, but I have rejected this view in n. 51 above. Though I do not, as I have acknowledged in that note, have a good account of what an *aitia* is for Aristotle generally, it seems clear to me that when an (irreducible) potential for some end is being realized, that end is responsible for the process leading up to it as that which the process is (irreducibly) *for*. That is to say, the end is a sort of intentional object of the process, much as the object of a desire (or perhaps intention) is the object of the action aimed at satisfying that desire. The end has a real status as aim, and was the end of the process even if the process failed to reach that end. Objects that perform such real functions clearly deserve the label '*aitia*', according to Aristotle; in fact, it could be said to be a condition on any successful account of Aristotle's conception of 'being responsible for' that it make clear why it should be appropriate to view such objects (of potentials, of desires or intentions) as actually *responsible* for their effects. (This is not a demand to collapse the final into the efficient cause. It is the potential (or its bearer *qua* bearer of that potential) which is the efficient cause, while the final cause is what the potential is for, and this distinction must be maintained (cf. the new part of n. 52 above).) Note 51 above, with its bracketed addition, contains, I think, some pieces of such a general account of an Aristotelian cause, but I do not yet know how to put them together.

So much for the first condition my account of Aristotelian teleological explanation must satisfy if it is truly to count as explanation for Aristotle. As for the second condition, if *A*'s being necessary for *B* explains *A*'s presence because an irreducible potential for *B* (which brings *A* along, as it were) is being realized, I will need to show that the presence of an irreducible potential for form is basic so far as explanation is concerned. For, otherwise, whatever explains the presence of such a potential will be more basic, and will be in fact what grounds teleological explanation. (For a view that there is something more basic, see John Cooper's interpretation in ch. 9 immediately following.) In arguing for irreducibility (claim (i)), I argued that the realization of *B* cannot be seen as the necessary consequence of the actualization of element-potentials alone, but I need also to show that my claim to the presence of an 'irreducible potential for form' is the most fundamental way to put the ontological consequences of irreducibility. That it is, is in part established, I think, by the argument for viewing natures and potentials as the fundamental explanatory concepts in Aristotle (as summarized two paragraphs above), but in part involves a crucial metaphysical claim – an ascription to Aristotle of a sort of ontological 'individualism'. The claim is, roughly, that the basic fact about the living world is the existence of individual living organisms with the capacity to produce other individuals like themselves. According to this view, other facts at this level of generality which might be thought to ground teleological explanation (e.g. the permanence of species, or the pervasive seeking of the good), are to be seen as *consequences* of the existence of self-sustaining, reproducing individuals. Some such view is defended by David Balme in chs. 10 and 11 below, and at least suggested by the argument of James Lennox's ch. 13 and his 1985a. If such a view can be made out, as I firmly think it can, then the fundamental analysis of teleological explanation will in fact be one in terms of 'irreducible potentials'.

Now, Charles Kahn (1985: 197–8 and n. 16) suggests that such a view gives only part of the picture, because one will need to 'build into the analysis of actualization the required normative component', and will need as part of one's analysis of teleological explanation an independent notion of the good. I have explained in the new portion of n. 18 above why I do not think this is right. I would like here to say just a little more on this issue. Supporters of what we might call 'the normative analysis' of Aristotelian teleology suggest that the basic pattern of a teleological explanation is something like:

A is there because it is good that *A* be there.

This is generally said to divide into two alternatives:

(a)   *A* is there because it is necessary for the presence of some good, *B*;
(b)   *A* is there because it is good (better, best) for some good, *B* (where *A* is not necessary for *B*).

The good, according to this view, thus enters independently into the analysis at two places. I have argued above (n. 18) that the goodness of the end is *not* an independent constituent of the analysis, nor what centrally establishes that end as the end. Rather the process really is towards a fully developed state, specifiable independently of its goodness, and establishable as an end without reference to its goodness. That all such ends are good is a separate fact about the world, itself a consequence of a 'metaethical' analysis of the good that analyzes it in terms of ends (and not ends in terms of it).

This view can be made more plausible by performing a thought experiment, in which one rejects the standard Aristotelian analysis of the good, and asks if teleological explanation will still be applicable. Let us imagine that the biological world is just as it is now, except that successful life was in no way a good thing. Let us suppose (*per impossibile* perhaps) that the existence of complexity was intrinsically evil, and the destruction of living bodies therefore intrinsically good (and *not* because of the will of some non-material being). In such a world, living organisms would seem to develop and function for the sake of outcomes that were in no way good, and yet, we may ask, if the production of these outcomes could not be explained by element-potentials alone, would not Aristotle still wish to offer teleological explanations for such developings and functionings? The 'evil' lung, for instance, forms because irreducible potentials for 'evil' viviparous land animals are being actualized, and such animals require lungs to function.

If the thought-experiment sits hard, it is because, as good Aristotelian ethical theorists, we cannot sustain this imaginary notion of the good. But *that* is because of something about the nature of the good, not something about the nature of ends as such. The 'normative analysis' of ends, then, which is perhaps 'first to us', is not 'first in nature'. 'First in nature' is an analysis in terms of potentials for complex living outcomes specifiable without reference to independent normative notions.

What, then, about pattern (b) above, where one explains *A*'s presence not because it is necessary for *B* but because it is the best of several things, one of which but no particular one of which is necessary for *B*? There are two points to make here. First, the operative notion of 'best for' in all cases here is something like 'greatest contribution to the life of', so that we do not have what I have been calling an independent notion of the good. (On this point, see above n. 18, with references.) Secondly, as others have pointed out (e.g. Sorabji 1980: 158–9), this pattern of explanation rests on the proposition, roughly, that 'nature always acts for the best'. I take this principle to state a basic fact about the sort of *ends* that exist in nature (and thus the sort of outcomes that the irreducible potentials are irreducible potentials *for*), viz. that in cases where there are options in the organization of living things, the ends aimed at are the 'best-possible organizations'. Both development and functioning are aimed at the realization and maintenance of an organism of maximum efficiency and capacity within what is possible to the basic nature of the organism in question. (That there is such a 'basic nature' against which such efficiency can be measured I argue in ch. 7 above.) In that way, pattern (b) has the same logical form as pattern (a). Explanations of the form '*A* is best for outcome *B*' are to be understood, at a deeper level, as being of the form '*A* is necessary for outcome *best-organized-B*', where 'best' has the fully naturalistic analysis I have indicated. That there are nonetheless *two* patterns of explanation derives, theoretically, from the fact that the second pattern requires an additional premise about nature, over and above the irreducibility premise needed for the first pattern, and practically, from the fact that the scientific work involved in producing explanations according to the different patterns is in some ways noticeably different.

Supporters of the 'normative analysis' of the form of Aristotelian teleological explanation point to Andrew Woodfield's analysis of teleology (Woodfield 1976) as one that captures important aspects of Aristotle's own analysis. For the reasons just given, I think rather that, so far as the basic form of analysis is concerned, Charles Taylor's account (cf. above, n. 10) is closer than Woodfield's. (On certain aspects Larry Wright's (1976) account is even closer: cf. section III of this Postscript below.)

II

In *Necessity, Cause, and Blame* (1980) Richard Sorabji argues that, according to Aristotle, a full material-level account of teleological processes is in principle available. One of the larger themes of his book is the relation between cause and necessity, and in that connection he explores the claim that the use of the final cause is incompatible with the existence of necessitating causes. He thinks it is not, and devotes one chapter to showing that, for the most part, Aristotle thought that individual outcomes in nature have necessitating (material) causes, and a second to showing that a proper understanding of how teleological explanations work reveals their compatibility with such causes.

In ch. 9 Sorabji sets out very nicely the problem that has engaged scholars: in several theoretical passages Aristotle appears to deny that individual natural outcomes have necessitating causes, while Aristotle insists time and again in the biology that outcomes are both for the sake of something *and* of necessity. Sorabji rightly objects to the view presented in Balme 1972 that material necessity is a disguised hypothetical necessity, presaging some of the objections developed more fully by John Cooper (below 260–2), and concludes that we in fact have conflicting claims here. We can only, he says, attempt to offer an explanation for the conflict, and the one he proposes is that Aristotle has confused weaker claims, primarily that necessitating causes do not explain, with the stronger claim that they do not exist (150–2, 162, 173–4).

This explanation does not seem possible, however. For, in one of the theoretical passages Sorabji cites in which Aristotle denies that individual natural outcomes occur of unhypothetical necessity (*PA* 639b21–640a8), Aristotle appears quite clear on the difference: one reason he gives for there being no explanation of natural outcomes in terms of simple necessity alone is precisely that such necessity does not exist in nature. This is not an unconscious slide but a deliberate move, and it is from non-existence to non-explanation, not the other way.

Himself convinced that individual outcomes in nature have necessitating causes according to Aristotle, Sorabji attempts in ch. 10 to show that this is fully compatible with their being for the sake of something. (Sorabji typically speaks of organs and processes having a 'purpose', a term I want to avoid for its (to me unavoidable) implication of design or intention.) Making use of the important *PA* 640a33ff., he finds three distinct patterns of teleological explanation, the first two of *parts* of animals (as necessary, given certain basic features of the organism, or as better, given such features), the third of *processes*, including organic development. In each case he seeks to show that the availability of a teleological explanation for an animal feature (part or process) does not preclude there being necessitating causes of that feature.

The first mode of teleological explanation, Sorabji argues, works according to the following generic pattern: Given *x*, it is only to be expected that *y*. He refers to Aristotle's explanation of the camel's extra stomachs (*PA* 674a28–b15), writing that

'The camel needs to eat tough and thorny food, and therefore it has an extra series of stomachs for digesting... The explanation seems to work by taking the existence of the camel, together with certain characteristics, such as the thorny diet, as given. Once these things are given, extra stomachs are *only to be expected*.' (156, italics in original).

But there is nothing in such an explanation that precludes the existence of necessitating causes (162–3), and even when these causes are fully known 'in many contexts, and for many purposes, we shall always want teleological explanations' (165).

My own view, mentioned in n. 19 above, is that this pattern (and the second, of which Sorabji gives a similar account, adding as given that 'nature does nothing in vain' (158)), works only when, and only because, the generation of that part was itself teleological. 'Coming to be for the sake of', on this view, is logically prior to 'being for the sake of'. My arguments for this perhaps paradoxical-sounding thesis are now presented below, in section III of this Postscript. If successful, they show that Sorabji's first two patterns are not independent of the third. And since this third pattern works, in the case of organic development, only because such development is not the result of material necessity alone (as I have argued above), the first pattern is *not* compatible with the existence of necessitating causes.

Sorabji himself thinks, however, that the third pattern *is* compatible with the existence of necessitating causes. He accepts, with his typical generous acknowledgment, the account of this pattern presented in the present paper. As he puts it, to say that the development of an organism, for instance, is for the sake of the mature organism which issues from it is to *identify* which of the various possible *dunameis* (of the whole organism, of the materials) is the one at work (171–2). But having said this, he soon qualifies it, in my view fatally. It is not that the material *dunameis* are not operative and necessitating, he says; it is that they are not considered explanatory (174). But that way of putting it is incompatible with his own formulation of my account of how these explanations work. If the outcome is of material necessity, then the material capacities, in sum, are sufficient, when actualized, to produce such an outcome, and in this case *have been actualized*. But this is just to say that *they* are the *dunameis* at work, and that the *dunamis* of the whole organism *is not*. My account of the *dunamis* of the whole allows for *dunameis* of the materials to be at work – anything hypothetically necessitated by the actualization of the *dunamis* for the form of the whole will be so necessitated only *given* the basic natures and potentials of the elements; but it does not allow that they be *sufficient* for the outcome. If they *are* sufficient, then there is simply no place for a *dunamis* of the whole.

Sorabji could modify my view to say that explanation here consists in selecting not which *dunameis* are *at work* but which are *explanatory*. But the result would largely be trivial. In fact, this exposes what I find to be another weakness in Sorabji's overall account of the relation of teleology and necessity. He says much about how outcomes might be the result of material necessity yet not be explained in that way but only teleologically. But he does little to show what features would make the one explanatory and the other not. Surely if an outcome is known to be of material necessity, then given the antecedents, it is 'only to be expected' that the outcome will occur. Why should that be sufficient for explanation in the case of parts, but not here? Sorabji refers several times to the relativity of explanation to the purposes of the questioner, but to many this will seem an un-Aristotelian thesis, and he mentions no passages which require it. (Cf. 11, 29–31, 56, 58–9, 158, listed in his index, s.v. 'explanation: ...relative to the question asked'; also 165–6.)

What, then, of the reservations Sorabji expressed (172–4) to my own interpretation of these matters? Following David Hamlyn, Sorabji objects first to calling the relevant *dunamis* by itself the explanation, since 'if anything explains, it is rather the whole *complex* of facts into which the [relevant] *dunamis* fits' (172). But I never denied this or implied the opposite. As Sorabji observes there, Aristotle himself is happy to call the relevant *dunamis* the efficient cause; the mistake would be in equating *cause* with *explanation*, which Sorabji does here probably because of the arguments to that effect which he has given earlier (40–2 and ch. 2 generally). The full explanation (*logos* or *apodeixis*, not *aitia*) would certainly involve more than just the efficient cause. As I have argued elsewhere, Aristotle views the various causes here as factors in one explanation, not as distinct explanations (cf. Gotthelf 1980: 373–4).

Sorabji then (173) objects to my thesis just mentioned that teleological explanation of parts is derivative from teleological explanation of development, offering a counterargument. I deal with this in section III below.

Finally, he objects to my treating the absence of a full material-level account as central to Aristotelian teleology, on grounds of his earlier argument that necessitating material causes *are* present even if not explanatory. Even this latter claim must be tempered, he observes, since 'Indeed, Aristotle uses a tattoo of words implying that the necessitating causes which he cites for biological arrangements really do explain them' (174, with nn. 62, 63). In the bracketed addition to n. 32 above, I responded to Sorabji's earlier claim that the pervasive language of 'both for the sake of...and of necessity' implies the existence of material-level causes sufficient to necessitate biological arrangements, referring to the contributions by Cooper and Balme below.

Sorabji himself provides, several chapters back (51 n. 24), the basis on which the explanatory language he points to here can be understood:

'... The denials [of explanatory value to material causes] are themselves sometimes nuanced: e.g. at *GA* v 8, 789b20, the word "through" (*dia*) seems to allow physiological causes explanatory value in producing biological parts in those cases where the parts serve no purpose; and even when the causes produce useful parts, they can be called explanations of the material kind (*hōs hulē aitia*, 789b8). Cf. *Phys.* II 9, 200a6, a9–10: things do not occur "through" (*dia*) material causes, "except in the sense of occurring through matter" (*plēn hōs di' hulēn*)...'

To be explanatory as matter is to be explanatory as that which, given its elemental natures and potentials, is necessary *if* some end not itself necessary is to be achieved – i.e. if some potential for form, not reducible to element-potentials, is to be actualized. This is a hypothetical, not a simple, necessity, and does nothing to imply that material factors explain (or even necessitate) *by themselves*.

III

'Hence we should if possible say that because this is what it is to be a man, therefore he has these things; for he cannot be without these parts. Failing that, we should get as near as possible to it: we should either say altogether that it cannot be otherwise, or that it is at least good thus. And these follow. And because he is such a thing, his coming-to-be necessarily happens so and is such. And that is why this part comes to be first, and then this. And this is the way we should speak of everything that is composed naturally.' (*PA* I.1 640a33–b4, tr. Balme)

In this well-known passage Aristotle describes the various patterns of explanation of animals' parts which a truly educated man should expect to find in a properly developed natural philosophy (cf. 639a1–15). The basic distinction is between (three types of) explanation of the being of parts – their being present in or possessed by certain animal kinds – and explanation of their coming to be, i.e. of the process by which they come to be present in or possessed by these animal kinds. Such explanations are teleological, establishing, respectively, that the part *is* or *came to be* for the sake of something.

Elsewhere, Aristotle speaks as if he recognizes that distinction. He concludes his first argument in support of the use of teleological explanation in *Physics* II.8, for instance, with the words: 'The "for the sake of something"', then, is present in things which by nature come to be and are' (199a7–8). In *GA* v.1 he excludes non-universal *pathē* from such explanation by writing that: 'Whatever features do not belong to the nature [of an animal generally] nor are peculiar (*idia*) to any particular [animal] kind – of features of this sort none either are or come to be for the sake of anything' (778a30–2). Of those things which do either belong to the nature of an animal generally or are peculiar to some animal kind, Aristotle says a few lines later that: 'Each one, then, is for the sake of something, and yet comes to be both on account of this cause and on account of the others [*sc.* material and moving causes: b9]...' (b10–12). And the division of labor between *PA* and *GA* pretty much mirrors this distinction, *PA* explaining the presence of parts teleologically, *GA* explaining their formation.*

---

* This is not to say that *PA* is unconcerned with generation. *PA* is concerned with why animals have the parts they do, and animals have the parts they do *partly* because some such parts are needed (or are best) for the functioning of the whole and *partly* because the available materials permit those parts: *tēi men heneka tou... tēi de ex anangkēs*. *PA* will thus have things to say about the 'necessary natures' of the available materials, and the constraints these natures place on what parts could be formed to fulfill a needed function,

In n. 19 above I suggested that *being for the sake of* was thought by Aristotle to be definable in terms of *coming to be for the sake* of, and have repeated this claim in section II of this Postscript. I want here to give my reasons. The idea has struck some people as peculiar, on grounds that Richard Sorabji well expresses, referring to my suggestion:

'This seems to me to *reverse* Aristotle's order of priorities. In the passage with which this chapter starts (*PA* I 1, 640a10–b4), reference to a *dunamis* occurs only in explaining processes, and the passage in question makes the explanation of processes *subordinate* to the explanation of why man has the parts he has.' (Sorabji 1980: 173)

Now, in the passage quoted above Aristotle says explicitly that it is 'because he is such a thing [that] his coming-to-be necessarily happens so and is such', so in one sense Sorabji is surely right. But that is only part of the story, and a part I shall argue which already *presupposes* that coming to be is for the sake of something.

The thesis I wish to defend is that a part, *A*, *is* for the sake of doing something, *B*, if, and only if, *A* in fact does *B*, *and* has *come to be* for the sake of doing *B*. Since coming to be for the sake of is explicated on my account without reference to being for the sake of (above 213), one can say, as I have, that the latter is defined in terms of the former.

Perhaps it should be stressed that this account is meant to hold only in those cases where giving what *A* is for the sake of is meant to give an *aitia*, and thus an explanation. When Aristotle says early in *Ph.* II.5 that 'among things which are neither necessary nor for the most part there are some to which it can belong to be for the sake of something' (196b19–21, after Charlton), and when he says of the tripod that fell open accidentally so as to be ready for sitting on that 'it was for the sake of sitting, but it did not fall for the sake of sitting' (196b17–18), one might wish to interpret him to be using a purely *descriptive* sense of 'is for the sake of' which merely labels some doing or capacity of the thing as useful in some way, without implying that that is why it is there. I think myself that these passages are to be read differently (cf. Gotthelf 1975: 62–72, 285 n. 119), but in any case want to make it clear that it is only explanatory uses of 'for the sake of' that are at issue here.

In fact, it is the chance cases that first bring out the plausibility of this thesis. One needs to ask whether, in cases where a part did something which contributed to life or well-being but had not come to be for the sake of doing so, Aristotle would be willing to say that the part *is for the sake of* that contribution, and thereby *explain* its presence in the organism. It seems not. To see this we might consider Empedocles' human-headed bull (n. 54 above). If, for instance, the neck muscles of the torso of the animal were strong enough (and the only muscles strong enough) to support the head that on the theory it accidentally joined up with, would Aristotle say that

but it will not focus on the generative process as such, and its timing and stages, and how these are necessitated by the nature of the result to be produced: those are the focus of *GA*. And *GA*'s initial focus is not so much the final cause of generation but its efficient cause: what antecedent movements (as it were) produce offspring one in form with their parents and how they do it. (Cf. *GA* I.1 715a11–18, II.1 733b23–32, etc.) Since the movements Aristotle identifies are those borne by the heat transmitted from the father, and involve, in addition to low-level material *dunameis*, a *dunamis* for form, teleological explanation will be inevitable, the end being what the *dunamis* that is the efficient cause is *for*. And teleological explanation does appear in *GA*, both for generation as such and its general features (II.1 731b18–732a11, 6 742a16–b17, 743a36–b3) and for particular formations, timings, and sequences (743b3–18, 744a35–b9, etc.). But it is introduced selectively and is not the primary focus of the work. Still, insofar as they are concerned with for-the-sake-of relationships, *PA* is primarily concerned with *being* for the sake of, *GA* with *coming to be* for the sake of.

those muscles *are* in that animal *for the sake of* supporting the head? If one imagines that one is Aristotle, the reaction is likely to be 'No'.

Aristotle too seems to say not. In the well-known first argument of *Ph.* ii.8 (above sec. xi), he generalizes from the case of teeth which arise by chance so as to be serviceable in some way, to all the parts in which 'the "for the sake of something" seems to be present' (198b27–9) but on this view would not. Now Aristotle's focus is on coming to be, and this sentence might well be speaking only of coming to be for the sake of. But it is perhaps more natural to read it as speaking of parts which appear to *be* for the sake of something, and in that case Aristotle (and his opponents, as he characterizes them) would seem to be assuming that, on the view under consideration, these parts cannot be said to *be* for the sake of something, precisely because they have not come to be for the sake of that but rather by chance.

The presence of *huparchein* here suggests this, as does the way Aristotle states the conclusion of his refutation of the opponents' view, at 199a7–8, the one place here where he explicitly mentions *being* for the sake of something:

The 'for the sake of something', then, is present in things which by nature come to be and are.

That is to say, the argument presented here establishes, and is apparently *needed* to establish, that things in nature *are* for the sake of something as well as come to be for the sake of something. Without the part's having *come* to be for the sake of something it simply isn't a candidate for *being* for the sake of anything.

But, *PA* ii–iv is full of arguments that conclude to some part's being for the sake of some function. Do these arguments refer to their parts having come to be for the sake of anything? On the face of it, no. Aristotle either takes as common knowledge, or argues to, the contribution a part makes to life or well-being, and from that concludes directly that the part is for the sake of making that contribution. He speaks, as noted, of the materially necessary factors in the part's coming to be but not of its having come to be for the sake of anything.

However, *PA* ii–iv is a study of animals, not of explanation. The theory of explanation which is at work in those books is itself developed, among other places, in *PA* i.1, and in that chapter, I would like to argue, Aristotle makes the dependence we have been discussing clear.

Much of i.1 is devoted to the final cause, in one way or another, and there is much argument in its behalf. It is striking that all of this argument, and most of this discussion, is devoted to the causes of *coming to be* and the notion of *coming to be* for the sake of. Richard Sorabji once suggested in correspondence that this can be explained by the preoccupation of Aristotle's opponents with coming to be and his concern to respond to them. But I think there is a deeper explanation, captured in the priority thesis I have been arguing for here. For, in the passage quoted at the head of this section, in which Aristotle presents the proper method for explaining parts, observe the 'hence' (*dio*). That this is the way to explain parts follows from something – from what?

As Balme notes, '"Hence" resumes the argument from a26' (1972: 87 *ad* 640a33; on a27–33 as parenthetical cf. 86 *ad loc.*). The argument begins at a15 in defense of an answer Aristotle gives to the question (a10–12) whether one should describe first an animal's coming to be, explaining the character of its being by reference to that, or the reverse. Aristotle's answer is, of course, the latter.

'For in house-building too it is more the case that *these* things take place because the form of the house is *such*, than that the house is such because it comes to be in this way. For coming-to-be is for the sake of being, not being for the sake of coming-to-be. Hence Empedocles was wrong in saying that many attributes belong to animals because it happened so in their coming-to-be, for instance that their backbone is such because it happened to get broken by bending. He failed to recognize, first, that the seed previously constituted must already possess this sort of capability (*toiautēn dunamin*), and secondly that its producer was prior not only in definition but in time; for it is the man that generates a man, and therefore it is because *that* man is such that *this* man's coming-to-be happens so. (a15–26, tr. Balme)

Hence we should if possible say that because this is what it is to be a man, therefore he has these things;...' (a33ff., my emphasis)

The appropriateness of teleological explanation of the presence of parts by reference to the animal's form or essence clearly derives from the appropriateness of teleological explanation of their coming to be. If parts came to be of material necessity (and thus animals were as they were because of the way they came to be – the force of the rejected alternative, 'being for the sake of coming-to-be'), teleological explanation of the presence of these parts by reference to their contribution to the being of the animals of which they are a part would not be warranted. Given that they *come to be* for the sake of such a contribution, their *being* can be *explained* by reference to that contribution.

Two questions, perhaps, arise at this point. First, what difference is there, then, between teleological explanation of the being or presence of a part and teleological explanation of its coming to be? And second, if the relationship is as I say, why does Aristotle speak so insistently in this context of the priority of being over coming to be?

The answer to the first question has been covered in my note above (237–8) on the difference of focus between *PA* and *GA*. A teleological explanation of the being of a part will make reference only to its current contribution to the being of the animal of which it is a part, and not to the stages by which that part is formed. As noted there, such an explanation may make reference to constraints on the character of the part that derive from the available matter, but will not attempt to explain why, for instance, 'this part comes to be first, and then this' (b2–3). Teleological explanation of coming to be will do that, and as noted, there are numerous such explanations in *GA*.

As for the second question, it is important to note that Aristotle's remarks about the priority of being over coming to be all have to do with the proper explanation of the *coming to be* of animals and their parts. The explanation of the parts' *being* is not involved at all. (*That* is what comes in the 'hence' passage.) To explain coming to be teleologically is to explain it by reference to (the needs of) the formed organism, and thus by reference to the organism's being. Since 'coming-to-be *is* for the sake of being, not being for the sake of coming-to-be', such teleological explanation is proper, and grasping the animal's being will be prior to engaging in such explanation.

Now, of course, one can show that a certain sort of animal must have a certain part, if it is to exist at all, or to exist well, without having shown that the coming to be of the animal is for the sake of something. And particular teleological explanations of coming to be will, as Aristotle says in the passage with which we began, build on such analyses. But it is important to see that such an analysis will not be a *teleological* explanation (or any other sort of *explanation*) of the part's presence, *if* the part has not come to be for the sake of the contribution the analysis shows it to make.

We can perhaps best see this by returning to Sorabji's account of these matters, quoted just above, and in particular to his rendering of the working of Aristotle's explanation of the additional stomachs in the camel (quoted in section II above, 235). 'The explanation seems to work by taking the existence of the camel, together with certain characteristics, such as the thorny diet, as given. Once these things are given, extra stomachs are *only to be expected*' (Sorabji 1980: 156; emphasis in original). The last sentence by itself is true enough. But why should it count as an *explanation*? If stalactites always produced stalagmites, and stalactites if they existed at all always existed, then given the existence of stalactites, it would be only to be expected that there were stalagmites. But what does the explaining is not the fact of universal correlation (compare Sorabji's barometer, 155), but our understanding of the *process* by which the one produces the other. Similarly with Aristotle's animals, it is the *process* by which the part comes to be that explains its presence; but *for him that process is irreducibly for an end*. The identity of the process is given by the capacity of which it is the actualization, and that capacity is an irreducible capacity for the production of an entity of the relevant kind, thus necessitating the relevant parts. Given that the process *is* irreducibly for the end, one is entitled to see the analysis of what parts are needed by that end as an *explanation* of the presence of those parts, and of course as a *teleological* explanation. Being for the sake of is thus to be defined in terms of coming to be for the sake of.

(The argument at 640a10–26 seems partly the basis for, and partly summarized in, the brief, difficult discussion of method at 645b14–28 in ch. 5. It is at an important stage in that later discussion that Aristotle makes what may be the most explicit statement of the thesis I am here ascribing to him. In Balme's translation: 'Consequently the body too is in a way for the sake of the soul, and the parts are for the sake of the functions in relation to which each has naturally grown (*pros ha pephuken hekaston*)' (b19–20). However, I cannot make sense of the argument of which this is an intermediate conclusion, and thus am not entirely sure how to take this statement.)

(Spontaneously generated organisms might appear to provide a counterexample to the thesis I have been arguing for in this section: their coming to be would seem to be of material necessity and not for the sake of anything, yet the presence of at least some of their parts get teleological explanations in *PA* iv. I discuss this in Gotthelf forthcoming 1987c.)

There is an interesting parallel between this analysis of 'being for the sake of' and a popular (and generally very plausible) contemporary analysis of the notion of the function of something. (Aristotle's notion of what something is for the sake of is pretty much equivalent to our notion of the function of something; 'is for the sake of' does more theoretical work in the biology than *ergon* does, though the latter is certainly present.) According to Wright's definition, 'The function of X is Z *iff*: (i) Z is a consequence (result) of X's being there, and (ii) X is there because it does (results in) Z.' (Wright 1976: 81; cf. 1973: 161.) Clause (ii) captures the distinction, important for the notion of a thing's function, between the function and anything the thing might do by accident. As we have seen, a similar distinction is important to Aristotle as well, and for him too, the function of X is Z only if 'X is there because it does (results in) Z'. (Cf. above 181 n. 40.)

While Wright elucidates the 'there because' in that condition in terms of natural selection, Aristotle, with his non-evolutionary perspective, can only speak of what 'the nature does' in embryonic development. He elucidates the 'there because' in the definition of function, as I have been arguing, in terms of another (and thus prior) teleological notion, that of 'coming to be for the sake of': the function of X is Z for Aristotle *iff* (i) Z is a consequence (result) of X's being there, and (ii) X came to be for the sake of doing (making possible, etc.) Z. Identifying the contribution to self-maintenance an organ makes thus identifies its function (and explains its presence) *only* on the condition that the organ came to be for the sake of making that contribution.

Since only individuals can come to be, the thesis defended in this section makes the individual prior to the species for purposes of explanation. This appears to be in harmony with David Balme's analysis of the general relation of individual to species, as presented below in ch. 11 (cf. above 233), and perhaps provides additional support for that analysis.

9

Hypothetical necessity and
natural teleology*

JOHN M. COOPER

In two places in his extant works, in *Physics* II.9 and three connected passages of the *Parts of Animals* I.1 (639b21–640a10, 642a1–13, 31–b4) Aristotle introduces and explains his notion of 'hypothetical necessity' (*anangkē ex hupotheseōs*).[1] Judging from this terminology one might think a hypothetical necessity would be anything that is necessary given something else, or something else being assumed to be so (cf. *APr.* I.10 30b32–40) – in effect, anything that follows necessarily from something else's being so, but that may not, taken in itself, be necessary at all. But this is not so: the necessity of New York's being north of Princeton given that it is north of New Brunswick and New Brunswick is north of Princeton, is not an example of what Aristotle calls a hypothetical necessity. This is because the hypothesis relatively to which a hypothetical necessity, in Aristotle's usage, is necessary is always a goal posited or set up (*hupotethen*) as something to be achieved.[2] Hence the necessity in question is always that of a

---

* This paper draws on two articles originally published elsewhere, as follows. Most of sections I and III come from Cooper 1982. Section II is taken from Cooper 1985. Aside from some condensation and a few bridge-passages, the present paper simply reproduces material contained in these articles.

[1] See also *GC* II.11 337b9–338a3, where in discussing necessary coming-to-be (e.g. of the sun's biennial 'turnings') he contrasts with such necessities the 'hypothetical' necessities that characterize comings-to-be of things in the sublunary world. Aside from these three places the expression *anangkē ex hupotheseōs* (and similar expressions) referring to a kind of necessity seems to occur in Aristotle only at *De Somno* 455b25–7, where Aristotle describes the necessity that animals go periodically to sleep as a 'hypothetical' one. There are further passages, especially in the *Organon*, where Aristotle refers to possibility or impossibility (or simply proof) *ex hupotheseōs* (see *Cael.* 1.11 281b2–9; *APr.* 1.23 40b23–9, 41a23–30; 29 45b15–28; 44 50a16–38; *APo.* 1.22 83b38–84a1; 11.6 92a20–4), but it is only in the context of natural processes and natural phenomena that he treats hypothetical necessity as a philosophically important special *kind* of necessity.

[2] Thus Aristotle regularly expresses the hypothesis in relation to which something is hypothetically necessary in the future tense: 'if this is to be' (see *PA* 642a32, ἡ δ' ἀνάγκη ὁτὲ μὲν σημαίνει ὅτι εἰ ἐκεῖνο ἔσται τὸ οὗ ἕνεκα, ταῦτα ἀνάγκη ἐστιν ἔχειν; similarly 639b27, 642a13, *Ph.* 200a12, 24, *De Somno* 455b26–7). It is important to observe that 'if there is to be' here refers not just to any potential event or outcome but (as τὸ οὗ ἕνεκα at 642a33 makes clear) only to events or outcomes that are goals of one sort or another. Obviously anything that exists or happens will generally have some conditions, not part of the thing's essence or nature, that must come about if it is to be, whether or not it is

means to some end. A hypothetical necessity, as Aristotle intends the term, is something necessary if some goal is to be attained. Thus, he says, a saw or an axe has to be hard in order to do its job of cutting or splitting, and in order to be hard it has to be made of bronze or iron:[3] hence it is necessary for a thing to be made of bronze or iron if it is to be a saw or an axe, and there must be bronze or iron to hand if one is to carry out the intention to make a saw or an axe.

Now Aristotle believes (and argues in the *Physics* in the chapter immediately preceding the one on hypothetical necessity) that nature, especially biological nature, acts for an end. This means that in his view the concept of hypothetical necessity will apply also to natural formations. Where one can identify and characterize in sufficient detail a natural end, for example the nature of a human being as an animal with certain particular capacities, one can ask, as with the saw and axe, what physical conditions must be realized – what a human body must be like – if an animal of that nature is to exist and exercise its natural capacities, that is, the ones mentioned in characterizing its nature. In answering this question one will be specifying various hypothetical necessities that characterize the human body. For example, as we shall see, Aristotle holds that human beings *must* have eyes (i.e. organs for sight) that are made mostly of fluid material and covered with flaps of flesh (in fact, eyelids), where the 'must' expresses a 'hypothetical' necessity. In this paper my aim is to give a systematic account of the uses to which Aristotle puts the notion of hypothetical necessity in his theory of nature, and the grounds on which he thinks he is justified in so applying it.

I

As just noted, anything necessitated hypothetically is necessitated as a means to some end or goal. Hence if there are in nature any

---

a goal of any sort. But (for good reasons) Aristotle does not speak of hypothetical necessity except where the outcome is also a goal: it may be true enough that my window wouldn't have broken when it did if there had not been a heavy wind blowing, but the wind did not blow by (hypothetical) necessity. That is because the window's breaking was no natural (or other) goal: where something is being pursued as a goal there is *some* reason to think it will come about, and this gives point to saying about the conditions necessary for the outcome in these cases, but not the others, that they come about by necessity. Aristotelian hypothetical necessity is not simply the necessity of conditions necessary for some outcome, for something to happen.

[3] *PA* 642a9–11, *Ph.* 200a10–13. Here I run together two presentations of what Aristotle obviously thinks of as the same illustration. The *Physics* passage says, obviously incorrectly, that a saw requires to be made of *iron*; I take this to be venially approximate for what the *PA* says more fully (but not quite fully enough – presumably the necessity is not for bronze or iron, as the *PA* has it, but only for bronze or iron or some other similar material).

hypothetical necessities, that implies that some products of nature are, or are for, goals. The first question we need to discuss, therefore, is why Aristotle thinks there are natural goals at all and what he thinks these goals are.

Aristotle understands by a goal (*hou heneka*), whether natural or not, something good (from some point of view) that something else causes or makes possible, where this other thing exists or happens (at least in part) because of that good.[4] So in holding that there are natural goals, he is holding that some things exist or happen in the course of nature because of some good that they do or make possible. Aristotle gives or suggests, at one place or another, several arguments in favor of this thesis. Some of these press the analogy between artistic activity, which is admittedly goal-directed, and natural processes, thus extending explanation by appeal to goals from human action to non-human, even non-animal nature. But these are not very good arguments and there are reasons for thinking that Aristotle did not think his view rested primarily on them.[5] So I will leave these arguments aside and concentrate on two lines of thought that argue directly from considerations of physical theory to the conclusion that there are goals in nature. The two lines of thought I want to discuss are found in *Physics* II.8–9, a connected discussion (see Aristotle's introduction to it, 198b10–16) that covers both natural teleology and hypothetical necessity. In this section I will discuss only the first of these two arguments, postponing the second until we have examined what Aristotle says here and elsewhere about hypothetical necessity.

Though it is only at the end of *Physics* II that Aristotle attempts

---

[4] See *Ph.* II.2 194a32–3; II.3 195a23–5; *Pol.* 1.2 1252b34–5; *EE* 1.8 1218b9–11, and the many passages where Aristotle routinely explicates 'that for the sake of which' by linking it with the good, the fine, the better, etc. (e.g. *Metaph.* A.3 983a31–2, *PA* 1.1 639b19–20). That the concept of a goal is the concept of something good is a view Aristotle inherited from Plato's *Phaedo* (cf. e.g. 97c6–d3, e1–4, 98a6–b3, 99a7–c7); unless one bears the connection between goal and good clearly in mind one will fail to understand much that Aristotle says about natural teleology, and many applications he makes of it. Andrew Woodfield (1976: 205–6) correctly notes that according to Aristotle all teleological explanations are claims that something happened *because it is good*, and makes this theme central to his own unifying account of teleological description.

[5] In *Ph.* II.8 the argument for natural teleology that Aristotle places first makes no appeal to the analogy between art and nature (198b32–199a8; see below, 250ff.). Only then does he add, for good measure, the three arguments (199a8–15, 15–20, 20–30) which do develop this analogy. As early as Philoponus one can find cogent objections to Aristotle's use of the analogy in at least the first two of these arguments (*CIAG* XVI 309.9–310.15 and 310.23–9). And since the first and most extensive argument Aristotle gives in this chapter is entirely independent of the art–nature analogy, one must reject the suggestion that is sometimes made that this analogy is central and fundamental to Aristotelian natural teleology.

to argue that there are goals in nature, he registers his commitment to this thesis at the very beginning of the book, where he argues (see 193a28–31) that there are two importantly distinct (kinds of) natures: material natures (the various kinds of *matter* things are made of) and formal natures (the various kinds of actual *things* there are – trees, plants, animals, etc.). For according to Aristotle explanations within physics refer to one or another of these two kinds of natures, and it turns out that explanations employing formal natures are teleological in character. According to Aristotle, it is due to a thing's form (its being, say, an apple tree) that it develops from the seed in certain particular ways and stages, and once full grown behaves in certain other particular ways (maintains a certain shape and size, grows certain kinds of leaves and fruit at certain seasons, etc.). And such explanations are teleological, since they postulate as a goal the formal nature that the behavior being explained serves to produce and thereafter maintain.[6] Why does Aristotle think there is this second level of facts and principles – facts about the natural kinds of living things and principles of a teleological sort governing their development and behavior – separate from and largely independent of the material level – facts about the various kinds of matter there are and principles of a non-teleological kind governing their behavior? His philosophical predecessors and contemporaries would all agree on the need for explanation at the level of matter, but many would deny the existence of a separate level of formal natures, not wholly dependent on and reducible to matter.

In answering this question one must begin by taking note of certain assumptions Aristotle makes about the character of physical reality. The most important of these is his belief that the world – the whole ordered arrangement of things, from outer heavens right down to the earth and its animal and plant life – is eternal. That the heavens are eternal and move at a fixed rate in daily rotation by strict necessity is, of course, not a mere assumption of Aristotle's; it is in fact the conclusion of certain a priori arguments in *Physics* VIII. This does not, however, immediately imply that the sublunary world has forever been arranged as it now is. That there has always been and always will be an annual cycle of warm and cold periods, as the sun moves round the ecliptic, is perhaps arguable on this basis. But that the distribution of land and water and air, and the kinds of plant and animal life that now exist, should be permanent parts of the world order seems clearly to need further argument; these features are certainly not determined merely by the constancy of the movements

---

[6] On this see further Cooper 1982: 200–1.

of the heavenly bodies. Nonetheless, Aristotle did believe that the world's climate and the existence of the animal and plant life that depends on it were further permanent structural facts – as it were, part of the given framework of the world, over and above that provided by the celestial movements.[7] Partly, no doubt, he thought that even fairly cursory acquaintance with the basic facts about animal and plant life should convince anyone that our world is a self-maintaining system, with a built-in tendency to preserve fundamentally the same distribution of air, land and water and the same balance of animal and plant populations as it had in his own time. The seasonal variation of hot and cold, wet and dry periods seems to have the effect that no permanent dislocation in the ecology takes place. Furthermore, every plant and animal species reproduces itself (or, in the case of spontaneously generated things, the conditions in which they are produced are regularly recurring); moreover, there

---

[7] In *GA* II.1 731b24–732a3 (cf. also *de An.* II.4 415a25–b7) Aristotle appeals to the permanence of animal and plant life to explain why there is sexual differentiation and animal reproduction in general. Living things are better than non-living and existence than non-existence, so the continuous existence of living things is an important good; but since individual animals and plants are all perishable it is only by constant replenishment that this good can be achieved. Since there cannot be eternal individuals, there is instead 'always a *genos* of human beings, of animals and of plants' (b35–6), and it is in order to sustain these genera in existence that reproduction through sexual differentiation takes place. It is true that in this argument Aristotle explicitly presupposes only that there are always plants and animals, not (except for human beings!) that there are always the *same* kinds. But the context shows that he is making this stronger assumption; for he goes on to speak of the arrangements which make possible the constant generation of the *existing* species. The stronger thesis is also found at *GA* II.6 742b17–743a1, where Aristotle takes Democritus to task for saying that if something is always (*aei*) so then that is sufficient explanation for it: what is *always* is infinite (*to d' aei apeiron*), i.e. lasts through infinite time, and there is no origin (*archē*) of the infinite, but to give an explanation of something is precisely to cite an origin (*archē* – but in another sense!) for it. If this were right, Aristotle says, we would be barred from seeking an explanation for why in animal generation we find just the organs and other parts we do find being formed in just the order in which they are actually formed. For the Democritean argument to be the threat he takes it to be Aristotle must be holding that the existing species of animals, whose structure and generation he is investigating, are existent through infinite time. The strict interpretation required for 'always' in this passage should put us on notice that when Aristotle speaks elsewhere of some arrangement as being so 'always or for the most part' (*aei ē hōs epi to polu*) he means to say that that arrangement is found existing eternally or recurring regularly throughout all time, with only the occasional exceptions implied in the 'for the most part' rider. Thus if he says that in some particular animal certain organic parts are formed always or for the most part in a certain way or order he does *not* just intend the hypothetical '*if* or *when* these animals are formed, this is the way it always happens'; he means to assert the categorical conjunction, 'these animals regularly are generated through all time, and this is the way it always happens'. Some rare, fortuitous event that nonetheless happened in the same way every time would not be counted by Aristotle as something that happens 'always or mostly' in a certain way; nor would he count animal generation as happening 'always or mostly' in some particular way if animals were found in the universe only in a certain finite period of its existence, even though *when* they exist they are always or mostly generated in that way.

appears to be an effective balance of nature, whereby no plant or animal is so constituted by its nature as to be permanently destructive of any other. Everything seems to fit together – the environment is permanently such as is needed to support the kinds of plants and animals there actually are, and the natural processes of generation and growth seem to maintain permanently a fairly fixed population of those same plants and animals. One observes in the world itself, then, no internal disharmony or imbalance that could lead to its eventual destruction; and since there is nothing outside it that could attack it and cause its disintegration, it seems only reasonable to believe that in these respects no change is to be anticipated. And if none is to be anticipated in the future, there is *pari passu* no reason to believe that things were ever any different in the past.

Now for Aristotle the fact, as he thought it, that the species of living things are permanent features of the natural world has a very special significance. It is not simply as if nature, by some mechanism or other, managed to keep in existence a stock of arbitrarily shaped and structured, but complex, objects (specially shaped and colored stones, for example). For each plant and animal is structured in such a way that its parts *work together* to make possible the specific form of life characteristic of its species, and (in almost all cases) so that they make possible the continuation of the species by enabling some appropriate kind of reproduction. It is important to realize that things might not have been this way. The organs and other internal parts of animals and plants might not have been as highly adapted to one another as in fact they are. Empedocles hypothesized that during one stage of the world's history all manner of animals were constantly being formed by chance collocations of varied animal parts more or less like those of animals known to us; some of these individual animals, having the parts necessary to make a go of it, survived to old age, others only for a short time if at all. While this situation continued all kinds of odd creatures were constantly being produced which clung to life with difficulty or not at all, and the adaptedness for life of the animals and plants known to us would be distinctly the exception, by no means the rule. If the world were permanently that way, one could perhaps speak of the permanence of all those weird kinds of 'animals', produced as they would continue to be by chance collocations of limbs springing up from the earth equally by chance, but in such a world the permanence of animal kinds would mean something very different from what it meant for Aristotle. For him, it meant the permanence of a set of well-adapted, well-functioning life forms. The preservation of the species of living things is therefore, as Aristotle understands it, the preservation of a fixed set of good things, things economically and efficiently organized so that they function in their environment for their own good.

The view that the world, together with its animal and plant life, is eternal was obviously quite a reasonable view in fourth-century Greece. But if it is *permanently* true that there *are* these given kinds of good, well-adapted plants and animals, and that the seasons follow upon each other in this given way, with those good effects, it becomes at once a condition of adequacy on any physical theory that it should be able to accommodate these facts. There are several possibilities. One might attempt to explain them by arguing, so to speak, from below: the materials of the world being what they are, and having the natures they do, the world naturally tends, by the operation of nothing but material principles, to produce and maintain just those kinds of living things that are actually observed. Or, one might attempt to explain them by arguing from above: for example, by claiming that it is a fundamental fact about nature, not to be further explained, that it tends toward maximal richness and variety, and then arguing that precisely the natural kinds that are actually observed, taken together with the environing inorganic stuffs, constitute the maximally rich and varied world. Thirdly, one might simply accept as a fundamental postulate of physical theory that the world *permanently has* whatever species it contains; that is, one might hold that it is an irreducible fact about the natural world, not further to be explained, that it so governs itself as to preserve in existence the species of well-adapted living thing that it actually contains. Of these alternatives Aristotle chose, and evidently thought one could not reasonably avoid, the last. He does not ever explicitly consider, so far as I can tell, a theory of the second sort. Perhaps he thought any such theory conflicts with well-established metaphysical principles, so that he could safely dismiss this alternative without discussion. For any such theory is committed to the idea that standards of goodness – in particular, of richness and variety – can be clearly conceived and specified in purely intellectual terms, in advance of study of the actual world, and that these standards can then be thought of as imposed on the world, as principles it must conform to, whether by its own inherent nature or by external compulsion. And Aristotle's metaphysics of the good rules out any such abstractly conceived standards. All our ideas about goodness, he thinks, are derived from familiarity with the actual world, and though we can extend these to conceive of possible arrangements that, if taken in isolation, might be better than actual ones, there is no Idea of the Good to provide us with absolute standards worked out by the pure intellect on its own, by which one might securely judge that the actual world either is or is not the best possible. In fact the world may *be* maximally rich and varied, but we cannot argue that it is by appeal to self-justifying standards independent of and prior to the good things we find in the world as it is actually constituted. Our best *idea* of richness and variety is, as a matter of fact, probably given by the actual world: in any event, we have no independent idea of these things by which to judge the world, so there cannot be any such principle of physics as this second sort of theory demands.[8]

Whether for this reason or another, Aristotle does not consider the possibility of deriving the permanence of the species in this Platonic sort of way, from above. He does, however, argue against the first sort of theory. He represents his materialist predecessors as having favored this sort of view: they supposed one could explain why there are the species there are, why they are preserved, and why the seasons follow one another as they do, in terms of nothing but the natures of the various materials the world contains and the ways in which, given their distribution at any given time, they interact with one another. In other words, they thought that ultimately only the first of Aristotle's two levels of facts and principles ever needs to be appealed to in explaining anything. His second level they proposed to account for entirely in terms of material causes and moving causes involving nothing but the motions that arise in matter, given its nature, under given conditions.

As I mentioned above, one can distinguish two lines of argument in Aristotle against any such supposition. One of these, which I shall explore in section III below, consists in an outright denial of the materialists' claim that their principles enable them to explain the occurrence of living things with the organic parts we actually observe them to have. But here I want to discuss a weaker line of argument, weaker in the sense that in it Aristotle grants, for the sake of argument, this major claim of his materialist opponents: even granted this outrageous claim, Aristotle argues, the materialists cannot explain *everything* that the fact of the permanence of the species involves.

This argument is found at *Physics* II.8 198b32–199a8 (and see *Metaph.* A.3 984b8–15). Interpreters have found this a difficult passage, but I believe the argument itself is rather straightforward.

---

[8] This line of thought explains why Aristotle's teleology does not extend to arguing that the good of the world as a whole requires any particular species or any particular interlocking arrangements among whatever species are to exist. He consistently takes the existing species as given; *they* are the good things by reference to which to explain those features of reality that he thinks need to be explained teleologically.

Without attempting a full-scale defense of my interpretation I shall simply state what I take the argument to be.

As I noted above, the animal and plant species we observe in nature are well-adapted. Their organs and other parts work together to promote their existence and functioning in their actual environments – a plant or animal's organs are, and do, good for it. Is there an explanation for this? The materialists argue that the various parts that are produced in the course of a creature's formation are produced by nothing but material necessity: the natures of the materials are such that *this* kind of tooth (a sharp one) necessarily comes up in the front of the mouth, and other material necessities result in *that* kind (a flat one) coming up in the back. But what explains the *fit* between these dental arrangements and the creature's need for food? The front ones, for example, are not just sharp, but useful for tearing food off, which is something the creature needs to do to survive and flourish. What account of *this* fact can the materialists give? Aristotle argues that the materialists' answer to this question is insupportable. (1) Where something occurs that in fact works to the advantage of someone or something, there are only two choices: either it is advantageous by coincidence or it happens for that reason, i.e. *because* of the good it does. If one admits that something is good, as the natural arrangements here in question indubitably are, one must either hold that this was a lucky coincidence, or grant that it happened that way (perhaps as a result of some agent's design, perhaps not) *for* the good of the person or thing in question. (2) Our materialists deny that in nature anything happens *for the sake of* any good that results, so they are forced to say, as Aristotle represents them as saying (198b16–32), that these good results are only coincidences: the teeth come up sharp in front by material necessity, but only *happen* to serve the creature's interests by doing so.[9] But, he argues, (3) a coincidence is necessarily an exceptional occurrence, and (4) animals' organs are *always* (with only occasional failures) formed in such a way as to serve the creature's needs. Hence it cannot be a coincidence, as the materialists say it is, that they do serve those needs. And if it is no coincidence, it must have the other explanation allowed: it happens that way *in order to* promote the creature's welfare. I.e., the creature's welfare is in such cases a natural goal.

---

[9] See 198b24–7; the sense of the ἐπεί clause in b27 is given by the expansion: ἐπεὶ οὐχ ἕνεκα τοῦ ἐπιτηδείους εἶναι, γενέσθαι τοὺς ὀδόντας ὀξεῖς, ἀλλὰ συμπεσεῖν τοῦτο ἐκείνῳ. It is essential for assessing this argument to notice that the opponents are represented as saying that the organs are *formed* as they are by necessity, but are *good* by coincidence. They do not claim they are *good* by necessity (whatever that would mean).

Aristotle's conclusion here does, clearly enough, follow from the premises he provides. Whether the opponents would have to grant all the premises is less clear. The premises about coincidences, (1) and (3), perhaps most often strike interpreters as questionable, though actually I believe each of them can be fairly vigorously defended.[10] What is quite certain, however, is that materialists like Democritus and Empedocles do not accept premise (4) in the sense in which Aristotle intends it (and the sense in which it must be taken to make the argument valid). It must be remembered (see n. 7 above) that when Aristotle says that the parts of animals and plants are *always* formed serviceably for the creature's needs he means that this has been going on *throughout all time*. And unless that is how (4) is taken the conclusion will not follow. If, for example, as Democritus is reported to have held, there have been infinitely many worlds (*kosmoi*), some of them larger than others, some with no sun or moon, some without plants and animals or even water (Hippol. *Haer.* 1.13 = DK 68A40), there have *not* always existed serviceably structured living things, reproducing themselves in the ways that now appear to be regular. And, as we have seen, according to Empedocles there are periods in the world's history during which all

---

[10] It might be objected, against (1), that while one may grant that any good outcome is either a coincidence or has *some* special explanation, this explanation *need* not be the teleological one asserted in (1). For if one has a run of heads in flipping a coin, and this is not a coincidence, it only follows that it has *some* cause (perhaps simply that the coin is untrue), not that it must have been produced for some purpose. But this reply overlooks that what premise (1) claims is not that *every* apparent coincidence that turns out not to be one must be explained teleologically, but only that when something *good* happens its being good must, if it is not a coincidence, have a teleological explanation. Thus the alleged counterexample must be expanded to make the run of heads a good thing for some reason (for example, because it means money for some particular person); but now we no longer have a counterexample, since this good that was done will remain a coincidence after the run of heads has itself been explained as due to the coin's weighting. Thus Aristotle's claim that if something good has an explanation and is no coincidence, the explanation must be teleological, is actually quite plausible. And even if it is not finally true, this will not give comfort to Aristotle's opponents. For certainly if some conjunction of phenomena is not a coincidence it must at least have an explanation that connects the conjoined phenomena in a single joint explanation (on this see Sorabji 1980: 10–11); and materialists driven to deny that the good done by the organs' arrangement is a coincidence surely cannot replace their separate explanations of how *each* organ is produced with a unified one claiming that the natures of the various materials in the world are in themselves such that this conjunction necessarily results every time.

The other premise, premise (3), can be seen to be perfectly unobjectionable if it is borne in mind that the criterion of the exceptional is defined against what happens throughout all time. For of course there is no assurance that any finite run of similar outcomes is not nonetheless a coincidence; but an *infinite* run with a preponderance of similar outcomes surely cannot be a coincidence but must have some special explanation. Strictly, perhaps, coincidences don't have to be exceptional, when taken in an infinite run, but they must not count for more than 50% of the cases, and that is good enough for the purposes of Aristotle's argument.

kinds of *un*serviceable combinations are produced (Simp. *in Ph.* 371.33–372. 9 = DK 31B61). On either of these views one could only hold the orderly and good arrangements presently prevailing to be an extended run of luck; viewed *sub specie aeternitatis* the good outcomes with which our experience makes us familiar are distinctly the exception, not the rule, and therefore the materialists' classification of them as coincidences would after all satisfy the requirements imposed by premises (1) and (3). Of course, Aristotle would insist that Democritus' theory of infinitely many world-orders and Empedocles' story about the alternating epochs of control by Love and by Strife are nothing but unsupported fancies, and that his own theory of the eternity of the actual world is more reasonable. One can well sympathize with this contention, and it is worth emphasizing that if one does accept Aristotle's theory, and I am right that premises (1) and (3) are defensible, then this argument provides quite a good defense of Aristotle's teleological hypothesis. It must at least be granted that Aristotle was on stronger ground than his actual materialist opponents, even if we would ourselves, for different reasons from theirs, side rather with them in rejecting Aristotle's thesis of the eternity of the actual kinds of living things.

II

This, then, is one argument by which Aristotle attempts to defend, against his materialist opponents, his own insistence that there are goals in nature and that some things that happen in the course of nature can only be correctly explained by reference to them. In this section I want to examine in detail Aristotle's views on the role of 'hypothetical' necessity in nature. What is the relation between something that is hypothetically necessitated and goal-directedness, on the one hand, and material causation, on the other? Once these questions are answered, we can return in section III to the second of Aristotle's two arguments for natural teleology.

I mentioned above that a hypothetical necessity is understood to be something necessary *if* some goal is to be attained. But not everything that is necessary if a goal is to be attained will qualify as necessitated hypothetically. For example, it is certainly true on Aristotle's view (cf. *PA* II.13) that human beings have to have both eyes and eyelids, but I take it that (he thinks) only the necessity for eyelids is or involves a hypothetical necessity. That is because hypothetical necessities are conditions *sine qua non* for ends (*Ph.* 200a5–6, *PA* 642a8), which is to say that they are things not already

254 *John M. Cooper*

included in the end in view, but rather things that are needed as external means to its realization. Aristotle warns in the *Eudemian Ethics* (1214b14–27) against the error of counting things like breathing or being awake, that are merely conditions *sine qua non* for human flourishing, as actual parts or constituents of the human good, and here the reverse error must be avoided, that of counting as merely a condition *sine qua non* what is in fact something essential to the animal nature in question. If for example it is part of human nature to have the capacity to see then having eyes of *some* sort is necessary to a human being as part of his nature (see *GA* v.1 778b16–17), and is not a mere hypothetical necessity. It is, to be sure, not clear where to draw the line between what is actually part of human nature and what isn't, but Aristotle's conception of hypothetical necessity depends upon observing the distinction at least in principle. He alludes to it at the end of *Ph.* ii.9 (200b4–8)[11] and observes it near the beginning of *PA* i.1 in describing the procedure to be followed in explaining an animal's parts:

Hence we should if possible say that because this is what it is to be a man (*tout' ēn to anthrōpōi einai*), therefore he has these things: for he cannot be without these parts. Failing that, we should get as near as possible to it: we should either say altogether that it cannot be otherwise, or that it is at least good thus. (640a33–b1, tr. Balme)

Following Balme,[12] I take it that the first necessity mentioned is the necessity of what follows directly from the human essence, as included in it, and it is only where, as Aristotle says, this kind of necessity cannot be claimed that the question of a hypothetical necessity arises.

The hypothetical necessity of certain animal parts is thus to be sharply distinguished from the necessity of those other parts the having of which is directly implied in the statement of the animal's essential nature.[13] What kind of necessity is this 'hypothetical

---

[11] Commentators, beginning with Simplicius and Philoponus, miss this connection. They interpret this passage simply as making the point Aristotle spells out at length in *de An.* i.1 403a29–b9 (see also *Metaph.* 1025b34–1026a6), that a complete account of the essence of a natural thing will make reference to the matter of which it is composed (or, in the case of an affection like anger, in which it is physically realized) (Philop. *CIAG* XVI 338.9–12, Simp. IX 392.20–7; Ross 1936: 533, Charlton, 1970: 128). But this overlooks the fact that here Aristotle argues not that matter must figure in the definition because these things' 'being is not without matter' but because, and to the extent that, having certain *parts* is essential to them: it is because a saw must have teeth and these have to be iron to do their job that Aristotle says the definition will refer to matter. The matter of other, non-essential parts (say, the handle) will not, on Aristotle's argument here, find their way into the definition. His point is, therefore, not the general one about natural things having to have a material constitution that the commentators have seen in it.

[12] Balme 1972: 87.

[13] In his detailed discussions Aristotle only rarely refers to some part as essentially necessary; but see *GA* ii.6 742a16–b17, esp. a34–5 and b1–3 (on why the heart is formed first) and v.1 778a34–5, b16–17.

necessity'? Aristotle's answer lies in the fundamental association, explicit in the *Physics* account (200a14, 30–2) and implicit in the *Parts of Animals* (cf. 639b26–30), between hypothetical necessity and matter. For assuming, as Aristotle does, that the various kinds of matter have their natures and properties independently at least of their role in constituting any *given* kind of living thing, it can reasonably be said that the actual physical features of any living thing will in very large part be the joint product of, on the one side, the creature's nature, specified in terms of capacities and functions, and on the other, the nature of the materials available to constitute a thing having that nature. Thus that we have eyelids, or anyhow eye-coverings of some sort, is a hypothetical necessity because given the materials that are available for making eyes, anyhow ones that see sharply and well as human eyes do, eyes must be fluid in character, with only a thin and fine skin (to allow light to get through); but being fluid and thinly covered they are easily injured. Eyelids are thus necessary to protect the eyes (*PA* II.13 657a30–5). Here there are two successive appeals to hypothetical necessity: first to the necessity for human eyes to be made mostly of fluid, and secondly to the necessity in that case for them to be covered with something solid and resistant to penetration, such as the skin that actually constitutes the eyelids. In such cases it is certain particular materials that are necessitated: since different kinds of matter have different properties and behave in different ways by their natures, not just any matter *can* do what eye-matter or eyelid-matter must do. In the end it is the nature of the material elements the world is made up from and the natural facts about how they do and don't combine with one another to form materials with specific properties and powers that necessitate this particular material constitution and arrangement for the human eye. But though matter is thus the seat, as one could put it (cf. *Ph.* 200a14, *en tēi hulēi to anangkaion*), of this necessity, its capacity to necessitate these arrangements is conditional on the production of human beings being something that occurs in nature. If this did not occur, then there would be none of these material formations that Aristotle says are necessary. Thus the *necessity* involved in hypothetical necessity is contributed by matter, and can therefore be called a material necessity; but this necessity only produces its effects given that there are to be the various kinds of living things that constitute the goals of natural production.

Aristotle's concept of hypothetical necessity thus unites two at first sight divergent ideas: the idea of matter as making some outcomes or arrangements necessary, and the idea of those outcomes and

arrangements as nonetheless means to a natural goal. It is important
to emphasize, however, that not every means actually employed in
nature in the material constitution of a living thing, but only *necessary*
ones, will count on Aristotle's view as hypothetically necessary. In
the passage quoted above where he summarizes the procedures to be
followed in the *PA* Aristotle distinguishes between saying 'altogether
that it cannot be otherwise' and 'that it is at least good thus'
(640a36–b1): to survive at all and perform its essential functions a
creature having the defining characteristics of a human being must
have certain parts, e.g. a heart and a liver, but (Aristotle thinks) it
does not have to have kidneys (the bladder being alone sufficient to
dispose of the urine), nor does the male of the species have to have
testicles in order to perform the reproductive function.[14] With a
kidney and testicles things go better for such a creature, but they are
not necessary. Here there is the same end in view in both classes of
means – namely, the good which consists in human beings living a
human life – but only those means to this end that are also indispensable for its being achieved at all count as hypothetically necessitated. The others, which allow this goal to be achieved more
efficiently or commodiously, though equally means to the end, are
not indispensable for its being achieved, and so are not hypothetically
necessitated. In short, 'hypothetical necessity' really is a kind of
necessity.

Up to this point I have been summarizing and attempting to
clarify the accounts Aristotle gives in *Physics* ii.9 and *Parts of Animals*
i.1 of what hypothetical necessity *is*. Summarily stated, an organ or
feature of a living thing is and is formed by hypothetical necessity
if, given the essence of the thing (specified in terms of capacities and
functions) and given the natures of the materials available to
constitute it, the organ or feature in question is a necessary means
to its constitution. Hence if some feature of an animal body is
explained as resulting from necessity hypothetically, it will be an
essential component of the explanation that the feature subserves the
good that is achieved by there being a well formed animal of the kind
in question. Explanation by appeal to hypothetical necessity is not
an alternative to explanation by reference to goals. It is a *special case*
of the latter kind of explanation, the case where the independently
given nature of the materials available for use in realizing the goal
makes precisely *one* possible means, or some narrowly circumscribed
set of possible means, to the end in question mandatory. Now

---

[14] I follow Balme's interpretation here: cf. 1972: 87. To the references given there add *GA*
1.4 717a14–21 (on testicles).

Aristotle does in his biological writings frequently enough offer to explain features of animal bodies in this way (e.g. the liquidity of the human eye and the possession of eyelids, mentioned above).[15] But in a large majority of the cases where he explains something as due to some necessity of or in the materials, the necessity invoked cannot be construed as a hypothetical one. I will cite some examples very shortly, but the general form of these explanations, and the fact that they are to be sharply distinguished from appeals to hypothetical necessity is already made clear at the end of *Parts of Animals* 1.1.

Here Aristotle gives a thumbnail account of the methods of argument to be employed in biology, using breathing as an example:

> Exposition should be as follows: for example, breathing exists for the sake of *this*, while *that* comes to be of necessity because of *those*. Necessity signifies sometimes that if there is to be *that* for the sake of which, *these* must necessarily be present; and sometimes that this is their state and nature. For the hot necessarily goes out and comes in again when it meets resistance and the air must flow in; so much is already necessitated.[16]

The first sentence here is admittedly not easy to understand, but that need not give us pause, since in the following sentences Aristotle states very clearly that while some material necessities are hypothetical ones – things that are necessary if an end is to be achieved – others are not, and the account he goes on to provide of the process of respiration illustrates this second kind of necessity. The nature of air and heat are such that when air gets heated it expands – their 'state and nature' is such that this must happen. The air in the lung does get heated (he does not say how or why, and for purposes of the example it does not matter); so, expanding by necessity, it goes up the windpipe and out of the mouth. Again, the surrounding air, which is colder, by the same kind of necessity of its 'state and nature', resists and (we are told) pursues the hot air back into the mouth and eventually down into the lung, where it gets heated, beginning the process all over again. I have filled out some details of this example, which Aristotle presents only sketchily, despite its telling a rather implausible story (it is not in fact the account of respiration Aristotle himself provides elsewhere), because it is important to see clearly how the explanation is supposed to work. It is plain that the behavior

---

15 See also *PA* 665b12–14 (blood vessels), 668b33–6 (lungs), 671a7–8 (bladder), 672b22–4 (diaphragm, i.e. *phrenes*), 674a12–15 (stomach).

16 642a31–7, tr. Balme. Peck (1961: 78n*b*) reasonably remarks that this passage looks like a displaced note, intended perhaps to follow 642a13 *ei ekeino estai*, somehow stuck on here at the end of the chapter. But there is no reason to doubt its authenticity. In fact the whole chapter seems to be composed of a series of disjointed discussions of points about methodology in biology, with little or no effort to impose a connected scheme of exposition on them.

of hot air here claimed to be necessary is represented as resulting from the nature of heat and air in exactly the same way as Aristotle says his materialist predecessors had offered to derive everything from the nature of the materials making up the world. Compare how Aristotle in *Physics* II.8 characterizes their view: 'since the hot is such and such by nature (*toiondi pephuken*)... these things are and happen by necessity' (198b12–14); *PA* 642a32–5: 'necessity sometimes means that this is their state and nature (*hoti estin houtōs echonta kai pephukota*)'. So, according to him in this *PA* passage, the hot air in the lung goes out by necessity, causing respiration. And since he here distinguishes this kind of necessity from what he elsewhere calls hypothetical necessity, in this passage Aristotle declares both that there is room in his own theory of natural explanation for appeal to material necessities of this pre-Socratic kind and that he does not construe them, or reconstrue them, as somehow hypothetical necessities after all.[17]

As I mentioned above there are many places in his biological works where Aristotle employs explanations parallel to that given here of respiration. The most fully elaborated case is that of the shedding of the front teeth and their replacement by new ones.[18] Aristotle says (*GA* v.8 789a8–b8, my translation):

Once [the front teeth] are formed, they fall out on the one hand for the sake of the better, because what is sharp quickly gets blunted, so that [the animal] must get other new ones to do the work [of tearing food off];...on the other hand they fall out from necessity, because the roots of the front teeth are in a thin part [of the jaw], so that they are weak and easily work loose....Democritus, however, neglecting to mention that for the sake of which [things happen in the course of nature], refers to necessity all the things that nature uses – things that are indeed necessitated in that way, but that does not mean they are not for the sake of something, and for the sake of what is better in each case. So nothing prevents [the front teeth] from...falling out in the way he says, but it is not on account of those factors (*dia tauta*) that they do, but on account of the end (*dia to telos*): *they* are causes as sources of motion and instruments and matter.

In this passage Aristotle does two things that are of interest from the present point of view: first, he explicitly invokes material necessity of what he himself describes as the Democritean sort, while explicitly

---

[17] *Contra* Balme 1972: 76–84. In ch. 10 below, Balme abandons this interpretation (see his n.33). On Balme's earlier view see below 260–2.

[18] Besides the passages cited in the text here and below, the following provide especially clear cases where Aristotle explains something as (materially) necessitated while distinguishing the necessitation in question from the 'hypothetical' necessitation of certain means for the achievement of a natural goal: *PA* 658b2–7 (why human beings have so much hair on their heads), 663b12–14 (why deer shed their horns), 672a12–15 (lard about the kidneys), 694a5–9 (the webbed feet of water birds), *GA* 738a33–b4 (the formation of menstrual fluid), 767b8–15 (female births), 776b31–4 (the formation of mammaries), 778a29–b19 (eye-color).

dissociating it from reference to natural goals. This shows that he accepts that there are material necessities of the Democritean kind, and that he is content to conceive them as operating simply alongside the kind of necessity that follows from the postulation of natural goals. But secondly, while admitting that both sorts of explanation for the falling out of the front teeth are correct – it happens both by necessity and for an end – he insists that the explanation by material necessity is nonetheless incomplete or defective in some respects not very fully specified: it is not *dia* the Democritean necessities referred to that the teeth fall out, but *dia* the end. Later on I will offer an interpretation of what Aristotle thinks justifies him in thus down-grading the Democritean explanation, even while accepting it.

Given the prominence and prevalence of appeals to what, follow-ing Aristotle's lead in this passage, I shall call Democritean necessity in Aristotle's biological writings, it is surprising that in his official expositions of hypothetical necessity he doesn't make it clear that in his own theory it continues to play a role. In fact in both expositions he contrasts the hypothetical kind of necessity which he champions with the kind of necessity invoked by his materialist predecessors in such a way as to give many interpreters the impression that he rejects the latter outright. Thus in *Parts of Animals*, while insisting (642a1–3) that many things in nature are formed by necessity, as indeed the materialists had maintained (639b22), he immediately adds:

But perhaps one might raise the question what sort of necessity is referred to by those who say 'by necessity'. For of the kinds of necessity distinguished in our philosophical writings neither of the two can be present; but the third *is* found in things that have coming-to-be. For we say that food is something necessary according to neither of the first-mentioned kinds of necessity, but because it is impossible for it to be without it. And this is as it were by hypothesis. (642a3–9)

In his account of necessity in *Metaphysics* Δ.5 Aristotle does in fact distinguish three principal kinds of necessity (cf. also *Metaph* Λ.7 1072b11–13); and he illustrates one of these by the same example of food as here, saying that this kind of necessity is that of what a thing cannot live without (1015a20–1).[19] The other two kinds of necessity are that of what is forced against a thing's choice or nature, and the necessity of 'what cannot be otherwise'. This last kind of necessity applies primarily (cf. *PA* 639b23–4) to eternal things, since it is absolutely impossible for these to be other in any respect than

[19] I believe Balme is wrong in suggesting (1972: 100) *APo.* ii.11 94b36 as the probable reference of 'in our philosophical writings' at *PA* i.1 642a5–6. That passage mentions only the two rejected types of necessity, whereas Aristotle's mention of *the* third (*hē tritē*) is most plausibly taken as indicating that he has in mind a place where a threefold distinction is deployed. In his extant writings only *Metaphysics* Δ.5 fits this description.

they are, but it is also sometimes made to cover the Democritean necessity by which physical materials act according to their natures: a thing of that nature cannot (at least, *usually* cannot) fail to act in some given way in given circumstances if not interfered with.[20] The apparent implication of the quoted passage is, therefore, that of the three kinds of necessity that there are, only one, hypothetical necessity, can be correctly appealed to when one says that something is formed in nature by necessity. Admittedly, Democritean necessity is not explicitly alluded to in this passage, but since hypothetical necessity and Democritean necessity are different things, and since at least sometimes the latter is ranged under the rejected necessity of 'what cannot be otherwise', it appears to be ruled out by implication.

The *Physics* chapter is more difficult to assess but it too seems, and has been thought, to deny the existence of Democritean necessity in the course of affirming that natural necessity is always *ex hupotheseōs*. So it is small wonder that, faced with this apparent inconsistency between Aristotle's scientific practice and his theory of scientific method, David Balme in his commentary on *PA* I should have exerted himself to show that, properly understood, even such cases of necessity as that by which the front teeth fall out can be construed as reducing to hypothetical necessities after all. I will not review here Balme's very complicated argument (as noted above, he has recently disclaimed it himself), but two brief comments may perhaps be ventured. First, since Aristotle repeatedly contrasts these necessities

---

[20] The *Metaphysics* chapter does not give examples of the necessity of 'what cannot be otherwise', but three considerations suggest strongly that it is meant to include Democritean necessity. First, it would be surprising if *no* place were made in a chapter officially devoted to saying how many 'senses' of 'necessity' there are for this sense of necessity, and it cannot be accommodated under either of the other two principal senses, at least not as they are presented here. Secondly, this sense is made the basic one (1015a35–b6), from which the other two are treated as extensions, so one seems to be invited to regard it as having the flexibility needed to accommodate this case of necessity. And thirdly, as Ross no doubt rightly points out (1924: I 299), at *APo.* II.11 94b37 Aristotle himself marks a twofold distinction of types of necessity that must be taken as parallel to the second and third of the *Metaphysics*' three senses, and the examples there ranged under the necessity of 'what cannot be otherwise' are of the Democritean type (light particles passing through a lamp 'by necessity', 94b27–30; thunder caused by quenching of fire 'by necessity', b32–3). Thus it seems in any event certain that in *APo.* II.11 Aristotle makes the necessity of 'what cannot be otherwise' (what the commentators refer to as 'absolute' or 'simple' necessity) cover material necessity of the Democritean sort. And if so, that is good reason to think the same classification is intended in *Metaph.* Δ.5 as well. (It should be observed that Aristotle's way of describing 'absolute' necessity at *APo.* II.11 94b37–95a1, *hē kata phusin kai hormēn*, is very close to the characterization he gives at *PA* I.1 642a34–5 of Democritean necessity: the inference to draw is that there too he means to classify Democritean necessity under the necessity of 'what cannot be otherwise'.) (I am indebted to Gisela Striker for helpful correspondence on the interpretation of *Metaph.* Δ.5 and its relation to the *PA* passage referred to in my main text.)

with what is necessary as a means to some natural goal (see the passages cited in n.18) it cannot in any event be said that Aristotle himself *classified* them as hypothetical necessities; Balme should rather be understood in his commentary as attempting to show how on Aristotle's own views about matter and its relationship to form Aristotle could have and should have described those necessities as hypothetical ones. That is, though in these passages Aristotle contrasts Democritean material necessity with things that are necessary as means to natural goals, his own views allow him to maintain that these material necessities are actually themselves necessary only as means to natural goals. This fact, I believe, already makes Balme's enterprise seem rather ill conceived. But secondly, I doubt very much that Aristotle's views about matter and its relationship to form do imply, as Balme in his commentary on *Parts of Animals* maintained, that whatever given materials do by a necessity of their own nature turns out on examination to be hypothetically necessitated only. In so interpreting Aristotle, Balme based himself on passages in the *Meteorology* (iv.12) and *Parts of Animals* (ii. 646a12–b10) (cf. also *GA* i.i 715a9–11) where Aristotle describes three stages in the constitution of a living thing: the non-uniform parts (organs) are the matter of the animal itself, the uniform parts (flesh, blood, bones, etc.) are matter for the organs, and, finally, the material elements (earth, air, fire and water) are matter for the uniform parts. Balme correctly took Aristotle to hold that the items at each of these three levels have the character that they have for the sake of the items at the level next higher. But he thought that that implies that, quite generally, the material elements themselves have the natural properties they do for the sake of the animal forms which are going to be made out of them, so that if, say, fire by a necessity of its nature causes certain changes in certain liquids, that necessity itself can be seen as holding only because an element that has these powers is needed if there are to be living things. This seems to me a mistaken interpretation of what Aristotle is saying in these passages. He is not discussing the question why in general the elements have the natures they do, but only why a *particular* animal is made up of the certain *particular* elements, and in the certain particular amounts and ratios, that it is. His point is just that if an animal of a certain kind is to be constituted these certain amounts of certain elements must be present for use: in effect, for *this* creature *those* elements are hypothetically necessitated. But plainly that presupposes, and does nothing to explain, the natural powers of the elements concerned. For it is only because the elements antecedently *do* have the particular powers they have of combining with and affecting one another, that *this* elemental combination (*so* much earth, *so* much air, etc.) rather than some other, is necessitated in this case. When properly understood, then, it seems to me that the passages to which Balme appeals show Aristotle actually presupposing as simply given the material elements and their natures, and arguing from them to the necessity of certain particular elemental combinations in order to constitute particular animal natures. So they tell against, rather than in favor of, Balme's thesis that for Aristotle the elements have the powers they do in order to make possible the world of living things.

It appears to me, therefore, that if the methods Aristotle actually employs in studying biological entities and explaining their structure and development are after all consistent with his pronouncements on the methodology of biology, this can only be shown by interpreting the latter so that they do not conflict with the former. On examination I believe such an interpretation does turn out to be correct. Let us turn first to *Physics* II.9. The topic for discussion in this chapter is first stated at the beginning of chapter 8, which together with chapter 9 constitutes a connected account of the respective roles of final causes and necessity in the natural realm, i.e. the realm of living things. In introducing it there he makes it clear that in asking how 'the necessary' operates in natural things (*peri tou anangkaiou pōs echei en tois phusikois*, 198b11–12), he means to be asking on what basis matter of various kinds can by its nature be said to necessitate natural outcomes. For he explains what he means by 'the necessary' here by referring to his predecessors' efforts to explain the formation of living things and their parts by appeal to the natural powers of matter-kinds as necessitating them (198b12–14). So when Aristotle returns to this question in chapter 9 and asks whether that which is by necessity (*to ex anangkēs*, 199b34) is found in nature (only) on a hypothesis or (instead) without any such qualification (*haplōs*, b35), he is asking whether *in* necessitating natural outcomes matter is to be thought of as doing so on a hypothesis, namely given that some natural goal is to be produced, or not, but simply on its own.[21] That is, I take the question from the outset to be not whether Democritean material necessity exists, but how it operates – on its own, or rather within the context and against the controlling background of some presupposed natural goal.

Aristotle's predecessors, denying goals in nature, thought of material necessitites as functioning entirely on their own to produce

---

[21] On this way of taking the opening lines of the chapter see further below 265–6 and n. 25.

the observed natural, living things. This, as Aristotle says (199b35–200a5), is as if one thought to explain a wall as having been produced by rocks and dirt and sticks assembling themselves by nothing but their natural tendencies, as materials of those kinds, to move and interact with one another under given environing conditions. In fact, of course, the wall came about because someone wanted to cover and protect some possessions, so that the natural interactions and movements that the materials themselves contributed only came into play because of the builder's intentions. Thus although, for example, the stones at the bottom of the wall hold up the superstructure and do so because, by a necessity of their nature as stones, they both stay put and do not contract under the weight as, for example, foam would do, this contribution they make to the being of the wall is only made by them because they have been placed there for the sake of the wall that the builder intends. In this case, then, stones or something very like them are necessary (i.e. hypothetically necessary) for the being of the wall (as Aristotle says, the wall could not have come to be without them, 200a5–6), but *that* is because these materials have by their nature as the materials that they are, certain powers to act and react with other materials in certain fixed ways, by a necessity that is other than hypothetical: in general, he says at 200a7–10, where a thing has an end, it cannot be without certain things that have a 'necessary nature', an *anangkaia phusis*, and by this he means things that by a necessity of their nature act and react in certain ways.[22] So, according to Aristotle in *Physics* II.9, Democritean necessity does play a role in nature, i.e. in the formation of natural, living things, but it does so only hypothetically – that is, only on the hypothesis that a living thing is to be produced. *Given* that a living thing is to be, certain materials are necessary (i.e.

---

[22] He certainly does not mean the tautology that it cannot be without what it cannot be without, i.e. without what has a nature that is *hypothetically* necessary for it to be. As *PA* III.2 663b23 shows (cf. b34), to have a 'necessary nature' is to have a nature that necessitates certain modes of action and reaction in given conditions, without reference to any end that may be achieved by its so acting. The reference in our text (200a31–2) to 'matter *and its movements*' as what in living things is necessary confirms that here too matter's necessity involves its behaving in certain ways by a necessity of *its* nature. Thus in this chapter Aristotle applies the predicate 'necessary' to the matter of a living thing in two senses: (a) it is hypothetically necessary for the being of the thing but (b) it is itself a necessary thing in the sense that it has a nature as a necessary result of which it behaves in certain more or less fixed ways. Perhaps one should take *ex anangkēs* at 200b2, 3, with the infinitives rather than with the main verb *dei*, as is grammatically certainly possible, and word order (especially in b3) rather suggests. In that case Aristotle will be saying here that in order for there to be health or a human being certain things must (*dei*), i.e. by hypothetical necessity, happen and be present by necessity (*ex anangkēs*), i.e. by the *materially* necessary action of matter; the distinction between the two applications of necessity will then be explicitly marked by the two modal expressions *dei* and *ex anangkēs*.

these materials are hypothetically necessary); this means that the presence of those materials is to be explained by reference to this goal. But once, for that reason, they *are* there, their nature, and the material necessity that belongs to it, will cause them to behave in various ways. They will act in those ways by necessity, and this necessity is not a hypothetical one.

An example may help to bring out the point. In *GA* II.4 Aristotle explains the fact that semen in congealing a portion of the menstrual fluid to form a fetus causes a membrane to form around its periphery as both due to necessity and happening for an end (739b26–30). It happens by necessity because, as can be observed when milk is heated, the surfaces of thickish fluids naturally do solidify when heated, and what the semen does is to heat up that portion of the *katamēnia*. (It happens for an end because the forming creature needs a solid periphery to mark it off from the surrounding fluids – if it were not in a fluid environment, things would be different.) Here the necessity is a Democritean, material necessity. But plainly there would be no congealing going on here even partly by that kind of necessity unless these materials (the semen, the *katamēnia*) were there, and *they* are there because they are necessary (this time hypothetically) for the formation of a fetus, which is a natural goal. Thus, as I interpret Aristotle in *Physics* II.9, he wants to say that Democritean necessity does indeed exist and has a role to play in the formation of living things, but that where it does make a contribution it only does so because the materials whose necessary action is in question are themselves necessitated hypothetically. On this interpretation it could be said that Aristotle 'subsumes' Democritean necessity under hypothetical necessity, in the explanation of living things.[23] But that does not mean that he *reduces* it to hypothetical necessity. Plainly, as in the passage just cited about the congealing of the fetus, the Democritean necessity appealed to is contrasted with appeal to final causation, as no hypothetical necessity could correctly be. It is subsumed under hypothetical necessity only in the sense that its operation in the case of living things presupposes the need for materials of that kind; it is that need, and not the natural powers of material stuffs themselves, acting by the necessities of their natures, still less by random chance, that explains their presence at the appropriate times and places. Nonetheless, *when* they are present they behave in certain ways by a necessity of their natures, and this necessity retains its character as non-hypothetical.

---

[23] It is important to keep this restriction clearly in mind; I do not mean to suggest that outside this context Aristotle subsumes Democritean necessity under hypothetical necessity in even the attenuated sense argued for here. See further below 267–8.

Aristotle's concern, then, is not to deny that some effects in the formation of living things are produced by Democritean material necessity, but to insist that the production of these effects by that necessity is contingent upon the forming plant's or animal's need for matter of the kind in question. But he insists on a second limitation as well. However much certain particular stages in the formation of a living thing may be materially necessitated, the end product, the finished living thing, is never the result of such necessitation: the end, he says (200a33–4), is the cause of the matter, but the matter is not reciprocally the cause of the end (nor does it necessitate it: 200a15–20). Democritean necessity does not suffice to explain the coming to be of any fully formed plant or animal; you cannot, starting from the presence of certain materials, trace a connected series of changes, resulting from nothing but necessities belonging to the natures and powers of the materials present, that leads up to the fully-formed living thing as its outcome. Thus Aristotle's view, as he explains it in *Physics* II.9, involves two limitations on the operation of Democritean necessity, where living things are concerned. First, it is not by material necessity that the materials needed to form a living thing come to be present at its formation; that happens by hypothetical necessity only. And, secondly, the materials, whatever else they do necessitate, do not necessitate the end-product of the process to which they contribute. In both these contentions, of course, Aristotle contradicts the determinist views of the materialist philosophers against whom his argument in the chapter is meant to be directed. But in neither of them does he deny that anything ever happens in the formation of living things by material necessity. Indeed, as I pointed out above, he approaches the discussion of hypo-thetical necessity in *Physics* II.9 having posed his question in such a way as to make clear his acceptance that Democritean necessity does play a role (198b11–16). His question is *how* this necessity figures, not whether it does; and the two limitations just discussed constitute the core of his answer to this question.

How, then, is it that so many readers come away from *Physics* II.9, as from *PA* I.1, thinking, even if unhappily, that Aristotle has rejected Democritean necessity altogether, in favor of hypothetical? The chapter begins with a question, translated by Hardie and Gaye as follows: 'As regards what is "of necessity", we must ask whether the necessity is "hypothetical", or "simple" as well.'[24] Now this is

---

[24] It is customary to take the *kai* (199b35), as Hardie and Gaye do, as meaning 'also', but there are good reasons to prefer the alternative 'actually', 'in fact' (cf. Denniston 1954: 317). Read with 'also' the Hardie and Gaye translation yields these two alternatives: (a) to suppose that only hypothetical necessitie: are to be found in nature and (b) to suppose that in addition to these there are also 'simple' necessities. So the two alternatives share

usually read as referring to two different kinds of necessity, Aristotle's hypothetical necessity (or necessity as a means to some goal) on the one hand, and the 'simple' or 'absolute' necessity of 'what cannot be otherwise' on the other; it is to this latter kind of necessity that the materialists are thought to have wished to reduce all the behavior of material things. Since in what follows Aristotle plainly argues that the necessity in natural, living things is hypothetical, the inference seems forced that he proposes to do away with all talk of the other kind of necessitation, where 'from certain conditions a certain result must follow' (Ross 1936: 531). That is, he rejects Democritean necessity altogether. Now on the interpretation I have presented there is no cause to reach this conclusion, since I have taken the opening question differently.[25] Instead of presenting as exclusive alternatives (explanation by) hypothetical necessity and (explanation by) material necessity, I take the contrast to be between two ways in which material necessity might be thought to operate. But, even if we adopt this interpretation in place of the usual one, we are not yet free of the difficulty. For we will face the fact that in *Parts of Animals* I (642a1–9, translated above p. 259) Aristotle insists that when things come about by necessity in living things and their formation this necessity is hypothetical, and refers to the other two kinds of necessity, including 'absolute' necessity, only to deny that they apply in this context. What can be made of this? Must Aristotle here (and in *Physics* II.9 if its opening question is read in the usual way) be construed as denying altogether the operation of Democritean necessity?

I do not think so. In interpreting Aristotle's rejection of 'absolute' necessity in the *Parts of Animals* passage one must bear carefully in mind the two limitations on the operation of Democritean necessity that I have argued form the core of his positive doctrine in the *Physics* chapter. First of all, the end product of a process of formation never

a commitment to hypothetical necessities, and so to teleological causation. In that case neither view represents the view of Aristotle's materialist opponents, as one might have expected. And it becomes hard to understand why in answering the question Aristotle spends so much time explaining and arguing for the presence of hypothetical necessity in nature, something the two views to be decided between share a commitment to, rather than simply discussing directly whether there are simple necessities in nature, the point over which the two alternatives differ. If *kai* is translated 'actually' the second alternative will express the opponent's view, and then it will be quite natural that Aristotle exerts himself to argue that the necessity that matter contributes is hypothetical, with the natural implication that (however this is then to be interpreted) it is not a case of simple necessity.

[25] I take *haplōs* closely with *huparchei* and parallel to *ex hupotheseōs*, so that (as given above 262) the alternatives are (a) that the (material) necessity in natural things is present hypothetically and (b) that it is present without that qualification, i.e. that it operates on its own and without any dependence on natural goals.

is, according to Aristotle, materially necessitated. This means that so far as the *whole* living thing is concerned, the flat rejection of absolute necessitation does fully accord with Aristotle's position; anything necessary there may be in such outcomes really is, on his view, hypothetically necessary only. But, secondly, where material necessity does function – in forming the membrane round an animal fetus, in making an eye blue or brown, and so on – it is on Aristotle's view at best a *proximate* cause of the necessitated feature. That a blue eye is produced depends upon the properties of the materials and their materially necessary interactions as the eye is being formed; but it is not, on Aristotle's theory, by material necessity that those materials, with their necessitating properties, are present in the first place. To say, therefore, in the contexts of the discussion in *Physics* II.9 or *Parts of Animals* I.1 642a1–9, that it is even partly by 'absolute' necessity that things happen in animate nature would be seriously misleading. Ultimately, on Aristotle's view, nothing that happens in the formation of a living thing *does* happen by 'absolute' necessity; if you trace back its conditions beyond the first step or two you do not find this kind of necessity operating at all.

When, therefore, one bears in mind the two limitations on the operation of material necessity for which Aristotle argues in *Physics* II.9 it is not too surprising that in discussing in general terms the role of necessity in the operations of animate nature he should deny a place to 'absolute' necessity, as he does in *PA* I.1 642a1–9 and would do in *Ph.* II.9 on the usual translation of its opening sentence. But this does not mean that, even here, he denies to Democritean necessity the sort of role which he assigns to it at the end of *PA* I.1, and for which he appeals to it at many places in the biological works; on the contrary, as we have seen, he actually insists on the necessitating character of matter in the course of his discussion in the *Physics*. It is just that *ultimately* what happens by that necessity only happens because it is hypothetically necessitated. Properly interpreted, therefore, in neither exposition of his theory of hypothetical necessity (even if the opening question of *Ph.* II.9 is understood in the usual way) does Aristotle imply that hypothetical necessity is the only kind of necessity ever found in the workings of animate nature.

Before concluding this section, I add two points of clarification. First, as I noted above in passing, Aristotle's discussions of hypothetical necessity in *Parts of Animals* and *Physics* deal only with the role of material necessity where animate nature is concerned. In the passages we have considered he does not discuss at all the behavior of the material elements or other stuffs outside of this context. He holds, of course, that material necessity operates wherever matter is found, but his claim (as I have interpreted him) that it operates only against the background of hypothetical necessity is limited to the formation and behavior of living things. If, for example, ice forms on a pond as a result of material necessities attaching to the natures of cold air and water, nothing he says in these passages commits him to seek some hypothetical necessity to explain why the air and water in question became conjoined, with that result.[26]

Secondly, I am now in a position to explain why Aristotle, even while accepting some explanations by Democritean necessity, downgrades them – why he says, for example (*GA* 789b6–8), that even though the front teeth do fall out in the way Democritus says they do, it is not on account of (*dia*) the material factors he appeals to, but on account of the end, the good they do the creature whose teeth they are, that they do so.[27] For, as our discussion has brought to light, Aristotle holds that it is only because of this end that the initial teeth form where and as they do, with the result that the front ones are vulnerable to the material forces which result in their loosening and eventual loss. These material forces are, Aristotle says, instruments (*organa*, 789b8–9) that nature, i.e. the nature of the whole animal here being brought to perfection, uses, and on the interpretation I have presented this metaphor is quite apt as an expression of Aristotle's theory. If there had not been a need for front teeth, there would have been none there for the material forces to work upon. By placing them where it does the nature of the animal therefore also brings it about that they eventually fall out; so *that* nature (and not the nature of the materials) is ultimately responsible for this loss. And because the animal nature is responsible for what happens in the course of an animal's development by functioning as the end or final cause of what happens, it is the completed animal nature as end that bears the ultimate responsibility for the teeth falling out at a certain stage of development. So, on Aristotle's theory, it is quite right to say, as he does, that though the teeth do indeed fall out by material necessity it is not *on account of* that necessity that they do, but *on account of* the end, i.e. on account of the completed animal nature that is being

---

[26] Still less is he committed to seek a hypothetical necessity to explain air and water's having these natures (see above 261–2). Aristotle does indeed hold (see *Mete.* IV.12) that even the simple physical elements have a formal as well as a material nature, and that the formal nature is to be defined in terms of some natural function, some end the stuff in question naturally achieves (389b28–9, with 390a3–9; a16–20). But this just refers e.g. to fire's tendency to heat things up, and offers no ground for saying that fire has the nature it does (including the natural tendency to warm things up) for the *sake* of anything further.

[27] See above, 258–9. Aristotle reiterates this complaint in *Physics* II.9, among other places: 200a6–7, 9–11, 26–7.

formed here. That end being absent, there would have been no teeth-falling-out-by-necessity to be explained; it is only *on account of* the fact that this end was being pursued that these teeth fall out by material necessity.[28]

It has frequently been remarked, and is obvious enough, that Aristotle developed the concept of hypothetical necessity in an effort to reconcile necessity with teleology in the explanation of animate nature. On the interpretation I have presented this concept turns out to be both a coherent and, given the science of his time, a remarkably effective way of achieving this result.[29]

III

Having offered an interpretation of Aristotle's account of hypo-thetical necessity in *Physics* II.9, I am now in a position to claim that Aristotle's argument in that chapter amounts to a second, stronger defense of his thesis that there exist goals in nature than the argument from *Physics* II.8 examined in section I. For his materialist opponents, as we have seen, claim that the given natures of the materials making up the world are such that under the conditions prevailing in animal generation they necessarily interact in such a way as to produce the organs we actually observe the living things to have, and in that arrangement which constitutes the normal, fully-formed specimen of the species in question. But, as we saw (p. 265), in *Physics* II.9 Aristotle argues that as a matter of fact it is not possible to complete the project of derivation thus envisaged. Acquaintance with the various kinds of matter there are and the ways in which by their natures they behave under various conditions does not permit one to think that there *are* any true principles at this level sufficiently strong and comprehensive to make any such derivation possible. The

---

[28] Thus I see no need to interpret Aristotle's preference for the teleological explanation over the material-necessity one as based on the thought that teleological explanations, where available, do more of what we want explanations to do, that they better assuage the discomfort that leads us to ask 'why?', and so on, than the appeal to material necessity does. Resort to such epistemological considerations is anachronistic and betrays a fun-damental misconception of the philosophical problems Aristotle faced and his way of addressing them.

[29] In working out my interpretation of Aristotle's views on hypothetical necessity I have concentrated on *Ph.* II.9 and *PA* 642a1–13 together with the discussion of respiration as a sample case for biological explanation which follows only 20 lines later, 642a 31-b4. These passages, I have argued, express the same view about hypothetical necessity and its relations to Democritean necessity, but they seem clearly written in mutual independence. The same cannot be said for the third of the three passages of *PA* I listed above (243), 639b21–640a10, which is in fact just a shorter and less full summary of *Ph.* II.9 (to which it refers back at 640a3). For that reason I have made few detailed references to it: the interpretation I have given of *Ph.* II.9 applies *a fortiori* to this passage as well.

Democritean hypothesis that there is a set of fixed, true principles specifying how material particles of different sizes and shapes behave under various conditions, and that everything that happens happens as a result of these principles ('by brute necessity') is mere fantasy. *Some* things do happen by this kind of necessity; but not very much does, and it is certainly not possible to start merely from a description in materialist terms of, say, a sperm and some female matter, together with a similar description of the environing conditions, and build up, step-by-step, with appeal only to material necessity, the complex and highly organized newborn animal that *always*, unless something specifiable goes wrong, results. If one actually studies how matter, as such, behaves, instead of inventing theories about such things, Aristotle thought, one will see at once that this is so.

It is easy for us, with the hindsight made possible by post-Renaissance experimental physics and chemistry to suppose that Aristotle's atomist opponents had the better of this dispute. But such an attitude is quite unhistorical. The ancient atomists had no *empirical* reason to think that the powers attributable to matter of different kinds were sufficient to determine any of the actually observed outcomes. No Greek theorist had any conception of what controlled experiment might show about the powers of matter; insofar as empirical evidence bearing on this question was available either to Aristotle or to his opponents it amounted to no more than what ordinary observation could yield. And there is no doubt that ordinary observation, so far from suggesting any universal necessitation of such outcomes by the inherent properties of matter, leads to Aristotle's more modest estimate of what can be explained by reference to the material and moving causes. Who, having observed what happens when fire is applied to a stick of wood, would suppose that the material characteristics of that stick and that fire, together with the prevailing conditions of air-flow, and so on, dictate that just *so* much ash will result, and in just *that* arrangement? That the stick will be consumed, that it will be turned to ashes – that is clear; but ordinary observation does not license the belief that the outcome is in further particulars determined one way or the other. Similarly, when wet warm stuff, such as fourth-century scientists thought gave rise to an animal fetus, was affected by the watery, mobile stuff of the male semen, there might be grounds, taking into account only what follows from their constitution as stuffs of a certain consistency, etc., for thinking that some congealing and setting effect will result. But that the congealing and setting should be precisely that which constitutes an animal fetus? There was no reason at all to believe that *this* was determined on *that* sort of ground. So insofar as either Aristotle or the atomists had an empirical basis for their views about the powers of matter, Aristotle's position was far stronger. I do not mean to deny, of course, the inherent theoretical strengths of the atomists' 'program'; but insofar as the dispute between them and Aristotle turned on actual evidence, Aristotle clearly had the better of this argument.

What then does account for the production of an animal fetus under the conditions in which we know such a fetus is produced? In his account in *Metaphysics* A of his predecessors' views on explanation, Aristotle remarks that some earlier philosophers (e.g. Anaxagoras) recognized that material necessity did not suffice, and also saw that one could not well say that there is no general explanation at all, that this outcome was due simply to chance – holding that *some* particular arrangement or other of the materials as they are congealed and set has to result, and that it just happens each time that what results is a properly constructed fetus of the appropriate kind (984b11–15). One might, I suppose, say that it is only a long run of luck that, so far as we know, has produced this regular-seeming result up to now, and that things may soon start turning out differently. But, as we have seen, Aristotle plausibly argued there was reason to believe that this is how things *always* have been and *always* will be. And if it *always* happens like this, throughout all time, some further explanation is required; it cannot be a matter of luck. So if this fact cannot be explained by deriving it from more basic natural facts about the material constitution of the world, then one must either invoke supernatural powers as responsible for it, or else posit as a second level of basic natural fact that the world permanently contains plants and animals (in addition to matter of various kinds), and indeed precisely the *same* plants and animals at all times. In other words: *if* one is determined to treat these regularities as a fact of nature, and they cannot be derived from other natural principles, one must take them as expressing a natural principle all on their own. Thus Aristotle's response, that it is an inherent, non-derivative fact about the natural world that it consists in part of the natural kinds and works to maintain them permanently in existence, is an eminently reasonable, even scientific, one.

But now – and this is the crucial point – by adopting the view that plants and animals are a basic, and not a derived, constituent of physical reality, one provides the theoretical background necessary to justify the appeal to goals in explaining the recurrent processes of animal and plant generation. For, on this view, there is inherent in the world a fundamental tendency to preserve permanently the species of living things it contains. But the living things in question are so structured that each one's organs and other parts work together to make it possible for it to achieve to a rather high degree its own specific good, the full and active life characteristic of its kind, including the leaving of offspring behind; the actual plant and animal life that is preserved is all of it *good*. One can therefore claim to discover in any given process of animal generation one of those processes in which the tendency to preserve the species of living things is concretely realized. And because the regular outcome of each such process is something good, one is also entitled to interpret the process itself as directed at that outcome as its goal. For if it is a fundamental fact about the world, not derivable from other natural principles, that it maintains forever these good life-forms, then the processes by which it does so, being processes by which something good is achieved, are for the sake of the outcomes. Thus, for example, fetal materials coming from a female dog and acted upon by a male dog's sperm are transformed by certain definite stages into a puppy. This transformation cannot be explained by reference to the material constitution of these antecedent stuffs; left to themselves these materials would not, or would not certainly, have produced just those formations in which the features and organs that characterize a dog are developed. What happens in this case needs to be explained by referring to the fundamental tendency of the natural kinds of living things to be preserved in existence, and recognizing that this process is one of those by which a species, the dog, preserves itself by reproduction. This tendency, which is not ultimately reducible to the powers and properties of matter-kinds, is irreducibly teleological; it is the tendency of certain materials to interact, be formed and transformed in certain ways, *so as* to produce a well-formed, well-adapted, viable new specimen of the same species as the animals from which they came. So, given his view that living things are basic to the permanent structure of the world, Aristotle can argue that those stages in the formation of a fetus in which one can discern the development of the features and organs of the mature animal being produced are *for the sake of* that animal nature which is the final outcome of the process.

This argument for natural teleology and the other one, from *Physics* ii.8, examined above (section i) are closely related. In both arguments the permanence of the natural kinds of living things figures prominently. In the first it is the fact that the permanent natural kinds are all of them well-adapted – that living things' organic and other parts serve their needs by enabling them to survive and flourish in their natural environments – that is said to demand teleological explanation, even if mechanical principles sufficed to explain everything else about them. In the argument just examined the focus is on the more elementary (alleged) fact that plants and animals are very complex objects whose regular and permanent production the natural powers of the matter-kinds are not sufficient to explain; that this nonetheless happens is only explicable, according to Aristotle, if we suppose the regular production of these objects is a fundamental goal (or rather, set of goals) in nature, so that the presence in nature of these goals is what makes the processes of animal and plant generation come about always in the way that they do.

It is worth emphasizing in conclusion that, as I have just implied, the teleological explanations that these arguments of Aristotle's are meant to endorse are best construed as causal explanations of a certain kind, whatever one may think of them so construed. On Aristotle's view, certain goals *actually exist* in *rerum natura*; there *are* in reality those plant and animal forms that he argues are natural goals. Their existence there is what controls and directs those aspects of the processes of generation that need to be explained by reference to them, and that, indeed, is why they need to be so explained. Thus one could put Aristotle's view by saying that *one* kind of causal explanation refers to antecedent material conditions and powers: what *makes* wood burn when fire is applied to it is that fire is hot and so has the power to act in this way on wood. The given material natures of fire and wood are simply such that this happens. But similarly what *makes* a particular series of transformations take place in the generation of a dog is that it is a fundamental fact about nature that each kind of living thing reproduces so as to preserve itself. That series is made to happen *because* what is being formed is a dog, and it is a dog's nature to have certain particular organs and other features. Here what Aristotle thinks of as the cause of what happens is located not in the material nature of anything but in a certain formal nature, that of the dog. The recent tendency to explicate and defend Aristotelian teleology exclusively by appeal to essentially epistemological considerations leaves out of account this crucial fact about Aristotle's theory, that he grounds his teleological explanations thus in the very nature of things. It is quite true, and important, as for example Richard Sorabji says, that we will certainly always need teleological explanations, no matter how much we learn about causal mechanisms, because, among other reasons, our interests in asking 'Why?' sometimes cannot be satisfied otherwise than by noticing some good that the thing inquired into does.[30] But it would be misleading to put such considerations forward as providing insight into Aristotle's theory or his reasons for holding it. For they leave out of account the fact that for Aristotle such explanations only *truly* explain where, and because, reality is *actually governed* in the ways the explanations claim; what our interests demand is only of significance where they may be satisfied by pointing to something about the actual workings of things. Here as elsewhere for Aristotle ontology takes precedence over epistemology. His commitment to teleological explanation is fundamentally misunderstood where this fact is not borne clearly in mind.[31]

[30] Sorabji 1980: 165–6. See the similar remarks of Martha Nussbaum 1978: 69–70, 78–80. Both authors record their indebtedness to Charles Taylor's work on teleological explanation.

[31] The difference between Aristotle and contemporary defenders of teleological (or, as people now for no very good reason say, teleonomic) argument in biology is well brought out by a comment of David Hull. Focusing on the issue of reductionism Hull points out that the dispute nowadays is over 'methodological reduction' and 'theory reduction', not 'ontological reduction'. 'Nowadays both scientists and philosophers take ontological reduction for granted...Organisms are "nothing but" atoms, and that is that' (Hull 1981: 282). When Aristotle opposes the reduction of teleological explanation to mechanical-efficient causation he is opposing ontological reduction just as much as methodological (and theory) reduction.

10

Teleology and necessity

D. M. BALME

The chief difficulty that final causes present to modern philosophers lies in reconciling them with what Aristotle calls 'necessity', that is the automatic interactions of the physical elements. It is difficult to see, first, how laws of nature can be directed towards goals and still remain 'necessary'; and, secondly, what could be the author and the means of such direction. The modern cybernetic model, and the concept of elaborate genetic coding, have not altered the problem; they have merely shown that some apparently teleological processes may in fact be necessary outcomes. It is arguable, as we shall see, that in the *GA* Aristotle himself was moving towards such a position. But there is no sign of it in *PA*, nor is there any sign in his writings generally that the relationship between finality and necessity could be a difficulty of the sort that we feel.

The novelty in Aristotle's theory was his insistence that finality is within nature: it is part of the natural process, not imposed upon it by an independent agent like Plato's world soul or Demiourgos. This is what allows him to claim that none of his predecessors had recognized the final cause with any clarity.[1] Anaxagoras called his primary cosmological cause 'Mind', and for this Aristotle likened him to a lone sober man among drunks;[2] Plato offered cosmic teleological causes in the *Timaeus*, *Philebus* and *Laws*; Xenophon argued for the popular belief in providential guidance of natural phenomena.[3] But such constructions are not what Aristotle meant by the final cause. Nor has his natural teleology anything to do with intentionality, the physiology of which in man and animals he explains in *MA*. There is no deliberating or purposing in most animals, he says; and it is by nature alone that roots and leaves grow for the sake of fruit; so that 'clearly the final cause is within the things that come about and exist by nature... It is absurd to deny that a thing comes about for the sake of something simply because one does not see that the cause of the change has deliberated. Art too does not

---

[1] *Metaph.* A. 988b6–16.   [2] *Metaph.* A. 984b17.   [3] *Memorabilia* I.4; IV.3.

deliberate. If the art of ship-building were present in the timber, it would be acting like nature... Nature is a cause in this way, namely for the sake of something' (*Ph.* II. 199a20, b26).

In *PA* II–IV Aristotle is occupied with exhibiting finality, but not with explaining how it works – that is to come in *GA*. Here he reviews every kind of tissue and organ found in animals, and argues that each part is as it is for two reasons: it exists for the sake of the animal's functions, while its development is both made possible and conditioned by the necessary actions of the materials out of which it grows. For example, horns grow for the sake of defense; but they grow out of earthy material which is necessarily flowing towards the animal's head; 'nature makes use of it for defense and advantage' (*PA* III. 663b34). In other animals nature uses the same material for teeth instead, which is why horned animals lack the upper incisors, not having enough material for both. While the material possesses the strength and density needed for horns and teeth, its natural action and movement will not produce the shapes and positioning of horns and teeth unless nature causes it to do so. The elements therefore are not absolute causes of the product, but contributory causes (*sunaitia*): 'for fire grows indefinitely so long as there is something to burn, but in everything constituted by nature there is a limit and definition (*logos*) of both size and growth; and these come from soul but not from fire, and from form rather than from matter' (*de An.* II. 416a4). The relationship appears clearly in *GA*: 'Heat and cold may make things hard, soft, tough, brittle, with all the other affections that belong to living things, but cannot go so far as to give them the definition in virtue of which one is now flesh and the other bone... Nature uses both heat and cold, which have power by necessity to do this and that; but in things that come to be the cooling and heating take place for an end;...they make flesh soft partly by necessity and partly not by necessity but for some end' (*GA* II. 734b31, 743a36, b16). The natural actions of the elements, taken by themselves, cannot deliver enough to account for animal parts. They do, however, account for many of the qualities of these parts, including possibly undesirable ones (bone is breakable) and irrelevant side-effects, upon which Aristotle comments: 'True, nature sometimes uses even excess products to advantage, but this does not justify our seeking a final cause in all – but while some things exist for the sake of an end, many other things necessarily come about too because of them' (*PA* IV. 677a17).

The analysis of causes into two kinds, those acting for the sake of an end and those acting by necessity, recalls Plato's *Timaeus* with its distinction between the two causes Mind and Necessity. In his account, which Plato says is only a 'likely myth', a divine intelligent Demiourgos puts order into a chaotic material. The material consists of air earth fire and water, which have their own powers but act in a 'wandering' manner until directed by Mind; they are the 'contributory cause' (*sunaition*).[4] Aristotle too expresses the distinction between the causes as between necessity and 'the better' or 'the good', although he makes it clearer than Plato does that 'good' is not an extrinsic value-judgment but means the useful or advantageous from the animal's viewpoint.[5] But because the *PA* shows Plato's influence more strongly than the other treatises, and because it does not explain how 'nature' controls the material interactions, nor what it means by 'nature', it has not surprisingly attracted interpretations which make nature into a cosmic and in fact supernatural force.

But these interpretations must be resisted, for there is no room in Aristotle's cosmology for any such force acting upon the sublunary region. The prime mover of the universe has no knowledge of the universe;[6] the stars are moved by causes within the spheres that carry them.[7] If there is 'teleology' in the movements of the heavens (though really this is a misuse of the word), it has no connection with natural teleology on earth.[8] For the stars, sun and planets consist of a separate element, *aithēr*, which does not exist on earth and naturally moves in circles.[9] Their movements cause the earth's seasons, and therefore exert a general influence upon growth, but nothing more detailed.[10] The sublunary elements, air earth fire and water, act teleologically only when they are part of a living body; outside that (for instance in the occurrence of rainstorms) there is no final cause acting on them (*Ph.* II. 198b18). Aristotle confines natural teleology to sublunary life. Each animal contains within itself its own sources of motion and direction (its *archai*, which are potential impulses[11]); these may be triggered by seasonal changes, but are not directed by anything external to themselves. The comparison which Aristotle draws between cycles of events on earth and astronomical cycles is drawn

---

[4] *Tim.* 46c, 48a.
[5] The useful: *PA* II. 654a19; III. 662a33, b3, 7; IV. 677a16, 678a4–16, 683b37, 684a3, 685a28, 687b29, 691b1; *Resp.* 476a12. Sometimes he gives precedence to 'the valuable' (*timion*: e.g. *PA* II. 658a22; III. 672b20; IV. 687a15). But the part's value derives from its usefulness, not vice versa: *IA* 706b14; *PA* III. 672b15.   [6] *Metaph.* Λ. 1072b18.
[7] *Cael.* II. 289b30.   [8] *Metaph.* Λ. 1072b2.   [9] *Cael.* I.2.
[10] *GC* II. 336a32, 338b3; *GA* IV. 777b28; *Mete.* I. 339a21.
[11] The extent to which nature's sources of motion are 'fresh starts' is discussed in Guthrie 1939: xviii; Ross 1924: lxxxi; Sorabji 1980: 143. See too *Metaph.* E. 1027b11; *Ph.* VIII. 253a11–20, 259b1–16. It is definitory that 'nature is a source of motion in itself' (*Ph.* II. 192b20; *Cael.* III. 301b17; *Metaph.* Θ. 1049b9; *GA* II. 735a3).

for the sake of contrast. The outer stars eternally repeat a perfect circle; sublunary beings, neither eternal nor perfect, tend towards cyclical order through reproduction (which is the individual's attempt to survive), but this tendency is disturbed by the matter's indeterminacy and by the mutual interference of the multifarious *archai*[12]. Therefore when Aristotle says (*Metaph.* Λ. 1072b4, 14) that nature depends upon the prime mover, he is referring to the general cause of motion but not to the individual processes whose direction is determined within the animals themselves. And when he compares the universe with a household in which 'all things are ordered together towards one end' (1075a18), he is not speaking of a control exerted by the prime mover but of a tendency to regularity in all living beings: this tendency is inherent in their natures, which of their own accord follow the regularity of the heavens. But in sublunary beings there is a laxity which prompts the question where is the goodness in nature. Aristotle answers that the contribution made to the common good by the stars is their orderliness, while that made by animals and plants is their cyclical dissolution and reproduction rather than their individual activities. 'For such a source of action (*archē*) in each is their nature' (1075a22), which seems to mean that the nature of the sublunary and superlunary realms respectively makes each act in its own way. The source and nature of animal actions must therefore be explained from the nature of animals.

Just as Aristotle provides no evidence for supernatural control, so he provides none for a natural force over and above the individual natures of living things. Although he speaks anthropomorphically of nature choosing and guiding and 'doing nothing in vain'[13], he offers no place for an actually hypostatized Dame Nature – any more than do those modern biologists who speak so freely of the 'purpose' of animal structures and indulge in anthropomorphic metaphors like 'information' and 'coding'. Interpreters who have believed that he intended an overall teleological control have pointed to two statements which at face value suggest that the good of some animals is subordinated to the good of others. *PA* IV. 696b26 says: 'Dolphins and selachians have their mouths underneath, and therefore turn on their backs to take their food. Nature seems to have done this not only for the sake of saving other animals (for while they delay in turning over, the others escape), but also to prevent them from suffering the consequences of gluttony; for if they got food too easily they would die of excess. In addition to these reasons, their snout is

---

[12] *GA* IV. 778a7.
[13] *PA* II. 658a9 and *passim*; even 'God and Nature' *Cael* I. 271a33.

round and thin and therefore not capable of easy division.' But what this account does is to replace a faulty teleological explanation (saving other animals) with a proper one (preventing gluttony); its expression is sarcastic, no doubt because the faulty explanation was of the sort favored by popular providentialists like Xenophon. The other passage is at *Pol.* i. 1256b16, where Aristotle says that plants exist to feed animals, and animals to feed and clothe men.[14] But it is impossible that he could have meant this literally. It comes in a rhetorical and popularizing account of the varieties in natural lifestyle, which argues that man is acting naturally and properly when he dominates other animals. But when Aristotle considers the final cause of living things, he says that the natural philosopher must explain 'how it is better so, not absolutely, but in relation to each thing's being' (*Ph.* ii. 198b9). This must rule out the face-value of *Pol.* 1256b16.

Nor does his analysis provide for 'vitalism' or any other 'extra factor' or nisus or conatus within animals.[15] Just as nature is not an independent entity but at most a generalization over the natures of individual beings, so soul is not an independent entity but is the form of the body.[16] It is the body's entelechy, its activity and actualization. In *GA* (as we shall see below) Aristotle equates the soul with 'movements' in the bodily tissues and blood, and because these movements form a self-limiting complex they control the body's constituents, so that the soul is at once the expression and the controller of bodily activity. This important idea is far from the 'mysterious entelechy' that some interpreters have imagined. Nor does Aristotle credit *pneuma* with the special powers that his medical contemporaries postulated. He defines it simply as 'hot air' (*GA* ii. 736a1), and confines its role to actions that can be explained from the natural properties of heat and air.[17]

A further difficulty, which has perhaps caused more misunderstanding of Aristotle's biology than any other, is the relation between individual and species. Some of his statements can be taken to imply that individuals may act not for their own good but for that of their kind, and even that the individual's form is the form of the species. The latter view will be examined in my discussion of essentialism.[18] With regard to the former, Aristotle says at *GA* ii. 731b35 that the reason why the kind is perpetuated is that the individual achieves

---

[14] Cf. *Pol.* vii. 1324b41 ('only the eatable should be hunted').
[15] For references to interpretations of this kind, see Sorabji 1980: 170.
[16] *De An.* ii.1.
[17] On *pneuma*, see my note at *GA* ii. 736a24 (1972: 158). For contrary views, giving a special meaning to *pneuma*, see Peck 1963: App. B; Solmsen 1957: 119.   [18] See ch. 11 below.

through reproduction the only eternality possible for it, namely in form.[19] He never says, however, that reproduction is for the sake of preserving the species, but leaves it that its preservation follows from the individual's attempt to preserve its own form – i.e. to survive. Again, he says that fishes are prolific because they live in a hostile environment and 'nature retrieves the wastage by quantity' (*GA* III. 755a31). Some animals cannot reproduce, but are generated spontaneously (*GA* III.11). In higher animals the sexes are separate because this benefits their intelligence; accordingly, to preserve their kind, nature ensures that enough females are produced even though a female birth is a deviation (*GA* II. 732a2; III. 767b9). What then is 'nature' in this context? The simplest answer is that nature is what is the case: here it is what survives, and the principle underlying it is the survival of those that are fit. This idea was already familiar from Empedocles. When Aristotle criticizes Empedocles at *Ph.* II. 198b29, it is not for saying that the fittest survive but for saying that they became fit by chance and through random material causes; to which Aristotle replies that this is impossible because nature is regular while random outcomes are irregular. Just as the very existence of species requires no deeper cause than the survival of those animals that fit best into a niche, so the preservation of species requires only the survival of the fit. If the fishes were not prolific, they would not survive in sufficient numbers; if the sharks could eat them quicker, they would not escape. This must seem to Aristotle mere common sense, not needing philosophical argument. The real problem is what ensures the reproduction of the individual: how is it that each fit animal produces equally fit offspring, fit to survive? Given that, the rest will follow. This is the problem that *GA* deals with, as will be seen. All the teleological explanations of the animals' parts in *PA*, at whatever level of generality they occur, refer to this individual development and to the individual's advantage: *this* is what benefits it in these circumstances. The explanations from 'nature's economy' refer to the economy within the individual body: the windpipe must be here because the heart is there...[20] What requires explanation, therefore, is how the individual's growth is directed towards these benefits, and what is meant by the 'soul' and 'nature' that control growth.

Lastly, at the opposite extreme from cosmic and overall teleology is the Kantian view that a teleological explanation is only an 'as-if' account: the final cause is a useful Reflexionsbegriff, but does not

---

[19] Cf. *de An.* II. 415a29; *GC* II. 336b30; and my note in 1972: 96.
[20] *PA* III. 665a7. Other examples in ch. 11 below, 300 n. 49.

actually exist.[21] Those who take this view hold that Aristotle's intention was to pick out the apparently teleological sequences because they draw attention to significant parts of the material-efficient process; but that process itself brings about the full result, and is scientifically explanatory without teleology. They hold that Aristotle indicates this by saying that every cybernetic process is also due to necessity, meaning that it is part of one physical interaction. The value of the teleological explanation then becomes purely heuristic. But this interpretation encounters two serious difficulties. First, as we have seen, Aristotle did not regard the automatic physical interaction as capable of producing animal tissues and organs; for when the elements act without being used by nature or soul, they do not impose limit and definition upon themselves.[22] This conception is hardly applicable to modern physical laws, which are envisaged as quantitatively precise on the observable scale in nature. Secondly, Aristotle always presents the four causes as four separate factors in a causal situation (*Ph.* II.3). They are not one factor plus three alternative descriptions or views of it. Nor does 'cause' (*aitia*) mean merely explanation, for which his word is *logos* or *apodeixis*. Modern translators, haunted by Hume, sometimes prefer 'explanation' to 'cause', but this risks a vicious ambiguity; for in Aristotle's usage explanations and reasons given are words and thoughts, whereas causes are objective things and events. Therefore if the efficient cause is one objective factor in nature, so too is the final cause another one.

If finality is not directed by an 'extra factor', whether within each animal separately or operating upon nature overall, and if it is not directed towards the good of anything other than the individual animal, it can only be part of the animal's natural growth. As such, the place for its explanation is the *GA*, and there indeed we find it. Aristotle explains how the animal inherits and reproduces its parents' forms. The sire implants his own form into the fetal matter (uterine blood, which itself has the dam's form implanted to a lesser degree – a complication which need not concern our present argument[23]). Actual form is the form of the matter at a given moment, therefore at conception the implanted form is simple; but it is potentially diverse, and it diversifies as the fetus grows. This is a logical analysis, which Aristotle now translates into physiological terms. The sperm

---

[21] For this view see Nussbaum 1978: 59–99; Wieland 1962: 261.
[22] *De An.* II. 416a15; *GA* II. 734b31.
[23] For a fuller outline of the account of generation see ch. 11 below, 293–4.

is secreted out of blood at the moment when the blood is being diversified within the sire's body into his parts and tissues.[24] The 'movements' or continuing changes (*kinēseis*) that the blood contains are transmitted to the sperm and thence to the uterine blood. These movements, like those in an automaton after it has been set going, become more complex and so bring about the progressive formation of the matter into tissues and parts. Nothing else but movements is transmitted to the fetus; for the sperm and its *pneuma* (the vehicle of the movements) evaporate;[25] moreover some animals transmit no sperm at all but simply movements directly implanted.[26] Now what the sire transmits is in fact soul,[27] which is therefore to be identified with the movements. At first it is merely nutritive soul in actuality, but potentially within it are the latent movements of sensitive soul, which become actualized in bodily parts as growth proceeds. From conception, therefore, the soul-movements are potentially the adult soul. At *GA* II. 740b29 Aristotle says:

The capability (*dunamis*) of the nutritive soul, just as later on in the actual animals and plants it makes growth out of food by using heat and cold as instruments (for its movements take place in them, and each part is formed according to a certain definition), so too from the beginning it forms the natural object that is coming to be... And this [*sc.* nutritive soul] is the nature of every one, present in plants and animals alike. The other parts of the soul are present in some but not in others.

This is Aristotle's physiological account of the teleological control which soul and nature exert. It shows the sense in which he says 'Nature is spoken of in two ways, as matter and as being; the latter is also nature as moving cause and as end; and such, in the animals, is either its whole soul or some part of it' (*PA* I. 641a27). In this context soul and nature are used synonymously to stand for a self-limiting complex of physiological interactions or 'movements' which control the body's development in conformity with the inherited parental forms.[28] In this way form and teleological direction are imposed by 'nature' upon the primary actions of the elements. The resulting complex interactions are 'reducible' to the primary actions of the elements only in the trivial sense that they consist of them, as a polygon consists of lines and angles, but not in the sense that they come about because of those primary actions and would have resulted automatically. The latter reduction was proposed by Epicurus, who argued that random atomic movements would sometimes throw up enclosed and self-limiting complexes; these

---

[24] *GA* I. 726b10; II. 737a18. [25] *GA* II. 737a11. [26] *GA* I. 729b27, 730b10.
[27] *GA* II. 735a5, 737a32.
[28] Potentiality in the sperm: *PA* I. 640a23, 642a1. Control of growth by soul-movements: *GA* II.1; II.3; II.4 740a8, 630.

would give off similar groups and so account for the reproduction of successful animals. Epicurus treated the problem too lightly in his haste to be rid of teleology (which he apparently understood only in a crude providential sense). Aristotle, like Plato and probably all the ancients, sees the primary actions of the elements as quantitatively indeterminate until limit is imposed upon them. If limit is naturally imposed, not at random but regularly and usually, it must come from a pre-existing source; this he interprets as an enclosed system of movements in air earth fire and water; and the only place where it can be is in the parent. In the long and brilliant argument of *GA* he assembles the evidence for this, and disposes of alternative theories. It is summed up in the cardinal principle that 'a man begets a man'. It follows (ironically, in view of later criticism) that the approach to a quantitative science, which is always more visible in Aristotle than in the atomists, is owed to his teleology. He shows this, for instance, when explaining why animals produce several embryos rather than one big one:

The fetus is formed out of spermatic material which is not indeterminate in quantity;...there must be a proportion between the male and female contributions;...for there is a limit set upon the capability of the material that is acted upon, and of the heat that acts upon it;...the product is a precise quantity out of a precise quantity (*poson ti ek posou tinos*). (*GA* IV. 772a2, 17, 29)

This idea of quantitative proportion often appears.[29] Nature's works are 'ordered and defined' (*GA* v. 778b4).

This is why the relation between teleology and necessity does not present a logical problem to Aristotle as it does to us. He sees the alternative to teleology not as a universal order mechanically determined by a nexus of physical causes and effect, in which each effect is both itself determinate and the cause of a further predictable effect, but as a chaos from which nothing amenable to scientific explanation could emerge.[30] The elements act in their own natural ways, but the actions are unlimited. This is the sense of the 'indeterminacy' (*aoristia*) that Aristotle attributes to proximate matter (*GA* IV. 778a6). It does not mean uncertain quality of action, nor an inscrutable intractability as some have suggested, but simply that the matter has not yet been formally determined into a precise state. The production of an animal therefore requires two material processes, which are of course combined in nature: there must be the primary actions of the elements, and there must be a limiting movement.

[29] *GA* I. 723a29, 727b11, 729a17; IV. 767a16, 772a17.
[30] *PA* I. 641b15; *Ph.* II. 198b35.

The primary actions are 'necessary' in the sense that they are necessitated by the nature of the elements, and themselves necessitate certain consequences. But they are also necessary in the sense that they are contributory causes without which the production could not take place. To express this, Aristotle borrows from his logical terminology the phrase 'on a hypothesis' (*ex hupotheseos*):[31] on the hypothesis that there will be this goal, such-and-such actions are necessary. In this sense necessity applies both to the primary material actions and to the limiting movement. At *Ph.* II. 199b34 he says:

Is the necessity 'on a hypothesis', or is it in fact absolute? Some suppose that the necessary exists in things that come-to-be in the way that one might think that a wall had come about necessarily because heavy things naturally go down and light things go up, so that the stones and foundations went to the bottom, the soil above them, and the timber to the top as being the lightest. Now the wall did not come about without these things, but nevertheless it was not because of them, except as matter, but for the sake of giving protection. Similarly with everything else that has a final cause: it is not without things that have a necessary nature, but on the other hand it is not because of them except as matter;...the necessary is in the matter, but the final cause is in the definition... (200a30) Clearly, then, the necessary in natural things is that which is spoken of as matter and the movements in it.

In saying that the material movements have their own necessary nature but are also necessitated on the hypothesis of the production, Aristotle would seem to imply one of two alternatives. The first, which would be trivial, is that if we hypothesize that a wall will be built, we may infer that wall-materials must first be assembled. This is the heuristic interpretation. The other alternative is that the materials are open to selection and control towards an end. This is the clear sense of the biology, and seems to influence Aristotle to speak at one point as though 'necessary on a hypothesis' covered all natural necessity:

There are then these two causes, the for-the-sake-of-which and the of-necessity – for many things come about of necessity. Perhaps the question might arise as to what kind of necessity is meant by those who say 'of necessity'. For neither of the two modes defined in our philosophical treatises can be present. In things that have coming-to-be, however, there is the third kind. For we say that food is a necessary thing not according to either of those modes but in that it is impossible to be without it. This is as it were 'on a hypothesis'. For just as there is a necessity that the axe be hard, since one must cut with it, and, if hard, that it be of bronze or iron, so too since the body is an instrument (for each of its parts is for the sake of something, and so is the body as a whole), therefore there is a necessity that it be such a thing and made of such things if that end is to be. (*PA* I. 642a1)

---

[31] *APr.* I. 45b16; *APo.* I. 72b15, 83b39; II. 92a7. The extension of this to natural science appears at *GC* II. 337b22–6. Generally, to distinguish contingent from unconditional: *Pol.* VII. 1332a10. Cf. Bonitz *Index s.v. hupothesis*.

The two modes distinguished in the 'philosophical treatises'[32] are evidently (i) movement necessitated by a natural state, as when a stone falls, (ii) movement necessitated by force, as when a stone is thrown up. Probably this extreme statement means that the proximate matter would not be present and active at all, were it not that a process of living nature was taking place (eating, digestion, etc.).[33] But apart from these two discussions Aristotle does not refer to 'hypothetical necessity' in his biology, but only to 'necessity'.[34] That he means necessity to cover both hypothetical and absolute necessity is clear in the little model explanation at the end of *PA* I.1 (642a31):

Exposition should be as follows: for example, breathing exists for the sake of this, while that comes to be of necessity because of those. Necessity signifies sometimes that if there is to be that for the sake of which, these must necessarily be present; and sometimes that this is their state and nature. For the hot necessarily goes out and comes in again when it meets resistance, and the air must flow in; so much is already necessitated.

Such an analysis would seem possible only because Aristotle regards the elementary actions as quantitatively undetermined when left to themselves. They are modified in the direction of natural goals. The modification is not an automatic interaction reducible to the primary actions of the elements, but is imposed upon them by the pre-established soul-movements. Nevertheless these limiting movements are movements only of the elements, and could therefore be regarded as an additional part of the whole efficient cause – taken in a wider sense than Aristotle uses. For what he is saying is that there is a cybernetic control in biological processes over and above the simple actions of air earth fire and water, but still consisting only of their interactions within the complex. It is only a step, in theory, to a quantitative analysis of such controls. But of course it demands a very long step from the state of observational science in his day. Meanwhile the significance of his analysis is his insistence that this control exists within nature itself, and so must come into the scientific account.

---

[32] An uncertain reference, possibly *APo.* II. 94b36. The account at *Metaph.* Δ.5 has been suggested (John Cooper, ch. 9 above, 259–60) but seems to me less close.

[33] Cooper, ch. 9 above, interprets it in this way, I think rightly. But this is not enough to 'reconcile necessity with teleology' as Cooper argues, for it still remains to be shown how nature brings the proximate matter to the goal-like state and position. I agree with Cooper in rejecting my former attempt (1972: 76) to subsume all 'necessity' within living bodies under 'hypothetical necessity'. *PA* I. 642a1 is the only passage that suggests it; moreover Aristotle's use of 'hypothetical' in this context is rare, whereas in the huge majority of cases he speaks only of 'necessity' and clearly refers to the automatic interactions of the primary powers.   [34] *De Somno* 455b26 is a rare exception.

PART IV

METAPHYSICAL THEMES

...for these most of all are substances.

(*Metaph.* Z. 1034a3–4)

Introduction

In their contributions to Part I, David Balme and Montgomery Furth have given us reason to think that Aristotle's systematic study of animals might help us to understand those concepts at the center of his metaphysical analysis of substance: form, matter, essence, substratum, kind, universal, differentia, actuality, potentiality, perhaps even *nous*. Each of the papers in this Part attempts to illustrate that thesis by bringing Aristotle's biological works directly to bear on such central themes of his metaphysics.

The keynote paper of Part IV is a slightly revised version of David Balme's rich and provocative 'Aristotle's biology was not essentialist', first published in *Archiv für Geschichte der Philosophie* in 1980. Balme argues that the essentialist identification of form and species traditionally attributed to Aristotle is not to be found in his biological works. According to *GA*, an animal's development is 'primarily towards the parental likeness, including even non-essential details, while the common form of the species is only a generality which "accompanies" this likeness'. Animal form includes material accidents and is to be distinguished from essence, which 'picks out only those features for which a teleological explanation holds'. Both are to be distinguished from species, which is a generalization over individual composites, over forms as actualized in matter. The question remains why there should be species, why the family lines generated by the principle of inherited resemblance should cluster into kinds as they do. Balme concludes by showing how this follows from the principle that animal forms are organized for maximum functional advantage.

The interpretation of the biology presented in this essay, Balme suggests, agrees closely 'with one plausible interpretation of the disputed books *Metaph.* ZH'. In two appendices, added for this volume, he elaborates his argument. Appendix 1 offers a fuller sketch of Balme's reading of ZH, and its connections with the biology. One topic only touched on there – Aristotle's use of 'the snub' to exemplify the form–matter relationship in natural substances – was discussed in greater detail by Balme in a recent article (1984), and at the risk of some overlap with Appendix 1 in the discussion of definition, we include this essay as Appendix 2.

The evidence collected in '*GENOS* and *EIDOS* in Aristotle's biology' (Balme 1962b), that these terms were taxonomically neutral, each applicable at virtually any level of generality, suggested to Balme a failure to carry out a taxonomic project implicit both in the logical, and in some theoretical portions of the biological, works. Pierre Pellegrin's recent study (Pellegrin 1982) has convinced most readers (including Balme) that in fact throughout Aristotle's works these concepts, at each level of generality, express the same logical/ontological relationship: *eidē* are always forms *of kinds* (*genē*), which are arrived at by division of the kind, i.e., by the specification of differentiae. In 'Logical difference and biological difference: the unity of Aristotle's thought', Pellegrin summarizes the argument of his book for this thesis and extends it to include the concepts of 'the more and the less', analogy, and differentia, or difference (as he prefers to translate *diaphora*). A central lesson of Pellegrin's research is that the reason why Aristotle's biology has seemed to its students to be so confused on these matters is that they have assumed that its aims and methods were similar to those of contemporary biology. This theme recalls the introductory remarks of Balme's 'The place of biology in Aristotle's philosophy' (ch. 1 above).

James Lennox's 'Kinds, forms of kinds, and the more and the less in Aristotle's biology' is a substantial revision and expansion of Lennox 1980, reflecting development of his thinking on its issues, and integrating the results of Pellegrin just described. The notion of kinds with forms varying by the more and less is a pervasive theoretical tool in Aristotle's biology. Lennox traces the theoretical development of this notion and its use to express the way in which *eidē* of a *genos* are related to each other, and examines the implications of its role in the biology for traditional views of Aristotelian essentialism. Like Balme, he concludes that the concept of form which emerges from these passages, and the attendant essentialism, appear quite unlike that usually ascribed to Aristotle by historians and philosophers of science.

Among the problems Aristotle grapples with in the central books of the *Metaphysics* is one that concerns the way matter and form are related in 'composite' natural substances, especially in living organisms. Does this relationship involve a unity of the sort required if organisms are to be proper objects of definition, and true substances? Balme's discussion shows how Aristotle's biological theory supports an affirmative answer to this question. Aryeh Kosman approaches the same issue by asking what distinguishes the being of organisms from that of artifacts, such that the former but not the latter are the paradigmatic substances. 'Animals and other beings in Aristotle' offers a reading of the main line of argument in the central books, not entirely unlike that of Balme's, but with more attention to the role in that argument of the analysis of potentiality and actuality in Book Θ.

Kosman's analysis of the form–matter relation builds on and illuminates the argument in his recent 'Substance, being, and *energeia*' (1984) in suggesting that, for the paradigmatic substances, the relation of matter to form is like the relation of first to second actuality. In organisms, as this view entails, the matter is essentially, and naturally, instrumental. Though an artifact can have parts, which lose their being as parts when they are separated from the artifact, ultimately its material has a nature of its own, specifiable independently of the artifact. While the craftsman makes use of the potentialities of his materials, these materials have no special, *natural* potentiality that leads to the artifact. The nature of the elements of which an animal's matter is constituted, on the other hand, is not exhausted by its independent potentialities; their nature includes, irreducibly, their instrumental potentialities. The elements, and the parts they compose, and the body these parts constitute, are 'a natural structure of potentiality for the higher functional being of animal life', and in that sense have no being independently of the organisms they constitute. Matter and form *are* 'one and the same, the one potentially the other actually'.

Though Kosman remarks on the notion of the matter *from which* an organism was made, his focus is on the matter *of which* it is presently constituted. Cynthia Freeland, in her contribution, explores the former. Biological generation has consistently proved an obstacle for those attempting to understand the place of matter in Aristotle's theory of unqualified coming into being. The uniform and non-uniform parts, which constitute the body of a living organism, and which *de An.* ii suggests are its matter, are clearly not that from which the organism has come to be. On the other hand, what an organism apparently does come to be from, viz. the seed, clearly does not persist through the change. One might think the embryo or zygote an appropriate choice, but Freeland shows that this is conceptually inappropriate as well. By stressing that matter embodies capacities to be things, which capacities *persist* in those things, Freeland develops a case for blood (or its nutritive analogue in the case of bloodless animals) being both the matter for and, in an important sense, the matter of, organic substances. But in so doing, she indicates the limitations of the 'bronze statue' paradigm in helping us to understand the generation of more complex, multi-layered beings. Her case rests firmly on a study of the place of blood in the generative and nutritive lives of organisms suggested by *Parts of Animals*, *Generation of Animals*, and *De Anima*. But her discussion also helps to illuminate the general account of matter and change in *Physics* i–iii and *Metaphysics* ZHΘ, through examining Aristotle's actual account of the unqualified coming-to-be of actual substances.

Part iv's treatment of metaphysical themes ends, perhaps appropriately, with a discussion of 'Aristotle on the place of mind in nature'. William Charlton considers evidence, much of it in the biological treatises and *De Anima*, for attributing a mind/body dualism to Aristotle. The evidence lies in three well-known Aristotelian theses about *nous*: that it is not an object of investigation for natural science (*PA* i); that it enters 'from outside' (*GA* ii); and that it is separable from matter (*de An.* iii, *Metaph.* Λ). Through a careful reconsideration of the texts in which these claims are made, Charlton provides us with a fresh understanding of each of these theses. A philosophy of mind emerges which is neither Cartesian nor materialist, on which the discussions in the biological works once again shed important light.

Aristotle's biology was not
essentialist

D. M. BALME

The kind of essentialism that has been attributed to Aristotle's biology either identifies form and species, or recognizes individual forms merely as variations from a basic specific form. The essentialist holds in particular that each animal's growth is directed primarily towards the form of the species; that its essence prescribes its form; and that animal form excludes material accidents such as eye color.

These views, although apparently supported by various statements in Aristotle's logic and metaphysics, are directly opposed to some of his most mature and carefully argued theories in biology. Moreover those theories agree closely with one plausible interpretation of the disputed books *Metaph.* ZH. In this paper I confine myself to the biology; but I would suggest that there is ground here for supporting those who have recently been questioning the 'essentialism' in the logic.[1] Here I argue that in the *GA* Aristotle holds that the animal develops primarily towards the parental likeness, including even non-essential details, while the common form of the species is only a generality which 'accompanies' this likeness. In *PA* he argues for teleology with the question 'What benefits an animal of this kind?', not with the question 'What benefits *all* animals of this kind?'. He treats species as merely a universal obtained by generalization. While it is true that species-membership may help to explain the features of individuals, this is not because species is an efficient cause of individual formation, but because individuals in like circumstances are advantaged by like features. He does not discuss the mechanism that brings about advantageous development, though it is possible to suggest a naturalistic mechanism for him; his concern is rather to show that 'the better' is a 'cause' which must come into biological explanation. The fact that individuals develop in their most advantageous way in given circumstances, within the limits of the form inherited from their parents, is enough to explain the existence of species in Aristotle's sense of it.

[1] See for instance Leszl 1972/3, White 1972/3, and now my Appendix, 'Note on the *aporia* in *Metaphysics* **Z**' below 302–6.

The control of an animal's growth

The embryo is formed by 'movements' which have been transmitted from the sire, usually via pneuma in the semen, but sometimes directly.[2] They are the same movements that are occurring in the sire's blood at the moment when the blood is being diversified into bodily parts.[3] This particularization may be distorted, so that the sire's likeness is lost.[4] If the sire's movements fail to control the fetal matter, the next most effective determination comes from the female's movements which are present in the fetal matter (blood in the uterus). If they too fail, movements inherited from ancestors exert control in turn. But if no individual influence proves dominant, but all are confused together, then Aristotle says that the offspring

resembles no one of its relations, but there remains only that which is common, e.g. it is a man. The reason is that this accompanies all the individuals; for man is a universal, while the Socrates who is the father and so-and-so the mother are individuals.[5]

To produce a female is already a distortion.[6] In a correct reproduction, therefore, the offspring will be a replica of the sire.

This primary orientation must continue through life, for the inherited movements become the offspring's own: they are potentially its adult soul.[7] They are coordinated in the heart, from where they steer the animal's development.[8] The model that Aristotle offers is the pre-set automaton, which goes through a prolonged routine once it has been triggered.[9] Therefore the soul-movements are a complex of self-limiting interactions: they are the changes that take place in the flesh and blood, and at the same time they limit these changes to conform with the inherited potentialities.

This explanation of inherited resemblance expresses in physical terms the theory that Aristotle has already argued in *GA* I. The male contributes the primary formal influence, while the female contribution is primarily material plus a secondary formal influence.[10] As the movements become more diversified, the embryo develops, progressively actualizing features which have been potentially present since conception. These potential features can only be the parents' individual formal details. In the whole account there is no mention of a form of the species: what Aristotle says is that

---

[2] 'Movements': *kinēseis*, which include physiological changes; cf. *GA* IV.3 *passim*; I. 730b8–32, 729b22.   [3] *GA* I. 726b10; II. 737a18.
[4] *GA* IV.3 767b15ff.   [5] *GA* IV. 768b10.
[6] *GA* IV. 767b7.
[7] *GA* II. 734b22ff., 736a29ff., 737a27–34, 738b26, 740b24–741a5.   [8] *GA* II. 740a1–9.
[9] *GA* II. 734b9, 741b9.   [10] *GA* I. 730a24–b32; IV. 768a10–20.

individual resemblance is accompanied by the universal. Both are actual movements in the semen,[11] but the universal is not the primary efficient cause but only a consequential.[12] His language is like that of his logic, where the universal is that which is common to the particulars.[13] He is saying, therefore, that the individual grows towards the general likeness of the species insofar as each species-member grows towards it. He does not say here why they grow towards it, nor what validates the animal universal as an 'actual movement' and as a real object of knowledge (so important in his theory of science). I think that his answer to this question is implicit in his theory that animals develop towards 'the better', which will be discussed below. Meanwhile the *GA* makes it clear that species-membership is a consequential, not a primary cause, in animal reproduction and growth.[14]

---

[11] *GA* IV. 768a12.   [12] *GA* IV. 767b32.

[13] *Int.* 7; *Metaph.* Z. 1038b11; *PA* I. 644a27.

[14] Some interpreters have held that the theory of family resemblance in *GA* IV.3, with its emphasis on individual forms, is an incidental addition to, and in fact not compatible with, the theory of the earlier books of *GA*. To show the contrary, one needs evidence from the earlier books (a) that the semen conveys movements which will impose the father's individual characteristics, not just a species-form, and (b) that the *katamēnia* is capable of conveying movements which will impose the mother's characteristics, if the semen's movements are weak. I suggest the following:

(a) *GA* I. 726b10: 'The seed is a residue of the nutriment which has become blood and is being distributed to the parts in its final stage. And because of this...the resemblance of offspring to parents is reasonable...'

GA II. 737a18: 'Since the seed is residue, and is being moved in the same movement as that with which the body grows when the final nutriment is being particularized, when it comes into the uterus it constitutes and moves the female's residue in the same movement in which it is actually moving.'

Here Aristotle uses the general theory to explain the resemblance of offspring. The semen's movements are the same as those in the sire's blood. The blood at that moment is becoming the sire's parts. Since there is no further intermediate stage of development, I infer that the movements in the blood conform at this point with the sire's bodily characteristics. If the sire's eyes are blue, for instance, then the offspring is getting blue-eye-making blood there, not just eye-making.

(b) *GA* I. 725b3: 'The residues in the female are "spermatic"' (cf. III. 750b4: 'spermatic matter').

728a26: 'The menses are seed that is not pure but needs working on; ...when it is mixed with semen...it generates.'

728b22: 'Evidence that the seed is in the menses...' (Aristotle proceeds to compare male and female).

II. 737a28: 'The menses are seed but not pure seed; for it lacks one thing only, the source of the soul. That is why in all animals that produce wind-eggs the egg that is being constituted has the parts of both...'

741a24: '[Wind-eggs] possess some soul potentially...and this is the nutritive soul...It does not bring the parts and the animal to completion, because they need to possess sensitive soul...Hence the need of the male's association.'

Generation is brought about by nutritive soul: *PA* I. 641b5, *GA* II. 740b35, *de An.* II. 415a26.

Essence may require a general morphology, but does not predict it

To account for animal features, Aristotle tells us to distinguish those that are for the sake of something from those that arise necessarily from the matter.[15] Eyes are for something; but their color is owed only to their matter and the movements of matter. Therefore the eyes are to be included in the animal's 'definition of being',[16] while their particular color is not. He makes the same distinction between features included in and excluded from the form (*eidos*): neither color nor sex is included in form by itself, but both are due to the matter in the composite form-in-matter.[17]

The form by itself is the essence, which in an animal would be soul by itself[18] (*per impossibile*). Essence therefore excludes some of the features that constitute inherited likeness, for example sex difference according to *GA* iv.3. Yet these are formal differences (as in fact all differences must be), for the sire contributes no matter but only form to the offspring. This apparent paradox is resolved by Aristotle in *Metaph.* ZH (discussed below), by distinguishing in the case of animals between their essence and their actualized form.

Further, it is not necessarily possible to infer the formal details from the essence. For not only does essence exclude some details, but Aristotle mentions the possibility that an essence might be realized in different matter: man, whose essence is rational soul, could conceivably be realized in matter other than flesh and bones.[19] He says that though the definition of a building process includes the definition of the house that is to be built, the definition of the house does not include that of the building process.[20] The building process is not merely the chronological order of building, but includes those details that are due only to matter and movement, which are not part of the definition of the house. In his comparison, the house stands for the animal's essence. Indeed, far from predicting all formal details, the essence need not be a morphological concept at all. At the most abstract level the essence of a man is just rational soul, of a house it is just shelter. If account is taken of matter, we may define the essence of house as 'shelter obtained through bricks or stones placed thus'.[21] But the definition of essence can never be the complete

---

GA iv.3 thus explicates what Aristotle has already implied, if not already asserted. Although he says that the male contributes the form and the female matter, this generality is only true when carefully qualified – as is often the case in Aristotle. (Cf. 'Nature always acts for the sake of something' (e.g. *PA* i. 641b12) with the more careful *PA* iv. 677a17.)

[15] *GA* v. 778a29–b19; *PA* i. 640a33–b4.   [16] *logos ousias*, *GA* v. 778a32–35.

[17] *Metaph.* I. 1058b2.   [18] *Metaph.* Z. 1035b14.

[19] *Metaph.* Z. 1036b2–7.   [20] *PA* ii. 646b3.   [21] *Metaph.* H. 1043a31.

formal description, for it must always exclude such material accidents as sex and color which *are* included in the form contributed by the sire.

The definition of an animal must include all its matter

Whatever is to be made of the discussion of definition in *Metaph.* Z it is at any rate clearly hostile to essentialism. For while essence is the proper object of definition wherever essence can be considered apart from matter, Aristotle argues that this is impossible for animals and all natural substances. They are composite like 'the snub'.[22] Whereas the circle can (indeed must) be considered without reference to the bronze that enmatters it, a man cannot be considered without flesh and bones. Aristotle is not saying that a man can only exist in matter, which would be trivial and would be equally true of the circle, but that unlike the circle the man's essence is not the same thing as the man. If his comparison with the snub is to hold, he must mean that it is logically impossible to prescind from matter when defining a man. But this causes the problem, for matter is posterior to form, and is itself unknowable because undetermined.[23]

In this discussion Aristotle treats the species Man as a universal generalized over individual men-in-flesh, and says that this universal is not the substance whose definition is sought.[24] The only two contenders for valid definition are Socrates' essence (soul) and Socrates in the flesh.[25] The discussion ends aporematically, apparently leaving the dilemma that an animal is not essence alone, and yet the composite which *is* the animal cannot be grasped because it contains matter. But a solution appears in the next book; at the moment of actualization matter is identical with the form realized in it, so that the composite is a definable unity (*Metaph.* H.6). It follows that a definition of Socrates includes a complete account of all his matter at a given moment. Aristotle makes no distinction here between substantial and accidental properties; the examples that he uses are soul and body, triangle and bronze, white and surface – the same composites that he used to illustrate the problem of *Metaph.* Z.

[22] *to simon*: *Metaph.* E. 1025b34; Z. 1036b29.
[23] *Metaph.* Z. 1035a8, 1036a8, 1036b22–32, 1037a27.
[24] *Metaph.* Z. 1033b25, 1035b28, 1037a6; Z. 13.
[25] *Metaph.* Z. 1039b20–31; cf. 1035a33, b14–31, 1036a1–9, 1037a24–33.

The equivocity of eidos; form as quantification

Critics have objected that Aristotle uses 'form' (*eidos*) equivocally for both universal and particular; first Zeller and recently Joseph Owens have considered it a fatal paradox.[26] But in fact the equivocity is both more extensive and more innocent. Besides referring to both individual and species, *eidos* can refer to more general composite universals[27] and also to the matterless essence at varying levels of abstraction.[28] *Eidos* indicates merely that a subject-matter is to be considered in the formal mode. A formal description can obviously vary from being quite general to quite precise, and the most precise possible must be that of the composite particular in the terms of *Metaph.* H.6.

Aristotle's chief contribution to logical division (*diairesis*) was his insistence on the progressive differentiation of a given generic differentia.[29] The movement from general towards particular should not proceed by adding new differentiae but by determining more and more precisely the forms with which the division began. So we cannot allow that man is animal *plus* two-footed.[30] Aristotle hints at a benign paradox: footed and two-footed are not the same property, yet if an animal possesses both he does not possess two properties thereby, but 'footed' becomes redundant.[31] In fact, footed is the same differentia regarded at a higher level of generality and less precisely quantified. Between genera at the highest level the differentiation is qualitative and analogous (feathers:scales), but between species it is quantitative 'according to the more and less' (long feathers:short feathers).[32] The determination of form is therefore a progressive quantification of matter.

Essence and species are explanatory in different ways

Since Porphyry, the traditional interpretation has tended to treat essence and species as synonyms referring to the first order of generality above particulars, and to regard this generality as an absolute form characterizing all the species-members alike. Ross even used the one word 'essence' to translate six different technical expressions in the *Metaphysics*, as though they were merely different ways of regarding the same absolute thing. It is true that such

[26] See also Edwin Hartman's well-balanced discussion in Hartman 1977.
[27] E.g. *GA* i. 719a7; *Ph.* v. 227b12.
[28] *Metaph.* Z. 1037a1, 1035b16, 32; H. 1044a36.
[29] *PA* i.2–3. [30] *Metaph.* H. 1045a15.
[31] *Metaph.* Z. 1038a21. [32] *PA* i. 644a19; *HA* i. 486a22.

expressions (normally distinguished as essence, form, universal, substance, the what, the what-is-it, etc.) stand for different ways of regarding, and that their object or factual reference can be the same. But it is not necessarily the same, for none of them is confined to an absolute level of generality. In the case of species, for which *eidos* often stands in the *Topics* and *Categories*, it is noticeable that Aristotle's use of the concept becomes altogether less in the metaphysics and biology. In these more mature works, when he refers to what we call a species, he more usually calls it the universal, while his use of *atomon eidos* ('indivisible form') is sometimes ambiguous between infima species and individual.[33] When he argues in biology from the 'kind' of animal, he may be referring to any level from infima species to super-genus.[34] It is often remarked that he has only the one word *eidos* for both form and species. But he does not need a technical word for species, since he does not hypostatize it into an entity or absolute; its status is merely that of a universal. True, his attitude to it is not nominalistic: the lowest universal especially, the infima species, has an objective validity which is important.[35] The question how it derives this validity is discussed below. But from the fact that it is objectively valid, it does not follow that it need also be formally precise or even unchanging.

Since Aristotle may refer to either essence or species when he speaks of *eidos* (or indeed to many other formal categories), only the context can tell us which he intends. Unfortunately the disjointed style of the *Metaphysics* often leaves this in doubt – for example the notorious remark that Socrates and Callias are the same thing in *eidos* but other because of the matter[36] (where *eidos* must refer to essence, and matter to the proximate matter in the composite). But the biological treatises lay out their arguments more explicitly, and these make clear the difference between essence and species. Essence picks out only those features for which a teleological explanation holds. Not only is it used at all levels of generality, but also of different categories, not necessarily of substances: for instance, essence of white and musical, of blood or flesh.[37] In the sense of *Metaph.* Z.17, essence is that which has made the matter PQR into an X. Eyes help to make a man, but their color is not part of the essence. Species on the other hand, since it is generalized over particulars, must include non-essential features

---

[33] E.g. *PA* I. 644a24. See my revised note on this passage quoted in Longrigg 1977.

[34] Essence of blooded animals *PA* IV. 678a34; of the insect genus 682b28; of fishes 695b18; of the lobster 684a34; of one kind of octopus 685b15.

[35] *APo.* II.19 100a15; *Metaph.* A.1.   [36] *Metaph.* Z. 1034a7–8.

[37] *Metaph.* Z. 1030a29; of white or musical 1031a27; of blood *PA* II. 649b22; of flesh *de An.* III. 429b17.

albeit in a generalized form: man has eyes that are colored (without restriction to a particular color). Species therefore picks out a class of composites as they are when materialized. What establishes this class, so that division of the genus must stop here?

Aristotle answers that we stop dividing when we cannot further distinguish the essence.[38] At each stage of division we should select the common feature which is necessarily entailed by the remaining features and which they follow as consequentials.[39] Two-footed and four-footed entail footed, while it is a consequential of footed that there be a particular number of feet. Rigidity entails bone or an analogous structure. These differences serve essential functions. But when we reach a point where the next differences (e.g. color) do not serve a different function, then they are to be attributed only to matter and movement without implying a different essence. In the *HA* Aristotle records many sub-specific variations due only to climate or nutrition, not constituting new species.[40] In Aristotle's usage a species is the universal generalized over all animals that have the same essence, as they appear in nature. The explanatory power of essence is that it reveals the teleological features. The account of the species gives this plus an explanation of the material appearances and accidents. This yields the double explanation which characterizes the *PA*. Taking over Plato's distinction between the good and the necessary causes in the *Timaeus*, Aristotle subsumes essence and teleology under the good, matter and movement under the necessary. At first sight this seems to confuse his analysis of four causes, since there must be movement under both headings. But he does not argue for two kinds of moving cause, one 'persuading' the other as Plato had it, but for a coordinated control of movements towards 'the best of what is possible'. This is the principle that will validate species.

Why do species exist and persist?

This brings his analysis to the crucial question. For in order that the universals which we perceive shall be objective, there needs to be a natural reason why an infima species exists at all. If all species-members were family relations, Aristotle's theory of reproduction would account for species. But this is not his belief. Nor has he the modern reason for believing in species, namely their reproductive isolation; for he believes that different species can produce fertile crosses (within practical limits of size and gestation-period).[41] If he

[38] *Metaph.* Δ. 1016a32; I. 1052a32.   [39] *APo.* II.14.
[40] *HA* v. 556a14; VIII. 605b22ff.; IX. 617b28, 632b14.   [41] *GA* II. 738b28, 746a30.

does not give the essentialist's answer, that species is an absolute form imposed upon individuals, then he needs some other hypothesis to validate the explanatory power of species and to show why the universal likeness must persist between unrelated families.

I want to argue that Aristotle's answer to this question is his constantly reiterated statement that natural growth is towards the best in given circumstances. The way that he expresses this, especially the way he personifies 'nature' and speaks anthropomorphically about nature choosing and guiding, has lent itself to various extravagant interpretations which there is no space to deal with here.[42] But it is necessary to point out the general improbability – indeed the philosophical enormity – of the essentialist interpretation of this principle. For if Aristotle meant that individual growth is directed *primarily* towards the specific form, and that individuals may do things primarily not for their own sake but for the sake of the species, then there is an intractable ontological problem: what directs them, and by what means? It is here that tradition lapsed into philosophy-fiction, inventing for Aristotle such *dei ex machina* as a hypostatized Nature supervising an overall teleology, or a cosmic control operated by the Unmoved Mover, or a living universe, or mysterious entelechies and magical pneuma within animals. But there is no room for such machinery in Aristotle's cosmology or theology. Therefore any statements (and there are only a few) that seem at face value to lead to such inferences, must mean something else. For example, the famous shark, whose mouth is underneath: Aristotle's comment is that nature seems to have done this not only to save the lives of other fishes, but to save the shark from over-eating – and besides its narrow snout has insufficient room for the mouth.[43] Rather than accept the horrendous consequences of overall finality, it is preferable to take this as a polite correction of popular teleology of the kind familiar in Xenophon. Similarly when Aristotle says that fishes in a hostile environment are prolific, 'for nature retrieves the wastage by quantity', he need only mean that if they were not prolific they would be extinct.[44] Aristotle gives no hint of drawing the conclusions that were drawn for him by Francis Bacon and others; on the contrary, in the overwhelming majority of cases his argument is based on what is good for this animal in these circumstances.[45] How then does he

---

[42] See ch. 10 above, 277ff.   [43] *PA* iv. 696b26.   [44] *GA* iii. 755a31.

[45] Aristotle's statements, which have been used to support the idea of *overall teleology* are collected and discussed in my note at *PA* i. 641b10 (Balme 1972: 93–8). The idea of *negative teleology* (surely contradictory?) was supported by Peck at *PA* ii. 648a16 (note in his Loeb edition). But there Aristotle's expression 'the better or worse' does not mean 'advantage or disadvantage' as Peck translates it, but a scale of relative advantages, just as 'the more

envisage this principle operating, and how do species come into the account?

The fundamental difference between animals, he suggests, is the difference in their natural heat. Because of this, they differ in perfectedness.[46] Then, given that each animal has a basic capability determined by its heat, the next determinant is environment and lifestyle, which together explain functions and organs.[47] But there are two limitations: one arises from actual conditions of matter and movement, the other from the inevitable self-limitation of a complex organism. For instance, since nutrition is limited, few animals can grow both horns and solid hoofs: therefore, instead of horns, horses rely on speed for defense.[48] Again, the windpipe's unsatisfactory position (vulnerable to choking, which necessitates the epiglottis) is due to the need for heart and lungs to be in front of the stomach.[49] Throughout these explanations, of which there are hundreds, Aristotle repeats that nature always does the best out of what is possible.[50] Whereas in the *GA* his problem is the growth of the individual animal towards the inherited form, in the *PA* his problem is the differences between the existing forms of animal. In an evolutionary context (which is of course inconsistent with his thought) he would be asking why animals evolved into their present forms. The equivalent

and less' means a scale of size or degree (cf. *PA* I. 644a15). See the discussion by Anthony Preus in 1975: 151. At *PA* II. 659a19 the backward-grazing cattle show the limitation imposed by horns, which are otherwise advantageous. At *PA* III. 663a8–18 *achrēstos* does not mean 'useless' in the sense of vain or pointless, but in the sense of not-useful or unsuccessful; cf. *PA* 659a29, 660b4, 685a29. The horns of deer, antelope, and bison are useful to some extent but not for every defense; hence they have other defenses too, 663a9. At *PA* IV. 694a20 the crooked talons, useful for predators, bring a limitation in that they impede walking. For other examples cf. *PA* IV. 685b15, III. 664a30; *GA* I. 717b14, 720b18.

[46] *GA* II. 732b26–32, 733a32–b11. Examples of 'unperfectedness', *ateleia*: insects *GA* III. 758b20; testaceans *IA* 714b10; crabs *IA* 714b16; fishes *PA* IV. 695b2.

[47] E.g. various birds' beaks *PA* III. 662b1–16; fishes' teeth 662a6; camel's stomachs 674a28; position of testacean head IV. 683b18; birds' necks and legs 693a3–19; webbed feet 694a6; longer legs in marsh birds 694b12; thick legs in birds of prey *GA* III. 750a4; neck of wolf and lion *PA* IV. 686a21; varied positions of insect sting 683a8; testacean shell 683b10; tail in crayfish but not in crabs 684a1.

Slight differences in lifestyle are reflected in slight changes of homologues: e.g. variations in the mouth *PA* III. 662a23ff. Or similar tissues may be diverted to form different organs for the animal's advantage: crabs, being more active than lobsters, spend more on feet than on claws *PA* IV. 684a15, 685a25. 'Nature always assigns each organ solely or chiefly to those that can use it, e.g. tusks, teeth, horns, spurs, and all such parts as are for help and defense' *PA* IV. 684a28.

[48] Cf. the discussion of the relation between horns, hoofs, teeth, stomachs, *PA* III. 662b23–664a12, 674a22–b13.

[49] *PA* III. 665a7–22. Cf. the discussions of eyelids *PA* II. 657b5–16, 30–5; tails 658a31; elephant's slowness 659a28; birds' lack of nostrils 659b13; quadrupeds' voice 660a31; fishes' teeth III. 675a7; wings and stings IV. 683a15; opposite relations of feet and bodies in squids and octopus 685a25; relative positions of head, heart, stomach 686a10–18; hooves 690a5ff.   [50] E.g. *PA* IV. 687a16; *Juv.* 469a28.

question for him is, why do animals differ? As he says in the introduction to *HA*, this is one purpose of zoological inquiry.[51]

His answer is the double explanation, 'necessity' and 'the better'. Given the necessary limitations of heat and environment, each animal form is the best possible: that is, the form which brings it the most functional advantage, what Aristotle often calls 'the useful'.[52] And no further premise is needed to show that this principle will produce species. For in given circumstances, animals that have the most useful form will all have the same functions and lifestyle, served by the same organs grown in the same field conditions, and will therefore be the same in all essential details in Aristotle's sense of essential: therefore they will fall under one kind, one universal. This is the reasoning by which modern biologists account for sibling species, when species originating from different orders come to resemble each other through occupying the same ecological niche.[53] The modern biologist explains such development through the mechanism of natural selection. What mechanism might Aristotle have in mind to explain why animals have the 'best possible' forms? He does not offer a physical explanation, no doubt because he was unable to. In this he would be no worse off than the Darwinians, who were invoking the principle of natural selection long before they could suggest how it might work in the biochemistry of genetics. The Aristotelian interpreter must therefore guess at this point. Some have guessed that he held vitalist or Lamarck-type views. But this would require 'nature' to be a metaphysical entity, which as I have argued would have implications too far-reaching to be plausible. It would be easier to suppose that he was presuming a vague 'survival of the fittest'; for this theory was already familiar in a primitive form in Empedocles,[54] and was shortly going to be elaborated in Epicurean atomism,[55] so that it was probably under discussion at Aristotle's time. For our purposes, however, it is enough to know that a naturalistic basis was available to Aristotle's teleology, and that there is no call for vaster speculations.

Aristotle's own concern was clearly not with this, but with establishing the hypothesis that 'the better' is a 'cause'. This is the theme of *PA*; he produces copious evidence for it, but characteristically does not speculate farther than his evidence takes him. His

[51] *HA* i. 491a9–11.
[52] E.g. *PA* ii. 654a19; iii. 662a33, b3, 7; iv. 677a16, 678a4–16, 683b37, 684a3, 685a28, 687b29, 691b1; *Resp.* 476a12.
[53] Cf. Mayr 1963: 34ff.
[54] *PA* i. 640a19, b4ff.; *Ph.* ii. 198b29.
[55] Lucretius *De Rerum Natura* i.1021–37, ii.707, 1050; iv.835; v.420–31, 855.

teleology therefore rests on the principles of *inherited form*[56] and *functional advantage*. His essentialism (if it can even be called that) goes only so far as accepting that animal universals are given in nature, and that they are the product of his two teleological principles. They in turn require the important distinction between teleological and 'necessary' features. But that distinction does not itself require there to be absolute specific forms, nor has it any wider ontological implication.

Appendix 1: Note on the *aporia* in *Metaphysics* Z

The editors have asked me to elaborate my suggestion (above 291) that *GA* confirms one possible interpretation of *Metaph* ZH. It concerns the problem of bringing matter into the definition of natural bodies.

Aristotle argues in Z that definition is confined to the matterless 'essence' (*ti ēn einai*), excluding mention of its material embodiment because matter is indeterminate and unknowable. This means excluding from apodeictic knowledge all the concrete objects which he declares to be real existents (*onta*), namely animals, plants and all natural bodies. The essence of a man is soul, so that only soul would be definable and scientifically knowable, not man's bodily parts. Obviously this is not Aristotle's real opinion, unless we are to believe that he is suddenly and uniquely expressing skepticism here, so that the question is what this *aporia* is intended to show. At the ends of both Z and H he gives ostensible solutions: the being (*ousia*) of these objects is to be expressed in a causal account of their 'nature' (Z.17); matter and form are one and the same thing when actualized (H.6). There is no evidence as to how in his actual lectures he filled out these solutions (assuming that that is what they are meant to be), and their import is much disputed.

The program of Z is to inquire what sense-perceived *onta* really are. A man's paleness is not part of what he really is. What formula then will pick out the being of *onta*? Aristotle proposes four possibilities: the essence, which in the case of man is soul; or the universal, Man, meaning that which is common to men; or the kind or genus, Animal; or the substrate, the underlying and persisting object which receives and loses accidental attributes. The *onta* under discussion are 'the bodies', primarily exemplified by animals, plants, their parts, and the elementary bodies air earth fire and water (1028b9); later he allows a doubt whether the parts and elements should be included, since they cannot exist independently (1040b6); but there is no doubt that 'man', represented by Socrates and Callias, is a prime object of inquiry. All that is doubtful here is whether Aristotle has in mind the human form common to men, or that of the individual Socrates, or whether – as I shall suggest – this distinction is not raised and *both* are the subject of this discussion. His aim is to show what sort of account (*logos*) of these *onta* would constitute apodeictic knowledge and not merely opinion (*doxa*, 1039b33). And he hopes that the inquiry will lead on from sense-perceived *onta* to the incorporeal, evidently referring to the Unmoved Mover.

At first sight the most attractive of the four candidates is the substrate, for it agrees with the *Categories* doctrine in distinguishing 'the what' from its attributes. But Aristotle disposes of it first (Ch. 3) by showing that the concept of substrate, when pressed in this way, becomes incoherent; for after every attribute that can be

---

[56] Strictly not yet actualized form, but what Allan Gotthelf has well explained as an 'irreducible potentiality' for form (above, ch. 8).

stripped away has been stripped, nothing remains but the object's matter, not the definiendum itself. During this argument, and again in chs. 7–9, he emphasizes his normal analysis of natural objects into form and matter and 'the combined whole', an analysis which is basic to ZH. These are the aspects under which an object may be truly described; they are not three more candidates to explicate the 'being' of the object. Ch. 3 shows that substrate as a candidate for *ousia* must not be confused with matter; and I shall suggest below that essence is not meant to be identified with form.

His discussion of the substrate brings out the significance of independent subsistence as a necessary mark of *ousia*. He proceeds to show that each of the other candidates, although none is actually equivalent to the being of these *onta*, contributes importantly to it. It is in examining the claim of essence that he sets up the problem which becomes a recurrent theme of Z, namely the apparent indefinability of sense-perceived *onta*. If chs. 5 and 6 are read together, the *aporia* is presented starkly. For ch. 5 argues that 'the snub' (a regular paradigm of the natural bodies) is indefinable, and ch. 6 then argues that *onta* are identical with their essences and that essence is the only object of definition. It must follow that an apodeictic account and knowledge of natural bodies is impossible (unless there is some other method, he says).

Ch. 5 argues that 'snub' cannot be defined without tautology, and that 'snub nose' involves either tautology or infinite regress. These arguments are in fact answered in *SE* 13 and 31 on the grounds that snubness is a species of concavity, not a species of nose, and that the snub can therefore be treated as a *pathos* or attribute of nose and not as itself a nose. Although Z.5 accepts that snub is a *pathos*, it does not use this escape route; the reason is seen in ch. 10 to be not logical but ontological: to be snub is not to be in a certain state, but to be flesh in a certain state, and so matter (flesh) is a part of snubness in a way that it is not part of concavity (1035a4). Aristotle often quotes the snub in other works, always to exemplify this point, that natural *onta* are 'thises-in-this' and cannot be isolated from their matter even in thought (*Ph.* 186b22, 194a6; *de An.* 429b14, 431b13; *Metaph.* E. 1025b34; *Cael.* 278a29).[57] The point is stressed in chs. 7–9, which were evidently written separately as an account of coming-to-be, but are relevant here to show that a natural being requires all four causes to explain it and can only be analyzed if regarded as a process in which matter is brought into a form. Chs. 10 and 11 (with the first section of 15) then bring out all the obstacles to defining natural bodies, showing that all are due to the presence of matter; for such bodies, like the snub, are what they are only when materialized – the essence of a man (soul) is not the man. The obstacles are:

(i) Matter cannot be brought into a definition because it is undetermined, capable of being other, and so unknowable (1036a5, 1037a27, 1039b28).

(ii) Some parts of a combined whole are posterior to the essence, therefore the definition would exclude some parts of the whole (1035b5ff.).

(iii) Definition of a natural being should include its movement (changing), but this would involve its matter (1036b29).

(iv) The definition can only be a unity if its subject is a unity, but a combined whole contains material parts (1037a19).

This last difficulty is left unanswered by ch. 12, which only shows that definition by genus and differentia preserves the unity of definition but does not show how the object itself is a unity, nor how to bring material parts into the form which is thus defined. Chs. 13–16, which are chiefly occupied with refuting the claims of universals and of Platonic Forms to be *ousia*, contribute an important point to the

[57] For further details see Appendix 2.

eventual solution, by showing that material parts and elements are only potentially part of a being unless they are united in the living animal (1040b5).

Z.17 announces a fresh start, and argues that the right way to state X's being is to 'dismember' X and show what caused its constituent material parts to become a combined whole possessing the essence of X. It asks for a causal explanation of X's 'nature', that is one that explains both the material and moving causes and the formal and final causes, in the normal manner of Z.7, *Ph.* II and the biological works. Finally H.6 argues that the object is a unity because its matter and form become one and the same thing when actualized.

These two chapters together answer all the difficulties raised in Z about defining natural bodies, but they raise the further possible question what kind of definition Aristotle intended. As to the difficulties, they have shown (i) that it is not illogical to include matter in a definition, so that the problem of the snub can be granted the solutions proposed in *SE* 13 and 31; (ii) the formal account of an actualized being would not distinguish form from matter, and would consequently assign no priority nor posteriority to parts (this explains the point at Z. 12 1038a33 that in nature there is no order in that sense); (iii) movement is brought into the account, for the object is presented as in process of change, and indeed can only be explained as part of a process; (iv) although the matter continues to be capable of being other, and will in nature immediately become other, at every given moment it is actualized in a definable form. This solution permits every material characteristic to be formalized as a differentia, so that our question is whether the human form should now be differentiated into forms of Socrates and of Callias. In favor of this is the clear statement of H.6 that the proximate matter is one with its form, making definition possible. The essence of Socrates is soul, and the soul of Socrates is separate and different from the soul of Callias. But against it is Aristotle's silence; to put words into his mouth is usually disastrous. It would conflict with many statements in other works, such as *Metaph.* I.9 1058a29 which argues that sex and color are not part of the formal difference but are due to matter, and *PA* 1.2–4 where the genus–differentia *diairesis* ends at Man. Z.8 itself contains the characteristic statement that Socrates and Callias are the same in form, for their form is indivisible (1034a8). If Aristotle had now intended to extend the *diairesis* by further differentiating man and horse, surely he would have said so. True, he does hint at 'another kind of definition' (1030a12, b13, 27, 1031a8), but no other is produced. (Ross's suggestion that 1037b27 points to definition by material constituents, as mentioned at B.998b13 and H.1043a20, cannot be sustained, for both those passages are hostile to such materialist methods.) Aristotle never suggests any method of defining animals other than by genus and differentia. It is likelier that these remarks are merely intended to reinforce the impasse: there would have to be another kind of definition...but there is none. The solutions in Z.17 and H.6 must therefore be taken as applying to Aristotle's own approved method of *diairesis*, given at *PA* 1.643b10–26: instead of trying to reach the definiendum through dividing the genus by its differentiae one at a time, all the differentiae should be applied simultaneously in the first instance. By this method the final cluster of differentiae will define the animal. Z.12 is not necessarily opposed to, nor attacked by, the critique in *PA* I, for the analysis in Z.12 can be read as a skeleton illustration aimed at the same conclusion, that the final differentia imports its predecessors together with the genus and so presents a unified definition. But the result of ZH is that differentiae formalizing every material constituent and accident can now be added without illogicality. If the differentiae are all applied together to the genus, as Aristotle says they should be (643b24), they can only be applied disjunctively, for as he often points out the genus divides into opposed differentiae: fish is not simultaneously scaly and not-scaly, but either/or. The material accidents could be added in the same way: man is blue-eyed or brown-eyed or... The definition would be of human, common to both Socrates and Callias, and at the same time it would define each individually if certain disjunctives were selected in each case. If the differentiae that are peculiarly applicable to Socrates were proved by a causal explanation, then the result would be a rigorous *apodeixis* of Socrates' own form, as perceived at a certain moment in the changing actualization of his matter. The definition itself would be both general and particular, and it would still be true to say that Socrates and Callias are the same in form. They differ because that form has been actualized in separate and different proximate matters, so that each has an individual form. Aristotle does not say that they are other *in* matter but *because of* matter (1034a7). Otherness must be formal, even when it is caused by matter and movement. The differences between proximate matters are formal, as he shows at 1036a32: the matters of circles – bronze, stone, wood – differ *in form*, *eidei*.

Although Aristotle can now logically validate a formal definition of an animal that would include every material detail, he does not extend the *diairesis* beyond the 'indivisible form' of man or horse. He treats the further differentiating details not as an extension of form to include matter, but as a bringing of matter into the account of form. And that is how he refers to it elsewhere – the bringing of matter and movement into the account of natural bodies (e.g. E. 1026a3). His reason is probably the teleological aspect. According to 1016a32 *diairesis* stops when the essence is no longer divisible. By itself this reason would hardly hold in view of H.6; moreover he can speak of 'the essence of Socrates' and 'your essence' (1029b14, 1032a8). But *GA* v.1 explains the point fully: the definition of being collects those functions and features which are common to that kind and are teleologically necessary to the animal, while the remainder are due only to matter and movement (778b10). Common sense would indeed suggest this, for not only is the difference between Socrates and a horse even more marked than that between Socrates and Callias, but Socrates' material details are in constant change while his more persistent characteristics are the human ones that he shares with Callias. Individuation is not an issue for Aristotle. If it were pressed, his analysis would show that Socrates and Callias differ in exact form, and so do their essences. But he uses both form and essence at varying levels of generality, according to convenience. The most convenient and usual level is that indicated by function, the level of human and equine. But form and essence do not necessarily pick out the same features: form is structural, essence is functional, and they do not always coincide. When Aristotle twice goes out of his way to say 'by form I mean the essence' (1032b1, 1035b32), the implication is that he does *not* always mean that, but here wishes to focus the reference upon essence; this is his normal and frequent use of 'I mean' (*legō*), namely it does not define a concept nor declare an identity between two, but limits the reference for immediate purposes (cf. 1032a14, b14, 18, 1033a25, 32, b13, 1036a3, 1037b3, and the passive *legomenon* ('in the sense of') at 1033b17).

This general interpretation of ZH agrees with the theory of *GA*. There he argues (see 292 above) that the male parent transmits nothing somatic but only form; it transfers movements from its blood into the female's uterine blood and thereby imposes its own personal characteristics upon the fetus. Similarly, but to a lesser extent, the female blood contains movements which impose her personal characteristics (IV. 768a10). So the male form contributes features that *Metaph.* Z treats as material parts of the combined whole, and the female matter contributes some formal qualities. The explanation of spontaneity in *GA* III.11, as in Z.9, supposes a sequence of formal changes in the proximate matter, taking place once the process has been started. In *GA* v the examination of *pathēmata* like coloration brings material accidents within the scope of formal description and causal explanation. These explanations in *GA* (like the attention given to material differentiae in *HA*) need not reflect a new-found materialism in Aristotle's view but a willingness to see formalization in matter.

In *GA* as in *Metaph.* Z, neither essence nor form corresponds to 'species', whether in its neoplatonist sense of an inner real form or in its modern sense of a class or population that has the same bodily structure and lifestyle. The nearest to the latter is 'Socrates generalized' (1033b25, 1035b28, 1037a6) which Aristotle emphatically denies to be *ousia*. The neoplatonist sense is not to be found in Aristotle. It is doubtful whether the translation 'species' is ever necessary in Aristotle, and if the word is used in English to indicate an inner real within a real (contrary to such denials as 1039a3) it is seriously misleading. The same must be said of 'essence', which one uses as a convenient label for the awkward 'that which has belonged to *X* so that it is *X*', but does not carry for Aristotle any of its English connotation of real essences. Equally the word 'substance', used unjustifiably for *ousia*, suggests a real within a real, and can mislead. Worst of all is the interchange of these words, as though Aristotle did not distinguish them. The extraordinary later misinterpretations of Aristotle, the magical entelechies and real specific forms, must be largely due to these imported concepts – Species, Essentia, Substantia – which presided like three witches over his rebirth in the Middle Ages, but should be banished to haunt the neoplatonism from which they came.

Appendix 2: The snub

Aristotle regularly uses 'the snub' (*to simon*) as the paradigm of a difficulty in defining certain objects, and treats it as critical.[58] At *Metaph.* E. 1025b34 he says that all living nature is like the snub nose, so that if we are to examine and define the what-is-it (*to ti estin*) of man and animals and plants, we must first solve this difficulty. It arises wherever a thing's form cannot be considered separately from considering its matter. Being snub implies being a nose; to define snub it is necessary to mention nose; it seems impossible to isolate and define the nose's snubness in the way that we can isolate and define its straightness or its color. The same is true of being a man: humanness cannot be isolated from flesh and bones with all their concomitant variables and potentialities – what Aristotle calls the indeterminacy of matter (*GA* IV. 778a6). His chief discussion of the problem is in *Metaph.* Z where he appears to leave it unsolved. But it seems clear that the following book is intended to offer a solution in its concluding words, rapid and sketchy though they are (*Metaph.* H.6 1045b17–23); and the solution can be seen put into practice in *GA*.

It should be said first that there is no question of this being merely a semantic trouble caused by a dead adjective, snub. For Aristotle produces other examples too, such as odd number and male animal, where odd and male need the understanding of number and animal in order to be conveyed themselves. Nor is it only a logical problem of predication. For he generates two distinct paradoxes – one logical but the other ontological – from the fact that snub implies nose. First, in *Metaph.* Z.5 he argues that when snub is predicated of nose, snub nose cannot be defined without vicious tautology. From this he draws the damaging conclusion that things like the snub have no definable essence, at least not properly or primarily. Then secondly in *Metaph.* Z.10, 11 and 15 he argues that snubness, considered as a form in matter, cannot be defined without bringing matter into the definition, which is impossible –

---

[58] *Metaph.* and *SE* as quoted below; *Ph.* I. 186b22, II. 194a6, 13; *de An.* III. 429b14, 431b13; *Metaph.* K. 1064a23; *Cael.* I. 278a29 (using 'aquiline' instead of 'snub').

for it contradicts the notion of matter. This again leads to the apparent conclusion that there can be no definition, and therefore no scientific knowledge (*epistēmē*), of snubness nor of the things like it.

In the first paradox the snub stands for subject plus attribute. It is examined also at *SE* 13 and 31, where solutions are proposed. *Metaph.* Z.5, however, treats it as insoluble. Ross thought Z.5 mistaken in ignoring those solutions.[59] But I would like to suggest instead that in Z Aristotle rightly sees that the solutions fail – the nose cannot be got rid of – and that this failure connects the logical paradox with the ontological problem: so at 1037a31 he refers to the tautology while speaking of the indefinability of matter.[60]

In the second paradox the snub nose stands for form in matter, as it usually does elsewhere in the treatises. The model's working parts act in the same way, but now of course it is more than a model: it is also a sample, one of great importance, if it is true that all natural substances are like the snub.

The tautology

In *SE* 13 and 31 Aristotle is considering how to avoid the fallacy of 'babbling' or 'saying the same twice'. His discussion shows that he means a tautology which vitiates a definition. He points to two classes of definiendum that are vulnerable to it: (i) relations, e.g., *double*; (ii) states or affections (*hexeis, pathē*), e.g., *odd* as applied to number.

(i) Having argued previously (*Top.* vi. 142a27) that we cannot know and define *double* without knowing and defining *half*, since relatives cannot be known without knowing their correlatives, he goes on at 173a35 to argue: if *double* signifies the same as *double-of-half*, then for *double-of-half* we may substitute *double-of-half-of-half*, and again for that *double-of-half-of-half-of-half*, and so babble. He extends this class to include e.g. *appetite*, presumably as a word which combines with an objective noun: if we say that our appetite is for something pleasant, but grant that appetite itself is desire for the pleasant, then it follows that *appetite-for-pleasant* is *desire-for-pleasant-for-pleasant*.

(ii) The *odd* is a number that has a middle; and there is an odd number; therefore there is a number-that-has-a-middle number. He calls this class

> 'things which are not necessarily relations but which have states or affections or suchlike, and the being (*ousia*) of the subjects is conveyed additionally in the definition of the states when these states are predicated of the subjects' (*SE* 173b5–7).[61]

Snubness is the state of a nose that is concave. But snubness is not adequately defined as concavity unless we convey that the concavity is that of a nose. This produces tautology. For if snubness is concavity of nose, and if there is a snub nose, then there is a concave-nose nose.

Aristotle ends this first discussion at 173b12 by saying that an apparent but unreal tautology may arise through failure to ascertain 'whether the *double* said by itself signifies something or nothing, and, if it does signify something, whether it signifies the same thing or different'. He fills this out later at *SE* 31: taken strictly by itself, *double* may not signify anything;

---

[59] Ross 1924; II 174.
[60] Ross (*ad Metaph.* Z. 1037a31) queried this text as 'irrelevant', i.e., assuming that the two paradoxes are unconnected; but all MSS and Alexander have it.
[61] There seems no reason to obelize this sentence as Ross does in his OCT; it is a careful formulation, which agrees with a similar statement at *Metaph.* Z. 1030b23.

'but if it does signify, it is still not the same as when it is in combination. Nor is the knowledge which is in the species (e.g. if medicine is a knowledge) identical with the universal. The latter was just knowledge of a knowable. And in the case of things predicated of subjects through which the predicates' meaning is conveyed, we should say that what is conveyed is not the same by itself as in the account (*sc.* the subject-predicate account). *The concave* as a universal conveys the same in the case of the snub and of the bandy; but when it is added (*sc.* to a subject) nothing prevents it from signifying different things, one for the nose and another for the leg. In the former it signifies the snub, in the latter the bandy, and there is no difference between saying *snub nose* and saying *concave nose*.' (181b33–182a2)

'Further, we should not concede the direct expression,[62] for it is untrue. For the snub is not concave nose, but this affection, say *of* nose; so there is no illogicality if the nose that is snub is a nose having concavity of nose.' (182a3–6)

There are two solutions here, the second of which appears to supersede the first. In the first at 181b38–182a2 the expression *concave nose* is allowed on the grounds that it gives a special sense to concave; in the second at 182a3–6 it is disallowed. But both solutions require the premise that *concave* when predicted of *nose* gains a specific determination which is not carried by the generic *concave* by itself. No doubt this corresponds with linguistic usage. For if you draw a concave nose and ask somebody what it is, he will say that it is a snub nose; if you now erase everything except the upper outline and ask what that is, he might say 'a concave curve' but he will not say 'a snub curve'. But this implicit premise destroys both solutions, if indeed we have to smuggle in some understanding that will determine the generic *concave* into its nasal species. The final formula in *SE* 31 succeeds only by repeating 'nose'. But at *Top* v. 130a34 Aristotle argues that it would be babbling to say 'fire is a body that is the lightest of bodies'. There he does not only object to the verbal repetition but says that the tautology would not be cured by substituting 'beings' for 'bodies', for they are one and the same thing; a valid formula would be in the pattern of 'Man is an animal receptive of knowledge'. He does not explain further, but what he has evidently done (just as in *SE*) is to place the definiendum under its genus and apply a proper differentia. Could we then cure the final *SE* formula by saying that, if snubness is concavity of nose, a snub nose is a nose having an appropriate concavity? No, for this would still offend against the *Topics*, since 'appropriate' or any such periphrasis is merely a verbal substitution for one and the same thing – 'belonging to noses'. The difficulty, therefore, has not been solved in *SE*.

In *Metaph.* Z.5 Aristotle deals first with *snub* and then with *snub nose*. First (1030b14–27) he argues that we cannot define *snub* without illicit *prosthesis* (smuggling *nose* into the definiendum). For snubness is an affection of nose per se, unlike for example color, which belongs per accidens and can be considered and defined without reference to its subject. The pale color of Callias can be spoken of and conveyed without necessarily conveying *pale man*; but *male* cannot be conveyed without conveying *animal*, nor *equal* without *quantity* – nor *snub* without *nose*. Although Aristotle allows here that snubness is an affection (*pathos*) as in the second solution in *SE*, he does not now use this to escape the difficulty. For snubness is what it is only in virtue of what a nose is. Affections that must include the presence of their subjects cannot be conveyed independently. Therefore if they have an essence and a definition at all, they must have them in some other way (*Metaph.* 1030b27).

In the second argument (*Metaph.* 1030b28–1031a1) he moves from *snubness* to *snub nose*. He argues by dilemma: 1030b28–32: the snub is not the same as the concave,

---

[62] 'Direct', *kat' euthu*, 182a3, may mean either (i) simple, unqualified, or (ii) grammatically uninflected, i.e. in the same case (but not necessarily the nominative case as LSJ suggest).

because *snub* cannot be said without (i.e. as if lacking) the thing of which it is an affection per se: for the snub is concavity-in-nose; 32–3 (the dilemma): therefore *snub nose* either cannot be said or will be the same thing said twice; 33–5 (taking the second horn first): for, accepting that the snub is concavity-in-nose, it follows that *nose-that-is-snub* is *nose-that-is-nose-that-is-concave*; hence it is absurd that the essence should belong to such things; 35–1031a1 (first horn): but if not (i.e. if we abandon the equation *snub = concavity-in-nose*, and return to the starting-point that snub cannot be said without nose), then it will go to infinity: for (*sc.* if there is a nose in the snub, there will be a second nose in the snub nose, and) there will be yet another nose in the nose that is a snub nose...

The dilemma lies between having two noses instead of one (which is absurd, 1030b34) and having an infinite series of nose within nose (which is unsayable, b32). To set up the dilemma, Aristotle posits that concavity-in-nose is equivalent to concave nose. Ross objects that he has thereby confused the quality of snubness with the thing that is snub; both indeed can be expressed simply as *to simon* in Greek. But while there is this well-known verbal ambiguity which the reader must guard against, the distinction in thought is so elementary that the inventor of the Categories is unlikely to have confused it; moreover it would not alter the case here. For Aristotle's point here is that there is no thinking of snubness without thinking of the flesh that is snub. To be snub is not to be in a certain state, but to be flesh in a certain state. In *Metaph.* Z.10 he says that the matter (flesh) is a part of snubness, in a way that the matter is not part of concavity (*Metaph.* 1035a4). In Z.11 he considers whether we could mentally isolate man from flesh if man were also embodied in other materials; for a circle can be in bronze or in stone, and this helps us to separate its form from its matter in thought (1036a31). But it would not help the case of man, for that is different, he says: man is a this-in-this or these things in this state (1036b23). It is this doctrine that invalidates the *SE* solutions. For if snubness must be regarded not simply as a shape imposed upon nose-flesh but as a shaped nose in nose-flesh, the definition of snub nose is incurably tautologous. The same difficulty must arise wherever there is a qualification that cannot be thought without also thinking its subject, that is wherever the embodiment is actually part of the quality. So the problem is not created by the logical method of subject-attribute predication but by the ontological analysis of things into form and matter. To solve it Aristotle re-examines this analysis, and produces a solution in *Metaph.* H.6 which is of radical importance, for it shows that the formal description of Socrates can – indeed must – logically include all material details and accidents.

Bringing matter and movement into the account

The ontological problem represented by the snub is: what is the definable unity of an object which is not formally abstractable like the circle (whose essence can be defined without reference to its embodiment), but is a 'combined whole' of form together with matter, e.g. a man? The man's form taken by itself (if that were possible) would be soul alone, to be considered by prescinding from the body of which soul is the functioning. But Socrates is not a bodiless soul. Yet body must presumably be excluded from the definition of man, on two grounds, which belong together. One is that body is matter. Matter is – *qua* matter – undetermined, unknowable (*Metaph.* 1036a8, 1037a27); it is not to be called something (1035a8); it is capable of being other, and therefore no *apodeixis* of it is possible (1039b29). The other ground is that body is not logically prior to soul, whereas the parts of a definition are only such as are prior to the definition (1034b21, 1035b4).[63]

---

[63] Aristotle explains at 1034b21 that by 'parts of the definition' he means what corresponds to the parts of the definiendum (not genus and differentiae as Ross interprets it).

Metaph. Z appears to leave the problem unsolved. On the one hand, the combined whole *(suneilēmmenon)* has no definable essence: in snub nose we can only define concavity; in man we can only define soul. On the other hand, Aristotle says (1036b23), we must not make the mistake of Socrates the Younger in supposing that a man can be defined as if lacking movement and parts capable of functioning. If man is to be defined, therefore, it will have to be in some other, non-primary way.

This repeated hint of non-primary definition *(allon tropon, ou prōtōs,* 1030a17, b7, 13, 27, 1031a8, 11) can hardly refer to another form or method of definition, for Aristotle never suggests that natural things should be defined otherwise than *per genus et differentiam.*[64] It may therefore be merely his way of emphasizing the impasse – for there is no other way of defining. Alternatively, it might refer to the *object* of definition: the primary object is essence, but Aristotle will now show that definitions of living nature must go beyond essence so as to include matter. Other references to the snub already imply this, e.g. at *Metaph.* E. 1025b30:

> 'among things defined, and among the what-is-it's of things, some are like the snub while others are like the concave;...all the natural things (animals, plants, and their parts) are like the snub...and their definition never presents them as lacking movement but always contains matter.'

And now at the end of *Metaph.* H.6 he indicates briefly how this can be achieved without illogicality; he gives it as his solution to the problem of the unity of definition, and although he refers immediately to H.3 he actually covers the cases mentioned in book Z (genus and differentia, substance and accident, matter and form) so that it may be taken as the reply to Z's *aporia.* He says that since matter is potentially form, at the moment of actualization matter and form are one thing (1045b18). The implication is that if an object is considered as at a moment, and not as in the process of changing, it has no matter: what was its matter has been determined *so* at this moment and can therefore be described formally, while its potentiality for further change does not come into the question at this moment. The difficulty in book Z was caused by considering objects at a moment as if they were changing, that is as if they had matter, but this creates a false problem. For, considered as if frozen at a moment, a man is not two items, body and soul or matter and form, but one: a complex but graspable form. On the other hand, considered as he is in nature (which H.6 assumes to be the right way to consider him), a man is a process, not a static subject-predicate state. The analysis of a man, therefore – or of a snub nose – should be either a causal account of the process or a complete description of every detail as at a given moment. Either will include matter and movement: the causal accounts will show them as factors in the process, the formal description will show their products.

While causal accounts of this kind exist in plenty in Aristotle's biological treatises, he has given no actual definitions of animals but only abbreviated paradigms and some discussions of method. From them, however, it is possible to infer the effect of *Metaph.* ZH upon definition. Following his discussion in *PA* 1.2–3, which appears to be his latest opinion, the method remains as a logical division *(diairesis)* in which all the characters of the definiendum must be shown to be determinations of characters of the genus. All characters proper to the genus must be stated together at the beginning; every genus divides into 'opposite' or disjunctive differentiae, e.g. Animal is terrestrial or marine, and blooded or bloodless, and legged or legless, etc.; the same is true at each stage of division, e.g. Bird is long-feathered or short-

---

[64] Ross suggests that 1037b27 may point to the kind of definition by material constituents that Aristotle mentions at *Metaph.* B. 993b13 and H. 1043a20; but this is unlikely, for both mentions are hostile.

feathered, etc. When the definiendum is reached, e.g. man, it is characterized by selecting the appropriate disjunctives, e.g. biped not quadruped, many-toed not hoofed, reasoning not unreasoning. The definition consists of the genus plus the whole cluster of final differentiae.

These differentiae which are not characters of soul only – such as biped – are admissible because of the admission of matter, and because it is legitimate in the terms of *Metaph.* H.6 to treat embodied man as a single formal object. The same solution has disposed of the snub paradox: for *snub* can now be defined as nose-flesh placed *so*. The tautology had been created by trying to present snub as a quality abstracted from nose-flesh, which is impossible. But treated as a description of nose-flesh in a certain state, it adds determinate differentiae to the genus without viciously repeating the definiendum. (If the fuller expression *snub nose* is still tautologous, that can now be treated as a case of redundant speech without logical implication.)

But this solution raises the question whether Aristotle now envisaged definition only at the level of the individual particular: to be valid, must the definition of 'man' be a definition of a Socrates at a moment? If so, it is a change of view from the *Topics*, where the definiendum is always a class, not a particular. And it would need accommodating with the view, say, of *Metaph.* Z. 1034a8 that Socrates and Callias are 'the same thing in form'. For whereas the definition of Socrates which is now legitimized will state that he is animal with two legs *so*, with blue eyes and arms thirty inches long...flesh of such constituents, blood *so*..., a definition of the human class will be stated in approximations and disjunctives (man is animal, biped, eyes blue or brown or..., arm length in the range *x–y* inches...). The latter definition will be true of both Socrates and Callias, without altering a word, but does it define either? Here we obviously need to distinguish. If we seek the definition of *being*, the answer must be 'no' in view of Aristotle's firm remarks in *Metaph* Z where he denies that any such generalization or universal can be the *being* to be defined (1035b28; cf. Z.13 on universals). In book Z the only two possibilities to be considered are man as soul and man as Socrates. But if it is man's *form* that is the definiendum, this can be considered at different levels of generality. In the biology 'form' (*eidos*) may refer to any level from the particular up to such general groupings as 'the bloodless' (e.g. at *GA* I. 719a7 viviparous and oviparous are each 'forms'). So Socrates and Callias share the general human form (1034a8); at *Metaph.* I. 1058a29 Aristotle excludes sex and color from formal differences and attributes them to matter; at Z. 1032b1 and 1035b32 he says 'by "form" I mean essence'. While, therefore, the *being* comprises all the characters that belong to Socrates' soul and body in actuality, his form may be grasped in greater or less particularity. A more general formal definition is useful provided that its validity can be guaranteed; and such a guarantee is now available, for the universal is 'that which is common to the particulars' (Z. 1038b11) and a complete formal description of the particular has been validated by H.6. Before considering why this universal Man, which cannot be the being of any actual man, is nevertheless both important and objectively real to Aristotle, it is useful to exclude certain meanings which it does *not* have for him. Being drawn from particulars, it is not merely the product of a prior division of larger genera; nor is it merely acquired by intuition; thirdly, and perhaps most important, it is not a precise 'specific form' of the sort posited by the neoplatonists, but it is a paper formula consisting largely of approximations and disjunctives. It refers to a combined whole made up from *this* definition (soul) and *this* matter (body) taken as a generality (Z. 1035b29), i.e. it is generalized over Socrates and Callias. Its closest reference in modern terms is 'species', when that is taken as meaning nothing more profound than the class of animals which have *XYZ* characters in common to the exclusion of other animals.

But this universal remains important to Aristotle for other reasons which only really become clear in his biology. The different classes of animal – man, horse – are primarily distinguished by essence (*to ti ēn einai*). Those with the same essence are in a way 'one' and indivisible (*Metaph*. Δ. 1016a32). Essence refers to those features which make a man a man, i.e *nous* above all. Again it is not a 'specific form', for it excludes material parts – hence much of the difficulty in book Z. Indeed, to specify man's essence is precisely what Z shows to be impossible, except in the case of the particular. Nevertheless, although Aristotle is occasionally willing to speak of the essence of particular men (Z. 1029b14, 1032a8) and although *nous* in Socrates must be formally distinguishable from the quality of *nous* in Callias, the more significant distinction lies between Socrates and Callias on the one hand and horses on the other. It therefore makes good pragmatic sense to halt the division of animals at the level of the lowest universal class, and there is no evidence that Aristotle changed his practice in this regard. His view of these concepts – form, essence, universal, being – is well demonstrated in his theory of animal reproduction in *GA*. The male semen contributes nothing somatic to the fetus, but only 'form' through the medium of 'movements' which it sets up in the uterine blood. Since the semen is drawn from the male's blood at the moment when it is about to be diversified into tissues and limbs (*GA* I. 726b10, II. 737a18), its movements control the embryo's development in conformity with the parent's individual attributes – including sex and coloration which are not part of the universal human *eidos* but are attributable to matter (*Metaph*. I. 1058a29). The contribution of 'form' therefore includes material accidents which have been formalized, just as *Metaph*. H.6 declares. So Aristotle explains family likenesses in *GA* IV.3, where he emphasizes the individuality of the parent's contribution but at the same time makes room for a real contribution by the universal:

> 'the generator is not merely male but such male, e.g. Coriscus or Socrates, and not merely Coriscus but also man' (767b24);' ... the individual and the particular has more influence upon generation' (b29);' ... both the particular and the kind (*genos*) are generators, but chiefly the particular because it is the being' (b32).

While the actual movements influencing the fetal growth are immediately those imported from the parents, movements derived from ancestors and the movement common to them all (the universalized movement) are potentially present and come into effect if the parental movements are frustrated (767b35ff.). The universal movement is therefore 'farther away' (767b27), weaker, and less precise, but nevertheless real: if the child bears no family resemblance, it should yet possess the common human characteristics (768b10). *GA* v goes on to explain characteristics such as hair quality and color, showing that although they are due to material causes they are amenable to scientific formalization. The introduction of *GA* v distinguishes them as 'affections' which are not attributable to essence and are not common to the whole class; for instance, both essence and the class would include eyes, but the eyes' color would be due only to matter and moving causes. It has been argued that Aristotle here excludes material and individuating accidents from 'form', but that is not what he says: rather he distinguishes them as non-teleological and therefore as not defined in the essence nor in the class (which is marked off by difference of essence). The analysis in *GA* therefore agrees closely with the solution of the *Metaph*. Z *aporia*. It would be interesting to determine which came first.

12

Logical difference and biological difference: the unity of Aristotle's thought

PIERRE PELLEGRIN*

1. In my book, *Aristotle's Classification of Animals*[1] I tried to show that there is no room at all for any animal taxonomy in the Aristotelian biological project. The various orderings of animals which we find in Aristotle are always relative to the point of view and the immediate objective of the inquiry at hand. Thus Aristotle can at one time order animals according to the growing complexity of their reproductive organs, at another according to the form and disposition of their nutritive organs. Certainly it seems obvious *to us* that such studies presuppose a distribution of animals into stable and recognized families. That is not how it is for Aristotle, and I tried to present the status, in the biological works, of his various classifications, relative to his different inquiries, none of which is able to claim priority over the others; these are purely empirical procedures, meant to facilitate the work of the biologist, but they remain outside properly epistemic research. I claim that the retrospective projection of the theoretical presuppositions of 'classical' natural history onto Aristotelian biology has prevented the best interpreters, and *a fortiori* the lesser, from grasping the exact functioning of these concepts in that biology. That is true of the notions of *genos* and *eidos* and of the relationships which, so to say, follow these two concepts, in particular the relation of *analogy*. I would like, taking up again some analyses and conclusions of my book, to say something about these concepts, and that will lead me to inquire about another notion, the notion of 'difference', *diaphora*.

2. The only hypothesis which I posited from the beginning – and it has seemed amply justified by its fecundity – is that of the unity of Aristotle's thought. There is no line of demarcation between Aristotle's logico-metaphysical work and the biological corpus. Of course biology is distinct at least in terms of its *object*, which gives it a certain *de facto* autonomy, but it remains a branch of 'physics', in

---

* Translated by Anthony Preus.
[1] Pellegrin 1982; rev. edn. 1986, in English translation by A. Preus.

Aristotle's system of the 'theoretical sciences'. In the case of the terms *genos* and *eidos*, although they assuredly have a properly biological *usage*, they do not have a properly biological *sense*. This unity of Aristotle's thought is only beginning to be taken really seriously by commentators. This delay has several causes, not the least of which is the reciprocal incompetence in each other's areas of the specialists of the logico-metaphysical corpus and the biological corpus; for a long time it has been thought that it was better, if one is to read the *Historia Animalium* or the *Parts of Animals*, to know zoology and its history than to know Aristotle's metaphysics. That was surely an error, though the best solution would be to know both areas; I do not dismiss history of zoology – in fact I have always been very interested in it. Another especially interesting cause of the misinterpretation of the theoretical unity of Aristotle's thought comes from the fact that the problem of the relationship between Aristotle's logic and his biology, when it has been posed, has almost always been framed in terms of *descent*. Thus J.-M. Le Blond thinks that the logical concepts have a biological origin, while for the notions of *genos* and *eidos*, D. M. Balme, as we will see, has thought the opposite.[2] Not that the question lacks interest, but I very much fear that given the present uncertainty surrounding the chronology of Aristotle's treatises, it is likely to remain for the time being unanswerable. In any case the question has had the unfortunate effect of pushing into secondary position, or even totally obscuring, what I take to be the real problem: that of the parallel functioning of these concepts in the different fields.

3. In the case of *genos* and *eidos*, the field of study has been thoroughly scouted by the many explanatory attempts of previous commentators. Not all of those attempts are equal: one was epoch-making, in that it reduced its predecessors to almost nothing and brought fully to light the true difficulties. That was the article by David Balme, published in 1962, '*GENOS* and *EIDOS* in Aristotle's biology'.[3] Let us begin by quickly recalling why commentators before Balme were so puzzled about Aristotle's use of the terms *genos* and *eidos*, and Balme's answers to that puzzlement.

4. Aristotle's biological corpus seems cut in two by an insurmountable textual shift concerning these concepts. In one group of texts, Aristotle actually *defines* the terms *genos* and *eidos* in themselves and in relation to each other in such a way that these two notions appear to us almost necessarily to be the paleo-taxonomic notions

[2] Cf. Le Blond 1939: 72; Balme 1962b: 98.
[3] On the same subject, see also part 1 of Balme, ch. 4 above.

from which evolved our concepts of genus and species. Balme counts
seven such texts (plus two more doubtful cases)[4] in the biological
corpus minus *Parts of Animals* I. From these texts one might extract
a kind of common classificatory doctrine according to which one
would call *genos* an animal family grouping living things which differ
by degree (thus, in the *genos* 'bird', the various species have wings,
feet, and so on, more or less long, the tongue more or less broad, etc.),
while animals would belong to the same *eidos* if all their parts are
similar (e.g. man, horse, and so on). On the other hand, analogical
relations could allow the establishment of relationships between
various *genē* (so feathers of the *genos* 'bird' are the analogue of scales
of the *genos* 'fish'). Even so Balme limits himself in his survey to
explicit and programmatic passages. We may add to his list passages
from texts which he did not examine, both in the biological works
(e.g., *PA* 1.4 644a17) and outside it, especially concerning analogical
relationships; we may also cite passages included in works surveyed
by Balme which seem to take this classificatory doctrine for granted
by *alluding* to it. Thus in *PA* IV.12 692b3:

> The difference which exists among the birds is that of the excess and defect of the
> parts, i.e. a difference of the more and the less. Some of them have long legs, others
> short; some have a broad tongue, some a narrow one; and similarly with the other
> parts. But each of them differs little from the others with respect to their parts.[5] In
> relation to the other animals, in contrast, they differ in the very form of the parts.
> (tr. after P.P.)

Although the word 'analogy' does not appear, the passage which
follows frequently makes implicit recourse to the analogy: feathers,
beak,...are to birds what scales, teeth, hands (trunk, tongue)...are
to other animals. I will return to this passage.

5. Nevertheless everything happens as if once he had posited this
taxonomically inspired rule, Aristotle proceeded to ignore it in the
practice of his biological research. There are very many supporting
texts: Balme and I have cited enough of them, and it is quite amusing
to see the hermeneutical contortions of the interpreters trying to
bring them under the canon cited above. So, limiting ourselves to
the cases in which *genos* and *eidos* designate animal families, we see
each of these terms successively designating classes of very different
extension. At *HA* II.15 506a9 (cf. *PA* III.4 666b19), Aristotle tells us

---

[4] Balme 1962b: 96; these passages are *HA* 486a16–b21, 488b30–2, (490b7–491a4?),
491a18–19, 497b9–12, (505b26–32?), 539a28–30, *GA* 784b21–3, *Long.* 465a4–7.

[5] At 692b7–8, Peck chooses the reading of MS Y (Vaticanus graecus 261): ἰδίᾳ δὲ μόρια
ὀλίγα διαφέροντα ἔχουσιν ἀλλήλων and consequently translates, 'Thus, as among
themselves they have few parts which differ from one another'. I prefer to follow the rest
of the manuscript tradition (except P), which has ἰδίᾳ δ' ἐπ' ὀλίγον διαφέρουσιν
ἀλλήλων τοῖς μορίοις.

that no animal has a bone in the heart except the horse and 'a *genos* among the cattle, but not all' (*genos ti boōn all' ou pantes*). *Genos* here designates what we would call a 'race' of cattle; at *HA* iv.1 523b28, Aristotle speaks of 'a *genos* of octopuses' (*henos genous polupodōn*), which does not have two rows of suckers, so that *genos* here designates a 'variety' (this passage is not cited by Balme; cf. *PA* iv.9 685b13). At the other end of the scale we have texts like the famous but distressing passage *GA* ii.1 732a1, which says that the uninterrupted succession of generations brings it about that there always exists 'a *genos* of man, of animals, of plants'. On the other hand, as Balme has noticed very well, some animal classes are sometimes called *genos* and sometimes *eidos*. I will cite only one example; it is, to be sure, quite remarkable: in three passages in the *Historia Animalium* not very distant from each other, Aristotle writes that there are 'many *eidē* of cicadas' (iv.7 532b14), that 'a certain *genos* of cicada' makes noise by a friction of breath (iv.9 535b8), and that there are 'two *genē*' of cicadas, small and large (v.30 556a14). Finally *eidos* can designate a class larger than one designated by *genos*, even when the two terms are used in an identical direction: thus in the *Generation of Animals*, Aristotle declares that viviparous and oviparous animals form two *eidē* (i.11 719a7), before talking about 'the *genos* of oviparous fish' (i.21 729b34). The conclusion which comes almost irresistibly to the mind of the commentator is that Aristotle does not apply the rules of usage which he himself enunciated for the terms *genos* and *eidos*.

6. Balme's solution is lucid and desperate. First, he refuses subterfuges, for example that of explaining the discord of the texts by saying that some use *genos* and *eidos* in a 'technical' sense, and others in a 'vulgar' or 'common' sense. Nevertheless it remains true that Balme ends up concluding that there is a contradiction *within* the Aristotelian biological corpus. In this respect Balme differs greatly from his predecessors, who supposed that there was an opposition between the logico-metaphysical books on the one hand, and the biological treatises on the other. For Balme, some biological texts conform to the schemata which regulate the use of *genos* and *eidos* as logical concepts, while other texts do not conform. I hope that I do not here misrepresent Balme's thought (in its 1962 form...) when I say that for him Aristotle indeed had the objective of showing that all the rigor of the logical functioning of the concepts of *genos* and *eidos* penetrates into biology, but he was not able (or did not know how) to accomplish this project. Another point which seems to militate in favor of a gap between the rigorous theoretical project and a biological practice which does not succeed in integrating this

rigor, is the fact that the programmatic texts picked out by Balme, at least those of the *Historia Animalium*, all belong, as Marjorie Grene remarks,[6] to 'introductory sections,' i.e. to methodological expositions. What a gripping vision Balme offers us, in which this biological 'continent' begins to be invaded by concepts developed in a quite different theoretical context – I noted above that for Balme Aristotle imported the logical concepts of *genos* and *eidos* into biology – but has not yet been conquered and thus we are given, in the texts which have come down to us, the image of an incomplete penetration, full of gaps, of logic into the world of life!

7. By importing into the biological corpus itself the supposed contradiction which his predecessors had located between the logical and biological works, Balme thus commits a 'felix culpa' in that he has put his successors on the road toward a unitary conception of Aristotle's thought. But as for the concepts which he examines, I said in my book that he 'cannot help falling at last into the errors of his predecessors whom he had so rightly criticized' (1982: 116). On this point Balme, with the honesty of the great scholar that he is, has recognized the validity of my (friendly) criticisms. I still think that the root of these errors is now and has always been taxonomy; in 1962, Balme was not yet freed from the idea that a taxonomy, at least approximate, ought to be one of the necessary bases of Aristotelian biology. In reading the next-to-last paragraph of Balme's article one sees what a frustrating image of Aristotle as biologist he finally comes to: the *Historia Animalium*, a long and painstaking collection of animal resemblances and differences, is the interminable gestation of a systematic which was never born.

8. Nevertheless, even if we find in Aristotle's biology only seven passages in which, according to Balme, 'the technical distinction between genus and species appears obligatory' (1962b: 96), a perspicacious reading of these passages will show that they are not sustained by a project of animal taxonomy, and that it is not the distinction between genus and species which they disclose. Thus in the last text in the list given by Balme we read:

I say that two things differ according to *genos* when they differ as man and horse do (for the *genos* man is longer-lived than that of horse), but differ according to *eidos* as man differs from man. (*Long.* 1 465a4, tr. after P.P.)

Here man and horse differ between each other according to *genos*, while two men (or two horses) differ between each other according to *eidos*. Other texts in Balme's list support a different viewpoint: for

[6] Grene 1974: 110.

example, at the beginning of the *Historia Animalium* (486a19) we read about horses that 'we say that they are the same in *eidos*' (*tōi eidei tauta*), a passage consonant with many others, notably that in the *Metaphysics* which I mention because it cites the same example, but taxonomically 'shifted', as the passage in the *De Longitudine*, and because I will refer to it again below:

> For by *genos* I mean that by which two things can be said to be one and the same and which does not have any accidental difference in it, whether conceived as matter or otherwise. For not only must something common belong to the two things, e.g. both animals, but this very animality must also be different for each, for example in the case of horse and man. (I.8 1057b38, tr. after P.P.)

These texts, which are programmatic in that they *posit* ('I say', 'we say', 'I call'), i.e. *define* the relations between *genos* and *eidos*, are not even in agreement with each other if one imagines that there might be drawn from them a taxonomic conception – or even a 'paleo-taxonomic' conception – of the pair *genos–eidos*.

9. To escape the difficulties which we encounter within the Aristotelian biological corpus it seemed to me necessary to step outside this 'region' of Aristotle's thought and to detour by way of the texts which I have called 'logico-metaphysical'. I must repeat again that this detour entails no position concerning chronology: I do not argue that the concepts of *genos* and *eidos* used in biology were first developed in the logical and metaphysical works. Nor do I argue the contrary. But in the logico-metaphysical works we find these concepts in their more 'formal' aspect and functioning, that is to say more disengaged from the constraints of a particular 'material'. Let us therefore quickly review the notions of *genos* and *eidos* in themselves and in relation to each other. Each of these terms has, for Aristotle, meanings in several directions, for us of unequal importance.

10. To define *genos* Aristotle uses, notably in *Metaphysics* I, formulas which, as I said in my book, 'ring with a Hegelian sound in our modern ears' (1982: 81). For example: 'for I call difference in *genos* the otherness which makes itself an other…' (*legō gar genous diaphoran heterotēta hē heteron poiei touto auto*: I.8 1058a7). The Aristotelian *genos* is, both in properties and in functioning, a *unity of contraries*. For the *genos* is characterized simultaneously by identity and by difference.

11. In the catalogue of the different senses of *genos* given in *Metaphysics* Δ.28, the first to be mentioned makes of *genos* 'the uninterrupted generation (*genesis*) of beings having the same *eidos*', which is to say that the *genos* is the locus of conservation of this *eidos* in time through the course of generations. I have shown elsewhere[7]

---

[7] See Pellegrin 1985.

that the interpretation of this term *eidos* ought to be located between two extremes: that which is conserved in the *genos* is at least a similarity of look, and it is at most the 'form' contained in the sperm of the male founder of the lineage. That the second interpretation is the more exact seems confirmed by the second sense given to *genos* by this passage, that of a *collection* of individuals descended from the same progenitor, i.e. the same male, although sometimes a lineage may, in a derived and weakened sense, take the name of a female founder, as in the case of Pyrrha. The *genos* is thus fundamentally a *patri-lineage*, a 'genetic space' of transmission of a kinship as well as a collection of individuals bound together by participation in the *eidos* of an ancestral male founder. We can easily see that this fundamental sense has both etymological and social roots;[8] in conformity with it, Aristotle gives as the primary function to his concept of *genos* that of the closure (de-fining) of a class in relation to other classes of objects. That function does not give any privilege to any degree at all of generality, but rather weaves a *horizontal* relationship between a class and one or more others from which it is distinguished. Thus in biology every animal family, no matter what its degree of generality, can be called a *genos*, from the moment that Aristotle intends, explicitly or implicitly, to de-fine it vis-à-vis other classes: the *genos* of living things is opposed to that of non-living, the *genos* of birds to that of fish, the *genos* of blackbirds to that of falcons.

12. The other side of Aristotle's *genos* is its capacity for accepting otherness within the very heart of its identity. That can be understood in a chronological sense: because *genesis* occurs within a *genos*, the *genos successively* includes contraries which transform into each other (cf. *Metaph.* I.4 1055a8). But it is the logical aspect of this property of *genos* which interests us most here. The *genos* is, for Aristotle, a *determinate* mixture of same and other, in that the otherness which it can harbor within it without dissolving itself is situated very precisely on the scale of possible othernesses: the *genos* includes in itself the *diaphora*, a concept which we are used to interpreting as 'specific difference'. That is to say that that which differs within the *genos* can differ to the extreme limits of difference, provided that it continues to relate itself to a 'same', which implies that the *diaphora* is not a pure otherness:

Difference is not the same as otherness. For the other and that which it is other than need not be other in some definite respect..., but that which is different is different from some particular thing in some particular respect, so that there must be something identical whereby they differ. (*Metaph.* I.3 1054b23, tr. Ross)

[8] Cf. Benveniste 1969: 'We have three groups, in order of increasing importance: *genos*, *phratra*, *phyle*, which are the three concentric circles of ancient Greek society'. (257).

In 'technical' Aristotelian terms, the maximum otherness which a *genos* can accept within itself is contrariety (*enantiōsis*), which in his doctrine of the different forms of opposition Aristotle places between the opposition of possession–privation (*hexis–sterēsis*) and the opposition of relatives (*pros ti*). In other words every *genos* is divisible into *contrary eidē*. If the *eidē* are only relative to each other (for example in the *genos* 'number', double and half) the *genos* does not actualize all its potentialities. But the opposition of possession–privation is too strong to be enclosed within the limits of a *genos*.[9]

13. Without treating it for its own sake, I nevertheless must say a few words about *contrariety* in Aristotle. *Categories* 10 gives valuable indications of the distinctions made by Aristotle (or by his school, if the *Categories* are not or not all by Aristotle himself) between the different forms of opposition, and more precisely between these two forms which are closely related, at least in certain cases, the opposition of 'contraries' and that of 'possession–privation'. We know that this distinction is made especially difficult by the fact that two sorts of contraries must be taken account of: those which have no intermediary (e.g., odd/even) and those which have (e.g., vice/virtue). This duality of contraries will help us a little later in our analysis. Of the distinctions in question, I will note just one: while the contraries can reciprocally change into each other (the black can become white and then turn back to black), the movement which goes from possession to privation is irreversible (when one has really become blind one does not recover one's sight).[10] I would like to make three remarks on the subject of the relationship between contrariety and 'specific difference'.

(i) Considered in relation to *genos–eidos* pairs, contraries can be encountered in three cases: either as *eidē* of the same *genos* (e.g., black/white are *eidē* of the *genos* 'color'), and that is the case which is most interesting for us; or as *eidē* of contrary *genē* (e.g., justice, *eidos* of the *genos* 'virtue' / injustice, *eidos* of the *genos* 'vice'); or as contrary *genē* (e.g., good/bad). Although this doctrine is presented thus in the *Categories*, I do not believe that it implies that one ought to deduce

[9] Thus I have argued in my book (Pellegrin 1982: 87) that Aristotle's criticism of the Platonists, because they divide 'according to privation' (*PA* 1.3 642b22), should be understood in the light of this logical doctrine according to which a *genos* does not include oppositions of possession and privation.

[10] A solid study of the different sorts of opposition in Aristotle may be found in Hamelin 1920: 'Neuvième leçon: l'opposition des concepts'. But the most complete study of the contrariety relation in Aristotle remains Anton 1957, a brilliant and detailed study which especially restores both the historical and the theoretical foundations of contrariety. The problems in which we are interested here are treated in Chapter VI. In a way, my study completes that of Anton, in that he has very little to say about biology.

that all these terms are definitively and in all cases categorized as either *genē* or *eidē*. If it were not beyond the limits of my topic, I would reread this passage in the light of what will be said below about the relativity of the terms *genos* and *eidos*.

(ii) The real *diaphora* can be attributed only to two things which have between them a contrariety in their essence (their *logos*, says Aristotle at *Metaph.* I.9 1058b1), and not to those whose contrariety is accidental or produced by the material. Thus a concrete man, whether black or white, would be specifically different from a horse no matter what its color, because the *logoi* of man and horse have a specific difference. But on the one hand a black man will not be specifically different from a white man, although white and black are contraries, and on the other, the difference of sexes, in that it is (according to Aristotelian doctrine) produced by movements of material, will not be a *diaphora*.

(iii) Finally, another feature is in danger of being masked simply by the translation of the term *enantia* by 'contraries'. In fact a term can have only one contrary *in a given direction*, but it can have contraries in several directions. That must have seemed strange even to Aristotle's contemporaries, since we read in the *Physics*:

And there is no need to be disturbed (*tarattesthai*) by the fact that there may be more than one contrary to the same thing, that a particular motion will be contrary both to rest and to motion in the contrary direction. We have only to grasp the fact that a particular motion is in a sense the opposite both of a state of rest and of the contrary motion, in the same way as that which is of equal or standard measure is the opposite both of that which surpasses it and of that which it surpasses, and that it is impossible for the opposite motions or changes to be present to a thing at the same time. (VIII.7 261b16, tr. Hardie and Gaye, with minor changes)

In biology, as I tried to show in my book (1982: 88ff.), 'terrestrial', 'winged', and 'aquatic', for example, can form three pairs of contraries when these terms are applied to the manner of life and of the local movement of animals.

14. I must also notice, to end this brief review of the logical concept of *genos*, a relation of the greatest importance in biology. We have seen that *genos* is defined above all by its closure on itself, the result of which is that 'the things which differ according to *genos* have no path (*hodos*) from one to the other, but are too distant, and without common measure (*asumblēta*)' (*Metaph.* I.4 1055a6). In my book, I commented at some length on the word *asumblēta* (1982: 80–1). It is the lack of a path between one *genos* and another which, in the theory of knowledge, is the basis of the doctrine of 'the incommunicability of genera' which has the consequence that there is only one

science per *genos*. Nevertheless there is a possible relation between the *genē*, and that is the relation of *analogy*. As Pierre Aubenque has already pointed out,[11] the only kind of analogy in Aristotle is the analogy of 'proportion', i.e. that in four terms. Thus, leaping over the generic closure, analogy posits: that which is *a* in *genos A* is *b* in *genos B*.

15. Now let us say a few words about *eidos*. When Aristotle integrates this term into his system it is determined by a double origin: the immemorial etymological origin, and the near origin, theoretically and emotionally charged, of its use by the Academy. Going back to its etymology, the *eidos* is the visible aspect of a thing. But this visible aspect is not principally opposed to a hidden aspect which encloses the truth of the thing, as would become the case in later Western thought. On the contrary: in that it appears, the *eidos* is fullness, and we must doubtless concede to Heidegger that for the Greeks visibility is a promise of truth. That has as consequence that Plato can use the word *eidos*, among others, for fully real being, that of the Forms, just as Aristotle will call *eidos* the 'form' of a being, its own structure which makes it be what it is. But I want to use these etymological remarks not so much to oppose, as Balme does, *genos* and *eidos* as 'kinship' and 'form', but rather to mark the contrast between the *eidos* as an *immediate* presence of one or several determinations, and the *genos* as a logical space within which the *process* of its own realization takes place. This can be seen very clearly in the Aristotelian doctrine according to which, at least in certain conditions, the *genos* is the matter of its *eidē*.[12]

16. It is striking to find in Plato and Aristotle, besides a profound difference of problematics, the permanence of that which one could call a 'terminological framework'. For whether one believes in the fundamental unity of Platonism or thinks that at about the time of the *Phaedrus* and/or *Parmenides* there was a radical break which called the 'first' Platonism into question, the texts show us that Plato used the same term to designate the Idea toward which one must climb to resolve the contradictions of the sensible world, and (at least from

[11] Aubenque 1978.
[12] This doctrine has been examined in, among other studies, Rorty 1974. It is against this interpretation that the passage from Grene 1974, quoted above (n. 6), is directed. Grene's arguments do not seem to me to lack force, but from this dispute I came to the conclusion that neither camp has a sufficiently extended conception of the Aristotelian notion of 'matter', no doubt because they have been too much influenced by the modern concept. To see how polymorphic Aristotle's concept of matter really is, consider this passage:

'The letters are the causes of syllables, the material of artificial products, fire, etc., of bodies, the parts of the whole, and the premises of the conclusion, in the sense of "that from which"' (*Ph.* II.3 195a16).

the *Sophist* on) the 'species' to which dichotomous division makes us descend. Similarly Aristotle calls both 'form' and 'species' *eidos*. In both philosophers, division, which was for a long time wrongly believed to be an instrument of classification, is a *definitional* method, which through an opposition of terms at each of its steps furnishes, when one arrives at the last indivisible *eidos*, the *definition* which is not just a name, but the *logos* of the thing.[13] Certainly at first sight the Platonic texts do not seem to make the *eidos* a subdivision of the *genos*, but to use these two terms indifferently in the course of the division. J. Stenzel believed that he could assert that the hierarchical relation of the terms *genos* and *eidos* was established by Speusippus, but the textual bases of his theory seem to me very uncertain.[14] In fact a more precise reading of the Platonic texts would seem to suggest the existence of a *tendency*, from the moment that the diaeretical method is fully developed, i.e. from the *Sophist* on, to designate with the word *genos* the groups which are susceptible to division and with the word *eidos* the groups which are the results of division.[15] But that does not imply an *absolute* formal subordination of one term to the other: a given reality can be by turns *genos* or *eidos* according to the point of view from which one considers it. In the descending scale of division *genē* can very well *follow eidē*, and it is doubtless that which has given interpreters the impression that Plato used the two terms *indifferently*, which is to my way of thinking an excessive assertion. Thus Plato would be closer to Aristotle than the tradition says in his usage of the terms *genos* and *eidos*. Nonetheless it is Aristotle who codified the order in which these concepts are 'located' with respect to each other.

17. From the *Topics* on, in fact, Aristotle posits unambiguously *eidos* as a sub-class of *genos*. Even more, in the *Topics* it is essentially by their *relative extension* that the terms *genos*, *eidos*, and *diaphora* are defined: the dialectician should be especially careful that his adversary does not improperly overturn the relative extensional order,

---

[13] That the purpose of *diairesis*, for both Plato and Aristotle, is definition and not classification is argued also by David Balme in ch. 4 above.

[14] Stenzel 1929.

[15] Plato would thus have been sensitive – how could he not be? – to the etymological baggage carried by the two terms. Among the 20 uses of *genos* and the 12 uses of *eidos* in the *Sophist*, one seems remarkable to me:

> *Stranger*: And of persuasion there may be said to be two kinds (*ditta legōmen genē*)?
> *Theaetetus*: What are they?
> *Stranger*: One is private, and the other public.
> *Theaetetus*: Yes, let each of them form a class (*gignesthon gar oun eidos hekateron*). (222d3–6)

It is as if the division were not really complete until the class obtained has lost its character of a *genos* and acquired the character of an *eidos*.

and thus the formal hierarchy, which should exist between these terms (cf. e.g. IV.I I2IbII). The text of the *Topics* as we have it does not, however, permit an indisputable decision about whether Aristotle already, at that stage of his career, thought of a *genos* as divided into *contrary eidē*.[16] But the terms *genos* and *eidos* preserve in Aristotle a fundamental Platonic trait – they do not qualify *absolutely* a class of objects, they do not mark a fixed level of generality. Every *eidos* can in its turn be taken as a *genos*, so long as the division has not yet arrived at the *atomon eidos*:

> There is nothing in the definition except the first-named *genos* and the *diaphorai*. The other genera are constituted by the first *genos* and along with this the *diaphorai* which are taken with it, e.g. the first *genos* may be 'animal', the next *genos* 'animal which is two-footed', and again 'animal which is two-footed and featherless', and similarly if the definition includes more terms. (*Metaph.* Z.12 1037b29, tr. Ross, with alterations)

18. Thus we see, by way of our examination of its logical functioning, that the pair *genos–eidos* is not destined to serve as a basis for a 'stable' classification of the objects to which it is applied, in contrast to our concepts of genus and species. This conceptual pair functions as a universally applicable schema: one finds it at work with physical qualities and colors, as well as with mathematical properties such as evenness, corporeal dispositions like health, and ethical and political notions like the virtues, command, and so on. Thus there is no reason to imagine, before we open the biological corpus, that the pair *genos–eidos* will have there a usage radically different from that which it has in other domains. This pair activates the Aristotelian definitional division which, as we have seen, took up again at the terminological level the Platonic project of *diairesis*, elsewhere strongly criticized by Aristotle. In biology too the division which 'descends' from the *genos* to its *eidē* has a definitional goal, not a classificatory one: Balme said so long ago, and I have tried to show that in more detail in the first chapter of my book. In the analyses which I will now carry out on the subject of the Aristotelian biological corpus, I will use the expression 'conceptual schema of division of the *genos* into *eidē*' (or more simply 'conceptual schema of *genos–eidos*') to indicate the process of division of the *genos* into contrary *eidē* which produces the 'specific difference', i.e. to name the method, in the

---

[16] Properly speaking, there is no definitional division in the *Topics*, but that is because the establishment of definitions is not the objective, nor one of the objectives, of that treatise; rather it proposes to uncover the dialectically exploitable vices of definitions proposed by an adversary. But we see the trace of the theory in that these definitions have been established by definitory division, proceeding by division of the *genos* into contrary *eidē*. Cf. v.6 136b3: *ek tōn antidiēirēmenōn*, and vi.4 142b7: *palin ei tōi antidiēirēmenōi to antidiēirēmenon*, b12: *ton dicha diairoumenon*.

etymological sense of *methodos,* which leads to the *definition* of the *atomon eidos.*

19. My first remark concerning the biological corpus goes beyond the terms *genos* and *eidos* alone and seems to me fundamental for the understanding of Aristotelian biology and indeed for Aristotle's thought in general. In fact the texts reveal that no term exists in his biology (and perhaps elsewhere, but I don't want to broaden the discussion that much) which designates a fixed level of generality. In the case of the terms *genos* and *eidos* themselves, all commentators have been forced to admit that Aristotle does not use them to designate classes of fixed generality. Thus Balme (1962b: 86) cites five examples of animals which, in the biological corpus, are called sometimes *genos,* sometimes *eidos.* As for *genos,* I have given examples showing that it can designate animal classes from the smallest variety to what one used to call a 'kingdom' (animal, vegetable) or even a more general class when Aristotle speaks of the *genos* of living things, or of the *genos* of beings subject to generation and corruption. I have also explained why the term *genos* was called upon to signify the closure of a class on itself, simultaneously de-fining it in relation to other classes. But, as one might expect after our study of the logical properties of the pair *genos–eidos,* things are different in the case of the term *eidos.* Quantitatively, in the first place, this term is little used by Aristotle in the biological corpus to designate an animal class. I have written in my book, perhaps maliciously, that one consequence of this rarity of use has been that most interpreters have had less difficulty accommodating *eidos* than *genos* to their opinions.[17] To give an idea of the phenomenon, the *Generation of Animals* uses the word *eidos* 32 times (Balme counts 33, and I'll give him the benefit of the doubt), but never to designate a class of animals, while of the 122 uses of *genos* many designate animal families of variable generality. On the other hand, when in the other biological works *eidos* designates a class of animals, it is always a sub-class obtained by division of a larger class, whether that is explicit or understood. There are perhaps two exceptions to that rule, as well as several debatable occurrences; I have discussed them in my book.[18] On this topic, I would like to refer to two passages, interesting

---

[17] Pellegrin 1982: 120. I made the remark about Louis 1956b, in which the author declared that 'the sense of the word *eidos* is thus clear enough' (148), i.e. that the word designated our *species.*

[18] *HA* VIII.3 592b7: there are two *eidē* of vultures of different color and size; *HA* IX.20 617a18: there are three *eidē* of thrushes. Perhaps in the first case one should assume that Aristotle takes the family of vultures as a *genos,* and in the second case *eidos* in the 'common' sense of 'visible appearance'. In Balme 1962b, Balme counts 13 passages in which *eidos* designates 'animal-types' (86). Among them appear the two uses cited above. I have discussed all these cases in my book (127ff.). Cf. Pellegrin 1985, and 1982: 126–30.

because they form limiting cases. In *Parts of Animals* iv.5 680a15, Aristotle writes that there are several *genē* of sea-urchins and adds: 'for there is no one unique *eidos* for all the sea-urchins' (*ou gar hen eidos tōn echinōn pantōn esti*).[19] I believe that this manner of expression, at first sight astonishing, can be explained by the fact that in this passage the word *genos* successively designates two classes of different extension, which is not at all astonishing. First Aristotle says that there are several kinds of sea-urchins, and naturally designates these kinds by the word *genē*. Then he considers the whole group of sea-urchins as a *genos* (that proposition is understood, but it is demanded by what follows). Thus Aristotle, when he says that there is no one unique *eidos* of sea-urchins, only asserts that the sea-urchins form a *true genos*, within which specific difference comes into play. The second passage (*HA* 1.6 490b15–18) has been studied in detail by A. Gotthelf,[20] who has kindly chided me for not having used it in my book. We read:

> Among the remaining animals [i.e., other than those listed previously] we find no large groups (*genē megala*), for an *eidos* does not include several *eidē* (*ou gar periechei polla eidē hen eidos*), for sometimes the *eidos* will be simple, showing no specific difference, for example, man; sometimes the groups have within them a specific difference, but the *eidē* are unnamed (*ta d' echei men, all' anōnuma ta eidē*). (Tr. after P.P.)

The phrase *ou gar periechei polla eidē hen eidos* has much intrigued the commentators. Gotthelf, though he recognizes that this use goes in the direction of my thesis in showing that *eidos* can be used at several levels of generality, thinks that this phrase, while cast in Aristotle's technical terminology, reports the state of everyday language. I prefer to see in this expression a *negative definition of 'eidos'*: in a given context, an *eidos* cannot be divided into *eidē*. The last phrase, however, includes an obscurity which, because of the elliptical turn of expression, cannot be totally dissipated. Gotthelf, against the tradition, thinks that it is the containing forms and not the contained forms which are called 'unnamed'. That seems to me difficult simply because Aristotle would then call a class an *eidos* at the same time that he says it is divisible, which he does nowhere else. To be coherent with the rest of the corpus, this passage ought in fact to situate 'those having difference' (*ta d' echei diaphoran*) at the level of the *genos* divisible into *eidē* according to specific difference.

20. Thus in regard to *genos* and *eidos* the biological corpus is

---

[19] P. Louis translates: '...il existe plusieurs genres d'oursins (en effet tous les oursins n'appartiennent pas à la même espèce)' (Louis 1956a: 117); Peck purely and simply jumps right over the parenthesis in his translation (though of course he retains it in the text).

[20] Gotthelf unpublished (1).

completely compatible with the logico-metaphysical texts both in terms of the level of generality, and in terms of the order of intervention of these two concepts. That is why I would like now to turn to two notions which interpreters have often believed to designate a fixed level of generality. These two notions are those of the 'greatest *genē*' and of analogy.

21. With delightful confidence, tempered however later on, Pierre Louis writes: 'In Aristotle's classification of animals the expression *ta genē megista* (or *megala*) has a precise sense; it designates the great divisions of the animal kingdom, the classes'.[21] We quote three passages:

Here are the greatest families (*genē megista*) among which the animals have been divided: one is that of the birds, another that of the fish, another that of the cetaceans…Another is that of the testaceans…, another that of the crustaceans…, another that of the molluscs…, another that of the insects…For none of the other animals do there exist greatest families (*genē megala*).' (*HA* 1.6 490b7; the passage which follows has been quoted above. Tr. after P.P.)

This is the feature in which the greatest families differ from the rest of the animals: they are blooded whereas the others are bloodless. (*HA* 11.15 505b26)

There are four greatest families (*genē megista*) [i.e., of crustaceans]: they are called lobsters, spiny lobsters, crayfish and crabs. Each of these families has many *eidē* which differ not only in form but especially in size. (*PA* iv.8 683b26, tr. after P.P.)

We may say that in these three passages the notion of *genos megiston* is classificatory, but not taxonomical: in each passage it indeed designates a class included in a nesting of classes more or less large, but far from designating a fixed class of extension, it designates each time a different taxonomic level. In my book I asserted that 'the expression *ta genē megista* designates a group large enough to be divided several times in a row' (1982: 121). James Lennox has proposed a related interpretation, but starting from the point of view of the concept's intension rather than its extension:

Aristotle's zoological *megista genē* are distinguished from one another *not* by one trait that is necessary and sufficient for membership in a kind, but by an organized set of general traits. Birds are oviparous, feathered, beaked, two-legged, and winged. Fish are cold-blooded, gilled, scaled, aquatic, oviparous, and so on.[22]

In view of the third passage quoted I would no longer go so far in the determination of the concept of *megista genē*. In fact it designates

[21] N. 5 to p. 13 of Vol. 1 of his translation of the *Historia Animalium* (Louis 1964–9: 1 162), about the beginning of *HA* 1.6. Eleven years later, in Louis 1975, he was much more circumspect: 'he [Aristotle] tried to express the idea of an order or family with the expression "great genus", which one finds in several passages in the biological treatises. It is sometimes applied to simple genera, but can also designate more vast groups, as the entire group of testacea or that of insects' (155). [22] Lennox 1980: 338.

quite simply those *genē* of animals which are *important* because they have many *eidē*: I believe that the superlative *megista* does nothing beyond signifying this profusion of *eidē*. But when he considers these classes as a whole, Aristotle normally designates them by the term *genos*: e.g., the crustaceans, of which he says several times that they form one of the four *genē* of non-blooded animals (*HA* IV.1 523b1, *PA* IV.5 678a30, *GA* 1.14 720b4).

22. Might one find in the notion of *analogy* – which does not designate a class of animals – the fixed point which would permit attributing to Aristotle at least the outline of a project of taxonomic construction? What we have seen of this notion with respect to the logical usage of concepts would seem to indicate that the answer must be 'no', since analogy is a way of going from one *genos* to another *genos*, and *genos* denotes classes of variable level. Nevertheless one finds in Aristotle a doctrine which, in the biological corpus, opposes analogical difference to difference 'according to the more and the less'. Thus at *PA* 1.4 644a16:

> For those kinds (*genē*) which differ by degree, i.e. according to the more and the less, have been linked under a single *genos*, while those which are analogous have been separated. I mean, for example, that a bird differs from another bird by the more and the less, i.e. by degree (one has the wings longer, another shorter), while a fish differs from a bird by analogy (for that which is feather in one is scale in the other). (tr. after P.P.)

As parallel texts confirm, *genos* is thus characterized by the fact that it admits within it a difference 'according to the more and the less'. I will return to this latter expression, but I want to make two remarks immediately. First, Aristotle uses the same word *genos* in two succeeding lines to designate classes of different extension; second, the doctrine presented in this passage – we ought to have begun the quotation from the beginning of chapter 4 – is not presented by Aristotle as a personal discovery, but as a generally accepted distinction. And I think that in the 'common consciousness' (although it may be difficult to determine what Aristotle means by the words *hoi anthrōpoi* at 644a13, and especially how much 'specialization' in biology these people may have had) there was a tendency to *fix* the levels of generality of the relations of the more and the less and of analogy, a kind of spontaneous tendency toward taxonomy, if one may put it that way. But in the Aristotelian conception, as we have seen, such a fixing is *logically* impossible. Thus as I have just said analogy ought to be just as variable as *genos*. For, from the Aristotelian point of view, it is impossible to say that the analogy feather–scale fixes the *genos* at the level of 'bird' or 'fish', but we must understand that feather and scale can be called analogous as soon as one has decided to take 'bird' and 'fish' as *genē*. But if the level called *genos* changes, which by definition it can do, analogy also changes level. That is shown by a comparison of two passages, noted by Balme, located a few pages apart in the *Parts of Animals*:

The animals which do not have [bone] have something analogous: in the fishes, for example, in some there are spines, in others cartilage. (II.8 653b35, after P.P.)

The nature of cartilage is the same as that of bone, but they differ according to the more and the less. (II.9 655a33, after P.P.)

Is there between cartilage and bone an analogical difference or a difference of degree? That is not an Aristotelian question. In the first case we have two *genē*, bony animals and cartilaginous animals, which have between them an analogical relationship; but in the second case the point of view is not the same. Chapter 9 studies the nature and functions of the skeleton: from this perspective bone and cartilage are two different 'species' of matter employed by nature as 'support' of the body (cf. 654b29: nature makes an armature, as do the sculptors who work with a soft material like clay). Within the *genos* constituted by 'parts' assuring the 'support' of flesh, there are variations of degree, particularly according to size and hardness, which relates, among others, to the difference between bone and cartilage. And one may find other examples of these changes in perspective which have the effect of 'declassing' the analogical relationship, even if these examples are less explicit from a terminological point of view. Compare these two texts:

In some animals the parts are not of the same *eidos* and do not differ by excess and defect, but differ by analogy: that is the case, for example, of bone in relation to spine, of nail in relation to hoof...(*HA* I.1 486b17, after P.P.)

We have here an example very close to the doctrine which we found above at *PA* 644a16: that which is nail for *genos A*, is hoof for *genos B*. But, as in the example given above, the point of view can change:

There are some parts which to the touch resemble bone, for example nails, hoofs, claws of lobsters, horns, beaks of birds. All these parts are possessed by animals for their defense. (*PA* II.9 655b2)

Although he does not say so explicitly, Aristotle now considers these different parts as *eidē* of the *genos* 'organs of defense', and from this perspective nail and hoof are no longer analogous. One may even suppose that when a little later Aristotle reminds us that these parts are all composed of earth (655b11), that is a way of saying that they form one *genos*.

23. In order to grasp correctly the philosophical import of the doctrine of analogy in Aristotle, we may make two remarks. First, analogy is not limited to the morphological or functional domain. Thus in *HA* VIII.1 588a25, Aristotle asserts that the psychological faculties of man and other animals differ from one another either by the more and the less or by analogy. The second remark is developed in my book: analogy 'does not serve so much to set apart natural families of living things as to relate one group of animals to another by some point of reference, and ultimately to relate all living things to one unique being, taken as a model of intelligibility, Man' (1982: 110). That is an essential thesis, and has been independently taken up since the appearance of my book by G. E. R. Lloyd:[23] Aristotelian biology is not only hierarchical, but, more exactly, anthropocentric, though not without some difficulties.[24] And if the secret spring of analogy in Aristotle's biology is ultimately the exaltation of human perfection – man being 'the most natural' animal (*IA* 4 706a19) – it is not surprising that the relation of analogy can operate at several levels. Thus we read in a passage of the *Metaphysics*:

Things that are one in number are also one in *eidos*, while things that are one in *eidos* are not all one in number; but things that are one in *eidos* are all one in *genos*, while things that are so in *genos* are not all one in *eidos* except by analogy; while things that are one by analogy are not all one in *genos*. (Δ.6 1016b36, after Ross)

We see in this passage that a relation between *eidē* within one *genos* can be called analogical. At the level of *terms* such a declaration is formally anti-Aristotelian, since the relation of analogy is a relation between *genē*. Perhaps one ought to see a shortening of the expression, a familiar procedure for Aristotle: if the *eidē* of a *genos* are taken in turn as *genē*, then they can enter into analogical relations. Man and horse are *eidē* of the *genos* 'animal', but one may weave between them relations of analogy which make them able to be called 'one': in a sense they have the same foot if one considers that that which is nail in the one is hoof in the other, and so on. In contrast, the last use of the term analogy in the passage quoted returns to the habitual sense which makes of analogical unity a unity above the *genē*.

24. None, then, of the classificatory concepts of Aristotelian biology is taxonomic, because none of them defines a constant level of generality to which a taxonomic construction, in fact or even in intent, could refer. An examination of the *logical* functioning of the

---

[23] Lloyd 1983, esp. §3: 'Man as model'.

[24] I have recalled in my book (113) that Aristotle recognized that on certain points, notably sensory performances, man was outclassed by some animals. See the summary which Lloyd gives of the difficulty with the thesis of man's preeminence, Lloyd 1983: 31ff.

schema *genos–eidos* would by itself suggest that. But the theoretical
unity which I presupposed by beginning between the logico-metaphysical works and the biological works does not seem sufficiently
established at this stage of our route, and we will collide, on the
subject of the concepts *genos* and *eidos*, with a formidable double
problem. In fact, on the one hand a (perhaps *the*) fundamental property of the conceptual schema *genos–eidos* is that in the same *genos*
the *eidē* are *contraries*: what is there in biology of this fundamental
property? On the other hand, it seems that Aristotle developed a
criterion of distinction between *genos* and *eidos* specific to biology: it
is the doctrine, of which I spoke above, according to which while the
differences from one *genos* to another are analogical, the differences
within the *genos* are differences 'according to the more and the less',
or 'according to excess and defect'.

25. Let us begin with the question of the more and the less, which
has been made much easier to discuss by an important article by
J. G. Lennox, already cited in relation to another topic.[25] This article
shows perfectly how difficult it is to reconcile the *logical* doctrine of
the division of *genos* into *eidē*, with the thesis, apparently peculiar to
the biological corpus,[26] that within a *genos* the various *eidē* differ
according to the more and the less. Lennox shows that these two
disparate descriptions of generic unity are reconcilable, primarily by
deriving the 'difference of degree' doctrine from another doctrine to
which Aristotle is committed (and noted above), according to which
the *genos* is the matter for the differences which come into play within
it, and then by appealing to teleology for the establishment of the
unity of each animal species:

Differentia by differentia, compared out of context, the species of a genus differ only
by 'excess and defect', or 'the more and the less'. But when the balanced unity of
those differentiae in each species is studied, and when it becomes clear that the

[25] Above n. 22. A substantially revised version of Lennox's essay appears below as ch. 13.
[26] While recognizing that the complete doctrine of the more and the less within a *genos*
properly belongs to the biological corpus, Lennox (1980: 330) quotes at least one passage
outside that corpus which seems to allude to it. It comes from the *Physics*, and Lennox
translates it thus: 'Within the same genus, but with respect to the more and the less'
(*Ph.* v.2 226b1–2) (it's a matter of qualitative changes), but the text has: ἡ δ' ἐν τῷ αὐτῷ εἴδει
μεταβολὴ ἐπὶ τὸ μᾶλλον καὶ ἧττον ἀλλοίωσίς ἐστιν. Again, there is a passage from the
Nicomachean Ethics (viii.1 1155b12) which he ought to have quoted:

'Those who think that there is only one *eidos* of friendship because it admits the more
and the less have relied on an inappropriate indication; for the same things can differ
both in the more and the less and in *eidos*. We have discussed this matter previously.'

This passage seems to show that the doctrine of the difference of degree within a *genos* had
been discussed outside the biology in domains more 'dialectical', as are the moral
problems, and that Aristotle had treated them in a work or passage today lost, since the
reference in the last words of this passage designates no known location in the corpus.

possession of just this degree of length of beak is needed for the members of this species to get their food, Aristotle insists that the forms of a genus are indeed different in form, and not merely in degree. (Lennox 1980: 344)

For my purposes the remarks which follow are sufficient. Aristotle never anywhere identifies specific difference and difference according to the more and the less. On the contrary some passages oppose these sorts of difference. Lennox (1980: 326 n. 15) cites, as unique, a passage from the *Politics* (1.13 1259b36) which says that to command and to be commanded are different *eidei* and not according to the more and the less. Lennox could also have cited the beginning of that same book 1 of the *Politics* where Aristotle writes, against the Platonists, that there is between the statesman, the king, the head of a family, and the master of slaves a difference *eidei* and not only of more and less, according to the number of people over whom power is wielded (1.1 1252a9).

26. We can then establish the following distinction: among the *genē* which all, by definition, can be divided into *eidē*, some admit *at the level* of their *eidē* variations of degree, others do not; there is thus an opposition between difference of degree and difference according to *eidos*. The 'physical characters' of the 'parts' of animals are of the first kind, for it is to these characters and parts that variation according to the more and the less within a *genos* is applied:

[In each *genos*] the parts differ, not in having an analogical relation (as in man and fish the relation of bone and spine), but rather by the physical characters (*tois sōmatikois pathesin*), as largeness and smallness, softness and hardness, the smooth and the rough, and properties of that sort, in a word they differ by the more and the less. (*PA* 1.4 644b11, tr. after P.P. Cf. *PA* IV.12 692b3, translated above p. 315)

It is entirely Aristotelian to say that some relations accept the more and the less, and others do not. An object can be more or less clear, while a number cannot be more or less even. And Lennox is right to put in parallel the biological texts treating the difference of degree and the passages of the *Categories* (for example, *Cat.* 8 10b26) which relate to the more and the less. But I believe that we must go a bit farther than Lennox and notice that the passages in the *Categories* tell us that certain *contraries* admit the more and the less and certain others do not. This should be put in relation with Aristotle's analysis, recalled above, according to which some contraries accept intermediaries between them, when others do not accept them. Thus in certain cases one passes from one extreme (contrary) to the other by a continuous variation of degree, which is impossible in other cases. But even in the first figure the extremes themselves remain true contraries which cannot be said to differ according to the more and the less. Thus, man may imperceptibly, in becoming better, pass from vice to virtue, but vice and virtue are true contraries and do not differ from each other according to the more and the less (cf. *Cat.* 10 13a22). Thus the relation of degree within the *genos* is not absolutely incompatible with the contrariety of *eidē* within the same *genos*, a fundamental property of the conceptual schema *genos–eidos*.

27. One may then wonder what status to attribute to this difference of degree in biology. I think that a beginning of an answer is given us by the passage in the *Parts of Animals* cited above (1.4 644a16) and by the remark which I made there concerning it: Aristotle is not the author of the doctrine which opposes difference of degree and analogical difference – even if we imagine that he applies to it a terminology which refers to concepts functioning elsewhere in his own philosophy – but he has taken it from 'common sense'. I am thus rather inclined to believe that differences of degree, which serve as a basis of the traditional distinction between animal classes taken up by Aristotle for his own use, ought to be struck with the same 'theoretical devaluation' as this distinction itself and as all the various classifications of animals found in the biological corpus; I have tried to show that these classifications were empirical and preliminary to science. I am of the same opinion as Lennox but for different reasons: the doctrine of the more and the less as applied in biology does not legitimate the view that this branch of knowledge can be held to account for peculiar concepts. Therefore we must consolidate the bridge which we have stretched between the logico-metaphysical usage and the biological usage of the concepts of *genos* and *eidos*. We will see that our preceding remarks concerning the differences of analogy and of degree will be useful for the project.

28. Let us return now to the first difficulty noted above (§24). Are there in Aristotle *two* doctrines of division of *genos* into *eidē*? For how can we reconcile the fact, frequently affirmed, that horse, man, and dog are *eidē* of the *genos* 'animal', with the thesis which cuts the *genos* into contrary *eidē*? *Textual considerations* absolutely forbid us to adopt this point of view of 'two doctrines'. I will call attention to two texts. At *Metaphysics* I.8 1058a3 (already cited, §8) Aristotle gives as explicit examples of *eidē* of the *genos* 'animal' man and horse, while in that same Book I, *both before and after* this passage, he establishes, develops, and incessantly reaffirms that the 'specific difference' is established within a *genos* between *contrary eidē*. On the other hand, at Δ.6 1016a25–7, we are reminded that the *genos* is divided according to contrary determinations (*antikeimenais diaphorais*), while the example given, in the following line, to illustrate this thesis is that of

the *genos* 'animal' divided into 'horse, man, dog'. I believe that our present embarrassment can be considered as the Parthian shot of the traditional taxonomic interpretation which I am trying to destroy. To escape this embarrassment a detour appears necessary.

29. Until now I have been assuming, like other commentators, that in biology the words *genos* and *eidos* serve the purpose of indicating animal classes. But that is quantitatively and, one may also say, qualitatively false. For while, as I noted above, *genos* is the normal term for designating an animal class of any level of generality, we have seen that the word *eidos* was much less used to indicate a class of animals. Equally, the *conceptual schema genos–eidos* ultimately is applied very little to classes of animals. But that is not at all surprising, since to apply this pair to animal classes is necessarily to undertake a classification, no matter how embryonic, of animals. Yet even without making reference to what I believe are the certain results of my book, we notice from a simple reading of the texts that such orderings of animals are rare in Aristotle, and far from having a value *in themselves*, they simply put in order the zoological given for purposes of a particular study. For example:

> We must now go on to describe the arrangement of the internal parts, and first of all those of the blooded animals, because this is the feature in which the greatest *genē* differ from the rest of the animals: they are blooded, whereas the others are bloodless. The former [greatest *genos*] includes man, those of the quadrupeds that are viviparous, as well as those of the quadrupeds that are oviparous, bird, fish, cetacean, and any other anonymous group there may be, [anonymous] because the *eidos* is not a *genos*, but an [*eidos*] which is simple in relation to the individuals, for example the serpent and the crocodile. Thus all the viviparous quadrupeds have an esophagus and a windpipe. (*HA* II.15 505b25, after P.P.)

The ordering of living things, visibly relying on a pre-existent 'common' knowledge, is simply a preamble to the 'serious' study, that of the 'internal parts'. Here the word *eidos* is used of a group which cannot be subdivided any more. But, and this is absolutely fundamental, *it cannot be subdivided in relation to the object of the study in progress, that of the internal parts.* Thus it is the identity – in his eyes and with his criteria and means of observations – of the internal organs which makes Aristotle say that serpents form an *eidos* but the cetaceans form a *genos*, while one may presume that Aristotle knew a greater number of species and varieties of serpents than of cetaceans. (Cf. Pellegrin 1986: 95ff., correcting my 1982: 120.)

30. But I want to go farther, to show that the use of the conceptual schema *genos–eidos* for designating animal classes is a *derivative use* which, for that very reason, undergoes what I have called, apropos of other concepts, a 'theoretical devaluation'. For if one reads the

biological corpus simultaneously putting aside taxonomic presuppositions and paying attention to the properties of the conceptual schema *genos–eidos*, one cannot fail to notice that this conceptual schema is applied preponderantly and *fully* not to animal classes but to the 'parts' of animals. We find that this practice is both announced and assumed in some of the passages generally thought to be 'taxonomic', where with remarkable intricacy, the schema *genos–eidos* is applied in turn to animal families and to the 'parts' of animals. Thus the famous passage, often cited, at the beginning of the *Historia Animalium* (1.1 486a14):

Some animals are the same in all their parts, and others are not the same; some parts are the same in *eidos*, as the nose or eye of a man in relation to the nose or eye of another man, flesh in relation to flesh and bone in relation to bone; and it is also in this way that we say of horses, as of other animals, that they are the same in *eidos*...Some parts are the same although differing according to the more and the less in animals which belong to the same *genos*.

Here it is the identity in *eidos* of the parts which is the basis of the identity in *eidos* of animal classes. That is not very surprising if one recalls that Aristotelian biology is fundamentally a 'moriology', a study of parts. I formulate this latter assertion prior to any possible polemic, simply appealing both to the biological corpus itself, which does not study species but *moria* or the functions of those *moria*, and Aristotle's own explicit declarations of intention, as when he declares, at the beginning of the *Parts of Animals*, in a passage too well known to be quoted, that it is better to study the common properties of animals than particular species. The polemic begins only with the interpretation of the *reasons* which Aristotle has for proceeding thus.[27] In Aristotle's biological treatises, then, whether in passages which present facts or in passages which try to explain them, we are dealing with *parts*: Aristotle divides into *eidē*, according to contrary determinations, the *genē* of blood, stomach, uterus, organs of local movement...And we see just from the vocabulary used that the division of the *moria* appeals to all the logical content of the conceptual schema *genos–eidos*. Aristotle in fact uses to describe the difference between the parts the 'technical' terms by which, in the logico-metaphysical works, he designates 'specific difference'. Thus, in the last three books of the *Parts of Animals*, if one eliminates the debatable and unclear cases, difference between the parts is expressed 11 times by the verb *diapherein*, 21 times by the word *diaphora*, seven times by the explicit mention of contraries (*enantia*

---

[27] My theses on Aristotle's 'moriology' are presented in my book, and more completely although on a more specific point in Pellegrin 1985.

and related words), this latter figure not including the much more
numerous cases where Aristotle resorts to particular contraries –
hot/cold, long/short, wide/narrow – to describe the *moria*, without
saying formally that it is a question of contraries.

31. I have shown elsewhere that there were precise theoretical
reasons, presented by Aristotle himself (particularly in Book I of the
Parts of Animals), why the correct division of a *genos* into *eidē* can only
be applied to *moria*.[28] The only examples which one may find in
Aristotle of a continued division of classes which would be, at least
from a distance, formally comparable to the division of the animal
and vegetable kingdoms practiced by the taxonomists of the classical
era, is applied to the *moria* and not to animal classes. Even so these
divisions remain very short (thus: footed→split-footed→polydactyl-
ous). In a more general way, although many of my colleagues remain
opposed to these views, I am convinced that the *moria* constitute the
cardinal level of Aristotelian biology, and that for Aristotle the
animal world is not thinkable – i.e., cannot be torn away from a
chaotic diversity – except in so far as, behind the flourishing diversity
of living forms, the biologist can find a repertoire of combinable parts
whose variations are themselves thinkable by the intermediary of
conceptual tools, the best example of which is perhaps the conceptual
schema *genos–eidos*. This of course does not mean that the *moria*
are the last stage of conceptual decomposition which the natural
philosopher – remember that biology is a branch of natural philosophy – can impose on the real: that is ultimately composed of the
four elements.[29]

32. In the end we see then that the conceptual schema, *genos–eidos*,
is indeed applied in biology, to animal classes and to *moria*. Thus
when it is applied to animal classes the pair *genos–eidos* rigorously
maintains the rules of subordination which regulate the relations of
these two concepts in the logico-metaphysical treatises: the *eidos* is

---

[28] The chief one of these reasons is that which I have called, in Pellegrin 1985, the 'rule of
homogeneity' which ought to regulate correct definitory division: it ought to function in
a homogeneous domain (in my book I called that an 'axis of division') excluding the
intersection of several domains. Thus the Platonists are subject to criticism because they
divide animals first into terrestrial and aquatic and then into wild and tame (*PA* 1.3
643b23), for from the point of view of the location of life, it is accidental for an animal
to be wild or not.

[29] In ch. 2 above (30–7) M. Furth distinguishes six steps in this conceptual decomposition:
(1) the simple bodies, i.e. the four elements which are themselves made of combinations
of primordial qualities (earth is cold and dry, water is cold and wet...); (2) the composite
bodies (*suntheta sōmata*) like metals, stones, 'pure' liquids; (3) the homoeomerous parts of
animals; (4) a level which Furth calls 'uniform to non-uniform': some of the viscera which
although having a complex structure (i.e., they are not amorphous) have a uniform
material (cf. *PA* II.1 646b30) – the heart is an example (*PA* II.1 647a31); (5) the
anhomoeomerous parts of animals; (6) whole animals.

always a sub-class of a *genos*. But it is only when the conceptual schema *genos–eidos* is applied to *moria* that it must have recourse to all the 'logical information' which it contains and that the division of the *genos* can be made according to *contrary eidē*. This distinction, which reminds us of the one which modern logicians make between 'strong logic' and 'weak logic', is not very surprising for the habitual reader of Aristotle, but in the end it is paradoxical. In the first place, it has resonances in the Aristotelian corpus, for in a 'system' fundamentally characterized, like that of Aristotle, by the multiple meanings of its concepts, the use of a notion not only in several senses, but also in *several degrees* is a normal and current practice. I will give only one example, apropos of the central concept of Aristotelian ontology, that of *ousia*. While he gives as characteristic of *ousia* to be 'separate' Aristotle qualifies as *ousiai* certain things which are not separated because, although they do not have that characteristic property of *ousia*, they have others equally characteristic of *ousia*. One may say that these things draw less than others from the logical content of the notion of *ousia*. Thus the substratum is *ousia* (*esti d' ousia to hupokeimenon, Metaph.* H.1 1042a26), but it is *less* that than the concrete composite of matter and form. One might say that the division of the parts according to the conceptual schema *genos–eidos* is 'more' a definitional division in the Aristotelian sense of the word than is the division of animal classes. Nevertheless it is paradoxical to discover that, by a sort of compensation, if it is to *moria* that the conceptual schema *genos–eidos* is applied the most *completely*, it is to animal classes that it is applied the most *explicitly*. Except for a few rare and ambiguous passages, discussed in my book, it is in fact only outside the biological corpus that Aristotle uses the words *genos* and *eidos* to speak of *moria*, while within the biological corpus he constantly applies to *moria* the 'technical' terminology of difference, differentiating, division according to contraries, etc. In fact it is in a passage like *Politics* iv.4 1290b25, which I have elsewhere analyzed in detail,[30] that we witness what could be called a full reconciliation, in regard both to content and to terminology, between the fields of application of the conceptual schema *genos–eidos*. This schema is applied sometimes to animal classes, sometimes to *moria*, with the latter level being determinant since it is the conjunction of the *moria* which makes possible animal diversity. I quote once more this passage:

If we were going to take (*labein*) the different kinds (*eidē*) of animals, we should first of all determine the organs which are indispensable to every animal, as for example

---

[30] Both in Pellegrin 1982 and in Pellegrin 1985.

some organs of sense and the instruments of receiving and digesting food, such as the mouth and the stomach, besides organs of locomotion. Assuming now that there are only so many kinds of organs, but that there may be differences (*diaphorai*) in them – I mean different kinds (*genē*) of mouths, and stomachs, and perceptive and locomotive organs – the possible combinations of these differences will necessarily furnish many varieties of animals. (For animals cannot be the same which have different kinds (*diaphoras*) of mouths or ears.) (Jowett tr., with minor alterations)

13
Kinds, forms of kinds, and the more and the less in Aristotle's biology*

JAMES G. LENNOX

I

Aristotle is often characterized, by both philosophers and evolutionary biologists, as the fountainhead of a typological theory of species that is absolutely inconsistent with evolutionary thinking.[1] D'Arcy Thompson, on the other hand, in his remarkable *On Growth and Form*,[2] claimed that the idea of using quantitative methods to help understand morphological relationships among animals of different species took root in his mind during his work on Aristotle's biology:

> Our inquiry lies, in short, just within the limits which Aristotle laid down when, in defining a genus, he showed that (apart from those superficial characters, such as colour, which he called 'accidents') the essential differences between one 'species' and another are merely differences of proportion, or relative magnitude, or as he phrased it, of 'excess and defect'.[3]

---

* The following is an attempt to integrate ideas originally presented in 'Aristotle on genera, species and "the more and the less"' (Lennox 1980) with ideas about the notion of being one in form which appear in 'Are Aristotelian species eternal?' (Lennox 1985a), a paper which was contributed to the Festschrift for David Balme (Gotthelf 1985a). A number of scholars have reached the conclusion recently that translating *genos* and *eidos* as 'genus' and 'species', unless these terms could be understood by all readers as merely conventional renderings of the Greek, is a dangerously misleading practice. Faced with this difficulty, I have opted in some contexts to transliterate and in others to render *genos* 'kind' and *eidos* 'form' (as in 'form of a kind'). This makes for some harshness, but the arguments presented by David Balme and Pierre Pellegrin has convinced me that some such move is required. The new title is not simply due to this change in translation, however. This paper represents a reconsideration of the issues and texts of its ancestor, rather than a 'revision' of it.

[1] Sir Karl Popper's verdict is perhaps more strongly worded than most: '...every discipline, as long as it used the Aristotelian method of definition, has remained arrested in a state of empty verbiage and barren scholasticism' (Popper 1952: II 9). Among philosophers of biology, David Hull has argued for precisely the same conclusion (Hull 1965–6). This position has been orthodoxy among neo-Darwinians, cf. Mayr 1963: 4; Dobzhansky 1970: 351; Simpson 1961: 46; Ghiselin 1969: 50–2. Recently, Professor Mayr has moderated his position considerably in the light of Professor Balme's research (cf. Mayr 1982: 11, 87–9, 149–54, 254–6, 636–8). Indeed, Mayr's is perhaps the most sympathetic treatment of Aristotle's biology by a historian of biology in this century. Mayr has separated Aristotle's non-evolutionary stance from his theory of natural kinds, whereas the texts noted above all assume that a typological essentialism on the latter topic was the primary reason why Aristotle adopted a non-evolutionary view of the zoological world.

[2] Orig. edn 1917; rev. edn 1942; abrdgd. edn 1971.   [3] Thompson 1971: 274.

A theory that asserts that species of a genus differ only in the relative magnitudes of their structures sounds very different, and might be thought to be incompatible with, a theory that claims that there are complete discontinuities between one *eidos* and all others. Can Aristotle consistently have held both these views? He can, and he did. To understand how he did so, one must understand the way in which he used the Academic technical notion of 'the more and the less' in his biology. It will be demonstrated that Aristotle treats variations between one form of a kind and another as differences of degree. Such a move conflicts with the sort of typological thinking traditionally ascribed to Aristotle by biologists and philosophers.[4] It will here be argued that Aristotle preserves the objective nature of biological kinds by stressing the teleological requirements of the lives of different organisms.

Being one in form and being one in kind are two ways in which numerically distinct entities can be the same, according to Aristotle. His many discussions of unity[5] lead us directly into the issue of how forms of a kind are differentiated from one another.

An individual is numerically one in virtue of being either naturally (e.g., a cat), artificially (e.g., table) or accidentally (e.g., a pool of water) physically continuous.[6] Two or more numerically distinct individuals may, nonetheless, be one in form (*hen eidei*). By this Aristotle seems to mean that they are structured or function in some sense identically, though the organization and functioning occur in discontinuous, self-subsistent bodies.[7] Organisms of different forms may yet be one in kind (*hen genei*).

In the next three sections of this paper (II–IV), I take up the issue of how Aristotle distinguishes forms of a kind; then I shall return to the question of the nature of the identity of animals that are one in form.

---

[4] By 'typological essentialism' I intend a view that there is some one identical feature or set of features in which individuals of a kind share or 'participate', and in virtue of which the individuals are said to belong to the kind. Indeed, on this view the species name might be viewed as having primary application to this essence, and only secondary reference to individuals. Aristotelian forms are occasionally taken to be such shared essences. Thus one aim of this paper is to discuss the evidence in Aristotle, and especially in his biology, for a non-typological essentialism which might be referred to as 'teleological essentialism'.

[5] *Metaph.* Δ.6 1016b32ff.; Δ.9 1018a7ff.; *Metaph.* I.1 1052a15ff.; *PA* 1.4 644a15–23, 644b1–16; *HA* 1.1 486a15ff.; *Top.* 1.7 103a6–16.

[6] *Metaph.* I.1 1052a15–30. Natural things, which have an inherent source of their remaining one, are one in a more unqualified way than artificial unities or heaps.

[7] *Metaph.* Δ.6 1016a32–1017a7; Z.8 1034a1–7; I.3 1054b16–17; 9 1058b6–12.

II

Aristotle offers two different, and not obviously related, accounts of what it is for different sorts of organisms to be one in kind. In the *Metaphysics* the *genos* is often described as the matter or substratum for differentiation into sub-kinds, *eidē*. In the *PA* and *HA* on the other hand, *eidē* are said to be one in kind provided their parts for the most part only differ in degree, that is, by 'the more and the less'. If their differences are predominantly greater than this, they may be described as one only by analogy.[8]

It is only in the biological works that Aristotle uses the concepts of 'the more and the less' or 'excess and deficiency'[9] to express the nature of the relationship between biological (i.e., substantial) *genē* and *eidē*, though the basis for this application is established in the *Metaphysics*.[10] The logic of these concepts is clear in the *Categories* and plainly derives from the *Philebus*. I shall contend that these two apparently quite different accounts of the *genos–eidos* relationship are in fact closely related to one another. As a consequence of this argument, it should become clear that Aristotle's essentialism is *not* typological, nor is it in any obvious way 'anti-evolutionary'.[11] Whatever it was that Darwin was up against, it was not Aristotelian essentialism.

Here are two passages from the biology which make use of the notions of 'excess and defect' and 'more and less' in characterizing the relationship that holds among forms of a kind.

Parts of Animals 1.4 644a16–21: For all kinds that differ by degree (*kath' huperochēn*) and by the more and the less have been linked under one kind, while all those that

[8] Lungs and gills, which are both used for cooling on Aristotle's understanding, are analogous structures (*PA* 1.5 645b8); as are bone and cartilage (*PA* 11.8 653b32ff.). In distinguishing extensive kinds from one another, this term usually refers to a relationship between structures which at a very abstract level perform a similar function for their possessors, but do so by different means, and are not structural variations on a common theme, i.e. are not open to more/less comparison.

[9] *Huperochē kai elleipsis* is often rendered 'excess and defect', which has unfortunate connotations of a norm which properties 'fall away from' or 'overreach'. As will be clear, all Aristotle means by this phrase is variation *in degree* rather than by *discrete units*. Likewise with *to mallon kai hētton*. The former phrase possesses greater generality and may have come into use later than the latter. Cf. *Metaph.* H.2 1042b32–5; *PA* iv.12 692b3–6; *HA* 1.1 486a1–16.

[10] Especially, as I shall argue, in *Metaph.* H.2.

[11] Let me stress that what I mean by this is that his theory of natural kinds is not in any obvious way 'anti-evolutionary'. As I have argued elsewhere ('Are Aristotelian species eternal?') there are many deep reasons for his not holding an evolutionary theory with respect to the origins of living things, but these do not include his theory of natural kinds, nor are they implications of it. I am not, as I have sometimes been taken to be, arguing that Aristotle could have easily adopted an evolutionary theory. He knew of a number of such theories, and (quite rightly, I believe, given the context) rejected them as implausible.

are analogous have been separated. I mean that bird differs from bird by the more or by degree (for one is long-feathered, another is short-feathered)...

> *Parts of Animals* 1.4 644b8–15: The kinds have been marked off mainly by the shapes (*ta schēmata*) of the parts and of the whole body, wherever they bear a similarity as the birds do when compared among themselves and the fishes, cephalopods and testaceans. For their parts differ not on the basis of analogous likeness, as bone in man is to spine in fish, but rather by bodily affections such as largeness and smallness, softness and hardness, smoothness and roughness, and such – in general by the more and the less.[12]

According to the account of kinds and forms of kinds in *PA* I and *HA* I, a kind is to be viewed as constituted of a set of general differentiae (*katholou diaphorai*),[13] features common to every bird or fish, *qua* bird or fish. What distinguishes the members of one form of a kind from another is the way in which these general differentiae are further determined. The length, width, texture, density, arrangement, even the number[14] of this general feature may differ in measurable ways from one member of the kind to the next. Birds, *qua* birds, have beaks, for example. Different sorts of birds may have beaks of differing length, width, hue, hardness, curvature. It is these sorts of differences, throughout all the differentiae of the general kind, which differentiate one form of bird from another. Along any parameter one may choose, then, each organ will differ only by shades and degrees from one kind to the next. Aristotle's works don't come supplied with pictures, but Figures 1 and 2 beautifully illustrate Aristotle's account of the relationship among the features of different forms of a kind.

Aristotle's use of these concepts has its roots in Plato's *Philebus*. During the provocative discussion of the mixture of the limit and the unlimited, Socrates contrasts features of the world which are without qualification unlimited from those which can be said to possess limit. The former group include,

> drier and wetter, higher and lower, quicker and slower, greater and smaller, and everything that we brought together a while ago as belonging to that kind of being which admits of the more and the less. (25c5–8)

---

[12] Cf. *HA* I. 486a21–b16; II. 497b1–15, 500b5; III. 516b4–34, 517b22–3; IV. 528b11–23; VIII. 588a24–31; *PA* IV. 692b3–6.

[13] *PA* I.3 642b24–6. The contrast, well brought out in Balme's translation, is between *general* differentiae and their more determinate forms at a more particular (*kath' hekaston*) level.

[14] Cf. *HA* I.1 486b7–12. A clear example of Aristotle treating many/few variations as variations in degree of a common organ is *HA* II.13 505a8–20, which provides examples of fish that have one, two, four, five and eight gills per side, a discussion which begins: 'And again, some fish have few gills, others a great number; but all have an equal number on each side.'

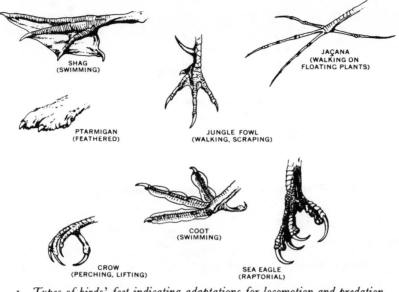

SHAG
(SWIMMING)

JAÇANA
(WALKING ON
FLOATING PLANTS)

PTARMIGAN
(FEATHERED)

JUNGLE FOWL
(WALKING, SCRAPING)

COOT
(SWIMMING)

CROW
(PERCHING, LIFTING)

SEA EAGLE
(RAPTORIAL)

1. *Types of birds' feet indicating adaptations for locomotion and predation.*
Source: *J. A. Thomson,* The Biology of Birds, *as reprinted in*
The Encyclopaedia Britannica, 14*th edn., Chicago* 1970.

The latter

don't admit of these terms, but admit of all the opposite terms like 'equal' and
'equality' in the first place, then 'double' and any term expressing a ratio of one
number to another, or one unit of measurement to another... (*Phlb.* 25a6–b1; cf.
Plt. 283c3–284b2)

In the *Topics*, the phrase *to mallon kai hētton* has the flavor of a
technical expression, and is one of the *topoi* under which various
opinions can be challenged or supported.[15]

In the *Categories*, 'more and less' plays a central role in explicating
and distinguishing the categories of substance, quantity and quality.
For example,

Substance, it seems, does not admit of a more and a less... For example, if the
substance is a man, it will not be more a man or less a man either than itself or
than another man.[16]

Qualities, on the other hand, 'admit of a more and less; for one thing
is called more or less pale than another' (*Cat.* 10b26–8). This is true
when 'both [things] admit of the account of what is under discussion'

[15] *Top.* II.11 115b3–11; III.3 118a27–b10; IV.6 127b18–25; V.8 137b24.
[16] *Cat.* 5 3b33. This seems to echo the suggestion of *Phaedo* 93d1–e2, 93a14–b6, that a soul
taken by itself can't be more or less a soul than any other.

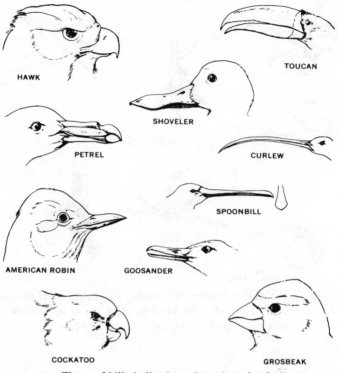

2. *Types of bills indicating adaptations for feeding.*
Source: *J. A. Thomson*, The Biology of Birds, *as reprinted in*
The Encyclopaedia Britannica, 14*th edn., Chicago* 1970.

(*Cat.* 11a11),[17] i.e. both are pale, though different shades of pale. Given that Aristotle treats the color spectrum as itself a continuum between dark and pale, one could presumably refer to an object, insofar as it was colored, as more or less dark or pale as well. Thus the claim is that, while Socrates cannot be more or less *human* than Callias, he may be more or less pale than Callias.

The *Categories* is innocent of the matter/form distinction, and free of the close association between *eidos* and *diaphora* which is so central to the *Metaphysics*. Indeed, the categorical status of *diaphora* in the *Categories* is left entirely unclear.[18] Like *genē*, differentiae and their accounts may be said of *eidē* and of individuals, but they are not granted even secondary substancehood. Nor are they ever mentioned as belonging to any other category.

[17] Cf. *Ph.* v.2 226b3; *Sens.* 7 448a13–16.
[18] *Cat.* 5 3a21–b9; cf. Ackrill 1963: 85–7. The *Topics*, however, states quite clearly that the differentia signifies a certain qualification of the *genos*; cf. *Top.* iv.2 122b20–3; iv.6 128a25–9.

It is probably with the *Categories'* discussion of substance and the more and less in mind that *Metaphysics* H.3 notes that,

> just as a number does not possess the more and the less, neither does the substance in virtue of the form (*kata to eidos*), but if it does possess the more and less, it is substance with the matter that does so. (1044a10–11)

The picture of natural substances as unities with material and formal aspects, the achievement of *Metaph.* H, suggests that the *Cat.* statement needs qualification: Socrates cannot be more or less a human than Callias *kata to eidos*. That is, the account which refers to them in abstraction from the different ways in which they actually embody human characteristics will not mention the more/less variations between them. But Socrates and Callias are 'this matter and this form here, and humans are such taken generally' (*Metaph.* Z.8 1033b24–6, 10 1035b28–32, 11 1037a5–7); and as such – as substances with matter (*ousia meta tēs hulēs*) – they can differ by the more and the less.

Indeed, this conclusion is implicit in the chapter immediately preceding, *Metaph.* H.2. Assuming that being a substrate or matter is potential being, Aristotle turns to an exploration of the *actual being* of sensible things (1042b9–11). Taking a hint from Democritus, he notes that the same material substrate is able to *be* different things. The chapter is an exploration of the *differences* which make the same material *be* different sorts of things. 'Excess and defect'[19] is introduced as a general term for the ways in which sensible affections (*pathēmata*) can differ (1042b22–5), and in this context *animal parts* are discussed.

> In some cases their being will be defined in all these ways, by being mixed in some cases, blended, contained, and condensed in others, and by having the other differentiae as well, just as a hand or a foot is. So we must grasp the kinds of differentiae, for these will constitute the origins of being: differences in respect of the more and less, density and rarity, and the other such differences. For all these are excess and defect. (*Metaph.* H.2 1042b29–35)[20]

The parts of animals are ultimately constructed out of the four elements, constituted of the qualities hot, cold, wet and dry.[21] *PA* II.1 notes that the other *pathē* of bodies – lightness, heaviness, density, rarity, roughness and smoothness and so on – follow from these (646a13–21). Uniform parts are constructed out of the four elements with these various second-order differentiae, and in turn such

---

19 *Huperochē kai elleipsis*. From here on I will freely exchange this full but misleading translation for the less misleading paraphrase 'variation in degree'. Cf. n. 8 above.
20 Cf. Furth forthcoming: §24.
21 The following is highly schematic. For a fuller discussion, cf. Furth, ch. 2 above, 30–7.

non-uniform parts as hand and foot are constructed out of these. Throughout, the relation of the less complex to more complex constituents in the process is teleological, the qualities acquired by the various parts at each stage being appropriate to and required for the functions to be performed by these parts in the organism's life (646b11–19). The uniform parts will differ along a limited number of qualitative parameters: harder/softer, more liquid/more solid, more flexible/more brittle – while the non-uniform parts constructed from them may have many such differentiae in various combinations for different ends.

for a different power (*dunamis*) will be useful to the hand relative to pressing and to grasping. (646b24–5)

The parts of animals, then, are materials differing with respect to the sorts of perceptible qualities acquired during development. And it is just these qualities which are said to differ by excess and defect, or the more and the less. But animal parts are also among the differentiae which constitute the nature or being of an animal. Thus, should one wish to distinguish one sort of bird from another, it will be in part by noting the differences in degree between the parts of one and the parts of another – thicker or thinner bone or blood, heavier or lighter body, thicker or thinner beak, and so on. The discussion of *Metaph.* H.2 then, suggests treating animal differentiae as constituted of just those qualitative features which the *Categories* had shown to differ by the more and the less.

Between *Categories*, *Metaphysics* H.3 and *Parts of Animals* 1, we have four distinct statements about the relationship between substances and the more and the less.

1. Socrates is not more or less a human than Callias.
2. Socrates *qua* form does not have more and less, but Socrates *qua* form with matter does.
3. Socrates may be more or less pale than Callias, but only if both are, in general, pale.
4. One bird may differ from another bird by more and less, though both are birds.

There is a position Aristotle could have adopted which is able to incorporate all four of these claims, namely, the following.

For two individuals to differ in degree, they must both be the same general sort of thing. With respect to that *sort* they do not differ in degree. But the general sort is constituted of *features with range* – any sub-kind may have those features exemplified by different specifications of that range.

With this position in hand, our four claims can be dealt with in the following manner: there is a general *logos* of human being which applies equally to Socrates and Callias; but the precise way in which Socrates is the realization of one of the features specified in that *logos* may differ in degree from the way in which Callias is; for example, while the flesh of each is equally human, Socrates' may be more or less pale or soft than Callias';[22] and this is true at any level of generality – sparrows and eagles have the same *logos qua bird*, but the *logos* of bird specifies *features with range*; thus, while sparrow and eagle may not differ with respect to having wings, beaks, or feathers, they may differ in having the sensible properties of those organs specified on a different region of that range.

It will be my contention that the elements of such a position are to be found in the *Metaphysics* but only explicitly stated in the biological works.

There are, of course, differences in the three discussions of the more and less I've examined. *Metaph.* H indicates a willingness to speak of features which make something what it is – differentiae – as differing in degree from those which make something *else* what it is. The *Categories* is mute on whether this could be the case. Again, *Metaph.* H introduces the notion of an organ as an organized *complex* of all sorts of such differences. *PA* I takes the further step of referring to the substances themselves (e.g., birds, fish, crustacea) as differing in degree relative to some general kind to which they belong. Thus not only can the differentiating features be said to differ in degree from one form of a kind to another – the forms of the kind themselves can be said to differ by degree, or by the more and the less, from each other.

III

The suggestion I wish to put forward now is that the standard *Metaphysics* account of the relationship between a kind and its forms underlies Aristotle's willingness to see forms of a kind as differing only by the more and less from one another.

Aristotle's account of *genos* in the *Metaphysics* is anything but extensional – that is, a *genos* is not primarily a class with members. Typically, a *genos* is represented as a substratum (*hupokeimenon*) or material (*hulē*) for differentiation.[23] Richard Rorty has suggested that the motivation for this account of *genos* is Aristotle's concern to stress the material/formal unity of his primary substances.[24] A second,

---

[22] Compare *Metaph.* I.9 1058b1–16.

[23] Cf. *Metaph.* Δ.6 1016a27, 28 1024b8; Z.12 1038a6–7; H.6 1045a35; I.3 1054b30; 8 1058a23–4; *PA* I.3 643a24–7.

[24] The role of the notion of *genos* as matter in the *Metaphysics* was the subject of an exchange between Richard Rorty and Marjorie Grene some years ago. Cf. Rorty 1973; Grene 1974;

related motivation, as *Metaph.* I strongly suggests, is the need to account for the identity of individuals which are different in form. What is the basis of our ability to see birds *as* birds, however different in form they may be?

Recent work on the concepts of *genos* and *eidos* can, I believe, illuminate, and in turn be illuminated by, the doctrine of *genos* as matter.

As Professor Balme has argued, the alleged equivocity of the term *eidos* is 'both more extensive and more innocent'[25] than is commonly supposed. In fact, the research of Pierre Pellegrin suggests that 'equivocity' is an inappropriate description of the fact that *eidos* (or *genos*) can refer to organisms at different levels of generality. To be a form is to be a *determinate realization* of a kind. Socrates is a determinate realization of human nature, as water-fowl is a determinate realization of bird. The fact that things at various levels of generality can be, according to this account, *eidē* does not render the concept equivocal.[26]

The claim that a kind is 'as matter' is the other side of this coin. Organisms which differ in form can be seen as different progressive determinations of a more general kind. To refer to a parrot and a blue jay as birds is to ignore (i.e., remove from my account) the way in which beak, feather, wing, legs, crop, etc., are differently realized in each. Similarly when I refer to two individual birds as parrots; in doing so I leave out of account the peculiar ways in which each realizes his parrot features. The *genos* is that which can be determined in various different ways – the generic potential, to use Montgomery Furth's expression. But this is just to say that the account of the *genos* will list what I previously referred to as *features with range* relative to

Rorty 1974. Grene finds a common thread in the work of Rorty, A. C. Lloyd and David Balme which sees in the notion of *genos* as matter no mere metaphor, but an integral part of Aristotle's account of natural substances. She argues that one possible 'interpretation of *genos* [i.e. category] as "material"...pertinent to the study of nature...is that "matter" is simply the unity of categoreal context open for distinctions of more and less – a very metaphorical meaning, which can not be identified with the concrete, worked up matter "out of which" the sculptor makes his bronze statue or the father his son' (120). I can't see why the first meaning of 'matter' is very metaphorical or how 'bronze', as the name for what can become many different sorts of (bronze) thing and which is common to them all, is matter in any sense radically different from 'bird' as the name for what can become many different sorts of bird and which is common to them all. I think it is extremely important that the 'lexicon' entry under *genos* (*Metaph.* Δ.28) does *not* distinguish these two cases, nor do the discussions of being one in *genos* – nor do the passages in *Metaph.* I that Grene relies on for the first sense. Balme's reply to Grene, quoted in n. 10 of her paper, seems to belie the necessity, at least for natural kinds, of the sort of distinction she wishes to find.

[25] Ch. 11 above.
[26] Cf. Pellegrin 1982: ch. 2, and ch. 12 above.

the next stage of realization or actuality. Understood in this way, it is clear that the term has no fixed taxonomic reference.

The doctrine of *genos* as matter is introduced in three distinct contexts in the *Metaphysics*: in the discussions of levels of unity in *Metaph.* Δ.6 and 8, and I.3; in the discussions of the relationship between forms and their kinds in *Metaph.* Z.12 and I.7–8; and in the discussion of the meaning of *genos* in *Metaph.* Δ.28. The summary of this last passage will serve as a useful starting-point.

> *Genos*, then, is used in all these ways, in virtue of a continuous generation of the same form, in virtue of the first mover being like in form, and as matter (*hōs hulē*); for that thing of which the differentiae and the quality are such is the substrate, which we call matter. (1024b7–10)[27]

Similarly in *Metaph.* I.8 the *genos* is referred to as the matter of the things of that *genos*, and in a context which is of direct relevance to our discussion.[28] The subject of this chapter is the relationship between things which are different in form (*to heteron tōi eidei*). It opens by declaring that

> That which is different in form from something is different in respect of something,[29] and this must be common to both; for example, if an animal is said to be different in form [from some other animal], both must be animals. Therefore the things which are different in form must be in the same kind. (1057b35–7)

The notion of kind as matter is introduced to clarify the role played by the kind which is common to its different forms, yet differentiated in each (1058a1–5). The animal itself, as he says, is both a horse and a man. Each is a different articulation of the features with range that constitute the nature of the *genos* animal.

The significance of this picture of the *genos–eidos* relation can be grasped by contrasting it with an alternative picture which commits the error Aristotle wishes to avoid. Horses and humans, according to this alternative model, would be identified as animals in virtue of one set of absolutely identical features in each, and distinguished from one another by an entirely different set of completely unrelated features. Certain aspects of modern technology exemplify this model, or could quite easily. Imagine, for example, that there was a 'basic' Porsche 911, and that the different 'models' of it consisted of this basic automobile onto which different features, *not present at all* on the basic model, are appended (FM radio, automatic transmission, air

---

[27] As Pellegrin has noted (Pellegrin 1985) the analysis in this chapter makes *genos* the most appropriate word for stressing the historical continuity of a kind: 'the continuous generation of things with the same form'. As Balme and Pellegrin document fully, *genos* is by far the most common term to denote animal groups in the biological works.

[28] Cf. *Metaph.* I.8 1058a23–5.

[29] Following Ross 1924: 301, I take the *ti* here as an accusative of respect.

foil, racing stripes, mud flaps, etc.). That is, the kind does *not* consist
of features with range, but rather completely determinate features;
and the features of the forms of the kind are *not* determinate
realizations of the generic features, but features 'added on' to the
generic features. There is no unity to the genus and differentiae, of
the sort Aristotle is seeking. The *genos* and differentiae appear in an
account of a substance as two distinct elements, and a major concern
of *Metaph.* Z-H is to explain how substances are unities in spite of
this apparent duality in the account of their being. *Metaph.* Z.12
introduces its discussion of definition by division with the *aporia*,
'That of which we say the account is a definition – why is it one; for
example "the animal biped" as definition of the human (for this is
the *logos* of man) – why is this human one and not many, animal and
biped?' (1037b12–14). And in *Metaph.* H.6 it is clear whom he takes
to have held such a splintered view of substance.

What is it, then, which makes the human one, i.e. why is it one but not many, for
example both the animal and the biped, especially if there is, as some say, some
animal itself and some biped itself. (1045a14–17)

On this view, it will be noted, the *genos* could exist without its *eidē*.
But this is just what Aristotle wishes to deny:

If then the kind does not exist without qualification apart from the forms as forms
of a kind, or if it exists it exists as matter (for the voice is a kind and matter, but
the differentiae produce the forms, i.e., the syllables, from this), it is apparent that
the definition is the account which derives from the differentiae. (*Metaph.* Z.12
1038a6–9)[30]

Aristotle insists on the parasitic nature of kinds because they
constitute simply the potential for a number of distinct realizations.
This is the conception of the *genos–eidos* relation which emerges from
Metaphysics Z.12. Aristotle stresses that division ought to proceed by
treating each previous stage of a division as the 'substrate' for the
next stage – 'divide by the differentia of the differentia' as he puts
it (1038a10–11). If being footed is a differentia of animal, the next
division should be into sorts of footed animals, not into footed animals
that are winged or wingless – look for the differentia of footed animal
qua footed (*Metaph.* Z.12 1038a10–16).[31]

The *Metaphysics* works throughout with simple, schematic examples which in certain ways suggest that Aristotle has not yet integrated the idea of a *genos* as the substratum of distinct realizations
in its different forms, with the doctrine that the differentiae of
animals within a kind vary only by the more and the less. The typical

[30] Compare *Phlb.* 17a–c.
[31] Cf. Balme, ch. 4 above, 73–80, on the methodological importance of this idea.

genos is 'animal', rather than the extensive kinds (*megista genē*) such as bird or fish of the biology – and the organs of forms of *this* kind will *not* typically vary only in degree. The *genos* itself is not said to be constituted of many general differentiae, and therefore the corollary of this conception, division proceeding simultaneously through many axes of differentiation, is never discussed.[32] Finally, in the biology the distinction between 'one in kind' and 'one by analogy' is typically drawn in terms of whether the majority of organs differ only in degree, or more extensively. The same distinction is drawn in the *Metaphysics*, but not on these grounds.[33]

The account of the relationship that holds among animals different in form but the same in kind which is so carefully worked out in *PA* 1.2–4 is based both on the concept of a *genos* as a substratum for differentiation into its *eidē*, and on the concept of organic parts as materials differentiated by a complex of more/less variations in their perceptible affections. But while in the *Metaphysics* these ideas are introduced in different contexts and are not obviously related, in *PA* 1.2–4 these two conceptions are integrated into a richer and more realistic understanding of the *genos–eidos* relationship.

IV

The general picture of division adopted by Aristotle in *PA* 1.2–3, which is developed in the context of pointing out the errors involved in dividing dichotomously by one differentia at a time, is clear from the following.

If man were merely a thing with toes, this method would have shown it to be his one differentia. But since in fact he is not, he must necessarily have many differentiae not under one division. Yet more than one cannot belong to the same object under one dichotomy, but one dichotomy must end with one at a time. So it is impossible to obtain any of the particular animals by dichotomous division. (644a6–10)

This indicates the artificiality of the *Metaph*. Z.12 discussion, and points the way to a more complex methodology.

One should try to take the animals by kinds in the way already shown by the popular distinction between *bird* kind and *fish* kind. Each of these has been marked off by many differentiae, not dichotomously. (*PA* 1.3 643b10–13)

These are general differentiae – the natures of the various forms of these kinds must be grasped by seeing how each of these general differentiae is realized distinctly in those forms.

---

[32] Cf. Balme, ch. 4 above, 73.
[33] Cf. *Metaph*. Δ.6 1016a31–5; Δ.8 1018a12–15.

But the general differentiae must have forms, for otherwise what would make it a general differentia and not a particular one? Some differentiae certainly are general and have forms, for example *featheredness*: the one feather is *unsplit*, the other *split*. And footedness similarly is *many-toed*, *two-toed* (the cloven-hoofed), and *toeless* and undivided (the solid-hoofed). (*PA* 1.3 642b25–31)

This picture of the differentiation of the general kind into its various forms is not viewed as a replacement of the idea that the kind is the substrate of differentiation, but rather an enrichment of it. In the midst of his discussion of the problems of 'dividing as the dichotomists do' he pauses to remind us that

It is the differentia in the matter that is the form. For just as there is no part of animal that is without matter, so there is none that is only matter...(*PA* 1.3 643a24–5)

Balme comments:

Aristotle may be referring to the physical matter or to the logical genus. But it makes no difference here (does it anywhere?). Each is one way of considering *that which is potentially X*.[34]

Having introduced multiple divisions of general differentiae as the way to achieve an account of biological kinds, he next, in the passages I noted on pp. 341–2, notes that these differences will be in degree.

And thus we have returned to those passages from *PA* 1.4 with which I began. To those, I now add a passage from *HA* 1.1 which brings out clearly the relevance of *Metaphysics* H.2 to the biological discussion of forms of a kind.

Some things are, on the one hand, the same, yet differ by excess and defect, namely those for which the *genos* is the same. And I call such things as bird and fish a *genos*; for each of these has a generic difference, and there are many forms of fish and birds. Now on the whole most of the parts in these cases differ besides by oppositions of their affections, e.g., color and shape, by the same feature being affected in some cases more and in some less, again by [the parts] being more or fewer, and larger and smaller, and generally speaking by excess and defect. For some are soft-fleshed and others hard-fleshed, some have long beaks and others short beaks, some have many feathers and some few feathers. What is more some even among these animals have different parts belonging to different animals; some have spurs while others don't, and some have crests while others don't. But speaking of the majority of cases, from which the entire body is composed, these parts are either the same or differ in the oppositions and according to excess and defect; for the more and less one might place under excess and defect. (486a23–b16)[35]

[34] Balme 1972: 114 *ad* 643a24.
[35] At 486b1 I have taken *para* as setting apart the class of affections with opposition from those differences which follow, although aware that sensible affections are also cases of features which can differ in degree. The primary reason for doing so is that the examples which follow correspond to the other three forms of difference, more/less, more/fewer, larger/smaller, while the examples for affections with opposition come immediately after the *para tas tōn pathēmatōn enantiōseis*. Both Thompson and Peck take the datives in lines 6–8 to be governed by this phrase, although Thompson's paraphrase in *On Growth and Form*

A number of the details of this passage are worth noting, for they are crucial to the actual comparisons among animals which Aristotle makes in practice, yet are not stressed in the more theoretical passages in *PA* 1.4. First, it is stressed that not *all* the parts of animals of different forms within a kind need differ by the more and less, or in degree. Some parts may be undifferentiated from one form to another, others may appear in some forms and not at all in others. Second, there is an attempt to distinguish between various sorts of difference in degree – between variations in affective quality, in magnitude, and in number, and examples are provided of each. Aristotle could have chosen the same part to exemplify all of these types of variations. Bird feathers will be many in some forms, few in others, longer in some, shorter in others, harder in some, softer in others, and so on. Once this sinks in, the complexity of the study of animal differentiae upon which he is here embarking reveals itself.

V

Based on ideas about the nature of kinds, forms of kinds, and differentiation explored in the *Metaphysics*, the zoology builds a rich and complex picture of how different forms of a kind may be related to one another – how, though animals may be different *eidei*, they may be one *genei*. But that picture may suggest that there is no clear, objective means of identifying organisms that are one in form. Two closely related forms *A* and *B* will differ only in degree from one another, and one might draw the conclusion from this fact that distinctions between members of *A* and members of *B* might be quite arbitrary. Groupings below the level of extensive kinds such as bird or cephalopod might plausibly be viewed as mere conventions.

Nonetheless Aristotle does maintain on the one hand that the organisms of an extensive kind differ only in degree among themselves, *and* on the other that they fall into *indivisible forms*, groups of numerically distinct organisms which are *hen eidei*. Having dwelt on the non-typological aspects of Aristotle's thinking, I now wish to argue that he maintains the notion of sub-groups within kinds which are *formally identical*, which I take to be a sort of essentialism.[36]

(Thompson 1971) makes the *para* even more contrastive than I have. The three cases Aristotle gives of variation in degree do not well suit the description 'by oppositions of affection'. I would suggest he gives this as one sort of variation, and then goes on to list three others. At the end of the passage he may be suggesting a unification of all four under 'excess and defect'.

[36] The following material in this section is excerpted from 'Are Aristotelian species eternal?' (Lennox 1985a) with the kind permission of Mathesis Publications. The argument

Let us begin by asking Aristotle to be more precise about what it is for the members of a sub-kind to be one in form. Why should we not treat the organisms of an extensive kind as 'just one big happy family'?

It is certainly not that at a certain level of generality organisms cease differing in degree from one another. Aristotle does not restrict the notion of being one in form to perfectly identical twins. In fact, he is quite explicit that things which are one in form may nonetheless differ in degree, by the more and less, from one another.[37]

In the *Metaphysics*, in discussing the notion of being one in form, Aristotle makes this notion dependent on that of indivisibility in conception (*hē noēsis* – 1016b2, 1052a32, 35) or indivisibility in account (*ho logos* – 1016b33, 1052a33, 36), in contrast to things numerically one which are physically indivisible.

Again, things are called one the account of the essence (*ho logos ho to ti ēn einai*) of which is indivisible relative to another which reveals the thing's essence. For just by itself every account is divisible. (1016a33–5)[38]

This passage indicates that it is not having just any account in common that makes many things one in form – the account must also reveal what it is to be the thing in question. An account of the kind would do this, of course, but it is *divisible* (into accounts of its various forms). Among accounts which make clear what a thing is, there is one which relative to the kind being defined is not further divisible and which is common to many things. Those things which share such an account are one in form.[39]

This passage makes another important point. We are told that by itself every account is divisible. 'By itself' in this passage is placed

developed there is that individuals secure eternality of a sort for themselves through reproduction, by creating something one in form with themselves. Crucial to this argument, and to the acceptability of the material reproduced here, is an understanding of what it means to be one in form. I argue that Aristotle is strongly opposed to a theory which explicates formal unity in terms of participation in numerically one form, and that he would find the suggestion of Albritton and others that forms of individuals may themselves be one in form unacceptable because open to 'Third Man' objections. I argue that it is matter/form unities, *sunola*, that may be one in form, meaning that they share an account which specifies their essence, an account which, were it more precise, would not reveal anything further about their essence. Thus there is, to use Professor Balme's language, a level of formal description which is privileged from the *scientific* point of view. We may as well stop division at that point, for we will not learn anything by further divisions about that thing relevant to its being what it is.

37 Cf. *Metaph.* I.3 1054b6, *NE* VIII.1 1155b11–15; Balme, ch. 11 above, 296–7.

38 At 1016a34 all the manuscripts read *ti ēn einai to pragma*. Ross finds only one other parallel of the accusative with *ti ēn einai* at 1029b14 which he says 'is suspect'. But the manuscripts are again unanimous, and Ross relies on his mistrust of 1016a34 to alter *that* text. Thus I translate the manuscripts.

39 Compare *PA* I. 642b7–20, 643a8–12, 643a24–6; *Metaph.* Z.8 1034a5, 12 1038a16.

in opposition to 'relative to another account which reveals the thing's essence'. That is, this account may be further divisible, but not into further 'essence-revealing' accounts. In any division, a point will be reached beyond which further division will not further reveal features essential to the kind in question.

Can we provide any concrete, taxonomic specification of that point? I think not. Two principles of Aristotle's approach to definition militate against doing so. The first is his willingness to seek definitions for kinds at various levels of generality.[40] What is incidental to being a bird may be essential to being a wading bird, or a crane, or a sandhill crane. Thus a feature is 'essential' or 'incidental' only relative to the kind being defined, not in itself.

Take the example of a bird's legs as part of what it is to be a bird again. Birds are by nature bipedal, but bipedal in a particular way: their legs bend at the 'knee' in the opposite direction to the other, true bipeds, human beings. Birds may have long or short legs, legs with webbed feet or unwebbed feet, and so on. Having *long* legs or *webbed* feet is not essential to being a bird – and if we were giving an account of what it is to be a bird, dividing down the leg axis further than 'backward-bending biped' would reveal nothing further about what it is to be a bird. On the other hand, if we were seeking to give an account of what it is to be a crane, reference to the length of leg would be crucial and thus 'backward-bending biped' would be divisible into a 'more revealing' account of the crane's nature.

In the above example division stopped short of quantitative (more/less) differentiation. One might think this is precisely the point at which division would cease to reveal anything but inessential variations. But we have seen that Aristotle treats the *eidē* of his extensive kinds as, for the most part, differing only in this way. And this is not a merely theoretical claim which is ignored in practice. Take the opening remarks of his chapter on the external part of Birds in *PA* IV.12.

Among the birds, the differentiation relative to each other is in the excess and deficiency of the parts, that is, according to the more and the less. For some are long-legged, some short-legged, some have a broad and some a narrow tongue; and similarly as well in the other parts. (692b3–6)

If such distinctions were, in some absolute sense, incidental, Aristotle would be unable to offer an account of anything below the level of the nine extensive kinds he recognized.

The second principle which rules out the possibility of specifying in advance a taxonomic level below which division will descend to

[40] Cf. the evidence for this collected in Gotthelf 1985b, summarized above, ch. 7, 190–2.

the incidental also tells against more/less variations being necessarily incidental. It is that, at least in regard to living things, the 'essence/ accident' distinction is a distinction between those features which are required by the kind of life an animal lives and those which aren't. If a crane is to survive and flourish, it *must* have, not simply 'long' legs, but legs of a certain length, defined relative to its body, neck length, environment, feeding habits, and so on.

Whichever birds live in swamps and eat plants have a broad beak, this sort being useful for digging and for the uprooting and cropping of their food. (*PA* iv.12 693a15–17)

Certain of the birds are long-legged. And a cause of this is that the life of such birds is marsh-bound; and nature makes organs relative to their function, not the function relative to the organ. (694b12–15)

At a slightly more specific level, similar explanations are offered in this chapter for a number of features of 'the crook-taloned birds' and the 'water fowl'. The stress is constantly on the way in which the differentiation of a feature is related to its possessor's life. For example, the discussion of beak variations begins, 'Beaks differ according to the lives lived' (*PA* iv.12 693a11), following which are teleological explanations in terms of feeding habits, why some are sharp and curved, others straight, others broad and others long (693a12–22).

Aristotle usually does not consider lower levels of functional 'fine-tuning' to the environment than this, though he does occasionally. But these examples are sufficient to show that specific quantitative variations in the qualitative affections of their organic structures will often be part of an account of the *being* of an animal of a certain kind.

In *GA* v.1, Aristotle makes the essential–incidental distinction in just this manner. He is reviewing the affections (*pathēmata*) by which the parts of animals are differentiated – that is, just those features which vary by the more and less. He insists that if the feature is neither a part of the kind's nature nor proper to each kind, then it neither came to be nor is for the sake of anything – nor should it be included in an account of the animal's being (*ho logos tēs ousias*).[41] He makes it quite clear, however, that what sort of feature fits the above description can not be specified out of context.

For an eye is for something, while being blue is not, *unless* (*plēn*) this affection is a property of the kind. (*GA* v.1 778a33–4)

Aristotle apparently used the fact that a feature was a property (*idion*) of a biological kind as prima facie evidence that it exists for the sake

---

[41] *GA* v.1 778a29–35. On this teleological notion of essence, cf. Balme, ch. 11 above, 297.

of something. The above suggests that if a kind of animal were universally blue-eyed, being blue-eyed would in all likelihood have functional value. To take another example, while most forms of clawed crustacea have the right claw larger than the left, one group has the larger claw randomly distributed. Aristotle offers a teleological explanation for the difference in the former cases, but in the latter treats the size variation as a matter of chance, and not for the sake of anything (*PA* IV.8 684a25–32).

For two or more organisms to be one in form, then, they must all fall under one account, which is not further divisible into more specific accounts which specify features which are required by the organism's life. For any kind less general than Aristotle's nine extensive kinds, this will often include reference to increasingly narrow ranges on more–less continua. Whether an account is indivisible will depend on the generality of the kind in question relative to that account. And what ought to be included in such an account is to be determined by a study of teleological adaptation.

These last two points are tightly connected. For example, if the form under consideration is 'duck', an account common to all birds will not be indivisible, for it will not mention the peculiar adaptations to a duck's way of life – the bill, the webbed feet, the placement of the legs, the lack of tail feathers, the dense, more oily nature of the feathers, and so on. Suppose these were specified, however, yet we wanted an account of what it is to be a *mallard duck*. The account indivisible relative to 'duck' would be further divisible relative to 'mallard duck', provided only that its life required peculiar features not possessed by other ducks leading different lives.

At some point in divisions within a kind, while we may still wish to distinguish groups of animals on various grounds, these will no longer be teleological. There is, for example, a reason why some humans are red-haired, some blond, and some brown-haired; but being one or the other is not a teleological requirement of blond, red-haired and brown-haired humans. Unlike other levels, this is not a division which is non-essential only relative to the form under investigation, but essential to the more specific kind. In this case, the division is non-essential *tout court*. Again, however, there is no a priori means of determining what this level might be – being a blond, might, under certain conditions, be a crucial adaptation to a specific lifestyle.

The same account of being one in form holds when one takes the activities (*praxeis*) of animals into consideration.

Therefore we must first state the activities, both those common to all and those that are generic and those that are specific (*ta kat' eidos*). (I call them common when they belong to all animals, generic when they belong to animals whose differences among each other are seen to be in degree. For example, I speak generically of 'bird' but specifically (*kata eidos*) of 'man' and of every animal that has no differentia in respect of its general definition (*kata ton katholou logon*). What they have in common some have by analogy, some generically, some specifically.) (*PA* 1.5 645b21-7)

The addition of the phrase *kata ton katholou logon* to the notion of having no differentia is meant to indicate that there may be further sub-divisions (say into those who farm and those who hunt), but these will not be part of the account of what it is to act in a specifically human manner.

Ultimately, then, the 'formal unity' of a number of animals turns on their having just the proper conformation of each part, and just the proper range of activities, for the life they have to live in a specific environment. This will involve their having a fully coordinated set of structures and activities suited to that life. Thus, while individuals of one form of a kind may differ with respect to one affection of one organ only by degree (or even not at all) from the individuals of another form of that kind, the overall unity of their differentiae will suit them to their life and no other, and distinguish them from the individuals of other forms suited to other lives in different environments.

VI

Let me provide a brief summary of the *genos–eidos* relationship sketched in this paper. Below the level of analogical likeness every *eidos* of a *genos* may serve as a *genos* for further division. Second, at every level, the variations in the differentiae among forms of a kind will be predominantly the more/less variety. Third, at every level, the *genos* is 'matter' for its *eidē* – and an *eidos* relative to the more general or common kind may be the matter/*genos* for further differentiation. This picture incorporates the research of David Balme and Pierre Pellegrin on the variable reference of *genos* and *eidos* in Aristotle's biology into the research that was reported in this paper's ancestor. The account of *genos* as matter and form as differentia, and of the more and the less, there presented was still implicitly wedded to a taxonomic understanding of *genos* and *eidos* which I have now abandoned. The wedding was a mismatch, and I find the basic thrust of the earlier paper is much better suited to the 'level neutral' divisional account of these concepts provided by Pellegrin's *La Classification*.

What, finally, of Aristotle's essentialism? He appears to have seen every individual of a kind as having every feature of every structure quantified (in Professor Balme's sense) precisely, and to have viewed every kind from the most extensive to the most specific as a range of potential quantifications for the next more specific kind. To look at Socrates *qua* human is to ignore those (relative to being human) inessential details of his organic nature – snubness of nose, bulge of eye, bandiness of leg. Those all represent *possible* ways in which human noses, eyes and legs may be realized.

Yet at each level there will be an organization among the allowable ranges for each feature of each differentia which is essential to an animal's life, particularly its mode of feeding, cooling itself, and rearing its young.[42] This is not typological essentialism, if by that one means that members of a kind share in some bundle of qualitatively indistinguishable features and differ in certain other incidental features. Nor does it rule out the possibility of environmental changes requiring slight changes in the acceptable ranges of variations. Aristotle seems not to have considered this a serious possibility, and therefore did not discuss how it might possibly occur, and this is hardly surprising. The range and subtlety of the evidence needed to make natural evolutionary change plausible is extremely difficult to come by, and in fourth-century Athens could only have been a wild cosmological speculation.[43] Aristotle took the (then) much more reasonable view that organisms well-suited to stable environments breed true to form – that is, variation is maintained within the limits established by the requirements of that organism's life.[44]

[42] Cf. the use of the concept of the more and the less with respect to psychological and physiological states at *HA* VIII.1 588a25–b2.

[43] Such views were held by Anaximander (DK12 A10, A30), Xenophanes (DK11 B33), and Empedocles (DK31 B9, B12, B17, B26).

[44] Cf. Balme, ch. 11 above, 298–301. I wish to thank Allan Gotthelf for written comments and helpful discussions concerning the reworking of this material, and in particular concerning how to integrate the ideas from Lennox 1985a with those of this paper's ancestor.

14

Animals and other beings
in Aristotle

L. A. KOSMAN

I

Animals, in Aristotle's view, are paradigm instances of substance-being. We may wonder whether Aristotle began with that conviction and shaped his ontology in the light of it, or arrived at it as a result of what his ontology revealed the nature of substance to be, and that question in turn may be related to our views about when and with what attitude he did his biological work. But whatever we decide to say on these questions, our answers will have to take account of his clear conviction that natural living things are 'above all substances'.[1]

We should therefore expect that Aristotle thought the most important features of substance to be exemplified in the case of living entities. This need not mean that he claimed that only animals are substances. On the whole, Aristotle was less concerned with the correct identification of a class of entities which are substances than with the proper understanding of the principles and modes of being by virtue of which those entities which we commonly understood to be substantial beings are substantial. He was, we might say, less interested in substances than in substance-being, less concerned with the question of what beings are substances than with the question of what it is to be a substance. But among the beings that Aristotle saw as commonly (and therefore in some sense correctly) understood to exemplify substance-being, animals caine first, and those features which metaphysics reveals as characteristic of substance-being should therefore be evident in the being of animals.

Recognition of this fact should not only contribute to our understanding of Aristotle's biology and of his metaphysics, but should also show, as it is part of the intention of this volume to show, why the biological writings are of interest not just intrinsically and thus separately, but as an integral part of the larger corpus of Aristotle's writing on philosophy.

[1] *Metaph.* Z.7 1032a19, 8 1034a4; cf. also *Metaph.* Θ.2 1043a4, 3 1043b22ff.

In this essay I will consider some features of the being of animals considered as substance-being, particularly in relation to the concepts of potentiality and actuality. I hope to explore some congruences between animal-being and substance-being according to Aristotle, as well as some differences Aristotle sees between animals and other entities. Moreover, by exposing some features of what we might think of as the conceptual background to Aristotle's biological writings, I hope to shed some indirect light on the modes of reasoning and explanation characteristically found in those writings, and so to provide something like a metaphysical prolegomenon to their study.

I begin with some preliminary remarks concerning certain of Aristotle's metaphysical notions, starting with matter and form.[2]

II

The concepts of matter and form, like those of potentiality and actuality, play an important role in the argument of the *Metaphysics* concerning substance. But to appreciate that role, we have to resist the temptation to think of matter and form solely in terms of *change* and *becoming*. There is a reasonably straightforward story to tell about matter and form if we concentrate on contexts of change: the matter of some entity, say a threshold, is the *ex quo* of the threshold, what the threshold is made or comes to be *out of*, while the form is the principle by virtue of which (through the agency of an efficient cause) that which the threshold is made *out of* comes to be or is made *into* (specifically) a *threshold*. This is the story Aristotle likes to tell in the *Physics* (which is after all about nature as the matrix and principle of change) and in the early introductions of matter and form in the dialectical argument of the *Metaphysics*.[3]

But the governing concern of the *Metaphysics* is not with contexts of change; it is with the larger and prior context of *being*, independent of change and becoming. And for this concern, a somewhat different account will be appropriate. The matter of a threshold is what the threshold is made *up* of; it is what *is* the threshold materially, or as we might say in order to bring out continuity with the previous account, what *constitutes* the threshold. The form, on the other hand, is the principle by virtue of which what is the threshold in this

---

[2] I have discussed many of these issues at greater length in Kosman 1984.

[3] The argument of the *Physics* is much more complicated than this account suggests, particularly in terms of the relation between matter and privation as the sources *from which* of change. In what follows I have systematically ignored those ambiguities that Aristotle attends to in the *Physics*, and so the analysis of matter sounds more general than it really is.

material sense is (actually and specifically) a *threshold*. These are the terms in which the discussion of the varieties of form in *Metaphysics* H.2 is cast. The matter of a threshold is the beam which is, as we might say, at work being the threshold, while its form, that which makes it *be a threshold* rather than a *lintel*, is the position in a house in which the beam is placed (*Metaph.* H.2 1042b19–20).

There are, then, two importantly related but different notions of matter as well as of form in Aristotle's ontology, depending on whether we take *becoming* or *being* as our primary context. Matter may on the one hand be thought of as the *ex quo*, the separated from-which of change and generation, and on the other, as the proximate underlying substratum of constitutive being. These are, as we shall see, often (although not always) only distinct *notions*, i.e. different modes of description of the same entity; it is after all the same beam out of which is made a threshold and which is as a result at work constituting a threshold.

There is another and perhaps more important respect in which matter ought properly to be said to be a 'notion'. The term 'matter' refers to entities taken a certain way; matter is a *principle of being* or nature, and not a *category of entity* in nature. The world does not divide up into instances of matter and of form; matter and form are ways of thinking about the entities of the world relative to an explanatory or descriptive context. To say that a beam is *matter* can therefore be misleading; for when we consider the beam as matter, it is in a sense the *threshold* which is being considered, either (a) as material, i.e. in terms of what it is made up of, or (b) as the end term in a process of change of which the beam is the first term. In a manner of speaking, then, a beam is never matter; for when it's still a beam, it's not yet matter, and when it is matter, it's no longer a beam, but a threshold. It is for this reason that Aristotle insists that a threshold is not a beam, but beamy. And it is for this reason that there is, strictly speaking, no being which is matter, no matter, in other words, that *is* anything:

By matter I mean that which is per se neither this nor so much nor said in any of the other categories by which being is determined. (*Metaph.* Z.3 1029a19ff.)

Matter is a principle of indeterminacy relative to some actual being. When we speak, therefore, of beams or of bronze or of bricks and stones as matter, we are speaking of entities which may be thought of in terms of such indeterminacy relative to other determinate entities; we are speaking of entities which can serve as matter, but which are not themselves per se matter. This is not to deny the appropriateness of the simple assertion that bronze, for example, is the matter of a statue; it is only to stress the fact that in so being considered, bronze loses the determinate being it has *qua* bronze, and comes to be thought of as indeterminate relative to another being.

Corresponding to these distinct ways of thinking of matter, there are distinct ways in which we may think of form; form may be thought of, on the one hand, as that which explains the coming to be or production of a being out of some matter, and, on the other hand, as the determining principle that explains why some matter constitutes this rather than that being.

When we think of the relation between matter and form in this larger context of being, we are able to recognize its affinity to the relation between subject and predicate or substratum and being – the relation, that is, between something which is a being and the being which that something is. So here, for example, the distinction between matter and form parallels the distinction between the thing which is a threshold, and its lying in such and such a position, since, as Aristotle makes clear in his discussion of the variety of forms at the beginning of *Metaphysics* H, the thing's lying in such a position is (part of) its being a threshold: ' [something] ' is a threshold because it lies in such and such a position, and its being a threshold means its lying in that position' (*Metaph.* H.2 1042b26–7).

The *Metaphysics* is an essay devoted, on the one hand, to understanding the relation between a subject and its being, and, on the other, to situating the concept of substance-being with respect to that relation. In *Metaphysics* Z, Aristotle leads us carefully through the arguments that recommend an account of *ousia* in terms of subject or substratum (beginning in chapter 3), and those that recommend an account in terms of the being of a subject, the what-it-is (beginning in chapter 6). But as Book Z progresses, it becomes increasingly clear that these accounts must surrender to the more obvious fact that *ousia* is a *synthesis* of these two principles and must therefore in some sense be understood as the *compound* of matter and form.

But in *what* sense? and how could substance be a compound or synthesis, and still be *primary* being? These are the questions to which the *Metaphysics* turns at the end of Book Z, and they are the questions that inform the argument of the next two books. In one sense they are merely technical questions; but in another they may be considered at the very heart of Aristotle's inquiry into substance and being.

Central to that inquiry is the project of rescuing substance from collapsing into either of the poles explored dialectically in Book Z, and this project concerns not merely substance but the nature of being in general. For the project is not simply about differing views concerning substance; it is about an important competing theory of being with which Aristotle is faced. On that theory, which we might call platonist (although without the implication that it is Plato's), entities in the world of nature are instances of a relation between a subject and its being. As a consequence, *being* properly understood belongs only to the Form to which the subject thus stands in relation; the so-called 'being' of an entity is in fact only an instance of such a relation.

One might counter this theory by insisting that being belongs most properly to subjects. This is essentially the strategy of atomists and other such materialists, and the strategy that is considered in the dialectical moves of *Metaphysics* Z.3. But in the developed argument of the *Metaphysics*, Aristotle employs a different strategy; he allows the relational theory of being as an account of the nature of *accidental* being, but shows it to be basically misleading with respect to substance-being. For in substance there is no relation of being to a substrate that can be defined and identified independently of that being. It is a human being who is white or in the Lyceum or able to laugh, and in each of these cases some being is said of an individual human being as of a subject. But that individual human being is not in turn a case of something being said *kath' hupokeimenou*, being said, that is, of an independently identifiable subject; for the thing which is said to be human is nothing other than the human being who is being human, and it is that human being being human that is the primary being, the *ousia*, described as *ho tis anthrōpos*, a particular (instance of) human being. Substance, in other words, is the primary and paradigm mode of per se being.

In order to understand this distinction between per se and accidental being properly, it is important to remember that in the *Metaphysics* Aristotle is attending to distinctions among three kinds of being: (1) accidental being, such as a *human being being white*, (2) per se being in categories other than substance, such as *being white*, and (3) substance-being, such as *being human* (or as we say in English with an ambiguity I feel sure would have delighted Aristotle, *the human being itself*). Being in category (2) is sometimes referred to as accidental being, since it is the belonging of such being to substance that constitutes the accidental being of category (1). Discussions of the *Metaphysics* then make it sound as though the distinction between per se and accidental being were primarily concerned with accident in this secondary sense of category (2), and as though the distinction between being in category (2) and being in category (3) were the central distinction in the argument of the *Metaphysics*.

But although that distinction is indeed important, since it continues the mode of ontological classification from the *Categories* and forms the center of the theory of *pros hen* predication so critical to the understanding both of being and of essence, it is not the primary distinction. Of equal importance to Aristotle's ontology, and of greater importance to what we might call his ousiology, that is, to his theory of the nature of substance itself, is the distinction between, on the one hand, being in category (1), and, on the other hand, being in categories (2) and (3), the distinction, that is, between per se and accidental being in the stricter sense of category (1). This is the distinction drawn in *Metaphysics* Δ.7 (1017a8ff.), and it is the distinction that Aristotle is working to articulate and to save with respect to substance-being.

An easy ontology would be one in which per se being were identified both with substance-being and with being in the other categories, provided only that we restrict the being in question to predicate being, to the being which some subject is, and not to the predicative whole including both subject and predicate. Being white and being in the Lyceum are, as the discussion in *Metaphysics* Δ.7 makes clear, thus instances of per se beings. Of course they are only derivatively per se, because they are fundamentally dependent for their being on the being of substance, which means not only on the existence of substance, but on substance's mode of being. So the primary per se being must remain, for example, being human.

But even if we make that important qualification, such a theory, although more textured than a platonist ontology which does not distinguish between different sorts of per se being, nor therefore between different categories of essence and of form, remains in all important respects a platonist theory, in the sense outlined above. What Aristotle is concerned to articulate is a theory in which the per se being of substance includes the subject as well; the substance which is to be a human being is not merely the Form of being human which an individual subject is, but that *individual subject's being human*. This however seems intractably to be a case of accidental being, and so it has always seemed to platonists; for it is a synthesis of a subject and its being, and can be shown to be a case of per se being only if these can be shown in some important respect to be one and the same thing.

At the end of *Metaphysics* H, Aristotle claims that this respect will become clear to us if we understand substance-being in terms of the concepts of potentiality and actuality. Speaking of the perplexity concerning the unity of being, he writes:

Clearly then, if we go on defining and speaking in this manner, it will not be possible to explain and solve this difficulty; but if, as we say, there is on the one hand matter and on the other form, the one potential and the other actual, what we are after will no longer seem to be perplexing. (*Metaph.* H.6 1045a20ff.)

Here again we must not suppose that the concepts of potentiality and actuality invoked by Aristotle are necessarily to be understood in terms of motion. For there are, as Aristotle makes clear and explicit throughout the argument of *Metaphysics* Θ, two senses of potentiality and actuality, just as there are two senses of matter and form. Potentiality and actuality are in one sense relative to motion and change, while in another they are relative simply to being.

Indeed, the concept of motion itself is defined in terms of a prior concept of actuality that is independent of motion and that is realized with respect to its potentiality not, as Aristotle stresses in *On the Soul*, by a change from one state to another, but by the *making manifest* of a state which is present but dormant. In this sense of actuality, since the actualization of a potential represents not a change in an entity but the making manifest of an entity's latent and unmanifest being, actuality and potentiality are one and the same thing. Actuality in this sense is in fact, as Aristotle says, the *sōtēria* – the preservation – of its potentiality; potentiality is not, as in the case of motion, consumed or used up, but is precisely preserved and made manifest, called forth into the full and active presentation of its being (*de An.* II.5 417b2ff.).

It is this sense of potentiality and actuality, as he makes clear in *Metaphysics* Θ (1046a1ff.), that Aristotle thinks most important to understanding substance, and particularly to understanding the unity of matter and form or subject and being in substance. Motion and substance are different modes of actuality relative to different potentialities, and in the latter case but not in the former the potentiality and actuality are the same being. For motion is the actuality of a potentiality that is the capacity and possibility of an entity *to be other than it is*, of matter which can be made into or become something else. Motion, in other words, is the principle of *change*. But substance is the principle of *being*; it is the actuality of its proximate matter considered as a potentiality for *being itself*: this human body actually *being* human.

The distinction between kinds of potentiality may, as we might have expected from Aristotle's constant linking of matter and potentiality, be expressed in terms of the distinction we have noted between kinds of matter. For a beam thought of as *ex quo* is potential in the first sense, since it may be *made into* a threshold, while a beam thought of as proximate matter is potential in the second sense. These facts are of course related; to describe a beam as *ex quo* matter of a threshold is merely to say that it can serve as proximate matter, that is, that it potentially (*dunamei*) *is* a threshold.

III

In the course of these preliminary remarks, I have introduced, in a somewhat roundabout way, a distinction between substances and accidental entities. The being of an accidental entity is relative to a substratum which is what it is independently of constituting the substratum of that being; a human being-who-is-in-the-Lyceum is a human being prior to and independently of being in that location, and it remains a human being whether or not it is, so to speak, at work being in that location. But the being of a substance is not thus relative to an independent substratum; for substance-being is not said of something that enjoys an independent being as that thing prior to constituting or being made into a substance. It is not, in other words, said of anything as of a subject. There is no substratum which is at work being a human being that is independent of the human being that it is being.

The distinction we are discussing is not, as I said earlier, the categorial distinction between a substance and what were later to be called its modes – quantities, positions and the like – but the distinction between a substance and an *accidental being* such as a white horse (*a horse being white*) or a six-foot human being (*a human being six feet tall*).

Or such as a bronze statue, or a house, or the threshold of our earlier discussion. For consider how, returning to that threshold, we may reenter the discussion by stating the distinction between substance and accidental entity in terms of matter and form. A wooden beam which is a threshold can be moved and still remain what it is *qua* wooden beam; it therefore has a being (being a wooden beam) independent of being a threshold. The matter of a threshold, in other words, is something other than a threshold, and it is that something which is the matter relative to the form 'lying in such and such a position as such and such a functional part of a house' that makes it a threshold. But in the case of a human being, for example, there is nothing that is human which is what it is independently of being human; for the body of a human being is itself the human being. If, in other words, substance is to be truly per se being, it can exhibit no radical distinction between material and formal being, such as there is between that which is the threshold and its position; there can be no separation between what is a substance and what a substance is.

But in order to extend in this fashion the distinction between per se and accidental being, we will have to suppose that an entity like a threshold or a house or a statue is in the same class with such obvious accidental beings as *a horse being white* or *a horse being in the field*. Why should we suppose this, and why should we suppose that interesting distinctions are to be made by contrasting things like thresholds and houses with things like horses and human beings? We are familiar with the sorts of argument that recommend an ontology distinguishing horses, dogs, human beings and other such self-subsistent, independent and identifiable individuals from sounds, locations, colors and the like, thought to be parasitic and dependent for their being and individuality upon entities of the first class. But the distinction we are here considering is between two classes of entity, *both* of which we should normally suppose to be entities of the first sort: independent, self-subsistent etc. Tables, chairs, houses, statues, thresholds and books seem not to be accidental unities, and to be no less substantial individuals, no less subsistent and independent in their (admittedly less complex) being than are horses, hounds, hawks and humans. So it is, as I suggested earlier, that we so often focus our reading of the *Metaphysics* on the arguments for the categorial distinction between substance and accidental mode; it is (at least relatively) easy to see the considerations that lead to Aristotle's doctrine of the categories, but more difficult to understand how the categorial distinction between substance and accident might lead to distinguishing between horses and thresholds, or between horses and houses.

But consider what a threshold is. It is a wooden beam (for example) which is in a certain position in a house; its being – *a wooden beam being in a certain position as such and such a part of a house* – is therefore exactly analogous to that of a white horse – *a horse being white*. And just as a *white horse* is not a substance so the threshold which is a *thus and so positioned wooden beam* is not a substance.

If, of course, we are seduced by an ontology that recognizes no significant differences among beings that are numerically identical, this fact will be hard to recognize even in the case of white horses. For since, in the case of a particular white horse, the horse and the white horse are one and the same individual entity, it will appear that if one is a substance the other must be a substance as well. In this way we will be lured into thinking of white horses as substances, as though substance were a category of *entity* rather than a category of the *being* of entities.

But this is not Aristotle's view. Aristotle's view – indeed, we may think of it as one of the cornerstones of his ontology – is that numerical identity does not entail equivalence of being. *A* and *B* may be one and the same individual entity – 'the same in number' as Aristotle often puts it – and yet be different beings: what it is to be *A* (*to A einai*) different from what it is to be *B* (*to B einai*). Thus although a white horse is a horse, the being of a white horse and the being of a horse are not the same; and since substance is a category of being, it may be the case (and indeed is the case) that the latter is a substance while the former is not.[4]

But once we are clear that a white horse, even though it is a substantial-looking thing, is not a substance on Aristotle's view, we will be able to recognize that the apparent independence and self-substantiality that characterize thresholds, houses, or statues in comparison with such entities as colors, sounds, or locations are not sufficient to constitute them as substances in Aristotle's ontology. Substances are not simply *things*.

Accidental entities such as white horses, and such as I am claiming thresholds and houses to be, are not, insofar as they are considered as composite wholes, in any single category of predicative being. For that which they are *qua hupokeimenon* – that which the predicate being is said *of* – may be in one category, while the predicate which is *said* of the *hupokeimenon* and constitutes the formal principle by virtue of which the being is specifically what it is may be in another. This indeed is part of what it means for them to be *accidental beings* (or *accidental unities*); it is also why, as accidental beings, they do not, strictly speaking, have an essence:

each of these predicates, if either it is said of itself, or if its genus is said of it, signifies *what it is* (*ti esti sēmainei*). But when it is said of something other, it does not signify *what it is*, but *how much* or *of what sort*, or one of the other categories. (*Topics* 1.10 103b35ff.)

---

[4] The important arguments of *Metaph.* Z.6 1031a19ff. rest upon these distinctions. Notice that in this case a substance (the horse) is in a sense the matter of a non-substance entity (the white horse), for a white horse *consists of* a horse formally qualified in such and such a way, that is, by being white. Similarly, if a wooden beam were a substance, a threshold would be a non-substance whose matter was, in this same sense, a substance. And although a wooden beam may not be a substance, *its* matter, the wood, may be; and if we feel uncomfortable about saying this because the wood is dead, the elements which we will eventually reach in an iterative material analysis are, for reasons I shall suggest in a moment, substances. Thinking this way may help us understand the initial plausibility of the view that being in general has substance as its matter, as well as the plausibility of the view that the proper analysis of substance is therefore as substratum and matter. It might, that is to say, help us to understand the plausibility of the arguments that are given consideration in *Metaphysics* Z.3.

Although the entire entity defined by an instance of accidental being is thus not in any single category of predication, the predicate itself may be. The predicate of a horse *being white* or of a wooden beam *being a threshold,* and therefore the formal principle of *being what it is* for such an entity as a white horse or a threshold, may be in a single category; but it is a category other than substance.

This fact is obvious in many cases of non-substantial being immediately predicated of a substance: the horse, for example, being white or being in the field. For in each of these cases the form by virtue of which the entity is what it is – *white* horse or horse *in a field* – is obviously in one of the categories other than substance: quality and location. But this is no less true, though perhaps less obvious, in the case of entities like our threshold. For a threshold, as the argument of the *Metaphysics* makes clear, is an entity whose being is in part in the category of position, since it is *being in a certain position* which, among other things, makes a wooden beam a threshold. Breakfast, on the other hand, is determined as breakfast by a mode of being in the category of time; for it is by virtue of being eaten (or served) *at a certain time* that a quantity of food constitutes breakfast rather than dinner. The north wind, to use another of Aristotle's examples, is in the category of place; and in general the predicates by which such accidental beings are determined in their being are in one or another of the categories other than substance. (*Metaph.* H.2 1042b15ff.).

These two facts about an accidental entity – that it spans, as it were, more than one category of being and that the form that defines it in its being is in a category other than substance – are obviously related. For since the ultimate subjects of predication are substances, predications in other categories of being will eventually reveal themselves to be instances of non-substance-being predicated of an instance of substance-being.

The situation is more complicated with more complex and highly structured entities such as beds or houses or statues, for here the proximate matter may be more easily understood as related per se to the form. But, as we shall see, there is eventually a matter which is not by virtue of itself a bed or what is a bed. It is that matter which, as Aristotle remembers Antiphon having argued, would sprout if one were to plant a bed, a fact which shows that the arrangement by virtue of which such matter constitutes a bed is an accidental attribute of it (*Ph.* II.1 193a12ff.).

The use of artifacts in the *Metaphysics* as *models* for the consideration of substance may tend to make us forget the fact that thresholds, beds, houses and statues are more appropriately to be classified with white horses than with horses. For their use sometimes makes it seem that Aristotle did wish to count as substances statues as well as animals, bronze spheres as well as the more divine celestial spheres. But we need only remember the subjunctive axe of *On the Soul* (II.1 412b13) to be reminded of the fact, with which I began, that for Aristotle such entities are not in an unqualified sense substance-beings. They are introduced into the discussion of the *Metaphysics* not as examples of substance, but as entities whose material and formal principles are more clearly visible, precisely because they are *non*-substantial beings, and therefore beings whose matter and form are separable.

IV

In our discussion so far, I have been considering the relation of these facts about horses and thresholds to another fact; the nature of matter, or alternatively of substratum, and the role which it plays in relation to form, or alternatively to being, is different, I have suggested, in the substance-being that characterizes entities such as horses and in the accidental being that characterizes entities such as thresholds and houses.

Prima facie, however, there might seem to be no such important distinction between the two cases with respect to the relation of matter and form. There will of course be differences between the *being* of the two entities, between *what it is to be a threshold* and *what it is to be a horse*. But why should there be thought to be any critical distinction with respect to the relation of the subject which is the being to its being what it is, or to the principle by virtue of which it is what it is? Why, in other words, should we think that there is a difference between (a) the relation of the beam that is the threshold to its being a threshold or to the principle by virtue of which it constitutes a *threshold* and (b) the relation of the body that is the horse to its being a horse, or to the principle by virtue of which it constitutes a *horse*?

To help us answer this question, I want to consider some smaller simple-minded questions and some trivial answers about matter and form, first in the case of entities like thresholds and houses, which I have argued are for Aristotle accidental unities, and then in the case of animals. First then about thresholds.

I begin by asking what we may call the *material question*: What is the matter of a threshold? or, What is a threshold materially? The answer to this first question is (for example) *the wooden beam out of which the threshold is made.* It is important, as I have urged, to understand this not simply in a genetic sense; 'out of which the threshold is made' is also to mean *which constitutes*, or *of which consists*, or as I have suggested, *which is at work being* a threshold.

Consider next the *formal question*: What is the form of a threshold? or What is a threshold formally? In asking this question, we must remember that *form* is for Aristotle always specific to a *being under a particular description*; every being has a form, and has a form under its description as *that being*. Since furthermore any particular individual entity is in fact many different beings, that is, is capable of many different descriptions, it will have as many forms, each form relative to the individual entity under that description, or as we say in an older idiom, *qua that being*. Inquiring concerning the form of a threshold is clearly to ask for the form of the entity *qua* threshold, that is, *qua* its *being a threshold*, and not *qua* any of the other beings in terms of which the threshold might be described: made out of a wooden beam, part of an obscure marriage ritual, a particularly fine example of Early American carpentry, etc. Asking for the form of a threshold in this sense is therefore asking: What is it for an entity *to be a threshold*, or as we might ask of a particular threshold, *ti estin autōi to oudōi einai*?[5]

The simplest Aristotelian answer to this question is clear and trivial; to be a threshold is to be actually doing what a threshold does. It is, in other words, to be acting out the liminal function, performing the *ergon* of thresholds: being, that is, *energeiāi* a threshold. The specification of what constitutes this liminal *ergon* is the subject matter not of philosophy, but of oudology, the science of thresholds. Oudologists will consider the formula for being-a-threshold (*to oudōi einai*), which formula will, as we have seen, include essentially some reference to the position in a house of the entity constituting the threshold; for the *ergon* or characteristic activity of a threshold and therefore the form by virtue of which that entity is a threshold includes, among other things, *being in a certain position in a house*. Suppose we call that formula the Liminal Logos, since it is the logos of a threshold. We can then use it to specify the formal account of a threshold: what it is to be a threshold is to be *energeiāi* what is specified in the Liminal Logos.

Suppose now that we ask the same series of questions about the matter itself, that is, about *that which constitutes* the threshold. Post-

---

[5] I think that just such a question, an example of which is to be found in *PA* II.3 649b22, is the origin of Aristotle's technical locution for the essence of a being *X*, *to X einai*, with '*X*' in the dative. The dative is by attraction to *autōi*, and the phrase is then detached to serve as a variable for the answer to the question. A similar story may be told about the origin of *to ti ēn einai* in the more formal question: *ti estin autōi to ti ēn einai*?

pone for the moment the material question about the matter: What constitutes or of what consists the wooden beam that is the matter of the threshold – What in other words is *its* matter? – and consider only the formal question: What is it to be that which is the matter of a threshold?

This question immediately reveals itself as ambiguous. For since the concept of form is relative to an entity *qua* a particular being, in asking What is it to be that which is the matter of a threshold? we might be asking either of two different questions. We might be asking What is the form of the beam *qua* matter-of-a-threshold, that is, insofar as it is thought of as an entity out of which is made a threshold, or which is serving as a threshold, or which is at work constituting a threshold. Here the beam is being considered specifically as the matter of a threshold, and we are asking to specify the formal nature of the matter$_1$ (let's call it) *qua* such matter.

But we may also think of the beam simply as a wooden beam; for since that which constitutes a threshold, independent of thus being the threshold's proximate matter, is also actually whatever it is, it will have a form that determines it not as that matter, but as the being that it is, so to speak, in its own right. We may therefore be asking the formal question with respect to *that* very being: What is it to be (in this case) *a wooden beam*, that is, What is the formal account of the wooden beam out of which a threshold is made, not *qua* that out of which a threshold is made, but *qua* what it happens to be? Here we are being asked to specify the formal nature of the matter$_2$ (let's call it) not *qua* matter, but simply *qua* wooden beam.

The answer to this question will then specify whatever we might think to be a reasonable formal account of a wooden beam; we might, for example, think of such an account in terms first of what it is to be a beam, and then what it is for such a beam to be made out of wood, or we might think straightaway in terms of what it is to be a transformed part of (say) an oak tree. But in any case, the formal account that it will here be appropriate to give is different from the formal account that we will want to give of the beam *qua* matter. For the one account, that of the beam$_2$ (*qua* beam), will not refer essentially to a threshold, while the other, that of the beam$_1$ (*qua* matter), will. There is revealed, in other words, to be two different beings when we consider that which is the matter of a threshold; it is one thing to be simply *a wooden beam* and another thing to be *the matter of a threshold*, even though it is just the wooden beam that *is* the matter of the threshold.

We may think of this fact as the ontic duplexity of accidental matter, for it is simply another face of the fact that a threshold is an accidental being; what has been revealed is that what is a threshold is not per se a threshold, and this is to say that it is such per accidens. An accidental being is thus a case of something being predicated of a subject which is independent of and other than the predicated being. A substance, however, is the same being in both subject and predicate; so Aristotle makes clear in somewhat of an aside in the *Posterior Analytics*:

> Expressions which signify substance signify that either the predicate or some particular form of the predicate is *just* what that of which it is predicated *is*. Those that do not signify substance, but are said of a different underlying subject (*kat' allou hupokeimenou*) so that neither the predicate nor any particular form of the predicate is just what it is, are accidental, as for example, *white* predicated of *human being*. Neither *white* nor any particular *form of white* is just what a human being is. *Animal*, however, is; a particular form of animal is just what a human being is. Expressions which do not signify substance must be predicated of some underlying subject; nothing is white that is not some *other* thing that is being white. (*APo.* 1.22 83a24ff.)

A wooden beam is a threshold not by virtue of itself, but by virtue of being in a certain position, which is not part of what it is *to be a wooden beam*. Indeed, to consider a wooden beam as a threshold is already in a sense no longer to consider it as a wooden beam, but rather as a (wooden-beamy) entity-in-a-position; it is for this very reason that a threshold, as Aristotle argues in *Metaphysics* Z.7 (1033a5ff.) and Θ.7 (1049a19ff.), is said not to be wood, but wooden.

We may now begin to think our way back into the nature of animals by noting how different thresholds are from horses in this respect. A threshold is wooden because it is made out of wood. A horse, however, is not bodily, for it is not in any sense *made out of* a body; it just *is* a body – a living body. This will become clearer if we turn our attention back to animals.

Consider then the same series of questions concerning our specimen living being, the horse. Once more we first ask what we have called the material question: What is the matter of a horse? It is easy to suppose that the proper answer to this question is *the horse's body*. It is the body of an animal that appears throughout Aristotle's discussions of *On the Soul* as matter relative to psychic form; the body, he writes at the beginning of the discussion in Book II, is not to be thought of 'as something predicated of a subject, but rather as itself subject, that is, matter (*hupokeimenon kai hulē*)' (*de An.* II.1 412a19).

This answer, however, reveals a particular and determinate understanding of the material question; for *the horse's body* is an appropriate answer to the question What is the *constitutive* matter of a horse? that is to say, What *constitutes* a horse? or Of what does a horse *consist*? But it is an inappropriate answer to a different question that we might pose concerning *ex quo* matter: Out of what does a horse come to be? For there is no sense in which a horse is *made out* of its body; there is no sense, in other words, in which a horse is generated *from* its body. The body of a horse *constitutes* the horse as its proximate matter, but it is not something that in any way *gets made into* a horse. It is for this reason that Aristotle sometimes describes not the body, but the *katamēnia* as an animal's matter.[6] Here clearly he must mean matter *for generation*: the *ex quo* matter out of which the animal comes to be, and not the matter that the animal is in any constitutive sense.

For if there is any sense in which the *katamēnia* is the matter for a horse and in which a horse may be said to be made out of *katamēnia*, it isn't one in which the horse would be said to be, if there were such a word, '*katamēnikon*', any more than we should want to say, given a contemporary understanding of generation, that it is eggy; a horse, in other words, doesn't bear the same relationship to the *katamēnia* which is its matter as it does to the body which is its matter.[7] It must be, then, that two different senses of matter, parallel, as we have seen, to the two different senses of potentiality that Aristotle distinguishes in *Metaphysics* Θ, are here operative, and lead, in the case of animals, to two quite different answers to the material question.

Now ask the formal question, What is the form of a horse? specifying as above that we mean to be asking about the form and definition of a horse *qua horse*, and not *qua* any of the accidental beings the horse might happen to be: white, in the field, worth a kingdom, etc. We are in other words asking: What is it for an entity *to be a horse*? Again the answer is: to be a horse is to be actually acting as horses act, that is, to be performing the *ergon* of horses in leading an equine life and therefore to be *energeiāi* a horse. The details of this activity are contained in the formula for being-a-horse (*to hippōi einai*). If again we call this formula the Equine Logos, then what it is to be a horse is to be *energeiāi* what is specified in the Equine Logos.[8]

---

[6] *GA* 1.19 727b31; *Metaph.* H.4 1044a35. In a strict sense of the word, *katamēnia* may be thought to refer only to the monthly menstrual flow of humans, and indeed most of Aristotle's examples are of human menses. But he commonly uses the term as well to apply to the *annua* of non-primate animals. Cf. *GA* 1.19 727a21; iii.1 750b12; *HA* iii.19 521a26; Bonitz, *Index* 327b23ff.

[7] Of course one might *make up* a sense in which a horse could be said to be *katamēnikon*, since it's a blooded animal, and the *katamēnia* is blood; but this is at best an accidental and weak sense: we wouldn't be monthly even if we were made out of the monthlies. (The common derivation of *Mensch* from *menses* is clearly an imaginative folk etymology.)

[8] It is a fact of interest about animals, and of considerable importance for the doctrine of substance, that the being *energeiāi* in terms of which animals are defined is capable of further discrimination into first and second actuality. This fact, that the soul is itself a functional

We now ask once more these questions concerning the matter itself, and for reasons that will become clear, I want to focus on questions concerning the *constitutive* matter, that is, concerning the horse's *body*. We may postpone again the iterated material question: what constitutes or of what consists the body of a horse, what is *its* matter? And here let us postpone as well, though we will see that this is no easy task, the formal question concerning the body of a horse *qua* matter-of-a-horse. We said that since the matter of an entity is also actually what it is, it will therefore have a form which determines it not as matter, but as the being that is the matter. Suppose again that we ask the formal question with respect to *this* being: What is it to be a horse's body? What is the formal account of being the body of a horse?

I suggest the following answer to this question: the body of a horse is the instrument by virtue of which a horse is able to do what it does in the acting out of its function, the *organ*, in other words, for the actual living of an equine life. An animal body, according to this suggestion, is a being whose formal account is a *hou heneka* account, since it is a being that essentially is a *heneka tou*; its very being is to be a telic instrument, an *organon* for the sake of the *ergon* which is the life of a horse.

The essential instrumentality of an animal's body is made explicit in Aristotle's repeated descriptions of the body as the instrument or organ of the animal's life. 'The body', he writes at the beginning of the *Parts of Animals*, 'is an instrument (*organon*); for just as each of its parts is for the sake of something, so with the body as a whole' (*PA* I.1 642a11). In his discussion of the soul, he repeats, relative to the soul as principle of an animal's life, this account of the body: 'all natural bodies are instruments (*organa*) of soul'.[9]

This point is again made clear in the definition of *psuchē*, given in *On the Soul*, as the 'first actuality of a natural body capable of having life (*dunamei zōēn echontos*)'. A body of this sort, he goes on to remark, 'is one which is instrumental (*ho an ēi organikon*)'.[10] It is common, at least as early as Alexander,[11] to render *organikon* here as 'having parts that are organs'; but this is a strained reading of *organikon*, suggesting for it a meaning nowhere else to be found in the corpus. Aristotle

potentiality relative to the more complete *energeia* of actual living, will necessitate a greater complexity in our account of what it is to be a horse; but since soul and living are both forms of *energeia*, it will not affect the structure of analysis I've here suggested.

[9] *De An.* II.4 415b18. Cf. also *EE* VII.9 1241b22.

[10] *De An.* II.1 412a28; compare the shorter definition a few lines later of the soul as first actuality of a *sōmatos phusikou organikou*.

[11] *Aporiai kai luseis* 54.9 and *De Anima* 16.11ff.

commonly refers to parts themselves as *organikon* and means by this simply that they are instrumental in nature.[12] And so here with the body as a whole; an animal's body considered as such is an instrument or organ, a *tou ergou heneka*, whose being is to be for the sake of the activity which is the animal's life.

So the formal account of a horse's body is the following: to be a horse's body is to be an organ which is *dunamei* that which is specified in the Equine Logos, that is, it is to be an *instrument capable of being* (or doing) that, the *actual* being (or doing) of which is specified in the formal account of being a horse.

The sense of *dunamei* invoked in thus defining an animal body as *dunamei* the animal is that sense, described by Aristotle in the *Metaphysics* as more important for the understanding of substance (*Metaph.* Θ.1 1046a1ff.), in which to say that something is *dunamei* A does not mean that it is capable of *becoming* A or of *changing into* A, but that it *is* A, although only as latent capacity. This means that the body that is *dunamei* living is not something that can *become* alive, but something that *is* alive, considered as a potentiality; as Aristotle states explicitly in *On the Soul*, 'it is not that which has lost its soul which is thus potentially living, but that which has it' (*de An.* II.1 413a2). The body, in other words, is always proximate matter, never matter *ex quo*; as we have seen, although animals are made *up* of their bodies, they are never made *out* of their bodies, but out of the *katamēnia*.[13]

Notice now what has happened. We set out to postpone the question concerning the formal account of a horse's body *qua* matter and to consider only what we might give as the formal account of a horse's body *qua* what it actually is. But that formal account has emerged as precisely an account of the horse's body *qua* proximate matter. To be a horse's body, as it turns out, is essentially nothing else than to be the matter of a horse.

V

I now want to consider some conclusions that may seem provisionally to emerge from these questions and their answers. Consider first some points about matter and form. A horse's form and its matter are seen to differ only as *energeia* and *dunamis* differ, for a horse and its body are defined formally by the same account, the Equine Logos, which

---

[12] Cf. for example *PA* II.1 646b26; III.1 661b29; *GA* II.4 739b14; II.6 742b10; *EN* III.1 1110a16.
[13] In fact, animals are not strictly speaking *made out* of anything at all; they are grown from seed. But this is another story.

specifies a single being that the one is *energeiāi* and the other *dunamei*. Our simple-minded questions have thus exposed that very identity between a substance's form and matter which Aristotle introduces in his difficult remarks at the end of *Metaphysics* H, but in a way that may help us to explicate these remarks.

Secondly, there seems to be no difference for the body of an animal, in contrast to the matter of accidental beings such as thresholds, between the two alternative questions concerning the matter: What is the formal nature of the matter of an entity *qua matter of that entity*? and What is the formal nature of that matter *qua what it happens actually to be*? There seems to be, in other words, no distinction for the body similar to the distinction between the beam$_1$ and the beam$_2$; the body of an animal does not exhibit two beings, one *qua* matter and one *qua* what it is actually, for the actual being of that which is the matter just is its being *qua* matter. This is why the body appeared to us as an organ; we might think of an animal's body as its *global organ*: that organ which is to its general living as the eye is to its seeing, or the hand to its manual activities.

But while in this sense, animals appear to exhibit a unity of material being relative to what I fancifully termed the 'ontic duplexity of accidental matter', in another sense, as we have seen, the concept of matter appears to be divided in the case of horses, relative to a different material unity that thresholds enjoy. For there is only one entity, the wooden beam, out of which is made a threshold and which then constitutes a threshold. We may wish to distinguish between importantly different descriptions of this entity, as I have here distinguished between the beam$_1$ and the beam$_2$, but it is important that these are different descriptions of the same entity. A beam$_2$ may be made into a threshold and we may then talk about it as the beam$_1$ that constitutes the threshold, but there is only one entity; the two descriptions are descriptions of one and the same wooden beam. But the case with animals seems very different; just as there is no *distinction* between the body$_1$ and the body$_2$, so there is no *single* entity in the case of animals that plays both material roles, that of *ex quo* matter and that of *constitutive* matter.

What is there about Aristotle's understanding of animal ontology that has led to these conclusions? It is basically, I suggest, that animals, as paradigm substances, exhibit most manifestly the fact that form and matter in substance-being is linked to the concepts of activity and the structures of potentiality which empower that activity. For the being of an animal consists in its life functions, in the characteristic activities and modes of living in which it engages.

The specific form of an animal's being is therefore, as we might say, its *lifestyle*; what it eats, how it gets its food, where it lives, the manner of its reproduction, sensation, movement, etc.: the entire complex of characteristic activities, in other words, that constitute the manner of its *bios*, and which it is the task of the biologist to describe, understand and explain.

The bodies of animals in turn are what they are by virtue of their power (*dunamis*) to perform these functions (or as we might prefer to say: their ability to empower the organism to perform these functions). An animal's body is thus, as we have seen, essentially an organ or instrument; its being *as a body* is that of a *heneka tou*, a for-the-sake-of, defined in terms of its instrumental ability to perform (or make possible the performance of) those life functions by which the being of the animal is determined.

An animal's body may therefore be thought of as 'essentially material'; it has *qua* body no formal being other than that of serving as telic and proximate matter, that is, as the specific and adequate instrument for the actuality that is the animal's life. It is this 'simple materiality' of the body which we saw expressed in the fact that an animal does not exhibit the duplexity of material being found in artifacts and other accidental entities, and which we saw witnessed in Aristotle's designation of it as essentially an *organon*.

For an *organ*, as is made clear by Aristotle in his discussion of biological organs at the beginning of Book II of the *Parts of Animals*, is just an entity whose essential nature is to be telic, an entity whose being is to be for the sake of that activity of which it is the organ.[14]

That the body may be thought of as an organ follows from our earlier recognition that the body of which we have been speaking is the living body, and not an animal's corpse; the body is the animal and not something out of which an animal is made. In this sense in which an animal's body *qua* organ *is* the animal, an animal's corpse is no longer its body, except in name only; a corpse is an animal's remains, not its body. As a dead eye is only homonymously an eye, so a dead body, that is, a dead animal, is only homonymously an animal. On this understanding, the nature of an animal's death reveals an important fact about its body; dying is not a change in a substratum, but the destruction of an entire being, a *phthora*, so that when an animal gives up the ghost, it dies together with its body, and neither continues to exist.

When a beam is removed from its position, however, and ceases to be a threshold, it does not stop being a beam; accidental beings

[14] *PA* II.1 646a25ff.; *Mete.* IV.12 389b23ff.

do not die, but merely suffer dissolution, and their matter, having a being other than that as matter, survives that dissolution. But when an animal is no longer alive, its body thought of this way as a 'global organ' is no longer a body, nor any of the animal's other more local organs any longer organs; no longer being instruments for the performance of certain functions, they no longer exhibit that mode of instrumental being that once constituted them essentially as the body and organs of an animal.

It is also because of this view of an animal's body that explanations of it and of its organic parts are teleological or functional in nature. I mean *teleological* here in the broad sense in which an explanation might be said to be teleological which specifies a *formal* though not necessarily *genetic* account of a body and its organs in terms of their being as a *heneka tou*. Since the formal account of an animal's body will form a part of an Aristotelian account of that animal's genesis, teleological explanation in the narrower and more common sense will, of course, also be involved. But teleology in Aristotle is not about the evolutionary (or any other historical) genesis of the fact that such and such a type of animal has such and such organs. It is a given that animals have the kinds of lives and biological practices they have, and therefore that they have the kinds of bodies and organs they have; for it is in terms of the former that the latter receive teleological, that is to say, functional explanations. It is the project of providing exactly such explanations, revealing the complex structure of biological phenomena by revealing the fit and join of bodies and their organs to lives and their practices, that Aristotle justifies theoretically at the beginning of *Parts of Animals* and carries out, with his usual complexity and subtlety, in the course of that treatise.

Any difficulty which we may feel with teleological explanations in the narrower sense is thus not an indictment of Aristotle's teleology. For, on the contrary, it is only because our diachronic and genetic explanations are undertaken against the background of a synchronic and formal understanding which is inescapably functional that there is a difficulty; it is because organs so clearly are entities whose formal nature demands a for-the-sake-of account that we feel perplexed by questions of whether teleological genetic accounts are necessary or possible.

It is an obvious consequence of these facts that body and soul are related as potentiality and actuality, and that the matter of an animal is a structure of instrumental capacities directed toward the life of the animal as its *telos*; an animal is therefore unified as potentiality and actuality are unified.[15] It is just this story that Aristotle clearly means to tell in his treatise on the soul, when he claims that the definition of *psuchē* quoted above as the 'first actuality of a natural body *which is instrumental in nature (sōmatos phusikou organikou)*' makes clear that it is ridiculous to ask if body and soul are one (*de An.* II.1 412a28; 413a4ff.). We know that they are; eye and sight, more generally organ and faculty, and finally body and soul exhibit not the mere accidental unity that characterizes a subject and its accidental predicates, but the per se unity that characterizes the matter and form of substance-being.

The essential instrumentality of animals' bodies in contrast to the matter of accidental unities such as I have been arguing thresholds and houses to be is at the heart of Aristotle's discussion of the 'subjunctive axe' mentioned earlier. In his introductory discussion of soul in Book II of *On the Soul*, Aristotle offers the following analogy:

It is as if some instrument, for example an axe, were a natural body; then *what it is to be an axe* would be its substance, and this would be its soul. For if this were removed, it would no longer be an axe, except homonymously.

But he immediately goes on to point out the respects in which the analogy is merely an analogy:

In fact, however, it is [still] an axe; for it is not *this* kind of body of which the essence and definition (*to ti ēn einai kai ho logos*) is a soul, but only a certain kind of natural body which has within itself a principle of motion and rest. We ought rather to think of what has been said in relation to the parts [of the animal]. If the eye were an animal, sight would be its soul; for this is the eye's formal substance (*ousia kata ton logon*). The eye is the matter for sight, lacking which it is no longer an eye, except homonymously, like a stone 'eye' or a painted 'eye'. We now have to apply [what is true] of the parts to the whole living body; for as part [of soul] is to part [of body] so is the whole of consciousness to the whole conscious body, as such. (*de An.* II.1 412b13ff.)

And, we may generalize, so is the whole of life to the whole living body. Here Aristotle clearly thinks of the body as an *organ* of the living

---

15 The fact about animals that they *rest*, that they have the capacity, that is, to turn off their activities temporarily without dying, and that the soul is therefore itself a being defined in terms of potentiality, will, as I suggested in an earlier note, necessitate a further refinement in an Aristotelian animal ontology. This refinement will have to account for the relation between soul as first actuality and actual living as second actuality. But it is a false problem to ask whether substance-being is most properly situated in first or second actuality, for these are on Aristotle's view the same being; substance-being is the being that entities of substantial complexity exhibit, of which first and second actuality differ merely as potentiality and actuality at a higher level than that exhibited by body and soul. In any case this question will not affect the fundamental fact that the matter of an animal is a structure of instrumental capacities directed toward the life of the animal as its *telos*, and that an animal is therefore unified as potentiality and actuality are unified.

animal, on analogy with the eye, and differing from that organ only as the whole differs from the part, or as a 'global' organ for the animal's general life functioning differs from a 'local' organ for the specific and limited function of sight. It is because he here thinks of the body as an analogue to the eye that he reminds us in the next line, as we earlier noted, that 'it is not that which has lost its soul which is thus potentially living, but that which has it' (de An. II.1 412b26–7).

Occasionally Aristotle speaks of the body not on analogy with the eye itself understood as an organ that makes up the animal, but on analogy with the matter of the eye, the 'stuff' out of which the eye is made and which, when combined with sight, yields an eye. So several lines later, we read that 'just as an eye is pupil and sight, so is an animal body and soul' (de An. II.1 413a2ff.). There is clearly some looseness in Aristotle's mode of talking about the body on this issue. It is not that he confuses the body with the ex quo matter of generation, which clearly remains the katamēnia or its analogue; but he sometimes speaks of the body primarily as the stuff of an animal, in keeping with the notion of matter as that which makes up an entity, while at other times, when he focuses upon the body as a locus of potentiality and dunamis, he speaks of the body as analogous to an organ.

It is the view of the body implicit in this latter mode of speaking that is, I would suggest, finally dominant in Aristotle's thinking. And it is this view that finally shapes his understanding of the matter–form relationship in general. For just insofar as animals and their bodies serve as paradigms of substance-being and its matter, this view of the body enables Aristotle to entertain a concept of matter not simply as stuff, but more importantly as dunamis, as the locus of dynamic potentiality relative to actual being.

It is in turn this concept of matter, in conjunction with the more sophisticated theory of potentiality and actuality elaborated in Metaphysics Θ, that provides the key to the problem of substance developed in the earlier books of the Metaphysics, and therefore to the general theory of being that constitutes its larger project.[16] The consideration of animals and their bodies, then, proves to be not merely of local, but of general interest. For in providing us with a model for a powerful rather than a stuffy theory of matter, it speaks to the theory of being as a whole and not simply to the theory of animal being.

[16] This is discussed in some detail in Kosman 1984: n.2.

VI

This recognition may help us think our way through an objection to the interpretation I've been developing. Suppose someone argued in the following way: there is nothing surprising in the fact that a horse's body should thus turn out to be essentially material in the sense suggested. For to refer to a horse's body under the description *body* is already to specify it as something that serves as matter for a more structured functional entity. But we can as well refer to the *body of a house*, and thus specify our reference to that entity in such a way that *under just that description*, it might equally be seen as 'essentially material'. We may want to think of such talk as metaphorical, but if so, it is surely justifiably metaphorical; the wood and stones which make up a house and which are, so to speak, at work as the substratum of a house, can surely be reasonably thought to constitute something importantly analogous to the body of the house, and with even greater ease we may think of the functional parts of a house – window, threshold, lintel, etc. – as making up its body.

If, however, we can speak of the body of a *house* in such a way that it appears 'essentially material', doesn't the distinction that we have been arguing for begin to vanish? For it turns out to be not merely the bodies of animals but the matter of complex entities like thresholds and houses as well that are essentially instrumental. In fact, isn't Aristotle led to think of the being of matter *in general* in terms of instrumental potentiality? Consider his discussion of material being at the end of the *Meteorology*: 'The uniform parts', he there writes,

> are composed of the elements, and the products of nature as a whole are in turn composed of these parts as their matter. But while all these parts are thus composed materially from the elements we have mentioned, what they are substantially has to do with their formal definition. This is always clearer in the case of higher beings and, in general, those that are instrumental and for the sake of something. It's clear, for example, that a corpse is a human being only homonymously, and similarly that the hand of a dead person is a hand only homonymously; each is said to be a human being or a hand in much the same way as we might say of a stone flute that it is a flute, since, that is, even these appear to be a sort of instrument.

This is a familiar story; the fact, which Aristotle will shortly make explicit, that instrumental beings deprived of their instrumental capacities can only equivocally be said to be such beings is offered as evidence that their being does not consist in what they are made of, but in what they are capable of. The argument at first appears to concern only beings of a high degree of instrumental complexity;

but it is at once generalized to apply as well to simple homoeomerous parts and to the elements of which they in turn are composed:

> It is less clear that the same thing is true in the case of flesh and bone, and even less clear in the case of fire and water.

Aristotle then immediately offers an explanation of our difficulty in recognizing the fact that even the elemental parts of an animal's body exhibit the mode of instrumental being exhibited by the more complex parts of the body or by the body itself.

> For the that-for-the-sake-of-which is least clear where we have gone furthest in material analysis, as if, taking the extreme cases, matter were nothing beyond itself and substance-being nothing other than its formal account, while intermediate beings were analogous to each of these extremes in terms of their proximity to each.

The presupposition of this explanation is that all the entities under discussion in fact exhibit this mode of instrumental being. The hypothetical analogy Aristotle offers (as the rhetorical tone in which he introduces it also makes clear) is therefore just that – a hypothetical analogy. We are not to suppose that the elemental matter of animal being – earth or fire, or the hot or cold – is in fact 'nothing beyond itself'. For, as he immediately goes on to make clear,

> any one of these is a for-the-sake-of-which, and is by no means simply fire or water, any more than is flesh or intestines; and this is even more so in the case of a face or of a hand. All of these, in fact, are defined in terms of function, for it is being able to perform its respective function that makes each of them what it truly is, as the eye is an eye when it can see; if it is not able to perform its function, it is what it is said to be only homonymously, like a dead eye, or a stone eye, which is no more an eye than a wooden saw is a saw, but simply an image of one. Well, the same is true of flesh; but its function is less clear than that of, say, the tongue. And it's equally true even of fire; but its function naturally is even less clear than that of flesh. And it is equally true even in the case of plants and of the non-living bodies, such as bronze or silver; for all of these are what they are by virtue of their capacities to do and to undergo certain things, just as much as flesh and sinew; it's simply that the formal account of them [in terms of these capacities] is not clear to us. (*Mete.* IV.12 389b27ff.)

Surely all of this should cause discomfort; for if matter *in general* is defined as a potential for-the-sake-of-which and thus exhibits the 'essential materiality' I have been ascribing to animal bodies, the distinction I have been arguing for vanishes; for that distinction was based on the notion that there is a fundamental difference in just this respect between the bodies of animals and plants and the like and the matter of all other entities.

One answer to this objection might go like this: there is nothing in the story I have been telling which should lead to such discomfort, for there is nothing in that story that argues against the possibility of describing the matter of an entity such as a house as its body, nor indeed against the possibility of describing matter in general in this way. On the contrary, the force of such a description derives from the light that an understanding of animals and their bodies sheds on the general structure of form and matter in other entities. It is in recognizing an animal's matter not simply as that of which the animal *consists*, but as a complex structure of *instrumental potentiality* by virtue of which it is enabled to enact its life and formal being, that we are able to think in general of the matter of active being in terms of instrumental potentiality.

Insofar as animals are paradigmatic of substance-being, the fact that the material being of artifacts may come to be understood in the light of the material being of animals from which it is initially distinguished is an instance of a more general feature of Aristotle's *Metaphysics*. Think about the relation between substance-being and being in general. The project of the central books of the *Metaphysics* is not simply to reveal the nature of substance-being, but to reveal how that particular primary mode of being illuminates the nature of being as such; these books explore the per se being of substance, as revealed through the concepts of matter, form, actuality and potentiality, with the end of explaining the nature of being in general.

It is this project of explanation that Aristotle announces at the beginning of *Metaphysics* Z when he claims that we understand quality, quantity, place and the like only when we know *what* each of these things *is*, that is to say, only when we understand the per se essential being that characterizes each of them (*Metaph.* Z.1 1028a37ff.). Note that the claim here, which is the claim of the priority of substance-being, is not the claim that we understand quality, quantity or place when we know the underlying substance of which these beings are predicated; it is the claim that we understand these modes of being insofar as we see them as exemplifying, even if only in a qualified fashion, the being of substance.

The argument of the *Metaphysics* then, which begins with a *distinction* between substance-being and all other modes of being, ends with a revelation of the respect in which all being *is* substance-being, substances themselves unqualifiedly, all other beings in a qualified sense. It is the understanding of this sense in which all being is substance, though not unqualifiedly, that fulfills the promise of the *Metaphysics* to explain being by explaining substance.

In much the same manner, the distinction that Aristotle marks between *kinēsis* and *energeia* is not undermined by his claim that *kinēsis* is itself an *energeia*, though an incomplete one (*Ph.* III. 1 201b31ff.), nor is the distinction that he marks between *ti esti* and other modes of being undermined by his claim that all being is *ti esti* being, but not unqualifiedly (*Metaph.* Z.4 1030a18ff.). In these cases, it is precisely Aristotle's claim that *kinēsis* will be properly understood only when it is recognized as an incomplete mode of *energeia*, and accidental being properly understood only when it is recognized as qualified *ti esti* being.

Here as well, the distinction between the matter of animals and that of artifacts does not preclude the fact that we will understand the one more subtly when we understand it in terms of the other. What began as the marking of a radical distinction between two modes of material being thus emerges as a theory that promises to illuminate one mode of being in the light of the other. To see the bodies of animals as paradigmatic of matter in general is to see the sense in which matter is not simply that of which an entity consists, but is a locus of instrumental capacity that enables an entity to exhibit its complex *energeiai*.

VII

But in what respect is this an *answer* to the objection? We were concerned that the distinction I have been worrying would vanish if we were to find that matter is a locus of dynamic potentiality for animal and artifact alike; and doesn't that concern now seem well-founded, for doesn't the generality that we have seen Aristotle accord the instrumental view of matter in the *Meteorology* collapse any such distinction?

In a sense this is right; in a sense the distinction with which we began has been negated by (or, as other philosophers might say, taken up into) the idea of identity which it has engendered. The response I imagined to the objection was not meant to deny that fact, but rather to reveal it as part of a positive and philosophically interesting strategy on Aristotle's part. But there is one further chapter to the story that must be told.

The text we read earlier from *On the Soul* (II.1 412b13ff.) highlights Aristotle's sense of there being a distinction between living things and artifacts such as the 'subjunctive axe'. But it also suggests that the features to which I have been drawing attention (and which now seem to us problematic) are indeed not for Aristotle the salient differentiating features of those beings, nor the features on which that sense of distinction is most importantly based.

What primarily characterizes the difference between animal and artifact in Aristotle's view is the fact that an animal contains within itself a *natural principle of motion and rest*, whereas an artifact does not. A horse has a nature, a natural principle of motion and rest, for its being is *by nature*; but although a bed has a form and being and is what it is, a bed does not itself have a natural principle of motion and rest. For the being of a bed, precisely insofar as it is an *artifact*, is not by nature.

But we might also say, and perhaps should rather say, that an artifact has a nature per accidens; for it has a nature, but only insofar as it is the natural matter out of which it is made and not insofar as it is an artifact. A bed, in other words, has no natural principle of motion and rest *qua bed*, but the bed's natural matter, the wood out of which it is made, has a nature and the bed could therefore be said to have that nature per accidens, since it happens to be made out of that wood. If for instance, we throw a bed into the air, it will fall down, but *qua* wood, not *qua* bed; if we were to plant it, it might sprout into a sapling, though never into a cot.

Aristotle describes this understanding of the distinction between animal and artifact clearly at the beginning of *Physics* II:

> Natural beings include animals and their parts, plants, and the simple bodies, earth, fire, air, and water; for these and things like them are what we call 'natural'. All of these clearly differ from things which are not constituted naturally. For each of them has within itself a principle of motion and rest. A bed or a cloak, on the other hand, and anything of the same sort, *qua* having acquired that characteristic, that is, insofar as it is an artifact (*apo technēs*), has no innate impulse for change. But *qua* happening to be made of stone or earth or of a mixture of these, and just in that respect, it does. (*Ph.* II.1 192b9ff.)

It is for this reason that Aristotle is sympathetic to those who hold the view (although it is finally a misleading view) that the nature of a statue is bronze and the nature of a bed is wood.[17]

Once we have described the situation this way, however, the claim that the matter of an artifact is like the body of an animal can be seen to require qualification, just as the claims that motion is a kind of *energeia* or that all being is a mode of substance-being require qualification. The qualification was foreshadowed for us when much earlier we briefly considered the matter of complex and highly organized beings other than animals.[18] Then I claimed that although the proximate matter of a complex entity such as a bed may be understood as related per se to its form, there is *eventually* a matter which is not by virtue of itself the bed or what is the bed. We may now want to redescribe that fact and say that there is in the case of

---

[17] *Metaph.* Δ.4 1014b27ff.; *Physics* II.1 193a11ff.   [18] Above, p. 370.

a bed some matter which, unlike the bed, has a nature and which is naturally other than what it has been made into. An artifact, we may say, consists (eventually) of a matter which has a nature, but the artifact in itself lacks a nature except the nature of the matter which it has merely *kata sumbebēkos*.

But we may now recognize the features of substances and artifacts we have been considering as a consequence of this more basic fact that some beings have by nature a principle of motion and rest within themselves, while others do not. For it is insofar as an artifact consists of a matter which *has* a nature, but in itself lacks a nature except per accidens, that the artifact is an accidental being in the sense we earlier explored. And it is in terms of this understanding that we will want to qualify our claim that the biologically-based instrumental view of matter is an appropriate account of matter in general.

Consider again what happens when we ask about the matter of the several entities we have been discussing. In the case of a relatively simple accidental being such as a threshold, we said that a threshold consists of matter that exhibits a being of its own independent of its potential to be a threshold; the wood which is a threshold, for example, is what it is independently of being the matter of a threshold. We may redescribe this fact as well and say that a threshold consists of matter which, unlike the threshold, has a nature, which the threshold it is made out of shares only accidentally.

In the case of a more complex entity such as a house, this fact may not be immediately apparent; for we may, as we have seen, first specify the house's functional parts – window, threshold, lintel, etc. – using descriptions that mark them as potentially a house in just the sense that would lead us to think of them as importantly like the house's body. But if we continue with an iterative material analysis, and ask for the matter, say, of the threshold, or perhaps of the beam which is the threshold, the answer, either immediately or eventually, will resemble that of the first case: wood or some similar constitutive material which has an independent natural being of its own. Eventually, in other words, a material analysis in the case of an artifact will reveal a matter which has a nature of its own, and which exhibits no *natural* potentiality that leads to the artifact out of which it is made; an artifact is made by *technē* and not by nature (*Ph.* II.1 192b14ff.).

The situation in the case of an animal, however, is subtly but importantly different. Here again a first answer may refer to the organs (that is, the differentiated instrumental parts) that make up the animal's body, and a material analysis of these organs in turn will reveal the uniform parts that make up the various organs, and finally the elements that make up the uniform parts. But in each of these cases, the relation of matter to that of which it is the matter will be the same as that of an animal's body to the animal; it will be one of natural instrumentality, in which matter and that of which it is the matter share the same nature. At no point will the telic instrumentality of the matter be solely accidental to its essential and natural being.

The relation between an animal and its body is thus reproduced at every stage of an iterative material analysis with respect to the elements that make up an animal. At no stage do we find the distinction of matter into two beings, one with a nature other than that exhibited by that of which it is the matter, such as occurs in the case of artifacts, for at every stage the being of organs and of their constituent elements alike are *naturally* devoted to their telic instrumentality.

This is not to say that what constitutes an animal's matter has no nature independent of its thus constituting the matter of the animal. Unless, after all, it did have some independent nature, there would be no sense to Aristotle's arguments concerning the hypothetical necessity that explains why animals need to be made out of such and such a matter, nor for that matter to explanations in terms of standard Democritean necessity. Flesh as well as wood has gravity, so that a horse will also fall if thrown into the air, and the nature of the elements is whatever nature fire has *qua* fire, earth *qua* earth, and so on. But these characteristics are all part of a complex of being which constitutes for Aristotle a *natural structure of potentiality* for the higher functional being of animal life.[19]

There is lurking here, I suspect, a deep if problematic aspect of Aristotle's biological ontology. It is as though, in viewing the elements themselves as essentially instrumental for the higher forms of organic life, Aristotle sees the entire range of being as naturally constituted for the sake of the complex modes of animal activity; motion, perception and mind itself are on his view the natural manifestations of modes of capacity and potentiality embedded in even the most elemental forms of nature. This fact may represent an aspect of Aristotle's thought most alien to a post-modern, or for that matter post-classical, philosophy of nature, for which the emergence

---

[19] This is why Aristotle claims that outside the actual unity of substance-being the elements, like the parts of animals, are only potentialities, *dunameis* for the fully realized substantial being which is animal life: *Metaph.* Z.16 1040b5ff.

of higher forms of animal life from brute and dumb matter remains a puzzle, or at least a phenomenon demanding the active intervention of a living creative god.[20]

But in another sense, it is simply the recognition that Aristotle's ontology is rooted in a theory of nature; so it is not surprising that we have been led by a tortuous path from being to *phusis*. Where that path might lead us next in the explanation of the complex relationship between being and nature is another story.

VIII

I close with some general conclusions I think should be drawn from the story we have been attending to.

(1) Central to an understanding of Aristotle's ontology is the concept of accidental beings in the sense we have explored. Unless we recognize that artifacts are, at least as understood by Aristotle, instances of accidental being in much the same sense as *a horse being in the field*, or *Socrates being in the Lyceum*, we will understand properly neither the nature of artifacts nor the argument of the *Metaphysics*.

(2) A proper understanding of Aristotle's most important philosophical notions depends upon an intensional and not merely extensional reading of being. These two points are connected; failure to recognize that Aristotle is concerned with a theory of *being* and not a classification of *entities* may tempt us into supposing that a white horse is a substance, or that a threshold is not an accidental being. It is a part of this fact that we have been attending in this essay not to a distinction between kinds of entity at all, but to a distinction between modes of being, not, in other words, to differences between animals and artifacts, but to differences between the substance-being Aristotle takes to be exemplified in animals and the accidental being he takes to be exemplified in artifacts. Furthermore, and I have suggested that this is a general feature of Aristotle's philosophical strategy, it is not so much the differences that Aristotle thinks important as the fact that one mode of being is prior to and explanatory of the other; it is for this reason that an understanding of being in general has roots in an understanding of animal being.

(3) A proper understanding of animal being in turn depends upon an understanding of the relationship of actuality and potentiality that obtains between animals and their bodies. On the one hand, the notions of biological function and behavior as the patterns of actual

---

[20] Myles Burnyeat makes a similar point in the course of a challenging although problematic discussion in an unpublished essay 'Is Aristotle's philosophy of mind still credible?'

animal life are important for understanding the formal nature of animal being. On the other hand, understanding the animal body as an organ or set of potentialities for those functions is equally important to Aristotle's theory of such being, and, I have argued, to his theory of matter in general. Above all, central to the whole of Aristotle's biological metaphysics, as we may call it, is the functional identity of body and life in animal being.

An appreciation of this last item may help us to understand Aristotle's biological writings in a clearer light. It may help us to understand why the explanations and descriptions of animal being in those writings exhibit a constant and untroubled play among bodies, organs, life functions and biological practices as explanatory principles, and it may help us to appreciate properly the role that teleology plays as an explanatory principle. In general, it may remind us of why Aristotle thought that the complex structure of biological phenomena might be explained by revealing the fit and join of bodies and their organs to lives and their practices.

Such an appreciation should also lead us to recognize, as I suggested at the opening of this essay, that Aristotle's biological works are of interest to the philosopher and historian of philosophy as well as to the antiquarian or historian of science, and constitute part of a larger fabric of Aristotelian philosophical thought. But carrying out the promise implicit in that recognition is the subject for other studies by other people, to which I offer this essay merely as prolegomenon.[21]

---

[21] This essay has benefited greatly from the helpful comments and criticisms of Allan Gotthelf, James Lennox and Charles Kahn. Gotthelf's comments have been particularly helpful; he has been generous with both his time and his knowledge of Aristotle and ruthless in his demands that I rethink issues on which I have been confused.

15
Aristotle on bodies, matter, and potentiality

CYNTHIA A. FREELAND

In this paper I want to explore the application of some of Aristotle's central metaphysical notions to the analysis of living things. Commentators have often remarked that the conceptual pairs of matter/form and potentiality/actuality apply best to the analysis of Aristotle's favorite example, the bronze statue, but fit organic creatures – the true substances – less well. Two distinct problems arise for these more complex cases.

First, it seems impossible to point to something which serves as both matter 'for' and matter 'of' a living creature, as bronze does for statues. In *Physics* 1.7 Aristotle tells us that in any change some underlying thing or substratum persists, and it is easy to see that the bronze persists when a statue is molded, the gold continues in the bangle, etc. But what exists before a person, duck, or oak tree comes to be is an embryo, egg, or acorn (cf. *Ph.* 1.7 190b3–5) – and these surely do not remain in the finished creatures as their matter. This disanalogy is the target of William Charlton's criticism in his commentary on *Physics* I and II:

> It ought to be flesh and bone which is the material factor. It is what, we would say loosely in English, a dog is made of... Aristotle's argument in *Physics* I will not disclose a factor like flesh and bone. Flesh and bone do not become or turn into a dog: they are not, under any description, a *terminus a quo* of the change to a dog, but rather the *terminus ad quem*. It is the seed which is the *terminus a quo*...[1]

Second, it is difficult to understand Aristotle's claim in the *De Anima* that soul is a form or first actuality of 'a natural body which has life potentially'.[2] J. L. Ackrill, for example, has this complaint about Aristotle's description of the body as 'potentially capable of living' (412b25–6):

> Unless there is a living thing...there is no 'body potentially alive'; and once there is, its body is necessarily actually alive.[3]

[1] Charlton 1970: 76–7.
[2] 412a19–21, 27–8. Unless otherwise indicated, translations are those of the Oxford series, except for *Parts* and *Generation of Animals* where I use those of Peck in the Loeb editions. On this definition of soul, and soul–body relations generally, see also Charlton 1980.
[3] Ackrill 1972/3: 132.

392

Part of the puzzle here is about why Aristotle refers to the completed body – rather than to its matter, or an embryo – as potentially alive; but it is also strange that he calls the apparently actual body of an actual living creature 'potentially alive'. We can understand this move more readily in the case of the bronze statue, since the bronze now in the statue once had the potential to become that statue; but, as Charlton's remarks make clear, a person's (or dog's) flesh and bones, or its body as a whole, do not exist before the person (or dog) comes into being – so were not potentially alive in this way.

In the *Metaphysics*, despite his confident claims that matter *is* potentially, form actually (cf. 1042a27–8, b9–11, 1043a5–28, and 1045a25–b23), Aristotle still seems at times hesitant about the proper analysis of living things. Richard Rorty thinks, for instance, that he is 'thoroughly at sea'[4] over what to identify as potentially a person in this passage from *Metaphysics* Θ.7:

Is earth potentially a man? No – but rather when it has already become seed – and perhaps not even then. (1049a1–2)

If we are puzzled about Aristotle's answers to these questions, then the obvious place to turn for help is to the biological works, and to the *Generation of Animals* in particular. Unfortunately no easy answers are forthcoming; metaphysical insights threaten to vanish amidst a myriad of biological details. To sift through these details so as to glean an understanding of the actual *theory* of reproduction presented here, we must approach these texts with an awareness of Aristotle's background assumptions. Hence I will begin by making some preliminary observations about Aristotle's other favorite metaphysical examples, houses and hatchets, with the aim of showing how these serve as useful analogues for true, living natural substances. Later I will also draw upon the doctrine of powers in *Metaphysics* Θ.1–5 and the analysis of change in *Physics* III. With this help, and if we allow for the enormous complexity of living beings, we will find answers to our questions in the biology. There is a plausible candidate for the matter which both pre-exists and persists in human beings, namely, blood. Embryos, eggs, and acorns ought not to be considered as competing candidates because, in Aristotle's view, they have a 'process-like' nature. Finally, we can make some sense of the claim that a living substance's body is potentially alive.

My investigation presupposes the work of my co-contributors in various ways, some more obvious than others. In particular I will have occasion to make use of Cooper's clarification of hypothetical necessity (ch. 9 above), Furth's catalogue of layers of construction

[4] Rorty 1974: 77.

in Aristotle's ontology (ch. 2 above), and Kosman's reading of *dunamis* and *energeia* in *Metaphysics* Θ (Kosman 1984; cf. ch. 14 above).

I. Preliminaries: houses and hatchets

The *Metaphysics* links form with activity and function in ways that make nonsense of the statue paradigm. (Even a half-hearted attempt at specifying some decorative, inspirational, or educative function of bronze sculptures would have helped, but Aristotle does not bother.) In discussing the forms or actualities of more complex artifacts, such as houses and hatchets, Aristotle mentions functions: sheltering chattels, dividing wood, etc. (*Metaph.* H.2 1043a16–18; *de An.* 1.1 403b3–5; *Ph.* 11.9 200a30–b8). Let us pursue some details of the analysis of such artifacts, to get clues about Aristotle's understanding of the claim that a substance's matter is potentially that thing.

The *Metaphysics* argues that the form and *ergon* or work of a thing constitute its end or completion (*telos*): and Aristotle maintains that 'the actuality is the work' (*hē de energeia to ergon*, 1050a21–2: cp. 1023a34). Form is more than mere shape (*morphē*): although they have the right shapes, animals carved from wood or metamorphosed into stone are not real (*PA* 1.1 640b35–641a6, 641a14–21). Similarly, though a corpse preserves the shape of a person, it is unable to continue its operations (640b33–5). By calling form the actuality (*energeia*) of a thing Aristotle clearly means to emphasize these functional specifications.

Now, obviously, the association of form with function must have important implications for our understanding of matter. Aristotle often says that some matter (or material configuration) is hypothetically necessary for a certain end or goal to be realized.[5] E.g.:

For just as there is a necessity that the axe be hard, since one must cut with it, and if hard that it be of bronze or iron, so too since the body is an instrument (for each of its parts is for the sake of something, and so is the body as a whole), therefore there is a necessity that it be *such* a thing and made of *such* things if that end is to be. (*PA* 1.1 642a9–13, tr. Balme)[6]

Thus Aristotle's schema for understanding form–matter relations looks straightforward. *First*, identify a substance's function or natural activity, say, sawing or dividing wood. (He seems confident we can do this job, even in the case of living creatures and their parts;

[5] For useful discussion of this notion, see Cooper, ch. 9 above.
[6] Cooper's discussion of this and related passages considers some points I represent here in oversimplified form, namely Aristotle's view that materials have their own necessary properties (a 'Democritean necessity') which may *also* – once present for a particular presumed end – be made use of for further purposes in the functioning of the creature. See Cooper, above 257–9.

cf. the opening statement of strategy at *PA* i.i 640a33–b1.[7]) *Second*, identify the *sort* of thing needed to carry out this function – here, stuff that is quite hard, yet not brittle. *Third*, and finally, look about in the world for something suitable. Iron fills the bill because it has the right dispositional property, hardness. So does bronze, as the passage just cited indicates. Butter, wool, or wood wouldn't do (cf. *Metaph.* H.4 1044a27–9).

Following this same schema, we could reason that a window must be made of something transparent, a soup pot of something that conducts heat, etc. Similarly Aristotle explains that particular matters are suitable for constructing various organs, e.g. bone for the skeleton, because of their dispositional properties, such as bone's lightness and hardness (*PA* ii.8 653b33–5; ii.9 654b28ff.).

Aristotle, in Book ii of *Generation and Corruption*, offers a quite elaborate theory of the dispositional properties of various materials. In short, he says there that any sort of matter or stuff has a certain ratio of the basic elements, and that as a result of their combination in this ratio, it has certain characteristic properties.[8] These include numerous familiar dispositional properties, such as softness, viscosity, dampness, brittleness, and so forth (ii.2). Elements combined in various ratios, then, are responsible for such compounds as flesh, bone, etc. (ii.7).[9]

Interestingly, Aristotle holds that certain materials which serve as the tissues of various bodily parts only achieve their peculiar dispositional features when they are actually *in* a living substance. (That is, only then are the ratios correct.) This explains numerous familiar changes we observe when tissues or residues are removed or exuded from the body, altering in thickness, liquidity, etc. (*PA* ii.2 647b10–14; ii.3 649b27–34). Formal or dispositional characteristics of such materials thus parallel the functional characteristics of higher-level bodily organs, since Aristotle believes that these organs too do not count as genuine once they are removed from a living creature and lose their capacities to function (*PA* i.i 640b33–5, 641a3–5, and 654a32ff.).

---

[7] See also Balme's detailed discussion of Aristotle's procedures in ch. 11 above, 300–1.

[8] It is interesting to compare the accounts of the *Generation and Corruption* with those of *Meteorology* iv, especially chapters 4 and 8ff. *Mete.* iv.12, after making a familiar Aristotelian point about corpses ('A corpse is a man in name only', 389b31, tr. H. D. P. Lee in the Loeb edition), remarks that uniform parts (such as flesh) have functions too, only less obvious ones (390a14–15). The comparison between the purposes of instrumental parts and those of their subordinate materials – at varying layers of complexity – is made explicit in *PA* ii.i 646b11–647a2. For a reading of *Meteorology* iv as the 'biochemistry' of the biology, see Furley 1983.

[9] For detailed discussion of how Aristotle builds up numerous, ever more complex layers from the basic elemental building-blocks, see Furth, ch. 2 above, 30–7.

I had a reason for marking out three stages in the explanatory schema involving the hatchet (just above 394–5): this makes it clear that Aristotle does not say that any particular matter is called for, or included in, the definition of a thing.[10] What is required is rather a certain sort of matter possessing the right dispositional properties. It is natural to understand these properties as themselves quasi-functional. That is, iron and bronze are materials which can hold their shapes and comprise a blade hard enough to divide wood (but not, say, diamonds). Following Aristotle's advice, in explaining form–matter relations we should first describe an artifact's (or organ's) function, and then list the subordinate functions its material constituents must perform. If a window is to allow light to enter a building, then its material must be able to transmit light (i.e. must be transparent) and able to be contained in a frame (making water an unlikely choice). Aristotle does not explicitly set out any one method for determining which subordinate functions or dispositional properties are hypothetically necessitated by the supposition of some particular end. He presumes we can complete this explanatory task; our lists may well be open-ended enough to permit alternative realizations. (Thus wood, straw, stones, or bricks can be matter for a house; copper or iron can be matter for a soup pot, etc.)

With this clearer understanding of Aristotle's way of linking form and function, we are now in a position to begin to interpret his claim that the matter of a thing is potentially that thing. Too often, I believe, readers take the Aristotelian notion of potentiality to have a strictly temporal application, indicating 'mere' potentiality or prior existence. Kosman's reading of *Metaphysics* Θ reminds us of the integral connections between Aristotle's term *dunamis* and the verb *dunasthai*, 'to be able'. For Aristotle a given matter's potentialities are its capacities to become or to be certain things – i.e. to be formed into, and serve in, artifacts (or organs) having particular functions. Aristotle is willing to call the matter actually in a thing 'potential' because it preserves its capacities.[11] Let me return to the hatchet example to illustrate this point.

---

[10] This point is controversial, and needs the support of an interpretation of *Metaphysics* Z, and of the apparent conflict between 1036a34–b7 and 1036b22–9. I incline to read the second passage as indicating that a definition of man would require reference to organic parts rather than to materials. But for a different view, see Kirwan 1971: 185. See also Balme's discussion, ch. 11 above.

[11] My discussion here and in the following three paragraphs should be read in the light of the study of *dunamis* and *energeia* in *Metaphysics* Θ in Kosman 1984. I will flag specific references as I proceed. On the sorts of actualization which preserve, rather than destroy, capacities, see his §3, 'Motion as a kind of actuality'.

Aristotle says that bronze is potentially a hatchet (meaning, presumably, that it is potentially a hatchet blade). As I interpret this, it means not that bronze itself is a thing capable of chopping (which it obviously is not, in, say, lumps), but rather that it can form a thing which is able to chop – a blade. Bronze has this capacity or potentiality, which it shares with iron, because it has the dispositional property of hardness (due to its constitution by the elements in ratios). Perhaps bronze is potentially a soup pot because of a different dispositional property, conductivity.

Now clearly bronze preserves its capacity to *be* a hatchet blade while it actually is one – just as a soprano preserves, and manifests, her capacity to hit high notes when she sings high 'C'.[12] Indeed, the bronze (or some alternative matter) must be present, with its peculiar dispositional or quasi-functional properties, for there to be an actual blade at all, rather than merely a drawing or idea of a blade. But this reading allows for the explanatory force of Aristotle's *dunamis*-claims in temporal contexts as well. Bronze's potential to become a hatchet – a capacity it has *qua* movable, changeable thing (*hēi kinēton*) is carefully distinguished from its capacity to be a hatchet (a capacity it has 'in itself', *hēi chalkos*) in *Physics* III.1 (201a25–b15). The former potential, to become a hatchet, disappears once the bronze has been formed.[13] Whether that potential is present depends in part upon contingent facts about its current state – upon, e.g., whether it is unformed rather than already in a hatchet. Its capacity to become a *hatchet*, as opposed to, say, a soufflé – like its capacity to become a statue or soup pot – depends upon certain of its dispositional properties. These same dispositional properties account for the bronze's capacity or potential to be the hatchet, statue, or soup pot.

Thus Aristotle calls matter potential because it has capacities to become and be certain things; these capacities vary according to the varying compositions and dispositional properties of the matter itself.[14] What holds true of hatchets is equally true of living substances and their organic parts. I will turn to these cases in more detail below, but for now we might note the parallel between, say, the glass in a window and the liquid in an eye. Given that the eye's function is to transmit light (or colors) from without to an animal, then it must contain something liquid and transparent, to fulfill the subordinate

---

[12] Compare Kosman 1984: §4, esp. 134.

[13] Cf. 201b11–12. Bronze's potential to *become* a hatchet is the self-destructive capacity for a motion; on such potentials, see Kosman 1984: §2, esp. 127.

[14] On the role of such necessary properties of matter within Aristotle's teleology, see Cooper, ch. 9 above, e.g. his discussion of respiration, 257–8.

function of transmitting the motion (*energeia*) of light within the organ.[15] The liquid in the eye is correctly identified as able to comprise an eye, exactly as glass is able to comprise a window. Thus the claim that eye-liquid is potentially an eye need not imply that it is available in lumps or puddles somewhere waiting to be scooped into eyes; rather, it means that this material, in particular, has the right capacities (dispositional properties) to be an eye, i.e., to satisfy the hypothetically necessitated requirements of transparency and susceptibility to motion. It may be thought puzzling that Aristotle does not think that eye-liquid exists outside of eyes with the potential to become eyes, as bronze awaits its mold; to that, and related puzzles, I turn next.

II. Human blood and other matters

Having noted what Aristotle does and does not intend by his claim that matter *is* potentially, we can now return to our first question: what, if anything, is both matter for and matter of a living creature, such as a person? Here we must delve into the details of Aristotle's account of sexual reproduction, observing the central role of blood in that account. (There are close analogues for other creatures, but for now I will concentrate on people.) I will also devote some attention to the nature of embryos, to show why they are not potentially living creatures; Aristotle holds subtle views on their ontological status. Below, in section III, I will turn to our second question – Ackrill's puzzle about why Aristotle calls a body potentially alive.

A brief review of the doctrine of powers in *Metaphysics* Θ is essential preparation for studying Aristotle's theory of sexual generation in the *Generation of Animals*. The first five chapters of this book of the *Metaphysics* deal with 'primary' potentialities, or powers (active and passive) to interact with other things (1046a9–15). Such powers include fire's capacity to burn oil, as well as oil's capacity to be burned (1046a24–8). Only in chapter 6 does Aristotle turn to the 'most useful' (*chrēsimōtatē*; cf. 1045b35–1046a1) notion of potentiality, which involves its connection with matter.[16] This chapter begins with the clear announcement of a new topic: 'Since we have treated of the kind of potency that is related to movement...' (1048a25–6). Hence we would not expect to find anything in

---

[15] *GA* v.1 779b21–34. I ignore the fine points here about the usefulness of various accidents of eye color, etc. See v.1 779b35ff.

[16] He does so in a puzzling analogy, in 1048a35–b4. For discussion, see Kosman 1984: 135ff.

Book Θ's earlier chapters, on powers, to help illuminate the study of matter-potentialities.

It seems, however, that in his biological works Aristotle regards matter- and form-potentialities in accordance with his account of active and passive powers in *Metaphysics* Θ, especially Θ.5. In that chapter Aristotle explains that when the given conditions for the operation of any particular power obtain, then, if an active and passive power are brought together, they both must *of necessity* be actualized:

When the agent and patient meet in the way appropriate to the potency in question, the one must act and the other be acted upon.[17]

That is, if the oil and fire are joined – in the right conditions – the fire necessarily ignites the oil.

Similarly, in the *Generation of Animals* Aristotle distinguishes active and passive factors in the generation of living substances, and remarks upon the inexorability of their operation when brought together in the right conditions:

When a pair of factors, the one active and the other passive, come into contact in the way in which the one is active and the other passive (by 'way' I mean the manner, place, and time of contact), then immediately both are brought into play, the one acting and the other being acted upon. In this case it is the female which provides the matter, and the male which provides the principle of movement.[18]

Generally, then, Aristotle uses his account of active and passive powers to discuss and analyze male–female inputs in animal generation. A father through his sperm introduces active powers into an appropriate female material, with correlated passive powers. The process of co-actualization of these powers starts off the generative process resulting in a new member of the species.

In a bit more detail, for the case of human reproduction we may distinguish the following two principal factors:

(1) The father's semen, which provides the embryo with its form – a replication of his own; it does this in virtue of containing a hot, foamy, gaseous substance, the *pneuma*. Aristotle stresses that the semen conveys motions to the embryo, but not matter; after its initial work is done, it dissolves or evaporates away. (Cf. II.2 735b32–5; II.3 736b33–737a10)

---

17 1048a5–7. The account in Θ.5 is complicated by Aristotle's distinction between rational and non-rational powers. I ignore here the rational powers, whose operation is not inevitable even in the right circumstances; these are surely irrelevant to a discussion of matter-potentialities and generative processes. See 1047b35–1048a8.

18 *GA* II. 740b21–25. The Greek reads:...καὶ ὅτι τὸ ποιητικὸν καὶ τὸ παθητικόν, ὅταν θίγωσιν, ὃν τρόπον ἐστὶ τὸ μὲν ποιητικὸν τὸ δὲ παθητικόν (τὸν δὲ τρόπον λέγω τὸ ὡς καὶ οὗ καὶ ὅτε), εὐθὺς τὸ μὲν ποιεῖ τὸ δὲ πάσχει. ὕλην μὲν οὖν παρέχει τὸ θῆλυ, τὴν δ' ἀρχὴν τῆς κινήσεως τὸ ἄρρεν.

(2) The matter for an embryo is the *katamēnia* or menstrual fluid, a residue of the mother. It is said to be 'potentially the same in character as the body whose secretion it is'. (II.4 738b3–4; cf. 738b20–7)

Now, in any case of sexual reproduction, the active powers in the seminal fluid must be exactly suited to operate upon the corresponding passive powers in the mother's residue.[19] Aristotle offers numerous analogies to explain the generative-constructive process. A male animal is compared to a craftsman directing the production of some sort of artifact – variously, a hatchet, saw, sword, flute, or house. Each of these must be made from the right sort of material; so too for a human being: 'The heat to produce flesh or bone does not work on just any material whatsoever at just any place or at just any time' (743a21–2; cf. *de An.* II.2 414a25–7). Aristotle continues,

And so it could not happen that a carpenter would make a chest which was not made from wood; nor, without the carpenter, will there be a chest from that wood. This heat resides in the seminal residue having a movement and activity suited in amount and character to each of the parts. Insofar as it is too little or too much, it will make the thing being produced either inferior or deformed. (743a23–30, tr. Peck, with alterations)

Pursuing one of these artifactual analogues in more detail will help us answer our question about what serves as human matter. In *Generation of Animals* 1.22 (cf. 730b5–32) Aristotle draws the following extended parallel between a human father and a carpenter working in wood:

Agent	Tools	Motions	Result	Material
Carpenter	Saw, etc.	Sawing, etc.	House	Wood
Father	Semen	Heating, etc.	Baby	*Katamēnia*

One very important fact about human reproduction is omitted from this chart: this concerns the nature of the *katamēnia*, or material element in human reproduction. In Aristotle's view the menstrual residue, like the semen, is a residue of blood (*GA* I.19 726b3ff., b31ff.). Unlike the semen, the *katamēnia* by itself lacks 'generative motions' (II.3 737a28–30; cf. II.1 734b8–9 and ff.). Both male and female adults are enabled, by their hearts as vital organs and life-principles, to maintain their being and nourish themselves, while the embryo, of course, requires impetus and nourishment from without to launch its being and sustain its growth. The menstrual residue serves as the first basis for the embryo's construction and growth, with later nourishment entering through the umbilical cord from the mother. The

[19] That is, barring certain unusual cases of cross-species mating or monstrosities. Even here the male and female contributions must be suited to one another. See 743a28; also 738b27–35, 769b10ff.

embryo is said to have its own blood once the *katamēnia* has been 'set' by the semen's heat (*GA* II.3 737a18–24, II.4 739b20ff., IV.1 765a34–b35).

Now this specifically human blood of the embryo is quite a promising candidate to consider in seeking to identify human matter. Unlike mere earth and water, and unlike the semen, blood is close enough to actual human matter to count as potentially human, quelling Aristotle's doubts in *Metaphysics* Θ.7. (Indeed, he lists it as human matter at H.4 1044a15–20.) Blood is an actual material part of a person, with its own functional role (*PA* II.4). However, blood is unlike other actual human materials, such as bone and flesh, in that it is the first material in the embryo, and exists outside of, and before the coming-to-be of, the infant (though in the mother). Blood alone comprises the embryo's heart, its first organ, which provides it with a minimal life-principle and identity of its own (*GA* II.4 740b3–4, 17–19; II.6 743b25–6; *PA* II.1 647b4–7; III.4 665b9–17).

Blood is suitable, then, as an answer to the question of what serves as the matter *for* – matter which becomes – a human. But is it also the matter *of* a person? It would be absurd to say that humans, or their bodies, are made up solely of blood – as absurd as saying that ducks are made up of egg-yolks all somehow stuck together. But perhaps it is too much to expect the same strict identity in these more complex cases as can be found for the far simpler bronze statue.

In fact, according to Aristotle blood does play a unique and pre-eminent role in the construction of human bodies. It is the material underlying all other human matter. Blood is called 'the final form of food' (*PA* II.3 650a34–5) and also 'the material out of which the whole body is constructed' (III.5 668a1ff.; cf. 651a15). Aristotle further remarks,

The material which supplies nourishment and the material out of which nature forms and fashions the animal are one and the same. (*GA* IV. 8 777a5–6; cf. II.4 740b34–6)

Again,

It is from the blood, when concocted and somehow divided up, that each part of the body is made. (726b5–7; cf. 751a34–b1 and 744b13ff.)

Thus, for Aristotle blood is the matter of such more complicated materials as flesh and bone, and, more directly, of the heart and viscera (*PA* II.1 646b31–4, 647a34–5). Blood is potentially bone, flesh, and so on. Aristotle allows that in certain complex cases 'there come to be several matters for the same thing', explaining that this is so,

...when the one matter is matter for the other: e.g. phlegm comes from the fat and from the sweet, if the fat comes from the sweet. (*Metaph.* H.4 1044a20–3)

In sum, we can identify a sort of halfway candidate for human matter; blood, unlike flesh and bones, exists before there is an actual human infant, but also, unlike the embryo itself, persists in the infant and adult as part of, and the basis for, their material parts.

A question may yet remain concerning the place of the embryo itself in this account of human reproduction. Why not say that the embryo is potentially a person (or is matter for a person) since it is what exists before there is, and turns into, a baby? This suggestion, I am convinced, reflects a misconception about the ontological status of embryos; so at this point it is appropriate to turn to the second extra-biological text mentioned earlier, the *Physics* III discussion of change. Aristotle emphasizes in his carpenter analogy in *Generation of Animals* 1.22 that neither the carpenter nor the art of carpentry 'passes into' the wood; instead a certain shape or form (*hē morphē kai to eidos*) is transferred. These, he says, 'come into being by means of the movement in the material' (*GA* II.4 740b14–15). The *Physics* provides the explanation for these claims.

In *Physics* III.3 Aristotle argues that the actualization of an agent's power is *in* the patient (202b5–10). Thus a teacher's power to instruct, as well as the pupil's capacity to learn, are realized *in* the student acquiring knowledge. These are the same in fact, though not in definition (202b11–22).

Furthermore, Aristotle distinguishes between two ways in which powers may be actualized.[20] The potential of bricks and stones to become a house is realized incompletely, or as a potentiality (*hēi toiouton*, 201a9–11) in the process of a housebuilding; it is also realized completely, of course, in the house itself. In parallel, the carpenter's active power to build may be manifested both in the process of building and in the house itself, as Aristotle notes in *Physics* II.3. If we describe the cause of a house as 'the builder building', we refer to the incomplete exercise of the carpenter's power, or to that power's incomplete actualization in the house-being-built. This cause will disappear once the house is finished, since the builder then ceases building (II.3 195b4–6 and 17–21). Processes (*kinēseis*) aim at their own cessation.

We should get clearer about what Aristotle thinks processes in fact are. He has no conception of events dislocated from substances; a housebuilding is simply the sawing, planing, hammering, etc. *of* some

<hr>

[20] My discussion here is indebted to Kosman 1969 as well as Kosman 1984.

wood *by* some skilled agent. In addition he maintains that the active and passive aspects of such an event are identical: the process of a housebuilding is the same as the process of a house-being-built: soufflé-cooking is one with the soufflé-being-cooked, etc. Such processes may be identified in terms of their intended end-results even though, obviously, those results do not yet exist. I can, in other words, point to several bowls and a mound of cheese, saying 'here's tonight's soufflé', though nothing appropriately browned and fluffy yet exists. What I have pointed to is merely some stage, incompletely beaten and mixed, of a soufflé-being-cooked.

The lesson for our reading of human reproduction should be clear if we recall Aristotle's frequent analogies between generation, building, and cooking. We can understand the true nature of embryos with the aid of the following illustrative chart (a modification of the one given earlier, p. 400):

Agent	Tools	Movements	Product	Process	Matter
Carpenter	Saw	Sawing, etc.	House	Housebuilding; house-being-built	Wood
Father	Semen	Cooking, etc.	Baby	Embryo-being cooked	*Katamēnia* (Blood)

Housebuilding is one with the process of a house-being-built, so also is 'baby-building' identical in being with a baby-being-built. I want to suggest that 'embryo' is just our name for what exists at any stage of this complex process. No similar designation is available for stages of those processes in which we have, understandably, less interest – housebuildings, soufflé-cookings, etc., but we certainly could invent and apply terms in a parallel way ('house-sprouts', 'avant-soufflés', etc.). For Aristotle the embryo is simply not the right sort of thing to count as a *bona fide* entity; it constantly changes, does not remain any one thing,[21] and aims at a certain conclusion. An embryo is a constantly shifting result of the being-cooked, -set, -hardened, etc. of some *katamēnia* by some paternal motions – as a house-stage is a phase in the being-sawed, -planed, etc. of some wood by a skilled agent. Both processes will cease when they reach their intended conclusion. The carpenter's skill is manifested in the finished house; similarly, the father's form is replicated in his progeny. At this stage, the organizational movements launched by the semen have stopped:

[21] The embryo is merely a 'quasi'-entity, in spite of the presence in it of its own life-principle (cf. *GA* II.4 739b34ff.), because it can at best be called *plant-like* – *not* an entity with the nature of a plant, because no plant will subsequently change into a human being (or any other animal).

Now semen, and the movement and principle which it contains are such that, as the movement ceases, each one of the parts gets formed and acquires soul. (*GA* II.1 734b22–4)

An embryo, then, is no more the *material* which exists before, and turns into, a baby than is a house-sprout the *matter* for a house. Both are, rather, the incomplete stages of construction of some final product; both possess formal as well as material aspects. Aristotle emphasizes this in frequent analogies, as when, for example, he compares the embryo's developing system of blood vessels to the skeletal walls of a house-being-built (II.6 743a1ff.).

Although my attention has been directed so far almost exclusively to the case of human reproduction, the general account given here holds for all viviparous blooded animals. Much the same pattern applies to oviparous animals too, since their generative matter – the analogue of *katamēnia* – is always some form of the parent animal's nourishment (III.1 751a33ff., 762b6ff., 26ff.). We can thus avoid calling the (fertilized) egg itself matter for a duck, since it is, like an embryo, a stage of a construction process. Neither are we forced to maintain that only specifically duckish 'goo'[22] (i.e. flesh and feathers) is potentially a duck, since we can point instead to the matter *in* the egg. Similarly, the seeds of plants, which contain in themselves both male and female principles (1.23 731a1–29), are parallel to embryos and eggs. Thus acorns contain a sort of matter which is able to *become* the matter of an oak and also able, within parent or adult trees, to *be* their matter.

III. People and their bodies

In concentrating so far on the roles of blood and embryos in the constitution and generation of persons, I have neglected to discuss *bodies*. As noted earlier, Aristotle links bodies, as well as matter, with potentiality, saying in the *De Anima*, for example, that organic bodies potentially have life. We must now turn to the second major question I raised at the start of this paper, namely, what does Aristotle mean by this claim? Why is an actually existing – and for that matter, living – body said to be potentially alive, and why is a body which cannot pre-exist its substance linked to potentiality at all?

I tried earlier (p. 396 above) to disentangle Aristotle's potentiality-claims from their temporal applications by emphasizing the meaning of *dunamis* as *capacity*. I noted that in Aristotle's view bronze, for

[22] The term is Richard Rorty's; see Rorty 1974.

example, has capacities both to become and to be hatchet blades or soup pots because it has the right dispositional characteristics, hardness and conductivity. The bronze *in* a blade or pot both preserves and manifests its capacity to be the blade or pot. In much the same way, we will see, the body 'in' (or better, *of*) a person both preserves and manifests its capacity to be a person.[23] As Aristotle quite sensibly remarks,

We must not understand by that which is potentially capable of living what has lost the soul it had, but only what still retains it.[24]

Being a person is, of course, a complex business, because we are capable of all sorts of things. Aristotle says in *De Anima* 1.4, for example, that a man pities, learns, or thinks with his soul (408b13– 15) – and this list can be considerably extended. People also walk, see, converse, reproduce, and behave courageously with their souls: human souls encompass these capacities because they are the souls of – i.e. actualizations of – certain very complex bodies. The human leg is potentially a moving, walking leg, the eye potentially a seeing organ, the uterus potentially a reproducing organ, etc. These and other human parts have the capacity to be alive (or better 'be lived' by the actual person) in a specifically human way. My eye cannot see eagle-fashion, my legs don't have the potential to do a duck-walk, and my uterus is not capable of producing lions.

Still we might well wonder whether Aristotle believes that there is ever a time when a human body is merely a sum of capacities, all dormant – whether a body is ever merely potentially (and not also actually) alive.[25] Although he believes that nothing which is not in fact already alive would count as a body, still, actual bodies closely approximate a level of purely potential being during sleep, when most vital functions are either shut off or greatly reduced (*de An.* II.1 412b25–413a3). Aristotle goes so far as to call sleep 'as it were a border-land between living and non-living', adding that 'a person who is asleep would appear to be neither completely non-existent nor

---

[23] See again Kosman 1984: §3.
[24] *De An.* II.1 412b25–6. He continues, b26–7,...τὸ δὲ σπέρμα καὶ ὁ καρπὸς τὸ δυνάμει τοιονδὶ σῶμα. These, I take it, are able to *become* such a body.
[25] This concerns Ackrill, as I noted above (392). One might also wonder whether a corpse ought to count as such a body, though Aristotle denies that it could. In *Metaph.* H.5 he denies that a living man is potentially dead; rather, 'it is the *matter* of the animal that is in virtue of its corruption the potency and matter of a corpse' (1045a1–2, my emphasis). A corpse, since its matter is decayed, can no longer see, walk, etc., as a body can. Its eyes would no longer be fluid enough, its legs too heavy, etc. (On the other hand a modern-day 'technically dead' person revived by emergency efforts perhaps did have (was?) a corpse-body potentially alive.)

completely existent' (*GA* v.1 778b29–31).[26] Since the body is capable of functioning in characteristically human ways, it remains 'potentially' alive even when it is actively functioning.

It seems to me likely that Aristotle's belief that there are no bodies alive *purely* potentially stems from contingent facts about his world and its technology, and not from logical or conceptual reasons. That is, I do not doubt that he would regard the eye, cornea, heart, or kidney in a donor bank as purely potential organs. So also would frozen sperm (or, for that matter, eggs) count as potential reproductive residues. In the event of advances permitting the deep-freeze of whole persons we could have ice-boxes full of bodies potentially alive.[27]

IV. Conclusion

In the preceding discussion I have suggested how Aristotle might respond to two key questions about the analysis of living substances: (1) What is the matter for and of – the persisting substratum of – a human being or other organic creature? and (2) Why is it appropriate to describe a body as potentially alive? I sought out answers to these questions in Aristotle's biology, keeping in mind certain of his views about form and function, active and passive powers, and the ontology of processes. I also emphasized that, for Aristotle, *dunamis*-claims concern a thing's capacities or abilities.

In response to question (1) I pointed out that the *Generation of Animals* theory of human reproduction identifies blood as the material from which an embryo begins, and out of which the fully-formed human infant comes to be. Blood persists as the matter of human adults, at least of certain of their parts; for other, more complex, parts it serves as building and nourishing material. Since humans are, obviously, constituted of materials other than blood itself, the simple analysis of change in *Physics* 1.7 must be modified. People, like other complicated organic substances, involve an extra stage of material transformation both in their coming-to-be and in their continued existence. Though blood persists in the organism when a living being is generated, it must be further worked up to become suitable material for complex tissues and organic parts. Something similar holds true even of many artifacts as well; wet clay and straw must set and harden to become strong brick walls; raw timber must be

---

[26] For a more thorough discussion, see Sprague 1977/8.
[27] My acquaintance with science-fiction visions of such a development leads me to believe that such bodies would 'hibernate', i.e. continue some metabolic functioning, and so, alas, would not be *purely* potentially alive.

sawed, planed, and smoothed before serving as a table, etc. Aristotle acknowledges the need to refine raw materials when he speaks in *Physics* II.2 of the helmsman's knowledge of useful woods and of how they should be finished. True, he proceeds to remark that *we* make the material in such cases, while in nature 'the matter is there all along' (194b7–8). We must, I think, reject this claim as overly simple, and in fact false, in light of the far more elaborate, qualified theory of the *Generation of Animals*. Of course there remains a crucial difference between productive processes of art and nature, namely that in the latter the self-directed unfolding organism manufactures *its own* matter, as it is needed, in order to make – and replenish – its parts. We can see, then, how this matter – blood, in the human case – provides a parallel to the bronze which is both matter *for* and *of* the statue, and provides a better answer to question (1) than candidates heretofore considered, embryos or flesh-and-bones. The latter do not come before the substance, as blood does; and the former, I have shown, are stages of processes, and not materials.

As for question (2), Aristotle holds that a body is potentially alive because in it reside capacities for life-activities. These capacities exist and even flourish in the actually living being, though never, as a contingent fact, in a purely potentially living thing.

A final question remains, namely, why did Aristotle serve himself so badly with that example of the lumpish bronze statue, not even, as I complained before, decorating the *agora* or inspiring young warriors? Perhaps, despite his own delight in the glories of the lowly, he remained mindful of the potentially squeamish audience at his metaphysical lectures (cf. *PA* I.5 644b22–645a37). Houses and hatchets are more mundane, but useful, exemplars, and indeed these too turn up more often in the biology. They incorporate, far better than the still statue, varieties of possible functioning, as well as intricacies of layering in form–matter relations. Artifactual analogues like these serve usefully to model the even more complex and subtle interweavings of form and matter, function and organ, which characterize the true, vital, self-perpetuating living substances, from rational animals down to the lowliest of insects. We may not share Aristotle's enthusiasm for mud-flies, but we must admire the ingenious way in which they are caught up in the strands of his metaphysical web.[28]

[28] Jim Lennox has helped with discussions and comments at every stage of the writing of this paper. I am also grateful to John Cooper, Allan Gotthelf, Alexander Nehamas and Willem de Vries for their suggestions.

16
Aristotle on the place of
mind in nature

WILLIAM CHARLTON

In the last chapter of her book *Physicalism* K. V. Wilkes writes:

Aristotle (and all Greek philosophers before him) lacked the concept of 'a mind', and would not have wanted it had it been explained to them; lacking any such notion, they lacked, too, the concept of 'the mental'; and hence they had no mind–body problem. Within Aristotle's psychology the relation of the mental to the physical cannot even be posed. (1978: 115)

This view is developed also by D. W. Hamlyn in the introduction to his *Aristotle's De Anima* (1968): it certainly has the charm of paradox. The common Greek word *nous* appears to express our concept of a mind. Aristotle speaks of *nous* as 'part of the soul' and says it differs from other parts in three ways: it is not the concern of the natural scientist, it comes in 'from outside', and it is 'separable' from the body. If that does not give him a mind–body problem, what would? The fact is that while Aristotle's account of psychological concepts generally, his doctrine that soul and body are related as form to matter or actuality to possibility, is attractively undualistic, when he comes to *nous* dualism seems to seep back. J. L. Ackrill in *Aristotle the Philosopher* remarks:

The idea of a pure intellect literally separable from the body is difficult to understand, and difficult to reconcile with the rest of Aristotle's philosophy. (1981a: 62)

In what follows I do not promise to effect a complete reconciliation. Anyone who can reconcile a hylomorphic account of the soul–body relation with a doctrine of personal immortality wins a jackpot beyond the dreams of Aristotelian scholarship. But I shall consider the three peculiarities Aristotle attributes to *nous* and argue that Aristotle is not committed to placing mind and body in completely different realms, like the seventeenth-century realms of thought and extension.

First, however, a word about what Aristotle's conception of *nous* is a conception of. Most of his readers take *nous* to be a capacity, and the distinction in *de An.* III.5 between a *nous* that makes and a *nous* that becomes all things as a further distinction between two intellectual faculties. That doctrine that *nous* is separable ought then to be the very unaristotelian-sounding doctrine that a capacity can exist without there being anything that has it. In fact everyone correctly understands it as the doctrine that there can be a bodiless thinker. In *de An.* II. 414a4–14 Aristotle says that we know things 'by' the soul in the way in which we are healthy 'by' the body. The dative inflection, which I just now rendered by the word 'by', clearly introduces here not *that by means of which*, but *that which*: the subject of health or knowledge. When in *de An.* III.4 429a10 Aristotle announces he is going to discuss 'that by which' the soul knows and thinks, it is easiest to suppose he is going to discuss that which thinks. In 429b14–18 he suggests that *nous* and *to aisthētikon* may be 'the same thing differently disposed': an odd suggestion if those expressions signified faculties and not subjects. If the *de An.* III.5 distinction is between a material and a formal aspect of *nous*, *nous* is better taken as that which thinks than as a faculty. It is 'part of the soul' in that a description of it is part of the description of the human soul, or in that a thinker is part of what a man, in his formal aspect, is.

The first peculiarity of *nous*, that it is not the concern of natural science, has gone almost unnoticed by recent commentators. Perhaps that is because we are used to a division of reality, or at least of concepts, between science and religion. Our division, however, hardly goes back beyond Hegel and Kant. The Aristotelian notion of natural science, of *phusikē*, is pretty much the creation of Plato and Aristotle. Before Plato thinkers do not seem to have distinguished at all clearly between scientific and philosophical (let alone religious) questions. Plato and Aristotle were in the position of being able to draw the boundaries of intellectual disciplines wherever it seemed to them appropriate. Now although Plato really does advocate the dualistic account some of Aristotle's remarks about *nous* suggest, Plato does not (in the *Timaeus* or elsewhere) distinguish two fields of inquiry, one containing human bodies and another containing minds. Why should Aristotle do this? In *Top.* I. 105b19–25 he distinguishes three sorts of problem: ethical problems, like whether we should obey our parents rather than the laws, logical, like whether knowledge of opposites is the same, and physical, like whether the universe is eternal. On this view questions about minds which were not ethical or logical would have to pertain to *phusikē*. It is true that *Metaph.* E. 1026a18–19 provides an alternative academic cartography: theoretical philosophy divides into mathematics, *phusikē* and theology. It might be conjectured that *nous*, as the most divine part of us, is the business of the theologian. But does Aristotle, like Hegel, conceive theology as wholly separate from *phusikē*? In *de An.* 1. 402b5–7 he wonders whether different accounts should be given of the souls of different living things, 'horse, dog, man and god', suggesting that theology, like anthropology, is a branch of zoology.

Perhaps it will be said that if we give a Cartesian account of the mind it follows at once that minds are not the concern of science; and hence that Aristotle's first point is a strong indication that he conceives minds as Cartesian thinking substances. But why are Cartesian minds not the business of science? We are tempted to imagine that an account of a spiritual substance would be just like an account of a body except that it was of something non-bodily: the accounts would be different in content but not in form, like accounts of an eagle and an octopus. The reason why a scientist cannot study minds would be like the reason why an ornithologically-minded octopus cannot study eagles: they live in an inaccessible realm. But if this were the position, minds *would* be the business of science. If an account of minds were to tell us how they are produced, how they affect other things, and how other things affect them, they would be material objects. Unless we gratuitously read back our confusions into Aristotle, his first point is prima facie evidence that his minds are *not* Cartesian substances.

Although in his introduction to *Aristotle's De Anima* Hamlyn says Aristotle has no concept of a Cartesian self, or at least no 'proper concept of a person or of consciousness', in his paper 'Aristotle's Cartesianism' (1978) he argues that Aristotle anticipates Descartes' idea that the thinking self is exempt from the laws of physical nature. Below the level of *nous*, says Hamlyn, everything is mechanically determined, but 'the ordinary principles of Aristotelian physics' cannot apply to thinkers because there is no organ of thought. If that were right, Aristotle might think that *nous* falls outside the scope of science precisely because of this lack of causal determination. In fact, however, (as I have argued against Hamlyn elsewhere: cf. Charlton 1985) Aristotle is just as little a determinist about the movements of subhuman animals, and indeed about all biological processes, as he is about the deliberate actions of men: none of them is determined by external causes. On the other hand biological processes generally and parts of the soul other than *nous are* the concern of *phusikē*. The exclusion of *nous*, then, must be for a different reason.

The doctrine that *phusikē* deals with some parts of the soul but not with *nous* is developed in *PA* 1. 641a17–b10 (cf. *Metaph.* E. 1026a5–6, *de An.* 1. 403a29–b16). Aristotle gives two arguments for excluding *nous.* The first may be presented as follows. *If* (a) *phusikē* covers *nous*, (b) *nous* and *noēta*, things thought of, are correlatives, and (c) correlatives must be studied together in the way perception and objects of perception are, *then* (d) *phusikē* will cover all objects of thought. But (d) is absurd (implied in a35–6). So let us reject (a). This argument is defective. Instead of (a), why not reject (b) or (c)? An account of perception has to take in objects of perception because perception involves causal action on the perceiver (cf. *De Sensu* 436b6–8). But according to *de An.* III.4 thought does not involve causal action on the thinker in the same way. Why, then, should an account of it have to include any account of objects of thought?

Aristotle's second argument is in b4–8. Natural science deals with soul only insofar as soul is nature. Soul is nature only insofar as it is a source of change. That which thinks (*to noētikon*) is not a source of change. So natural science does not deal with it. Formally this argument is unimpeachable, but as D. M. Balme remarks (1972: *ad loc.*), it is surprising to hear that *nous* is not a source of change or a part of nature. Aristotle does, indeed, give an argument. The changes which are due to nature *qua* form are growth, alteration and locomotion, and *nous* is not responsible for any of these. But we know from two famous passages, *de An.* III. 433a13–14 and *EN* VI. 1139a35–6, that practical *nous is* responsible for locomotion. Besides, a thing's form or soul seems to be responsible for natural change chiefly as that for the benefit of which the change occurs. Do not my limbs, or at least (see below p. 414) my heart and brain, develop for the benefit of me as a thinker? In *Pol.* VII. 1334b15, Aristotle declares that our mind is the 'end of nature' (*tēs phuseōs telos*). This argument too, then, is unsatisfying. I shall later suggest a different reason for excluding *nous* from *phusikē*, but we may note here that Aristotle does not in *PA* I.1 appeal to the fact that *nous* is a non-material substance.

The second peculiarity of *nous* is that it comes 'from outside' (*thurathen*). This doctrine is expounded in *GA* II.3. The manuscripts carry a further reference to a mind 'from outside' in 744b21–2, but as it stands that text is barely intelligible, and I agree with those who consider it corrupt. H. J. Drossaart Lulofs (1965) obelizes it; P. Moraux (1955) emends the word *nous* away. The earlier passage cannot be so easily dismissed, partly because there is testimony to it in Theophrastus. It is, however, very puzzling.

In *GA* I Aristotle has argued that animals generate through the male's acting with semen (*gonē* or *sperma*) on material (*katamēnia*) provided by the female. In *GA* II.1 he asks what causal agent is responsible for the development of parts in the embryo (733b32). His answer (734b4–17, 735a13–14) is that once conceived, the embryo is itself responsible for the development of parts, but the agent responsible for its coming into being in the first place is the semen. In 735a13 he speaks of this as coming from outside (*exōthen*), and in a5–9 he says that it has soul in the same way as the parts of a living thing, a way he calls, a little confusingly, 'potentially' (*dunamei*).

In *GA* ii.2 Aristotle considers a couple of purely physiological questions about the material aspect of semen; in *GA* ii.3 he turns, it seems, to the formal aspect, and asks what kinds of soul are present in semen and fetuses (*kuēmata*). Clearly they have nutritive soul (736a35–6), but what about the perceptive and intellective souls? Having declared that 'all souls must be possessed potentially before actually' Aristotle continues:

And either they must all be produced in the body without existing beforehand, or they must all pre-exist, or some must but not others; and they must be produced in the matter either without having entered in the male's seed, or having come from there; and in the male they must either all be produced from outside (*thurathen*), or none from outside, or some but not others. Now it is evident from the following that they cannot all pre-exist: all principles whose actuality [or activity: *energeia*] is bodily are clearly unable to be present without body (for example walking without feet). Hence too they cannot enter from outside. For they can neither enter by themselves, since they have no separate existence, nor enter in a body; for the seed is a residue produced by a change in the nutriment. It remains, then, that the intellect alone enters additionally from outside and alone is divine; for bodily actuality is in no way associated with its actuality. (736b15–29, tr. Balme.)

In this passage Aristotle certainly seems to say that *nous*, in the words of Zeller, 'is not born into existence like the other parts of the soul' and 'since it is said to enter the body from without, it must have existed previously' (1897: ii 95–6, 99–100). Moraux, feeling this to be too much at variance with the rest of Aristotle's teaching, suggests that the passage expresses not Aristotle's own view but the second half of an antinomy. On the one hand, the appearance of *nous* is 'conditionnée…par le développement des organes corporels', on the other, in its activity it is 'radicalement indépendent du corps' (1955: 283). Aristotle goes on to say:

The capability of all soul seems to be associated with a body different from and diviner than the so-called elements. (b29–31)

This is hot stuff analogous to the material of the stars which is contained in semen (736b33–737a1). Moraux holds that Aristotle's solution to the antinomy is that *nous* is 'en connexion avec' this hot stuff and can therefore, like our other psychological powers, be 'contenu potentiellement par le sperme' and transmitted to the embryo by it (pp. 269, 285).

Unfortunately it is not at all easy to read Moraux's antinomy into the text of 736b15–29 and the preceding lines. Later commentators have not accepted his interpretation, although A. Preus (1975: 83–5) expresses sympathy with it. Balme and Charles Lefèvre (1972: 269–80) think that some kind of substantial *nous* comes into the semen 'from outside' and is passed on by it. According to Lefèvre, this is included in a 'germe du principe psychique' (277), a phrase which translates *to sperma to tēs psuchēs archēs* in 737a7–8. The word *sperma*, however, seems to be wrong – Lulofs obelizes it – and there seems to be no filling for the gap which will give a satisfactory sense for the whole relative clause running from a8–11. Balme suggests that Aristotle might conceive the semen as conveying intellect by 'movements superimposed on the heat's own movements – perhaps as a liquid conveys waves' (1972: 161). This, however, renders otiose the semen's carrying a substantial *nous*, and brings us back to a view like Moraux's.

The testimony of Theophrastus sheds no appreciable light on our chapter. It is not wholly certain even that it refers to it. Theophrastus uses the word *exōthen*, not *thurathen*; according to Themistius, to whose commentary on the *De Anima* (*CIAG* v.3 107–8) we owe the relevant fragments, Theophrastus is talking about a *dunamei nous* – identified by Themistius with the *pathētikos nous* of *de An.* III.5 – and his question is one which does not appear in *GA* II.3, the question in what way *nous* is 'from outside' and in what way 'connate', *sumphuēs*. His tentative reply is that it is not added, *epithetos*, but co-embraced, *sumperilambanomenon*, a word which may echo *emperilambanetai* in 737a9–10, but which is not illuminating as an answer to the question. All we can infer with confidence from Theophrastus is that the phrase *ho thurathen nous* was not associated with any special Aristotelian theory. The same thing is shown by Aristotle's use of the phrase in *Juv.* 472a22 to refer to the hot mind-stuff in the air postulated by Democritus.

I find it extremely hard to believe that Aristotle in *GA* II.3 is saying that the intellect, in the sense of a capacity for intellectual thought, is transmitted at conception. Nothing of the sort is suggested anywhere else in his work. Even in our chapter embryos 'do not become simultaneously animal and man or animal and horse' (736b2–5), that is, *nous*, which is peculiar to men, comes after the ability to perceive, which is shared by all animals; and Aristotle is not sure that the perceptive soul is present in any way except 'potentially' at conception (741a11–12), though it seems to be there actually at birth (cf. *de An.* II. 417b16–18). His regular view is that

the capacity for intellectual thinking develops after birth, via perception, memory and experience: so *APo.* II.19 (where *nous* means
a capacity, not a thinker), cf. *Pol.* 1334b20–4.

On the other hand *nous* of some kind ought to belong to embryos.
In *Metaph.* Z. 1035a25–7 Aristotle says that certain parts of an
organism are neither prior nor posterior to the whole but simultaneous with it, namely:

such as are in control and are the primary thing in which the account (*logos*) and
substance (*ousia*) are, such as the heart, perhaps, or the brain, it makes no difference
which it is.

Not only cannot there exist a man without this essential part; if a
human embryo has this part (and it does have both heart and brain)
it must have all the essential characteristics of a member of the human
species: will not that include some kind of *nous*?

The same conclusion emerges from more biological considerations.
It is not just by chance that we have *nous* and horses do not. We are
more sagacious than other animals because we have a nicer sense of
touch (*de An.* II. 421a21–3), because we walk erect (*PA* IV. 686a27),
and above all because the heat in our hearts is the purest, and this
heat is balanced and controlled by an exceptionally large and moist
brain. The brain, in Aristotle's view, is not the center of the
perceptive system, but it nevertheless performs an indispensable
function (*PA* II. 652b6–7): all vital activities depend on heat, and the
brain controls the heat in the system (652b10–23; the physiology
sounds crude, but it would be surprising to find an intelligent species
which did not have a mechanism for keeping the blood at a high and
constant temperature). Now in 741a10–12 Aristotle reasons that an
embryo could not develop parts peculiar and useful to perceivers, like
a face and hands, unless it in some way possessed a perceptive soul.
How could it develop the big, wet human brain and the pure human
heart without having an intellective soul?

Aristotle has, then, a mild antinomy of the kind Moraux describes,
even if it is not expressed in *GA* II.3, and it is fairly clear that he solves
it by saying that embryos have an intellective soul 'potentially'
(736b14–15, 737a16–18). The formula '*x* has a φ-ive soul potentially'
may be taken to mean '*x* is, in its formal aspect, a thing which can
become a φ-er', and this implies that *x* is capable of developing the
parts of a φ-er. Aristotle probably has in mind in 736b29–737a7 the
biological theories about *nous* which I have just mentioned. At any
rate we can understand the point of this section to be that hot stuff
in the semen can and does cause an intellective soul to be present
'potentially' in the embryo.

This interpretation does not explain the relative clause a8–11 in the next section, a7–16, which Balme translates:

But the body of the semen, in which also comes the portion of soul-source – partly separate from body in all those in which something divine is included (and such is what we call intellect) and partly inseparate – this body of the semen dissolves and evaporates.

As I said, however, this clause seems incurably corrupt. It is irrelevant to the question the whole sentence is answering, namely, what becomes of the corporeal element of the semen, given that 'that which enters is no part of the fetus produced' (736a24–6); and even if Aristotle did think that a non-material but substantial *nous* came away from the male (*sunaperchetai*) with the semen, it would not be a 'portion', a 'germe' or anything else of the 'soul-source', which must be the hot stuff referred to in a5 and a7. (The phrase likeliest to have *to men chōriston on...to d' achōriston* in apposition to it is *morion* or *moria tēs psuchēs*; if, therefore, what we have is genuine, it looks as if at least a whole line of text has dropped out.)

On my interpretation, 736b29–737a7 allows the intellective soul just as much as the perceptive to come to be present in the embryo through the action of semen. That, indeed, is what we should expect from the opening words *pasēs psuchēs*, 'all soul'. On the other hand, 736b15–19 contrasts *nous* with other kinds of soul. Now this passage can hardly, I think, be correct as it stands. Aristotle is made to say that *nous* comes 'from outside' not into the embryo but into semen. Nowhere else does he raise the absurd question how psychological powers come to be in semen, and the suggestion that semen contains a substantial intellect has a wildness beyond anything in Descartes. I suggest that the text is at fault at least in lines b19–20. In b19 *ē* is most naturally construed with *thurathen*, and we expect another contrasting adverbial phrase: 'in the male they arise either from outside or...' Balme takes it (as does Lefèvre) with *hapasas*: 'they must either all be produced from outside, or none...' But we still want some alternative to coming from outside, and none is stated. A simple solution is to take *ē thurathen* as a gloss on *en tōi arreni*, since anything which enters in the semen enters from outside the body of the female, the natural sense of *thurathen*. We can then paraphrase: 'Either the various kinds of soul are present in the female all along, or they come to be in the embryo; in the latter case, either they come into being in it without having entered with the semen, or they enter with the semen, i.e. from outside. They cannot be there all along, and no kind of soul of which the functioning is corporeal can enter from without, either in the semen or by itself. (Such kinds of soul, the nutritive and the perceptive, arise in the embryo through the action of semen, but do not enter with it.) The only kind of soul left to enter from outside is *nous*.'

This interpretation gives 736b15–19 a reasonable sense. Its weakness is that it leaves the final sentence hanging in the air; Aristotle does not say definitely whether or not *nous* does come in from outside, but passes in 736b29ff. to a completely separate line of thought. This unevenness, however, is not untypical. There are parallels to it in *GA* II.1, as Moraux notes. If we could press Aristotle, he might say that *nous* does differ from other kinds of soul in coming in from outside, but not in the way 736b15–29 suggests. Actual *nous* arises only when, as we grow up, we take in forms of things without their matter, as stated in *de An.* III.4.

Mention of that chapter brings me to the last peculiarity of *nous*, its separability from the body.

Aristotle recognizes degrees of separability. Objects of mathematics like a sphere are separable in that we can give an account of a sphere without mentioning any particular kind of material; but they are not separable to the extent that there can exist a sphere which is not composed of any material at all. Aristotle uses *logōi*, 'in account', chiefly, though not exclusively, for things which are separable as objects of mathematics are. The forms of natural things and artifacts, though separable in account to some extent (*Metaph.* H. 1042a29, cf. *de An.* II. 413b29), are less separable than these (*Ph.* II. 194a1). That, it seems, is because things which satisfy ordinary sortal concepts have to be composed of certain kinds of material. A saw must be made of iron (*Ph.* II. 200b7); a dog must be able to perceive, and for that needs sense-organs composed of certain materials (cf. *Sens.* 436a6–8). Still less separable than forms of natural things, if not inseparable in a different way altogether, are things like the infinite (*Metaph.* Θ. 1048b15). The things which are most separable are said to be separable *haplōs*, 'simply', *topōi*, 'in place', or *kata megethos*, 'in magnitude' (*de An.* III. 429a12): I do not think these expressions mark distinct classes of separables. As this survey shows, the word I translate 'separable', *chōristos*, does not have a precisely limited sense in Aristotle. I suspect it is derived from Plato's formulation of the core of the Theory of Ideas: 'Separately (*chōris*) there are certain forms themselves, and separately the things which participate in these' (*Prm.* 130b); here Plato is saying little more than that the forms are not identical with the things that participate in them. It is not immediately clear, then, what Aristotle means when he says that *nous* is separable. Nobody can doubt that he thinks it is more separable than forms of natural things generally. It is hard not to interpret 430a22–3 as claiming that *nous*, and not just some mysterious divine *nous*, but that *nous* which 'each of us seems to be identical with' (*EN* x. 1178a2, cf. IX. 1168b35), can exist without the body. Not only, however, does that appear to conflict with the rest of his philosophical psychology; the arguments he brings to bear on the question of separability seem able to show at most that *nous* is separable in the same way as objects of mathematics. That *nous* is separable in that way would be consistent with the rest of his teaching, and is a vital postulate of modern science fiction. Intelligent agents in science fiction do not have to have any particular bodily structure, but they do need some bodily structure or other. Bodiless thinkers belong not to scientific but to theological fantasy.

We can distinguish three arguments for the separability of *nous* in *de An.* III.4. The slightest is in 429a24–7. Aristotle argues that if *nous* were 'mixed' with the body, it would have a temperature and even an organ; but there is no organ of thought. That there is no organ of thought may be agreed. We do not think with our brains, or use them in thinking, in the way in which we write with our hands or use them in writing. But what does that prove? There is no organ for turning over in bed; nevertheless, there could not be a turner-over-in-bed without a body.

In 429a29–b5 we have the consideration that 'very perceptible things' like deafening noises and blinding lights make us less capable of perceiving, whereas after thinking of something 'very thinkable' we are not less but more capable of thinking of inferior objects of thought. What are the very thinkable things? 'Pure form' says Hamlyn. I should rather bet on examples or models such as (cf. Plato, *Plt.* 277d–278e) we use to illuminate obscure concepts in philosophy. Whatever view we take, it is true that nothing in thought exactly corresponds to the over-stimulation of a sense-organ. But it is a big step to infer that a thinker does not require any bodily apparatus whatever. In *de An.* I. 408b18–24 Aristotle says:

Nous seems to come to be in us as a kind of substance (*ousia*), and not to be destroyed. For it would be destroyed above all by the decline involved in old age; but in fact the situation is perhaps the same as over the sense-organs: if an old man got a certain sort of eye he would see like a youth. We age through a change not in the soul but in that which has it, as when we are sick or drunk.

In noting the effects of drink and disease, and comparing *nous* with sight, Aristotle in fact implies that *nous* does require bodily apparatus – something recognized, as we have seen in his biological works.

Aristotle's principal argument is as follows. (a) Thinking is like perceiving: it consists in receiving the form of the thing thought of and becoming like it (429a13–17, cf. 424a17–25). (b) If that which thinks already has a form of its own, it cannot acquire that form or think of it. (This premise is attributed to Aristotle by Hamlyn, and it is certainly required, though not easily extracted from the difficult parenthesis 429a20–1, which Hamlyn and Ross understand as 'The intrusion of anything foreign interferes with it.') (c) There is nothing of which we do not think (429a18). (d) Therefore that which thinks has no form of its own except this, that it is capable of receiving forms (429a21–2).

Prominent as this argument is, only Hamlyn among recent commentators takes it seriously. In Hamlyn 1978 he challenges (c). In Hamlyn 1968, however, he questions (a), and that is certainly the most surprising part of the argument. We can accept that when we see a red object, some part of us, the retina, becomes red, and when we hear a note played on the piano, the wave-motion caused by the piano in the air is reproduced by the ossicles and membranes of the middle ear in the liquid in the so-called labyrinth. But surely when we think of elephants, there is no part of us that becomes elephantine. Some readers may have taken Aristotle to mean that we acquire, not the form of the thing we get to know about, but a concept of that form. To say that, of course, is not to explain 'how thinking comes about' (Aristotle's declared purpose: 429a13), but merely to restate what needs explaining. In fact, however, Aristotle says nothing about *concepts* of things known. Instead he emphasizes that *nous* becomes these things: 429b6, 431b17, b21–8. In 429b30–430a1 he says:

nous is potentially the things thought of...: potentially as things are potentially on a tablet on which nothing is actually written.

This is not to say that concepts are like words or pictures. The analogy is not: as a tablet is to physical pictures of houses, dogs, etc., so the mind is to mental pictures of them. Rather it is: as a tablet is to a physical picture, so *nous* is to things depicted. Aristotle continues:

In the case of things without matter, thinker and thing thought of are the same; for theoretical knowledge and what is so known are the same. (430a3–5, cf. a19–20)

Today we should not readily say either that astronomers are the same as stars or that astronomy is. Aristotle's equation of the three is intelligible only if he believes that a thinker really does acquire forms thought of. If a form known is a form acquired by the knower, the astronomer's knowledge of the form of a star will be a kind of knowledge of himself. That becoming an astronomer is becoming starry seems intended not as a truism but as a powerful positive account. But how, then, could Aristotle think it true?

Thinking about a triangle involves imagining a triangle (*Mem.* 449b30–450a5). Imagining a triangle involves a physiological process like the process which is caused by a perceived triangle and correlated with it (428b10–17). Hence thinking of a triangle involves something quasi-triangular in the perceptive system. Is this why Aristotle says it involves taking on the form thought of? This explanation (which was originally suggested to me by Richard Sorabji) is ingenious but has two defects. It readily fits only objects of geometry, rather a restricted division of the intelligible world. More serious, the acquiring of the form of an *f* which Aristotle identifies with acquiring knowledge of *f*s is acquiring the ability to imagine *f*s in their absence (429b5–9). It accounts for this imaginative activity, and cannot, therefore, be identified with it.

If someone were to say that Aristotle's theory of thought is now an insoluble mystery, he would be hard to refute. If, however, the mystery is soluble, the solution should surely be sought in the passages outside *de An.* III where Aristotle tries to explain the genesis of knowledge.

In *APo.* II.19 Aristotle discusses our knowledge of 'primary and immediate principles' (99b21). He gives no examples of such principles in that chapter, but probably has in mind items like: 'An eclipse is privation of light through the interposition of a heavenly body' (90a16), 'Longevity is caused by having no gall' (cf. *APr.* II. 68b19–24), 'A straight line is duality in a continuum' (429b18–20). He raises two questions about these principles: 'How do we come to know them?' and 'What is the disposition which knows them?' (99b18). The disposition, we learn at 100b12, is *nous*. The word is here used, not for a thinker, nor for some special intuitive faculty (an interpretation well criticized by Jonathan Barnes (1975a)), but merely for dispositional knowledge of some primary, undemonstrated proposition. Aristotle's position is simple but at the same time striking. He posits no general capacity for grasping first principles. Instead he recognizes a plurality of specific capacities, identified with dispositional knowledge of specific principles. There is, for instance, no general ability to discern causal connections, but only the ability to make causal inferences from the movements of heavenly bodies, the ability to make causal inferences from the presence or absence

of gall, and so on. And these specific capacities are not innate
(99b26–7); they are acquired through perception, memory and
experience:

From perception comes memory, and from memory of the same thing occurring
many times, experience...And from experience or from the coming to rest of the
whole universal in the soul, the one over the many, which is one and the same for
all of them, originate art (*technē*) and knowledge, art if about coming to be,
knowledge if about that which is. (100a3–9)

The later part of this process is illustrated in *Metaph.* A.1:

Art arises when from the many thoughts of experience there comes to be one
universal understanding about similar things. Understanding that this benefited
Callias when he was sick of this disease, and also Socrates, and many individuals
in the same way, belongs to experience. It belongs to art to understand that it benefits
all people of a certain sort, grouped together by accordance with a single form, when
sick of such and such a disease, e.g. the phlegmatic or bilious when suffering from
fever. (981a5–12)

To flesh out the example, the experienced but illiterate Thracian
medicine-man remembers that when Callias and Socrates felt
wretched they were cured by bark soup, so when the next travelling
Hellene, Coriscus, feels wretched, he gives him bark soup and expects
him to recover. The qualified Asclepiadic doctor, in contrast, thinks
of Callias and Socrates not as travelling Hellenes but as bilious types;
the important but unobvious characteristic of biliousness has come
to rest in his soul. He identifies their malaise as fever; and he expects
bark soup to cure them by purging them of bile, the excess of which
constitutes the fever. He has acquired a disposition to expect bilious
types to be cured of fever on taking bark soup, when in fact bark soup
cures fever. To generalize: A has art concerning fs (say cures or
eclipses) where there is a g such that gx causes fx, and A is dis-
positionally the sort of man that, knowing or having it appear that
gx, expects fx. Men of art 'know the why and the cause' (981a29–30).
The sort of man to whom it would be a reason for expecting the Moon
to be eclipsed, that the Earth is getting between it and the Sun, is
an astronomer.

This account of knowledge-acquiring may be defensible, but does
it illuminate the puzzling statements in *de An.* III.4? My tentative
suggestion is this. We have no general and non-formal concept of
knowledge or skill. We have no concept of medical skill apart from
our concept of health, no concept of astronomical knowledge apart
from our concepts of phenomena like eclipses. A doctor is not a man
who satisfies something called 'the concept of skill'. He is a man to
whom the concept of health applies in a special way. It takes a doctor

to tell whether another man is a doctor: my judgment that you have (or lack) medical skill is an application of my own medical skill. More specifically I apply the concept of a doctor to you if, for the reason that Coriscus is bilious and feverish, I expect you to give him bark soup. I think of you as an astronomer if, for the reason that the Earth is getting into a position between the Moon and the Sun, I expect you to lay on an eclipse-watching party the night of the next full moon. Both these expectations, of course, involve attributing to you a certain character as well as certain technical knowledge. Nevertheless my attributing that knowledge to you is no more than my applying my knowledge of health or eclipses to you in a special way. In what way? I do not expect you yourself to become eclipsed, or even healthy. It is as if you somehow had the form of health or an eclipse without the matter. And since my notion of you as a thinker, as a thing which acquires and possesses knowledge of other things, is simply the notion of you as a thing to which knowledge of other things can apply in this special way, could it not be said that a thinker is a thing with no nature of its own except this, that it is capable of taking on the forms of other things without the matter?

Among the most baffling lines in *de An.* III.4 are 430a2–5:

[*Nous*] is itself an object of thought as its objects are. For in the case of things without matter, thinker and thing thought of are the same.

In *PA* I. 640a31–2 (see also *Metaph.* Z. 1032b5–6, b13–14) Aristotle says 'Art is the account of the work without the matter'. As I point out in Charlton 1981, Aristotle recognizes two distinct types of form-description, descriptions in functional terms like 'a shelter' and physical or mathematical descriptions like 'the ratio of two to one'. The forms relevant here are the mathematical ones. The builder knows the physico-mathematical structure he must impose on bricks and beams if there is to be a shelter, or desires this structure in a house he buys. The musician, for the reason that the strings are in the ratio $2:1$, expects them to be consonant. The suggestion about self-knowledge could be that the knowledgeable man's awareness of these mathematical forms as objectives, desiderata or reasons is at the same time an awareness of himself as a man of skill. Such a suggestion would not be unreasonable. My consciousness of myself as a person is not separate from my knowledge of what I am aiming at and my causal monitoring of my progress; and a musician's knowledge that he is about to produce a consonance is not separate from his knowledge of the causal factors on which this effect depends.

This interpretation of *de An.* III.4 may seem far-fetched. Certainly there is no direct support for it in the text. On the other hand I can see no alternative interpretation which both makes Aristotle's remarks intelligible and fits the text better. If it is right, Aristotle can hold that *nous* is separable in the same way as objects of mathematics. To become disposed to think that *q* for the reason that *p* when in fact *q* because *p*, it is not necessary, or at least it is not logically necessary, to be composed of any particular kind of material. But I do not think it can be inferred that a thinker need not be composed of material at all.

Can we go further and say that the doctrine of total separability is inconsistent with the rest of Aristotle's philosophical psychology? Conflict is usually located at two points. First, Aristotle says that thought involves imagination (*de An.* III. 432a8–9, *Mem.* 449b31) and imagination physical processes (428b10–16); as he himself recognizes (*de An.* I. 403a8–10) it follows that without a body thought would be impossible. This difficulty, perhaps, is not itself insuperable. Aristotle is deeply committed to holding that the existence of a thinker involves judging and wanting for reasons, and these reasons must 'appear' to the thinker; their appearing is what Aristotle calls *phantasia*, the word we translate 'imagination'. I do not think he is so deeply committed to holding that all appearing, including the 'deliberative' kind of *de An.* III. 434a7, involves a body. If there were no other objections to bodiless thinkers, they might have some body-independent way of having reasons appear to them. The other difficulty, however, is more grave. The concept of a thinker, a thing with beliefs and desires, is supposed to be a concept of the form or formal aspect of a human being: how can there be a formal aspect which is not an aspect of anything, a form which is not the form of anything?

Although he usually writes as a dualist, in at least one place (*Reply to Objections VI*, ed. Adam and Tannery VII.442 ll. 1–3, 445 ll. 3–6) Descartes suggests that a human thinker is a thing which is at present a material body but not essentially so; we are now composed of flesh and bones, but could cease to be composed of anything. Aristotle may have toyed with a similar idea: that men start as material objects, but when they develop intellectual powers it is possible for them to separate themselves as thinkers from their bodies. That sounds whimsical or even mystical, but Aristotle uses language which suggests it:

We should not listen to those who say that as men we must think human thoughts and as mortals, mortal ones. So far as possible we should go immortal (*athanatizein*) and do everything to live up to what is best in us. Even if it is small in bulk, in power and worth it far exceeds all the rest; and it is this which each person seems to be (*EN* x. 1177b31–1178a2).

A speculation like this, even if it is unsound, need not introduce any incoherence into a philosophical system so long as it remains an isolated speculation, without other arguments tying it in. We have seen that the arguments actually offered in *de An.* III.4 for the separability of *nous* do not yield the conclusion that there can be a bodiless thinker.

On the other hand Aristotle's theory of 'how thinking comes about' (429a13) does provide a refreshing explanation of the doctrine that *nous* is not the business of the natural scientist. It falls outside the scope of science not because it falls within the scope of some other kind of first-order knowledge (as it might be, theology), but because thinking of a man as a possessor of knowledge is applying one's ordinary knowledge of other things to him in a special way. The concept of *nous* is not a scientist's concept because it is a kind of formal concept.

List of works cited

Ackrill, J. L. 1963. *Aristotle's Categories and De Interpretatione*. Clarendon Aristotle Series. Oxford.
—— 1972/3. 'Aristotle's definition of *psuchē*', *Proceedings of the Aristotelian Society* LXXIII, 119–33.
—— 1981a. *Aristotle the Philosopher*. Oxford.
—— 1981b. 'Aristotle's theory of definition: some questions on *Posterior Analytics* II 8–10', in Berti 1981, pp. 359–84.
Anton, J. 1957. *Aristotle's Theory of Contrariety*. London.
Aubenque, P. 1978. 'Les origines de la doctrine de l'analogie de l'être: sur l'histoire d'un contresens', *Les Etudes philosophiques*, 3–12.
Ayala, F. 1972. 'The autonomy of biology as a natural science' (orig. 'Biology as an autonomous science', *American Scientist* LVI (1968) 207–21), in A. D. Breck and W. Yourgrau, eds., *Biology, History and Natural Philosophy* (New York 1974), pp. 1–16.
Balme, D. M. 1939. 'Greek science and mechanism 1. Aristotle on nature and chance', *Classical Quarterly* XXXIII, 129–38.
—— 1941. 'Greek science and mechanism 2. The Atomists', *Classical Quarterly* XXXV, 23–8.
—— 1962a. 'Development of biology in Aristotle and Theophrastus: theory of spontaneous generation', *Phronesis* VII, 91–104.
—— 1962b. 'ΓΕΝΟΣ and ΕΙΔΟΣ in Aristotle's biology', *Classical Quarterly* N.S. XII, 81–98.
—— 1965. *Aristotle's Use of the Teleological Explanation*. Inaugural Lecture. Queen Mary College London.
—— 1972. *Aristotle's De Partibus Animalium I and De Generatione Animalium I (with passages from II. 1–3)*. Clarendon Aristotle Series. Oxford.
—— 1975. 'Aristotle's use of differentiae in zoology' (in Mansion 1961, pp. 195–212), in Barnes, Schofield and Sorabji 1975, pp. 183–93.
—— 1982. Review of M. C. Nussbaum, *Aristotle's De Motu Animalium* (Princeton 1978), *Journal of the History of Philosophy* XX, 91–5.
—— 1984. 'The snub', *Ancient Philosophy* IV, 1–8.
—— 1985. 'Aristotle, *Historia Animalium* Book Ten', in J. Wiesner, ed., *Aristoteles: Werk und Wirkung*, 2 vols. (Berlin 1985), pp. 191–206.
—— Forthcoming. *Aristotle, Historia Animalium, Books VII–X*. Loeb Classical Library. London and Cambridge, Mass.
Barnes, J. 1975a. *Aristotle's Posterior Analytics*. Clarendon Aristotle Series. Oxford.
—— 1975b. 'Aristotle's theory of demonstration', in Barnes, Schofield and Sorabji 1975, pp. 65–87.
—— 1980. 'Aristotle and the methods of ethics', *Revue Internationale de Philosophie* XXXIV, 490–511.

424

—— 1981. 'Proof and the syllogism', in Berti 1981, pp. 17–59.

—— 1982. *Aristotle*. Oxford.

Barnes, J., Schofield, M. and Sorabji, R., eds. 1975. *Articles on Aristotle I: Science*. London.

Benveniste, E. 1969. *Le Vocabulaire des institutions indo-européennes*, Vol. 1: *Economie, parenté, societé*. Paris.

Berti, E., ed. 1981. *Aristotle on Science: the Posterior Analytics*. Proceedings of the 8th Symposium Aristotelicum. Padova.

Bolton, R. 1976. 'Essentialism and semantic theory in Aristotle: *Posterior Analytics* II.7–10', *Philosophical Review* LXXXV, 514–44.

—— 1978. 'Aristotle's definitions of the soul: *De Anima* II.1–3', *Phronesis* XXIII, 258–78.

Bourgey, L. 1955. *Observation et expérience chez Aristote*. Paris.

Bradie, M. and Miller, Fred D., Jr. 1984. 'Teleology and natural necessity in Aristotle', *History of Philosophy Quarterly* I, 133–45.

Brunschwig, J. 1967. *Aristote Topiques I (livres I–IV)*. Collection...Budé. Paris.

Burnyeat, M. F. 1981. 'Aristotle on understanding knowledge', in Berti 1981, pp. 97–139.

—— Unpublished. 'Is Aristotle's philosophy of mind still credible?'

Byl. S. 1980. *Recherches sur les grands traités biologiques d'Aristote: sources écrites et préjugés*. Académie Royale de Belgique, Mémoires de la Classe des Lettres, 2nd ser. 64, 3. Bruxelles.

Charles, D. Unpublished. 'Meaning, natural kinds, and natural history'.

Charlton, W. 1970. *Aristotle's Physics Books I and II*. Clarendon Aristotle Series. Oxford.

—— 1980. 'Aristotle's definition of soul', *Phronesis* XXV, 170–86.

—— 1985. 'Aristotle and the *harmonia* theory', in Gotthelf 1985a, pp. 131–50.

Cherniss, H. F. 1935. *Aristotle's Criticism of Presocratic Philosophy*. Baltimore.

—— 1944. *Aristotle's Criticism of Plato and the Academy*. Baltimore.

Collingwood, R. G. 1945. *The Idea of Nature*. Oxford.

Cooper, J. M. 1982. 'Aristotle on natural teleology', in Schofield and Nussbaum 1982, pp. 197–222.

—— 1985. 'Hypothetical necessity', in Gotthelf 1985a, pp. 151–67.

Cornford, F. M. 1937. *Plato's Cosmology: the Timaeus of Plato translated with a running commentary*. London.

Coutant, V. 1971. *Theophrastus, De Igne: a post-Aristotelian view of the nature of fire*. Assen.

Denniston, J. D. 1954. *The Greek Particles*, 2nd ed. Oxford.

Dobzhansky, T. 1970. *Genetics of the Evolutionary Process*. New York.

Drossaart Lulofs, H. J. 1965. *Aristotelis De Generatione Animalium*. Oxford Classical Texts. Oxford.

Düring, I. 1943. *Aristotle's De Partibus Animalium: Critical and Literary Commentaries*. Göteborg.

Evans, J. D. G. 1977. *Aristotle's Concept of Dialectic*. Cambridge.

Ferejohn, M. 1981. 'Aristotle on necessary truth and logical priority', *American Philosophical Quarterly* XVIII, 285–93.

—— 1982/3. 'Definition and the two stages of Aristotelian demonstration', *Review of Metaphysics* XXXVI, 375–95.

Freeland, C. A. Unpublished. 'Scientific method in Aristotle's *Meteorology*'.

Furley, D. J. 1983. 'The mechanics of *Meteorologica* IV: a prolegomenon to biology', in Moraux and Wiesner 1983, pp. 73–93.

—— 1985. 'The rainfall example in *Physics* II.8', in Gotthelf 1985a, pp. 177–82.

Furth, M. 1985. *Aristotle, Metaphysics VII–X: Zeta, Eta, Theta, Iota*. Indianapolis.

—— Forthcoming. *Substance, Form and Psyche: an Aristotelean metaphysics*. Cambridge.

Gallop, D. 1975. *Plato's Phaedo*. Clarendon Plato Series. Oxford.

Ghiselin, M. T. 1969. *The Triumph of the Darwinian Method*. Berkeley.

Gotthelf, A. 1975. *Aristotle's Conception of Final Causality*. Columbia University Dissertation. Ann Arbor.

—— 1976/7. 'Aristotle's conception of final causality', *Review of Metaphysics* xxx, 226–54.

—— 1980. Review of M. C. Nussbaum, *Aristotle's De Motu Animalium* (Princeton 1978), *Journal of Philosophy* LXXVII, 365–78.

—— 1981/2. Review of M. C. Nussbaum, *Aristotle's De Motu Animalium* (Princeton 1978), *Review of Metaphysics* xxxv, 619–23.

—— Ed. 1985a. *Aristotle on Nature and Living Things: philosophical and historical studies presented to David M. Balme on his seventieth birthday*. Pittsburgh and Bristol.

—— 1985b. 'Notes towards a study of substance and essence in Aristotle's *Parts of Animals* II–IV', in Gotthelf, ed. 1985a, pp. 27–54.

—— Forthcoming 1987a. *Historiae* I: *Plantarum* et *Animalium*', in *Theophrastean Studies*, ed. W. W. Fortenbaugh (New Brunswick, forthcoming 1987).

—— Forthcoming 1987b. 'Professor Furley and the rainfall in Aristotle's *Physics* II.8'.

—— Forthcoming 1987c. 'Teleology and spontaneous generation in Aristotle: a discussion'.

—— Unpublished (1). '*Historia Animalium* 1.6 490b7–491a6: Aristotle's *megista genē*'.

—— Unpublished (2). 'Philosophical lessons of Aristotle's *Historia Animalium*'. (The bulk of this paper will be published as part of Gotthelf forthcoming 1987a.)

Grene, M. 1974. 'Is genus to species as matter to form?' *Synthèse* xxviii, 51–69; repr. in M. Grene, *The Understanding of Nature* (Dordrecht and Boston 1974), pp. 108–26.

—— 1985. 'On the division of the sciences', in Gotthelf 1985a, pp. 9–13.

Guthrie, W. K. C. 1939. *Aristotle, On the Heavens*. Loeb Classical Library. London and Cambridge, Mass.

—— 1965. *History of Greek Philosophy*, Vol. II: *The Presocratic Tradition from Parmenides to Democritus*. Cambridge.

Hamelin, D. 1920. *Le Système d'Aristote*. Paris.

Hamlyn, D. W. 1968. *Aristotle's De Anima Books II and III (with certain passages from Book I)*. Clarendon Aristotle Series. Oxford.

—— 1978. 'Aristotle's Cartesianism', *Paideia* 2nd special issue, 8–15.

Hartman, E. 1977. *Substance, Body and Soul: Aristotelian Investigations*. Princeton.

Heath, T. L. 1949. *Mathematics in Aristotle*. Oxford.

—— 1956. *Euclid: The Thirteen Books of the Elements*, 3 vols. London.

Heiberg, J. L. 1919. *Euclidis Elementa*. Leipzig.

Hull, D. 1965–6. 'The effect of essentialism on taxonomy – two thousand years of stasis', *British Journal for the Philosophy of Science* xv, 314–66; xvi, 1–18.

—— 1981. 'Philosophy and biology', in G. Fløistad, ed., *Contemporary Philosophy: a new Survey*, vol. II (The Hague 1981), pp. 281–316.

Jacob, F. 1973. *The Logic of Life: a history of heredity*. New York.

Jaeger, W. 1948. *Aristotle: Fundamentals of the History of his Development*. Oxford.

Joachim, H. H. 1922. *Aristotle on Coming-to-be and Passing Away*. Oxford.

Kahn, C. H. 1985. 'The place of the prime mover in Aristotle's teleology', in Gotthelf 1985a, pp. 183–205.

Kirwan, C. 1971. *Aristotle's Metaphysics Books* Γ, Δ and E. Clarendon Aristotle Series. Oxford.

Kosman, L. A. 1969. 'Aristotle's definition of motion', *Phronesis* XIV, 40–62.

—— 1973. 'Understanding, explanation, and insight in the *Posterior Analytics*', in Lee, Mourelatos and Rorty 1973, pp. 374–92.

—— 1984. 'Substance, being, and *energeia*', *Oxford Studies in Ancient Philosophy* II, 121–49.

Kühner, R. and Gerth, B. 1898. *Grammatik der Griechischen Sprache*, 2 vols. Hanover and Leipzig.

Kullmann, W. 1974. *Wissenschaft und Methode: Interpretationen zur aristotelischen Theorie der Naturwissenschaft*. Berlin and New York.

—— 1985. 'Different concepts of the final cause in Aristotle', in Gotthelf 1985a, pp. 169–75.

Landor, B. 1981. 'Definitions and hypotheses in *Posterior Analytics* 72a19–25 and 76b35–77a4', *Phronesis* XXVI, 308–18.

Le Blond, J.-M. 1939. *Logique et méthode chez Aristote*. Paris.

Lear, J. 1980. *Aristotle and Logical Theory*. Cambridge.

Lee, E. N., Mourelatos, A. D. P. and Rorty, R. M., eds. 1973. *Exegesis and Argument: studies presented to Gregory Vlastos*. *Phronesis* suppl. vol. I. Assen.

Lee, H. D. P. 1948. 'Place-names and the date of Aristotle's biological works', *Classical Quarterly* XLII, 61–7.

—— 1985. 'The fishes of Lesbos again', in Gotthelf 1985a, pp. 3–8.

Lefèvre, C. 1972. *Sur l'évolution d'Aristote en psychologie*. Louvain.

Lennox, J. G. 1980. 'Aristotle on genera, species, and "the more and the less"', *Journal of the History of Biology* XIII, 321–46.

—— 1982. 'Teleology, chance, and Aristotle's theory of spontaneous generation', *Journal of the History of Philosophy* XX, 219–38.

—— 1985a. 'Are Aristotelian species eternal?', in Gotthelf 1985a, pp. 67–94.

—— 1985b. 'Theophrastus on the limits of teleology', in W. W. Fortenbaugh, P. Huby, and A. A. Long, eds., *Theophrastus of Eresus: on His Life and Work*, Rutgers University Studies in Classical Humanities, vol. II (New Brunswick 1985), pp. 143–63.

—— Forthcoming 1987. 'Between data and demonstration: the *Anal.* and the *HA*', in A. C. Bowen, ed., *Science and Philosophy in Classical Greece*.

Lesky, E. 1951. *Die Zeugungs- und Vererbungslehren der Antike und ihr Nachwirken*. Akademie der Wissenschaften und der Literatur, Mainz, Abhandlungen der geistes- und sozialwissenschaftlichen Klasse, Jahrgang 1959, 19. Wiesbaden.

Leszl, W. 1972/3. 'Knowledge of the universal and knowledge of the particular in Aristotle', *Review of Metaphysics* XXVI, 278–313.

Lewes, G. H. 1864. *Aristotle: a chapter from the history of science*. London.

Lloyd, G. E. R. 1968. *Aristotle: the Growth and Structure of his Thought*. Cambridge.

—— 1973. 'Right and Left in Greek philosophy' (*Journal of Hellenic Studies* LXXXII (1962), 56–85), in *Right and Left*, ed. R. Needham (Chicago 1973), pp. 167–86.

—— 1979. *Magic, Reason, and Experience*. Cambridge.

—— 1983. *Science, Folklore and Ideology: studies in the life sciences in Ancient Greece*. Cambridge.

Lones, T. E. 1912. *Aristotle's Researches in Natural Science*. London.

Longrigg, J. 1977. Review of Balme 1972, *Classical Review* XXVIII, 38–9.

Lonie, I. M. 1981. *The Hippocratic Treatises "On Generation", "On the Nature of the Child", "Diseases IV": A Commentary*. Berlin and New York.

Louis, P. 1956a. *Aristote, Les parties des animaux*. Collection...Budé. Paris.

—— 1956b. 'Observations sur le vocabulaire technique d'Aristote', in *Mélanges de philosophie grecque offerts à Mgr. Dies* (Paris 1956), pp. 141–9.

—— 1964–9. *Aristote, Histoire des animaux*, 3 vols. Collection...Budé. Paris.
—— 1975. *La Découverte de la vie, Aristote*. Paris.
Maier, H. 1896–1900. *Die Syllogistik des Aristoteles*, 3 vols. Tübingen.
Manquat, M. 1932. *Aristote naturaliste*. Paris.
Mansion, A. 1946. *Introduction à la physique aristotélicienne*, 2nd ed. Louvain and Paris.
Mansion, S., ed. 1961. *Aristote et les problèmes de méthode*. Communications présentées au Symposium Aristotelicum tenu à Louvain du 24 août au 1ᵉʳ septembre 1960. Louvain and Paris.
Mayr, E. 1963. *Populations, Species and Evolution*. Cambridge, Mass.
—— 1982. *The Growth of Biological Thought*. Cambridge, Mass.
Meyer, J. B. 1855. *Aristoteles Thierkunde: ein Beitrag zur Geschichte der Zoologie, Physiologie und alten Philosophie*. Berlin.
Moraux, P. 1955. 'A propos du *nous thurathen* chez Aristote' in *Autour d'Aristote: recueil d'études offerts à Mgr. A. Mansion* (Louvain 1955), pp. 255–95.
—— 1979. *Le Commentaire d'Alexandre d'Aphrodise aux 'seconds analytics'*... Berlin.
Moraux, P. and Wiesner, J., eds. 1983. *Zweifelhaftes in Corpus Aristotelicum: Studien zu Einigen Dubia: Akten des 9. Symposium Aristotelicum*. Berlin and New York.
Nagel, E. 1961. *The Structure of Science*. New York.
Nehamas, A. 1979. 'Self-predication and Plato's theory of Forms', *American Philosophical Quarterly* XVI, 93–103.
Nussbaum, M. C. 1976. 'The text of Aristotle's *De Motu Animalium*', *Harvard Studies in Classical Philology* LXXX, 111–59.
—— 1978. *Aristotle's De Motu Animalium: Text with Translation, Commentary, and Interpretive Essays*. Princeton.
—— 1980. Review of E. Hartman, *Substance, Body, and Soul: Aristotelian Investigations* (Princeton 1977), *Journal of Philosophy* LXXVII, 355–65.
—— 1982a. 'Aristotle', in T. J. Luce, ed., *Ancient Writers* (New York 1982), pp. 377–416.
—— 1982b. 'Saving Aristotle's appearances', in Schofield and Nussbaum 1982, pp. 267–93.
—— 1983. 'The "common explanation" of animal motion', in Moraux and Wiesner 1983, pp. 116–56.
—— 1984. 'Aristotelian dualism: reply to Howard Robinson', *Oxford Studies in Ancient Philosophy* II, 197–207.
Ogle, W. 1882. *Aristotle on the Parts of Animals*. London.
—— 1897. *Aristotle on Youth and Old Age, Life and Death and Respiration*. London.
—— 1912. *Aristotle: De Partibus Animalium*. The works of Aristotle translated into English under the editorship of J. A. Smith and W. D. Ross, vol. V. Oxford.
Owen, G. E. L. 1968. 'Dialectic and eristic in the treatment of the Forms', in *Aristotle on Dialectic*, ed. G. E. L. Owen (Oxford 1968), pp. 103–25.
—— 1970. 'Aristotle: method, physics, cosmology' in C. C. Gillispie, ed. *Dictionary of Scientific Biography*, vol. I (New York 1970), pp. 250–8.
—— 1975. '*Tithenai ta phainomena*' (in Mansion 1961, pp. 83–103), in Barnes, Schofield and Sorabji 1975, pp. 113–26.
Peck, A. L. 1961. *Aristotle, Parts of Animals*. Loeb Classical Library. London and Cambridge, Mass. (Original edn. 1937.)
—— 1963. *Aristotle, Generation of Animals*. Loeb Classical Library. London and Cambridge, Mass. (Original edn. 1942.)
—— 1965–70. *Aristotle, History of Animals*. Vol. I: Books I–III (1965), vol. II: Books IV–VI (1970). Loeb Classical Library. London and Cambridge, Mass.
Pellegrin, P. 1982. *La Classification des animaux chez Aristote: statut de la biologie et unité de l'aristotélisme*. Paris.
—— 1985. 'Aristotle: a zoology without species', in Gotthelf 1985a, pp. 95–115.

—— 1986. *Aristotle's Classification of Animals*, tr. A. Preus. Berkeley. (Rev. edn. of Pellegrin 1982.)

Popper, K. 1952. *The Open Society and Its Enemies*, 2nd ed., 2 vols. London.

Poschenrieder, R. 1887. *Die naturwissenschaftlichen Schriften des Aristoteles in ihrem Verhältnis zu den Büchern der hippokratischen Sammlung*. Bamberg.

Preus, A. 1975. *Science and Philosophy in Aristotle's Biological Works*. Hildesheim and New York.

Randall, J. H., Jr. 1960. *Aristotle*. New York.

Rist, J. M. 1965. 'Some aspects of Aristotelian teleology', *Transactions and Proceedings of the American Philological Association* xcvi 337–49.

Robinson, H. 1983. 'Aristotelian dualism', *Oxford Studies in Ancient Philosophy* i, 124–44.

Rorty, R. M. 1973. 'Genus as matter: a reading of *Metaphysics* Z–H' in Lee, Mourelatos and Rorty 1973, pp. 393–420.

—— 1974. 'Matter as goo: comments on Grene's paper', *Synthèse* xxviii, 71–7.

Ross, W. D. 1924. *Aristotle, Metaphysics: a revised text with introduction and commentary*, 2 vols. Oxford.

—— 1936. *Aristotle, Physics: a revised text with introduction and commentary*. Oxford.

—— 1949. *Aristotle, Prior and Posterior Analytics: a revised text with introduction and commentary*. Oxford.

—— 1955. *Aristotle, Parva Naturalia*. Oxford.

Ross, W. D. and Fobes, F. H. 1929. *Theophrastus, Metaphysics*. Oxford.

Scaliger, J. C. 1619. *Aristotelis Historia de Animalibus*. Toulouse.

Schaffner, K. F. 1974. 'The peripherality of reductionism in the development of molecular biology', *Journal of the History of Biology* vii, 111–18.

Schofield, M. and Nussbaum, M. C., eds. 1982. *Language and Logos: studies in ancient Greek philosophy presented to G. E. L. Owen*. Cambridge.

Simpson, G. G. 1961. *Principles of Animal Taxonomy*. New York.

Solmsen, F. 1929. *Die Entwicklung der aristotelischen Logik und Rhetorik*. Neue Philologische Untersuchungen 4. Berlin.

—— 1957. 'The vital heat, the inborn pneuma and the aether', *Journal of Hellenic Studies* lxxvii, 119–23.

Sorabji, R. 1980. *Necessity, Cause, and Blame: Perspective on Aristotle's Theory*. London.

Sprague, R. K. 1977/8. 'Aristotle and the metaphysics of sleep', *Review of Metaphysics* xxxi, 230–41.

Stenzel, J. 1929. 'Speusippos', in *Pauly-Wissowa Real-Encyclopädie der classischen Altertumswissenschaft*, 2nd ser., vol. iii.2, cols. 1636–69.

Taylor, C. 1964. *The Explanation of Behaviour*. London and New York.

Thompson, D. W. 1910. *Aristotle: Historia Animalium*. The works of Aristotle translated into English under the editorship of J. A. Smith and W. D. Ross. Oxford.

—— 1971. *On Growth and Form*, abridged edn, ed. J. T. Bonner. Cambridge. (Original edn Cambridge 1917; rev. edn 1942.)

Tiles, J. E. 1983. 'Why the triangle has two right angles *kath' hauto*', *Phronesis* xxviii, 1–16.

Toulmin, S. and Goodfield, J. 1966. *The Architecture of Matter*. New York.

Vlastos, G. 1969. 'Reasons and causes in the *Phaedo*', *Philosophical Review* lxxviii, 291–325.

Waitz, T. 1844–6. *Aristotelis Organon*, 2 vols. Leipzig.

Waterlow, S. 1982. *Nature, Change, and Agency in Aristotle's Physics*. Oxford.

Weil, E. 1951. 'La place de la logique dans la pensée aristotélicienne', *Revue de métaphysique et de morale* lvi, 283–315; English transl. in Barnes, Schofield and Sorabji 1975, pp. 88–112.

Whewell, W. 1837. *History of the Inductive Sciences*, 3 vols. London.

White, N. P. 1972/3. 'Origins of Aristotle's essentialism', *Review of Metaphysics* XXVI, 57–85.

Wieland, W. 1962. *Die aristotelische Physik*. Göttingen.

Wilkes, K. V. 1978. *Physicalism*. London.

Woodfield, A. 1976. *Teleology*. Cambridge.

Wright, L. 1973. 'Functions', *Philosophical Review* LXXII, 139–68.

—— 1976. *Teleological Explanations*. Berkeley.

Zabarella, J. 1597. *Opera Logica*. Köln.

Zeller, E. 1897. *Aristotle and the Earlier Peripatetics*, tr. B. F. C. Costelloe and J. H. Muirhead, 2 vols. London.

Index locorum

Historia Animalium (*HA*) (cont.)

9 535b8 316
11 538a22ff. 57
  538b15ff. 57
v–vii. 104
v. 15
  1 539a28–30 315
  5 540b15ff. 57
    541a2 15
  6 541b8ff. 54
  12 544a12ff. 54
  16 548a23 84
    548b10 15
    549a8 15
  19 552b15ff. 54
    552b20 15
  30 556a14 11, 298, 316
vi.
  1 559a1 83
  2 560a28 16
  3 561a6 58
  10 565a12–13 97
    565a22–8 15
  11 566a6–8 54
    566a14–15 97
  12 566b3–26 109
  18 573a11ff. 54
  20 574b15ff. 54
  24 577b23 15
    577b24 15
  29 578b31 16
  31 579b2ff. 54
    579b5ff. 54
  35 580a19–22 54
  36 580b1 15
vii. 16, 53
  2 582b28ff. 57
    583a4ff. 57
  3 583b2ff. 57, 59
    583b5ff. 57, 59
  4 584a12ff. 57
  6 585b35ff. 61
viii. 16, 53
  1–2 110–11, 193
  1 588a25–b2 359
    588a25 330
    588b4–589a2 52
    588b20 15
  2 76, 110
    589a5–8 193
    589a10ff. 85
    589a29–590a12 193
    589b12 86
    589b13 84
    589b27–9 106
  3 592b7 325
  3a 593a15 83
  12 596b20–8 192

    597a32ff. 54
    597b25 83
  13 598a15 86
  28 605b22ff. 298
    605b22 11
    606a8 54
    606b14ff. 54
ix. 16, 53
  20 617a18 325
  25 617b20 16
  27 617b28 11, 298
  37 621a1 83
  39 623a3 116
  40 623b5–629a28 123
    623b5 83, 85
  42 629a24 85
  49 632b14 11, 298
x. 53

Parts of Animals (*PA*) 5, 9, 10, 11, 12, 15,
  16, 17, 31, 33, 67, 68, 86, 90, 103, 106,
  108, 109, 111, 112, 114, 116, 167, 168,
  169, 170, 238, 240, 275, 277, 280, 290,
  291, 300, 314, 335, 341, 380
i. 6, 9, 13, 17, 69, 78, 79, 89, 114, 170,
  175, 188, 200, 232, 315, 336, 342, 346,
  347
  1 197–8, 204, 220, 225, 226, 256, 265
    639a1–15 237
    639a3 170
    639a13 114
    639a15–b7 115
    639a16–19 114
    639a16 28
    639a23 115
    639b5–10 140
    639b5ff. 125
    639b5 115
    639b8ff. 55, 62
    639b11ff. 38
    639b14 157
    639b19–20 245
    639b21–640a10 243, 269
    639b21–640a9 40, 171–2, 197–8
    639b21–640a8 235
    639b22 188, 259
    639b24 188, 197
    639b26–30 255
    639b27–30 206
    639b27 243
    640a10–12 239
    640a1 197, 198
    640a2 170
    640a3–4 198
    640a3 269
    640a4–5 198
    640a6–9 198
    640a10ff. 38

General index

division (*cont.*)
Aristotle's reforms of, 49, 66, 69, 71–8, 80
and explanation, 66–7, 97–9
not by accidents, 75, 76
by opposites, 75–6
Platonic, *see* Plato and Platonism: on division
by privations, 75
and the specification of form, 296, 298, 348–53
stopping-point of, 298, 304–5, 310–12, 353–8
via successive differentiation, 69, 70–1, 73–4, 350–1
Dobzhansky, T., 339 n. 1
Drossaart Lulofs, H. J., 411
dualism, 408, 409, 422–3
dualizing, *see* tending to both sides
Düring, I., 12, 120 n. 2, 122 n. 5

eclipse, 134 n. 29, 135 n. 30, 141–2, 144; definition of, 134–6
eidos, see form(s); species
elemental blend, see *krasis*
element(s)
material natures and potentials of, 24–5, 30–4, 42–6, 176–7, 183, 185–6, 188–9, 193–4, 202, 211–26, 230–1, 234–7, 246, 249, 255, 257–73, 276, 283–5, 394–5; *see also* matter; nature(s): material; necessity, material
formal natures and potentials of, 230–1, 388–90
Empedocles, 24–6, 30–3, 43–6, 155 n. 49, 225–6, 238, 248, 252–3, 301, 359 n. 43
empeiria, 123 n. 10, 126 n. 17, 420–1
empiricism, in science, *see* biology: empirical character of
endoxa, 122–30, 150, 158–9; *see also* dialectic
end(s), 33; as essentially good, 202, 210 n. 13, 214 n. 18, 231, 233–4; as not necessitated, 220 n. 32, 236–7, 265, 266–7; unrealized, 213 n. 18; *see also* final cause; good, the; necessity, material; teleological explanation; teleology
Epicurus, 282–3, 301
epiglottis, 300
epistēmē: biology as, 1–2, 170–2; Platonic interest in, 116 n. 50, 118; unqualified vs. incidental, 90–7, 118, 119; *see also* demonstration
esophagus, 56 n. 19, 59, 179
essence(s), 11, 28 n. 9
definition of an, 294–5, 297–8, 302, 303
distinguished from form, 294–5, 303, 304, 305

distinguished from species, 295–8, 306
explanatory role of, 189, 240, 254, 298, 395
includes only teleological features, 294, 297–8, 302, 355–9
of individuals, 295, 304, 305, 312
of natural entities, 254 n. 11
of non-substances, 297
as translation of *ti ēn einai*, 306
see also essentialism
essential accidents, 19, 75, 87–8
essentialism: defined, 291, 340 n. 4; limited, 302; not a feature of Aristotle's biology, 291–302, 305–6, 312; teleological, 340 n. 4, 353, 356 n. 41, 358–9; typological, 339–40, 359
Euclid, 115 n. 49, 118
Eudoxus, 115 n. 49
Eustratius, 138 n. 33
Evans, J. D. G., 121 n. 4
evolution, 44; Aristotle and, 241, 280, 300–1, 339, 341, 359
excess and defect, *see* 'more and less, the'
existence, awareness of, 132–7, 152–4
explanation(s)
Aristotle's general approach to, 55–6, 200–1, 209–11, 236, 240–1, 281
'A-type', 92–7, 98–9, 108, 109–14
'B-type', 92–7, 99, 108, 109–14
in subordinate sciences, 175–6, 183
teleological explanation as form of, 207–8, 231–3, 240–1
see also cause(s); demonstration; final cause; teleological explanation; teleology

eye color, 258 n. 18, 267, 291, 297

female, 56, 57; nature of, 292; role in generation, 292, 293 n. 14, 400–1
Ferejohn, M., 93 n. 7, 99 n. 19, 119 n. 60
final cause, 1, 2, 55, 56, 210 n. 13
analysis of, 204–6, 213, 226 n. 51, 230, 231–2, 245, 282–3, 285
priority of 'coming to be' over 'being', 207 n. 8, 214 n. 19, 235, 237–42
relation to efficient cause, 226 n. 51, 227 n. 52, 232
as type of cause, 205 n. 2, 216 n. 21, 226 n. 51, 232, 236, 273–4, 281
see also end(s); teleological explanation; teleology
first principles, *see* axiomatic structure
fish, 191; prolific character of, 299
Fløistad, G., 274 n. 31
Fobes, F. H., 178 n. 33
food, 182–3
'for the most part', 247 n. 7

heat: of fire, 217, 218; generative or vital, 10, 163–4, 216 n. 20, 218–19, 220 n. 32, 399, 412, 414; productive of qualitative features, 173, 176, 218–19
Heath, T. L., 115 n. 49
Hegel, G. W. F., 318, 409, 410
Heiberg, L., 115 n. 49
Heidegger, M., 322
Heraclitus, 28
Herodotus, 53, 54
Hippocratics, 16, 53, 58, 59 n. 51
historia, 97 n. 16, 101–2; *see also* Aristotle: *Historia Animalium*, aims of
homoeomerous bodies, *see* parts, animal: uniform; uniform inanimate bodies
homonymy, 34 n. 22
horn(s), 35 n. 24; formation of, 276, 300; shedding of, 258 n. 18
hou heneka, see final cause
Hull, D., 274 n. 31, 339 n. 1
Hume, D., 205 n. 2, 281
hypothetical necessity, *see* necessity, hypothetical

identity, *see* form(s): and matter, unity of; sameness
immediates, 138 n. 32, 138 n. 33, 141 n. 38
indeterminism, 410
individuals: definitions of, 295, 296, 304–5, 309, 310–12; essences of, 295, 304, 305, 312; forms of 6, 7, 18–20, 302, 304–6, 309; priority relative to species, 28 n. 8, 44 n. 50, 201–2, 233, 242, 279–80, 298–301, 304–5, 311–12
individuation, 21–2, 73, 305, 311
indivisibility, relative to essence, 297, 298–301, 304–5, 310–12, 353–8
insects, 15, 190–1; copulation of, 61
intellect, see *nous*
intestines, 56 n. 19, 179, 180, 181–3
irreducibility, 25 n. 3, 206–7, 208–12, 230–1, 232, 235–6, 249, 282–5; as grounding teleological explanation, 188–9, 231–4, 240–1, 250–3, 269–74, 282–5
'irreducible potential for form', 201–2, 230–4, 240–1, 302 n. 56
Italiano, L., 197 n. 66

Jacob, F., 29 n. 11
Jaeger, W., 12, 13, 17, 120
Joachim, H., 16
Joachim H. H., 38 n. 32, 43 n. 45

Kahn, C. H., 210 n. 13, 213 n. 18, 233, 391 n. 21
Kant, I., 280–1, 409
katamēnia, 258 n. 18, 375, 382, 400, 403, 404

kidneys, 258 n. 18
kind(s), 69, 78–9
  absence of intermediate, 80–5
  as basic group concept, with variable level, 71–4, 314–31, 334–5, 358–9
  as explanatory, 89; *see also* explanation(s): 'A-type'
  as having contrary forms, 320–1, 331, 333–8
  as matter or potentiality, 322, 341, 347–51
  and 'the more and the less', 328–9, 331–3, 347–51
  as not a taxonomic concept, *see* kind(s): as basic group concept
  oneness or sameness in, 340, 341–2, 348
  recognizing, 78–9, 187 n. 49
  unnamed, 91, 97, 115–18, 187 n. 49
  see also analogy; definition(s); form(s); *megista genē*; species
kinēsis, 216 n. 20; *see also* motion; 'movements'
Kirwan, C., 396 n. 10
knowledge: genesis of, 419–23; possession of, 420–1; scientific, see *epistēmē*
Kosman, L. A., viii, 119 n. 60, 195, 196; (1969), 402 n. 20; (1973), 91 n. 4; (1984), 38 n. 35, 361 n. 2, 382 n. 16, 394, 396, 397 n. 12, 397 n. 13, 398 n. 16, 402 n. 20, 405 n. 23; (ch. 14 above), 38 n. 35, 209 n. 11, 231, 394
krasis, 25 n. 2, 38 n. 31, 43 n. 46, 193; *see also* mixture
Kühner, R., 132 n. 26
Kullmann, W., 69 n. 1, 76 n. 6, 90 n. 2, 98 n. 17, 171, 189 n. 56, 197 n. 66, 210 n. 13
Kung, J., xiii, 197 n. 66

lard, 258 n. 18
law, scientific, 209, 211
Le Blond, J.-M., 53 n. 3, 121 n. 4, 314
Lear, J., 118 n. 58, 195–6
Lee, H. D. P., 13, 395 n. 8
left/right/up/down, 17, 56, 57, 59 n. 49, 174 n. 15
Lefèvre, C., 413, 415
Lennox, J. G., viii, xii, xiii, 76 n. 6, 100–1, 166 n. 63, 197 n. 66, 230 n. 57, 391 n. 21, 407 n. 28; (1980), 327, 331–2; (1982), 223 n. 38, 231; (1985a), 210 n. 13, 233, 353 n. 36, 359 n. 44; (1985b), 178 n. 33, 213 n. 18; (ch. 5 below), 66–7, 68, 146 n. 42, 170 n. 3, 171, 174, 196 n. 65; (ch. 13 below), 91 n. 5, 113 n. 46, 233, 288–9
Lesbos, 13, 17
Lesky, E, 59 n. 51